AI for a Just World

Power, Liberation, and the People Left Behind

Edited by
Christo El Morr, Rachel da Silveira Gorman,
Elham Dolatabadi, and Laleh Seyyed-Kalantari

CRC Press
Taylor & Francis Group
Boca Raton London New York

CRC Press is an imprint of the
Taylor & Francis Group, an **informa** business
A CHAPMAN & HALL BOOK

Designed cover image: Shutterstock

First edition published 2027
by CRC Press
2385 NW Executive Center Drive, Suite 320, Boca Raton FL 33431

and by CRC Press
4 Park Square, Milton Park, Abingdon, Oxon, OX14 4RN

CRC Press is an imprint of Taylor & Francis Group, LLC

ISBN: 978-1-041-23697-9 (hbk)
ISBN: 978-1-041-23741-9 (pbk)
ISBN: 978-1-003-73781-0 (ebk)

DOI: 10.1201/9781003737810

Typeset in Times
by codeMantra

For communities everywhere—especially in the Global South and Indigenous worlds—who teach us that liberation is made together, and whose knowledge and struggles illuminate the path to collective care and shared flourishing.

For liberation, always unfinished—and always worth fighting for.

In that spirit of love and solidarity, we dedicate this also:

***To Valentina and Alexi**, for your love and unwavering support.*

***To Ehsan, Elin, and Aila**—your love reminds me to hope and to work toward a just world where no one is left behind.*

***To Ali, Borna, Arvin, Azam, and Mohammad Ali**, for your patience and love.*

***To Carlos, Emre, Chloe, Sage, Chase, Miles, Genevieve, Abigail, Vivienne, Alastair, Zithembe, Zwakalile, Oisín, and Avşin**—you are already imagining a new world.*

Contents

Preface

This book began as a conversation—a conversation among scholars, artists, engineers, and activists who refused to accept that artificial intelligence (AI) must mirror the injustices of the world that produced it. The *Equity and Artificial Intelligence Symposium: Possibilities for Justice and Liberation*, held at York University in November 2025, became the seedbed of that conversation. Supported by the Social Sciences and Humanities Research Council of Canada (SSHRC) through a Connection Grant, and by the Connected Minds Program funded by the Canada First Research Excellence Fund, the symposium gathered an extraordinary constellation of participants who understood that equity in AI is not a technical adjustment but a political commitment.

Over two intense days of dialogue and co-creation—across panels, workshops, and art interventions—we witnessed how differently the language of justice sounds when spoken in many disciplinary tongues. Computer scientists spoke of architectures and benchmarks; disability scholars spoke of access and embodiment; philosophers and artists spoke of being and relation. Out of these plural grammars emerged a shared conviction: justice in AI cannot be achieved by one field alone. It requires a coalition of knowledge, a practice of listening across the boundaries of expertise, and a willingness to let the most affected communities define what equity means.

The essays collected in *AI for a Just World: Power, Liberation, and the People Left Behind* are the continuation of that collaborative project. Some originated as symposium papers; others were developed in the months that followed, shaped through the working groups and virtual meetings that kept the conversation alive. Together, they offer both critical diagnosis and creative imagination. They expose how algorithms replicate racial capitalism, ableism, patriarchy, and colonial domination—but they also point toward alternative futures grounded in co-design, participatory governance, and decolonial ethics.

We have organized this book to move from the concrete to the philosophical. **Part 1** examines health and medical contexts, where algorithmic decision-making can quite literally determine life and death. **Part 2** explores disability, education, techno-ableism, and disability-centered AI policy, showing how the politics of access, participation, and governance are inscribed in code, curriculum, and institutional decision-making alike. **Part 3** turns to gender, labor, and social reproduction, tracing how AI reshapes intimacy, care, and work. **Part 4** interrogates governance, trust, and bias, extending the discussion to borders, geopolitics, and colonial infrastructures of surveillance. **Part 5** closes with decolonial and philosophical reflections that ask us to reimagine both the human and the nonhuman foundations of technological ethics. (A chapter on education, to appear in the final version, will bridge **Parts 4 and 5**, highlighting the role of pedagogy in cultivating public responsibility for AI.)

The making of this book was itself a collective process of translation, among disciplines, between technical and narrative languages, and between academic and community knowledge. Many of the contributors write from lived experience as well as professional expertise. Some are engineers who turned to philosophy; others are social scientists who now build models or advise on policy. Their diversity is not incidental: it is the condition of possibility for the intellectual and ethical project we call *AI for Justice*.

We are indebted to the communities and institutions that made this work possible. The SSHRC recognized the urgency of these questions through its Connection Grant, which enabled the symposium and the collaborations that followed. The Connected Minds Program—a joint initiative supported by the Canada First Research Excellence Fund—provided both financial and intellectual infrastructure, encouraging cross-faculty partnerships that are rare in Canadian academia. The Centre for Feminist Research (CFR) at York University offered administrative home and moral compass, reminding us that equity work begins with care. We are grateful to York's Health Equity and AI Lab (HEAL Lab), School of Health Policy and Management, and the many research assistants, students, and volunteers who sustained the project through months of preparation and editing.

Our deepest gratitude goes to the contributors who entrusted us with their work and to the reviewers who offered guidance with rigor and generosity. We also thank the readers, including scholars, practitioners, students, and citizens, who approach this book not only for information but also for inspiration. You are part of the ongoing experiment this volume represents: an experiment in building technologies that are accountable to the communities they serve.

This preface is written in the plural because the project has always been plural. There is no single author of *AI for a Just World*. It belongs to a network of thinkers committed to making technology answer to the demands of justice, liberation, and human dignity. If the chapters sometimes disagree, that disagreement is a form of integrity. It signals a field that remains alive, becoming, and capable of self-critique.

We hope that the pages that follow will serve as a record of research and a call to action. To design equitable and liberatory technologies is to participate in world-building. It asks us to imagine systems rooted in relation rather than extraction, in solidarity rather than surveillance. May this book offer both the vocabulary and the courage to do so.

Christo El Morr, Rachel da Silveira Gorman, Elham Dolatabadi, and Laleh Seyyed-Kalantari (Editors)
York University, Toronto

Contributors

Mohamed Abdalla is an assistant professor in the Department of Medicine at the University of Alberta. He received his PhD in Natural Language Processing from the Department of Computer Science at the University of Toronto. He has previously worked with multiple hospitals and health-care systems across Canada and internationally.

His research interests lie at the intersection of natural language processing, clinical informatics, and AI ethics. He is specifically interested in identifying and addressing gaps in the translation of academic AI research to real-world clinical deployments. His work has received international media coverage from publications such as *WIRED magazine*, *The Washington Post*, and *Fast Company*, among others.

Mehdi Adda is a full professor in the Department of Mathematics, Computer Science, and Engineering at Université du Québec à Rimouski (UQAR), Lévis, QC, Canada, and an affiliated researcher at the Research Centre of the CISSS (Centre intégré de santé et de services sociaux) de Chaudière-Appalaches. He received two PhD degrees in Computer Science in 2008, jointly conferred under a cotutelle agreement by Université de Montréal (Canada) and Université des Sciences et Technologies de Lille 1 (France), for work on knowledge representation, discovery, and data mining.

His research lies at the intersection of artificial intelligence (AI), data science, and the Internet of Things, with applications to Smart Health, Smart Homes, Smart Cities, and Industry 4.0. He is particularly interested in explainable and trustworthy AI, access control and security-by-design, and the development of resilient intelligent systems that meaningfully serve the people who depend on them.

In the context of health, his work increasingly engages with questions of equity, transparency, and inclusion—examining how AI systems can be designed to reduce, rather than reproduce, existing disparities in care. He is the recipient of an NSERC Discovery Grant and collaborates actively with clinical and community partners in Quebec.

Monish Ahluwalia is a diagnostic radiology resident at Queen's University. He completed his MD at the University of Toronto with a combined MSc in Systems Leadership and Innovation through the Institute of Health Policy, Management, and Evaluation. He completed an HBSc at McMaster University in Integrated Science. His research interests are wide ranging but include health economics, health systems, and machine learning.

Arash Asgari, an MSc student in Computer Science at York University's Responsible AI Lab, is a Machine Learning researcher advancing AI fairness and safety. His current research focuses on LLM safety evaluation metrics and post-training debiasing methods. He also holds an MSc in Computer Engineering from Sharif University of Technology, where he curated crowdsourcing-based metrics for software artifact code understandability and evaluated computationally efficient deployment scenarios for ML inference pipelines.

Arash's commitment to ethical AI innovation is further underscored by his work as a research intern at the Vector Institute, where he evaluated LLM knowledge editing methods. Bridging academia and industry, his applied experience includes serving as a Machine Learning engineer at Drivee in California, where he architected serverless computer vision pipelines and developed autonomous LLM-based conversational agents.

With recent publications in top-tier venues such as ACL and AAAI, Arash's expertise in NLP, computer vision, and MLOps, paired with his academic and practical insights, positions him as a versatile researcher dedicated to equitable and responsible AI development.

Melanie Baljko's research focus is on interrogating and intervening in the complex relationships among technology, disability, and ableism. Her work focuses on situated, contextual, and experiential aspects of human interaction with technology, with efforts toward innovation in co-creation and participatory design approaches to digital and social technologies. She does this work as Associate Professor of Computer Science in Human-Computer Interaction (HCI), with graduate appointments to Science and Technology Studies, Critical Disability Studies, and Digital Media. She directs the Practices in Enabling Technologies (PiET) research lab, an interdisciplinary research lab at York University which focuses on research projects that seek to intervene in technoableism.

Katherine Barron (BA, BEd, MEd) is a Vanier scholar and PhD candidate in the Faculty of Education at York University in Ontario, Canada. Her research examines how systems produce educational experiences for students, particularly how policy and technology shape educational decision-making. Her dissertation investigates how decisions to enact curriculum modifications in Individual Education Plans (IEPs) are produced, and her second line of inquiry explores how educators' use of generative AI for lesson planning, grading, and classroom materials transforms—for better and for worse—educational practices.

Amir Bayat is a fourth-year undergraduate student in Health Studies at York University, specializing in Health Policy, Management, and Digital Health. He is currently focused on completing his degree while engaging in academic and professional development opportunities within the university. Amir has developed a strong interest in the intersections of social sciences, health systems, and economics, with a particular focus on how these fields inform public policy and population health outcomes. He is especially intrigued by the growing influence of artificial intelligence and its potential to reshape healthcare delivery, economic systems, and broader social structures. Through his studies, Amir aims to contribute to interdisciplinary conversations that address complex health challenges in an increasingly digital and interconnected world.

Elizabeth Marie Borycki is a professor in the School of Health Information Science at the University of Victoria and an internationally recognized leader in digital health, patient safety, and artificial intelligence in healthcare. She directs the Global Lab for Digital Health and AI Innovation, where her work focuses on improving the safety, quality, and effectiveness of health technologies used by clinicians and patients. With a career spanning research, education, and policy, Borycki has contributed significantly to understanding how health information systems—particularly electronic health records and AI-driven tools—impact clinical decision-making and patient outcomes.

A recipient of the Michael Smith Health Research BC Health Professional Investigator Award, she has led numerous funded research initiatives and collaborated with interdisciplinary teams across Canada and internationally. Her scholarship bridges human factors, health informatics, and health system design, emphasizing the importance of safe and ethical technology integration.

Borycki is widely published and has played a key role in advancing training and knowledge translation in digital health. Through her work, she continues to shape the future of healthcare by ensuring emerging technologies support safer, more efficient, and patient-centered systems.

Hannah Bullock is a visual artist, writer, and researcher whose work explores contemporary issues through interdisciplinary artistic practice. She is currently pursuing a PhD in Critical Disability Studies at York University, where she also completed a Master of Fine Arts (MFA) in Visual Arts. Her work engages with visual culture and critical theory through artistic inquiry and autotheoretical writing.

Jenna Cappello (they/she) holds a Bachelor of Health Studies (Spec. Hons. Health Informatics) from York University, and is an incoming Masters of Arts in Health student specializing in Health Systems Management and Health Data Analytics at York University for September 2026. This chapter represents their first ever contribution to a published academic work, completed in their final year of study as an undergraduate student. Their scholarly interests lie at the intersection of artificial intelligence and health equity, with a particular passion for exploring how digital health innovations may be designed to promote inclusivity, accessibility, and trust in healthcare systems.

Leo Anthony Celi is the principal investigator behind the Medical Information Mart for Intensive Care (MIMIC) and its extensions (MIMIC-CXR, MIMIC-ED, MIMIC-ECHO, MIMIC-ECG), resources that serve nearly 100,000 users worldwide and have enabled over 10,000 publications, significantly shaping machine learning in healthcare. At the Massachusetts Institute of Technology, he leads MIT Critical Data, a global consortium dedicated to building local AI capacity in healthcare through open data, collaborative software, and community engagement via datathons and workshops, with a strong focus on equity and access.

Celi's research advances process-based approaches to algorithmic fairness that move beyond conventional demographic metrics, emphasizing culturally grounded human–AI systems that integrate diverse knowledge traditions, including Indigenous epistemologies and faith perspectives. In partnership with global institutions, his team has organized over 100 health data science events across more than 40 countries, broadening participation and addressing structural inequities in knowledge production.

More recently, he has developed DOJO (Distributed Open Justice Oversight), alongside complementary frameworks such as BODHI, SAKSHI, and LTARC, which support community-driven evaluation and accountability in health AI. As Editor-in-Chief of *PLOS Digital Health*, he advocates for reform in scientific publishing and leads initiatives that reimagine medical education through inclusive, interdisciplinary collaboration.

Kathleen Cherrington is a PhD Candidate in Gender, Feminist, and Women's Studies at York University. Her research examines the intersections of sexual technologies, artificial intelligence, and the political economy of sex work, with a focus on how emerging "erobotic" systems are reshaping labor, intimacy, and regulation within human-to-human sexual economies. Drawing on feminist ethnography and autoethnography, her work explores issues of consent, stigma, safety, and governance in digital sexual cultures.

Cherrington engages in research-creation through visual art and interactive media. Her painting series on cyborg femininities and AI intimacy has been exhibited at Academy of Fine Arts Vienna, Austria, and at the Love and Sex with Robots Conference at UQAM in Montreal, Canada. She is also the creator of *Porn Trivia*, an interactive board game exploring sexual cultures and knowledge production, which was showcased at The New School in New York. She was the research assistant for an arts-based performance ethnography project, *Sex Worker Diaries... Spoken and Sung*, which explores stigma and public perception through community-engaged methods.

Her work advances critical, sex worker-informed approaches to AI ethics, digital labor, and technological futures.

Ryan B. Collis is a PhD candidate in the Faculty of Education at York University, working at the intersection of education, critical disability studies, and science and technology studies. Autistic, and the father of an autistic son, Ryan focuses his research on how to improve the academic and social support provided to autistic high school students.

Ryan is a high school teacher who loves teaching and learning. He has collected a variety of degrees to make his email signature look more impressive. Ryan holds a BScH in Computer and Information Science and a BA in English Language and Literature from Queen's University, a BEd from OISE/University of Toronto, and a BScH and MA in Science and Technology Studies from York University. His PhD research is funded through a Canada Social Science and Humanities Research Council doctoral fellowship and uses cultural probes, the shared reading of science fiction, and collaborative worldbuilding with autistic participants to examine how autistic students navigate a world that was not designed for them.

Outside of his own work, Ryan is a founding co-editor of the *Canadian Journal of Autism Equity*. He lives in Ajax, Ontario with his wife, and his son studies business at Trent.

Sonia D'Angelo is a feminist sociologist and contract faculty member at Wilfrid Laurier University. Her scholarship focuses on the sociology of gender, grounded in critical femininities scholarship and intersectional feminist theory. Sonia's work addresses fundamental questions of power, inequality, and political subjectivity, with particular emphasis on how femininities are constructed, negotiated, and enacted in contemporary socio-political contexts. Her research also explores digital cultures and emerging technologies, particularly the dynamics of digital misogyny and gender-based violence within the manosphere. Sonia has taught a wide range of courses in sociology, criminology, and research methods at universities across Ontario. Her research and teaching are rooted in anti-racist and feminist approaches, demonstrating a strong commitment to critical pedagogy and community-engaged learning. Sonia envisions academia as a site of collaborative knowledge production oriented toward social transformation.

Christopher Dietzel, PhD (he/him), is an affiliate assistant professor at Concordia University, postdoctoral fellow at Western University, and research associate in the Centre for Feminist Research at York University. His research program explores the sociology of technology, with a focus on safety, health, gender, and sexuality. Dietzel is Principal Investigator of a SSHRC Insight Development Grant that examines AI in online dating, and a SSHRC Partnership Engage Grant that investigates AI-enabled bad actors in community-based digital research. He is also Co-Investigator of DIY: Digital Safety, funded by SSHRC, which examines technology-facilitated violence among youth, and Co-Investigator of the Collaboratory on Digital Equity Research, a project that studies digital harms in online dating.

Elham Dolatabadi, PhD, is an assistant professor and Tier 2 Connected Minds York research chair in Safe AI for Health Equity at York University. She is an emerging leader in machine learning (ML) for health and an affiliated faculty member at the Vector Institute. She also serves as the Lead of the Research Committee for Connected Minds. Dolatabadi has led multiple large-scale projects with hospitals, government bodies, and private-sector partners across Ontario and Canada. Her contributions to date have advanced the development of advanced ML and foundation models across six key areas: clinical diagnostic models, conversational AI, public health surveillance, algorithmic fairness, multimodal learning, and health-sensing technologies. Her research has been recognized through publications in *Nature, JAMA, JMIR, TMLR*, and *IEEE Transactions*, as well as top-tier machine learning conferences, including ACL, ICML, and MICCAI, and has received media coverage in outlets such as the *National Post*. Dolatabadi's contributions have also been supported by numerous grants and awards, including the NSERC Discovery Grant, the CIHR Special Call from the Centre for Research on Pandemic Preparedness and Health Emergencies, the Long COVID Web Seed Grant, and the Connected Minds Seed Grant.

Yahya El-Lahib is a long-time disability justice activist from Bedouin Arab background. His research, teaching, and practice center on interrogating colonial power dynamics, relations, and structures as they shape everyday realities of marginalized and oppressed social groups. Yahya's academic work questions the intersection of disability and displacement to interrogate the manifestation of settler colonialism and challenge the hegemony of Western imperialism. Yahya's current research focuses on epistemic dominance manifested through algorithmic imperialism where he calls into question the deployment of artificial intelligence as a tool for Western imperial and colonial dominance.

Christo El Morr is a global authority in health informatics and equity-driven digital health. A professor at York University and director of the Centre for Feminist Research, his scholarship sits at the critical intersection of technology and social justice, with a pioneering focus on AI and Equity. He is the author and editor of several volumes examining artificial intelligence through both technical and critical lenses. Beyond his scientific work, El Morr is a prolific voice in Arabic literature and thought; a novelist, poet, and theologian, he has published ten books on theological subjects—most notably regarding Palestine—and is a regular contributor to the Arabic press. Across all disciplines, his work remains a unified project of liberation from oppression and exploitation and a celebration of life.

Vanessa Ferguson is a PhD Candidate in Health Policy and Equity in the School of Health Policy & Management at York University. Her research examines the ethical, social, and policy implications of artificial intelligence (AI) in healthcare, with a particular focus on sickle cell disease (SCD). Drawing on interdisciplinary frameworks across health equity, science and technology studies, disability studies, and critical race scholarship, her work interrogates how emerging health technologies can reproduce or challenge existing health inequities. Vanessa's research explores issues such as bias, data justice, and patient inclusion. Her work combines critical policy analysis and community-engaged research to highlight the perspectives of those most impacted by health inequities.

Sabine Fernandes is a PhD Candidate in Critical Disability Studies at York University, where their research examines disability, care, and social reproduction through a historical materialist lens. Their dissertation, *Care as White Property*, analyzes how dominant ideas of solidarity are shaped by imperial relations of unequal exchange.

More broadly, their research experience sits at the intersection of disability justice, migration, and digital health, with a particular focus on how artificial intelligence and data systems reproduce inequities in healthcare. They are currently a research coordinator with the AI and Medical Bias project, and a collaborator on the Mobilizing Collective Inclusion Pathways to Access project.

Fernandes has published on accessible and inclusive AI, disability justice, and care work, and has presented their research at international conferences in medical informatics, disability studies, and critical policy spaces. Grounded in community-based and co-design methodologies, their work aims to develop practical tools and political strategies to challenge exclusionary systems in healthcare and education.

Benjamin Fine is an assistant professor at the University of Toronto (Temerty Faculty of Medicine), a radiologist at Trillium Health Partners, and Quality and Informatics physician lead for Diagnostic Imaging. He obtained his medical degree, residency, and fellowship training from the University of Toronto, and holds a master's degree in Engineering from the Massachusetts Institute of Technology.

Fine's research focuses on artificial intelligence (AI) in medical imaging, healthcare quality improvement, and clinical informatics. His work includes machine learning applications for radiology workflow optimization, such as automated imaging protocol selection, as well as frameworks for the evaluation and safe deployment of AI systems in clinical practice. He has also contributed to research on challenges in AI implementation, including data quality and labeling limitations, and on generalization gaps in clinical imaging models. More recently, his work has explored data drift detection in real-world medical imaging systems.

Anoop George, PhD, is an associate professor at the Indian Institute of Technology Palakkad. His research expertise lies in continental philosophy, phenomenology, existentialism, and philosophy of technology, with a particular focus on Heideggerian perspectives on the human condition.

Judy Wawira Gichoya is the William and Kay Casarella Professor of Radiology at Emory University and leads the HITI (Healthcare AI Innovation and Translational Informatics) lab. Her work is centered on using data science to study health equity. Her group works in 4 areas—building diverse datasets for machine learning (for example, the Emory Breast dataset); evaluating AI for bias and fairness; validating AI in the real world setting; and training the next generation of data scientists (both clinical and technical students) through hive learning and village mentoring. She serves as the program director for Radiology: AI Trainee Editorial Board and the Emory University medical students machine learning elective. She has mentored over 60 students across the world (now successful faculty, post doc, PHD and industry employees) from several institutions around the world. She has received several awards including the most influential radiology researcher in 2022, and is a 2023 Emerging Scholar in the National Academy of Medicine.

Rachel da Silveira Gorman is Professor and Program Director in the Graduate Program in Critical Disability Studies at York University. Gorman is an interdisciplinary scholar, working across fine arts, humanities, and sciences. Gorman's current projects focus on disability movements and community-based AI applications; disability and community-defined medical violence; and dance, disability arts, and research-creation. Gorman currently holds funding from the New Frontiers in Research Fund for a project titled *Training an AI to detect medical bias and unmet health needs through critical race and disability theory and community-generated data*. In 2024–2025, Gorman was a visiting professor at the Dalla Lana School of Public Health, University of Toronto; in 2019, Gorman held the Albrecht Global Lectureship on Disability at the University of Illinois at Chicago; and in 2017–2018, Gorman was the Lillian Robinson scholar-in-residence at the Simone de Beauvoir Institute in Montréal.

Hassan Hamidi is a PhD Candidate in Computer Science at the York University, specializing in computer vision with a focus on diffusion models and their applications in medical image analysis. His current research aims to improve the performance and explainability of medical image classification systems through the use of synthetic data, addressing key challenges related to data scarcity and model transparency in healthcare. He completed his master's degree in Artificial Intelligence at the Sharif University of Technology, where his research focused on semantic segmentation, 3D computer vision, and knowledge distillation. During this time, he developed a novel framework to enhance point cloud semantic segmentation in data-limited scenarios by integrating complementary modalities, such as images, and transferring their knowledge into point cloud-based models. This work contributed to improving both the accuracy and efficiency of 3D vision systems. His research interests include generative AI, fairness in machine learning, and AI applications in medical imaging. He is a recipient of support from the VISTA program.

Yoonmee Han (she/her) is a PhD Candidate in Science and Technology Studies at York University. She completed a master's degree in Critical Disability Studies at York University in Canada. She is a disability scholar whose work focuses on the intersection of mental health, legal safeguards, digital media, community-based research, and design justice, specifically within the context of blind studies and research by the blind and partially sighted community.

Carolina A. M. Heming, MD, is a board-certified radiologist specializing in body and oncologic imaging, advanced MRI applications, and artificial intelligence in radiology. She earned her medical degree from the Universidade Federal do Rio de Janeiro, Brazil, and completed her Diagnostic Radiology residency at the Hospital Federal dos Servidores do Rio de Janeiro. She pursued fellowships in Magnetic Resonance Imaging and in Abdominal and Pelvic Imaging at Universidade Corporativa Fleury/Labs, Brazil.

Modena Heming completed postdoctoral research training at the Radiomics and Machine Learning Laboratory, Lunenfeld-Tanenbaum Research Institute, Mount Sinai Hospital, Toronto (2021–2023), focusing on quantitative imaging, radiomics, federated learning, and AI applications in prostate MRI, later expanding into gynecologic oncology research at the University of Iowa.

She is currently a clinical assistant professor in the Department of Radiology at the University of Iowa Hospitals and Clinics, where she served as MRI Medical Director (2024–2025) and now holds the role of Interim Body Division Director. Her academic interests include oncologic MRI, imaging biomarkers, artificial intelligence, fairness in AI, and radiology education. She has published in leading journals, reviewed for *Radiology: Artificial Intelligence*, and received recognition from RSNA.

InChan Hwang is Assistant Professor of Cybersecurity at Montreat College, where he teaches courses in data mining/machine learning, AI agent development, data analytics, and applied statistics. He received PhD in Data Science & Analytics from Kennesaw State University, Kennesaw, GA, USA, where he was recognized with the Outstanding Student Award.

Hwang's research interests vary across machine learning explainability, medical image analysis, credit risk modeling, and AI-assisted diagnostics. He has collaborated with medical professionals at Emory University on AI-driven breast cancer detection and with industry partners including Truist Bank and Southern Company on applied data science projects. His work has been published in outlets such as *PLOS Digital Health*, *Frontiers in Radiology*, and *IEEE*, with over ten peer-reviewed publications to his name.

His broader interests include the intersection of AI, ethics, and society, including an AI-based text-mining study of cultural and religious discourse supported by the Atlanta Interdisciplinary AI Network. Hwang brings both academic rigor and industry experience to his interdisciplinary work on technology's impact on human communities.

Amanie Issa, a Palestinian native, is a PhD researcher jointly based at the Irish Centre for Human Rights and the Centre for Disability Law and Policy at the University of Galway. Funded by Research Ireland, her doctoral research examines the intersection of gender and disability within the framework of settler colonialism, focusing on Palestine as a case study. She holds a BA in Human Rights and International Law from Al-Quds University in Palestine, and an LLM in International Human Rights Law from the University of Galway. Alongside her academic work, Amanie serves on the Disability Advisory Committee of the Irish Human Rights and Equality Commission.

Before commencing her doctoral studies, Amanie worked with a range of NGOs and grassroots initiatives focusing on human rights, environmental justice, human trafficking, and period poverty. She also worked as a Legal Consultant with the World Bank's Women, Business and the Law project, contributing to research on advancing the rights of women with disabilities across 190 economies.

Her broader research interests and work include disability justice, artificial intelligence in armed conflict, gendered disablement, the right to health, and the agency of women and girls with disabilities, particularly within settler colonial and conflict-affected contexts.

Naleni Jacob is PhD Student in the Critical Disability Studies program at York University and an independent consultant specializing in disability and care. Her research focuses on inclusive education, with particular attention to advancing accessible and meaningful accommodations for students, newcomers, and their families.

Born in Guyana and immigrating to Canada in the 1990s, Naleni brings a rich cultural and lived perspective to her work. She studied at Loyalist College and Toronto Metropolitan University (TMU), where she continues to contribute as a guest lecturer.

A lifelong advocate for disability justice, her work is informed by her lived experience as a mother raising her son, Emeal, who has cerebral palsy. Her current research explores the intersection of artificial intelligence, social media, and disability, critically examining both the risks of stigmatization and the potential for amplifying disabled voices in digital and academic spaces.

Sammy Jo Johnson (she/her), is a PhD Candidate in the Critical Disability Studies program at York University. She also works at the Writing Centre at York, where she primarily supports deaf and disabled students. In her research, she uses community-based and participatory approaches and focuses on making universities more accessible. She doesn't think that the work of access should fall to individuals. Outside of research and teaching, she spends most of her time walking her dogs and lifting weights.

Jude Kadri is a political sociologist, researcher, and university instructor based in Montreal, Canada. She is currently a research associate at York University and a sessional lecturer at McGill University's Institute of Islamic Studies. She earned her PhD from the University of Ottawa, where her dissertation offered a socio-historical analysis of the war in Yemen. Prior to her current academic roles, she worked as an advisor on Yemen at the United Nations Economic and Social Commission for Western Asia (UN-ESCWA).

Her research centers on the war on terror, the religious dimensions of conflict, the historical transformations of capitalism, and the growing role of artificial intelligence in warfare. She has published widely in peer-reviewed journals, including *Middle East Critique*, *Labor and Society*, *Comparative Sociology*, the *International Review of Sociology*, *World Review of Political Economy*, *Cultural Logic*, *Arab Studies Quarterly*, *Digest of Middle East Studies*, and *Contemporary Arab Affairs*. Her book *Socio-Historical Roots of Yemen's War* was published by Palgrave Macmillan in May 2023. Her forthcoming book, *Historical Materialism for the Middle East*, is scheduled for publication by Brill in 2026.

Maimuna S. Khan is a PhD candidate at the School of Social Work, McMaster University and a sessional instructor at the Faculty of Social Work, University of Calgary. Her academic work relies on epistemologies of the Global South, transnational feminisms, and disability justice. Her PhD dissertation analyzes how legacies of colonialism and imperialism have continued through state care and how social work as a profession sanctions anti-Muslim racism and violence through its practice. Maimuna's current research also examines how artificial intelligence operates as a tool of colonial modernity, manifesting in imperial and colonial violence in the Global South.

Mojtaba Kolahdouzi is a postdoctoral fellow in the Department of Computer Science at the York University and a visiting researcher at the Vector Institute for Artificial Intelligence. His research focuses on fair and safe artificial intelligence, with particular emphasis on understanding how training dynamics influence fairness and safety, developing label-free fairness-enhancing frameworks, and designing methods for deepfake detection and facial expression recognition. He received his PhD in Computer Engineering from the Queen's University, where his dissertation introduced novel approaches to improving fairness in machine learning and examined the impact of optimization algorithms on group fairness in deep learning models. His work has been published in leading venues, including NeurIPS, Transactions on Machine Learning Research (TMLR), IEEE Transactions on Artificial Intelligence, ICMI, FG, and IJCB. Kolahdouzi's research has been recognized through several competitive awards, including the Connected Minds Postdoctoral Fellowship and the VISTA Postdoctoral Fellowship.

Salamata Konate is a postdoctoral researcher in Computer Science at the York University, where her work focuses on improving the interpretability and explainability of machine learning models, particularly in computer vision and healthcare applications. Her research aims to bridge the gap between complex AI systems and human understanding, enabling more transparent, trustworthy, and clinically reliable decision-making in domains such as medical imaging and diagnostics. She received her PhD from the Queensland University of Technology, where she developed visual interpretability techniques for machine learning models. Her doctoral research contributed to advancing methods that clarify how AI systems process and analyze visual data, with a particular emphasis on improving the reliability and accountability of AI-driven tools in healthcare. Konate's research interests include explainable and interpretable

AI, fairness in machine learning, and AI applications in medical imaging. She has contributed to projects that enhance both the transparency and performance of AI systems in critical, real-world settings.

Nolan Krahn (he/him) is an MA candidate in Sociology at York University, set to defend his MA thesis in August 2026. His research interests span social movements, disability justice, and AI discourse. Placing theories from political sociology and critical disability studies into dialogue, his thesis focuses on the potential for disability justice to expand the tactical repertoires of multi-issue, intersectional social movements. Nolan's analyses are informed by historical literature on Canadian disability rights movements, public documents found on the websites of two disability justice organizations in Southern Ontario, and publicly available blog posts written by disabled activists. The insights from these writings suggest that current sociological conceptions of social movement tactics neglect the activities of disability justice activists. Nolan is a member of York's Disability Justice Research Cluster, and plans to continue working with the cluster as he pursues a PhD in Sociology at McMaster University.

Andre William Kushniruk is a professor in the School of Health Information Science at the University of Victoria. He holds undergraduate degrees in Psychology and Biology, an MSc in Computer Science, and a PhD in Cognitive Psychology. An elected member of the International Academy of Health Sciences Informatics, the Canadian Academy of Health Sciences, he is a fellow of the American College of Medical Informatics. He conducts research in several areas, including evaluation of the effects of technology, human-computer interaction in health care, human-centered AI, and usability engineering.

Kushniruk's research focuses on developing new methods for evaluating information technology and conducting video analysis of computer users. He has extended this research to remote studies of e-health applications, virtual healthcare, and advanced information technologies, including electronic health record systems and AI applications. He has been a key researcher on many national and international collaborative projects and has held academic positions at several Canadian universities. Besides his research with the publication of over 300 scholarly peer-reviewed articles and as a co-editor of several books in health informatics, Kushniruk has mentored numerous students and is actively involved in teaching, bridging academia to industry.

Andrea Lachmansingh is a PhD candidate at York University. As a Canada Graduate Scholarship—Doctoral (CGS D) fellow, her interdisciplinary research examines the politics of AI-driven surveillance technologies. Through her framework, Infrastructures of Securitization, she analyzes how transnational vendor dependencies, commercial data extraction, and algorithmic threat construction are reconfiguring security and sovereignty, particularly across policing and intelligence institutions.

Mina Mir is an ABD PhD candidate in the Department of Politics at York University, assistant editor at Big Data & Society, and Gale Digital Humanities fellow. Her doctoral research investigates the socio-technical construction of algorithms and artificial intelligence (AI), with particular attention to datafication, platformization, and the infrastructures of biometric surveillance technologies such as computer vision and facial recognition. Her MA research, "The Securitisation of Facial Recognition Technology: The Case of Clearview AI", analyzed how private firms become entangled with state security bureaucracies and integrated into wider infrastructures of security governance. She has presented her work at international conferences across Canada, the UK, the EU, and Brazil. Her research has also contributed to policy debates on data privacy in Canada and the UK, highlighting the risks of third-party tracking in 'mHealth' (mobile health) applications and the governance of intimate data infrastructures. Her recent publications include an article in New Media & Society and forthcoming chapters on biometric visual technologies.

Shahram Mohanna is an academic in the Department of Electronics and Electrical Engineering at the University of Bath, UK. He previously served as a Research Associate at the Responsible AI Research Lab at the University of York, where he contributed to research on responsible and ethical artificial intelligence, with a particular focus on healthcare applications.

Mohanna has over ten years of teaching experience in higher education across several international institutions. He received his PhD in Electronic Engineering from the University of Manchester in 2006. From 2012 to 2016, he was an associate professor at the University of Nottingham Malaysia and then continued his academic career at the University of Sistan and Baluchestan.

He has published 31 articles in indexed journals and presented 18 papers at international conferences. His early research focused on impedance tomography and microwave imaging, while his current work centeres on responsible and trustworthy AI, particularly in healthcare. His interdisciplinary research spans electronic communication systems, fairness, and bias in AI for health applications.

Amirreza Naziri is a machine learning engineer and researcher specializing in the development and scaling of sophisticated deep learning architectures. Having recently graduated with an MSc in Computer Science from York University, he currently works in the AI industry, focusing on translating advanced research into production-ready solutions.

His technical expertise is centered on Generative Models, including Diffusion Models and Variational Autoencoders (VAEs), as well as Large Language Models (LLMs). Amirreza has extensive experience applying Graph Neural Networks (GNNs) and Transformers to high-dimensional foundation models, achieving significant improvements in data interpretation accuracy.

Fouâd Oveisy is a PhD Candidate in Political Science at York University and a former Lecturer in Artificial Intelligence at the University of Toronto. He previously completed a PhD in Critical Theory at the University of California, Irvine. His current research examines how the strategic cultures of Canadian, American, and Chinese foreign-policy institutions become embedded in their AI models, and how Canada can influence global AI governance and promote value-aligned regulation to de-escalate the AI arms race. Drawing on consultation work for Global Affairs Canada and a two-pillar research design that combines comparative fieldwork with training a publicly accessible foreign policy model, he proposes a "Third Option" framework that grounds Canadian digital sovereignty in equity, Indigenous rights, and rules-based multilateralism. His research is rooted in a commitment to public scholarship and in blending strategic analysis with the prototyping of open-source AI tools for civic use. A former SSHRC, CGS, and IPIC fellow, he currently supports Professor Jennifer Pybus's project on democratic digital governance.

Artur Parkhimchyk is a Master's Student in Computer Vision and Artificial Intelligence at York University. He earned his Bachelor's degree in Physics from York University and went on to work as a lead developer at RBC Capital Markets.

Prateeksha Pathak is a PhD candidate in the Department of Geography at York University and a research assistant at Athabasca University in Canada. Her research interests include Political Geography, Visual Culture, AI & Equity Studies, and Gender Studies.

Ayissha Pavakopethan is a Master of Health Industry Administration candidate at the Schulich School of Business. She holds a Bachelor of Health Studies (Specialized Honours) in Health Management, Policy, and Digital Health from York University. Her academic work is situated at the intersection of health systems management, digital health, and health equity, with a particular focus on the social and ethical implications of emerging technologies in healthcare.

Her research interests include artificial intelligence in healthcare, health inequities, digital governance, and the ways technological innovation can both mitigate and reproduce structural disparities in access, quality, and health outcomes. She has contributed to research examining AI-based epidemic early warning systems, the ethical deployment of data-driven technologies, and the implications of digital transformation for equity-deserving populations.

In addition to her academic work, Ayissha has held roles in health system strategy and analytics at Trillium Health Partners and Reconnect Health Services, where she has supported organizational planning, performance analysis, and system improvement initiatives. Her work reflects a broader commitment to advancing equitable, evidence-informed health policy and organizational decision-making.

Janise Peters is an adjunct lecturer at the University of Toronto's Institute of Health Policy, Management and Evaluation and a recognized Leader in Health Informatics and Operations. Currently serving as the Director of Operations for The Black Fathers Alliance, Janise drives strategic alignment and community advocacy to support fathers and families.

Her scholarly work sits at the critical intersection of artificial intelligence and health equity. Janise specifically investigates the implications of AI deployment in clinical settings, examining how these technologies may reinforce or mitigate systemic biases in health quality. A committed educator, she recently developed the "Responsible AI in Healthcare" micro-credential course and is a frequent speaker on the potential for AI to scale inequities within healthcare systems.

Janise holds a Master of Health Informatics from the University of Waterloo and an Honours Bachelor of Science in Psychology from the University of Toronto. She resides in Simcoe County, Ontario, where she is a devoted wife to her partner and proud mother to their four boys.

Krystal A. Porter is Doctoral Student in Systems Engineering at the University of Virginia and holds a Master of Engineering degree. Her work focuses on the intersection of artificial intelligence, systems engineering, healthcare, and defense, with an emphasis on responsible innovation and mission-critical applications. She is particularly interested in how emerging technologies can be designed, governed, and deployed in ways that are ethical, equitable, and effective. Her broader research interests include AI lifecycle systems, human-centered technology, and the policy and organizational considerations that shape responsible AI adoption. Porter brings a multidisciplinary perspective informed by technical expertise, applied research, and a commitment to translating complex ideas into practical impact. Her contribution to this edited volume reflects her dedication to exploring how AI can be developed and used in service of a just and equitable world.

Shruti Raji-Kalyanaraman is Doctoral Candidate in Gender, Feminist and Women's Studies at York University, and a community college professor at Seneca Polytechnic. Her doctoral dissertation is titled "Social Reproduction, Governmentality and Resilience: First Generation Immigrant Women's Narratives on Community Food Work".

Her doctoral fieldwork, conducted in partnership with food advocacy organizations, examines unpaid and underpaid labor among first-generation immigrant women volunteers, revealing how community care work sustains non-profit operations and immigrant wellbeing. This work informs her emerging research on AI literacy, ethics, and responsible adoption in immigrant social reproduction, building on her accepted book chapter on AI and household care.

Her research spans 18 years of qualitative and feminist economic inquiry, focusing on gendered labor, social reproduction, immigrant community work, and the future of work with artificial intelligence. She has led research projects in the areas of feminist economics, gender and work, sustainability, economic democracy, and community advocacy. She has extensive training across psychology, management, gender studies, and AI ethics.

A first-generation immigrant woman and educator, Shruti brings lived experience, interdisciplinary expertise, and strong community networks to her scholarship. Her work is supported by major institutional, provincial (Ontario Graduate Scholarship), and federal (SSHRC Doctoral Fellowship) awards of over $200,000 CAD.

Aaron Richmond, PhD, is a visually disabled independent researcher whose work is located at the intersection of literary disability studies and disability studies in education. Recently Aaron and his co-authors have published an article in the Harvard Educational Review (2025), and contributed a chapter to the (2025) edited collection Beyond Tech Fixes: Towards an AI Future Where Disability Justice Thrives. Additionally, Aaron and his coauthors' work will be published in the upcoming edited collection Rewiring for Artificial Intelligence: Education, Contemporary Issues, and Futurities. In each of their publications Aaron and his coauthors have critically examined the representation of disability in AI-generated flash fiction stories through which they have developed the theory of disability evasiveness. Aaron is currently employed as a resource facilitator at the Happy Valley-Goose Bay Campus of the College of the North Atlantic in Labrador Canada.

Courtney C. Rogers, PhD, MPH, is an epidemiologist and systems engineer whose work sits at the intersection of health equity, human-centered design, and social justice. She holds a PhD in Systems Engineering and a Master of Public Health from the University of Virginia. As an Epidemic Intelligence Service Officer with the U.S. Centers for Disease Control and Prevention, she led studies on structural drivers of health inequity and provided technical assistance to international partners on integrating health equity principles into public health programs. Her research spans digital health, maternal health access, disability inclusion, and community-based participatory methods, with a consistent focus on centering the experiences of marginalized communities.

Vaibhav Sawhney is a PhD Student in Health Systems Management and Data Analytics at the School of Health Policy and Management, York University. His research examines the ethical, fair, and equitable use of artificial intelligence in healthcare and public health. He holds a Master's degree in Health System Management and Analytics and a Bachelor's degree in Health Studies, graduating summa cum laude.

Vaibhav has interdisciplinary experience in public health practice, program evaluation, and data analysis. He currently serves as a health promoter and evaluation analyst at the Alliance for South Asian AIDS Prevention (ASAAP), where he contributes to community-based health initiatives and equity-driven programming. His research interests include decolonizing digital health, algorithmic bias and fairness, disability justice, and the role of AI in shaping health systems and policy.

His work aims to advance inclusive, accountable, and community-centered approaches to the design and governance of AI in health.

Gabi Schaffzin is an artist, educator, and researcher based in Toronto. He is currently an associate professor in the Department of Design at York University's School of Arts, Media, Performance, and Design. He holds a PhD in Art History, Theory, and Criticism from the University of California San Diego and an MFA from the Massachusetts College of Art & Design's Dynamic Media Institute. His current project combines design history, disability studies, and a history of computing to trace the history of designed pain scales in the United States throughout the 20th century.

Julia Scialla, School of Medicine, University of Virginia, Charlottesville, Virginia, USA

Laleh Seyyed-Kalantari is an assistant professor at York University's Lassonde School of Engineering and a faculty affiliate at the Vector Institute. She earned her PhD in Electrical Engineering from McMaster University and completed her NSERC Postdoctoral Fellowship (2019–2022) at the Vector Institute and the University of Toronto. Her research centers on AI safety, risk, bias, and interpretability, aiming to mitigate bias and prevent digital exclusion across cultural, social, and healthcare domains. At her Responsible AI Lab, she leverages generative AI and foundation models with adaptive design strategies to improve model performance for underrepresented groups and promote equitable access, representation, and cultural inclusion in AI systems. While her work often applies to health and societal contexts, her broader goal is to develop AI systems that embed cultural and ethical awareness, ensuring technology serves diverse communities responsibly. Seyyed-Kalantari also contributes to policy efforts through the AI Insights for Policymakers Program, initiated by CIFAR and Mila—Quebec Artificial Intelligence Institute (2024–2025). Her accolades include the Google Research Scholar Award (2024), two York University Research Award (2025) for Outstanding Early Career and Significant Knowledge Mobilization & Impact, NSERC Postdoctoral Fellowship (2018), and the Banting Postdoctoral Fellowship (2022, declined). Her pioneering work on fairness in medical imaging has been featured in several prominent technology news outlets.

Michael G. Sherbert is an Algonquin of Pikwàkanagàn First Nation and a postdoctoral fellow with the Connected Minds initiative at Queen's University, where his research explores the ethical, religious, and cultural dimensions of emerging technologies, including artificial intelligence. His work brings Indigenous perspectives into critical dialogue with technological development, with a particular focus on relationality, responsibility, Indigenous data sovereignty, and the socio-cultural assumptions embedded in contemporary AI systems.

Sherbert's interdisciplinary scholarship sits at the intersection of religion, culture, and the philosophy of technology. His research examines the ideological and quasi-religious dimensions of transhumanism, culminating in his recent book *Deconstructing Transhumanism: A Religion Without Religion* (Routledge). He is also engaged in projects exploring technology in relation to disability, embodiment, and ethics, including contributions to the Canadian Space Agency's Health Beyond Initiative, where he has worked on inclusive and culturally grounded approaches to healthcare technologies.

His work has been published in academic journals and edited volumes, and he regularly contributes to conversations on AI ethics, Indigenous futurisms, and the social implications of emerging technologies. Through his research, Sherbert advocates for more inclusive, critically reflexive, and relational approaches to technological development.

Damanjot Singh is a multidisciplinary professional based in Ontario, Canada, with a background in healthcare, data analytics, and applied research. He holds a Bachelor of Health Studies (Honours) with a major in Health Informatics from York University and a postgraduate diploma in Chemical Laboratory Technician from Seneca College.

He has worked as a data analyst with Preyra Solutions Group, where he supported projects focused on data-driven insights and business decision-making. He also gained valuable experience at Scarborough Health Network, contributing to healthcare analytics and helping teams make more informed decisions. During his time at York University, he worked as a research assistant under Christo El Morr, exploring the role of technology in shaping health and social outcomes.

His interests lie in how data and emerging technologies, such as artificial intelligence, can be used to create fairer and more accessible systems. He brings a practical and thoughtful approach to his work, shaped by real-world experience, curiosity, and a strong commitment to continuous.

Maverick Smith is a PhD Candidate in Critical Disability Studies in the Faculty of Health at York University who focuses on realizing disability futurity by creating accessible futures. Maverick is an academic, activist, and author who has both an MEd and an MA, the latter of which won the 2022 Bengt Lindqvist Human Rights Prize in Critical Disability Studies. In addition to disability justice and intersectionality, their interdisciplinary research interests include social policy, critical disability theory, human rights, and social justice.

Seyed Matin Tavakoli Afshari is a PhD Student in Computer Science at York University, specializing in Responsible AI with a particular focus on bias, fairness, and reliability in AI systems. He earned his MSc in Software Engineering and Intelligent Systems from the University of Alberta and his BSc in Computer Engineering from Amirkabir University of Technology.

His research spans autonomous driving, object detection, and multimodal learning, aiming to address critical issues of reliability and transparency in AI models. His current work emphasizes developing parameter-efficient techniques and fairness-aware representations to ensure AI transparency in high-stakes applications.

Elizabeth U. Thompson is a PhD Candidate in Systems Engineering at the University of Virginia. Her research is conducted in collaboration with the UVA School of Medicine under the guidance of Rupa Valdez and Julia Scialla. Her work focuses on healthcare AI, fairness, and how clinical decision-support systems interact with real-world care conditions. Her recent work examines how care instability can influence the behavior of EHR-trained AI systems for treatment recommendations in in-center hemodialysis. More broadly, her work examines how AI systems should be designed and evaluated when the constructs they aim to measure are socially, clinically, and contextually dependent, particularly in settings where no ground truth exists.

Hari Trivedi is Associate Professor in the Department of Radiology and Imaging Sciences with joint appointment in the Department of Biomedical Informatics. As co-director of the HITI Lab, his research areas include the application of machine learning (artificial intelligence) to solve problems in radiology, including development of large, multi-modal datasets and developing algorithms related to breast imaging.

Rupa S. Valdez is an interdisciplinary researcher whose work focuses on understanding and designing solutions to support how people manage health at home and within their communities. Drawing on methods from human factors engineering, cultural anthropology, health informatics, and related fields, her research examines how social networks, physical environments, community resources, and information technologies shape patient experiences and health management practices. Her work emphasizes participatory and co-design methodologies, with particular attention to equity and the lived experiences of underserved populations, including low-wealth communities, rural populations, communities of color, and people with disabilities.

In addition to her applied research, Valdez is actively engaged in methodological development for research and teaching in health and technology contexts. She has testified before the U.S. Congress and holds leadership and advisory roles across multiple national organizations. She serves as Associate Editor for *Ergonomics* and *JAMIA Open*, sits on the Board of Directors for the American Association of People with Disabilities, and advises organizations including the Agency for Healthcare Research and Quality, the National Committee for Quality Assurance, and the National Academy of Sciences, Engineering, and Medicine. She previously served on Patient-Centered Outcomes Research Institute's Patient Engagement Advisory Panel and is the Founder and President of the Blue Trunk Foundation

Ellouise Van Berkel is a PhD candidate in the Faculty of Education at York University in Toronto; her work sits at the intersections of education, critical access studies, technology, artificial intelligence, inclusion, and critical disabilities studies. Her research draws on critical disability studies and critical access studies to examine the relationships between students, technology, and schooling that shape educational experiences.

Jessica Vorstermans (she/her) is an associate professor in the School of Health Policy & Management and School of Global Health at York University. Her research interests include critical AI refusal, transnationalism, and critical disability approaches to transformative change, equity, and solidarity. Her geographical focus is on Latin America, Cuba in particular. She is an interdisciplinary scholar with plural threads of inquiry rooted in relationship with transnational communities and activists doing equity, anti-racism, anti-colonial, and anti-capitalist work and resistance. Her research is guided by multiple lines of inquiry that, together, works to understand how the processes of colonization and disablement have organized, and continue to organize, our world and the ways this is hidden, erased, and pushed out of our systems of knowledge.

MinJae Woo, PhD, is Assistant Professor of Data Science in the Department of Public Health at Clemson University. His work sits at the intersection of artificial intelligence, public health, and information systems, with a focus on fairness, transparency, and the responsible deployment of predictive models. Woo's research emphasizes the necessity of moving beyond performance metrics to make sure that AI systems deliver meaningful, real-world impact for patients, consumers, and underserved populations. His recent work explores methods to identify and mitigate bias in machine learning systems, as well as frameworks for aligning AI innovation with ethical, clinical, and societal needs. He has led multi-institutional collaborations across academia and industry, developing explainable and equitable AI applications in healthcare and finance.

Woo earned his PhD in Biomedical Data Science and Informatics through a joint program between Clemson University and the Medical University of South Carolina, and holds a BS in Mathematics and Economics from the University of California, Los Angeles

Huan Wu is a Master of Computer Science student at York University, where he conducts research under the supervision of Laleh Seyyed-Kalantari in the Responsible AI Lab. He is also affiliated with the Vector Institute as a faculty affiliate researcher. His research focuses on AI fairness, responsible AI, and natural language processing, with a particular interest in dialect bias in large language models.

His current work studies how language models process dialectal variation, especially the differences between African American English and Standard American English. His recent work on bias benchmarking in large language models was accepted to the ACL 2026 Main Conference. More broadly, his research aims to develop evaluation methods and mitigation strategies that make NLP systems fairer, more reliable, and more inclusive for diverse linguistic communities.

Linglin Zhang received her BS in Biological Sciences from Hubei University in 2016. She then pursued graduate studies in the United States, earning an MS in Chemical Biology from the University of Michigan in 2017, an MS in Bioinformatics from Georgia Institute of Technology in 2020, and a PhD in Data Science and Analytics from Kennesaw State University in 2024. She is currently a data scientist at Equifax. Her research interests include responsible AI, model robustness, and fairness-aware machine learning, with a focus on AI-driven decision-making.

Nicole Zhang is a Bachelor of Health Studies student at York University in Toronto. Her research interests span digital health, health informatics, and health policy, with a focus on how technology shapes clinical workflows and the patient experience. Drawing on her experience as a diagnostic medical sonographer, as well as her perspective as a patient, she brings a practical, patient-centered approach to her work. She is particularly interested in how health systems can better serve the people who use them, and plans to pursue graduate studies in the health sciences.

Acknowledgments

We would like to express our sincere gratitude to the reviewers who generously gave their time and expertise to evaluate chapters in this volume. Their careful readings, constructive critiques, and thoughtful suggestions significantly strengthened the clarity, rigor, and coherence of the contributions. This book is substantially improved thanks to the reviewers' engagement and scholarly insight.

We gratefully acknowledge the following reviewers (listed alphabetically):

- Abeer Badawi, PhD
- Habiba Rahman, PhD (Candidate)
- Hirut Melaku, MA
- Julian Wee Tom, MA
- Lynn LaCroix, MA
- Matin Tavakoli (Candidate)
- Mohammad Khair Nahhas, PhD
- Mojtaba Kolahdouzi, PhD
- Nedward WD Rehanek, MA
- Pedram Noghani Ardestani, PhD (Candidate)
- Prateeksha Pathak, PhD (Candidate)
- Puja Chauhan, MA
- Sabine Fernandes, PhD (Candidate)
- Salamata Konate, PhD
- Sepideh Nahali, PhD (Candidate)
- Shahram Mohanna, PhD
- Stanley Abhadiomhen, PhD
- Vanessa Ferguson, PhD (Candidate)

Beyond the Myth of Neutral Machines

Christo El Morr, Rachel da Silveira Gorman, Elham Dolatabadi, and Laleh Seyyed-Kalantari

Artificial intelligence (AI) has been celebrated as a symbol of progress: faster, smarter, and more efficient than any previous human-made tool. Yet behind the glow of innovation, there's a question as old as modernity—who benefits, and who is left behind?

AI for a Just World: Power, Liberation, and the People Left Behind brings together scholars, engineers, artists, clinicians, educators, and community organizers who reject the myth of technological neutrality. Across disciplines and regions, the contributors share a core belief: AI systems are never just technical artifacts. They are shaped by histories of colonialism, racial capitalism, patriarchy, ableism, and settler violence. Their logics of optimization and prediction do not simply mirror society—they actively reproduce and reinforce its hierarchies.

This volume is not only an account of harm but also an act of collective imagination. Together, these chapters explore pathways toward technologies rooted in care, relationality, accountability, and liberation. They inquire what it would mean to design, govern, and evaluate AI systems that redistribute power instead of consolidating it and that see justice not as a technical constraint but as a political commitment.

FROM FAIRNESS TO LIBERATION

Public discourse on "ethical AI" has primarily focused on fairness metrics, transparency tools, and accountability frameworks. While important, these strategies remain inadequate. Fairness does not undo structural injustice, and transparency alone does not ensure justice. As the chapters in this volume demonstrate, bias is not a technical glitch—it is a social legacy embedded in data, institutions, and ways of knowing.

This book therefore advances a shift from fairness to liberation. Fairness asks whether outcomes are evenly distributed; liberation asks who defines the outcomes, whose knowledge counts, and who holds power over design and governance. Fairness refines algorithms; liberation reimagines systems. Justice in AI demands rejecting what Ruha Benjamin describes as the "default settings" of inequality—a rejection that is carried out through ongoing collaboration between technical experts and communities historically excluded from technological decision-making.

The architecture of *AI for a Just World* reflects this commitment to relational knowledge and shared accountability. This book is organized across six interlinked parts, each grounded in a sector of practice—health, disability, education, labor, governance, and decolonial critique—while remaining in active dialogue with the others. Rather than treating disability, race, gender, or colonialism as "applications" of AI ethics, this volume positions them as epistemic anchors for understanding how AI systems operate in the world.

A defining contribution of this volume is its sustained engagement with Disability Justice, not merely as an ethical concern but as a policy, governance, and design imperative. Building on the 2025 edited volume *Beyond Tech Fixes: Towards an AI Future Where Disability Justice Thrives*, the addition of a section on *Disability, Education, and Techno-Ableism* deepens this commitment to radical anti-ableism. The section opens with our chapter "Disability-centered Policy Opportunities and Challenges for Accessible and Inclusive AI: A Scoping Review", which moves us beyond individual tools or accommodations to examine the policy infrastructures that shape whose access, participation, and expertise are recognized across the AI lifecycle. Drawing on Disability Justice and participatory governance, it demonstrates that accessibility cannot be retrofitted—it must be structurally embedded from inception to outcomes.

OVERVIEW OF THIS VOLUME

Part 1: AI, Equity, and Health Justice situates AI within healthcare systems where data, diagnosis, and care are unevenly distributed. These chapters interrogate racialized norms, proxy fairness, institutional barriers, benchmarking practices, foundation models, and clinical simulation, reframing health justice as a design principle rather than a downstream outcome.

Part 2: Disability, Education, and Techno-Ableism expands this book's engagement with disability beyond critique to policy, pedagogy, and participatory design. In addition to analyses of sickle cell disease, STEM education, social media, and techno-ableism, the newly added disability-centered policy chapter foregrounds the structural conditions under which AI can either reproduce exclusion or enable collective access. Together, these chapters insist that disability is not a deficit to be corrected but a site of political knowledge, methodological innovation, and governance reform.

Part 3: AI in Society—Gender, Labor, and Social Relations examines how AI mediates social reproduction, intimacy, and violence. From epistemic injustice and misogynistic infrastructures to dating platforms and global labor regimes, these chapters demonstrate how algorithmic systems reconfigure power in everyday life.

Part 4: Governance, Power, and Bias in AI Systems confronts the institutional and geopolitical dimensions of AI. Chapters address higher education under generative AI, cognitive usability, leftist approaches to geopolitical analysis, border securitization, settler-colonial violence, and algorithmic disablement. Governance emerges not as a neutral administrative task but as a terrain of struggle.

Part 5: Decolonial and Philosophical Critiques of AI turns to ontological and ethical foundations. Drawing on Indigenous relational ethics, posthumanism, animism, Marxist analysis, and phenomenology, these chapters unsettle dominant assumptions about intelligence, agency, and technological progress.

TOWARD AN AI FOR JUSTICE FRAMEWORK

Across its parts, *AI for a Just World* advances a shared proposition: AI justice will not emerge from better code alone. It requires redistributive politics, participatory governance, disability-centered policy, Indigenous sovereignty, and care-based design practices. This volume emphasizes leadership by those most impacted—disabled people, racialized communities, migrants, and colonized populations—not as consultees but as decision-makers.

This book is grounded in the recognition that data are never raw, that technologies are never neutral, and that justice is not an add-on. To pursue equity in AI is to confront history directly and to choose repair over repetition.

LIVING OTHERWISE

We live in a moment when algorithmic systems decide who receives care, who is surveilled, who is employable, and who disappears into statistical invisibility. The choice before us is stark: to allow AI to deepen extraction and control, or to claim it as a site of liberation.

AI for a Just World takes the second path. It is both diagnosis and blueprint—a collective refusal of inevitability and a rehearsal of alternative futures. It invites readers not only to critique AI, but to build, govern, and live otherwise.

In this spirit, this book is not a final word but an opening: a living manifesto for co-creation, shared responsibility, and justice in the age of the machine.

ACKNOWLEDGMENT

The authors acknowledge the use of ChatGPT version 5 and Grammarly 1.147.1 for assistance with English-language editing, including the improvement of sentence structure and clarity.

Part 1

AI, Equity, and Health Justice

This section examines how artificial intelligence (AI) is being developed and deployed across health systems, with particular attention to its implications for equity, access, and clinical decision-making. The chapters move beyond narrow accounts of algorithmic bias to interrogate how data practices, design assumptions, and institutional contexts reproduce health inequities. Together, they establish health as a foundational site for evaluating whether AI can meaningfully support justice-oriented care.

DOI: 10.1201/9781003737810-1

1 Artificial Intelligence and the Pursuit of Equity

A Scoping Review of Benefits, Harms, and Gaps

Prateeksha Pathak, Nicole Zhang, Ayissha Pavakopethan, Amir Bayat and Christo El Morr

INTRODUCTION

AI has moved from the field of technical research to become a significant presence across different sectors of society (El Morr, 2022), including health (Rajpurkar et al., 2022), education (Nagi et al., 2023), disability (El Morr et al., 2027; Gorman et al., 2024), finance (Svetlova, 2022), and governance (Gasser, 2023). Systems once confined to experimental laboratories are now embedded in routine practices, shaping eligibility for loans, prioritization of healthcare, allocation of social resources, and access to education. This rapid diffusion has intensified the urgency of examining not only whether AI systems are technically efficient but also whether they are equitable (Nong et al., 2024). AI systems often operate in opaque ways; therefore, the influence of these systems is not always immediately visible, yet their effects can be far-reaching. A systematic review of this terrain is essential to assess the extent to which AI has become a tool that either narrows or widens social gaps.

The importance of equity in AI cannot be understood without recognizing the ways in which data and algorithms intersect with existing socioeconomic structures. Historical patterns of discrimination and inequality are often embedded within the data used for training AI systems (Prince & Schwarcz, 2019). In turn, these systems risk reinforcing stereotypes, magnifying disadvantages, and legitimizing disparities under a veneer of technical neutrality (Xavier, 2025). Equity-oriented analysis thus requires a dual lens: one that examines the internal mechanics of AI development and another that considers how these technologies interact with broader social, economic, and political inequalities. By addressing both, scholarship can move beyond narrow metrics of "fairness" and instead interrogate the deeper societal consequences of algorithmic decision-making.

At the same time, questions of equity in AI are increasingly entering the domains of policy, governance, and public debate. International organizations, regional regulators, and national governments are beginning to articulate frameworks for "trustworthy" and "responsible" AI, often with equity as a central concern (Barletta et al., 2023). Discussions around accountability, transparency, and inclusiveness have become prominent, reflecting growing recognition that AI systems cannot be left to market forces alone. This broader discourse underscores the timeliness of this review, as it situates empirical and conceptual research within an evolving landscape of societal expectations and governance efforts. By doing so, it contributes both to academic understanding and to the practical challenge of shaping AI systems that are consistent with values of justice and inclusion.

The aim of this scoping review is to systematically map the existing literature on the interplay between artificial intelligence (AI) and equity, with a particular focus on how AI technologies impact equity across various domains such as healthcare, employment, education, and social services. The review seeks to: (1) identify how AI systems have been shown to either promote or undermine equity in different contexts; (2) examine the definitions and conceptualizations of "equity"

DOI: 10.1201/9781003737810-2

as used in the literature on AI; (3) explore the mechanisms, pathways, or design choices through which AI influences structural, procedural, and outcome-based equity; (4) map the populations, settings (e.g., urban, rural, clinical, educational), and sectors (e.g., health, finance, governance) where equity-related impacts are most commonly studied; and (5) highlight gaps in the literature to inform future research, policy, and practice that seek to ensure AI contributes to justice and inclusion.

METHODS

Search Strategy

The Population, Concept, and Context method was used to guide the search strategy for this scoping review. A systematic search was conducted across six online databases: IEEE Xplore, ACM Digital Library, Web of Science, PubMed, EBSCO, and ProQuest.

Population: The search targeted studies addressing human populations in relation to equity impacts of AI, with no restrictions on population type.

Concept: The search aimed to identify research related to "artificial intelligence," including terms such as "artificial intelligence," "AI," "machine learning," and related technologies.

Context: The review encompassed a broad range of domains, including healthcare, employment, education, social services, and governance, where AI's impacts on equity are examined.

The search terms were refined in consultation with the research team to ensure comprehensive coverage of relevant scholarly and grey literature. The search yielded 3,628 records, of which 954 duplicate records were removed. A total of 2,674 records were screened. The complete search strategies are provided in Appendix A.

Eligibility Criteria

We included studies that examined the relationship between AI technologies and equity, addressing how AI systems promote or undermine equity in domains such as healthcare, employment, education, social services, and governance. Eligible studies engaged with the concept of *equity* (structural, procedural, or outcome-based) and included empirical research, conceptual or theoretical papers, systematic, scoping, or narrative reviews, and relevant grey literature. The included studies spanned publications from approximately 2019 to 2025, reflecting the rapid growth of scholarship on AI and equity during this period. No geographic restrictions were applied; only English-language publications were included.

Studies were excluded if they did not substantively address AI or its equity implications, focused solely on technical performance without discussing equity, or addressed algorithmic fairness without linking it to real-world equity impacts or justice considerations. We also excluded purely computational studies without human or social relevance, as well as opinion pieces and non-English publications.

Selection Process

The inclusion and exclusion criteria were applied to 2,674 records screened after duplicate removal. Two authors (PP and NZ) used Rayyan software to screen 2,674 records, of which 234 were identified as potentially eligible and assessed for eligibility through full-text review. No records were unretrievable. Both authors reviewed the full-text version of the 234 articles retrieved for eligibility; 2 could not be retrieved, and 110 articles met the inclusion criteria and were retained for further analysis (Figure 1.1). During full-text screening, additional exclusions were applied, including studies that were reviews, not on machine learning, or not addressing equity. The literature search and article collection were conducted by a single author (PP), while the full-text review and data collection from articles were conducted collaboratively by four authors (PP, NZ, AP, AB). In case of ambiguities or disagreements, consensus was reached through discussion and consultation with the fifth author (CEM). The PRISMA diagram (Figure 1A.1) and the studies found (Table 1A.1) are listed in the Appendix.

KEY FINDINGS

Bias and Mitigation

Bias: Across the included studies, common findings highlight that AI systems often reflect existing biases and can inadvertently perpetuate inequities if not carefully managed (Duarte et al., 2024; Hong et al., 2023; Hutchinson et al., 2020; Jenks et al., 2024; J. D. Kong et al., 2023; Y. Kong, 2022; La Fors & Meissner, 2022; Lalor et al., 2024). For instance, Suresh and Guttag (2021) identify seven potential sources of downstream harm throughout the machine learning pipeline (from data collection to deployment), demonstrating that bias can enter at many stages and cause two main types of harm: unequal distribution of opportunities (*allocative harm*) and distorted representation of groups (*representational harm*). This is reflected in studies covering several sectors, including health, public opinion, border control, education, finance, and hiring.

Health: Xu et al. (2024), for example, found that deep learning models for medical imaging can produce unfair diagnostic outcomes for underrepresented patient groups if fairness issues are not addressed, potentially leading to underdiagnosis and harm.

Opinion: Chen et al. (2024) highlight that conversational AI systems like GPT-3 often deliver worse user experiences to opinion-minority groups (e.g., climate deniers, racists) and education-minority groups (e.g., those with lower levels of formal education), reinforcing inequities in knowledge access and expression. Their audit of 20,000 dialogues revealed that marginalized users faced more negative tone in AI responses and had disproportionately higher attitude change, raising concerns about manipulation and cognitive equity.

Border control: La Fors and Meissner (2022) critique border AI systems for prioritizing control over migrant safety.

Education: Jenks et al. (2024) advocates for cocreating AI education policies with disabled students to prevent ableist exclusions. Studies in education by Jiang and Pardos (2021) demonstrate how adversarial learning and equity-based sampling can improve fairness, though trade-offs persist.

Finance and hiring: Jorgensen et al. (2023) explore the financial sector and illustrate that loan repayment models adjusted to satisfy fairness constraints sometimes produced worse outcomes for disadvantaged groups compared to unmitigated models. Chauhan and Kshetri (2022) discuss that AI can both reveal and exacerbate inequities in hiring, promotion, and retention, especially when datasets lack representation. They highlight that disaggregated data analysis can uncover systemic bias and enable targeted interventions for marginalized job seekers.

Fairness

Consequently, there is a need for *fairness* metrics, such as measuring the percentage of correct predictions across different demographic or social groups, as well as approaches to mitigate AI models' biases.

However, many studies emphasize that fairness is highly context-dependent and that an overarching definition will be inadequate and often harmful (Calvi & Kotzinos, 2023; Caton & Haas, 2024; Horna-Saldaña et al., 2025; Inuwa-Dutse, 2023; Lee, 2019; Thomasian et al., 2021; Uddin et al., 2024; Vishwanatha et al., 2023). However, beyond biased training data and fairness metrics, unequal access to technology and culturally specific definitions of fairness are also crucial. Bias, fairness, context (e.g., culture), and access to technology are dimensions that must be considered together to understand AI's impacts (Molamohammadi et al., 2023). For example, in domain-specific settings such as healthcare, researchers warn that AI can reproduce racial, gendered, and historical inequities unless participatory and corrective practices are built into design (Bearman & Ajjawi, 2025; Iloanusi & Chun, 2024; Joshi, 2024; Nong et al., 2024). Giovanola and Tiribelli (2023) argue that fairness in healthcare must extend beyond bias mitigation to include relational and distributive justice, recognizing patients as particular persons with context-sensitive needs.

Also, scholarship highlights how algorithmic inclusion must also account for cultural, linguistic, and structural inequities. Horna-Saldaña et al. (2025) show how AI tools like Quispe Chequea can empower indigenous communities through multilingual fact-checking, but only when designed with cultural sensitivity and indigenous data sovereignty in mind. Additionally, survey research by Sanchez et al. (2024) uncovered that stakeholders' perceptions of AI's equity impacts differ by demographics. For example, older professionals were more skeptical about AI's benefits, and women showed more optimism about AI reducing bias than men—reflecting varied levels of trust and concern among end users.

Hence, fairness alone is not sufficient. To meaningfully address AI's social impacts, we must also confront the structural inequities that shape how technologies are designed, developed, deployed, and experienced.

Fairness Frameworks and Colonialism

One of the most entrenched, yet often obscured, dimensions of structural inequality is colonialism. While fairness frameworks in AI have been developed to address issues of bias and discrimination, they often operate within paradigms that assume neutrality, ignoring the colonial histories and global asymmetries that shape data infrastructures, design practices, and deployment contexts. Since AI outcomes are never neutral, relying heavily on data quality, design choices, and human interpretation, these systems can either mitigate or reinforce historical injustices (Mhasawade et al., 2021; Smith, 2021; Vishwanatha et al., 2023).

Most AI fairness frameworks are developed in the Global North, embedding assumptions that may not reflect the realities of low- and middle-income countries (LMICs). This imbalance, rooted in colonial legacies, such as outdated, biased data for the AI training, unequal data ownership, infrastructure dependence on foreign providers, and the use of models poorly suited to local contexts, detrimentally impacts the local populations who remain under-represented, under-heard, and marginalized (Alami et al., 2020; Anawati et al., 2024; Asiedu et al., 2024; Benthall & Haynes, 2019; Dankwa-Mullan, 2024; Dankwa-Mullan et al., 2021; Inuwa-Dutse, 2023; Qadri et al., 2023).

Without codesign and capacity building, and a decolonial approach, such deployments risk technological neocolonialism, where benefits flow outward while local communities remain dependent, or that the outcomes of such AI models are not effective or equitable. Recognizing this, some scholars have begun to call for fairness frameworks that are not only technically rigorous but also historically informed, culturally situated, and anti-colonial in orientation.

From Fairness to Justice

While all approaches to fairness converge on the aim of mitigating bias and ensuring AI systems do not unduly favor already-privileged groups, conceptions of equity should go beyond strict mathematical criteria to deal with broader social justice and liberatory frameworks. Critical theoretical work expands this view.

Kasirzadeh (2022), Hort et al. (2024), and Keswani and Celis (2025) argue that fairness frameworks must move beyond distributive metrics to address *structural injustice* and historical subordination. Another study by Klein and D'Ignazio (2024) also endorses feminist, community-driven approaches to counter extractive AI practices. Tools for *accountability* and governance are also emerging; for example, Krafft et al. (2021) developed a tool for community-led audits, while Kraft and Soulier (2024) exposed how "neutral" AI models, especially those trained on curated knowledge sources, actually reinforce deep inequalities in whose knowledge counts, by sidelining marginalized perspectives and contributing to epistemic injustice. Other studies also revealed interplay between human and algorithmic biases; for instance, Sühr et al. (2021) showed that while a fair-ranking algorithm increased the selection of minority candidates in online hiring, the benefit was dampened when employers held strong preexisting gender biases, indicating that human decision-makers can reinforce or undermine algorithmic fairness efforts. Similarly, Kelan (2024) and Biju and Gayathri (2024) emphasize that inclusion is shaped not only by technical design but also by decisions, where human–algorithm interactions must be continuously audited and regulated.

Taken together, these dimensions, from bias and fairness to coloniality and justice, highlight that inequities in AI unfold differently across institutional contexts. The following section offers a comparative synthesis of these patterns across major sectors.

COMPARATIVE INSIGHTS

Common Patterns

Across sectors, a consistent pattern emerges that inequities in AI are rooted in biased data, limited representation, and the absence of participatory design (Cachat-Rosset & Klarsfeld, 2023; Chauhan & Kshetri, 2022; Chen et al., 2023; Suresh & Guttag, 2021). Whether in healthcare (Abràmoff et al., 2023; Ali et al., 2023; Bearman & Ajjawi, 2025; Xu et al., 2024), education (Jenks et al., 2024; Jiang & Pardos, 2021; Roscoe, 2023), employment (Baum, 2023; Chan, 2024; Kelan, 2024; Tyagi & Tyagi, 2024), or governance (Anawati et al., 2024; Biju & Gayathri, 2024; La Fors & Meissner, 2022), these structural gaps reproduce existing social hierarchies by embedding discrimination into technical systems. Data that reflect historical exclusion lead to models that privilege dominant populations (Asiedu et al., 2024; Benthall & Haynes, 2019; Hong et al., 2023; Kraft & Soulier, 2024), while fairness frameworks, often grounded in narrow statistical parity, fail to capture the lived realities of marginalized groups (Binns & Kirkham, 2021; Buyl & De Bie, 2024; Caton & Haas, 2024; Kasirzadeh, 2022; Kong, 2022; Tomasev et al., 2021). Across contexts, AI systems tend to obscure rather than resolve structural inequities when they are developed without critical engagement from affected communities (Duarte et al., 2024; Krafft et al., 2021; Solyst et al., 2023; Vishwanatha et al., 2023). This convergence suggests that the core problem lies less in algorithmic malfunction than in the social conditions and governance structures that shape data creation, model design, and deployment (Holzmeyer, 2021; Klein & D'Ignazio, 2024; Lalor et al., 2024; Santos et al., 2025; Siala & Wang, 2022).

Sectoral Differences

Despite these shared mechanisms, sectoral variations are evident. In healthcare, inequity appears through diagnostic misclassification, unequal clinical representation, and the reinforcement of historical biases in medical research (Cary et al., 2025; Deo, 2024; Joshi, 2024; Xu et al., 2024). Educational applications of AI raise distinct concerns about access, fairness in evaluation, and the reproduction of systemic disadvantage through predictive analytics and automated tutoring systems (Jenks et al., 2024; Jiang & Pardos, 2021; Roscoe, 2023; Roshanaei, 2024). In employment contexts, inequities manifest through biased hiring algorithms, exclusion of disabled or racialized candidates, and unexamined human–machine decision dynamics (Chan, 2024; Goretzko & Israel, 2022; Kelan, 2024; Tilmes, 2022). In governance and public policy, challenges relate to accountability, opacity, and the concentration of decision-making power in private actors, often without democratic oversight (Biju & Gayathri, 2024; Holzmeyer, 2021; Krafft et al., 2021; Teixeira et al., 2022). Each domain, therefore, reflects its own nexus of social relations and institutional constraints, revealing the need for domain-specific but ethically coherent strategies for intervention (Lewicki et al., 2023; Molamohammadi et al., 2023).

Implication

The above findings demonstrate that inequity in AI is not a technical anomaly but a systemic outcome of social, institutional, and epistemic structures (Kasirzadeh, 2022; Kraft & Soulier, 2024). Advancing equity across sectors requires moving beyond corrective bias mitigation toward structural reform, inclusive governance and accountability, decolonial frameworks, and sustained community participation (Asiedu et al., 2024; Kong et al., 2023; Nong et al., 2024; Rubeis et al., 2022). Equity-enhancing design principles, such as participatory cocreation, inclusive data governance, and fairness auditing, yield more trustworthy outcomes when integrated from the earliest stages of development (Calvi & Kotzinos, 2023; Raji et al., 2020; Solyst et al., 2023; Suresh & Guttag, 2021). Achieving justice in AI demands a coordinated, cross-sectoral approach that aligns technical innovation with the ethical and political imperative to redistribute power, representation, and accountability in sociotechnical systems (Giovanola & Tiribelli, 2023; Klein & D'Ignazio, 2024; Lyons et al., 2023; Santos et al., 2025).

Table 1.1 provides a comparative summary of AI equity dynamics across sectors.

TABLE 1.1
AI Equity Dynamics across Sectors

Sector	Common Bias Sources	Distinct Challenges	Emerging Equity Strategies
Healthcare/ public health	• Underrepresentation in clinical datasets; historical bias in medical research; one-size-fits-all diagnostic models	• Misdiagnosis and underdiagnosis among marginalized populations; inequitable access to AI-driven care	• Inclusive data governance; participatory design with patients and clinicians; outcome-oriented fairness frameworks
Education/ higher learning	• Narrow performance metrics; data reflecting structural inequality; algorithmic opacity in learning analytics	• Biased student profiling; unequal access to AI-enhanced tools; reinforcement of institutional hierarchies	• Equity-based sampling; transparency in learning algorithms; inclusive AI pedagogy and digital literacy initiatives
Employment/ labor	• Biased recruitment and performance data; use of proxy variables for protected attributes	• Exclusion of disabled, racialized, or gender-diverse candidates; reinforcement of workplace hierarchies	• Bias-mitigation ranking models; accessible hiring algorithms; human oversight and continuous audit of AI systems
Governance/ public policy	• Centralized control of data; lack of public oversight; private-sector dominance in AI infrastructure	• Opaque decision-making; accountability gaps; inequitable policy implementation	• Public auditing and algorithmic impact assessments; stakeholder participation; transparency and open data mandates
Disability/ accessibility	• Invisibility of disability data; exclusion from dataset labeling and design processes	• Incompatibility of fairness metrics with disability rights; accessibility gaps in digital tools	• Codesign with disability communities; universal and assistive design standards; adaptive fairness auditing
Finance/ economics	• Discriminatory credit scoring data; profit-driven algorithmic optimization	• Financial exclusion of women and low-income groups; unmonitored lending bias	• Fair-lending regulations; demographic parity audits; inclusive financial data practices
Cross-sector/ theoretical	• Western-centric fairness metrics; neglect of structural and historical inequities	• Technological colonialism; epistemic injustice; dominance of Global North frameworks	• Decolonial AI design; feminist and community-led governance; global equity partnerships

EQUITY DEFINITIONS

The included literature uses varied definitions of "equity" and fairness in the context of AI. Some papers adopt formal metric-based definitions: for instance, Uddin et al. (2024) define fairness such that a machine learning model is fair if *protected and unprotected groups have equal true positive rates, false positive rates, and related error ratios.* Similarly, Tyagi and Anuj (2024) operationalize gender equity in hiring algorithms as achieving balanced error rates between male and female applicant groups.

In contrast, other studies frame equity in terms of access and outcomes for disadvantaged groups. Rubeis et al. (2022), for example, define equity in "AgeTech" as *fairness and equality of access to assistive technologies regardless of one's social disadvantages*, emphasizing that older adults of all backgrounds should benefit equally. Ganesh et al. (2023) also operationalize group fairness to ensure equitable treatment across demographic groups. Goyal et al. (2024) also define equity and fairness in terms of demographic parity and user perception, exploring impacts of proxy versus protected features. Another study by Tomasev et al. (2021) advocates for AI systems to be designed in a way that the benefits and burdens of automated decisions are distributed justly across society, including for groups whose protected attributes may be *unobserved* (e.g., sexual orientation or gender identity). Likewise, Trewin et al. (2019) stress an equitable approach to AI must *neither exclude nor disadvantage people with disabilities* at any stage, which requires both procedural justice (inclusive design, ability for disabled users to contest decisions) and distributive justice (ensuring outcomes don't reinforce disability-based disparities).

Other studies such as Friedler et al. (2019) refer to equity in terms of fairness and define accuracy and fairness as conditional probabilities of outcomes with respect to variables like predicted and actual results. Goretzko and Finja et al. (2022) emphasize algorithmic equity through bias detection, transparency, and procedural fairness. Grote and Keeling (2022) argue that fairness should be evaluated based on final decisions arising from human-ML collaboration rather than only algorithmic statistics. Similarly, Holzmeyer (2021) and Mhasawade et al. (2021) emphasize equity in terms of social determinants of health and community-driven interventions.

Notably, one study highlights the distinction between equality and equity: Solyst et al. (2023) found that Black adolescent girls initially equated "fairness" with everyone being treated the same (a notion of equality) and only after guided discussion did the idea of meeting different needs to achieve fairness (equity) emerge and gain acceptance. In summary, conceptions of equity range from strict mathematical criteria to broader social justice frameworks, but all converge on the aim of mitigating bias and ensuring AI systems do not unduly favor already-privileged groups.

CHALLENGES

Achieving equity in AI deployment comes with numerous challenges, as documented across the studies. A pervasive issue is data bias and underrepresentation: many authors note that marginalized groups are often not adequately represented in training datasets, leading to models that perform poorly for those populations (Dychiao et al., 2024; Ellen et al., 2024; Ganesh et al., 2023; Kumar et al., 2024; Mhasawade et al., 2021; Morris, 2020; Roscoe, 2023; Suresh & Guttag, 2021; Upadhyay et al., 2023). For example, Suresh and Guttag (2021) point out that historical and sampling biases can result in systematic underrepresentation of certain groups in data, which in turn yields algorithms that allocate resources unfairly or stereotype those groups. Neumann and Wolczynski (2023) demonstrate that even when systems are designed with diverse sampling and labeling, the benefits still accrue disproportionately to majority groups, leaving minority groups comparatively at risk.

In the healthcare domain, scholars similarly warn that if biases in clinical data are not addressed, AI diagnostic tools may systematically misdiagnose or underdiagnose patients from overlooked communities, causing serious harm (Ali et al., 2023; P. Chen et al., 2023b; Jiang & Pardos, 2021; Liu et al., 2023; Ueda et al., 2024). Liu et al. (2023) argue that AI fairness frameworks that equate equality with fairness in healthcare can overlook clinically relevant differences and must be reframed contextually where equitable treatment decisions require considerations beyond metrics used in general AI fairness. Lee (2019), Kasirzadeh (2022), and Keswani and Celis (2025) also critique the overreliance on narrow fairness metrics and technical neutrality, which can legitimize systemic inequities.

Another key challenge is that bias can creep in at multiple stages of the AI life cycle. Both technical and social factors contribute to this; models may have design or algorithmic biases, developers and users can introduce their own assumptions, and institutional practices can amplify inequities (Biswas & Rajan, 2020; Santos et al., 2025; Varanasi & Goyal, 2023). Scholars have noted that AI systems apply a "one-size-fits-all" approach to diverse population groups, risking the exacerbation of power inequalities and inequities (Baum, 2023; Buyl & Bie, 2024; Lewicki et al., 2023). Studies also demonstrate that removing protected attributes (e.g., race) often fails because proxy variables carry bias (Barton et al., 2023; G. Chan, 2024; S. C. C. Chan et al., 2024; Delecraz et al., 2022; Desiere & Struyven, 2021; Embi, 2021).

Challenges specific to sensitive attributes were also noted. Disability-focused studies highlight the difficulty of collecting and using data about disability status: Trewin et al. (2019) discuss a "data representation gap" where disability is heterogeneous and often invisible in data, making it hard for AI to treat disabled users fairly, especially under privacy constraints. Tilmes (2022) adds that many standard fairness metrics (e.g., demographic parity) can be incompatible with disability rights laws and can inadvertently "flatten" the diverse experiences of disabled individuals into a single category, thus failing to capture intersectional disadvantages. Chemnad and Othman (2024) argue that while AI has made strides in digital accessibility, especially for vision impairments, there is a critical neglect of users with speech, neurological, or cognitive disabilities. Equity-advancing tools face regulatory and business-model hurdles that can limit uptake despite clinical promise (Deo, 2024).

Studies also raise concerns about the "digital divide" and organizational readiness. Binns and Kirkham (2021) emphasize that UK equality law, particularly around disability, demands anticipatory obligations and reasonable adjustments beyond generic fairness metrics. They show how legal protections, like "discrimination arising from disability" can reshape how fairness should be implemented for disabled communities within AI systems. Roshanaei (2024) points out that unequal access to technology and AI literacy can skew who actually benefits from AI interventions—for example, if only well-resourced schools implement fairness-driven AI tools, already-advantaged students may gain more, widening gaps. Teixeira et al. (2022) identify the opaqueness of AI systems and the lack of accountability, privacy, explainability, and interpretability as factors that hamper the creation of a responsible AI framework.

Sanchez et al. (2024) found that many transportation professionals were not fully prepared to use AI or were unconvinced of its equity benefits, citing worries about transparency, data privacy, and even job displacement. Omotubora (2024) also observes that while AI technology in financial sectors promises greater inclusion for women, profit-driven deployment often prioritizes lucrative markets over underserved groups. For instance, in Nigeria, AI systems trained on historically exclusionary data may reinforce rather than reduce gender gaps to financial access. In sum, common challenges include biased or incomplete data, the complexity of socio-technical bias propagation, tensions between fairness and privacy or legal constraints, and a lack of awareness or capacity among practitioners, all of which can hinder the goal of equitable AI.

BENEFITS

Despite the challenges, many studies identify significant benefits and opportunities of AI when it is developed and applied with equity in mind. In healthcare, developing fair and unbiased AI systems is expected to improve outcomes for underserved populations. For instance, Ueda et al. (2024) note that "fair" AI, defined as providing accurate diagnoses and treatments regardless of patients' social or ethnic background, could help reduce disparities in clinical care. Another study by Grote and Keeling (2022) also demonstrates that fairness-focused AI in clinical settings can reduce pain underdiagnosis among Black patients and increase eligibility for surgical interventions, showing that outcome-oriented approaches have practical benefits. Joshi (2024) and Clark et al. (2021) highlight that AI can improve diagnostics, personalized medicine, and early intervention for women's health, enhancing both efficiency and equity. Kumar et al. (2024) similarly note that AI can support personalized medicine, equitable trial access, and improved health outcomes when developed inclusively.

In employment settings, Sühr et al. (2021) provide evidence that algorithmic fairness interventions can counteract human biases to a degree; their experiment with hiring algorithms showed that using a bias-mitigation ranking strategy increased the selection of underrepresented candidates, suggesting AI tools can promote diversity in hiring when properly designed. Trewin et al. (2019) and Zhuang and Goggin (2024) suggest that well-designed AI can unlock new opportunities in employment and daily life for individuals with disabilities by reducing prejudice and accessibility hurdles: for example, AI-driven hiring platforms, if designed with disability inclusion in mind, could focus on candidates' skills and provide accommodations, thereby opening pathways to jobs that might otherwise be closed.

Several papers focusing on disability highlight AI's role as an assistive enabler: Rosa (2025) describes how AI-powered technologies, from smart prosthetics and personalized training apps to alternative communication interfaces, can help dismantle barriers in sports and physical exercise, allowing people with disabilities to participate on more equal footing with their peers. Hutchinson and Mitchell (2019) and Delgado-Rodríguez et al. (2023) raise awareness of how ML models can improve accessibility tools.

In education, researchers argue that bias-mitigated AI tools (for example, in university admissions or advising systems) could broaden access for underrepresented students and enhance trust in institutional decision-making (Ramos & Wilson-Kennedy, 2024; Roshanaei, 2024). Long and Palmer (2024) also suggest that publicly funded AI systems can offer clear, tailored legal guidance, helping individuals overcome financial obstacles and cultural stigma when pursuing justice. This, in turn, enhances legal trust, encourages social inclusion, and supports wider economic engagement.

Bano et al. (2024) propose a structured method for embedding diversity by using persona-based elicitation integrated with generative AI tools. This approach not only surfaces hidden equity concerns early on, such as socioeconomic and intersectional accessibility barriers, but also enhances traceability of equity-related design choices. These benefits illustrate AI's promise to advance equity, from more inclusive healthcare and hiring to greater accessibility, provided that the technology is intentionally developed and governed to serve marginalized as well as majority groups. LLM-supported interpretation can reduce access barriers for limited-English-proficiency patients when coupled with human oversight (Bakdash et al., 2024; R. Chen et al., 2023).

DISCUSSION AND RECOMMENDATIONS

To address these challenges, the literature converges on several recommendations for promoting equity in AI design and implementation. A recurring theme is inclusive and participatory design: many scholars urge involving diverse stakeholders, especially those from marginalized communities, throughout the AI life cycle. For example, Trewin et al. (2019) recommend embedding disability experts and end-users in the design, testing, and deployment of AI systems to catch bias and accessibility issues early. Similarly, Qadri et al. (2023) and Solyst et al. (2023) suggest codesigning AI solutions with the communities affected to ensure the technology accounts for those users' needs and lived experiences. Zhuang and Goggin (2024) call for involving disabled workers into the development of workplace AI and automated decision-making tools, rather than treating disability only as an afterthought in algorithm auditing. Ueda et al. (2024) emphasize improving data collection by including members of overlooked groups in healthcare datasets and conducting long-term monitoring to ensure biases are identified and mitigated. Likewise, Park (2024) and Cary et al. (2025) call for increased involvement of nurses in the design, development, and implementation of AI, alongside patient education, to maintain transparency and inclusivity to ensure that the benefits of AI are realized equitably across all populations within clinical settings.

Another set of recommendations centers on data diversity and bias auditing. Nyariro et al. (2022) advocate for diversity in not only clinical datasets but also involving diverse stakeholders (especially those at risk of being marginalized by AI tools) at all stages of the AI life cycle in order to mitigate downstream harm. Roshanaei (2024) likewise advocates for curating more representative training data in higher education algorithms and performing regular bias audits with accountability mechanisms, so that any emerging inequities can be corrected.

Scholars highlight the need for fairness approaches that recognize intersectionality and multidimensional discrimination, recommending that future work adopt a holistic view of bias (so that improving fairness for one group doesn't unintentionally harm another) (Friedler et al., 2019; Ganesh et al., 2023; Kelan, 2024; Roy et al., 2023). In terms of practice, several papers stress education and guidance for AI practitioners, urging translating high-level AI ethics principles into concrete best practices, checklists, and "audit trails" that development teams can easily implement to prevent harm (Abràmoff et al., 2023; Bird et al., 2019; Cheng et al., 2021; Nong et al., 2024; Raji et al., 2020; Shneiderman, 2021).

Bird et al. (2019) echo the need for early fairness integration, reporting that many fairness-aware ML systems fail when fairness is treated as a post-hoc patch rather than a core design constraint. Their industry-based analysis advocates a "fairness-first" paradigm, where stakeholder impacts guide system architecture from the outset. Raji et al. (2020) and Cachat-Rosset and Klarsfeld (2023) recommend that accountability in AI should rest with organizations through strong governance structure to ensure systems are not only technically reliable but also ethically compliant. They stress the need for practical methods to translate ethical principles into action, with clear mechanisms for human oversight and bias prevention. Similarly, Lyons et al. (2023) emphasize that the responsibility for ethical AI lies not in the technology itself but in its responsible use, where education, transparency, and oversight should be built into development and deployment.

Siala and Wang (2022) suggest adopting SHIFT framework, where developers must focus on five thematic ideas: sustainability, human-centric development, inclusiveness, fairness, and transparency, to ensure AI development and usage are governed by an ethical framework. Finally, domain-specific recommendations were noted: for example, healthcare AI calls for regulatory oversight and validation to ensure algorithms are safe and effective for all groups (echoing a general "responsible AI" call to action in the health sector), and in hiring, aligning algorithmic practices with legal protections to avoid conflicts with disability rights and anti-discrimination laws (Tilmes, 2022). Overall, the recommendations across studies converge on fostering a more socially aware AI ecosystem—one that prioritizes transparency, inclusivity, stakeholder engagement, bias mitigation, and continuous monitoring to ensure that AI technologies actively advance equity rather than inadvertently undermining it.

LIMITATIONS

This scoping review has several limitations that should be acknowledged when interpreting its findings.

First, while the review followed a systematic and transparent search strategy across six databases, it was restricted to English-language publications, which may have excluded relevant studies published in other languages, particularly from regions in the Global South. Second, because scoping reviews are designed to map the breadth rather than assess the quality of evidence, the included studies were not subjected to formal critical appraisal; as a result, the reliability of individual findings may vary. Third, the rapid evolution of AI technologies means that newer developments, especially in generative and multimodal AI, may not yet be represented in the literature synthesized here. Additionally, domain boundaries were sometimes fluid, and certain studies could be classified under more than one sector, introducing minor subjectivity into domain categorization. Finally, most of the evidence originates from high-income countries, limiting the generalizability of conclusions to low- and middle-income contexts where infrastructural and governance conditions differ.

Despite these limitations, the review provides a comprehensive and timely mapping of the intersection between AI and equity, identifying key patterns and research gaps that can inform more inclusive and context-sensitive policy and design frameworks.

CONCLUSION

In conclusion, this scoping review reveals that AI holds substantial potential to advance equity across domains such as healthcare, education, employment, and public governance. However, realizing this potential requires deliberate attention to structural inequalities embedded in data, design, and institutional contexts. The findings demonstrate that technical fairness measures alone are insufficient to redress systemic bias; equity must be built into every stage of the AI life cycle through inclusive governance, participatory design, and sustained accountability mechanisms.

At the same time, significant research gaps remain. Empirical evidence is still limited on how fairness interventions perform across different sociocultural and economic settings, particularly in LMICs. Few studies assess the long-term impacts of AI systems on marginalized communities or track how fairness metrics translate into tangible social outcomes. There is also a lack of comparative, cross-sectoral research examining how equity frameworks can be adapted between fields such as healthcare, education, and labor. Moreover, existing scholarship rarely integrates intersectional and community-led methodologies, leaving critical questions about power, voice, and representation underexplored. Finally, the absence of standardized metrics for measuring equity outcomes constrains the ability to evaluate progress or compare interventions across contexts.

Addressing these gaps requires interdisciplinary collaboration between technologists, social scientists, and affected communities, supported by policies that promote open data governance, equitable participation, and context-sensitive evaluation. By combining technical innovation with structural reform and global inclusivity, future research and policy development can ensure that AI technologies not only perform efficiently but also advance justice and social well-being for all.

ACKNOWLEDGMENT

Portions of this chapter were developed with the assistance of ChatGPT and Grammarly in an editing capacity to improve clarity and flow. All intellectual contributions, interpretations, and final editorial decisions are the authors' own, and the authors take full responsibility for the content. Any AI-assisted or AI-generated material was reviewed and verified by the authors.

REFLECTION QUESTIONS

1. How does the concept of garbage in, garbage out explain the relationship between historical medical education and modern AI diagnostic errors?
2. The author describes how AI can perpetuate the erasure of darker skin tones. How might the lack of visual representation in training data lead to specific material harms for patients with skin of color?
3. Reflect on the proposed Checklist for AI Procurement. Do you believe mandatory clinician overrides and pilot studies in diverse settings are sufficient to mitigate algorithmic bias, or are deeper structural changes needed?
4. Why is it critical to include race-based data collection in patient health information, despite the potential risks of surveillance or discriminatory application?

APPENDIX A

SEARCH TERMS

IEEE Xplore

(((Document Title:AI) OR (Document Title:neural networks) OR (Document Title:deep learning) OR (Document Title:machine learning) OR (Document Title:artificial intelligence) OR (Document Title:predictive analytics) refined by:"Content Type":Conferences, "Content Type":Journals; Year:2019–2025)) AND ((Document Title:equity) OR (Document Title:accountability) OR

(Document Title:parity) OR (Document Title:access) OR (Document Title:fairness) OR (Document Title:equality) OR (Document Title:equal opportunity) OR (Document Title:responsible) OR (Document Title:accessibility) OR (Document Title:inclusion) refined by:"Content Type":Conferences, "Content Type":Journals; Year:2019–2025)

Additional Filters: Journal Articles

Web of Science

#8 AND #9 and Article (Document Types) and English (Languages) and Article (Document Types)

#9: ((((((TI=(AI)) OR TI=(Artificial Intelligence)) OR TI=(Machine Learning)) OR TI=(Deep learning))) OR TI=(Predicitive Analytics)) OR TI=(neural networks)

#8: (((((((((TI=(accessibility)) OR TI=(accountability)) OR TI=(inclusion)) OR TI=(access)) OR TI=(parity)) OR TI=(fairness)) OR TI=(equity)) OR TI=(equality)) OR TI=("equal opportunity")) OR TI=(responsible)

Additional Filters: Article, 2019-Present

PubMed

(((((((((equity[Title]) OR (equality[Title])) OR (responsible[Title])) OR (fairness[Title])) OR (access [Title])) OR (accountability[Title])) OR (inclusion[Title])) OR ("equal opportunity"[Title])) OR (parity[Title])) OR (accessibility[Title]) AND ((classicalarticle[Filter] OR comparativestudy[Filter] OR editorial[Filter] OR introductoryjournalarticle[Filter] OR systematicreview[Filter]) AND (english[Filter]) AND (2019:2025[pdat]))) AND ((((((AI[Title]) OR (Artificial Intelligence[Title])) OR (Neural networks[Title])) OR (predictive analytics[Title])) OR (deep learning[Title])) OR (machine learning[Title]) AND ((classicalarticle[Filter] OR comparativestudy[Filter] OR editorial[Filter] OR introductoryjournala rticle[Filter] OR systematicreview[Filter]) AND (english[Filter]) AND (2019:2025[pdat])))

Additional Filters: Classical Article, Comparative Study, Editorial, Introductory Journal Article, Systematic Review, English

Proquest

((title(AI) OR title(Artificial intelligence) OR title(Machine learning) OR title(deep learning) OR title(predictive analytics) OR title(neural networks) AND title(accountability) OR title(equity) OR title(equality) OR title(fairness) OR title(access) OR title(parity) OR title(equal opportunity) OR title(responsible) OR title(accessibility) OR title(inclusion)))

EBSCO

Search: (TI AI) OR (TI neural networks) OR (TI deep learning) OR (TI artificial intelligence) OR (TI machine learning) OR (TI predictive analytics)) AND ((TI equity) OR (TI accountability) OR (TI equality) OR (TI fairness) OR (TI access) OR (TI parity) OR (TI equal opportunity) OR (TI responsible) OR (TI accessibility) OR (TI inclusion))

Limitations: English Language; Peer Reviewed; Research Article; Exact search terms

ACM Digital Library

[[Title: ai] OR [Title: artificial intelligence] OR [Title: deep learning] OR [Title: machine learning] OR [Title: neural networks] OR [Title: predictive analytics]] AND [[Title: equity] OR [Title: equality] OR [Title: access] OR [Title: parity] OR [Title: responsibility] OR [Title: fairness] OR [Title: equal opportunity] OR [Title: accessability] OR [Title: accountability] OR [Title: inclusion]] AND [E-Publication Date: (01/01/2019 TO 31/12/2025)]

Additional Filters: Research Articles

PRISMA Diagram

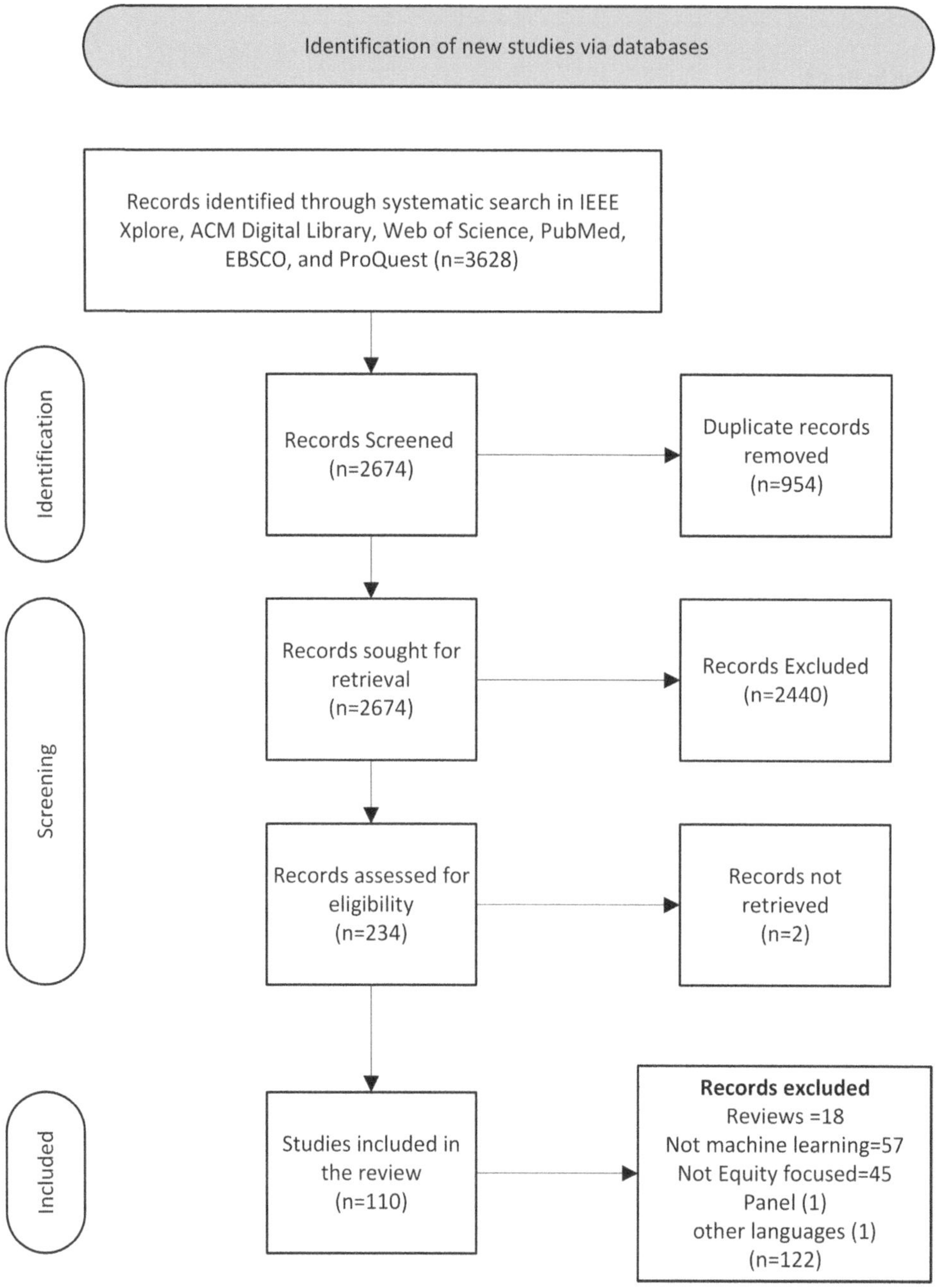

FIGURE 1A.1 PRISMA flow diagram showing the study selection process for the scoping review of artificial intelligence and equity, from database identification to final inclusion of 110 studies.

Included Studies

TABLE A1.1
Included Studies

Author(s)	Year	Study Title
Abramoff et al.	• 2023	• Considerations for addressing bias in artificial intelligence for health equity
Alami et al.	• 2023	• Artificial intelligence in health care: laying the Foundation for Responsible, sustainable, and inclusive innovation in low- and middle-income countries.
Ali et al.	• 2023	• Addressing ethnic and global health inequalities in the era of artificial intelligence healthcare models: a call for responsible implementation
Anawati et al.	• 2024	• Artificial intelligence and social accountability in the Canadian health care landscape: A rapid literature review.
Asiedu et al.	• 2024	• The Case for Globalizing Fairness: A Mixed Methods Study on Colonialism, AI, and Health in Africa
Bakdash et al.	• 2024	• Chatting Beyond ChatGPT: Advancing Equity Through AI-Driven Language Interpretation.
Bano et al.	• 2024	• A Vision for Operationalising Diversity and Inclusion in AI
Barton et al.	• 2023	• Racial Equity in Healthcare Machine Learning: Illustrating Bias in Models With Minimal Bias Mitigation
Baum	• 2023	• AI CHALLENGES IN THE WORKPLACE: ARE ARTIFICIAL INTELLIGENCE POLICIES MEETING DIVERSITY, EQUITY, AND INCLUSION THRESHOLDS?
Bearman and Aijawi	• 2025	• Artificial intelligence and gender equity: An integrated approach for health professional education
Benthal and Haynes	• 2019	• Racial categories in machine learning
Biju and Gayathri	• 2024	• Algorithmic solutions, subjectivity and decision errors: a study of AI accountability
Binns and Kirkham	• 2021	• How Could Equality and Data Protection Law Shape AI Fairness for People with Disabilities?
Bird et al	• 2019	• Fairness-Aware Machine Learning: Practical Challenges and Lessons Learned
Biswas and Rajan	• 2020	• Do the machine learning models on a crowd sourced platform exhibit bias? an empirical study on model fairness
Buyl and Bie	• 2024	• Inherent Limitations of AI Fairness
Cachat-Rosset and Klarsfeld	• 2023	• Diversity, equity, and inclusion in artificial intelligence: An evaluation of guidelines
Calvi and Kotzinos	• 2023	• Enhancing AI fairness through impact assessment in the European Union: a legal and computer science perspective
Cary et al.	• 2025	• Empowering nurses to champion Health equity & BE FAIR: Bias elimination for fair and responsible AI in healthcare
Caton and Haas	• 2024	• Fairness in Machine Learning: A Survey
Chan	• 2024	• AI employment decision-making: integrating the equal opportunity merit principle and explainable AI
Chan et al.	• 2024	• Bridging the equity gap towards inclusive artificial intelligence in healthcare diagnostics.
Chauhan and Kshetri	• 2022	• The Role of Data and Artificial Intelligence in Driving Diversity, Equity, and Inclusion
Chemnad and Othman	• 2024	• Digital accessibility in the era of artificial intelligence-Bibliometric analysis and systematic review.
Chen et al.	• 2024	• Conversational AI and equity through assessing GPT-3's communication with diverse social groups on contentious topics
Chen et al.	• 2023	• Algorithmic fairness in artificial intelligence for medicine and healthcare

(Continued)

TABLE A1.1
(Continued)

Author(s)	Year	Study Title
Chen et al.	• 2023	• AI Fairness in Data Management and Analytics: A Review on Challenges, Methodologies and Applications
Cheng et al.	• 2021	• Socially Responsible AI Algorithms: Issues, Purposes, and Challenges
Clark et al.	• 2021	• Health Care Equity in the Use of Advanced Analytics and Artificial Intelligence Technologies in Primary Care.
Dankwa-Mullan	• 2024	• Health Equity and Ethical Considerations in Using Artificial Intelligence in Public Health and Medicine
Dankwa-Mullan et al.	• 2021	• A Proposed Framework on Integrating Health Equity and Racial Justice into the Artificial Intelligence Development Lifecycle
Delecraz et al.	• 2022	• Making recruitment more inclusive: unfairness monitoring with a job matching machine-learning algorithm
Delgado-Rodríguez et al.	• 2023	• Immersive technology and artificial intelligence to improve attention to diversity, equity and inclusion of students: Case study with augmented reality
Deo	• 2024	• Artificial Intelligence and Health Equity: Opportunities and Obstacles.
Desiere and Struyven	• 2021	• Using Artificial Intelligence to classify Jobseekers: The Accuracy-Equity Trade-off.
Duarte et al.	• 2024	• GranDIHC-BR 2025–2035- GC6: Implications of Artificial Intelligence in HCI: A Discussion on Paradigms Ethics and Diversity Equity and Inclusion*
Dychiao et al.	• 2024	• Artificial intelligence and global health equity.
Ellen et al.	• 2024	• Participant flow diagrams for health equity in AI
Embi	• 2021	• Algorithmovigilance—Advancing Methods to Analyze and Monitor Artificial Intelligence–Driven Health Care for Effectiveness and Equity
Friedler et al.	• 2019	• A comparative study of fairness-enhancing interventions in machine learning
Ganesh et al.	• 2023	• On The Impact of Machine Learning Randomness on Group Fairness
Giovanola and Tiribelli	• 2023	• Beyond bias and discrimination: redefining the AI ethics principle of fairness in healthcare machine-learning algorithms
Goretzko and Finja Israel	• 2022	• Pitfalls of machine learning-based personnel selection: Fairness, transparency, and data quality
Goyal et al	• 2024	• The Impact of Explanations on Fairness in Human-AI Decision-Making: Protected vs Proxy Features
Grote and Keeling	• 2022	• Enabling Fairness in Healthcare Through Machine Learning
Holzmeyer	• 2021	• Beyond 'AI for Social Good' (AI4SG): social transformations-not tech-fixes-for health equity
Hong et al.	• 2023	• Evaluation of targeted dataset collection on racial equity in face recognition
Horna-Saldaña et al.	• 2025	• Artificial intelligence in the preservation of native languages and bridging the information access gap for indigenous peoples
Hort et al.	• 2024	• Bias Mitigation for Machine Learning Classifiers: A Comprehensive Survey
Hutchinson and Mitchell	• 2019	• 50 Years of Test (Un)fairness: Lessons for Machine Learning
Hutchinson et al.	• 2020	• Unintended machine learning biases as social barriers for persons with disabilities
Iloanusi and Chun	• 2024	• AI Impact on Health Equity for Marginalized, Racial, and Ethnic Minorities
Inuwa-Dutse	• 2023	• FATE in AI: Towards Algorithmic Inclusivity and Accessibility
Jenks et al.	• 2024	• Emergent questions of access: disability and the integration of generative AI in teaching and learning
Jiang and Pardos	• 2021	• Towards Equity and Algorithmic Fairness in Student Grade Prediction
Jorgensen et al.	• 2023	• Not So Fair: The Impact of Presumably Fair Machine Learning Models
Joshi	• 2024	• Big data and AI for gender equality in health: bias is a big challenge
Kasirzadeh	• 2022	• Algorithmic Fairness and Structural Injustice: Insights from Feminist Political Philosophy

(Continued)

TABLE A1.1
(Continued)

Author(s)	Year	Study Title
Kelan	• 2024	• Algorithmic inclusion: Shaping the predictive algorithms of artificial intelligence in hiring
Keswani and Celis	• 2025	• Algorithmic Fairness From the Perspective of Legal Anti-Discrimination Principles
Klein and D'Ignazio	• 2024	• Data Feminism in AI
Kong	• 2022	• Are "Intersectionally Fair" AI Algorithms Really Fair to Women of Color? A Philosophical Analysis
Kong et al.	• 2023	• Leveraging Responsible, Explainable, and Local Artificial Intelligence Solutions for Clinical Public Health in the Global South.
Krafft et al.	• 2021	• An Action-Oriented AI Policy Toolkit for Technology Audits by Community Advocates and Activists
Kraft and Soulier	• 2024	• Knowledge-Enhanced Language Models Are Not Bias-Proof: Situated Knowledge and Epistemic Injustice in AI
Kumar et al.	• 2024	• AI in Biomedicine—A Forward-Looking Perspective on Health Equity
La Fors and Meissner	• 2022	• Contesting border artificial intelligence: Applying the guidance-ethics approach as a responsible design lens
Lalor et al.	• 2024	• Should Fairness be a Metric or a Model? A Model-based Framework for Assessing Bias in Machine Learning Pipelines
Lee	• 2019	• Context-conscious fairness in using machine learning to make decisions
Lewicki et al.	• 2023	• Out of Context: Investigating the Bias and Fairness Concerns of "Artificial Intelligence as a Service"
Liu et al.	• 2023	• A translational perspective towards clinical AI fairness
Long and Palmer	• 2024	• AI and access to justice: • How AI legal advisors can reduce economic • and shame-based barriers to justice
Lyons et al.	• 2023	• Responsible (use of) AI
Mhasawade et al.	• 2021	• Machine learning and algorithmic fairness in public and population health
Molamohammadi et al.	• 2023	• Unraveling the Interconnected Axes of Heterogeneity in Machine Learning for Democratic and Inclusive Advancements
Morris	• 2020	• AI and accessibility
Neumann and Wolczynski	• 2023	• Does AI-Assisted Fact-Checking Disproportionately Benefit Majority Groups Online?
Nong et al.	• 2024	• Equity and AI Governance at Academic Medical Centers.
Nyariro et al.	• 2022	• Integrating Equity, Diversity, and Inclusion throughout the lifecycle of Artificial Intelligence in health
Omotubora	• 2024	• AI for women's financial inclusion—analysis of product design and policy approaches in Nigeria
Park	• 2024	• Harnessing Artificial Intelligence to Promote Health Equity.
Qadri et al.	• 2023	• AI's Regimes of Representation: A Community-centered Study of Text-to-Image Models in South Asia
Raji et al.	• 2020	• Closing the AI accountability gap: defining an end-to-end framework for internal algorithmic auditing
Ramos and Wilson-Kennedy	• 2024	• Promoting equity and addressing concerns in teaching and learning with artificial intelligence
Rosa	• 2024	• The potential role of artificial intelligence to promote the participation and inclusion in physical exercise and sports for people with disabilities: A narrative review
Roscoe	• 2023	• Building Inclusive and Equitable Artificial Intelligence for Education
Roshanaei	• 2024	• Towards Best Practices for Mitigating Artificial Intelligence Implicit Bias in Shaping Diversity, Inclusion and Equity in Higher Education

(Continued)

TABLE A1.1
(*Continued*)

Author(s)	Year	Study Title
Roy et al.	• 2023	• Multi-dimensional Discrimination in Law and Machine Learning A Comparative Overview
Rubeis, et al.	• 2022	• Equity in AgeTech for Ageing Well in Technology-Driven Places: The Role of Social Determinants in Designing AI-based Assistive Technologies
Sanchez et al.	• 2024	• AI Applications in Transportation and Equity: A Survey of U.S. Transportation Professionals
Santos et al.	• 2024	• Software Fairness Debt: Building a Research Agenda for Addressing Bias in AI Systems
Shneiderman et al.	• 2021	• Viewpoint Responsible AI: Bridging From Ethics to Practice
Siala and Wang	• 2022	• SHIFTing Artificial Intelligence to be Responsible in Healthcare: A Systematic Review
Smith	• 2020	• Clinical AI: opacity, accountability, responsibility and liability
Solyst et al.	• 2023	• "I Would Like to Design": Black Girls Analyzing and Ideating Fair and Accountable AI
Sühr et al.	• 2021	• Does Fair Ranking Improve Minority Outcomes? Understanding the Interplay of Human and Algorithmic Biases in Online Hiring
Suresh and Guttag	• 2021	• A Framework for Understanding Sources of Harm throughout the Machine Learning Life Cycle
Teixeira et al.	• 2022	• An Exploratory Diagnosis of Artificial Intelligence Risks for a Responsible Governance.
Thomasian et al.	• 2021	• Advancing health equity with artificial intelligence
Tilmes	• 2022	• Disability, fairness, and algorithmic bias in AI recruitment
Tomasev et al.	• 2021	• Fairness for Unobserved Characteristics: Insights from Technological Impacts on Queer Communities
Trewin et al.	• 2019	• Considerations for AI fairness for people with disabilities
Tyagi and Anuj	• 2024	• Promoting Gender Fair Resume Screening Using Gender-Weighted Sampling
Uddin et al.	• 2024	• A novel approach for assessing fairness in deployed machine learning algorithms
Ueda et al.	• 2023	• Fairness of artificial intelligence in healthcare: review and recommendations
Upadhyay et al.	• 2023	• Call for the responsible artificial intelligence in the healthcare
Varanasi and Goyal	• 2023	• "It is currently hodgepodge": Examining AI/ML Practitioners' Challenges during Co-production of Responsible AI Values
Vishwanatha et al.	• 2023	• Community perspectives on AI/ML and health equity: AIM-AHEAD nationwide stakeholder listening sessions.
Xu et al.	• 2024	• Addressing fairness issues in deep learning-based medical image analysis: a systematic review
Zhuang and Goggin	• 2024	• New possibilities or problems for disability and inclusion? The case of AI and ADMs across work

REFERENCES

Abràmoff, M. D., Tarver, M. E., Loyo-Berrios, N., Trujillo, S., Char, D., Obermeyer, Z., Eydelman, M. B., & Maisel, W. H. (2023). Considerations for addressing bias in artificial intelligence for health equity. *NPJ Digital Medicine*, *6*(1), 170. Nursing & Allied Health Collection; Publicly Available Content Database. https://doi.org/10.1038/s41746-023-00913-9

Alami, H., Rivard, L., Lehoux, P., Hoffman, S. J., Cadeddu, S. B. M., Savoldelli, M., Samri, M. A., Ag Ahmed, M. A., Fleet, R., & Fortin, J.-P. (2020). Artificial intelligence in health care: Laying the Foundation for Responsible, sustainable, and inclusive innovation in low- and middle-income countries. *Globalization & Health*, *16*(1), 1–6. CINAHL Plus with Full Text. https://doi.org/10.1186/s12992-020-00584-1

Ali, M., Lawson, C., Wood, A., & Khunti, K. (2023). Addressing ethnic and global health inequalities in the era of artificial intelligence healthcare models: A call for responsible implementation. *Journal of the Royal Society of Medicine*. https://doi.org/10.1177/01410768231187734

Anawati, A., Fleming, H., Mertz, M., Bertrand, J., Dumond, J., Myles, S., Leblanc, J., Ross, B., Lamoureux, D., Patel, D., Carrier, R., & Cameron, E. (2024). Artificial intelligence and social accountability in the Canadian health care landscape: A rapid literature review. *PLoS Digital Health*, *3*(9), 1–17. CINAHL Plus with Full Text. https://doi.org/10.1371/journal.pdig.0000597

Asiedu, M. N., Dieng, A., Haykel, I., Rostamzadeh, N., Pfohl, S., Nagpal, C., Nagawa, M., Oppong, A., Koyejo, S., & Heller, K. (2024). The case for globalizing fairness: A mixed methods study on colonialism, AI, and health in Africa. In *Proceedings of the 4th ACM Conference on Equity and Access in Algorithms, Mechanisms, and Optimization*, San Luis Potosi (p. Article 10). Association for Computing Machinery. https://doi.org/10.1145/3689904.3694708

Bakdash, L., Abid, A., Gourisankar, A., & Henry, T. L. (2024). Chatting beyond ChatGPT: Advancing equity through AI-driven language interpretation. *Journal of General Internal Medicine*, *39*(3), 492–495. https://doi.org/10.1007/s11606-023-08497-6

Bano, M., Zowghi, D., & Gervasi, V. (2024). A vision for operationalising diversity and inclusion in AI. In *Proceedings of the 2nd International Workshop on Responsible AI Engineering*, Lisbon (pp. 36–45). Association for Computing Machinery. https://doi.org/10.1145/3643691.3648587

Barletta, V. S., Caivano, D., Gigante, D., & Ragone, A. (2023). A Rapid Review of Responsible AI frameworks: How to guide the development of ethical AI. In *EASE '23: The International Conference on Evaluation and Assessment in Software Engineering*, Oulu, June 14–16 (pp. 358–367).

Barton, M., Hamza, M., & Guevel, B. (2023). Racial equity in healthcare machine learning: Illustrating bias in models with minimal bias mitigation. *Cureus*, *15*(2). Publicly Available Content Database. https://doi.org/10.7759/cureus.35037

Baum, B. (2023). AI challenges in the workplace: Are artificial intelligence policies meeting diversity, equity, and inclusion thresholds? *Journal of Business and Behavioral Sciences*, *35*(3), 3–15. ABI/INFORM Global.

Bearman, M., & Ajjawi, R. (2025). Artificial intelligence and gender equity: An integrated approach for health professional education. *Medical Education*. https://doi.org/10.1111/medu.15657

Benthall, S., & Haynes, B. D. (2019). Racial categories in machine learning. In *Proceedings of the Conference on Fairness, Accountability, and Transparency*, Atlanta, GA (pp. 289–298). Association for Computing Machinery. https://doi.org/10.1145/3287560.3287575

Biju, P., & Gayathri, O. (2024). Algorithmic solutions, subjectivity and decision errors: A study of AI accountability. *Digital Policy Regulation and Governance*. https://doi.org/10.1108/DPRG-05-2024-0090

Binns, R., & Kirkham, R. (2021). How could equality and data protection law shape AI fairness for people with disabilities? *ACM Transactions on Accessible Computing*, *14*(3), Article 17. Association for Computing Machinery.

Bird, S., Hutchinson, B., Kenthapadi, K., Kıcıman, E., & Mitchell, M. (2019). Fairness-aware machine learning: Practical challenges and lessons learned. In *Companion Proceedings of the 2019 World Wide Web Conference*, San Francisco, USA (pp. 1297–1298). Association for Computing Machinery. https://doi.org/10.1145/3308560.3320086

Biswas, S., & Rajan, H. (2020). Do the machine learning models on a crowd sourced platform exhibit bias? An empirical study on model fairness. In *Proceedings of the 28th ACM Joint Meeting on European Software Engineering Conference and Symposium on the Foundations of Software Engineering*, Virtual Event USA (pp. 642–653). Association for Computing Machinery. https://doi.org/10.1145/3368089.3409704

Buyl, M., & Bie, T. D. (2024). Inherent limitations of AI fairness. *Communications of the ACM*, *67*(2), 48–55. Association for Computing Machinery.

Cachat-Rosset, G., & Klarsfeld, A. (2023). Diversity, equity, and inclusion in artificial intelligence: An evaluation of guidelines. *Applied Artificial Intelligence*, *37*(1), 2176618. https://doi.org/10.1080/08839514.2023.2176618

Calvi, A., & Kotzinos, D. (2023). Enhancing AI fairness through impact assessment in the European Union: A legal and computer science perspective. In *Proceedings of the 2023 ACM Conference on Fairness, Accountability, and Transparency*, Chicago, IL (pp. 1229–1245). Association for Computing Machinery. https://doi.org/10.1145/3593013.3594076

Cary, M. P., Bessias, S., McCall, J., Pencina, M. J., Grady, S. D., Lytle, K., & Economou-Zavlanos, N. J. (2025). Empowering nurses to champion Health equity & BE FAIR: Bias elimination for fair and responsible AI in healthcare. *Journal of Nursing Scholarship, Suppl. Special Issue: Transformative Role of Artificial Intelligence in Nursing*, *57*(1), 130–139. Applied Social Sciences Index & Abstracts (ASSIA); Nursing & Allied Health Collection; Public Health Database; Sociology Collection. https://doi.org/10.1111/jnu.13007

Caton, S., & Haas, C. (2024). Fairness in machine learning: A survey. *ACM Computing Surveys*, *56*(7), Article 166. Association for Computing Machinery.

Chan, G. (2024). AI employment decision-making: Integrating the equal opportunity merit principle and explainable AI. *AI & Society*, *39*(3), 1027–1038. https://doi.org/10.1007/s00146-022-01532-w

Chan, S. C. C., Neves, A. L., Majeed, A., & Faisal, A. (2024). Bridging the equity gap towards inclusive artificial intelligence in healthcare diagnostics. *BMJ (Clinical Research Ed.)*, *384*, q490. https://doi.org/10.1136/bmj.q490

Chauhan, P., & Kshetri, N. (2022). The role of data and artificial intelligence in driving diversity, equity, and inclusion. *Computer*, *55*(4), 88–93. https://doi.org/10.1109/MC.2022.3149017

Chemnad, K., & Othman, A. (2024). Digital accessibility in the era of artificial intelligence-Bibliometric analysis and systematic review. *Frontiers in Artificial Intelligence*, *7*, 1349668. https://doi.org/10.3389/frai.2024.1349668

Chen, K., Shao, A., Burapacheep, J., & Li, Y. (2024). Conversational AI and equity through assessing GPT-3's communication with diverse social groups on contentious topics. *Scientific Reports (Nature Publisher Group)*, *14*(1), 1561. Publicly Available Content Database. https://doi.org/10.1038/s41598-024-51969-w

Chen, P., Wu, L., & Wang, L. (2023). AI fairness in data management and analytics: A review on challenges, methodologies and applications. *Applied Sciences*, *13*(18), 10258. https://doi.org/10.3390/app131810258

Chen, R., Wang, J., Williamson, D., Chen, T., Lipkova, J., Lu, M., Sahai, S., & Mahmood, F. (2023). Algorithmic fairness in artificial intelligence for medicine and healthcare. *Nature Biomedical Engineering*, *7*(6), 719–742. https://doi.org/10.1038/s41551-023-01056-8

Cheng, L., Varshney, K. R., & Liu, H. (2021). Socially responsible AI algorithms: Issues, purposes, and challenges. *The Journal of Artificial Intelligence Research*, *71*, 1137–1181. Coronavirus Research Database; Publicly Available Content Database. https://doi.org/10.1613/jair.1.12814

Clark, C. R., Wilkins, C. H., Rodriguez, J. A., Preininger, A. M., Harris, J., DesAutels, S., Karunakaram, H., Rhee, K., Bates, D. W., & Dankwa-Mullan, I. (2021). Health care equity in the use of advanced analytics and artificial intelligence technologies in primary care. *Journal of General Internal Medicine*, *36*(10), 3188–3193. https://doi.org/10.1007/s11606-021-06846-x

Dankwa-Mullan, I. (2024). Health equity and ethical considerations in using artificial intelligence in public health and medicine. *Preventing Chronic Disease*, *21*. Nursing & Allied Health Collection; Public Health Database. https://doi.org/10.5888/pcd21.240245

Dankwa-Mullan, I., Scheufele, E. L., Matheny, M. E., Quintana, Y., Chapman, W. W., Jackson, G., & South, B. R. (2021). A proposed framework on integrating health equity and racial justice into the artificial intelligence development lifecycle. *Journal of Health Care for the Poor and Underserved*, *32*(2 Supplement), 300–317. Applied Social Sciences Index & Abstracts (ASSIA); Black Studies Center; Nursing & Allied Health Collection; Public Health Database; Sociology Collection.

Delecraz, S., Eltarr, L., Becuwe, M., Bouxin, H., Boutin, N., & Oullier, O. (2022). Making recruitment more inclusive: Unfairness monitoring with a job matching machine-learning algorithm. In *Proceedings of the 2nd International Workshop on Equitable Data and Technology*, Pittsburgh, PA (pp. 34–41). Association for Computing Machinery. https://doi.org/10.1145/3524491.3527309

Delgado-Rodríguez, S., García-Fandino, R., & Carrascal-Domínguez, S. (2023). Immersive technology and artificial intelligence to improve attention to diversity, equity and inclusion of students: Case study with augmented reality. *Dialogia*, *47*. https://doi.org/10.5585/47.2023.25204

Deo, R. C. (2024). Artificial intelligence and health equity: Opportunities and obstacles. *JACC. Advances*, *3*(9), 101045. https://doi.org/10.1016/j.jacadv.2024.101045

Desiere, S., & Struyven, L. (2021). Using artificial intelligence to classify Jobseekers: The accuracy-equity trade-off. *Journal of Social Policy*, *50*(2), 367–385. CINAHL Plus with Full Text. https://doi.org/10.1017/S0047279420000203

Duarte, E. F., Palomino, P. T., Falcão, T. P., Porto, G. L. P. M. B., Portela, C. dos S., Ribeiro, D. F., Nascimento, A., Aguiar, Y. P. C., Souza, M., Gasparotto, A. M. S., & Toda, A. M. (2024). GranDIHC-BR 2025–2035—GC6: Implications of artificial intelligence in HCI: A discussion on paradigms ethics and diversity equity and inclusion*. In *Proceedings of the XXIII Brazilian Symposium on Human Factors in Computing Systems*, Brasília (p. Article 22). Association for Computing Machinery. https://doi.org/10.1145/3702038.3702059

Dychiao, R. G., Nazer, L., Mlombwa, D., & Celi, L. A. (2024). Artificial intelligence and global health equity. *BMJ (Clinical Research Ed.)*, *387*, q2194. https://doi.org/10.1136/bmj.q2194

El Morr, C. (Ed.). (2022). *AI and Society: Tensions and Opportunities*. CRC Press Taylor & Francis.

El Morr, C., Fernandes, S., Singh, D., Sawhney, V., Gorman, R., & El-Lahib, Y. (2027). Disability-centered policy opportunities and challenges for accessible and inclusive AI: A scoping review. In C. El Morr, R. Gorman, E. Dolatabadi, & L. Seyyed-Kalantari (Eds.), *AI for a Just World: Power, Liberation, and the People Left Behind* (pp. 108–122). Chapman and Hall/CRC.

Ellen, J., Matos, J., Viola, M., Gallifant, J., Quion, J., Celi, L., & Hussein, N. (2024). Participant flow diagrams for health equity in AI. *Journal of Biomedical Informatics, 152*. https://doi.org/10.1016/j.jbi.2024.104631

Embi, P. J. (2021). Algorithmovigilance—Advancing methods to analyze and monitor artificial intelligence–Driven health care for effectiveness and equity. *JAMA Network Open, 4*(4). Publicly Available Content Database. https://doi.org/10.1001/jamanetworkopen.2021.4622

Friedler, S. A., Scheidegger, C., Venkatasubramanian, S., Choudhary, S., Hamilton, E. P., & Roth, D. (2019). A comparative study of fairness-enhancing interventions in machine learning. In *Proceedings of the Conference on Fairness, Accountability, and Transparency*, Atlanta, GA (pp. 329–338). Association for Computing Machinery. https://doi.org/10.1145/3287560.3287589

Ganesh, P., Chang, H., Strobel, M., & Shokri, R. (2023). On the impact of machine learning randomness on group fairness. In *Proceedings of the 2023 ACM Conference on Fairness, Accountability, and Transparency*, Chicago, IL (pp. 1789–1800). Association for Computing Machinery. https://doi.org/10.1145/3593013.3594116

Gasser, U. (2023). An EU landmark for AI governance. *Science (New York, N.Y.), 380*(6651), 1203. https://doi.org/10.1126/science.adj1627

Giovanola, B., & Tiribelli, S. (2023). Beyond bias and discrimination: Redefining the AI ethics principle of fairness in healthcare machine-learning algorithms. *AI & Society, 38*(2), 549–563. https://doi.org/10.1007/s00146-022-01455-6

Goretzko, D., & Finja Israel, L. S. (2022). Pitfalls of machine learning-based personnel selection: Fairness, transparency, and data quality. *Journal of Personnel Psychology, 21*(1), 37–47. APA PsycArticles®. https://doi.org/10.1027/1866-5888/a000287

Gorman, R., Creighton, A., Dada, S., Maret, P., Mgwigwi, T., Muhlenbach, F., Kundi, B., Tadesse, R., Dharmalingam, D., Clarkson, A., Stanley, A., Buettgen, A., Dinca-Panaitescu, M., Bangash, M., Brown, Z., Corfield, D., Getfield, J., Gray, Y., Gunraj, P. D., … El Morr, C. (2024). Disability data justice from the ground up: A practice-led, participatory co-design approach to building an AI search engine and data repository for local, national, and transnational disability organizations. *Critical Studies, 18*(1), 28–43. https://doi.org/10.51357/cs.v18i1.229

Goyal, N., Baumler, C., Nguyen, T., & III, H. D. (2024). The impact of explanations on fairness in human-AI decision-making: Protected vs proxy features. In *Proceedings of the 29th International Conference on Intelligent User Interfaces*, Greenville, SC (pp. 155–180). Association for Computing Machinery. https://doi.org/10.1145/3640543.3645210

Grote, T., & Keeling, G. (2022). Enabling fairness in healthcare through machine learning. *Ethics and Information Technology, 24*(3), 39. ABI/INFORM Global. https://doi.org/10.1007/s10676-022-09658-7

Holzmeyer, C. (2021). Beyond 'AI for Social Good' (AI4SG): Social transformations-not tech-fixes-for health equity. *Interdisciplinary Science Reviews, 46*(1–2), 94–125. https://doi.org/10.1080/03080188.2020.1840221

Hong, R., Kohno, T., & Morgenstern, J. (2023). Evaluation of targeted dataset collection on racial equity in face recognition. In *Proceedings of the 2023 AAAI/ACM Conference on AI, Ethics, and Society*, Montréal (pp. 531–541). Association for Computing Machinery. https://doi.org/10.1145/3600211.3604662

Horna-Saldaña, C. J., Perez Perez, J. E., & Toro Galeano, M. L. (2025). Artificial intelligence in the preservation of native languages and bridging the information access gap for indigenous peoples. *Journal of Enabling Technologies, 19*(1), 63–75. Applied Social Sciences Index & Abstracts (ASSIA); Linguistics and Language Behavior Abstracts (LLBA); Nursing & Allied Health Collection; Sociology Collection. https://doi.org/10.1108/JET-09-2024-0063

Hort, M., Chen, Z., Zhang, J. M., Harman, M., & Sarro, F. (2024). Bias mitigation for machine learning classifiers: A comprehensive survey. *ACM Journal on Responsibible Computing, 1*(2), Article 11. Association for Computing Machinery.

Hutchinson, B., & Mitchell, M. (2019). 50 years of test (Un)fairness: Lessons for machine learning. In *Proceedings of the Conference on Fairness, Accountability, and Transparency*, Atlanta, GA (pp. 49–58). Association for Computing Machinery. https://doi.org/10.1145/3287560.3287600

Hutchinson, B., Prabhakaran, V., Denton, E., Webster, K., Zhong, Y., & Denuyl, S. (2020). Unintended machine learning biases as social barriers for persons with disabilities. *SIGACCESS Accessibility and Computing*, (125), Article 9. Association for Computing Machinery, New York.

Iloanusi, N.-J., & Chun, S. A. (2024). AI impact on health equity for marginalized, racial, and ethnic minorities. In *Proceedings of the 25th Annual International Conference on Digital Government Research*, Taipei (pp. 841–848). Association for Computing Machinery. https://doi.org/10.1145/3657054.3657152

Inuwa-Dutse, I. (2023). FATE in AI: Towards algorithmic inclusivity and accessibility. In *Proceedings of the 3rd ACM Conference on Equity and Access in Algorithms, Mechanisms, and Optimization*, Boston, MA (p. Article 13). Association for Computing Machinery. https://doi.org/10.1145/3617694.3623233

Jenks, A., Onufer, L., & Guberman, D. (2024). Emergent questions of access: Disability and the integration of generative AI in teaching and learning. *Higher Education Research & Development*. https://doi.org/10.1080/07294360.2024.2442611

Jiang, W., & Pardos, Z. A. (2021). Towards equity and algorithmic fairness in student grade prediction. In *Proceedings of the 2021 AAAI/ACM Conference on AI, Ethics, and Society*, Virtual Event USA (pp. 608–617). Association for Computing Machinery. https://doi.org/10.1145/3461702.3462623

Jorgensen, M., Richert, H., Black, E., Criado, N., & Such, J. (2023). Not so fair: The impact of presumably fair machine learning models. In *Proceedings of the 2023 AAAI/ACM Conference on AI, Ethics, and Society* (pp. 297–311). Association for Computing Machinery, Montréal. https://doi.org/10.1145/3600211.3604699

Joshi, A. (2024). Big data and AI for gender equality in health: Bias is a big challenge. *Frontiers in Big Data*, *7*. https://doi.org/10.3389/fdata.2024.1436019

Kasirzadeh, A. (2022). Algorithmic fairness and structural injustice: Insights from feminist political philosophy. In *Proceedings of the 2022 AAAI/ACM Conference on AI, Ethics, and Society*, Oxford (pp. 349–356). Association for Computing Machinery. https://doi.org/10.1145/3514094.3534188

Kelan, E. K. (2024). Algorithmic inclusion: Shaping the predictive algorithms of artificial intelligence in hiring. *Human Resource Management Journal*, *34*(3), 694–707. ABI/INFORM Global. https://doi.org/10.1111/1748-8583.12511

Keswani, V., & Celis, L. E. (2025). Algorithmic fairness from the perspective of legal anti-discrimination principles. *Proceedings of the 2024 AAAI/ACM Conference on AI, Ethics, and Society,* San Jose, CA (pp. 724–737).

Klein, L., & D'Ignazio, C. (2024). Data feminism for AI. In *Proceedings of the 2024 ACM Conference on Fairness, Accountability, and Transparency*, Rio de Janeiro (pp. 100–112). Association for Computing Machinery. https://doi.org/10.1145/3630106.3658543

Kong, J. D., Akpudo, U. E., Effoduh, J. O., & Bragazzi, N. L. (2023). Leveraging responsible, explainable, and local artificial intelligence solutions for clinical public health in the Global South. *Healthcare (2227-9032)*, *11*(4), 457. CINAHL Plus with Full Text. https://doi.org/10.3390/healthcare11040457

Kong, Y. (2022). *Are "Intersectionally Fair" AI Algorithms Really Fair to Women of Color? A Philosophical Analysis* (rayyan-194881767). 485–494. https://doi.org/10.1145/3531146.3533114

Krafft, P. M., Young, M., Katell, M., Lee, J. E., Narayan, S., Epstein, M., Dailey, D., Herman, B., Tam, A., Guetler, V., Bintz, C., Raz, D., Jobe, P. O., Putz, F., Robick, B., & Barghouti, B. (2021). An action-oriented AI policy toolkit for technology audits by community advocates and activists. In *Proceedings of the 2021 ACM Conference on Fairness, Accountability, and Transparency*, Virtual Event Canada (pp. 772–781). Association for Computing Machinery. https://doi.org/10.1145/3442188.3445938

Kraft, A., & Soulier, E. (2024). Knowledge-enhanced language models are not bias-proof: Situated knowledge and epistemic injustice in AI. In *Proceedings of the 2024 ACM Conference on Fairness, Accountability, and Transparency*¸ Rio de Janeiro (pp. 1433–1445). Association for Computing Machinery. https://doi.org/10.1145/3630106.3658981

Kumar, D., Malin, B. A., Vishwanatha, J. K., Lang, W., & Hedges, J. R. (2024). AI in biomedicine—A forward-looking perspective on health equity. *International Journal of Environmental Research and Public Health*, *21*(12), 1642. Public Health Database; Publicly Available Content Database. https://doi.org/10.3390/ijerph21121642

La Fors, K., & Meissner, F. (2022). Contesting border artificial intelligence: Applying the guidance-ethics approach as a responsible design lens. *Data & Policy*, *4*. International Bibliography of the Social Sciences (IBSS); Politics Collection. https://doi.org/10.1017/dap.2022.28

Lalor, J. P., Abbasi, A., Oketch, K., Yang, Y., & Forsgren, N. (2024). Should fairness be a metric or a model? A model-based framework for assessing bias in machine learning pipelines. *ACM Transactions on Information Systems*, *42*(4), Article 99. Association for Computing Machinery.

Lee, M. S. A. (2019). Context-conscious fairness in using machine learning to make decisions. *AI Matters*, *5*(2), 23–29. Association for Computing Machinery.

Lewicki, K., Lee, M. S. A., Cobbe, J., & Singh, J. (2023). Out of context: Investigating the bias and fairness concerns of "artificial intelligence as a service". In *Proceedings of the 2023 CHI Conference on Human Factors in Computing Systems*, Rio de Janeiro (p. Article 135). Association for Computing Machinery. https://doi.org/10.1145/3544548.3581463

Liu, M., Ning, Y., Teixayavong, S., Mertens, M., Xu, J., Ting, D. S. W., Cheng, L. T.-E., Ong, J. C. L., Teo, Z. L., Tan, T. F., RaviChandran, N., Wang, F., Celi, L. A., Ong, M. E. H., & Liu, N. (2023). A translational perspective towards clinical AI fairness. *NPJ Digital Medicine*, *6*(1), 172. Coronavirus Research Database; Nursing & Allied Health Collection; Publicly Available Content Database. https://doi.org/10.1038/s41746-023-00918-4

Long, B., & Palmer, A. (2024). AI and access to justice: How AI legal advisors can reduce economic and shame-based barriers to justice. *Zeitschrift Fuer Technikfolgenabschaetzung in Theorie Und Praxis – Tatup*, *33*(1). https://doi.org/10.14512/tatup.33.1.21

Lyons, J. B., Hobbs, K., Rogers, S., & Clouse, S. H. (2023). Responsible (use of) AI. *Frontiers in Neuroergonomics*, *4*, 1201777. APA PsycInfo®. https://doi.org/10.3389/fnrgo.2023.1201777

Mhasawade, V., Zhao, Y., & Chunara, R. (2021). Machine learning and algorithmic fairness in public and population health. *Nature Machine Intelligence*, *3*(8), 659–666. https://doi.org/10.1038/s42256-021-00373-4

Molamohammadi, M., Taïk, A., Roux, N. L., & Farnadi, G. (2023). Unraveling the interconnected axes of heterogeneity in machine learning for democratic and inclusive advancements. In *Proceedings of the 3rd ACM Conference on Equity and Access in Algorithms, Mechanisms, and Optimization*, Boston, MA (p. Article 33). Association for Computing Machinery. https://doi.org/10.1145/3617694.3623256

Morris, M. R. (2020). AI and accessibility. *Association for Computing Machinery. Journal of the Association for Computing Machinery*, *67*(3), 35. ABI/INFORM Global. https://doi.org/10.1145/3356727

Nagi, F., Salih, R., Alzubaidi, M., Shah, H., Alam, T., Shah, Z., & Househ, M. (2023). Applications of Artificial Intelligence (AI) in medical education: A scoping review. *Studies in Health Technology and Informatics*, *305*, 648–651. https://doi.org/10.3233/SHTI230581

Neumann, T., & Wolczynski, N. (2023). Does AI-assisted fact-checking disproportionately benefit majority groups online? In *Proceedings of the 2023 ACM Conference on Fairness, Accountability, and Transparency*, Chicago, IL (pp. 480–490). Association for Computing Machinery. https://doi.org/10.1145/3593013.3594013

Nong, P., Hamasha, R., & Platt, J. (2024). Equity and AI governance at academic medical centers. *American Journal of Managed Care*, *30*, SP468–SP472. CINAHL Plus with Full Text. https://doi.org/10.37765/ajmc.2024.89555

Nyariro, M., Emami, E., & Rahimi, S. A. (2022). Integrating equity, diversity, and inclusion throughout the lifecycle of artificial intelligence in health. In *13th Augmented Human International Conference*, Winnipeg (p. Article 11). Association for Computing Machinery. https://doi.org/10.1145/3532530.3539565

Omotubora, A. (2024). AI for women's financial inclusion—Analysis of product design and policy approaches in Nigeria. *Data & Policy*, *6*. International Bibliography of the Social Sciences (IBSS); Politics Collection. https://doi.org/10.1017/dap.2024.62

Park, J. I. (2024). Harnessing artificial intelligence to promote health equity. *Clinical Nursing Research*, *33*(7), 507–508. https://doi.org/10.1177/10547738241270546

Prince, A. E. R., & Schwarcz, D. B. (2019). Proxy discrimination in the age of artificial intelligence and big data. *Information Privacy Law eJournal*. https://api.semanticscholar.org/CorpusID:132118143

Qadri, R., Shelby, R., Bennett, C. L., & Denton, E. (2023). AI's regimes of representation: A community-centered study of text-to-image models in South Asia. In *Proceedings of the 2023 ACM Conference on Fairness, Accountability, and Transparency*, Chicago, IL (pp. 506–517). Association for Computing Machinery. https://doi.org/10.1145/3593013.3594016

Raji, I. D., Smart, A., White, R. N., Mitchell, M., Gebru, T., Hutchinson, B., Smith-Loud, J., Theron, D., & Barnes, P. (2020). *Closing the AI accountability gap: Defining an end-to-end framework for internal algorithmic auditing* (rayyan-194881684). 33–44. https://doi.org/10.1145/3351095.3372873

Rajpurkar, P., Chen, E., Banerjee, O., & Topol, E. J. (2022). AI in health and medicine. *Nature Medicine*, *28*(1), 31–38. https://doi.org/10.1038/s41591-021-01614-0

Ramos, J., & Wilson-Kennedy, Z. (2024). Promoting equity and addressing concerns in teaching and learning with artificial intelligence. *Frontiers in Education*, *9*. https://doi.org/10.3389/feduc.2024.1487882

Rosa, P. (2025). The potential role of artificial intelligence to promote the participation and inclusion in physical exercise and sports for people with disabilities: A narrative review. *Journal of Bodywork and Movement Therapies*, *42*, 127–131. https://doi.org/10.1016/j.jbmt.2024.12.024

Roscoe, R. D. (2023). Building inclusive and equitable artificial intelligence for education. *XRDS*, *29*(3), 22–25. Association for Computing Machinery.

Roshanaei, M. (2024). Towards best practices for mitigating artificial intelligence implicit bias in shaping diversity, inclusion and equity in higher education. *Education and Information Technologies*, *29*(14), 18959–18984. ERIC. https://doi.org/10.1007/s10639-024-12605-2

Roy, A., Horstmann, J., & Ntoutsi, E. (2023). Multi-dimensional discrimination in law and machine learning—A comparative overview. In *Proceedings of the 2023 ACM Conference on Fairness, Accountability, and Transparency*, Chicago, IL (pp. 89–100). Association for Computing Machinery. https://doi.org/10.1145/3593013.3593979

Rubeis, G., Fang, M. L., & Sixsmith, A. (2022). Equity in ageTech for ageing well in technology-driven places: The role of social determinants in designing AI-based assistive technologies. *Science and Engineering Ethics*, *28*(6), 49. Humanities Index. https://doi.org/10.1007/s11948-022-00397-y

Sanchez, T. W., Qian, Y., & Yan, X. (2024). AI applications in transportation and equity: A survey of U.S. Transportation Professionals. *Future Transportation*, *4*(4), 1161. ABI/INFORM Global; Publicly Available Content Database. https://doi.org/10.3390/futuretransp4040056

Santos, R. de S., Fronchetti, F., Freire, S., & Spinola, R. (2025). Software fairness debt: Building a research Agenda for addressing bias in AI systems. *ACM Transactions on Software Engineering and Methodology*, Association for Computing Machinery. https://doi.org/10.1145/3709357

Shneiderman, B. (2021). Viewpoint responsible AI: Bridging from ethics to practice. *Association for Computing Machinery. Communications of the ACM*, *64*(8), 32. ABI/INFORM Global. https://doi.org/10.1145/3445973

Siala, H., & Wang, Y. (2022). SHIFTing artificial intelligence to be responsible in healthcare: A systematic review. *Social Science & Medicine*, *296*, N.PAG-N.PAG. CINAHL Plus with Full Text. https://doi.org/10.1016/j.socscimed.2022.114782

Smith, H. (2021). Clinical AI: Opacity, accountability, responsibility and liability. *AI & Society*, *36*(2), 535–545. https://doi.org/10.1007/s00146-020-01019-6

Solyst, J., Xie, S., Yang, E., Stewart, A. E. B., Eslami, M., Hammer, J., & Ogan, A. (2023). "I would like to design": Black girls analyzing and ideating fair and accountable AI. In *Proceedings of the 2023 CHI Conference on Human Factors in Computing Systems*, Hamburg (p. Article 452). Association for Computing Machinery. https://doi.org/10.1145/3544548.3581378

Sühr, T., Hilgard, S., & Lakkaraju, H. (2021). Does fair ranking improve minority outcomes? Understanding the interplay of human and algorithmic biases in online hiring. In *Proceedings of the 2021 AAAI/ACM Conference on AI, Ethics, and Society*, Virtual Event USA (pp. 989–999). Association for Computing Machinery. https://doi.org/10.1145/3461702.3462602

Suresh, H., & Guttag, J. (2021a). A framework for understanding sources of harm throughout the machine learning life cycle. In *Proceedings of the 1st ACM Conference on Equity and Access in Algorithms, Mechanisms, and Optimization*, New York (p. Article 17). Association for Computing Machinery. https://doi.org/10.1145/3465416.3483305

Svetlova, E. (2022). AI ethics and systemic risks in finance. *AI and Ethics*, *2*(4), 713–725. https://doi.org/10.1007/s43681-021-00129-1

Teixeira, S., Rodrigues, J., Veloso, B., & Gama, J. (2022). An exploratory diagnosis of artificial intelligence risks for a responsible governance. In *Proceedings of the 15th International Conference on Theory and Practice of Electronic Governance*, Guimarães (pp. 25–31). Association for Computing Machinery. https://doi.org/10.1145/3560107.3560298

Thomasian, N. M., Eickhoff, C., & Adashi, E. Y. (2021). Advancing health equity with artificial intelligence. *Journal of Public Health Policy*, *42*(4), 602–611. Applied Social Sciences Index & Abstracts (ASSIA); Politics Collection; Public Health Database; Sociology Collection. https://doi.org/10.1057/s41271-021-00319-5

Tilmes, N. (2022). Disability, fairness, and algorithmic bias in AI recruitment. *Ethics and Information Technology*, *24*(2). ABI/INFORM Global. https://doi.org/10.1007/s10676-022-09633-2

Tomasev, N., McKee, K. R., Kay, J., & Mohamed, S. (2021). Fairness for unobserved characteristics: Insights from technological impacts on Queer communities. In *Proceedings of the 2021 AAAI/ACM Conference on AI, Ethics, and Society*, Virtual Event USA (pp. 254–265). Association for Computing Machinery. https://doi.org/10.1145/3461702.3462540

Trewin, S., Basson, S., Muller, M., Branham, S., Treviranus, J., Gruen, D., Hebert, D., Lyckowski, N., & Manser, E. (2019). Considerations for AI fairness for people with disabilities. *AI Matters*, *5*(3), 40–63. Association for Computing Machinery.

Tyagi, S., & Anuj, A. (2024). Promoting gender fair resume screening using gender-weighted sampling. In *Proceedings of the International Conference on Computing, Machine Learning and Data Science*, Singapore (p. Article 57). Association for Computing Machinery. https://doi.org/10.1145/3661725.3661786

Uddin, S., Lu, H., Rahman, A., & Gao, J. (2024). A novel approach for assessing fairness in deployed machine learning algorithms. *Scientific Reports (Nature Publisher Group), 14*(1), 17753. Publicly Available Content Database. https://doi.org/10.1038/s41598-024-68651-w

Ueda, D., Kakinuma, T., Fujita, S., Kamagata, K., Fushimi, Y., Ito, R., Matsui, Y., Nozaki, T., Nakaura, T., Fujima, N., Tatsugami, F., Yanagawa, M., Hirata, K., Yamada, A., Tsuboyama, T., Kawamura, M., Fujioka, T., & Naganawa, S. (2024). Fairness of artificial intelligence in healthcare: Review and recommendations. *Japanese Journal of Radiology*, *42*(1), 3–15. Nursing & Allied Health Collection. https://doi.org/10.1007/s11604-023-01474-3

Upadhyay, U., Gradisek, A., Iqbal, U., Dhar, E., Yu-Chuan, L., & Syed-Abdul, S. (2023). Call for the responsible artificial intelligence in the healthcare. *BMJ Health & Care Informatics*, *30*(1). Nursing & Allied Health Collection; Public Health Database. https://doi.org/10.1136/bmjhci-2023-100920

Varanasi, R. A., & Goyal, N. (2023). "It is currently hodgepodge": Examining AI/ML Practitioners' Challenges during Co-production of Responsible AI Values. In *Proceedings of the 2023 CHI Conference on Human Factors in Computing Systems*, Hamburg (p. Article 251). Association for Computing Machinery. https://doi.org/10.1145/3544548.3580903

Vishwanatha, J. K., Christian, A., Sambamoorthi, U., Thompson, E. L., Stinson, K., & Syed, T. A. (2023). Community perspectives on AI/ML and health equity: AIM-AHEAD nationwide stakeholder listening sessions. *PLoS Digital Health*, *1*(6), 1–18. CINAHL Plus with Full Text. https://doi.org/10.1371/journal.pdig.0000288

Xavier, B. (2025). Biases within AI: Challenging the illusion of neutrality. *AI & Society*, *40*(3), 1545–1546. https://doi.org/10.1007/s00146-024-01985-1

Xu, Z., Li, J., Yao, Q., Li, H., Zhao, M., & Zhou, S. K. (2024). Addressing fairness issues in deep learning-based medical image analysis: A systematic review. *NPJ Digital Medicine*, *7*(1), 286. Coronavirus Research Database; Nursing & Allied Health Collection; Publicly Available Content Database. https://doi.org/10.1038/s41746-024-01276-5

Zhuang, K., & Goggin, G. (2024). New possibilities or problems for disability and inclusion? The case of AI and ADMs across work. *Telematics and Informatics*, *92*. https://doi.org/10.1016/j.tele.2024.102156

2 Beyond White Skin
The Need for Equitable AI in Healthcare

Janise Peters

INTRODUCTION

My journey into this research began with a personal experience. As a Black mother of Black children, I've faced my fair share of hurdles. However, when my five-year-old son suffered from a fever accompanied by a bumpy full body rash, I gained a new interest in medical racism.

When he was initially seen by a physician, we were not given a diagnosis and were instructed to treat him at home with calamine lotion. Unsatisfied, we went to another walk-in clinic later that day for a second opinion. This time, we received an accurate diagnosis: scarlet fever due to strep throat. The characteristic reddish presentation of scarlet fever is often subtle or absent in highly melanated skin, which most likely led to the initial misdiagnosis (or lack thereof). He was subsequently prescribed antibiotics.

This experience fueled a desire in me to find less subjective means of obtaining healthcare, where practitioner bias—whether unconscious or conscious—would not affect diagnoses or treatment. Technology offers an objective view of healthcare where a patient's skin color would not impede access to fair and equitable care and treatment. Or so I thought. This chapter explores the scope of this issue through a review of relevant literature, highlights key examples, and proposes suggestions for future policy and practice.

Artificial intelligence (AI) offers great potential in transforming the delivery of healthcare. Traditional medicine is limited by the breadth of knowledge providers possess or are willing to acquire. By contrast, technology knows no bounds and AI is only limited by the amount of data available in the dataset from which information is drawn. AI has the ability to inform medical diagnosis, treatment and resource allocation. With performance accuracy and speed comparable to that of humans, AI's usefulness in healthcare is promising (Al Kuwaiti et al., 2023).

However, over all this hope looms the possibility that AI-generated healthcare brings with it the racial biases already ingrained in traditional medical data, education, and care. The long-standing focus has been patients with white skin. They make up most of our pool of research participants, visual illustrations in medical literature, and target market for product development. It is hard to extend the knowledge gained from research to all the population when it is generated based on the outcomes of a specific segment of the population. Further hampering accurate identification of conditions, the majority of clinical images in print and online show how conditions present on white skin leading to misdiagnosis or underdiagnosis in those with darker skin. Moreover, health products are being developed and designed with White people in mind (e.g., bandages, spirometer, pulse oximeter).

While there are no biological differences between races, disparities in healthcare access, care, and outcomes for those with dark skin tones are a direct consequence of systemic racism and the unequal distribution of social determinants of health. Therefore, for healthcare solutions generated by AI to be effective, equitable, and accurate, the inherent biases and forms of discrimination found in traditional medicine must first be dismantled.

Prior to contemplating the use of AI in assisting with diagnosis and treatment of patients, we must first explore the "garbage in, garbage out" (GIGO) effect. The GIGO concept is based on the

DOI: 10.1201/9781003737810-3

idea that if data is of poor quality, flawed or biased and it is put into a system that system's output will also be of poor quality (Hanson et al., 2023). This suggests that the effectiveness of AI for healthcare will be hindered and perpetuated by existing racial, gendered, and medical hierarchies (garbage in). This leads to adverse health outcomes that disproportionately affect marginalized groups (garbage out).

This review will examine the historical roots of visual and systemic bias in traditional medicine, exploring its direct manifestation in AI, and proposing multifaceted strategies for achieving diagnostic equity that extends beyond white skin.

METHODS

Search and Study Selection

Aspect	Description	Details/Criteria
Search strategy	A systematic search using the University of Toronto libraries system was conducted to identify relevant journal articles on the intersection of race, technology, and health.	Databases included Pub Med Central, Ovid, Wiley, Springer, Elsevier, and ProQuest.
Key terms	The following key terms and Boolean operators were used in the search:	• "Diagnosis AND skin color" • "Artificial intelligence AND healthcare" • "Artificial intelligence AND healthcare AND race"
Inclusion criteria	Papers were included based on a predefined set of criteria to ensure relevance and quality.	• Published in English • Journal articles published within the last ten years • Research conducted in multi-ethnic regions • Searches of peer-reviewed literature completed between April 14, 2025 and August 14, 2025
Exclusion criteria	Papers were excluded if they met any of the following criteria:	• Published more than ten years ago • Published in a language other than English • Books
Study selection	All identified papers were screened for eligibility.	20 papers were screened and 10 were selected for final inclusion in the review.

Following the initial comprehensive search and screening process, and in response to reviewer feedback, additional studies were identified. These articles were then subjected to the same inclusion and exclusion criteria as the initially identified studies. Three new articles met the criteria and have been incorporated into the review. This refined set of articles further strengthened the comprehensiveness of my findings by further validating the notion that bias exists in multiple health disciplines.

LITERATURE REVIEW

To further explore the GIGO concept and how it may have negative implications for the use of AI for healthcare, we must first determine the current impact of inequity in the healthcare system. Specifically, we'll look at how healthcare is experienced through the lens of racialized patients.

A focused literature review was conducted. Studies highlighting the disparities that currently exist in our healthcare system for those without white skin were examined. The scope of the review included journal articles published within the last ten years. The review specifically focused on multi-ethnic populations. Key terms used in the search included "diagnosis AND skin color", "artificial intelligence AND healthcare", and "artificial intelligence AND healthcare AND race".

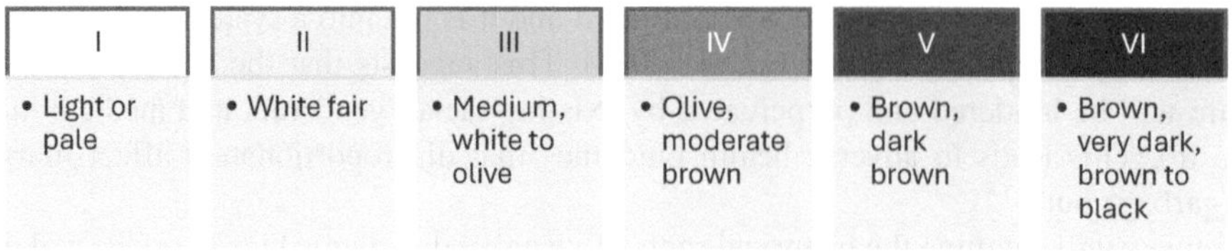

FIGURE 2.1 Fitzpatrick scale.

Examining Patient Outcomes in the Absence of Equitable Healthcare Delivery

The Fitzpatrick scale (FTS) is a numerical categorization system for human skin color. Thomas B. Fitzpatrick, an American dermatologist, created this classification scheme in 1975. It is a way to estimate the response of different types of skin to sunlight (Figure 2.1). Researchers who champion the use of more equitable methods of categorization suggest that this scale is often misused as a way to classify people by race or ethnicity and is therefore considered a biased scale (Okoji, Taylor, & Lipoff, 2021). The FTS assumes that white skin is the baseline, therefore suggesting that other skin colors are deviations from that norm. However, the perceived inherent biases of this scale will not be examined in this review. For the purposes of this review, the FTS will be used merely as a classification tool.

Diagnosis of skin conditions with "standard" skin presentations are often delayed in FTS skin types IV–VI. It is not that these cases are less common in types IV–VI vs. I–III, rather, it is that they go undetected for a longer period of time until they are finally diagnosed. This may be due to practitioners' unfamiliarity with the presentation of certain conditions in diverse patient populations. Sadly, the hold up in correct disease identification leads to a decrease in patient quality of life.

Diagnosis of diseases such as granular parakeratosis, a skin condition "characterized by erythematous scaly patches, papules, and plaques" (Ip & Li, 2022), is not easily distinguishable if skin redness (erythema) is used as the primary visual cue. A patient with FTS type V skin suffered from granular parakeratosis for nearly two years due to misdiagnosis which resulted in improper treatment. In this case, the patient endured many months of pain and discomfort (i.e., vulvar itching, burning) before receiving a proper diagnosis (McAleer, Powers, & Mauskar, 2025). This is evidence that supports the inclusion of a variety of skin types and descriptors when describing a dermatologic condition.

A study examining time to diagnosis in patients suffering from nail psoriasis found that patients with skin types IV–VI were diagnosed on average three years later than those with type I–III (59 vs. 24 months: $p = 0.009$). The individuals with darker skin also had more severe cases by the time they received their diagnosis (Chang, Lee, Desai, & Lipner, 2023). This is very significant given that nail psoriasis may be considered an indicator for patients at risk for future psoriatic joint damage. Also, treatment for psoriatic nail disease may take up to a year to show effectiveness, indicating that a timely diagnosis is crucial (Pasch, 2016).

Pressure injuries (PIs) like bed sores are categorized by stages based on depth and severity of damage to skin (Table 2.1). Studies have determined that more severe (stages 3–4) PIs are more frequently found in dark skin (11% vs 6.5%, 13% vs 6.5%) whereas stages 1 and 2 were found more commonly in patients with white skin (38% vs 13%). The authors suggest that this discrepancy may be occurring due to difficulties in identifying PIs in darker skin (Black et al., 2023).

Consequences of Bias in Traditional Medical Education and Educational Material

Visual underrepresentation of skin of color in medical textbooks, anatomical atlases, clinical images, and educational materials is a dominant theme. This disparity in representation has its roots based on over 2,500 years of history (Massie et al., 2021). Past prominent

TABLE 2.1
Pressure Injuries Stages

Stage	Description
1	• The skin is intact, but there is a persistent area of non-blanchable redness. • The area may be painful, firm, soft, warmer, or cooler compared to the surrounding tissue.
2	• There is partial-thickness skin loss involving the epidermis and/or dermis
3	• There is full-thickness skin loss. • Subcutaneous fat may be visible, but bone, tendon, or muscle is not exposed.
4	• There is full-thickness tissue loss with exposed bone, tendon, or muscle.

American medical scholars helped to create and spread the notion that the Black race was biologically inferior. But oddly enough, darker skinned individuals were thought to have a higher tolerance to pain. These theories were a standard part of the curriculum in U.S. medical schools from the 18th century through to the first half of the 20th century (Byrd & Clayton, 2001). In recent years, there has been a shift and while myths surrounding specific races have lessened, the need for representation remains.

One study reports that the lack of adequate visual representation of racial minorities in lecture slides and other course material is leading future healthcare providers to make incorrect inferences about pain tolerance for Black and Hispanic patients (Massie et al., 2021). Black people are thought to have "thick skin" and thus are given less pain medication even when they report feeling as much pain as their White counterparts. Hoffman, Trawalter, Axt, and Oliver (2016) report that Black patients compared to White patients were less likely to receive pain medication (57% vs. 74%) for extremity fractures. Kuwait University, College of Medicine surveyed students in preclinical and clinical programs and determined that not only were they overall less accurate in correct diagnosis of disease with visual presentations in types I–III vs IV–VI, they were also less confident in their identification when it came to darker skin (Ahmad et al., 2024).

A study specifically focused on examining skin type diversity in pediatric medical textbooks highlighted the need for diversity in medical educational material not only for dermatologist but also for pediatricians. These specialists are sometimes the first point of contact for young patients, which means that their providers need to be equipped to identify common conditions that present differently on different skin types (Gruver, Pruszynski, & Haugh, 2024).

The GIGO Effect: Built-in Bias in AI-based Diagnostic Tools

With bias inherent in modern medicine, it is only natural that bias will creep into AI-based medical solutions. Chakravorti (2022) examined the potential and ultimate failures of AI application during the COVID-19 pandemic. AI teams from around the globe mobilized and developed AI tools to diagnose COVID cases using algorithms trained on lung CT scans data, a separate team trained their AI to identify coughing sounds, and another trained their AI to predict which patients would develop severe respiratory disease. Chakravorti (2022) found that most AI-based decision-making tools created in response to the pandemic were of little use due to poor datasets as well as "automated discrimination". The latter refers to the idea that although datasets appear comprehensive, bias is already ingrained into datasets because of historical hierarchies.

Bias does not occur solely through visual data. In a key recent psychiatric study, researchers discovered a tendency for providers (and subsequently the resulting AI, specifically large language models) to over-diagnose Black individuals with schizophrenia while concurrently under-diagnosing them with conditions such as anxiety and depression, compared to their White counterparts. This disparity was significantly influenced by the patient's vernacular. Critically, when the AI analyzed the plain text and audio from clinical interviews, the model inferred the patient's race from their speech patterns and provided diagnoses that reflected these preexisting racial biases (Bouguettaya, Stuart, & Aboujaoude, 2025).

Another study tested four different AIs for race-based bias in medicine and determined the AI sometimes generated groundless race-based equations related to kidney function and lung capacity based on the explicit or implicit mention of patient race. In this instance, the AI again helped to perpetuate false and potentially harmful clinical conclusions (Omiye et al., 2023).

In cardiology, the American Heart Association's Heart Failure Risk Score, a score that arbitrarily categorizes all Black patients as being lower risk for in-hospital mortality when admitted as patients with heart failure, is another case where algorithmic bias can have very detrimental consequences (Vyas, Eisenstein, & Jones, 2020). These examples make it clear that disparities in diagnosis and treatment do not discriminate based on health specialty.

However, this phenomenon extends beyond skin color or race. If the AI algorithms exclude other marginalized groups such as youths, women, older adults, immigrants and refugees, and people with disabilities, the AI may not be able to accurately diagnose or treat that patient population either (Norori et al., 2021)..

STRATEGIES FOR ACHIEVING DIAGNOSTIC EQUITY THROUGH AI

Data Diversification and Ethical Collection

To achieve data diversification, a standard method for medical data collection and storage must be established. Data must also be maintained in a consistent format. We must advocate for the collection of data from diverse sources globally, ensuring it adheres to this set format. We must also take measures to ensure adequate representation from marginalized groups, particularly focusing on visual symptom presentation across the full spectrum of skin types.

Universal privacy and confidentiality measures are necessary and must be enforced to ensure patient data is not disclosed inappropriately. Laws under the Ontario Human Rights Code, the Canadian Human Rights Act, and the Anti-Racism Act, 2017, support the collection of race-based data but require that collection must be made with the patient's expressed consent, be de-identified when at all possible and be collected to promote equality. While these laws exist, the Canadian government does not impose that the collection of race-based patient data be done. Therefore, it may be up to provincial or municipal jurisdictions (e.g., public health units, hospitals) to enforce the collection of this data in order to ensure data diversification and in turn more equitable outcomes for their population.

The collection of race-based data poses legitimate concerns for patients. They may fear that this data may be used to exclude them from certain programing or dictate the quality of care they receive. Although there is always a risk of discriminatory application, a multilayered defense of safeguards may decrease this risk. These safeguards include technical protections (de-identification, access controls), policy requirements, legal accountability (privacy and human rights law), and data governance standards (OCAP/CARE principles). Adhering to these controls create a protected environment for ethical and equitable AI development.

AI Model Development and Bias Mitigation

Healthcare AI teams must ensure health equity-focused AI developers are included in team composition. They will create processes for actively identifying and mitigating bias during AI model design, training, and deployment, specifically targeting racial and visual biases. These AI-equity experts must also implement post-go-live monitoring and auditing processes to detect and correct emergent biases, with a focus on outcomes for diverse populations. With all measures in place, if it so happens that the dataset used to train an AI application does not accurately reflect the demographics of its target population, the tool should not be used, as it may be statistically biased.

Healthcare Professional Education and Anti-Racism Training

To increase the likelihood that we obtain better data and build good datasets in the future, it is imperative that medical educational material and curriculums become more inclusive. Certain medical schools are making efforts to include perspectives from marginalized communities (i.e., people with disabilities, 2SLGBTQ+, Black and Indigenous). Their goal should be to graduate culturally safe, anti-racist, and equity-minded physicians who are exceptionally prepared to address and reduce health disparities in marginalized communities and contribute to a healthier, more equitable society. We must also develop and deliver anti-racism training to those currently practicing in the medical field. This training should be focused on both the history that is contributing to these biases and also current equity focused best practices to care that might dispel long held stereotypes and myths. The medical education curriculum and anti-racism training should be cocreated along with people representing minority groups.

Policy, Governance, and Accountability

Racism in medicine is not new but it is something a bit taboo. The Tuskegee Syphilis study is a prime example of such racism. In the U.S. state of Alabama, approximately 600 Black men were targeted and used to study the progression of syphilis from 1932 to 1972. Treatment was withheld and they were misled about the gravity of their condition. This along with other examples are reasons why people of color have reservations about the intentions of White providers, the medical establishment, and research (Freimuth et al., 2001).

Mistrust and the fear of exploitation by the medical system have reduced throughout the years and efforts have been made to include racial and ethnic identifiers in U.S. research (Massie et al., 2021). However, policies and governing bodies are needed to oversee, review, and audit AI systems for racial bias. Additionally, information generated by AI for healthcare must be carefully regulated.

Policy Recommendation: Checklist for AI Procurement

The following checklist (or one like it) should be mandated and enforced by Health Canada during the procurement and use of all healthcare-related AI tools to ensure they align with principles of ethical judgment and equity. Additionally, any AI solution developed for the purposes of diagnosis and treatment must meet certification requirements set out by Health Canada.

Requirement	Description	Rationale for Inclusion
Mandatory clinician override	The system must always allow the treating clinician to override and document the rationale for deviating from the AI's recommendation.	Ensures human accountability remains paramount and prevents "automation bias" when the AI output conflicts with clinical judgment, especially in atypical patient presentations.
Provenance metadata	All AI models must be accompanied by comprehensive metadata detailing the demographic composition (race, ethnicity, gender, age) of the datasets used for training and validation.	Enables procurement teams to assess the model's generalizability and identify potential areas of bias before deployment in diverse, multi-ethnic healthcare settings.
Mandatory pilot in diverse settings	Before widespread adoption, the technology must undergo a mandatory, localized pilot study in clinical settings known for serving diverse and multi-ethnic patient populations.	Assesses real-world performance, safety, and equitable outcomes under different operational conditions, capturing failure modes missed during initial testing.
Remediation funding	The procurement contract must include a dedicated fund or contractual clause requiring the vendor to support rapid, cost-free remediation (retraining, patch deployment) if post-deployment audit reveals racial or ethnic disparities in performance or safety.	Ensures accountability and resources are available to address bias immediately upon detection, promoting continuous quality improvement in health equity.

DISCUSSION

To improve AI effectiveness in the administration of healthcare, we must take measures to ensure data diversification in order to train AI solutions on high quality datasets. To achieve a comprehensive dataset, data must be collected and stored electronically. This may present a challenge as access to electronic medical records is not widespread and it would be necessary for streamlined data collection and sharing.

Even though race and ethnic demographic information should be captured along with patient health information, when possible, patients may not want to self-identify thinking they may face discrimination or subpar care. This is also a documented fear for some who are from Indigenous communities. Some individuals are able to "pass" for White and use this privilege to increase their chances of receiving better care.

To further enhance the diagnostic capabilities of providers and technological diagnostic tools, conditions should have symptoms descriptors that can apply to a variety of patients, not just White ones. Additionally, culturally competent healthcare providers would not only make patients feel more comfortable but also ensure more equitable care.

This review was limited in that it was not focused on only Canadian sources but rather various multiethnic regions. To increase the validity of these findings it would be preferable to obtain data focused on a specific region, determine its current state, make the suggested changes, and evaluate outcomes.

Furthermore, the focus of this work was primarily a review of health conditions with visual representations. It is important to note that racial bias extends past dermatological conditions or those health conditions with symptoms that are commonly identified visually.

CONCLUSION

The evidence provided in this review supports the idea that there is inherent racism in medicine and that this can be replicated in AI solutions in healthcare. AI may even amplify existing racial biases, particularly those stemming from a predominant focus on white skin in traditional medical data and education.

Future research should focus on establishing guidelines to design, train, deploy, and monitor AI diagnostic solutions for healthcare. The following proposed agenda suggests the next critical steps to bolster effective real-world application of an equitable AI interventional framework for healthcare:

1. Identify and secure a hospital pilot site committed to advancing health equity. Within this site, select a department or clinical discipline with a known history of documented unequitable care (e.g., psychiatry, cardiology) to maximize the impact of the intervention.
2. Create of a multidisciplinary Advisory Board composed of clinicians, data scientists, policy experts, and community representatives to oversee the project.
3. Establish a baseline/current state of diagnostic and treatment disparities through chart audits.
4. Select an AI vendor partner and their specific diagnostic tool to pilot the new procurement framework.
5. Deliberate effort must be taken to ensure the AI is trained using a high-quality, demographically representative dataset. The advisory board must approve the provenance metadata before deployment.
6. The pilot's success must be evaluated comprehensively using a Health Impact Assessment. This mandated evaluation process will explicitly measure the technology's impact on health equity, algorithmic fairness, and patient outcomes across diverse demographic groups.

This structured approach ensures that the deployment and use of AI for healthcare is not only safe and effective but also proactively designed for equity from the initial procurement stage onward.

ACKNOWLEDGMENT

Portions of this chapter were developed with the assistance of Gemini AI for editing and proofreading (grammar and spell-checking). All intellectual contributions, interpretations, and final editorial decisions are the authors' own; the authors take full responsibility for the content. All AI-assisted or AI-generated material was thoroughly reviewed and verified by the authors.

REFLECTION QUESTIONS

1. How does the concept of garbage in, garbage out explain the relationship between historical medical education and modern AI diagnostic errors?
2. How might using poor-quality or biased datasets to train an AI system directly impact patient safety and health outcomes?
3. Reflect on the proposed Checklist for AI Procurement. Do you believe mandatory clinician overrides and pilot studies in diverse settings are sufficient to mitigate algorithmic bias, or are deeper structural changes needed?
4. The text mentions collecting "race-based patient data". What are the ethical considerations and potential risks and benefits associated with this practice? How can we ensure such data is used to promote equitable care rather than reinforce stereotypes?
5. How could practical experience—such as clinical placements in diverse communities, pediatric hospitals, institutes for the blind, or with under-housed and 2SLGBTQ+ communities—shape a provider's ability to deliver equity-informed care?

REFERENCES

Ahmad, G., Ghanem, R., Mahfouz, W. S., AlHaddad, S., AlHayyan, W., AlMoosa, A., Shehab, H. F., AlRasheid, A., Garashi, A., Kankouni, M. W., & Ziyab, A. H. (2024). Skin colour and disease diagnosis: A cross-sectional study of medical students in Kuwait. *Skin Health and Disease*, *4*(4), e396. https://doi.org/10.1002/ski2.396

Al Kuwaiti, A., Nazer, K., Al-Reedy, A., Al-Shehri, S., Al-Muhanna, A., Subbarayalu, A. V., … & Al-Muhanna, F. A. (2023). A review of the role of artificial intelligence in healthcare. *Journal of Personalized Medicine*, *13*(6), 951.

Black, J., Cox, J., Capasso, V., Bliss, D. Z., Delmore, B., Iyer, V., Massaro, J., Munro, C., Pittman, J., & Ayello, E. A. (2023). Current perspectives on pressure injuries in persons with dark skin tones from the National Pressure Injury Advisory Panel. *Advances in Skin & Wound Care*, *36*(9), 470–480. https://doi.org/10.1097/ASW.0000000000000032

Bouguettaya, A., Stuart, E. M., & Aboujaoude, E. (2025). Racial bias in AI-mediated psychiatric diagnosis and treatment: A qualitative comparison of four large language models. *NPJ Digital Medicine*, *8*(1), Article 332. https://doi.org/10.1038/s41746-025-01746-4

Byrd, W. M., & Clayton, L. A. (2001). Race, medicine, and health care in the United States: A historical survey. *Journal of the National Medical Association*, *93*(3 Suppl), 11S–34S.

Chakravorti, B. (2022). Why AI failed to live up to its potential during the pandemic. *Harvard Business Review*, *17*. https://hbr.org/2022/03/why-ai-failed-to-live-up-to-its-potential-during-the-pandemic

Chang, M. J., Lee, D., Desai, A. D., & Lipner, S. R. (2023). Disparities in time to diagnosis and disease severity in skin of colour patients with nail psoriasis: A retrospective analysis. *Journal of the European Academy of Dermatology and Venereology*, *37*(8), e1066–e1067. https://doi.org/10.1111/jdv.19110

Freimuth, V. S., Quinn, S. C., Thomas, S. B., Cole, G., Zook, E., & Duncan, T. (2001). African Americans' views on research and the Tuskegee Syphilis study. *Social Science & Medicine*, *52*(5), 797–808. https://doi.org/10.1016/S0277-9536(00)00178-7

Government of Ontario. (2017). *Anti-Racism Act, 2017*, S.O. 2017, c. 15. Ontario.ca.

Gruver, J. R., Pruszynski, J., & Haugh, I. (2024). Representation of diverse skin tones in Nelson's Textbook of Pediatrics. *Archives of Dermatological Research*, *316*(10), 733. https://doi.org/10.1007/s00403-024-03460-9

Hanson, B., Stall, S., Cutcher-Gershenfeld, J., Vrouwenvelder, K., Wirz, C., Rao, Y. D., & Peng, G. (2023). Garbage in, garbage out: Mitigating risks and maximizing benefits of AI in research. *Nature*, *623*(7985), 28–31. https://doi.org/10.1038/d41586-023-03316-8

Hoffman, K. M., Trawalter, S., Axt, J. R., & Oliver, M. N. (2016). Racial bias in pain assessment and treatment recommendations, and false beliefs about biological differences between blacks and Whites. *Proceedings of the National Academy of Sciences*, *113*(16), 4296–4301. https://doi.org/10.1073/pnas.1516047113

Human Rights Code, R.S.O. 1990, c. H.19. Ontario.ca

Ip, K. H. K., & Li, A. (2022). Clinical features, histology, and treatment outcomes of granular parakeratosis: A systematic review. *International Journal of Dermatology*, *61*(8), 973–978.

Massie, J. P., Cho, D. Y., Kneib, C. J., Sousa, J. D., Morrison, S. D., & Friedrich, J. B. (2021). A picture of modern medicine: Race and visual representation in medical literature. *Journal of the National Medical Association*, *113*(1), 88–94.

McAleer, L., Powers, C. M., & Mauskar, M. M. (2025). Granular parakeratosis delayed diagnosis in skin of color. *American Journal of Obstetrics and Gynecology*. https://doi.org/10.1016/j.ajog.2025.01.043

Norori, N., Hu, Q., Aellen, F. M., Faraci, F. D., & Tzovara, A. (2021). Addressing bias in big data and AI for health care: A call for open science. *Patterns*, *2*(10), 1–9.

Okoji, S. C., Taylor, J. B., & Lipoff, J. B. (2021). Equity in skin typing: Why it is time to replace the Fitzpatrick scale. *British Journal of Dermatology*, *185*(1), 198–199. https://doi.org/10.1111/bjd.19932

Omiye, J. A., Lester, J. C., Spichak, S., Rotemberg, V., & Daneshjou, R. (2023). Large language models propagate race-based medicine. *NPJ Digital Medicine*, *6*(1), Article 195. https://doi.org/10.1038/s41746-023-00939-z

Parliament of Canada. (1985). *Canadian Human Rights Act* (R.S.C., c. H-6). Justice Laws Website.

Pasch, M. C. (2016). Nail psoriasis: A review of treatment options. *Drugs*, *76*, 675–705. https://doi.org/10.1007/s40265-016-0564-5

Vyas, D. A., Eisenstein, L. G., & Jones, D. S. (2020). Hidden in plain sight—Reconsidering the use of race correction in clinical algorithms. *The New England Journal of Medicine*, *383*(9), 874–882. https://doi.org/10.1056/NEJMms2004740

3 What the AI Doesn't See
On Fairness Proxies in Medical AI

Elizabeth U. Thompson, Courtney C. Rogers, Krystal A. Porter, Julia Scialla and Rupa S. Valdez

INTRODUCTION

Fairness in healthcare AI is frequently treated as statistical parity, aiming to ensure similar outcomes across diverse groups (R. J. Chen et al., 2023). However, algorithmic approaches that prioritize equal rates over equitable care can lead to substandard clinical decisions and ignore real differences in health risks rooted in structural inequalities. Fairness definitions are design choices, ones that can embed biases within seemingly objective technical decisions. A core component of design is the selection of proxy variables, which are quantifiable stand-ins for complex concepts like medical need or vulnerability (Nilsson et al., 2023). Proxy choice is not a neutral technical step; it is a justice decision that determines whose needs are visible to AI, how inequities are interpreted, and who is prioritized in care.

The risk stratification algorithm analyzed by Obermeyer et al. (2019) illustrates this vividly: by using prior healthcare spending as a proxy for need, it systematically underestimated risk for Black patients, who historically face barriers to care that suppress spending despite higher disease burden (Benjamin, 2019). Although the model satisfied fairness audits, the proxy itself encoded structural disadvantage. This shows that fairness metrics are only as reliable as the proxies they evaluate.

The effects are not abstract. Proxies such as appointment adherence often misclassify patients. Missed follow-up visits may reflect transportation gaps or unstable housing rather than disengagement, yet they can still lead to patients being dropped from care (Pickett & Wilkinson, 2015). We return to this issue in a dialysis case study, which illustrates a related risk: missed sessions can alter treatment exposure in ways that AI may misinterpret as variability in patient response.

When proxies are chosen without sustained engagement with those most affected, particularly disadvantaged populations including Indigenous, racialized, disabled, queer, impoverished, and other communities (hereafter, marginalized groups), they often reflect institutional priorities rather than lived realities, embedding structural inequalities into AI design (Braveman & Gottlieb, 2014). From a systems perspective, algorithmic infrastructures can reproduce racial disparities (Benjamin, 2019), spending-based proxies can underestimate Black patients' risk (Obermeyer et al., 2019), and broader social hierarchies shape both datasets and outcomes (Corbin & Marques, 2023; Pickett & Wilkinson, 2015). Raza et al. (2024) argue that equity-centered evaluation is necessary to make these systemic dynamics visible and actionable.

LITERATURE REVIEW: THE ROLE AND RISKS OF PROXY VARIABLES IN HEALTHCARE AI

Proxy variables are a foundational component of healthcare AI (R. J. Chen et al., 2022; Cross et al., 2024; Raza et al., 2024). Their ubiquity reflects the limits of healthcare data: many critical constructs cannot be directly measured, and electronic health records (EHRs) or insurance claims rarely contain key social or contextual details (Mhasawade et al., 2021; Secinaro et al., 2021). As a result, developers rely on proxies to approximate the clinical, behavioral, or structural factors that shape patient outcomes. While this practice is standard in applied modeling (Mitchell et al.,

DOI: 10.1201/9781003737810-4

2021), scholars increasingly warn that the assumptions behind commonly used proxies are rarely critically evaluated, particularly their social, cultural, or structural validity (I. Y. Chen et al., 2021; Giovanola & Tiribelli, 2023). Without such scrutiny, proxies risk misaligning with the concepts they are intended to represent.

In practice, proxy selection is often driven by what is most readily available in EHR or claims data, utilization rates, healthcare costs, and hospital readmission counts (Chin et al., 2023; Norori et al., 2021; Obermeyer et al., 2019). As Rowe (2021) demonstrates, these metrics are shaped by billing practices, documentation norms, and reporting frameworks that reflect institutional convenience rather than lived realities. Braveman and Gottlieb (2014) similarly show how structural and social determinants influence the data used as inputs. As a result, proxies frequently fail to capture the experiences of marginalized groups, whose interactions with healthcare are mediated by barriers such as lack of insurance, disinvestment in facilities, discrimination, and historical exclusion (Mercado et al., 2024; O'Neil, 2016; Pickett & Wilkinson, 2015; *Tuskegee Study – Timeline – CDC – OS*, 2022).

The consequences of these choices are tangible. Sargent (2021) shows that in population health management, spending-based proxies have deprioritized patients with high disease burden but historically low utilization, many of whom are Black, Indigenous, or living in poverty. In dermatology, Corbin and Marques (2023) and Guo et al. (2022) demonstrate that classifiers trained on datasets dominated by lighter skin tones can pass fairness audits yet still produce worse diagnostic accuracy for darker-skinned patients. These examples, alongside the Obermeyer study, demonstrate that even models that satisfy statistical fairness definitions can still encode inequity when their proxies fail to capture the realities of marginalized groups.

Despite growing interest in fairness evaluation Yang et al. (2023) demonstrate that proxy selection in medical AI has continued to cause unfair outcomes and recommend developing algorithmic methodologies for improving fairness. Chen et al. (2022), in their review of algorithmic fairness in medicine, emphasize that while numerous technical definitions and mitigation strategies exist, few standardized methods are available to ensure that measures are valid across diverse populations. Even fewer approaches involve leadership from the patients or communities most affected. By contrast, King et al. (2024) show that incorporating patient and clinician perspectives into proxy definition improves both the face validity of measures and their alignment with clinical goals. Yet in AI development, such engagement remains rare.

Building on this critique, emerging work in AI ethics, health equity, and systems thinking has argued for reframing proxy development as a justice-oriented practice (National Academies, n.d.). These scholars contend that fairness work must extend upstream, beyond auditing outputs, to interrogate the variables that stand in for core health constructs. When marginalized communities are centered in this process, proxies can be designed to reflect lived realities, capture structural barriers, and hold systems accountable for inequities in care.

Taken together, this literature suggests one conclusion: proxies are technically indispensable but ethically consequential. Without equity-informed design, they risk becoming instruments of exclusion. To address these risks, we outline five principles for equity-informed proxy design that move beyond technical expediency toward structural accountability.

Rethinking Proxy Design in Healthcare AI

Flawed proxy design is not simply a data quality problem, it is a structural equity problem. Many current approaches rely on institutional convenience rather than clinical validity or structural relevance, embedding inequities into AI systems and forming the foundation of fairness infrastructure. This section outlines five principles for a justice-oriented approach to proxy design, treating selection as both a technical and equity decision, and shows how centering marginalized communities in proxy development can transform these variables from instruments of exclusion into tools for accountability and structural change (Figure 3.1).

Five Principles for Equity-Informed Proxy Design

Transforming healthcare AI variables from instruments of exclusion to tools for accountability

	1 Ground Proxies in Real-World Care Dynamics	2 Make Structural Barriers Explicit	3 Validate Proxies Against Marginalized Experience	4 Challenge Institutional Defaults	5 Allow for Proxy Imperfection, But With Transparency
PROBLEM	Many EHR-derived variables are assumed to directly represent patient behavior or need, but they are shaped by billing codes, documentation norms, and institutional processes.	Common proxies, such as utilization or adherence rates, can mask systemic barriers, like transportation gaps, rigid work schedules, or lack of insurance, by treating low use as low need.	Proxies are often selected and defined by technical teams without input from the communities they impact.	Many default proxies serve institutional goals (e.g., efficiency, cost reduction) rather than patient outcomes.	No proxy perfectly represents its intended concept, yet most models lack transparent documentation of their selection, meaning, and limitations.
WHY IT MATTERS	Without grounding in the lived context of care delivery, proxies risk misrepresenting need and embedding structural biases into models.	When structural factors are invisible in proxy definitions, they are also invisible in AI-driven decisions, reinforcing inequitable care patterns.	Without participatory design, proxy decisions can misinterpret need, vulnerability, or quality of care.	Adopting these measures uncritically embeds institutional priorities into AI systems, often at the expense of those facing the greatest barriers.	Without transparency, stakeholders cannot identify hidden harms, challenge flawed measures, or improve them over time.
RECOMMMENDED ACTIONS	Convene co-design workshops with patients, frontline clinicians, and care coordinators before selecting proxies Use mixed data sources (e.g., patient-reported outcomes, community service utilization) to validate EHR-derived measures Audit existing proxies to compare recorded data patterns with actual care experiences	Identify likely structural determinants for each candidate proxy through patient interviews and social determinant data Embed these factors directly into proxy definitions (e.g., "adherence adjusted for transportation reliability") Work with EHR vendors to create fields for recording key structural determinants in a standardized, interoperable format	Establish patient advisory boards or community review panels to assess proxy definitions before modeling begins Use participatory design cycles with multiple rounds of feedback, revision, and re-testing, rather than one-off consultations Compensate community participants for their expertise to avoid extractive engagement	For each candidate proxy, ask "Whose interests does this serve?" and "Does it reflect patient-centered outcomes?" Compare institutional metrics with patient-defined quality indicators, replacing or supplementing defaults where necessary Document the decision-making process for retaining or rejecting default proxies, including expected impacts on different groups	Maintain multi-tiered documentation for each proxy: plain-language public summaries, operational briefs for clinicians, and full technical specifications for researchers Publish proxy design rationales and limitations alongside model documentation Establish periodic review cycles to re-evaluate proxies as structural conditions, policy environments, and available data evolve

FIGURE 3.1 Five principles for equity-informed proxy design.

Principle 1: Ground Proxies in Real-World Care Dynamics

Proxies must be grounded in real-world care dynamics, not just institutional records. As discussed in the literature review, measures drawn from billing or documentation often misrepresent patient experience because they reflect administrative priorities rather than clinical realities. To correct this, proxies should be designed with input from patients, clinicians, and care teams and validated against the actual rhythms and practices of care. Incorporating diverse data sources, such as patient-reported outcomes or community service use, anchors proxies in the lived dynamics of care rather than the convenience of institutional data systems.

Principle 2: Make Structural Barriers Explicit

Common proxies such as utilization or adherence rates frequently mask structural barriers by treating low use as low need. As noted earlier, this risks penalizing patients facing transportation challenges, unstable housing, or inflexible work schedules. Proxies should therefore be explicitly adjusted to account for these barriers. Embedding social and structural factors directly into proxy definitions makes inequities visible rather than hidden within the data.

Principle 3: Validate Proxies against Marginalized Experience

Existing methods rarely validate proxies across diverse populations and even less often involve the leadership of the communities most affected. As highlighted in prior research, participatory approaches improve both the validity of measures and their alignment with clinical goals. Proxy development should therefore include patient and community review processes, such as advisory boards or feedback cycles, to ensure measures accurately reflect marginalized experience.

Principle 4: Challenge Institutional Defaults

Default proxies often serve institutional priorities like efficiency or cost containment rather than patient outcomes. As discussed earlier, spending-based proxies systematically deprioritize patients with high disease burden but low utilization. Developers should critically challenge each proxy by asking: Whose interests does this measure serve? Does it reflect patient-centered outcomes? Explicitly documenting the rationale for retaining or rejecting default proxies helps prevent institutional logics from quietly shaping AI decisions.

Principle 5: Allow for Proxy Imperfection, but with Transparency

No proxy perfectly captures its intended concept. Yet, as noted in the literature, proxy selection is often opaque, preventing stakeholders from recognizing limitations or identifying hidden harms. Transparency requires documenting the meaning, rationale, and limitations of each proxy in multiple formats, from plain-language summaries to technical specifications, and establishing review cycles to update proxies as conditions evolve. This practice acknowledges imperfection while creating accountability.

CASE STUDY: AI IN DIALYSIS

This case study demonstrates how justice-oriented design can apply the five principles to the use of proxies in healthcare AI.

In-center hemodialysis has unique care dynamics that shape both patient experience and the data available for AI:

1. **Rigid treatment schedules**: People on hemodialysis need treatment three times a week, about four hours per session, plus travel time that can be one to two hours each way in rural areas. Because the treatment requires surgical access to a large vein and a fixed machine connection, appointments are locked into Monday/Wednesday/Friday or Tuesday/Thursday/Saturday slots (Flythe & Watnick, 2024). This routine structures patients' daily lives and means that "attendance" in health records reflects structural constraints, not simply individual commitment.
2. **Medicare coverage and reporting**: In the United States, kidney failure qualifies most patients for Medicare, which sets the rules for dialysis care and requires clinics to complete standardized federal forms at enrollment and beyond (*End-Stage Renal Disease (ESRD) | CMS*, n.d.). Much of the data AI systems rely on comes from these administrative processes.
3. **Bundled payment system**: Dialysis is reimbursed as a monthly bundled fee based on the number of sessions, not the actual cost of care. Within this model, patients must have at least one comprehensive visit each month, including lab tests, nutrition and social work support, and a care plan developed by a team (*End Stage Renal Disease (ESRD) Prospective Payment System (PPS) | CMS*, n.d.).
4. **Quality oversight**: Federal Quality Improvement Programs monitor dialysis centers to prevent care reductions under the bundled system (*ESRD Quality Incentive Program | CMS*, n.d.). Metrics change annually but may include lab values, outcomes, and sometimes patient-reported measures like satisfaction or depression.
5. **Large provider networks and siloed data**: Most U.S. dialysis care is delivered by large dialysis organizations. Their EHR systems are frequently disconnected from hospitals or primary care providers, creating gaps in the broader clinical picture (*March 2024 Report to the Congress: Medicare Payment Policy – MedPAC*, 2024).

These features of dialysis care create both advantages and challenges for AI and for the use of proxy variables. On the one hand, the data is relatively complete and consistent because of federal reporting and quality programs. On the other hand, important information about patients' symptoms or social needs is often missing, since it is not directly tied to payment or required reporting. Regular, multidisciplinary visits are part of the dialysis structure, but unlike in other areas of healthcare, they don't necessarily signal higher or more complex medical needs. And because dialysis centers operate separately from other providers, information about hospital stays or external treatments may not be captured in their records.

Designing proxies in this context requires caution. For instance, using "missed sessions" as a proxy for nonadherence is misleading. Patients spend over 12 hours each week in dialysis, so absences may reflect transportation problems, unstable housing, or lack of childcare rather than disengagement. Complications with vascular access, such as poor blood flow or infection, can also prevent dialysis despite attendance. Hospitalizations, averaging 1.5 per patient per year, further disrupt treatment but are not always visible in dialysis records (*Annual Data Report*, n.d.).

Relying on missed sessions alone risks misclassifying patients and misinterpreting their needs. Alternatives are being explored: Medicare has piloted the Patient Activation Measure (PAM), which asks patients directly about their ability to manage their health (Hussein et al., 2022), and other efforts aim to capture structural barriers more systematically.

The applications of the five principles for equitable proxy development for patients with kidney failure treated with hemodialysis are shown in Table 3.1.

This case study illustrates how centering patient voices and acknowledging care dynamics can lead to more accurate proxies. It reframes "nonadherence" not as individual failure but as the product of structural barriers, shifting responsibility from patients to the systems that shape their care.

TABLE 3.1
Application of the Five Principles for Equitable Proxy Development for Patients with Kidney Failure Treated with Hemodialysis

Principle	Example in the Field
1. Ground proxies in real-world care dynamics	**Engagement with patients and clinicians in model design principles**[a] Including patient and caregiver voices, along with clinicians, in focus groups to support modeling decisions can improve understanding of model considerations from a variety of perspectives.
2. Make structural barriers explicit	**Incorporation of Social Determinants of Health (SDoH) Variables in electronic health records**[b] Throughout healthcare efforts to increase capture of SDoH may help address missing information on structural barriers. Capture of SDoH has recently been incorporated in hemodialysis quality metrics.
3. Validate proxies against marginalized experience	**Evaluate and report limitations of existing patient-reported measures**[c] The Patient Activation Measure-13 (PAM-13) was piloted in hemodialysis alternative payment models to improve assessment of self-management. Assessment of the PAM-13 scores suggested it may not function as anticipated in the unique hemodialysis care environment compared to other healthcare environments.
4. Challenge institutional defaults	**Collaboratives with patients and clinicians to set priorities on outcomes**[d] The Standardizing Outcomes in Nephrology-Hemodialysis (SONG-HD) Collaborative has convened patients, caregivers, and clinicians to identify key priorities for treatment in patients on hemodialysis. The group has expanded from traditional measures to incorporate important patient-centered considerations such as fatigue. **Incorporate patient-reported information on high-priority Outcomes**[e] Novel clinical trials in patients treated with in-center hemodialysis are evaluating the incorporation of symptom measures in clinical care to improve care and capture of high-priority features that may also improve equity of healthcare AI.

(Continued)

TABLE 3.1
(Continued)

Principle	Example in the Field
5. Allow for proxy imperfection, but with transparency	**Use of governance and life cycle management to promote transparency**[f] Institutional AI oversight committees can review the use and justification for proxies to ensure these variables convey more benefit than harm and reassess justification for their use over time.

Note:
[a] *(Sperling et al., 2025)*
[b] (Cantor & Thorpe, 2018; *ESRD QIP Payment Year 2025 Fact Sheet, n.d.*)
[c] (Cukor et al., 2021; Gopal et al., 2024)
[d] (Evangelidis et al., 2017)
[e] (Flythe et al., 2025)
[f] (Goldstein et al., 2024)

DISCUSSION

Fairness in healthcare AI is not simply a matter of passing statistical tests. It is shaped, and often constrained, by the selected proxy variables that define what the model "sees" as patient need. For marginalized communities these proxies often misrepresent reality because they are built from data produced in systems that have historically underserved, excluded, or mischaracterized them. Misaligned proxies can deprioritize those most in need, prolonging wait times or disrupting continuity of care, thereby reinforcing the very disparities fairness efforts aim to address.

Placing marginalized communities at the center of proxy design changes both the process and the outcome. When patients, frontline providers, and community advocates define the constructs and test the measures, proxies can be designed to surface inequities rather than conceal them. This approach shifts fairness from a reactive audit to a proactive, justice-driven design practice.

To sustain this shift, proxy redesign must also be evaluated over time. Monitoring indicators such as subgroup performance gaps, override rates, or changes in downstream outcomes helps ensure proxies remain aligned with equity goals. Clear thresholds for review are needed to trigger timely action when disparities emerge. Importantly, defining "success" in equity-informed proxy redesign is itself a proxy choice, embedding value judgments into evaluation metrics just as into model variables, and therefore requiring the same level of critical scrutiny. Oversight mechanisms, whether through community advisory boards, quality review committees, or vendor requirements, can provide accountability, but further work is needed to test their feasibility across different institutions. Existing pilots, such as the CMS Innovation Center's Accountable Health Communities model (Centers for Medicare and Medicaid Services et al., 2017) and NCQA's social needs-related HEDIS measures (Reynolds, 2022), illustrate the potential of linking structural data to clinical practice, though scaling these approaches will require further investment and policy alignment (Anderson et al., 2021).

By embedding these processes into AI development, proxy choice becomes an intentional act of accountability, aligning measurement with the realities of those most affected, and ensuring that fairness in healthcare AI is defined not by statistical thresholds but by its capacity to operate justly in structurally unequal systems.

LIMITATIONS

This chapter primarily synthesizes existing literature and proposes prescriptive tools, supplemented by a case study on dialysis care used to illustrate how proxy design can obscure or reveal structural barriers. While this case grounds the principles in a concrete clinical context, it remains illustrative and should not be interpreted as generalizable across all healthcare settings. Broader empirical validation of the proposed principles is still needed. In particular, evidence on post-deployment impacts of proxy redesign remains sparse, especially across equity dimensions such as gender, language access, immigration status, disability, and intersectionality. Governance and monitoring strategies are discussed at a conceptual level only; further research should test their feasibility within diverse institutional, technical, and policy contexts. Finally, this chapter focuses on healthcare proxies, due to the context-specific nature; comparative analysis with other sectors (e.g. finance or education) is beyond its scope but represents an area for future exploration. Future studies should evaluate the costs and benefits of equity-informed proxy redesign, compare governance models across health systems, and build empirical evidence on whether redesigned proxies improve both fairness metrics and real-world outcomes.

CONCLUSION

Fairness in healthcare AI depends as much on the choice of proxy variables as it does on the statistical metrics. Because proxies are drawn from data systems that often misrepresent marginalized communities, they encode value judgments that shape how inequities are interpreted and which patients become visible to AI.

As shown throughout this chapter, commonly used proxies, such as healthcare cost, utilization, or appointment adherence, often reflect institutional convenience rather than lived realities. This disconnect is most harmful in high-stakes settings like dialysis, emergency care, and chronic disease management, where those facing the steepest structural barriers are least visible in the data. For marginalized communities, such omissions distort model outputs and risk deepening the inequities AI is meant to reduce.

The five principles for equity-informed proxy design outlined here, grounding measures in real-world care dynamics, making structural barriers explicit, validating against marginalized perspectives, challenging institutional defaults, and embracing transparency, offer a roadmap for shifting from data-driven expediency to justice-oriented design. Applied in practice, these principles can transform proxies from silent carriers of structural inequity into tools for accountability and repair.

Future work should expand the empirical evidence base, testing these principles across diverse equity dimensions and institutional settings. If healthcare AI is to support, rather than sabotage, efforts toward equity, proxy design must be treated as an intentional act of governance and ethical responsibility. In systems meant to heal, doing no harm begins with deciding, deliberately and transparently, what, and who, counts.

REFLECTION QUESTIONS

There are many critical questions that still need to be answered. These are not merely technical or philosophical puzzles, they are design decisions that shape how care, risk, and recognition are distributed in healthcare systems influenced by AI. Addressing them requires acknowledging both the stakes of immediate outcomes and the long-term consequences of reinforcing unjust systems.

- If a model is technically unfair, meaning it performs better for some groups than others, but improves outcomes for all groups, including the most marginalized, is it ethical to deploy it?
    - Would it be more unethical not to deploy it, knowing it outperforms current practices?
- How should we weigh short-term lives saved against the long-term harm of proxies that reinforce structural inequities?
- When do performance trade-offs become ethically justifiable, and who gets to decide?
- The principle of do no harm is foundational in healthcare. If an AI system has the potential to save lives, but only for a particular subgroup, would withholding it be a greater harm?

- How can we ensure that our proxies, and our definition of fairness itself, are contextually grounded and equitable in each use case?

ACKNOWLEDGMENT

Portions of this chapter were developed with the assistance of ChatGPT for editing to improve clarity and flow. All intellectual contributions, interpretations, and final editorial decisions are the author's own, and the author takes full responsibility for the content. Any AI-assisted material was reviewed and verified by the author.

REFERENCES

Anderson, K. A., Dabelko-Schoeny, H., Koeuth, S., Marx, K., Gitlin, L. N., & Gaugler, J. E. (2021). The Use of Community Advisory Boards in Pragmatic Clinical Trials: The Case of the Adult Day Services Plus Project. *Home Health Care Services Quarterly*, *40*(1), 16–26. https://doi.org/10.1080/01621424.2020.1816522

Annual Data Report. (n.d.). USRDS. Retrieved March 3, 2023, from https://adr.usrds.org/

Benjamin, R. (2019). Assessing Risk, Automating Racism. *Science (New York, N.Y.)*, *366*(6464), 421–422. https://doi.org/10.1126/science.aaz3873

Braveman, P., & Gottlieb, L. (2014). The Social Determinants of Health: It's Time to Consider the Causes of the Causes. *Public Health Reports®*, *129*(1_suppl2), 19–31. https://doi.org/10.1177/00333549141291S206

Cantor, M. N., & Thorpe, L. (2018). Integrating Data on Social Determinants of Health into Electronic Health Records. *Health Affairs (Project Hope)*, *37*(4), 585–590. https://doi.org/10.1377/hlthaff.2017.1252

Centers for Medicare and Medicaid Services, Billioux, A., Verlander, K., Centers for Medicare and Medicaid Services, Anthony, S., Centers for Medicare and Medicaid Services, Alley, D., & Centers for Medicare and Medicaid Services. (2017). Standardized Screening for Health-Related Social Needs in Clinical Settings: The Accountable Health Communities Screening Tool. *NAM Perspectives*, *7*(5). https://doi.org/10.31478/201705b

Chen, I. Y., Pierson, E., Rose, S., Joshi, S., Ferryman, K., & Ghassemi, M. (2021). Ethical Machine Learning in Healthcare. *Annual Review of Biomedical Data Science*, *4*, 123–144. https://doi.org/10.1146/annurev-biodatasci-092820-114757

Chen, R. J., Chen, T. Y., Lipkova, J., Wang, J. J., Williamson, D. F. K., Lu, M. Y., Sahai, S., & Mahmood, F. (2022). *Algorithm Fairness in AI for Medicine and Healthcare* (No. arXiv:2110.00603). arXiv. https://arxiv.org/abs/2110.00603

Chen, R. J., Wang, J. J., Williamson, D. F. K., Chen, T. Y., Lipkova, J., Lu, M. Y., Sahai, S., & Mahmood, F. (2023). Algorithmic Fairness in Artificial Intelligence for Medicine and Healthcare. *Nature Biomedical Engineering*, *7*(6), Article 6. https://doi.org/10.1038/s41551-023-01056-8

Chin, M. H., Afsar-Manesh, N., Bierman, A. S., Chang, C., Colón-Rodríguez, C. J., Dullabh, P., Duran, D. G., Fair, M., Hernandez-Boussard, T., Hightower, M., Jain, A., Jordan, W. B., Konya, S., Moore, R. H., Moore, T. T., Rodriguez, R., Shaheen, G., Snyder, L. P., Srinivasan, M., … Ohno-Machado, L. (2023). Guiding Principles to Address the Impact of Algorithm Bias on Racial and Ethnic Disparities in Health and Health Care. *JAMA Network Open*, *6*(12), e2345050. https://doi.org/10.1001/jamanetworkopen.2023.45050

Corbin, A., & Marques, O. (2023). Assessing Bias in Skin Lesion Classifiers with Contemporary Deep Learning and Post-Hoc Explainability Techniques. *IEEE Access*, *11*, 78339–78352. IEEE Access. https://doi.org/10.1109/ACCESS.2023.3289320

Cross, J. L., Choma, M. A., & Onofrey, J. A. (2024). Bias in Medical AI: Implications for Clinical Decision-making. *PLOS Digital Health*, *3*(11), e0000651. https://doi.org/10.1371/journal.pdig.0000651

Cukor, D., Zelnick, L. R., Charytan, D. M., Shallcross, A. J., & Mehrotra, R. (2021). Patient Activation Measure in Dialysis-Dependent Patients in the United States. *Journal of the American Society of Nephrology : JASN*, *32*(12), 3017–3019. https://doi.org/10.1681/ASN.2021030315

End Stage Renal Disease (ESRD) Prospective Payment System (PPS) | CMS. (n.d.). Retrieved October 1, 2025, from https://www.cms.gov/medicare/payment/prospective-payment-systems/end-stage-renal-disease-esrd

End-Stage Renal Disease (ESRD) | CMS. (n.d.). Retrieved October 1, 2025, from https://www.cms.gov/medicare/coordination-benefits-recovery/overview/end-stage-renal-disease-esrd

ESRD QIP Payment Year 2025 Fact Sheet. (n.d.).

ESRD Quality Incentive Program | CMS. (n.d.). Retrieved October 1, 2025, from https://www.cms.gov/medicare/quality/end-stage-renal-disease-esrd-quality-incentive-program

Evangelidis, N., Tong, A., Manns, B., Hemmelgarn, B., Wheeler, D. C., Tugwell, P., Crowe, S., Harris, T., Van Biesen, W., Winkelmayer, W. C., Sautenet, B., O'Donoghue, D., Tam-Tham, H., Youssouf, S., Mandayam, S., Ju, A., Hawley, C., Pollock, C., Harris, D. C., … Craig, J. C. (2017). Developing a Set of Core Outcomes for Trials in Hemodialysis: An International Delphi Survey. *American Journal of Kidney Diseases*, *70*(4), 464–475. https://doi.org/10.1053/j.ajkd.2016.11.029

Flythe, J. E., Picataggio, C. B., Bernardo, L., Dalrymple, L. S., Kossmann, R. J., DeWalt, D. A., Hanson, L. C., Wang, V., Unruh, M. L., Hsu, J. Y., & Dember, L. M. (2025). Design and Rationale of the SMaRRT-HD Study: A Pragmatic, Randomized Trial of Symptom Monitoring for Individuals Receiving Maintenance Hemodialysis. *Contemporary Clinical Trials*, *157*, 108058. https://doi.org/10.1016/j.cct.2025.108058

Flythe, J. E., & Watnick, S. (2024). Dialysis for Chronic Kidney Failure: A Review. *JAMA*, *332*(18), 1559–1573. https://doi.org/10.1001/jama.2024.16338

Giovanola, B., & Tiribelli, S. (2023). Beyond Bias and Discrimination: Redefining the AI Ethics Principle of Fairness in Healthcare Machine-learning Algorithms. *AI & Society*, *38*(2), 549–563. https://doi.org/10.1007/s00146-022-01455-6

Goldstein, B. A., Mohottige, D., Bessias, S., & Cary, M. P. (2024). Enhancing Clinical Decision Support in Nephrology: Addressing Algorithmic Bias through Artificial Intelligence Governance. *American Journal of Kidney Diseases: The Official Journal of the National Kidney Foundation*, *84*(6), 780–786. https://doi.org/10.1053/j.ajkd.2024.04.008

Gopal, T., Chen, S., Weinhandl, E., & Hussein, W. F. (2024). Associations of Patient Activation with Outcomes among Patients on Chronic Hemodialysis: A Retrospective, Longitudinal, Observational Study. *Kidney360*, *5*(11), 1662–1668. https://doi.org/10.34067/KID.0000000591

Guo, L. N., Lee, M. S., Kassamali, B., Mita, C., & Nambudiri, V. E. (2022). Bias in, Bias Out: Underreporting and Underrepresentation of Diverse Skin Types in Machine Learning Research for Skin Cancer Detection—A Scoping Review. *Journal of the American Academy of Dermatology*, *87*(1), 157–159. https://doi.org/10.1016/j.jaad.2021.06.884

Hussein, W. F., Bennett, P. N., Abra, G., Watson, E., & Schiller, B. (2022). Integrating Patient Activation into Dialysis Care. *American Journal of Kidney Diseases*, *79*(1), 105–112. https://doi.org/10.1053/j.ajkd.2021.07.015

King, B. J., Read, G. J. M., Hulme, A., Chari, S., Clay-Williams, R., Plant, K. L., McCormack, L., Tresillian, M., & Salmon, P. M. (2024). Evaluating the Use of Systems Thinking Methods in Healthcare: A RE-AIM Analysis of AcciMap and Net-HARMS. *Ergonomics*. https://www.tandfonline.com/doi/abs/10.1080/00140139.2024.2423170

March 2024 Report to the Congress: Medicare Payment Policy – MedPAC. (n.d.). Retrieved October 1, 2025, from https://www.medpac.gov/document/march-2024-report-to-the-congress-medicare-payment-policy/

Mercado, C. I., Bullard, K. M., Bolduc, M. L. F., Andrews, C. A., Freggens, Z. R. F., Liggett, G., Banks, D., Johnson, S. B., Penman-Aguilar, A., & Njai, R. (2024). A Shift in Approach to Addressing Public Health Inequities and the Effect of Societal Structural and Systemic Drivers on Social Determinants of Health. *Public Health Reports*, 00333549241283586. https://doi.org/10.1177/00333549241283586

Mhasawade, V., Zhao, Y., & Chunara, R. (2021). Machine Learning and Algorithmic Fairness in Public and Population Health. *Nature Machine Intelligence*, *3*(8), 659–666. https://doi.org/10.1038/s42256-021-00373-4

Mitchell, S., Potash, E., Barocas, S., D'Amour, A., & Lum, K. (2021). Algorithmic Fairness: Choices, Assumptions, and Definitions. *Annual Review of Statistics and Its Application*, *8*, 141–163. https://doi.org/10.1146/annurev-statistics-042720-125902

Nilsson, A., Björk, J., & Bonander, C. (2023). Proxy Variables and the Generalizability of Study Results. *American Journal of Epidemiology*, *192*(3), 448–454. https://doi.org/10.1093/aje/kwac200

Norori, N., Hu, Q., Aellen, F. M., Faraci, F. D., & Tzovara, A. (2021). Addressing Bias in Big Data and AI for Health Care: A Call for Open Science. *Patterns*, *2*(10). https://doi.org/10.1016/j.patter.2021.100347

Obermeyer, Z., Powers, B., Vogeli, C., & Mullainathan, S. (2019). Dissecting Racial Bias in an Algorithm Used to Manage the Health of Populations. *Science*, *366*(6464), 447–453. https://doi.org/10.1126/science.aax2342

O'Neil, C. (2016). *Weapons of Math Destruction: How Big Data Increases Inequality and Threatens Democracy*. Crown Publishing Group.

Pickett, K. E., & Wilkinson, R. G. (2015). Income Inequality and Health: A Causal Review. *Social Science & Medicine*, *128*, 316–326. https://doi.org/10.1016/j.socscimed.2014.12.031

Raza, S., Shaban-Nejad, A., Dolatabadi, E., & Mamiya, H. (2024). Exploring Bias and Prediction Metrics to Characterise the Fairness of Machine Learning for Equity-Centered Public Health Decision-Making: A Narrative Review (No. arXiv:2408.13295; Version 2). arXiv. https://doi.org/10.48550/arXiv.2408.13295

Reynolds, A. (2022, November 2). Social Need: New HEDIS Measure Uses Electronic Data to Look at Screening, Intervention. *NCQA*. https://www.ncqa.org/blog/social-need-new-hedis-measure-uses-electronic-data-to-look-at-screening-intervention/

Rowe, R. (2021). *Social Determinants of Health in the Big Data Mode of Population Health Risk Calculation*. Big Data & Society. https://doi.org/10.1177/20539517211062881

Sargent, S. (2021). AI Bias in Healthcare: Using ImpactPro as a Case Study for Healthcare Practitioners' Duties to Engage in Anti-Bias Measures. *Canadian Journal of Bioethics/Revue Canadienne de Bioéthique*, *4*(1), 112–116. https://doi.org/10.7202/1077639ar

Secinaro, S., Calandra, D., Secinaro, A., Muthurangu, V., & Biancone, P. (2021). The Role of Artificial Intelligence in Healthcare: A Structured Literature Review. *BMC Medical Informatics and Decision Making*, *21*(1), 125. https://doi.org/10.1186/s12911-021-01488-9

Sperling, J., Welsh, W., Haseley, E., Quenstedt, S., Muhigaba, P. B., Brown, A., Ephraim, P., Shafi, T., Waitzkin, M., Casarett, D., & Goldstein, B. A. (2025). Machine Learning-based Prediction Models in Medical Decision-making in Kidney Disease: Patient, Caregiver, and Clinician Perspectives on Trust and Appropriate Use. *Journal of the American Medical Informatics Association: JAMIA*, *32*(1), 51–62. https://doi.org/10.1093/jamia/ocae255

The Intersections Between Health Disparities Disabilities and Health Equity A Workshop | National Academies. (n.d.). Retrieved January 8, 2025, from https://www.nationalacademies.org/our-work/the-intersections-between-health-disparities-disabilities-and-health-equity-a-workshop#resources

Tuskegee Study—Timeline—CDC—OS. (2022, December 20). https://www.cdc.gov/tuskegee/timeline.htm

Yang, J., Soltan, A. A. S., Eyre, D. W., Yang, Y., & Clifton, D. A. (2023). An Adversarial Training Framework for Mitigating Algorithmic Biases in Clinical Machine Learning. *Npj Digital Medicine*, *6*(1), 1–10. https://doi.org/10.1038/s41746-023-00805-y

4 Aligning AI for Health Equity
Successes, Gaps, and Barriers in the Canadian Healthcare System

Jenna Cappello, Christo El Morr and Elham Dolatabadi

INTRODUCTION

Artificial intelligence (AI) is rapidly emerging as a transformative force in Canadian healthcare, with applications ranging from predictive analytics in oncology, Clinical Decision Support Systems (CDSS), to population health planning tools. However, while AI offers opportunities to enhance efficiency, diagnostic accuracy, and patient-centered care, its implementation is unfolding against a backdrop of persistent inequities in the Canadian healthcare system.

Health equity, defined as the absence of avoidable, unfair, and unjust differences in health outcomes across population groups, remains a central challenge in the Canadian healthcare landscape (Gao et al., 2025; Ghanem et al., 2025). Indigenous, rural, and socioeconomically marginalized populations continue to encounter systemic barriers to care, experience poorer health outcomes, and often express mistrust in emerging health technologies. This raises a central and unresolved question: Will adopting AI in Canadian healthcare mitigate inequities, or risk entrenching and amplifying them (Davis et al., 2025; Anawati et al., 2024)?

At the core of this tension lies the issue of alignment: ensuring that AI tools are not only technically robust but also ethically grounded, contextually responsive, and explicitly designed with equity goals in mind (Badawi et al., 2025; Raza et al., 2025; Richardson et al., 2022). Evidence from representation learning and multimodal benchmarking demonstrates that data quality and diversity are essential for equitable performance (Baghbanzadeh, Fallahpour et al., 2025; Raza et al., 2024; Roy et al., 2024), whereas large medical corpora can broaden coverage but still demand careful curation to ensure fairness (Baghbanzadeh, Ashkezari et al., 2025). At the same time, studies document limited sociodemographic diversity in biomedical sources, constraining the detection of disparities and the generalizability of models (Medina Florez et al., 2025). Technical remedies such as fairness-aware optimization and surrogate reweighting show promise but are not yet routinely translated into clinical practice (Xu & Dolatabadi, 2025). In parallel, technologies such as AI-driven CDSS can not only personalize patient care but also risk perpetuating algorithmic bias when trained on minimal, incomplete, and/or biased datasets (Elhaddad & Hamam, 2024). Similarly, AI tools such as Natural Language Processing (NLP) models that attempt to extract social determinants of health (SDoH) data from electronic medical records (EMRs) may improve equity-driven planning, but they also raise serious concerns about privacy, consent, and the loss of a "human touch" in care experiences (Davis et al., 2025).

To address these complexities, this chapter synthesizes recent peer-reviewed literature on AI and health equity in the Canadian healthcare system, drawing on the expanded National Institute on Minority Health and Health Disparities (NIMHD) Framework for Digital Health Equity (Richardson et al., 2022). This framework enables a multilevel analysis of individual, interpersonal, community, and societal determinants of digital health equity, helping to classify where AI has advanced equity and where critical barriers persist. Two guiding research questions frame this narrative literature review:

1. Where do current approaches to AI alignment succeed or fall short in promoting health equity in the Canadian healthcare system?

DOI: 10.1201/9781003737810-5

2. What are the main technical, institutional, clinical workflow, and ethical barriers for aligning AI systems with health equity in Canadian healthcare settings?

By organizing findings through this framework, the review highlights both the opportunities for AI to support personalization, empowerment, and community-specific care, as well as the barriers posed by digital divides, workflow challenges, algorithmic bias, and governance gaps. Together, these insights aim to clarify the pathways through which AI might either narrow or widen existing inequities in Canadian healthcare. Since Canada's health services are provincially/territorially delivered, uneven electronic health record (EHR) interoperability, rural/northern broadband access, and Indigenous data sovereignty obligations create distinct equity risks and opportunities for AI.

METHODOLOGY

Study Design

We searched PubMed, OVID Medline, and the OMNI Catalogue (York University) using terms spanning AI/ML, health equity/SDoH, and Canada (searches completed: September 2025). A total of 34 full-text articles were assessed, 16 of which met all inclusion criteria. One additional study was identified through reference screening, and a further 10 were added through expert review. This resulted in a total of 28 studies that have been included in this review.

Scoping/Eligibility Criteria

Only peer-reviewed, academic sources were included in this analysis. Gray literature sources such as policy reports, preprints, or media publications were excluded. Eligible articles met the following criteria:

- Peer-reviewed, English-language studies.
- Focused on AI in Canadian Healthcare contexts *or* on international cases with clear relevance to Canada (e.g., governance frameworks, equity considerations of public health AI).
- Explicitly addressed themes of health equity, institutional or clinical barriers, or ethical implications of AI alignment in healthcare.
- Published within the last five years (2020–2025).

Search Strategy

The search strategy combined a number of terms related to *artificial intelligence* (e.g., "AI", "Machine Learning" or "ML", "predictive analytics", "Natural Language Processing", or "NLP"), *health equity* (e.g., "health disparities", "equity", and "social determinants of health"), and *Canada* (e.g., "Canadian healthcare" and "Canada health system"). Additionally, Boolean operators and database-specific filters were applied to refine results. Searches were limited to articles published within the past five years (2020–2025) to capture the most current evidence base.

Selection and Data Extraction

Articles were screened for relevance to the two guiding research questions. A final set was selected and annotated for key findings. Extracted data focused on successes and gaps in AI alignment with health equity, as well as barriers categorized as technical, institutional, clinical workflow, or ethical.

Framework for Analysis

The expanded NIMHD Framework for Digital Health Equity provides the analytical structure for classifying findings. The framework for Digital Health Equity is an extension of the NIMHD

Research Framework to incorporate the *digital environment domain*. This framework identifies Digital Determinants of Health (DDoH) and organizes them across four levels of influence:

1. **Individual** (digital literacy, technology access, self-efficacy, attitudes towards use)
2. **Interpersonal** (implicit tech bias, clinician–patient–tech relationships, interdependence)
3. **Community** (community infrastructure, health infrastructure, community tech norms, community partners)
4. **Societal** (tech policy, data standards, design standards, social norms and ideologies, algorithmic bias)

Using this framework enabled findings to be classified into multilevel barriers and facilitators of equitable AI adoption across Canadian healthcare (Richardson et al., 2022).

RESULTS

Findings from the reviewed studies were classified using the NIMHD-expanded Digital Health Equity Framework, which organizes determinants across individual, interpersonal, community, and societal levels. Within each level, studies revealed both enabling factors, contexts in which AI supports equity, constraining factors, and contexts in which inequities are reinforced or created. Below, we outline opportunities and barriers within each domain.

Individual-Level Determinants

Opportunities for Personalization, Empowerment, and Self-Management

AI-enabled tools have shown potential to empower patients by tailoring healthcare to individual needs. CDSS trained on patient histories have reduced diagnostic errors and enabled more personalized treatment planning (Elhaddad & Hamam, 2024). Patient-facing applications have also supported self-management by presenting complex health information in accessible formats, fostering independence and active engagement in care (Nesa et al., 2025). NLP approaches have extracted contextual SDoH from electronic records, allowing clinicians to anticipate nonclinical risk factors such as housing instability or unemployment, thereby enabling targeted interventions (Davis et al., 2025).

Lacking Technology Access, Digital Literacy, and Trust

Despite these benefits, inequities emerge when patients lack the skills, resources, or confidence to engage with AI-driven systems (Osonuga et al., 2025). Beyond basic digital literacy, digital self-sufficiency, the ability to use technology independently and with confidence, is unevenly distributed. Limited digital literacy, particularly among older adults, immigrants, and low-income Canadians, further restricts the uptake of AI-enabled tools such as patient portals and monitoring devices, with some patients requiring ongoing technical support to use these systems effectively (Anawati et al., 2024; Osonuga et al., 2025). Without such support, AI risks reinforcing dependence on caregivers or widening inequities among patients who cannot use systems autonomously (Osonuga et al., 2025).

Trust is another major barrier to equitable AI. A Canadian qualitative study by Davis et al. (2025) highlights that patients often express skepticism about whether AI will respect their privacy and whether sensitive sociodemographic information will be used ethically. Marginalized populations, in particular, have disproportionately reported heightened fears of surveillance or misuse of their data, which reduced their willingness to engage with AI-driven tools. Notably, in the same study, patients reported feeling worried about losing the element of "human touch" in their healthcare experiences and questioned whether AI would truly support rather than replace clinician judgment. These concerns reflect a broader mistrust of health systems among marginalized communities, who may fear that AI surveillance will exacerbate, rather than address, inequities (Davis et al., 2025).

Interpersonal-Level Determinants

Strengthening Patient-Clinician Relationships, Communication, and Trust

AI can also act as a bridge for communication between patients and providers. Qualitative research by Davis et al. (2025) found that when clinicians received AI-derived SDoH information from patient EMRs, it fostered deeper dialogue on social and economic barriers beyond just the biomedical indicators of patient needs. By fostering trust and validating patients' lived experiences, this could strengthen the therapeutic relationships between patients and clinicians. Automation of routine documentation and scheduling also has the potential to free up clinicians' time, creating more opportunities for meaningful patient interaction.

Clinical Workflow Integration Challenges and Patient-Provider Trust

Poor integration of AI into clinical practice often undermines these gains. A common concern is the "black box" nature of AI tools, where opaque outputs (i.e., those that lack explainability and clear reasoning) undermine clinician confidence and make it harder to explain decisions to patients (Nesa et al., 2025; Ghanem et al., 2025). Without transparency, both provider and patient trust in AI recommendations may erode, creating strain in the patient-tech-clinician relationship.

Moreover, a study by Darcel et al. (2023) highlighted concerns among Canadian clinicians that poorly designed systems may increase workload through duplicative documentation or workflow disruptions. These inefficiencies can ultimately reduce the quality of patient–provider interactions and strain relational trust.

Community-Level Determinants

Community Engagement and Context-Specific Applications

AI has been most effective at the community level when deployed through participatory approaches. In oncology, equity-oriented AI programs were more effective when codesigned with affected communities, ensuring that models accounted for local health needs and cultural contexts (Istasy et al., 2022).

AI-powered virtual care platforms also hold promise for rural and underserved communities, including Indigenous populations. For instance, pilot programs in Saskatchewan have shown that AI-powered virtual care platforms can reduce geographic barriers and extend access to primary care services (Khan et al., 2025). Similarly, two major hospitals in Ontario have implemented AI-driven emergency department surge prediction systems, enabling more effective resource allocation and improving access for diverse urban populations (Hassan et al., 2024).

Persistent Infrastructural Gaps and the Digital Divide

Despite these promising examples, however, several major systemic barriers persist. Many organizations lack interoperable EHRs or sufficient IT capacity, leading to fragmented data and underperforming models for marginalized groups (Darcel et al., 2023). Interoperability challenges are compounded by proprietary control of health data by major EHR vendors. Without shared standards and data-sharing agreements, AI applications risk being unevenly adopted across provinces, exacerbating inequities between communities (Darcel et al., 2023). Another major infrastructural barrier is the *digital divide*, a recurring theme in the literature that refers to unequal access to the internet, devices, and digital infrastructure. In Canada, this divide is most pronounced in rural and northern communities, where broadband connectivity remains inconsistent and expensive (Darcel et al., 2023).

These structural inequities create new barriers to AI-enabled care, especially as healthcare systems increasingly digitize (Anawati et al., 2024; Osonuga et al., 2025). Furthermore, recent survey evidence from Northern Ontario demonstrates how these barriers manifest in practice:

over half of healthcare providers in remote regions reported poor internet connectivity as a key obstacle, alongside shortages of support staff and underfunding of local facilities. Providers also noted that AI tools designed for urban contexts often fail to account for the linguistic and cultural realities of rural Indigenous and Francophone communities, reinforcing the need for community-engaged and context-specific AI development. As a result, AI-driven healthcare technologies may disproportionately benefit urban and affluent populations while leaving behind already marginalized groups (Zhang et al., 2025). Furthermore, research from Batista et al. (2024) showed that Ontario's administrative databases inconsistently capture patients' language, limiting the visibility of Francophone populations in the datasets that increasingly support AI tools. As Lee et al. (2025) argue, advancing equitable care requires linguistic inclusion and cultural humility, principles equally critical for AI design. Without attention to these factors, AI-driven innovations risk amplifying existing linguistic inequities across Canadian provinces and territories, reinforcing preexisting regional disparities in Canada's federated healthcare system.

Beyond infrastructure, community-level equity also depends on whether AI systems reflect the linguistic and cultural fabric of local populations. In many Indigenous and Francophone regions, language barriers intersect with data exclusion, as most clinical and administrative health datasets are collected and processed in English (Zhang et al., 2025). This omission reduces the representativeness of AI training data and may limit diagnostic and predictive accuracy for non-English-speaking communities (Anawati et al., 2024). Similarly, when AI interfaces and outputs are not culturally or linguistically tailored, they risk reproducing colonial assumptions embedded within biomedical data and eroding patient trust (Davis et al., 2025; Khan et al., 2025). Ensuring equitable AI deployment, therefore, requires attention not only to physical connectivity but also to linguistic and algorithmic inclusion, with models designed to account for language diversity, dialectal variation, and bilingual service delivery (Lee et al., 2025; Sasseville et al., 2025; Zhang et al., 2025). Together, these linguistic and cultural dynamics illustrate that responsible AI in healthcare cannot be separated from the diverse social and political landscapes in which it is deployed.

Societal-Level Determinants

Policy and Design Pathways towards AI Equity

At the societal level, policy and governance frameworks are essential for embedding equity into AI deployment. In Canada, some existing federal AI governance initiatives have introduced risk assessment frameworks, such as the recent *Algorithmic AI Assessment (AIA)* tool launched by the Government of Canada, recognizing that identifying and managing AI-related risks is a core aspect of responsible AI governance (Kim et al., 2025). Prior to this, the federal government had introduced the Pan-Canadian Artificial Intelligence Strategy in 2017, with an investment of CAD $125 million to advance AI research, creating opportunities to embed equity into research funding, policy design, and standards development in the future (Hassan et al., 2024).

Additionally, Kim et al. (2025) describe how a major university-affiliated Canadian hospital successfully implemented an operational governance framework for AI using a People–Process–Technology–Operations (PPTO) model. This approach translated high-level principles into approved policies, clearly defined roles, and formal oversight structures. The establishment of a standing AI governance committee illustrates that it is possible to institutionalize accountability mechanisms for AI within Canadian healthcare settings.

Furthermore, research demonstrates that AI can be explicitly designed to advance health equity. For example, Istasy et al. (2022) describe an ML-powered oral cancer screening program in British Columbia, which was developed to address the disproportionately high rates of oral cancer among the provinces' South Asian population. By using quantitative cytology to improve early detection in this high-risk group, this case illustrates how equity-focused design can be directly tailored to specific communities and reduce health disparities. Additionally, Hassan et al. (2024) describe how the Hospital for Sick Children and Humber River Hospital in Ontario have implemented AI systems to predict emergency department surges and optimize resource allocation. While the primary goal of these systems is to improve operational efficiency, such tools may also contribute indirectly to equity by helping reduce wait times and improve access to timely emergency care across patient populations. These cases demonstrate that when AI is intentionally designed around community context and equity principles, it can function as a practical tool for reducing health disparities, rather than reinforcing them.

Furthermore, Indigenous communities across Canada have advanced governance frameworks rooted in collective consent and data sovereignty, emphasizing community control over health information and its ethical use in research and care (Khan et al., 2025). These frameworks embody relational accountability and cultural safety, demonstrating how Indigenous-led oversight can operationalize ethical AI deployment within healthcare. Embedding such community governance models within federal or pan-Canadian AI strategies would help reconcile national policy ambitions with local ethical and cultural priorities (Bouabida et al., 2025; Zhang et al., 2025).

Algorithmic Bias, Governance Gaps, and Unequal Representation

Several systemic barriers currently exist at the societal level. A recurring issue noted across the literature is *Algorithmic Bias*: models trained on nonrepresentative data risk generating inequitable outputs, leading to disparities in diagnosis and treatment (Elhaddad & Hamam, 2024). For example, algorithmic bias can cause misdiagnoses, underdiagnoses, and limit access to resources for specific demographic groups, ultimately perpetuating patient harm (Kim et al., 2025).

Additionally, major regulatory and governance gaps exist that further exacerbate these risks. Canada currently lacks standardized guidelines for AI validation, approval, integration, deployment and monitoring across health systems (Bouabida et al., 2024; Darcel et al., 2023). Most existing AI-governance frameworks, including the *AIA* only provide broad, nonoperational guidance, leaving healthcare organizations without practical tools to govern AI equitably. Moreover, although Canadian privacy laws such as the *Personal Information Protection and Electronic Documents Act (PIPEDA)* and Ontario's *Personal Health Information Protection Act (PHIPA)* provide a foundational layer for the protection of patient data, these frameworks were not designed for AI-driven systems. Therefore, they do not adequately address emerging challenges in algorithmic accountability and equity (Bouabida et al., 2025). The lack of sector-specific governance models means that most Canadian healthcare organizations still face uncertainty around decision points, accountability, liability, and metrics for AI oversight (Kim et al., 2025).

These challenges are reflected in survey evidence, accumulated by Zhang et al. (2025), which found that over 40% of Northern Ontario providers identified insufficient regulation and unclear liability as barriers to adoption. Respondents also reported uncertainty and skepticism about AI, with high rates of "don't know" responses, suggesting both limited exposure and underlying mistrust (Zhang et al., 2025).

Finally, public perceptions of AI risks vary demographically. Studies report that older Canadians express greater discomfort with AI and lower trust compared to younger cohorts, while Canadian women consistently report lower AI literacy and higher skepticism than men (Li et al., 2024). These disparities may indicate the need for targeted outreach and education to build societal trust in AI. Table 4.1 summarizes the cross-level equity enablers and barriers identified across the reviewed studies.

TABLE 4.1
Summary of Equity Enablers and Barriers in AI Alignment within the Canadian Healthcare System, Organized by Level of Determinant

Level of Determinant	Equity Enablers	Equity Barriers	Proposed Solutions
Individual	Accessible, explainable tools; AI supporting self-management through SDoH-aware insights.	Digital literacy and access gaps; privacy concerns; fears of losing the "human touch"; uneven capacity for independent tech use.	• Deliver digital literacy and self-efficacy programs targeted to older adults, low-income Canadians, and other socioeconomically marginalized populations to reduce uneven capacity for AI use. • Design explainable, human-centered AI tools that preserve clinician oversight to sustain patient trust. • Embed equity-by-design features such as multilingual, accessible interfaces and adaptive supports. • Expand affordable device and broadband access initiatives to address structural digital divides affecting rural and low-income users.
Interpersonal	AI-prompted conversations about nonclinical barriers; automation that frees clinician time for patient interaction.	Opaque outputs undermining clinician–patient trust; workflow friction that adds documentation burden and narrows dialogue.	• Integrate explainable AI approaches to make AI reasoning interpretable for clinicians and patients. • Align tools with clinical workflows through codesign and usability testing to prevent duplication and overload. • Provide professional development and AI training that enable clinicians to interpret and communicate AI outputs, supporting relational trust.
Community	Codesign with local communities; virtual-care extensions for rural/remote settings; surge planning that redistributes resources.	Interoperability deficits; vendor lock-in; rural/northern broadband gaps; cultural and linguistic mismatch.	• Employ participatory and community-led design ensuring Indigenous data sovereignty and cultural tailoring. • Invest in rural and northern digital infrastructure, including broadband and telehealth capacity, to enable equitable access. • Implement open-standard interoperability and shared data-governance frameworks to overcome vendor lock-in. • Support context-specific AI adaptation for example, linguistic and cultural customization in Indigenous and Francophone communities.
Societal	Operational AI governance (e.g., PPTO models); national funding that embeds equity criteria in research and deployment.	Nonrepresentative data; limited validation or monitoring standards; unclear liability; privacy regimes not tailored to AI equity.	• Develop national AI-governance standards with enforceable validation, monitoring, and accountability mechanisms. • Mandate bias auditing and representativeness testing for training datasets before deployment. • Modernize privacy and consent frameworks (e.g., PIPEDA, PHIPA) to incorporate algorithmic accountability and equity safeguards. • Integrate equity metrics into funding, procurement, and regulatory processes, ensuring measurable equity outcomes. • Promote participatory and transparent AI governance to build public trust and accountability.

DISCUSSION

Across levels, equity outcomes are less dependent on model novelty than on governance, representation, and workflow alignment. Where data is representative, outputs explainable, and oversight operationalized, AI augments care; where interoperability, consent, and accountability are weak, AI amplifies existing inequities.

Cross-Cutting Themes and Findings: Successes and Shortfalls

This review shows that while Canadian health AI research increasingly acknowledges equity, its operationalization remains inconsistent. A central lesson is that governance and accountability are not abstract add-ons but core determinants of equity impact. The PPTO case demonstrates feasibility, yet its rarity underscores how few institutions have translated principles into practice. This gap reflects the broader challenge of moving from guidelines to enforceable standards, a tension that recurs across technical, institutional, and ethical domains (Kim et al., 2025).

Another recurring theme is trust (Li et al., 2024). The results suggest that technical literacy and data protection alone are insufficient to secure public comfort. Instead, trust is relational and contingent on transparent governance, explainable outputs, and evidence that AI augments, rather than replaces, the human aspects of care. This highlights a paradox: AI is most effective when invisible in the background, yet most equitable when visible, explainable, and accountable (Khattak et al., 2023).

Next, technical and workflow fit are crucial to ensure equitable impact. The results emphasize data quality and user-centered design, whilst stressing that AI must align with clinical tasks, remain explainable, and integrate smoothly into existing systems. When poorly integrated, these tools risk adding documentation burdens or reproducing inequities if privacy and interoperability are not addressed (Bouabida et al., 2025; Darcel et al., 2023; Elhaddad & Hamam, 2024).

Fourth, context and community structure shape who benefits from health technologies. Studies from Northern Ontario and other remote settings highlight that connectivity, education and training, cultural/linguistic tailoring, and community representation are essential. "One-size-fits-all" approaches risk excluding marginalized groups, whereas participatory design and community governance support alignment (Anawati et al., 2024; Khan et al., 2025; Zhang et al., 2025).

Finally, public health AI research cautions that without an explicit equity lens, implementing AI technologies might amplify preexisting structural oppression and the digital divide. Emphasis is placed on health equity being integrated into the full AI life cycle, from problem selection to evaluation (Ghanem et al., 2025).

Overall, it appears that successful AI alignment with health equity can be achieved if: AI tools are codesigned with affected communities in mind are explainable, task-fit, and embedded within robust governance structures. On the contrary, it may fall short when datasets are non-representative and/or biased, clinical workflows are disrupted, or accountability, governance, and consent pathways are unclear (Elhaddad & Hamam, 2024; Kim et al., 2025; Li et al., 2024; Zhang et al., 2025).

Barriers to Health Equity-Aligned AI

While the identified technical, institutional, workflow, and governance barriers are often treated as discrete categories, they are in fact interdependent. For example, the opacity of algorithms (technical) becomes consequential only when embedded in workflows (clinical) and unaddressed by accountability structures (governance). Similarly, limited institutional readiness and resource constraints magnify technical gaps, while inadequate governance frameworks exacerbate public mistrust of clinical adoption. Taken together, barriers can be summarized into four domains:

1. **Technical** – biased or unrepresentative datasets, algorithmic opacity, and fragmented IT systems with poor interoperability (Bouabida et al., 2025; Elhaddad & Hamam, 2024; Istasy et al., 2022; Nesa et al., 2025).
2. **Institutional** – limited leadership, organizational readiness, training, and funding (Hassan et al., 2024; Kim et al., 2025; Nesa et al., 2025; Zhang et al., 2025).
3. **Clinical workflow** – poor task fit, added documentation burden, and workflow disruption (Darcel et al., 2023; Elhaddad & Hamam, 2024).
4. **Ethical and governance** – privacy and surveillance concerns, unclear consent, weak accountability, and the absence of enforceable standards (Anawati et al., 2024; Bouabida et al., 2025; Davis et al., 2025; Khan et al., 2025; Kim et al., 2025; Zhang et al., 2025).

Implications for Practice and Policy

The analysis highlights that achieving health-equity–aligned AI is less about inventing new tools than about embedding existing ethical commitments into operational systems. Governance, procurement, and regulatory processes must be reengineered so that equity becomes a measurable deliverable rather than an aspirational value. The recommendations below identify practical pathways toward that goal.

- **Equity as a design principle, not an evaluation metric**: Too often, equity is assessed after deployment rather than embedded from the outset. Canadian institutions must shift toward equity-by-design approaches, aligning procurement, funding, and innovation incentives accordingly (Anawati et al., 2024; Ghanem et al., 2025; Richardson et al., 2022).
- **From principles to enforceable standards:** Governance frameworks such as AIA provide useful starting points, but without enforceable mechanisms for validation, monitoring, and accountability, they risk remaining symbolic (Bouabida et al., 2025; Darcel et al., 2023; Kim et al., 2025).
- **Trust-building as ongoing practice:** Trust is not achieved through education alone but through demonstrable accountability, participatory governance, and visible pathways for redress (Anawati et al., 2024; Davis et al., 2025; Li et al., 2024).
- **Context-sensitive deployment:** National strategies must account for regional inequities in infrastructure, culture, and language. What constitutes "equitable AI" in Toronto will differ from what is feasible in Nunavut or Northern Ontario (Khan et al., 2025; Zhang et al., 2025).
- **Redistributing power in innovation:** Equity requires not only technical fixes but also shifts in who designs, governs, and benefits from AI. Supporting Indigenous data sovereignty, community-led governance, and nonprofit innovation models may be as critical as algorithmic refinements (Anawati et al., 2024; Khan et al., 2025; Richardson et al., 2022; Zhang et al., 2025).

Limitations

This narrative review has limitations. The synthesis was based on a relatively small set of peer-reviewed articles (n = 25), reflecting the limited but gradually emerging body of Canadian-based/focused research on AI and health equity. Additionally, current evidence is disproportionately drawn from

Ontario, with comparatively limited analysis of regional contexts such as Quebec, where French–English bilingualism and distinct data governance laws influence how AI tools are integrated into health systems. The exclusion of gray literature (e.g., policy briefs and government reports) means that institutional strategies and real-world implementation cases and/or practices may be underrepresented. Additionally, the rapid pace of AI innovation means that new developments may not be fully captured. Finally, although the NIMHD-expanded Framework for Digital Health Equity provided a valuable structure for classifying the narrative review findings, its U.S.-based context may not capture all nuances of the Canadian health equity landscape.

CONCLUSION

In conclusion, the findings of this narrative review clearly indicate that the central challenge for AI in Canadian healthcare is not whether these tools can be deployed, but whether they are deployed effectively, in ways that advance health equity rather than deepen inequities. Across the assessed literature, the alignment of AI with health equity appears to succeed when AI systems are codesigned with communities, draw from representative datasets, and are built to be transparent, explainable, and task-fit. Models for AI governance, such as the PPTO framework, demonstrate how accountability can be embedded into organizational practice, ensuring that health equity principles effectively translate into operational reality (Kim et al., 2025). At the same time, however, barriers to AI alignment with health equity remain substantial. Nonrepresentative data, poor interoperability, and weak integration into clinical workflows threaten to reproduce structural inequities (Bouabida et al., 2025; Darcel et al., 2023; Istasy et al., 2022). Institutional gaps in readiness, education and training, as well as resourcing, leave many providers ill-equipped to adopt equity-aligned AI (Hassan et al., 2024; Nesa et al., 2025). Ethical concerns over privacy, consent, accountability, and Indigenous data sovereignty highlight that current legal frameworks, such as PIPEDA and PHIPA, while important, were not designed for more novel AI-specific equity challenges (Bouabida et al., 2025; Davis et al., 2025; Khan et al., 2025).

Ultimately, AI's value may not lie in its technical innovation and efficiency alone, but in its ability to reduce disparities in healthcare access, quality, and outcomes. To achieve this, however, there must be considerable investment in relevant infrastructure, participatory governance, bias auditing, and policy that prioritizes the needs of Canada's marginalized communities. Health equity, therefore, must be a measure of success for AI alignment in Canadian healthcare, or else the adoption of these technologies risks reinforcing the very inequities they're meant to address (Ghanem et al., 2025; Richardson et al., 2022).

ACKNOWLEDGMENT

Portions of this chapter were developed with the assistance of ChatGPT for brainstorming. All intellectual contributions, interpretations, and final editorial decisions are the authors' own, and the authors take full responsibility for the content. Any AI-assisted or AI-generated material was reviewed and verified by the authors.

REFLECTION QUESTIONS

1. How does the digital divide in rural and Northern Canada complicate the narrative that AI will inevitably improve healthcare access for all?
2. The authors identify trust as a major barrier to AI adoption. How is trust linked to the historical experiences of marginalized communities with the healthcare system?
3. In what ways does the current lack of interoperability between provincial data systems serve as a barrier to equitable AI deployment?
4. Reflecting on the concept of Indigenous data sovereignty, why is it essential for Indigenous communities to have governance over their own health data rather than just being subjects of data extraction?

REFERENCES

Anawati, A., Fleming, H., Mertz, M., Bertrand, J., Dumond, J., Myles, S., Leblanc, J., Ross, B., Lamoureux, D., Patel, D., Carrier, R., & Cameron, E. (2024). Artificial intelligence and social accountability in the Canadian health care landscape: A rapid literature review. *PLOS Digital Health*, *3*(9), e0000597. https://doi.org/10.1371/journal.pdig.0000597

Badawi, A., Laskar, Huang, J. X., Raza, S., & Dolatabadi, E. (2025). Position: Beyond Assistance – Reimagining LLMs as Ethical and Adaptive Co-Creators in Mental Health Care. https://arxiv.org/abs/2503.16456

Baghbanzadeh, N., Ashkezari, S., Dolatabadi, E., & Afkanpour, A. (2025). Open-PMC-18M: A High-Fidelity Large Scale Medical Dataset for Multimodal Representation Learning. ArXiv.org. https://arxiv.org/abs/2506.02738

Baghbanzadeh, N., Fallahpour, A., Parhizkar, Y., Ogidi, F., Roy, S., Ashkezari, S., Reza, K. V., Colacci, M., Etemad, A., Afkanpour, A., & Dolatabadi, E. (2025). Advancing Medical Representation Learning Through High-Quality Data. ArXiv.org. https://arxiv.org/abs/2503.14377

Batista, R., Hsu, A. T., Bouchard, L., Reaume, M., Rhodes, E., Sucha, E., Guerin, E., Prud'homme, D., Manuel, D. G., & Tanuseputro, P. (2024). Ascertaining the Francophone population in Ontario: Validating the language variable in health data. *BMC Medical Research Methodology*, *24*(1). https://doi.org/10.1186/s12874-024-02220-7

Bouabida, K., Chaves, B. G., Anane, E., & Navaal, J. (2025). Navigating the landscape of remote patient monitoring in Canada: Trends, challenges, and future directions. *Frontiers in Digital Health*, *7*. https://doi.org/10.3389/fdgth.2025.1523401

Bouabida, K., Lebouché, B., & Pomey, M. P. (2024). The paradoxes of telehealth platforms: What did we learn from the use of telehealth platforms?. *Frontiers in Digital Health*, *6*(1346039). doi: 10.3389/fdgth.2024.1346039

Darcel, K., Upshaw, T., Craig-Neil, A., Macklin, J., Carolyn Steele Gray, C. Y., Chan, T., Gibson, J., & Pinto, A. D. (2023). Implementing artificial intelligence in Canadian primary care: Barriers and strategies identified through a national deliberative dialogue. *PLOS ONE*, *18*(2), e0281733–e0281733. https://doi.org/10.1371/journal.pone.0281733

Davis, V. H., Qiang, J. R., MacCarthy, I. A., Howse, D., Seshie, A. Z., Kosowan, L., Delahunty-Pike, A., Abaga, E., Cooney, J., Robinson, M., Senior, D., Zsager, A., Aubrey-Bassler, K., Irwin, M., Jackson, L. A., Katz, A., Marshall, E. G., Muhajarine, N., Neudorf, C., & Garies, S. (2025). Perspectives on using artificial intelligence to derive social determinants of health data from medical records in Canada: Large multijurisdictional qualitative study. *Journal of Medical Internet Research*, *27*(1), e52244. https://doi.org/10.2196/52244

Elhaddad, M., & Hamam, S. (2024). AI-driven clinical decision support systems: An ongoing Pursuit of potential. *Cureus*, *16*(4). https://doi.org/10.7759/cureus.57728

Gao, J., Chou, B., McCaw, Z. R., Thurston, H., Varghese, P., Hong, C., & Gronsbell, J. (2025). What is fair? Defining fairness in machine learning for health. *Statistics in Medicine*, *44*(20–22). https://doi.org/10.1002/sim.70234

Ghanem, S., Moraleja, M., Gravesande, D., & Rooney, J. (2025). Integrating health equity in artificial intelligence for public health in Canada: A rapid narrative review. *Frontiers in Public Health*, *13*. https://doi.org/10.3389/fpubh.2025.1524616

Hassan, M., Kushniruk, A., & Borycki, E. (2024). Barriers and facilitators of artificial intelligence adoption in healthcare: A scoping review (Preprint). *JMIR Human Factors*, *11*, e48633–e48633. https://doi.org/10.2196/48633

Istasy, P., Lee, W. S., Iansavichene, A., Upshur, R., Gyawali, B., Burkell, J., Sadikovic, B., Lazo-Langner, A., & Chin-Yee, B. (2022). The impact of artificial intelligence on health equity in oncology: Scoping review. *Journal of Medical Internet Research*, *24*(11), e39748. https://doi.org/10.2196/39748

Khan, A., Galea, S., & Mendez, I. (2025). Five steps for the deployment of artificial intelligence-driven healthcare delivery for remote and indigenous populations in Canada. *Digital Health*, *11*. https://doi.org/10.1177/20552076251334422

Khattak, F. K., Subasri, V., Krishnan, A., Dolatabadi, E., Pandya, D., Seyyed-Kalantari, L., & Rudzicz, F. (2023). MLHOps: Machine Learning for Healthcare Operations. ArXiv.org. https://arxiv.org/abs/2305.02474

Kim, J. Y., Hasan, A., Kueper, J., Tang, T., Hayes, C., Fine, B., Balu, S., & Sendak, M. (2025). Establishing organizational AI governance in healthcare: A case study in Canada. *Npj Digital Medicine*, *8*(1). https://doi.org/10.1038/s41746-025-01909-3

Lee, S. H., Reaume, M., Fung, C., & MacLeod, K. K. (2025). Reflections on the value of Canadian multiculturalism in health care delivery. *Canadian Family Physician*, *71*(4), 238–240. https://doi.org/10.46747/cfp.7104238

Li, A. K. C., Rauf, I. A., & Keshavjee, K. (2024). Knowledge is not all you need for comfort in use of AI in healthcare. *Public Health*, *238*, 254–259. https://doi.org/10.1016/j.puhe.2024.11.019

Medina Florez, J. A., Raza, S., Lynn Ansell, R., Shakeri, Z., Smith, B. T., & Dolatabadi, E. (2025). Academic case reports lack diversity: Assessing the presence and diversity of sociodemographic and behavioral factors related to Post COVID-19 Condition. *PLOS One*, *20*(7), e0326668. https://doi.org/10.1371/journal.pone.0326668

Nesa, L., Karim, M., Chowdhury, S., Most. Baby Naznin, Halder, K., Ara, M. H., Akter, N. N., Kobory Mankhin, Jinat Mohasana Shabnur, Alam, J., Parvin, M. R., Alrazeeni, D. M., & Akter, F. (2025). Artificial intelligence in healthcare: A scoping review of medical professionals' acceptance and institutional challenges in implementation. *Journal of Evaluation in Clinical Practice*, *31*(4). https://doi.org/10.1111/jep.70170

Osonuga, A., Osonuga, A. A., Fidelis, S. C., Osonuga, G. C., Juckes, J., & Olawade, D. B. (2025). Bridging the digital divide: Artificial intelligence as a catalyst for health equity in primary care settings. *International Journal of Medical Informatics*, 106051. https://doi.org/10.1016/j.ijmedinf.2025.106051

Raza, S., Ghuge, S., Ding, C., Dolatabadi, E., & Pandya, D. (2024). FAIR enough: Develop and assess a FAIR-compliant dataset for large language model training? *Data Intelligence*, *6*(2), 559–585. https://doi.org/10.1162/dint_a_00255

Raza, S., Qureshi, R., Zahid, A., Fioresi, J., Sadak, F., Saeed, M., Sapkota, R., Jain, A., Zafar, A., Hassan, M. U., Zafar, A., Maqbool, H., Wu, J., & Shoman, M. (2025). Who is Responsible? The Data, Models, Users or Regulations? Responsible Generative AI for a Sustainable Future. ArXiv (Cornell University). https://doi.org/10.48550/arxiv.2502.08650

Richardson, S., Lawrence, K., Schoenthaler, A. M., & Mann, D. (2022). A framework for digital health equity. *Npj Digital Medicine*, *5*(1). https://doi.org/10.1038/s41746-022-00663-0

Roy, S., Parhizkar, Y., Ogidi, F., Reza, K. V., Colacci, M., Etemad, A., Dolatabadi, E., & Afkanpour, A. (2024). Benchmarking Vision-Language Contrastive Methods for Medical Representation Learning. ArXiv.org. https://arxiv.org/abs/2406.07450

Sasseville, M., Ouellet, S., Rhéaume, C., Sahlia, M., Couture, V., Després, P., Paquette, J.-S., Darmon, D., Bergeron, F., & Gagnon, M.-P. (2025). Bias mitigation in primary health care artificial intelligence models: Scoping review. *Journal of Medical Internet Research*, *27*. https://doi.org/10.2196/60269

Xu, W., & Dolatabadi, E. (2025). A Flexible Fairness Framework with Surrogate Loss Reweighting for Addressing Sociodemographic Disparities. ArXiv.org. https://arxiv.org/abs/2503.16836

Zhang, Y., Newbery, S., Savage, D., & Ross, B. (2025). Artificial intelligence and rural health equity: Perspectives from Northern Ontario. *Journal of Rural and Community Development/Revue Du Développement Rural et Communautaire*, *20*(3). https://journals.brandonu.ca/jrcd/article/view/2876

5 Benchmarking Bias

Expanding Clinical AI Model Card to Incorporate Bias Reporting of Social and Nonsocial Factors

Shahram Mohanna, Carolina A. M. Heming, Mohamed Abdalla, Monish Ahluwalia, Linglin Zhang, Hari Trivedi, MinJae Woo, InChan Hwang, Benjamin Fine, Judy Wawira Gichoya, Leo Anthony Celi and Laleh Seyyed-Kalantari

INTRODUCTION

Artificial intelligence (AI) models have been shown to suffer from fairness and bias in diverse applications (Brady et al., 2024; Ogbuokiri et al., 2025; Asgarimendejin et al., 2025; Subasri et al., 2025; Zadeh Khaki et al., 2025) and propagate the existing biases in real-world practice (Walker et al., 2024; Naziri et al., 2025; Banerjee et al., 2023; Zhang et al., 2023; Abdelmalek et al., 2024). Here, bias means disparate outcomes of an AI model across different subpopulations in the dataset for a given sensitive attribute. The sensitive attribute is a feature that may statistically correlate with the AI model's outcome, but there is no causal basis, leading to an unfair model performance, against or in favor of a subpopulation. As a result, the performance average across all test cases may be high, but the majority of the model failures may belong to particular subpopulations, e.g., Black patients, pointing to the model is not suitable for these groups of patients. In such a scenario, reporting the subgroup analysis outcome provides essential information that the reported performance average across all test cases cannot reveal. AI bias and unfairness are concerning, particularly in medical imaging applications, as it has been shown to impact marginalized patients (Bahre et al., 2025; Woo et al., 2025; Ahluwalia et al., 2023; Seyyed-Kalantari et al., 2020) and may lead to harm, such as underdiagnosis (Seyyed-Kalantari et al., 2021; Kalantari et al., 2022; Bahre et al., 2025) and potentially exacerbate inequities.

Using an AI "Model Card" or the "Model Facts Label" is a standard way to document AI model's purpose, training data, performance, limitations, and intended use and communicate the outcome to the end users (Sendak et al., 2020; Chen et al., 2022; Dan & Seeuws, 2024; Bracamonte et al., 2023). The purpose is to ensure that frontline clinicians know how to incorporate model output into clinical decisions, when, how not, and when not. We have performed a scientific review from 2018 to 2024, with the keywords: "Model Card", "AI Model Card", "AI model fact sheet", "AI model fact sheet in medical imaging" and "AI fairness in model fact sheet", while we are focusing on literature that consider bias and fairness applicable to healthcare and medical imaging. Recent research has highlighted various efforts aimed at improving transparency, accountability, and fairness in clinical AI systems, particularly through the development and implementation of model cards. In ophthalmology, standardized AI model cards have been proposed to improve transparency in clinical applications (Chen et al., 2022). Other work has focused on enhancing the reproducibility of machine learning (ML) studies by promoting structured model documentation (Dan & Seeuws, 2024). Studies have also explored how model cards are perceived in terms of information quality and effectiveness, shedding light on their usability and impact on stakeholders' understanding (Bracamonte et al., 2023).

DOI: 10.1201/9781003737810-6

These model cards often present the performance average across all test cases (Sendak et al., 2020; Chen et al., 2022; Dan & Seeuws, 2024; Bracamonte et al., 2023). The existing model fact cards proposed for healthcare applications do not include the bias and fairness assessment outcomes (Sendak et al., 2020). These cards typically report only overall performance metrics, without addressing potential biases. However, fairness analysis of AI models in medical imaging indicates that the model performance varies across subgroups of sexes, ages, or races (sociodemographic fairness factors) (Zhang et al., 2023; Abdelmalek et al, 2024; Bahre et al., AI4H 2025; Woo et al., 2025; Seyyed-Kalantari et al., 2020; Seyyed-Kalantari et al., 2021; Ahluwalia et al., 2023; Bahre et al., IEEE 2025). In other words, a model that has a high performance across all populations may have a higher underdiagnosis rate for Black patients and a much lower underdiagnosis rate for White patients (Seyyed-Kalantari et al., 2021). Then, reporting the performance average across all patients in the model card is not as informative as reporting the performance average across subgroups.

In this work, we propose the use of a model card for medical imaging that considers domain-specific attributes impacting disparate outcomes of AI models. We often evaluate bias concerning sociodemographic fairness factors (e.g., sex, race, socioeconomic status). In the context of medical imaging, disparate outcomes of AI models across sociodemographic fairness factors have been well-documented across many applications (Zhang et al., 2023; Seyyed-Kalantari et al., 2021; Bahre et al., 2025; Salvado et al., 2024; Konate et al., 2025); however, reporting such disparate outcomes in the model card has been overlooked (Sendak et al., 2020; Chen et al., 2022; Dan & Seeuws, 2024; Bracamonte et al., 2023). Moreover, we observed that there are domain-specific attributes, such as technical, environmental, and biological bias factors (e.g., disease-dependent, anatomical, instrumental factors) that highly impact disparate outcomes of AI models in medical imaging, which have not been explored much or reported in the model fact card. Expanding the model's fact cards in medical imaging to incorporate both types of factors supports the end users in distinguishing the models' caveats and realizing when and how to use the AI model.

To our knowledge, none of the existing proposed model cards for healthcare applications have discussed the importance of reporting through fairness analysis with respect to sociodemographic fairness factors or explored the importance of technical, environmental, and biological bias factors specific to medical imaging. Here, we demonstrate disparities with respect to both sets of factors.

ESSENTIAL FACTORS IN FAIRNESS AND BIAS ANALYSIS IN MEDICAL IMAGING

The AI model performance gap with respect to the sociodemographic fairness factors has been widely demonstrated in many applications. For example, race and sex bias have been reported in AI models developed for medical image disease diagnosis (Seyyed-Kalantari et al., 2021). Patients' self-reported race can be detected from their medical images alone (Gichoya et al., 2022) by AI algorithms, while AI models have worse performance for historically underserved races (e.g., Hispanic or Black patients) (Seyyed-Kalantari et al., 2021; Bahre et al., 2025). Such biases in healthcare AI-based decision-making tools are a critical issue that must be detected and, if not mitigated, at least communicated to the end user and addressed before large-scale adoption.

The bias and fairness analysis papers often explore sociodemographic fairness factors, with the main focus on race and sex (Gichoya et al., 2022; Zhang et al., 2022; Cirillo et al., 2020; Obermeyer et al., 2019; Larrazabal et al., 2020; Vyas et al., 2020), sensitive attributes. There is less attention to other sociodemographic factors that cause disparity, such as spoken language (Zhang et al., 2020), education (Pierson et al., 2021), income level (Pierson et al., 2021), age (Seyyed-Kalantari et al., 2021; Bahre et al., 2025), or insurance type (Seyyed-Kalantari et al., 2021; Bahre et al., 2025). Such a narrow focus misses other sources of bias and does not consider heterogeneity within members of a specific race/sex subgroup. For example, a research paper has shown that a commercial algorithm identified black patients as having fewer healthcare needs than white patients with similar medical conditions (Obermeyer et al., 2019). This occurred because the AI model used healthcare costs as a proxy for healthcare needs. Then, since black patients often spent less on healthcare than white patients due to lower socioeconomic status, the model flagged them as patients with less healthcare need. If this model were blindly debiased simply by correcting predictions for black patients, the model would still harm low-income patients of all other races, since income level has been the real source of bias, which cannot be universally attributed to race. In other words, for this case, race is the false bias factor to correct. Recognizing and addressing various sources of bias is essential for algorithmic debiasing, ensuring trustworthiness, and contributing to the just and equitable deployment of AI in medical imaging (Drukker et al., 2023; Chen et al., 2022).

A broader investigation is required to extend beyond known sociodemographic fairness factors in bias analysis, and a desire for reflection on model cards. These categories highlight the disparate outcomes of AI models across (1) anatomic factors (e.g., body habitus, anatomic variants), (2) disease-dependent factors (e.g., disease appearance), (3) instrumental factors (e.g., imaging devices), and (4) data sources. This topic has not been extensively explored in the healthcare domain and has not been reported in model cards, which we introduce and discuss in more detail in this paper.

A COMPREHENSIVE AI MODEL FACT CARD FOR MEDICAL IMAGING – INCORPORATING BIAS

This section describes the suggested more comprehensive AI Model Cards that are shown in Figure 5.1 (Ahluwalia et al., 2023) and Figure 5.2 (Zhang et al., 2023). These models demonstrate the disparate outcomes of both AI models for chest X-ray and mammography abnormality classification tasks (normal/abnormal) that are demonstrated across available sociodemographic fairness factors in the employed dataset. To create such models, more comprehensive set of factors is to be reported in model fact cards in the context of medical imaging. Our suggestions are inspired by Mitchell et al., who introduced a model card for non-healthcare applications, which includes a thorough fairness analysis and demonstrates the impact of instrumental and environmental factors on model bias and fairness (Bracamonte et al., 2023).

Combining the study of Mitchell et al., domain experts, and observed biases in AI models in medical imaging (Zhang et al., 2023; Abdelmalek et al, 2024; Bahre et al., AI4H 2025; Woo et al., 2025; Seyyed-Kalantari et al., 2020; Seyyed-Kalantari et al., 2021; Ahluwalia et al., 2023; Bahre et al., IEEE 2025), we have suggested that the model fact cards in medical imaging need to include a thorough bias and fairness analysis across:

(a) sociodemographic fairness factors (e.g., sex, race, socioeconomic status) in a broader range vs a conventional focus on sex and race.

(b) technical, environmental, and biological bias factors (e.g., disease-dependent, anatomical, instrumental factors). This includes anatomic factors (e.g., body habitus, anatomic variants), disease-dependent factors (e.g., disease appearance), instrumental factors (e.g., imaging devices), and data sources.

Following, we expand on the rationale for the proposed idea through two illustrative examples in chest X-ray and mammography abnormality classification.

The Impact of Sociodemographic Fairness Factors ON Disparate AI Outcomes

The impact of sociodemographic fairness factors, such as patient race and sex, on disparate outcomes of AI models in healthcare has been widely demonstrated (Gichoya et al., 2022; Obermeyer et al., 2019; Pierson et al., 2021; Bahre et al., 2024; Parkhimchyk et al., 2024; Zhang et al., 2021). However, other social factors such as patients' language (English vs. non-English speakers) (Zhang et al., 2020), education (Pierson et al., 2021), income level (Pierson et al., 2021), age (Seyyed-Kalantari et al., 2021), or insurance type (Seyyed-Kalantari et al., 2021) have received less attention. For instance, Seyyed-Kalantari et al. (2021) found that AI models in chest X-ray diagnostics, underdiagnose historically underserved patients, e.g., such as younger patients or patients with Medicaid insurance type, who are often low-income at a higher rate. Relatedly, in electronic health

Model Facts Card – Chest Radiograph Classification

Model Details:

- State-of-the-art convolutional neural network with a 121-layer DenseNet architecture developed by Kalantar et al., 2020 based on the CheXpert Image dataset
- Classifies chest radiographs into one or more of 14 classes: atelectasis, cardiomegaly, consolidation, edema, enlarged cardiomediastinum, fracture, lung lesion, lung opacity, pleural effusion, pleural other, pneumonia, pneumothorax, support devices, and no finding
- The no finding category was used to determine binary classes (normal if 1, abnormal if 0)

Intended Use:

- Chest radiograph classification for research purposes only

Factors:

- **Groups** include age, EHR-reported sex, and name-based ancestry (Greater European, Greater African/Indian, and Greater East Asian), and 12 pathology classes
- **Instrumentation factors** include 8 chest radiograph imaging systems
- **Environment factors** include patient location (emergency room, inpatient, outpatient, and ICU)
- **Other relevant factors** not studied include image quality and rotation

Metrics:

- **Evaluation metrics** include accuracy, positive predictive value (PPV), negative predictive value (NPV), sensitivity, and specificity for each factor and group; sensitivity is provided for pathology classes
- Metrics were calculated from respective confusion matrices
- Bootstrap resampling (n = 10,000) was used to generate 95% confidence intervals

Training & Evaluation Data:

- **Trained** on 224,316 chest radiographs from Stanford University Medical Center between October 2002 and July 2017 (Irvin et al., 2019); no retraining or threshold adjustment was performed
- **Evaluated** on 197,540 chest radiographs from Trillium Health Partners from January 2016 to December 2020 (Ahluwalia et al., 2023)

Caveats & Recommendations:

- Only applicable to Trillium Health Partners

Quantitative Analysis:

- Accuracy of 76% in binary classification with skewing to higher specificity vs. sensitivity
- Higher sensitivity in detecting pleural effusions; lower sensitivity in detecting cardiomegaly, fracture, and all pathologies when solitary
- Low sensitivity and high specificity in patients under 40 and in the emergency room
- High sensitivity and low specificity in patients over 65 and in the ICU
- Similar performance relative to sex and ancestry; variable performance on different equipment models

FIGURE 5.1 The suggested model card shows the model performance analysis across social and nonsocial factors. In this case, we analyzed a third-party classifier applied to 200,000 images from a tertiary care center (Ahluwalia et al., 2023). We plot the difference in performance as measured by multiple metrics to demonstrate disparities.

record data, Zhang et al. (2020) perpetuated undesired biases, resulting in performance discrepancies with respect to patients' spoken language (English vs. non-English), ethnicity, and insurance type. Besides, Pierson et al. (2021) demonstrate bias with respect to the patients' education and income level in pain severity measures.

Technical, Environmental, and Biological Bias Factors

Technical, environmental, and biological bias factors can contribute to AI model bias, but they are often ignored and have not been explored much. These factors may have a great impact on end-users' (e.g. doctors and nurses) ability to rely on the predictions of AI models in practice. Here,

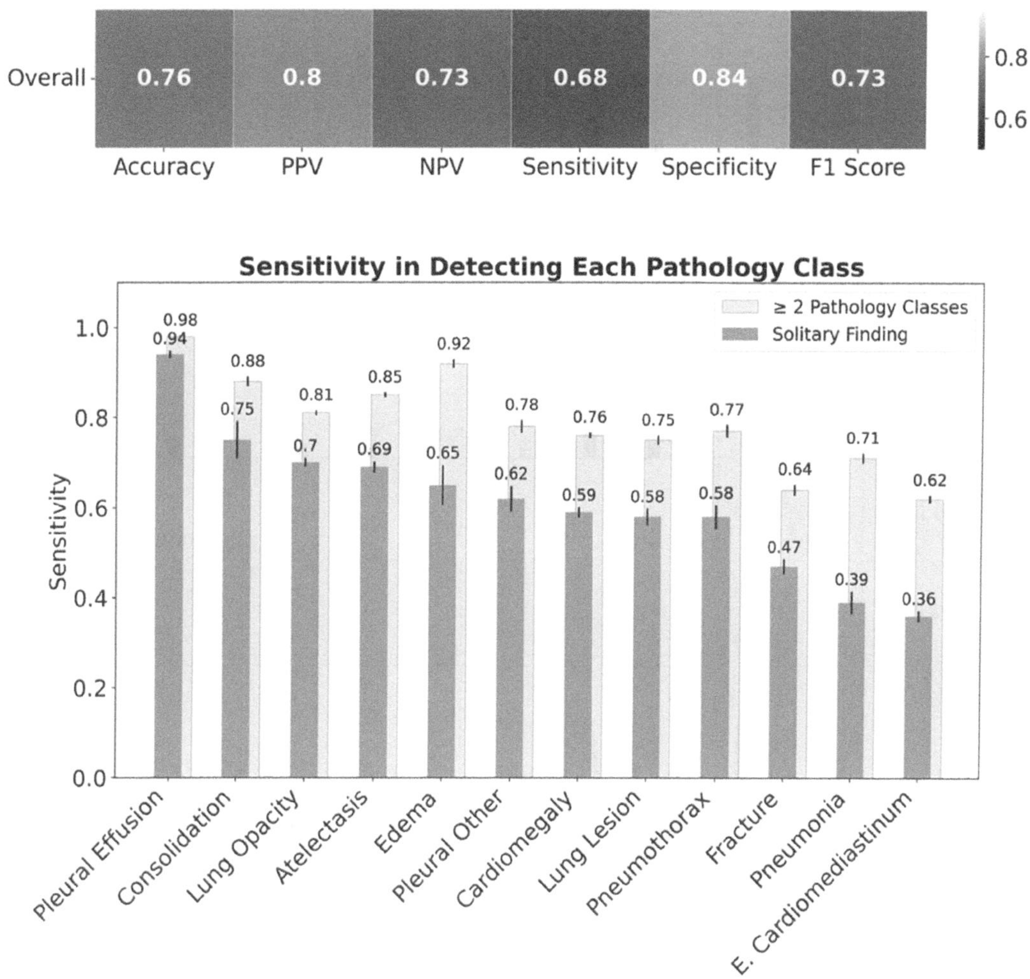

FIGURE 5.1 (Continued)

we list these factors that we suggest should be considered in the context of AI models for radiology applications.

Anatomic Factors

Anatomic variants may cause errors in diagnosis and treatment planning. For example, anatomic variants in the spine may be a source of inaccurate radiotherapy planning (Ford et al., 2020). Similarly, anatomic variants can also be a source of inaccuracy in ML models for organ or tumor segmentation (Bohlender et al., 2023). Oakden-Rayner et al. (2022) found that a classifier for hip fracture detection on frontal X-rays performed worst in cases with abnormal bone or joint appearance, such as Paget's disease of the bone. Additionally, differences in body habitus may affect model predictions. For instance, increased breast density is an independent risk factor for breast cancer (McCormack & dos Santos Silva, 2006) and simultaneously reduces mammography's sensitivity in breast cancer screening (Checka et al., 2012), which may challenge the use of AI in mammography (Nalla et al., 2024).

We have shown disparate outcomes of AI model across breast density in Figure 5.2 (Zhang et al., 2023). Here, the disparate outcomes of AI model across breast density demonstrate a lower AUC for patients with BI-RADS densities C and D. In practice, Asian and Black patients have a higher

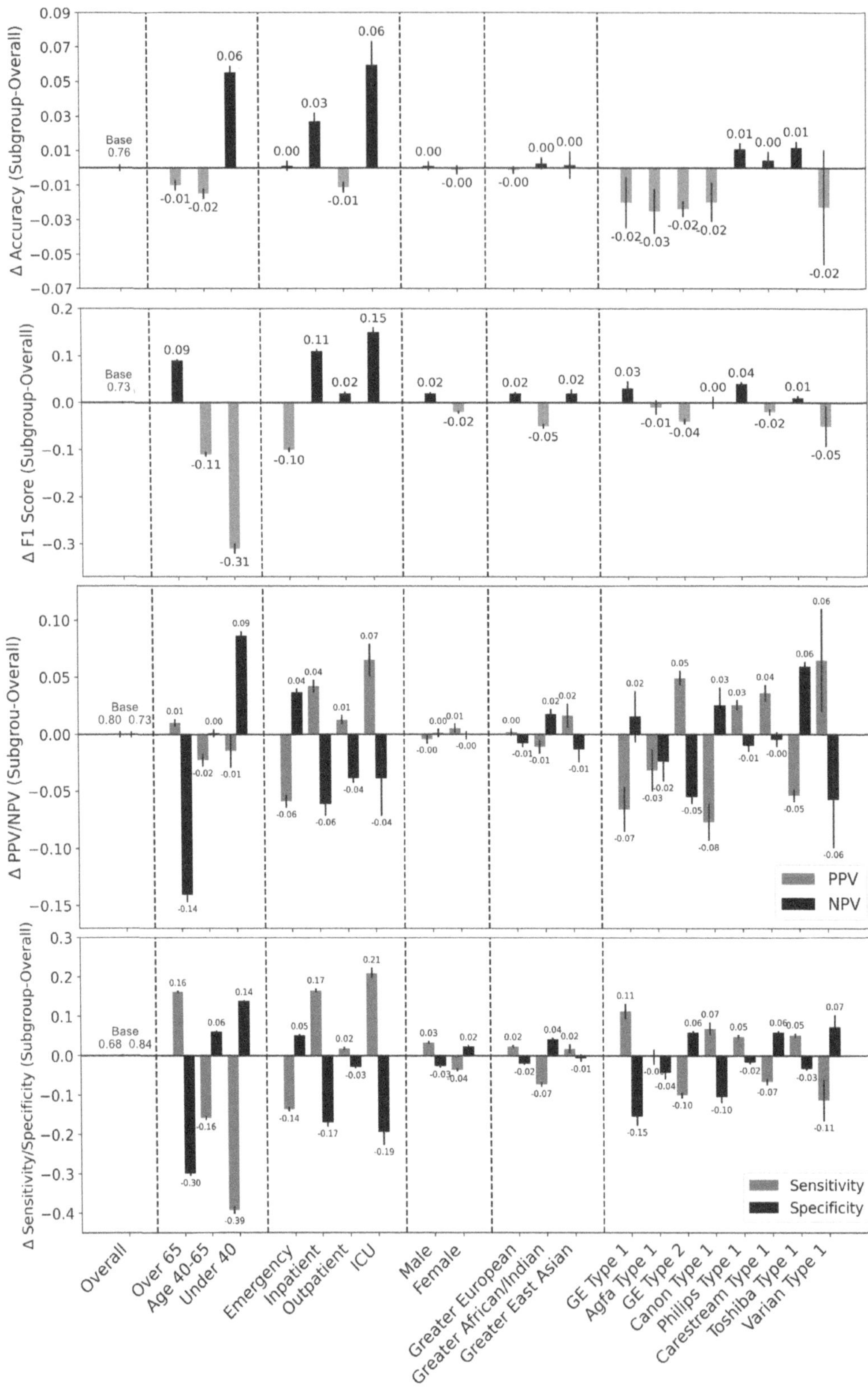

FIGURE 5.1 (Continued)

Model Facts Card – Abnormality Classification of Screening Mammograms

Model Details:
• A deep convolutional neural network enhanced by ResNet152V2 (He et al., 2016) pretrained on ImageNet (Deng et al., 2009), six additional dense layers were added
• Classifies screening mammogram patches as normal (BIRADS 1 or 2) or abnormal (BIRADS 0)
Intended Use:
• Screening mammograms classification for research purpose only
Factors:
• Groups include race (White, Black, other races), age, and 3 pathology classes (never biopsied, benign, and cancer)
• Anatomic tissue density
• Image Findings include mass, asymmetry, architectural distortion (AD), and calcification
• Instrumental Factors include 3 mammography device manufacturers
• Environmental Factors include screening mammography exam location
Metrics:
• Evaluation metrics include accuracy, area under the receiver operating characteristic curve (AUC), recall, precision, F1 score
• Bootstrap resampling ($n \in [1000, 13390]$) was used to generate 95% confidence interval (CI) Training & Evaluation Data:
• 52,444 mammogram patches extracted from Emory Breast Imaging Dataset (EMBED) between 2013 to 2020 (Jeong et al., 2023)
Caveats & Recommendations:
• Does not represent performance at institutions outside Emory University
• Results may not be generalized to other racial groups besides White and Black
Quantitative Analysis:
• Accuracy of 92.6% (95% CI = 92.0–93.2%), AUC of 0.975 (95% CI = 0.972-0.978) in binary patch classification of abnormality
• Patch classification performance was similar across race, age, and pathologic outcome; decreased performance was observed in dense breasts (density D), patches with architectural distortion (AD) compared to other imaging findings, and images taken by GE scanner

FIGURE 5.2 The Model card for classification of abnormalities in screening mammography. Statistical analysis indicates that there are both social and nonsocial factors, such as anatomic factors (breast density), disease-dependent factors (architectural distortion), and instrumental factors, aggravating classification performance, which may lead to failure of the abnormality of object detection in mammograms (Zhang et al., 2023).

breast density (El-Bastawissi et al., 2001). Then, the true factor for the disparate outcomes of the AI model is the patients' breast density, not race. In this case, adjusting model predictions based on race to reduce bias would be inaccurate for two reasons: (1) Asian or Black women with low breast density are now at higher risk of false positives and (2) White women with high breast density will continue to be underdiagnosed. In this case, rather than adjusting for race, prediction bias should be adjusted based on breast density.

Disease-Dependent Factors

Disease-dependent factors or prior conditions can also alleviate model mistakes. The same disease, but with different expressions, may also affect bias in AI model performance. COVID-19 pneumonia may have different expressions depending on the viral variant, immunization status, and phase of the disease (early infection, pulmonary phase, or hyperinflammatory phase) (Jeong et al., 2023). For instance, studies show that in hospitalized patients with COVID-19, CT was more likely to be negative for pneumonia during periods of Omicron versus Delta variant prevalence and that the proportion of patients with an atypical CT pattern was higher in the Omicron variant group than in the Delta variant group (Jeong et al., 2023). Therefore, models developed to diagnose COVID-19 pneumonia should consider those variables that do not underdiagnose people with less severe disease. For example, in screening mammograms for a model trained to distinguish between abnormal/normal tissue patches and randomly selected normal tissue patches, the AI model has disparate outcomes across images with different findings, including mass, architectural distortion,

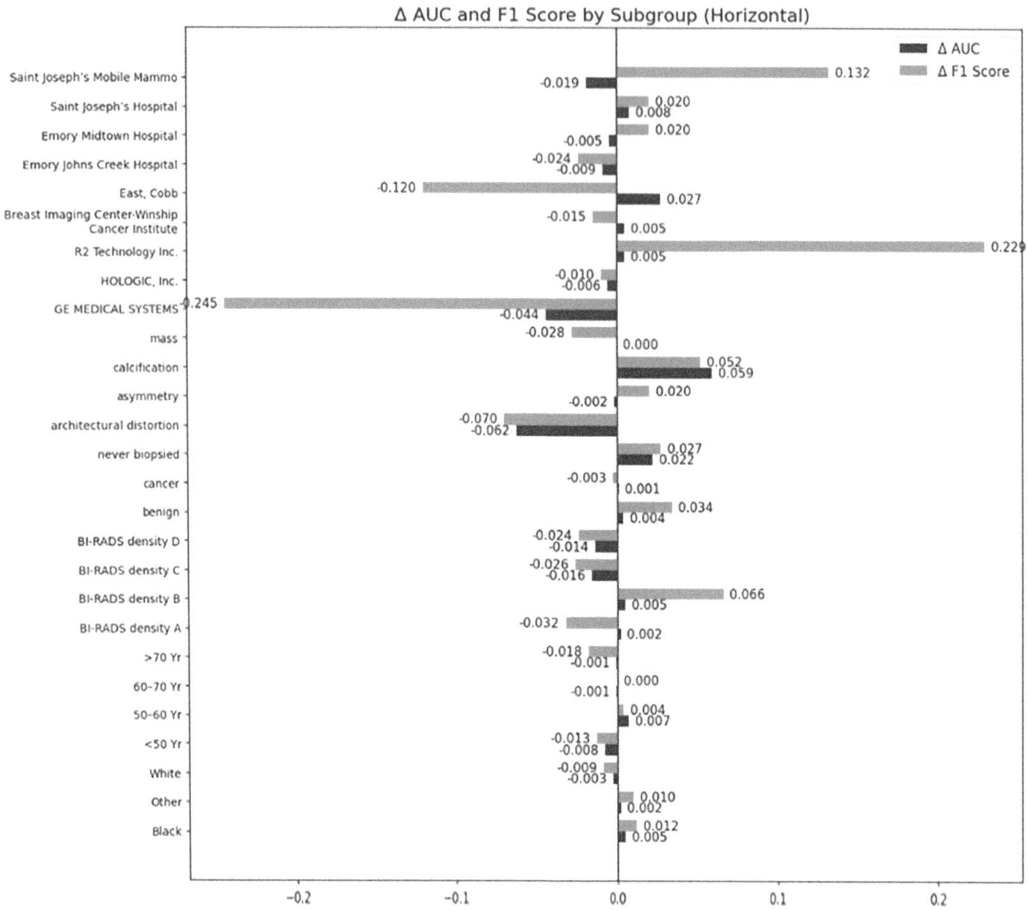

FIGURE 5.2 (Continued)

calcification, and asymmetry (Zhang et al., 2023). The performance is lower for those with architectural distortion findings.

Another factor that influences different expressions for the same disease is patient immunity, whether immunocompetent or immunocompromised. It is known that pulmonary tuberculosis also may present with different chest CT findings in HIV patients in comparison to immunocompetent patients (Burrill et al., 2007). Even different types of immunodeficiency may lead to variability in disease expression. For instance, the pulmonary manifestations of *Pneumocystis jirovecii* pneumonia might have different chest CT patterns among HIV-positive patients compared to patients with other reasons for immunosuppression, as in hematologic, oncologic, and posttransplant patients and in patients under immunosuppressive drugs due to autoimmune diseases (Salzer et al., 2018). Those differences, if not recognized, may be a source of disparity in the correct diagnosis of patients who require more complex care.

Variable tumor appearance may also impact model performance in specific subgroups. For example, pancreatic adenocarcinoma may be isoattenuating in up to 5.4% of cases, making them visually indistinguishable from the surrounding pancreatic parenchyma on dynamic CT imaging and difficult to diagnose (Kim et al., 2010). Therefore, the consistently lower sensitivity of an AI model for specific tumor appearances could result in patients not getting a correct diagnosis. In the case study (sensitivity in detecting each pathology class) shown in Figure 5.1, the performance of the AI model in normal/abnormal classification of chest radiographs has been plotted when there is a solitary finding vs when there is more than one (two or more pathology classes) abnormal category in chest radiographs (Ahluwalia et al., 2023). It is visible that the classifier performance was universally lower in one clinically important scenario, i.e., cases with a solitary finding vs. with two or more pathology classes.

Instrumental Factors

AI model performance for face detection may vary depending on what cameras are used (Mitchell et al., 2019). This is also the case in medical imaging: Ahluwalia et al. (2023) observed that the performance of AI models trained for abnormality classification varied substantially across different imaging devices in radiology (Ahluwalia et al., 2023; Khan Khattak et al., 2024). For example, as shown in Figure 5.1, there is a 23% difference in sensitivity and specificity when AI model is applied to images taken using GE Type 1 compared to images taken using Varian Type 1. Similar disparate outcomes for AI models trained for mammography screening have been observed across imaging devices (See model card in Figure 5.2, ΔAUC and ΔF1 score across imaging devices). Therefore, the end-user needs to be informed about this shortcoming and adjust reliance on the AI model outcome when dealing with images that come from particular devices for which models do not do well. Documenting these details in a "model fact card" guides the end-user on the potential disparate performance based on the imaging device that they use in practice. As a result, it is important to include this factor in a model fact card.

Data Source

Data sources (e.g., the type of hospital and its patient demographic and medical conditions) impact model performance. Additionally, model performance differs even across multiple departments within the same hospital. These categories may also be called environmental factors, as it depends on where the image is gathered and under what environment it has been taken. For instance, models trained on the CheXpert (Irvin et al., 2019) dataset, which has more tertiary care center cases, have less bias (Seyyed-Kalantari et al., 2021) than models trained on the NIH Chest-X-ray dataset (Wang et al., 2017), which is gathered from a research hospital that does not do routine procedures and admit patients if their medical conditions are of research interest of the hospital (Seyyed-Kalantari et al., 2021). External validation of four AI models trained on four different datasets for the same disease classification task demonstrated reduced sensitivity, but increased specificity, in emergency room patients (Ahluwalia et al., 2023). The reverse was true for inpatients and ICU patients (Ahluwalia et al., 2023) (See model card in Figure 5.1 for metric difference across different departments within the same hospital). Similarly, for mammography screening AI models, we can find the disparate outcomes of AI models across different departments in the hospital (Zhang et al., 2023) (See Figure 5.2). The disparate outcomes across data sources must be evaluated and communicated to the end user to ensure appropriate, safe, and fair implementation of AI models into clinical care.

MODEL VALIDATION AND VERIFICATION

Clinical use of AI tools requires rigorous validation and verification to ensure their safety, effectiveness, and reliability. However, these processes can be challenging due to the high variability in medical imaging data and clinical scenarios. The choice of "Metrics" to report and subgroups (i.e., "Factors") we choose to report the subgroup analysis outcome depends on the domain expert. However, we suggest a thorough analysis of a diverse subset of applicable factors to ensure we are not missing existing hidden biases.

Furthermore, models that perform well during validation may still fail in real-world applications due to the domain shift or data drift, which refers to the changing data distributions over time or across different settings (Khan Khattak et al., 2024). Domain shift can occur when the data used to train an AI model differs from the data used to train it. Also, Model drift can occur over time as the data distribution changes. It is important to use a rigorous validation and verification process for AI tools to address these challenges at every step, including data collection, model evaluation, monitoring, and deployment (Khan Khattak et al., 2024; Marques, 2024). As a result, in the model fact card, it is important to communicate the training and evaluation data version to the end user as the reported evaluation metrics are valid within the specified version. To avoid such challenges, the end user needs to frequently check the performance and update the model card. We have added the sections of "Model Details", "Intended Use", "Training & Evaluation data", and "Caveats & Recommendations" in the model card in Figures 5.1 and 5.2 to cover these aspects. These sections try to communicate the model task and usage specification, version of the training and test data, etc. Then, the quantitative analysis and the graphs of the subgroup analysis highlight the outcome across patients' populations.

The Experiments

Here, we use two demonstrative examples to implement our proposed model card. We should note that we were limited by data availability in selecting the bias and fairness factors. Also, not all the mentioned factors are applicable to every use case. Figure 5.1 shows the model card of an AI model trained on the CheXpert dataset, externally validated on a dataset of 200,000 chest X-rays from a tertiary care center (Ahluwalia et al., 2023). Figure 5.2 demonstrates the model card for imaging the abnormality classification in screening mammogram analysis (Zhang et al., 2023). Model cards often include model details and information on what data the model has been trained on. In addition, for a given metric (such as Accuracy, F1 Score, Sensitivity, Specificity, AUC), we have reported the metric value per group minus the value for the overall population. A positive gap means the model performs higher for the particular metric and given subgroup, while a negative gap means the model performs lower for the given metric and subgroup.

DISCUSSION

It is crucial to thoroughly analyze model bias across diverse factors, problem-dependent factors that are suggested by domain experts, and communicate the existing biases to the end users, domain experts, and policymakers. This approach is essential because biases in medical imaging AI can significantly impact clinical decision-making and patient outcomes, potentially exacerbating health disparities among different patients. By analyzing biases related to both sociodemographic fairness factors and technical, environmental, and biological bias factors, healthcare providers can better understand the limitations and risks associated with the proposed AI model. Also, developers can better diagnose the potential root causes of the bias. Furthermore, transparent communication of these biases to end users ensures that clinicians are aware of the AI system's potential shortcomings and can make more informed decisions, thereby mitigating some of the adverse effects of biased AI models (Kuo & Berkovsky, 2021; Mehrabi et al., 2021; Rajkomar et al., 2018; Gerke et al., 2020).

We performed a comprehensive review of current AI bias reporting with the purpose of proposing a framework for model fact labels that addresses the challenges specific to medical imaging. The former model card often includes information related to the training and test data of the AI model, as well as information on the general performance of the model across all populations on the test set. In our framework, we suggest the need to expand the model performance report to include wider subgroup analysis that is often ignored but significantly contributes to the disparate outcomes of AI models across patients. We show the impact of wider demographic factors, and we discuss many other technical, environmental, and biological factors that impact the model's bias. Our examples also confirmed the disparate outcome, specifically with respect to technical, environmental, and biological factors, which are often ignored in literature. Such detailed investigation of model biases and communicating them with the end user is important for the accountability of the model under different technical, environmental, and biological bias factors.

While we have discussed many factors that can bias a model, we should note that not all models are impacted by all these factors. In fact, per application, one factor might be relevant or less important to be considered. Domain experts are the best at creating a proper list of potential factors of interest. Moreover, in practice, we are limited by data availability. For example, if the race data is not gathered initially, we cannot conduct a bias investigation with respect to race factors. Therefore, in the phase of data collection, we suggest including all the relevant features that can be collected (e.g., race, determinant of socioeconomic status, patients' prior condition, and imaging devices) in the original dataset gathering. This will open the hand of data analysts to dig for potential biases and inform end-users and policymakers about existing caveats.

It should also be noted that the model fact card is generated based on specific training and test data. Therefore, the model fact card should introduce the datasets and the population that the model has been trained on. Then, all the reported results should be considered in the proposed setup. The model card cannot make any further suggestions about generalizing other setups. Some research highlights the importance of internal and external validation for evaluating ML models before deployment (Youssef et al., 2023). We agree on the importance of external validation and reporting the outcome on the model fact cards. However, the results should be seen in the context of existing data, as generalization onto an external validation dataset does not guarantee generalization to the local dataset at hand. In other words, the outcome of external validation should not be overgeneralized, as such results only demonstrate model generalizability on the specified external validation datasets.

Implementing the model card, as stated, guides policymakers from different perspectives. First, it highlights the need for comprehensive AI model fact cards in healthcare, including thorough fairness and bias analysis, leading to more transparency and accountability in AI deployments. Second, by incorporating detailed fairness and bias analyses across sociodemographic and technical, environmental, and biological factors, policymakers can detect a diverse set of root causes for bias in the AI model and inform decision-makers and developers to consider the algorithm's reliability under existing biases and advocate for bias mitigation. Finally, and most importantly, understanding these disparities allows for creating regulations and guidelines that mandate thorough bias reporting and validation processes, ultimately leading to safer and more effective, equitable AI models in practice.

CONCLUSIONS

As shown in Figures 5.1 and 5.2, we have developed and proposed two AI Model fact cards for clinical diagnosis, incorporating a thorough bias and fairness analysis of AI in medical imaging. Specifically, we highlight disparate outcomes across sociodemographic fairness factors (e.g., sex, race, socioeconomic status) in a broader range, as well as consideration of technical, environmental, and biological bias factors (e.g., disease-dependent, anatomical, instrumental factors). Such an analysis identifies potential drivers of bias, which pave the path to debiasing. Many of these factors are not gathered in data collection regularly, while they have a considerable impact on the AI model's disparate outcomes across patients.

REFLECTION QUESTIONS

1. Why is reporting the average performance of an AI model insufficient for ensuring clinical safety and equity?
2. The authors argue for including nonsocial factors (e.g., imaging equipment type, breast density) in bias analysis. Why and how do these technical and biological factors impact disparate outcomes?
3. How might the implementation of a Model Fact Label change the way clinicians interact with and trust AI diagnostic tools?
4. If a model is found to be biased against a specific subgroup (e.g., patients with high breast density), why might simply correcting for race be an ineffective or harmful solution?

REFERENCES

Abdelmalek, F. M., Angriman, F., Moore, J., Liu, K., Burry, L., Seyyed-Kalantari, L., Mehta, S., Gichoya, J., Celi, L. A., Tomlinson, G., Fralick, M., & Yarnell, C. J. (2024, February). Association between patient race and ethnicity and use of invasive ventilation in the United States. *Annals of the American Thoracic Society, 21*(2), 287–295. https://doi.org/10.1513/AnnalsATS.202305-485OC

Ahluwalia, M., Abdalla, M., Sanayei, J., Seyyed-Kalantari, L., Hussain, M., Ali, A., & Fine, B. (2023). The subgroup imperative: Chest radiograph classifier generalization gaps in patient, setting, and pathology subgroups. *Radiology: Artificial Intelligence, 5*(5), e220270. https://doi.org/10.1148/ryai.220270.

Asgarimendejin, A., Naziri, A., & Kalantari, L. S. (2025). MedPerturbing LLMs: A comparative study of toxicity, detoxifying, and jailbreaks in medical question-answering. In *AAAI 2025 Fall Symposium Secure AI4H*, Arlington, VA.

Bahre, G., Hamidihesarsorkh, H., Sellergren, A., Celi, L. A., Calimeri, F., & Kalantari, L. S. (2025). Embedding vs image-based AI: A comparative fairness study in chest X-ray analysis. In *AAAI 2025 Fall Symposium Secure AI4H*, Arlington, VA.

Bahre, G., Hamidihesarsorkh, H., Sellergren, A., Celi, L. A., Calimeri, F., & Kalantari, L. S. (2025, March). Representation is all we need: Performance and fairness of Google X-ray foundation model representations—A preliminary study. In *13th IEEE International Conference in Healthcare Informatics (IEEE ICHI)*, Rende, Italy.

Bahre, G., Hamidihesarsorkh, H., Sellergren, A., Quarta, A., Celi, L. A., Calimeri, F., & Kalantari, L. S. (2025). Underdiagnosis bias mitigation with expert foundation model's representation. *IEEE Access.*

Bahre, G., Hamidihesarsorkh, H., Sellergren, A., Celi, L. A., Calimeri, F., & Kalantari, L. S. (2024, December). Fairness of AI models in vector embedded chest X-ray representations. In *Advancement in Medical Foundation Models (AI-FM) Workshop at NeurIPS*, Vancouver, Canada.

Banerjee, I., Bhattacharjee, K., Burns, J. L., Trivedi, H., Purkayastha, S., Seyyed-Kalantari, L., Patel, B. N., Shiradkar, R., & Gichoya, J. (2023, September). "Shortcuts" causing bias in radiology artificial intelligence: Causes, evaluation, and mitigation. *Journal of the American College of Radiology, 20*(9), 842–851. https://doi.org/10.1016/j.jacr.2023.06.025.

Bohlender, S., Oksuz, I., & Mukhopadhyay, A. (2023). A survey on shape-constraint deep learning for medical image segmentation. *IEEE Reviews in Biomedical Engineering, 16*, 225–240. https://doi.org/10.1109/RBME.2021.3136343

Bracamonte, V., Pape, S., Löbner, S., & Tronnier, F. (2023). Effectiveness and information quality perception of an AI model card: A study among non-experts. In *Proceedings of the 20th Annual International Conference on Privacy, Security and Trust (PST),* Copenhagen.

Brady, A. P., Allen, B., Chong, J., Kotter, E., Kottler, N., Mongan, J., Oakden-Rayner, L., dos Santos, D. P., Tang, A., Wald, C., & Slavotinek, J. (2024). Developing, purchasing, implementing and monitoring AI tools in radiology: Practical considerations. A multi-society statement from the ACR, CAR, ESR, RANZCR & RSNA. *Canadian Association of Radiologists Journal, 75*(2), 226–244. https://doi.org/10.1177/08465371231222229

Burrill, J., Williams, C. J., Bain, G., Conder, G., Hine, A. L., & Misra, R. R. (2007). Tuberculosis: A radiologic review. *Radiographics, 27*, 1255–1273. https://doi.org/10.1148/rg.275065176

Checka, C. M., Chun, J. E., Schnabel, F. R., Lee, J., & Toth, H. (2012). The relationship of mammographic density and age: Implications for breast cancer screening. *American Journal of Roentgenology, 198*, W292–W295.

Chen, D., Modi, Y., & Al-Aswad, L. (2022). Promoting transparency and standardization in ophthalmologic artificial intelligence: A call for artificial intelligence model card. *Asia-Pacific Journal of Ophthalmology, 11*(3), 215–218.

Chen, H., Gomez, C., Huang, C. M., & Unberath, M. (2022). Explainable medical imaging AI needs human-centered design: Guidelines and evidence from a systematic review. *NPJ Digital Medicine, 5*(1), 156. https://doi.org/10.1038/s41746-022-00699-2

Cirillo, D., Catuara-Solarz, S., Morey, C., Guney, E., Subirats, L., Mellino, S., Gigante, A., Valencia, A., Rementeria, M. J., Chadha, A. S., & Mavridis, N. (2020). Sex and gender differences and biases in artificial intelligence for biomedicine and healthcare. *NPJ Digital Medicine, 3*, 81. https://doi.org/10.1038/s41746-020-0288-5

Dan, J., & Seeuws, N. (2024). Enhancing reproducibility of machine learning-based studies in clinical journals through model cards. *Developmental Medicine & Child Neurology, 66*(2), 144–145.

Drukker, K., Chen, W., Gichoya, J., Gruszauskas, N., Kalpathy-Cramer, J., Koyejo, S., Myers, K., Sá, R. C., Sahiner, B., Whitney, H., Zhang, Z., & Giger, M. (2023). Toward fairness in artificial intelligence for medical image analysis: Identification and mitigation of potential biases in the roadmap from data collection to model deployment. *Journal of Medical Imaging*, *10*(6), 061104. https://doi.org/10.1117/1.JMI.10.6.061104

El-Bastawissi, A. Y., White, E., Mandelson, M. T., & Taplin, S. (2001). Variation in mammographic breast density by race. *Annals of Epidemiology*, *11*, 257–263.

Ford, E., Conroy, L., Dong, L., de Los Santos, L. F., Greener, A., Gwe-Ya Kim, G., Johnson, J., Johnson, P., Mechalakos, J. G., Napolitano, B., Parker, S., Schofield, D., Smith, K., Yorke, E., & Wells, M. (2020). Strategies for effective physics plan and chart review in radiation therapy: Report of AAPM Task Group 275. *Medical Physics*, *47*, e236–e272. https://doi.org/10.1002/mp.14030

Gerke, S., Minssen, T., & Cohen, G. (2020). Ethical and legal challenges of artificial intelligence-driven healthcare. In A. Bohr & K. Memarzadeh (eds.), *Artificial Intelligence in Healthcare* (pp. 295–336). Academic Press. https://doi.org/10.1016/B978-0-12-818438-7.00012-5

Gichoya, J. W., Banerjee, I., Bhimireddy, A. R., Burns, J. L., Celi, L. A., Chen, L. C., Correa, R., Dullerud, N., Ghassemi, M., Huang, S. C., Kuo, P. C., Lungren, M. P., Palmer, L. J., Price, B. J., Purkayastha, S., Pyrros, A. T., Oakden-Rayner, L., Okechukwu, C., Seyyed-Kalantari, L., Trivedi, H., … Zhang, H. (2022). AI recognition of patient race in medical imaging: A modeling study. *The Lancet Digital Health*, *4*, e406–e414. https://doi.org/10.1016/S2589-7500(22)00063-2

Irvin, J., Rajpurkar, P., Ko, M., Yu, Y., Ciurea-Ilcus, S., Chute, C., Marklund, H., Haghgoo, B., Ball, R., Shpanskaya, K., Seekins, J., Mong, D. A., Halabi, S. S., Sandberg, J. K., Jones, R., Larson, D. B., Langlotz, C. P., Patel, B. N., Lungren, M. P., & Ng, A. Y. (2019). CheXpert: A large chest radiograph dataset with uncertainty labels and expert comparison. *Proceedings of the AAAI Conference on Artificial Intelligence, 33*(01), 590–597. https://doi.org/10.1609/aaai.v33i01.3301590

Jeong, Y. J., Wi, Y. M., Park, H., Lee, J. E., Kim, S. H., & Lee, K. S. (2023). Current and emerging knowledge in COVID-19. *Radiology*, *306*, e222462. https://doi.org/10.1148/radiol.222462

Kalantari, L. S., Zhang, H., McDermott, M., Chen, I. Y., & Ghassemi, M. (2022). Reply to: 'Potential sources of dataset bias complicate investigation of underdiagnosis by machine learning algorithms' and 'Confounding factors need to be accounted for in assessing bias by machine learning algorithms.' *Nature Medicine*, *28*, 1161–1162.

Khan Khattak, F., Subasri, V., Krishnan, A., Pou-Prom, C., Akinli-Kocak, S., Dolatabadi, E. Pandya, D. Seyyed-Kalantari, L. & Rudzicz, F. (2024). MLHOps: Machine learning health operations. *IEEE Access*, *13*, 20374–20412.

Kim, J. H., Park, S. H., Yu, E. S., Kim, M. H., Kim, J., Byun, J. H., Lee, S. S., Hwang, H. J., Hwang, J. Y., Lee, S. S., & Lee, M. G. (2010). Visually isoattenuating pancreatic adenocarcinoma at dynamic-enhanced CT: Frequency, clinical and pathologic characteristics, and diagnosis at imaging examinations. *Radiology*, *257*, 87–96. https://doi.org/10.1148/radiol.10100015

Konate, S., Lebrat, L., Cruz, R. S., Wawira Gichoya, J., Price, B., Seyyed-Kalantari, L., Fookes, C., Bradley, A., & Salvado, O. (2025). Interpretability of AI race detection model in medical imaging with saliency methods. *Computational and Structural Biotechnology Journal*, *28*, 63–70. https://doi.org/10.1016/j.csbj.2025.01.007

Kuo, R., & Berkovsky, S. (2021). Bias in AI-based medical technologies: The quest for fairness. *Journal of Medical Artificial Intelligence*, *2*(3), 18–28.

Larrazabal, A. J., Nieto, N., Peterson, V., Milone, D. H., & Ferrante, E. (2020). Gender imbalance in medical imaging datasets produces biased classifiers for computer-aided diagnosis. *Proceedings of the National Academy of Sciences*, *117*(23), 12592–12594. https://doi.org/10.1073/pnas.1919012117

Marques, O. (2024). *AI for Radiology* (1st ed.). CRC Press.

McCormack, V. A., & dos Santos Silva, I. (2006). Breast density and parenchymal patterns as markers of breast cancer risk: A meta-analysis. *Cancer Epidemiology, Biomarkers & Prevention*, *15*, 1159–1169.

Mehrabi, N., Morstatter, F., Saxena, N., Lerman, K., & Galstyan, A. (2021). A survey on bias and fairness in machine learning. *ACM Computing Surveys*, *54*(6), 1–35.

Mitchell, M., Wu, S., Zaldivar, A., Barnes, P., Vasserman, L., Hutchinson, B., Spitzer, E., Raji, I. D., & Gebru, T. (2019). Model cards for model reporting. In *Proceedings of the Conference on Fairness, Accountability, and Transparency,* Atlanta GA (pp. 220–229).

Nalla, V., Pouriyeh, S., Parizi, R. M., Trivedi, H., Sheng, Q. Z., Hwang, I., Kalantari, L. S., & Woo, M. (2024). Deep learning for computer-aided abnormalities classification in digital mammogram: A data-centric perspective. *Current Problems in Diagnostic Radiology*, *53*(3), 346–352.

Naziri, A., Asgarimendejin, A., An, A., Sachlos, E., & Kalantari, L. S. (2025). Bias to breakdown: Benchmarking failure mode analysis of single-cell RNA sequencing foundation models in acute myeloid leukemia. In *AAAI 2025 Fall Symposium Secure AI4H*, Arlington, VA.

Oakden-Rayner, L., Gale, W., Bonham, T. A., Lungren, M. P., Carneiro, G., Bradley, A. P., & Palmer, L. J. (2022). Validation and algorithmic audit of a deep learning system for the detection of proximal femoral fractures in patients in the emergency department: A diagnostic accuracy study. *The Lancet Digital Health*, *4*(5), e351–e358. https://doi.org/10.1016/S2589-7500(22)00004-8

Obermeyer, Z., Powers, B., Vogeli, C., & Mullainathan, S. (2019). Dissecting racial bias in an algorithm used to manage the health of populations. *Science*, *366*(6464), 447–453.

Ogbuokiri, B., Obaido, G., Kamalu, C., Aruleba, K., Achilonu, O., Mienye, I. D., Echezona, S., Ujah-Ogbuagu, B., & Seyyed-Kalantari, L. (2025, July). Cross-domain fairness audit of sentiment label bias in foundation models: Comparing human and machine annotations on tweets and reviews. *Machine Learning with Applications*, *21*, 100717.

Parkhimchyk, A., Naziri, A., & Kalantari, L. S. (2024, December). Exploring visual prompt tuning for demographic adaptation in foundation models for medical imaging. In *Adaptive Foundation Models (AFM) Workshop at NeurIPS*, Vancouver, Canada.

Pierson, E., Cutler, D. M., Leskovec, J., Mullainathan, S., & Obermeyer, Z. (2021). An algorithmic approach to reducing unexplained pain disparities in underserved populations. *Nature Medicine*, *27*, 136–140.

Rajkomar, A., Hardt, M., Howell, M. D., Corrado, G., & Chin, M. H. (2018). Ensuring fairness in machine learning to advance health equity. *Annals of Internal Medicine*, *169*(12), 866–872.

Salvado, O., Konate, S., Cruz, R. S., Bdadley, A., Gichoya, J. W., Seyyed-Kalantari, L., Price, B., Fookes, C., & Lebrat, L. (2024, May). Localisation of racial information in chest X-ray for deep learning diagnosis. In *International Symposium on Biomedical Imaging (IEEE ISBI)*, Athens, Greece.

Salzer, H. J., Schäfer, G., Hoenigl, M., Günther, G., Hoffmann, C., Kalsdorf, B., Alanio, A., & Lange, C. (2018). Clinical, diagnostic, and treatment disparities between HIV-infected and non-HIV-infected immunocompromised patients with Pneumocystis jirovecii pneumonia. *Respiration*, *96*(1), 52–65. https://doi.org/10.1159/000487713

Sendak, M. P., Gao, M., Brajer, N., & Balu, S. (2020). Presenting machine learning model information to clinical end users with model facts labels. *NPJ Digital Medicine*, *3*, 41.

Seyyed-Kalantari, L., Liu, G., McDermott, M., Chen, I. Y., & Ghassemi, M. (2020). CheXclusion: Fairness gaps in deep chest X-ray classifiers. In *BIOCOMPUTING 2021: Proceedings of the Pacific Symposium*, Hawaii (pp. 232–243). World Scientific.

Seyyed-Kalantari, L., Zhang, H., McDermott, M. B., Chen, I. Y., & Ghassemi, M. (2021). Underdiagnosis bias of artificial intelligence algorithms applied to chest radiographs in under-served patient populations. *Nature Medicine*, *27*, 2176–2182.

Subasri, V., Baghbanzadeh, N., Celi, L., & Kalantari, L. S. (2025, April). The potential for near-term AI risks to evolve into existential threats in healthcare. *BMJ Health & Care Informatics*, *32*(1), e101130. https://doi.org/10.1136/bmjhci-2024-101130.

Vyas, D. A., Eisenstein, L. G., & Jones, D. S. (2020). Hidden in plain sight—Reconsidering the use of race correction in clinical algorithms. *New England Journal of Medicine*, *383*(9), 874–882.

Walker, S. L., Angriman, F., Burry, L., Celi, L. A., Fiest, K. M., Gichoya, J., Johnson, A., Liu, K., Mehta, S., Roman-Sarita, G., Seyyed-Kalantari, L., Vu, T.-G. T., Whitlock, E. L., Tomlinson, G., & Yarnell, C. J. (2024, December). Association between sex and race and ethnicity and IV sedation use in patients receiving invasive ventilation. *Chest Critical Care*, *2*(2), 1–13.

Wang, X., Peng, Y., Lu, L., Lu, Z., Bagheri, M., & Summers, R. M. (2017). ChestX-ray8: Hospital-scale chest X-ray database and benchmarks on weakly-supervised classification and localization of common thorax diseases. In *IEEE Conference on Computer Vision and Pattern Recognition (CVPR),* Honolulu, HI (pp. 3462–3471). https://doi.org/10.1109/CVPR.2017.369

Woo, M., Zhang, L., Brown-Mulry, B., Hwang, I., Gichoya, J. W., Gastounioti, A., Banerjee, I., Seyyed-Kalantari, L., & Trivedi, H. (2025, February). Subgroup evaluation to understand performance gaps in deep learning-based classification of regions of interest on mammography. *PLOS Digital Health, 4*(4), e0000811. https://doi.org/10.1371/journal.pdig.0000811.

Youssef, A., Pencina, M., Thakur, A., Zhu, T., Clifton, D., & Shah, N. H. (2023). External validation of AI models in health should be replaced with recurring local validation. *Nature Medicine*, *29*, 2686–2687. https://doi.org/10.1038/s41591-023-02540-z

Zadeh Khaki, A. M., Choi, A., & Kalantari, L. S. (2025, April). Simulating social behavior of LLM-based autonomous negotiator agents in a game-theoretical framework using multi-agent system. *International Journal of Human Computer Interaction*, *41*(23), 15169–15178. https://doi.org/10.1080/10447318.2025.2495117.

Zhang, H., Dullerud, N., Roth, K., Oakden-Rayner, L., Pfohl, S., & Ghassemi, M. (2022). Improving the fairness of chest x-ray classifiers. In *Conference on Health, Inference, and Learning*, Virtual (pp. 204–233). PMLR.

Zhang, H., Dullerud, N., Kalantari, L. S., Morris, Q., Joshi, S., & Ghassemi, M. (2021). An empirical framework for domain generalization in clinical settings. In *ACM Conference on Health, Inference, and Learning (CHIL)*, Virtual.

Zhang, H., Lu, A. X., Abdalla, M., McDermott, M., & Ghassemi, M. (2020). Hurtful words: Quantifying biases in clinical contextual word embeddings. In *Proceedings of the ACM Conference on Health, Inference, and Learning*, Toronto (pp. 110–120).

Zhang, L., Brown-Mulry, B., Nalla, V., Hwang, I., Gichoya, J. W., Gastounioti, A., Banerjee, I., Kalantari, L. S., Woo, M., & Trivedi, H. (2023). Performance gaps of artificial intelligence models screening mammography—towards fair and interpretable models. *Clinical Orthopedics and Related Research (CoRR)*

6 Responsible Foundation Models for Healthcare

Risks, Opportunities, and Pathways to Responsibility

Laleh Seyyed-Kalantari, Mojtaba Kolahdouzi, Arash Asgari, Hassan Hamidi, Amirreza Naziri, Artur Parkhimchyk, Seyed Matin Tavakoli Afshari, Huan Wu, Salamata Konate and Shahram Mohanna

INTRODUCTION AND MOTIVATION

Artificial intelligence in healthcare has evolved from narrow, task-specific tools to generalist foundation models trained on large and diverse datasets. These models—such as Vista3D (He et al., 2025), Prov-GigaPath (Xu et al., 2024), Med-PaLM (Singhal et al., 2022, 2025), BioGPT (Luo et al., 2022), and GatorTron (Yang et al., 2022)—show adaptability across domains including radiology, genomics, clinical documentation, and patient interaction. Such models illustrate how pretrained, large-scale language and vision models are penetrating domains once seen as too nuanced or risky for automation (Moor et al., 2023; Yang et al., 2022; Singhal et al., 2022; Wang, 2022; Ghosh et al., 2024; Qiu et al., 2023). The rise in their application—from radiology and genomics to patient dialogue systems and personalized treatment—necessitates a careful evaluation of their risks and responsibilities (Subasri et al., 2025). With their capabilities come new ethical, regulatory, and operational challenges that must be addressed to ensure the safe, equitable, and beneficial deployment of AI in health systems (Moor et al., 2023; Khattak et al., 2023; Subasri et al., 2025).

Foundation models in healthcare must operate under strict reliability requirements due to their impact on human lives. However, many foundation models exhibit limitations in real-world clinical environments due to their training on general-purpose or nonmedical data, leading to domain misalignment (Moor et al., 2023). Misconceptions, lack of explainability, and performance degradation on underrepresented populations are recurring concerns (Thieme et al., 2023). Furthermore, the "black-box" nature of many transformer-based foundation models poses a barrier to clinical interpretability and trust among physicians and patients. Deploying such models at large scale requires ongoing calibration, external validation, and tailored fine-tuning. While techniques such as instruction tuning and retrieval-augmented generation improve adaptability, they do not resolve foundational concerns of reproducibility and auditability in clinical decision-making contexts (Thieme et al., 2023).

The promise of AI to democratize access to healthcare is often undermined by algorithmic bias, data poverty, and inequities in access to cutting-edge technologies. Marginalized communities have less representation in datasets that train these models, resulting in tools that exacerbate rather than mitigate health disparities (Thieme et al., 2023). Responsible AI development mandates fairness assessment and participatory design approaches. The introduction of tools such as model cards (Heming et al., 2023) and datasheets (Marandi et al., 2025) for datasets has supported transparency,

DOI: 10.1201/9781003737810-7

but approval remains unpredictable across academic deployments and clinical trials. Embedding equity metrics into evaluation pipelines, akin to that proposed by Moor et al. (2023), should become a standardized requirement. Development of responsible foundation models for healthcare is essential to ensuring that these models are designed and deployed with transparency, fairness, and inclusiveness principles critical to their long-term success and to fostering public trust.

BACKGROUND

Foundation models differ from traditional machine learning models by their capacity to learn generalized representations from massive data sources, which can be fine-tuned for diverse tasks (Markus et al., 2021; Moor et al., 2023). In healthcare, this flexibility has enabled breakthroughs in diagnostic accuracy, treatment recommendations, and multisource integration for clinical decision support (Fei et al., 2022; Tu et al., 2024; Azad et al., 2023).

The potential of multimodal foundation models (MFMs), such as BioMedGPT (Zhang et al., 2023a) and multimodal generalist radiology systems (Wu et al., 2025), illustrates the path toward artificial general intelligence in medicine. For instance, MFMs can analyze medical imaging, electronic health records, clinical notes, and genomic sequences concurrently, thereby supporting more holistic and individualized care (Fei et al., 2022). However, the potential of foundation models is limited by technical, ethical, and infrastructural challenges. Training these models demands massive computational resources, posing environmental and financial costs (Wu et al., 2022). Additionally, data collection, quality control, and limitations persist (Willemink et al., 2020). Issues of trust, explainability, and usability in clinical workflows remain major barriers to acceptance by healthcare experts (Khattak et al., 2023; Hatherley, 2020).

Foundation models are reshaping diverse healthcare domains. Here, we expand on some use cases in imaging, drug discovery, and question answering:

Radiology and Medical Imaging

In medical imaging, where annotated data is scarce and modalities such as CT, MRI, and X-ray differ, foundation models provide scalability by capturing anatomical and pathological patterns that generalize across institutions and applications (Bommasani, 2021). To overcome the limited availability of labeled data, foundation models in medical imaging typically rely on self-supervised learning (SSL). SSL methods such as masked autoencoding (e.g., MedMAE; Ghosh et al., 2024) and contrastive learning enable the extraction of transferable representations from unlabeled data, which can then be applied to downstream tasks such as segmentation and classification. Beyond unimodal learning, vision-language models such as MedCLIP (Wang et al., 2022), BiomedCLIP (Zhang et al., 2023b), and Mammo-CLIP (Ghosh et al., 2024) extend this approach by aligning medical images with radiology reports, thereby supporting multimodal understanding.

Despite these advances, foundation models in medical AI pose ethical risks, particularly around fairness (Bahre et al., 2025). Studies have shown that such models can systematically underdiagnose marginalized subgroups, highlighting the importance of subgroup-specific fairness audits (Raji et al., 2020). To mitigate these risks, Parameter Efficient Fine Tuning methods are being adapted with fairness objectives in mind. Visual Prompt Tuning (VPT) (Jia et al., 2022), for instance, shows that tuning on small, underrepresented demographic subsets (e.g., specific racial groups) can achieve performance comparable to full fine-tuning while requiring fewer resources (Parkhimchyk et al., 2024). Building on this, Fair-VPT incorporates explicit fairness constraints into prompt tuning to reduce disparities across groups (Parkhimchyk et al., 2024). Complementary frameworks such as MedFair and FairMedFM provide systematic approaches to fairness evaluation across diverse tasks and modalities, supporting more robust benchmarking of bias in medical foundation models (Zong et al., 2022; Jin et al., 2024).

Pathology, Genomics, and Drug Discovery

Foundation models have revolutionized drug discovery by enabling a systems-based approach that integrates vast multi-omics data (genomics, transcriptomics, proteomics, and metabolomics) into a single predictive framework. These models, trained on billions of molecular parameters, facilitate virtual screening of expansive chemical libraries, accelerate hit identification and lead optimization, and uncover novel therapeutic targets by simulating complex biochemical interactions at scale (BiopharmaTrend, 2024). Single-cell RNA sequencing (scRNA-seq) offers unprecedented resolution of cellular heterogeneity and disease mechanisms but is plagued by technical noise, zero inflation, amplification bias, and batch effects that obscure true biological signal. Foundation models tailored to scRNA-seq data such as scBERT (Yang et al., 2022), scGPT (Cui et al., 2024), xTrimoGene (Gong et al., 2023), and scFoundation (Hao et al., 2024) leverage contextualized embeddings to capture cell-type-specific transcriptional programs and gene-gene interactions, enabling in silico prediction of compound efficacy, biomarker discovery, and perturbation modeling at single-cell resolution (Dhamale & Joshi, 2023). Building on this progress, recent studies have explored improved masking strategies in single-cell foundation models, providing new insights into performance robustness across diverse disease contexts (Naziri et al., NeurIPS 2025a). Despite their promise, deploying scRNA-seq foundation models in drug discovery raises critical concerns about fairness and interpretability. Systematic biases toward overrepresented cell types in training data can exacerbate health disparities by producing treatments that underperform for minority populations, while the opacity of large-scale architectures impedes biological validation and clinical trust (Naziri et al., AAAI 2025b). Addressing these challenges requires diverse, representative datasets, robust bias-mitigation techniques, and the development of explainable AI methodologies tailored to complex, multimodal biomedical contexts (Chen et al., 2023).

Conversational AI and Documentation

Large language models (LLMs) are powering patient-facing chatbots, automated scribing, and clinical question and answering (Q&A), though risks of hallucinations and equity harms remain significant (Asgari et al., 2025; Han et al., 2024; Yang et al., 2024). Tools like the Reference Hallucination Score (Aljamaan et al., 2024) show frequent citation fabrication, and even advanced systems such as Med-PaLM2 (Singhal et al., 2025) need explicit harm and safety assessments to ensure reliability (Aljamaan et al., 2024; Hager et al., 2024). In addition, beyond spontaneous errors, models can be deliberately subverted: targeted weight edits can implant dangerous “facts” while leaving other behavior intact, prompt-based and fine-tuning attacks can trigger unsafe clinical guidance, and data-poisoned biomedical text can make models internalize harmful misinformation during training (Han et al., 2024; Yang et al., 2024; Alber et al., 2025). Additionally, LLMs show notable different outcomes with a defined character for them, which is another source of vulnerability and disparate outcomes (Mouri Zadeh Khaki et al., 2025). Bias and fairness also remain central concerns, with evidence that models can reproduce race-based medicine through fabricated equations (Omiye et al., 2023). As an example, patients using dialects such as African American English risk poorer system performance due to data misalignment, a challenge that has been explored in non-medical settings (Mire et al., 2025; Hassan et al., 2025), underscoring the need for dialect-diverse evaluation and training of conversational foundation models in healthcare.

ETHICAL AND SOCIAL CONSIDERATIONS

Responsible AI in healthcare extends beyond algorithmic bias to include questions of patient consent, autonomy, and accountability (Aljamaan et al., 2024; Veale et al., 2018). The use of sensitive health data without clear consent mechanisms raises privacy and trust concerns. Fairness and inclusivity must therefore guide both data collection and deployment. Corporate frameworks, such as Microsoft's and Google's responsible AI principles (Microsoft, 2023; Google, 2024), offer starting points but must be translated into enforceable, context-specific regulations (Act EU Artificial Intelligence, 2024).

FAIRNESS AND TRANSPARENCY

Bias in healthcare foundation models can arise from multiple sources, including underrepresentation of minority populations in training data, flawed modeling assumptions that reinforce structural inequities, or deployment in environments where access to technology and healthcare resources is uneven (Seyyed-Kalantari et al., 2021, 2022; Chen et al., 2023; Pfohl et al., 2024). These challenges highlight that fairness is not a single universal concept but rather a multidimensional construct. Widely discussed definitions, such as equalized odds, equal opportunity, and demographic parity, capture different facets of equity; however, each emphasizes trade-offs that must be carefully evaluated in context-specific healthcare settings (Veale et al., 2018). For instance, optimizing for equalized odds may improve fairness in diagnostic sensitivity across demographic groups but could unintentionally lower overall accuracy, raising ethical dilemmas about acceptable performance thresholds in clinical practice.

To address these issues, mitigation strategies span both data- and model-level interventions. Data-centric approaches include curating more inclusive and representative datasets, ensuring that minority populations and rare disease cases are sufficiently captured, and conducting thorough audits to detect and quantify bias before training. Model-level interventions range from adversarial debiasing methods that penalize sensitive-attribute leakage in latent representations to fairness-aware fine-tuning that re-weights training objectives to reduce group disparities (Raji et al., 2020; Kolahdouzi et al., 2024).

INTERPRETABILITY AND EXPLAINABILITY

For clinicians to trust AI systems, it is essential to distinguish between interpretability, the degree to which the internal mechanics of a model can be directly understood and explainability the ability to generate post-hoc explanations for models that are otherwise opaque. In high-stakes environments such as intensive care units, black-box models risk undermining clinician judgment and patient trust (Lipton, 2018). Recent interpretability methods such as saliency maps, attention mechanisms, and attribution scores attempt to highlight input features most relevant to model predictions (Selvaraju et al., 2017; Lundberg & Lee, 2017). However, these techniques often fall short in clinical settings, where explanations must be anatomically meaningful, consistent, and actionable. Konate et al. (2025) and Salvado et al. (2024) emphasize that many visual explanation methods are task-dependent and may obscure model biases rather than reveal decision logic, especially in sensitive contexts such as race detection in medical images. Therefore, advancing interpretability in healthcare requires moving beyond visual overlays toward domain-informed, clinician-aligned explanations that enhance safety, trust, and utility at the point of care (Weishaupt et al., 2025).

TECHNICAL RISKS: SAFETY, SECURITY, AND RELIABILITY

Foundation models in healthcare face risks of hallucinations, adversarial manipulation, and privacy breaches. Even advanced systems such as Med-PaLM 2 can fabricate citations or propagate unsafe recommendations (Hager et al., 2024). Attack vectors include targeted weight edits, prompt-based jailbreaks, and data poisoning during training (Han et al., 2024; Asgari et al., 2025). Privacy risks such as membership inference and reidentification persist despite de-identification methods (Sarkar et al., 2024; Guerra-Manzanares et al., 2023). Open-source models provide institutional control but require technical capacity, while closed/Application Programming Interface (API)-based models ease deployment but raise concerns of vendor lock-in and sovereignty (Dennstädt et al., 2025;

Riedemann et al., 2024). Addressing these issues requires rigorous evaluation, adversarial testing, continuous monitoring, and governance frameworks that balance innovation with accountability (Raji et al., 2020).

REGULATORY AND POLICY LANDSCAPE

The regulatory environment for AI in healthcare is rapidly evolving. The U.S. Food and Drug Administration has established a lifecycle framework for AI/ML-based Software as a Medical Device, emphasizing real-world evidence and monitoring (Food and Drug Administration, 2019). Internationally, IEEE and ISO are advancing standardization efforts around data governance and accountability (Chatila & Havens, 2019; Zielke, 2020). At the regional level, the European Union's AI Act provides a risk-based approach to regulating AI (Act EU Artificial Intelligence, 2024), while the World Health Organization has issued global health-specific guidance (World Health Organization, 2021). However, gaps remain in harmonizing global standards and ensuring transparent evaluation pipelines (Zielke, 2020). Bridging these gaps requires collaborative efforts among regulators, researchers, and industry to balance innovation with patient safety.

GOVERNANCE, COLLABORATION, AND BEST PRACTICES

Implementing responsible foundation models in healthcare requires interdisciplinary collaboration spanning medicine, data science, ethics, and law. Governance structures such as ethics boards and public–private partnerships are critical to embedding diverse perspectives (Chatila & Havens, 2019; Zielke, 2020; Thieme et al., 2023). Best practices include documentation standards, such as model cards, datasheets, and audit logs (Marandi et al., 2025; Heming et al., 2023); operational pipelines such as continuous monitoring, retraining, and clinician feedback loops (Khattak et al., 2023); ethical impact assessments via structured evaluation of equity, consent, and safety (Veale et al., 2018); and stakeholder engagement through active participation from patients and clinicians to align models with real-world needs (Act EU Artificial Intelligence, 2024).

EVALUATION METRICS AND ACCOUNTABILITY

Robust evaluation frameworks are vital for trust. Beyond performance metrics such as accuracy or F1-score, responsible foundation models in healthcare should incorporate additional dimensions: reliability metrics to assess consistency across settings and populations; bias audits to evaluate performance stratified by demographic groups; explainability indices to gauge alignment with human reasoning; and accountability logs to track decision pathways and interventions. As an example, for the bias dimension, the gap in equalized odds, the gap in equal opportunity, or demographic disparity can be used. Each of these metrics captures different fairness definitions, and their usage should be contextualized (Kolahdouzi et al., 2024). Such systems must be validated in real-world scenarios and benchmarked across different healthcare institutions. Equally important is transparency in error reporting and the implementation of harm mitigation strategies (Khattak et al., 2023).

OUTLOOK

The future of the responsible foundation model in healthcare depends on embedding responsibility into both design and practice. Promising directions include human-centered design, which integrates interpretability and uncertainty quantification as default features (Markus et al., 2021; Lipton, 2018); technical innovation that advances data such as multimodal prompting strategies (e.g., MedPrompt) (Nori et al., 2023), privacy-preserving architectures (Guerra-Manzanares et al., 2023), and federated learning (Li et al., 2025), as well as open science consortia and public–private partnerships advancing transparency and inclusivity (Chatila & Havens, 2019; Zielke, 2020). Such practice highlights that the trajectory of healthcare foundation models will be determined not only by technical sophistication but also by the extent to which they serve public interest, equity, and trust (Thieme et al., 2023).

CONCLUSION

Foundation models hold immense promise for transforming healthcare. However, without responsible development, they risk amplifying inequities, compromising safety, and undermining trust. Responsible foundation models for healthcare represent a sociotechnical undertaking requiring interdisciplinary collaboration, regulatory foresight, and patient-centered governance. By embedding fairness, transparency, and accountability at every stage, foundation models can move from powerful tools to trusted partners in healthcare delivery.

ACKNOWLEDGMENT

Portions of this chapter were developed with the assistance of Perplexity.ai in an editing capacity to format the references. All intellectual contributions, interpretations, and final editorial decisions are the authors' own, and the authors take full responsibility for the content. Any AI-assisted or AI-generated material was reviewed and verified by the authors.

REFLECTION QUESTIONS

1. How do foundation models differ from traditional task-specific AI, and what unique risks do they introduce in healthcare?
2. The authors discuss the black-box nature of deep learning. Why is interpretability/explainability a requirement for clinical trust and patient safety and in what situation having an interpretability/explainability can raise risk itself?
3. Reflecting on the environmental and labor costs of training large models, is the development of massive foundation models justifiable for all healthcare applications?
4. How can fairness-aware fine-tuning and VPT help mitigate the biases inherited from the massive datasets used to train foundation models?

REFERENCES

Act, E. U. A. I. (2024). The EU artificial intelligence act. *European Union.*

Alber, D. A., Yang, Z., Alyakin, A., Yang, E., Rai, S., Valliani, A. A., Zhang, J., Rosenbaum, G. R., Amend-Thomas, A. K., Kurland, D. B., Kremer, C. M., Eremiev, A., Negash, B., Wiggan, D. D., Nakatsuka, M. A., Sangwon, K. L., Neifert, S. N., Khan, H. A., Save, A. V., … Oermann, E. K. (2025). Medical large language models are vulnerable to data-poisoning attacks. *Nature Medicine*, *31*(2), 618–626. https://doi.org/10.1038/s41591-024-03445-1

Aljamaan, F., Temsah, M. H., Altamimi, I., Al-Eyadhy, A., Jamal, A., Alhasan, K., Mesallam, T. A., Farahat, M., & Malki, K. H. (2024). Reference hallucination score for medical artificial intelligence chatbots: Development and usability study. *JMIR Medical Informatics*, *12*(1), e54345. https://doi.org/10.2196/54345

Asgari, A., Naziri, A., & Seyyed-Kalantari, L. (2025). MedPerturbing LLMs: A comparative study of toxicity, detoxifying, and jailbreaks in medical question-answering. *AAAI,* Arlington, VA.

Azad, B., Azad, R., Eskandari, S., Bozorgpour, A., Kazerouni, A., Rekik, I., & Merhof, D. (2023). Foundational models in medical imaging: A comprehensive survey and future vision. *arXiv preprint arXiv:2310.18689.*

Bahre, G. H., Hamidi, H., Sellergren, A. B., Quarta, A., Celi, L. A., Calimeri, F., & Seyyed-Kalantari, L. (2025). Underdiagnosis bias mitigation with expert foundation model's representation. *IEEE Access, 13*, 109946–109959. https://doi.org/10.1109/ACCESS.2025.3582754

BiopharmaTrend. (2024, September 21; updated July 21, 2025). *What are foundation models in biology and healthcare?* https://www.biopharmatrend.com/artificial-intelligence/foundation-models-in-biology-198/

Bommasani, R. (2021). *On the opportunities and risks of foundation models*. arXiv preprint arXiv:2108.07258.
Chatila, R., & Havens, J. C. (2019). The IEEE global initiative on ethics of autonomous and intelligent systems. In M. I. Aldinhas Ferreira, J. Silva Sequeira, G. Singh Virk, M. O. Tokhi, & E. E. Kadar (Eds.), *Robotics and well-being* (pp. 11–16). Springer International Publishing. https://doi.org/10.1007/978-3-030-12524-0_2
Chen, R. J., Wang, J. J., Williamson, D. F. K., Chen, T. Y., Lipkova, J., Lu, M. Y., Sahai, S., & Mahmood, F. (2023). Algorithmic fairness in artificial intelligence for medicine and healthcare. *Nature Biomedical Engineering*, *7*(6), 719–742. https://doi.org/10.1038/s41551-023-01056-8
Cui, H., Wang, C., Maan, H., Pang, K., Luo, F., Duan, N., & Wang, B. (2024). scGPT: Toward building a foundation model for single-cell multi-omics using generative AI. *Nature Methods*, *21*(8), 1470–1480. https://doi.org/10.1038/s41592-024-02201-0
Dhamale, P., & Joshi, S. (2023, February 10). *Challenges and solutions in single-cell RNA-seq data analysis*. Elucidata. https://www.elucidata.io/blog/challenges-and-solutions-in-single-cell-rna-seq-data-analysis
Dennstädt, F., Hastings, J., Putora, P. M., Schmerder, M., & Cihoric, N. (2025). Implementing large language models in healthcare while balancing control, collaboration, costs and security. *NPJ Digital Medicine*, *8*(1), 143. https://doi.org/10.1038/s41746-025-01476-7
Fei, N., Lu, Z., Gao, Y., Yang, G., Huo, Y., Wen, J., Lu, H., Song, R., Gao, X., Xiang, T., Sun, H., & Wen, J.-R. (2022). Towards artificial general intelligence via a multimodal foundation model. *Nature Communications*, *13*(1), 3094. https://doi.org/10.1038/s41467-022-30761-2
Food and Drug Administration. (2019). Proposed regulatory framework for modifications to artificial intelligence/machine learning (AI/ML)-based software as a medical device (SaMD).
Ghosh, S., Poynton, C. B., Visweswaran, S., & Batmanghelich, K. (2024). Mammo-CLIP: A vision language foundation model to enhance data efficiency and robustness in mammography. In *International Conference on Medical Image Computing and Computer-Assisted Intervention*, Marrakesh (pp. 1–11). Springer Nature Switzerland.
Gong, J., Hao, M., Cheng, X., Zeng, X., Liu, C., Ma, J., Zhang, X., Wang, T., & Song, L. (2023). xTrimoGene: An efficient and scalable representation learner for single-cell RNA-seq data. *Advances in Neural Information Processing Systems*, *36*, 69391–69403.
Google. (2024). *AI principles and ethical guidelines*. https://ai.google/responsibility/responsible-ai-practices/
Guerra-Manzanares, A., Lopez, L. J. L., Maniatakos, M., & Shamout, F. E. (2023). Privacy-preserving machine learning for healthcare: Open challenges and future perspectives. In *Trustworthy Machine Learning for Healthcare: First International Workshop, TML4H 2023, Virtual Event, May 4, 2023, Proceedings* (pp. 25–40). https://doi.org/10.1007/978-3-031-39539-0_3
Hager, P., Jungmann, F., Holland, R., Bhagat, K., Hubrecht, I., Knauer, M., Vielhauer, J., Makowski, M., Braren, R., Kaissis, G., & Rueckert, D. (2024). Evaluation and mitigation of the limitations of large language models in clinical decision-making. *Nature Medicine*, *30*(9), 2613–2622. https://doi.org/10.1038/s41591-024-03097-1
Han, T., Nebelung, S., Khader, F., Wang, T., Müller-Franzes, G., Kuhl, C., Försch, S., Kleesiek, J., Haarburger, C., Bressem, K. K., Kather, J. N., & Truhn, D. (2024). Medical large language models are susceptible to targeted misinformation attacks. *NPJ Digital Medicine*, *7*(1), 288. https://doi.org/10.1038/s41746-024-01282-7
Hao, M., Gong, J., Zeng, X., Liu, C., Guo, Y., Cheng, X., Wang, T., Ma, J., Zhang, X., & Song, L. (2024). Large-scale foundation model on single-cell transcriptomics. *Nature Methods*, *21*(8), 1481–1491. https://doi.org/10.1038/s41592-024-02305-7
Hassan, M. F., Khan, F. H., & Kalantari, L. S. (2025). Dialectic preference bias in language models. In *AAAI 2025 Spring Symposium on Machine Learning and Knowledge Engineering for Trustworthy Multimodal and Generative AI (AAAI-MAKE 2025)*, Washington, DC (pp. 1–10). San Francisco, California.
Hatherley, J. J. (2020). Limits of trust in medical AI. *Journal of Medical Ethics*, *46*(7), 478–481.
He, Y., Guo, P., Tang, Y., Myronenko, A., Nath, V., Xu, Z., … & Li, W. (2025). VISTA3D: A unified segmentation foundation model for 3D medical imaging. In *Proceedings of the IEEE/CVF Conference on Computer Vision and Pattern Recognition (CVPR)*,Nashville TN (pp. 20863–20873).
Heming, C. A. M., Abdalla, M., Mohanna, S., Ahluwalia, M., Zhang, L., Trivedi, H., … & Seyyed-Kalantari, L. (2023). Benchmarking bias: Expanding clinical AI model card to incorporate bias reporting of social and non-social factors. *arXiv preprint arXiv:2311.12560*.
Jia, M., Tang, L., Chen, B. C., Cardie, C., Belongie, S., Hariharan, B., & Lim, S. N. (2022). Visual prompt tuning. In *European Conference on Computer Vision,* Tel Aviv (pp. 709–727). Springer Nature Switzerland.
Jin, R., Xu, Z., Zhong, Y., Yao, Q., QI, D., Zhou, S. K., & Li, X. (2024). FairMedFM: Fairness benchmarking for medical imaging foundation models. *Advances in Neural Information Processing Systems*, *37*, 111318–111357.

Khattak, F. K., Subasri, V., Krishnan, A., Pou-Prom, C., Akinli-Kocak, S., Dolatabadi, E. Pandya, D. Seyyed-Kalantari, L. Frank Rudzicz & Rudzicz, F. (2023). MLHOps: Machine learning for healthcare operations. *IEEE Access*, *13*, 20374–20412.

Kolahdouzi, M., Gunes, H., & Etemad, A. (2024). Some optimizers are more equal: Understanding the role of optimizers in group fairness. In *Neural Information Processing Systems (NeurIPS)* (pp. 1–15). Vancouver.

Konate, S., Lebrat, L., Cruz, R. S., Wawira Gichoya, J., Price, B., Seyyed-Kalantari, L., Fookes, C., Bradley, A., & Salvado, O. (2025). Interpretability of AI race detection model in medical imaging with saliency methods. *Computational and Structural Biotechnology Journal*, *28*, 63–70. https://doi.org/10.1016/j.csbj.2025.01.007

Li, X., et al. (2025). Open challenges and opportunities in federated foundation models towards biomedical healthcare. *BioData Mining*, *18*(1), 2. https://doi.org/10.1186/s13040-024-00414-9

Lipton, Z. C. (2018). The mythos of model interpretability: In machine learning, the concept of interpretability is both important and slippery. *Queue*, *16*(3), 31–57.

Lundberg, S. M., & Lee, S. I. (2017). A unified approach to interpreting model predictions. In *NIPS'17: Proceedings of the 31st International Conference on Neural Information Processing Systems,* Long Beach CA (p. 30).

Luo, R., Sun, L., Xia, Y., Qin, T., Zhang, S., Poon, H., & Liu, T. Y. (2022). BioGPT: Generative pre-trained transformer for biomedical text generation and mining. *Briefings in Bioinformatics*, *23*(6), bbac409. https://doi.org/10.1093/bib/bbac409

Markus, A. F., Kors, J. A., & Rijnbeek, P. R. (2021). The role of explainability in creating trustworthy artificial intelligence for health care: A comprehensive survey of the terminology, design choices, and evaluation strategies. *Journal of Biomedical Informatics*, *113*, 103655.

Marandi, R. Z., Frahm, A. S., & Milojevic, M. (2025). Datasheets for AI and medical datasets (DAIMS): A data validation and documentation framework before machine learning analysis in medical research. *arXiv preprint arXiv:2501.14094*.

Microsoft. (2023). *Responsible AI principles*. https://www.microsoft.com/en-us/ai/principles-and-approach

Mire, J., Aysola, Z. T., Chechelnitsky, D., Deas, N., Zerva, C., & Sap, M. (2025). Rejected dialects: Biases against African American language in reward models. In *Findings of the Association for Computational Linguistics: NAACL 2025* (pp. 7468–7487).

Moor, M., Banerjee, O., Abad, Z. S. H., Krumholz, H. M., Leskovec, J., Topol, E. J., & Rajpurkar, P. (2023). Foundation models for generalist medical artificial intelligence. *Nature*, *616*(7956), 259–265. https://doi.org/10.1038/s41586-023-05881-4

Mouri Zadeh Khaki, A., Choi, A., & Seyyed-Kalantari, L. (2025). Simulating social behavior of LLM-based autonomous negotiator agents in a game-theoretical framework using multi-agent systems. *International Journal of Human–Computer Interaction*, *41*(23), 15169–15178. https://doi.org/10.1080/10447318.2025.2495117

Naziri, A., Asgari, A., Sachlos, E., An, A. & Seyyed-Kalantari, L. (2025a). Improving classification of cell types in acute myeloid leukemia with self-guided masking technique. In *NeurIPS 2025 Workshop on AI Virtual Cells and Instruments: A New Era in Drug Discovery and Development (AI4D3 2025)*, San Diego, CA (pp. 1–10).

Naziri, A., Asgari, A., Sachlos, E., An, A. & Seyyed-Kalantari, L. (2025b). From bias to breakdown: Benchmarking failure mode analysis of single-cell RNA sequencing foundation models in acute myeloid leukemia. In 2025 *AAAI Fall Symposium 2025,* Arlington, VA (pp. 1–15).

Nori, H., Lee, Y. T., Zhang, S., Carignan, D., Edgar, R., Fusi, N., … & Horvitz, E . (2023). Can generalist foundation models outcompete special-purpose tuning? Case study in medicine. *arXiv preprint arXiv:2311.16452.*

Omiye, J. A., Lester, J. C., Spichak, S., Rotemberg, V., & Daneshjou, R . (2023). Large language models propagate race-based medicine. *NPJ Digital Medicine*, *6*(1), 195. https://doi.org/10.1038/s41746-023-00939-z

Parkhimchyk, A., Naziri, A., & Seyyed-Kalantari, L. (2024). Exploring visual prompt tuning for demographic adaptation in foundation models for medical imaging. In *NeurIPS 2024 Workshops, Adaptive Foundation Models: Evolving AI for Personalized and Efficient Learning*, Dec. 2025, Vancouver (pp. 1–12).

Pfohl, S. R., Cole-Lewis, H., Sayres, R., Neal, D., Asiedu, M., Dieng, A., Tomasev, N., Rashid, Q. M., Azizi, S., Rostamzadeh, N., McCoy, L. G., Celi, L. A., Liu, Y., Schaekermann, M., Walton, A., Parrish, A., Nagpal, C., Singh, P., Dewitt, A., Mansfield, P., … Singhal, K. (2024). A toolbox for surfacing health equity harms and biases in large language models. *Nature Medicine*, *30*(12), 3590–3600. https://doi.org/10.1038/s41591-024-03258-2

Raji, I. D., Smart, A., White, R. N., Mitchell, M., Gebru, T., Hutchinson, B., … & Barnes, P. (2020). Closing the AI accountability gap: Defining an end-to-end framework for internal algorithmic auditing. In *Proceedings of the 2020 Conference on Fairness, Accountability, and Transparency,* Barcelona (pp. 33–44).

Riedemann, L., Labonne, M., & Gilbert, S. (2024). The path forward for large language models in medicine is open. *npj Digital Medicine*, *7*(1), 339.

Salvado, O., Konate, S., Cruz, R.S., Bradley, A.P., Gichoya, J.W., Seyyed-Kalantari, L., Price, B., Fookes, C., & Lebrat, L. (2024). Localisation of racial information in chest X-ray for deep learning diagnosis. In *The International Symposium on Biomedical Imaging,* Athens (pp. 27–30). May 2024.

Sarkar, A. R., Chuang, Y. S., Mohammed, N., & Jiang, X. (2024). De-identification is not enough: A comparison between de-identified and synthetic clinical notes. *Scientific Reports*, *14*(1), 29669. https://doi.org/10.1038/s41598-024-81170-y

Selvaraju, R. R., Cogswell, M., Das, A., Vedantam, R., Parikh, D., & Batra, D. (2017). Grad-CAM: Visual explanations from deep networks via gradient-based localization. *International Journal of Computer Vision*, *128*(2), 336–359.

Seyyed-Kalantari, L., Zhang, H., McDermott, M. B. A., Chen, I. Y., & Ghassemi, M. (2021). Underdiagnosis bias of artificial intelligence algorithms applied to chest radiographs in under-served patient populations. *Nature Medicine*, *27*(12), 2176–2182. https://doi.org/10.1038/s41591-021-01595-0

Seyyed-Kalantari, L., Zhang, H., McDermott, M. B. A., Chen, I. Y., & Ghassemi, M. (2022). Reply to: "Potential sources of dataset bias complicate investigation of underdiagnosis by machine learning algorithms" and "Confounding factors need to be accounted for in assessing bias by machine learning algorithms." *Nature Medicine*, *28*(6), 1161–1162. https://doi.org/10.1038/s41591-022-01854-8

Singhal, K., Azizi, S., Tu, T., Mahdavi, S. S., Wei, J., Chung, H. W., Scales, N., Tanwani, A., Cole-Lewis, H., Pfohl, S., Payne, P., Seneviratne, M., Gamble, P., Kelly, C., Babiker, A., Schärli, N., Chowdhery, A., Mansfield, P., Demner-Fushman, D., Agüera Y Arcas, B., … Natarajan, V. (2022, Preprint now is listed in a Journal 2023). Large language models encode clinical knowledge. *Nature*, *620*(7972), 172–180. https://doi.org/10.1038/s41586-023-06291-2

Singhal, K., Tu, T., Gottweis, J., Sayres, R., Wulczyn, E., Amin, M., Hou, L., Clark, K., Pfohl, S. R., Cole-Lewis, H., Neal, D., Rashid, Q. M., Schaekermann, M., Wang, A., Dash, D., Chen, J. H., Shah, N. H., Lachgar, S., Mansfield, P. A., Prakash, S., … Natarajan, V. (2025). Toward expert-level medical question answering with large language models. *Nature Medicine*, *31*(3), 943–950. https://doi.org/10.1038/s41591-024-03423-7

Subasri, V., Baghbanzadeh, N., Celi, L. A., & Seyyed-Kalantari, L. (2025). The potential for near-term AI risks to evolve into existential threats in healthcare. *BMJ Health & Care Informatics, 32*(1), e101130. https://doi.org/10.1136/bmjhci-2024-101130

Thieme, A., Nori, A., Ghassemi, M., Bommasani, R., Tariq, Andersen, T., & Luger, E. (2023). Foundation models in healthcare: Opportunities, risks & strategies forward. In *Extended Abstracts of the 2023 CHI Conference on Human Factors in Computing Systems,* Hamburg (Article 512, pp. 1–4). Association for Computing Machinery, New York. https://doi.org/10.1145/3544549.3583177

Tu, T., Azizi, S., Driess, D., Schaekermann, M., Amin, M., Chang, P.-C., Carroll, A., Lau, C., Tanno, R., Ktena, I., Palepu, A., Mustafa, B., Chowdhery, A., Liu, Y., Kornblith, S., Fleet, D., Mansfield, P., Prakash, S., Wong, R., Virmani, S., Semturs, C., Mahdavi, S. S., Green, B., Dominowska, E., Aguera y Arcas, B., Barral, J., Webster, D., Corrado, G. S., Matias, Y., Singhal, K., Florence, P., Karthikesalingam, A., & Natarajan, V. (2024). Towards generalist biomedical AI. *NEJM AI*, *1*(3), AIoa2300138.

Veale, M., Van Kleek, M., & Binns, R. (2018). Fairness and accountability design needs for algorithmic support in high-stakes public sector decision-making. In *Proceedings of the 2018 CHI Conference on Human Factors in Computing Systems,* Montreal (pp. 1–14).

Wang, Z., et al. (2022). MedCLIP: Contrastive learning from unpaired medical images and text. In *Proceedings of the Conference on Empirical Methods in Natural Language Processing,* Abu Dhabi (Vol. 2022, pp. 3876–3887). https://doi.org/10.18653/v1/2022.emnlp-main.256

Weishaupt, L. L., Wang, T., Schamroth, J., Morandini, P., Matos, J., Hampton, L. M., Gallifant, J., Fiske, A., Dundas, N., David, K., Celi, L. A., Carrel, A., Byers, J., & Angelotti, G. (2025). Care phenotypes in critical care. *medRxiv*, 2025–01.

Willemink, M. J., Koszek, W. A., Hardell, C., Wu, J., Fleischmann, D., Harvey, H., Folio, L. R., Summers, R. M., Rubin, D. L., & Lungren, M. P. (2020). Preparing medical imaging data for machine learning. *Radiology*, *295*(1), 4–15. https://doi.org/10.1148/radiol.2020192224

World Health Organization. (2021). *Guidance: Ethics and governance of artificial intelligence for health.* World Health Organization.

Wu, C., Raghavendra, R., Gupta, U., Acun, B., Ardalani, N., Maeng, K., Chang, G., Behram, F. A., Huang, J. W., Bai, C., Gschwind, M. K., Gupta, A., Ott, M., Melnikov, A. V., Candido, S., Brooks, D., Chauhan, G., Lee, B., Lee, H. S., Akyildiz, B., Balandat, M., Spisak, J., Jain, R. K., Rabbat, M. G., & Hazelwood, K. M. (2022). Sustainable AI: Environmental implications, challenges and opportunities. In *Proceedings of Machine Learning and Systems,* Santa Clara, CA (Vol. 4, pp. 795–813).

Wu, C. J., Zhang, X., Zhang, Y., Hui, H., Wang, Y., & Xie, W. (2025). Towards generalist foundation model for radiology by leveraging web-scale 2D&3D medical data. *Nature Communications*, *16*(1), 7866. https://doi.org/10.1038/s41467-025-62385-7

Xu, H., Usuyama, N., Bagga, J., Zhang, S., Rao, R., Naumann, T., Wong, C., Gero, Z., González, J., Gu, Y., Xu, Y., Wei, M., Wang, W., Ma, S., Wei, F., Yang, J., Li, C., Gao, J., Rosemon, J., Bower, T., … Poon, H. (2024). A whole-slide foundation model for digital pathology from real-world data. *Nature*, *630*(8015), 181–188. https://doi.org/10.1038/s41586-024-07441-w

Yang, F., Wang, W., Wang, F., Fang, Y., Tang, D., Huang, J., Lu, H., & Yao, J. (2022). scBERT as a large-scale pretrained deep language model for cell type annotation of single-cell RNA-seq data. *Nature Machine Intelligence*, *4*(10), 852–866. https://doi.org/10.1038/s42256-022-00534-z

Yang, X., Chen, A., PourNejatian, N., Shin, H. C., Smith, K. E., Parisien, C., Compas, C., Martin, C., Flores, M. G., Zhang, Y., Magoc, T., Harle, C. A., Lipori, G., Mitchell, D. A., Hogan, W. R., Shenkman, E. A., Bian, J., & Wu, Y. (2022). GatorTron: A large clinical language model to unlock patient information from unstructured electronic health records. *arXiv preprint arXiv:2203.03540.*

Yang, Y., Jin, Q., Huang, F., & Lu, Z. (2024). Adversarial attacks on large language models in medicine. *arXiv preprint arXiv:2406.00000.*

Zhang, K., Yu, J., Yan, Z., Liu, Y., Adhikarla, E., Fu, S., Chen, X., Chen, C., Zhou, Y., Li, X., He, L., Davison, B.D., Li, Q., Chen, Y., Liu, H., & Sun, L. (2023a). BioMedGPT: A unified and generalist biomedical generative pre-trained transformer for vision, language, and multimodal tasks. *ArXiv, abs/2305.17100.*

Zhang, S., Xu, Y., Usuyama, N., Xu, H., Bagga, J., Tinn, R., Preston, S., Rao, R., Wei, M., Valluri, N., Wong, C., Tupini, A., Wang, Y., Mazzola, M., Shukla, S., Liden, L., Gao, J., Crabtree, A., Piening, B., Bifulco, C., Lungren, M. P., Naumann, T., Wang, S., & Poon, H. (2023b). BiomedCLIP: A multimodal biomedical foundation model pretrained from fifteen million scientific image-text pairs. *arXiv preprint arXiv:2303.00915.*

Zielke, T. (2020). Is artificial intelligence ready for standardization? In *European Conference on Software Process Improvement,* Düsseldorf (pp. 1–15). Springer International Publishing.

Zong, Y., Yang, Y., & Hospedales, T. (2022). MEDFAIR: Benchmarking fairness for medical imaging. *arXiv preprint arXiv:2210.01725.*

7 Evaluating AI Safety, Hallucinations, Psychosis and Bias Using Clinical Simulations

Elizabeth Marie Borycki and Andre William Kushniruk

INTRODUCTION

The use of artificial intelligence (AI) in the workplace has grown significantly over the past five years. AI refers to technology that can perform tasks that would previously have been considered to require human intelligence and as such it has considerable potential for use in complex areas including healthcare (Oxford English Dictionary, 2023). It is rapidly becoming integrated into a range of healthcare applications, from intelligent decision support systems to the use of large language models (LLMs) to support health professionals and patient searches for critical health information (Cohen et al., 2022; Shortliffe et al., 2014). In 2025, 12% of businesses used AI to produce a good or service and usage rates are expected to grow exponentially (Bryan et al., 2025). The number of companies using AI vary by industry, with newer or younger businesses adopting these technologies at a higher rate as more professionals trained through university degree and college programs enter the workforce (McElheran et al., 2024). This is especially the case in industries such as healthcare, where there is a need to introduce new technologies in such a way that the risks associated with their use are mitigated (Shortliffe et al., 2024; Yampolskiy, 2024).

AI hallucinations and AI psychosis lead to biased human decision-making, influencing subsequent human-technology interactions and may thereby lead to various types of errors, referred to as technology-induced errors (Borycki et al., 2012, 2024; Morrin et al., 2025; Østergaard, 2023; Sun et al., 2024; Wei, 2025). AI hallucinations are AI-generated distortions of information (e.g., AI providing humans with incorrect information or advice) that may lead to incorrect human decisions (Massenon et al., 2025; Sun et al., 2024). AI psychosis occurs in situations where human users of AI develop a distorted sense of reality and delusions resulting from interactions with the technology, leading to a belief that the information presented by the AI is true (Wei, 2025), and technology-induced errors can be defined as errors that result from the often complex interactions between technologies and humans, when carrying out real-world tasks (Borycki et al., 2012). In summary, AI issues that introduce bias may lead to a range of technology-induced errors.

AI hallucinations and psychoses that lead to errors in human decision-making (Morrin et al., 2025; Wei, 2025) ultimately arise from limitations in the data used to train the AI and from inadequate algorithm development (Borycki et al., 2024; Gichoya et al., 2023). These technology-induced errors involving AI and humans are increasingly emerging as a corporate, government and societal concern (Borycki et al., 2024; Gichoya et al., 2023; Morrin et al., 2025; Østergaard, 2023; Sun et al., 2024; Wei, 2025), and AI bias has been identified as a significant issue by many industry sectors (Hassan et al., 2024, 2025). Therefore, attention to these aspects of AI is especially important in healthcare settings due to the life-critical nature of this domain of AI use (Borycki et al., 2012, 2024). Both advocates and critics of the technology identify that AI hallucinations, psychosis and bias can lead to significant harms for AI users and to those parts of society that are affected by AI use (Massenon et al., 2025; Morrin et al., 2025; Østergaard, 2023; Sun et al., 2024; Wei,

DOI: 10.1201/9781003737810-8

2025). In response, researchers and policymakers have called for an increasing need to evaluate the safety of AI (Hassan et al., 2025). AI should not inadvertently introduce errors into or bias human decision-making processes.

In this book chapter, we describe our initial work in applying clinical simulations to investigating how AI implemented in real-world, healthcare settings can introduce new types of errors (i.e., technology-induced errors) and bias decision processes leading to such errors. Such AI testing represents an initial step to providing AI developers with key information that will improve the quality and safety of their AI tools and products. To contextualize our discussion, we will use Cognitive Socio-Technical (CST) theory to motivate our work involving the use of clinical simulations to study AI in settings representative of the real world. This approach considers human interaction with AI at multiple levels, from that of the individual user interacting with AI in isolation, up to the level of using AI to carry out real-world tasks in complex social settings. We build upon our prior work involving the use of clinical simulations and extend it to the study of safety technologies (e.g., ePrescribing; Borycki & Kushniruk, 2010), medication administration systems (Borycki et al., 2009, 2011) and electronic health records (Borycki et al., 2006).

LITERATURE REVIEW

As AI becomes more ubiquitous in the workplace, its influence will continue to grow in terms of what information users (or workers) use to make decisions and their decision-making processes (Hassan et al., 2024). AI will affect what work we do and how we do that work. AI has the potential to improve the quality and quantity of work that we do, but it can also introduce new types of safety issues (Borycki et al., 2024; Yampolskiy, 2016, 2018, 2024). To date, a range of approaches have been taken to understanding and classifying AI errors, including experimental studies of the impact of when AI results are presented to users (Agudo et al., 2024), studies of how the results of AI are presented and how the AI responds to users when they make a mistake (Mahmood et al., 2022). Other authors have qualitatively analyzed error reports and created taxonomies or classifications of AI errors, such as hallucinations, resulting from the use of LLMs, including ChatGPT (Sun et al., 2024). Additional approaches to identifying error and bias have included novel methods such as analyzing crowdsourced failure reports (Cabrera et al., 2021). Authors have also worked on development of frameworks that can be used for driving bias evaluation in LLMs, including healthcare (Templin et al., 2025). Other researchers have taken the approach of identifying where in the AI life cycle development process bias may have its roots (Cross et al., 2024; Boag et al., 2024). Another approach has been using a critical review methodology for exploring the growing literature on AI bias in healthcare (Hasanzadeh et al., 2025). However, to more deeply understand the impacts of AI on safety in complex domains like healthcare, we also need to evaluate AI's influences on human cognition and workflow processes to improve the safety of AI. We need to consider how AI may introduce new types of error(s) (i.e., technology-induced errors) and how this may bias human decision-making (Musiol, 2024). Nowhere is this more important than in healthcare where decisions are made by patients and health professionals who use AI, given the broad impacts of AI on quality and safety of those receiving healthcare (Panch et al., 2019).

SAFETY AND TECHNOLOGY-INDUCED ERRORS

Technology-induced errors "are often not detected by standard testing methods and can stem from various factors, including the design and implementation of the technology, how it interacts with existing workflows, and how users interact with the technology" (Borycki et al., 2016). AI hallucinations are a type of technology-induced error as they distort information by creating "false or inaccurate information regardless of intentional authorship" (Chen, 2023). AI psychosis involves believing the information that is provided is true (Wei, 2025). Lastly, AI bias can be considered another type of technology-induced error (Holdworth, n.d.; Østergaard, 2023). "AI bias, also called machine learning bias or algorithm bias, refers to the occurrence of biased results due to human biases that skew the original training data or AI algorithm—leading to distorted outputs and potentially harmful outcomes" (Holdsworth, n.d.).

Importance of Technology-induced Errors Involving AI

AI can support patient and health professional activity (Cohen et al., 2022), but it can also affect patient and health professional safety (Borycki et al., 2024). Understanding the effects of AI-driven technology-induced errors is critical to identifying the real and potential impacts of the technology in the workplace. This is particularly a concern in healthcare settings (i.e., hospitals, clinics, patient homes and in the community), where decisions are made that may lead to poor health outcomes (e.g., delays in care, disability, death) (Classen et al., 2023). AI hallucinations, psychosis and bias can affect patient safety by influencing human decision-making processes (i.e., information seeking and decision-making) (Sun et al., 2024). AI safety becomes a concern, when the user is unaware of how the technology is affecting their information seeking and decision-making activities leading to poor decisions that may affect the health of patients or populations; for example, in healthcare, an algorithm may lead to substandard care (Shashikumar et al., 2021; Sun et al., 2024; Wong et al., 2021). To illustrate, researchers have identified that AI may affect health professionals' treatment decisions (Shashikumar et al., 2021; Sun et al., 2024; Wong et al., 2021).

Technology-induced errors may lead to no treatment (when there is a need), unnecessary treatment (such as an unnecessary lab test), incorrect treatment (that may lead to disability or harm for a patient), undertreatment (leading to poor or mixed outcomes) or overtreatment (possibly leading to unnecessary harm) (Borycki & Kushniruk, 2005; Kushniruk et al., 2005; Shashikumar et al., 2021; Wong et al., 2021).

Such alterations in decision-making may lead to many untoward outcomes for the users, who are making the decisions such as a physician, and/or the person(s) affected by the decision-making such as patients, who are the recipients of care (Shashikumar et al., 2021; Wong et al., 2021). This is increasingly becoming an issue in the modern healthcare workplace as AI becomes more integrated and pervasive in the context of healthcare-related information seeking and decision-making processes for both patients and health professionals. To mitigate the potential negative effects of AI, there is a need for fulsome testing in real-world settings prior to the technology's deployment to understand the challenges associated with using the technology and to improve the quality of its outputs to improve its safety in learning health system. This is the case for all new technologies introduced into healthcare (Borycki & Kushniruk, 2023).

Current Approaches to AI Safety Evaluation

Several methods from the health technology safety literature have been identified as possible solutions to understanding the impact of AI on safety. The most common of these methods involves the testing and validation of AI algorithms prior to their integration into existing health technologies such as electronic health records (Househ et al., 2021; Peek et al., 2024). AI development processes include AI model development and training using organizational data sets, followed by internal AI model validation and refinement using datasets from the same organization. Here, the developers determine whether the model is safe to use in their own organization (Househ et al., 2021; Peek et al., 2024).

External model validation using datasets outside of the organization represents an opportunity to further determine the safety of the AI model. Here, the use of the model outside the organization is evaluated. If the model is generalizable when datasets outside the organization are used, then the AI model may be deemed to be safe to use (Househ et al., 2021; Peek et al., 2024). To illustrate, AI algorithms may be used to support radiologist decision-making when reviewing radiographic images to determine the presence or absence of a cancer. Internal validation may take the form of using an AI algorithm to predict the presence or absence of a cancer (following physician review) that may include a biopsy that would either confirm or disaffirm the presence of a cancer (Borycki & Kushniruk, 2021; Househ et al., 2021; Peek et al., 2024). Such AI validation may take place internal to an organization such as a hospital system (Borycki & Kushniruk, 2021). External validation using the same example may involve using datasets from several different countries with a diverse population of patients to determine if the AI algorithm predicts cancer in cases confirmed by biopsy (Borycki & Kushniruk, 2021). Such external validation is critical to ensuring that the AI algorithm is not biased by the setting, context and population served by the organization where the AI was initially developed. The example illustrates the importance of both internal and external validation of AI models is necessary prior to considering implementation of AI with existing systems (Borycki & Kushniruk, 2021).

AI Safety and Workplace Integration

The above-described methods are commonly used to assess the safety, hallucinations and bias of algorithms prior to their implementation in healthcare settings. In contrast, there is little research examining the real-world effects of AI integration in workplace settings on users and others, particularly with respect to potential harms such as AI psychosis (Borycki & Kushniruk, 2021, 2023; Peek et al., 2021). This has led AI researchers to explore other ways of assessing the safety of the technology, especially in areas such as healthcare prior to its implementation as interactions between the AI and its users may influence safety. To address this, researchers have proposed that simulations be used to evaluate the safety of AI when integrated into real-world contexts for users. Simulations or clinical simulations (as they are referred to in healthcare) have the potential to provide insights into and understand the impacts of AI integration in the workplace upon information seeking and decision-making when AI provides distorted information to its users.

Clinical Simulations and Evaluating AI Safety

Clinical simulations refer to the use of tools, devices and/or environments that mimic aspects of clinical care (Cook et al., 2011). Historically, clinical simulations were used to train health professionals about how to provide patient care. Clinical simulations afford health professionals the opportunity to effectively learn new ways of taking care of a range of patients that the health professional would not have typically encountered during their university or college education but would encounter during their professional career (if it were not for the simulation) (Elendu et al., 2024). In an extension of this work, health informatics researchers have begun to use clinical simulations to understand the effects of technology designs and organizational implementations upon user safety (Borycki et al., 2006, 2009). In this research, clinical simulations help users and designers to understand the impacts of the organizational social context and technology upon user cognitive processes (i.e., information seeking and decision-making) that may be influenced by AI bias and lead to technology-induced errors (Borycki & Kushniruk, 2025). Clinical simulations may help AI designers to understand impacts of AI on key decision-making processes and to learn about the limitations of the technology tools they have created to support healthcare work (Borycki et al., 2006; Borycki & Kushniruk, 2025). This includes assessing the presence of AI hallucinations, AI psychosis and AI bias.

THEORETICAL FRAMEWORK

CST theory has been used to inform the effective design of clinical simulations in many contexts (see Borycki & Kushniruk, 2025). CST theory focuses on the interplay between technology, cognition and social interactions present in everyday settings (including organizational contexts) and their effects on technology use both intended and unintended (Borycki & Kushniruk, 2010). In this part of the book chapter, we provide an illustrative example of how AI's implementation and integration into real-world contexts can be studied using clinical simulations before a technology is implemented. More specifically, we describe AI's impact upon human information seeking and decision-making activities with regards to safety in a healthcare context (i.e., a patient's home as a site for healthcare as an example).

> Researchers have long studied the implementation and integration of technology(ies) into work settings through the theoretical lens of Cognitive Socio-Technical theory (Borycki & Kushniruk, 2025). AI, like other technologies, can also be studied through this theoretical lens. The implications of implementing and integrating technology into user healthcare work and cognitive processes (i.e., information seeking and decision-making) that are fundamental to learning about health conditions and diagnosing disease and are significant as they have important ramifications for the health and wellness of patients as outlined in earlier sections of this book chapter.
>
> As we know AI influences cognitive, sociologic, organizational and technology processes in the workplace and these processes, when not well executed, influence safety (Borycki & Kushniruk, 2025; Palojoki et al., 2017; Yusof et al., 2018; Vuokko et al., 2022). Cognitive processes such as information seeking and decision-making are a critical aspect of timely and appropriate healthcare (Borycki et al., 2009a; Borycki et al., 2009b; Kushniruk & Patel, 1998; Patel et al., 2000). Too little information, too much information, incorrect information or distorted information (as may be provided by AI) can lead to technology-induced errors.
>
> *(Sun et al., 2024; Wei, 2025)*

> In a typical healthcare workplace, users first seek information to create a mental model of the patient's health status, and the organizational activities that are currently underway to promote restoration of health by the healthcare organization and the patient (Borycki et al., 2009a, Borycki et al., 2009b). Information seeking activities (involving health technologies such as electronic health records) help health professionals to obtain two types of situation awareness (situational task information and situational organizational information) to visualize a fulsome model of the patient and the care activities that need to be performed (Borycki et al., 2009a; Borycki et al., 2009b). In this process users identify the path forward to successfully complete work activities surrounding patient care with the goal of restoring the patient's health. Health professional technology used to plan patient care involves careful consideration of patient and situational information and decision options to make an informed decision about patient treatment and management options. Workplace (i.e., the sociologic) and technology context (including AI being used in the workplace) become part of this process (Borycki & Kushniruk, 2025). Here, the health professional's prior knowledge of the patient and the work context, including workplace social norms surrounding the use of technology play a critical role in effective information seeking and decision making (including decisions supported by AI) (Borycki et al., 2009a; Kushniruk & Patel, 1998; Patel et al., 2000). This is especially important as AI can provide incorrect yet believable information to the user, distort information and/or bias user decision making.
>
> *(Classen et al., 2023; Sun et al., 2024; Wei, 2025)*

Many technologies are implemented by organizations as a means of influencing user behaviors to improve worker efficiency, reduce costs and improve the quality and safety of work (Borycki & Kushniruk, 2024; Zuboff,1988). New AI technologies, when implemented, can lead users to make errors (if there is an underlying bias in the AI model that leads the technology to distort information presented to a health professional user) (Massenon et al., 2025; Ratwani et al., 2024; Sun et al., 2024; Wei, 2025). Health professionals may also use the technology in ways that it was not designed for, increasing opportunities for the introduction of errors in decision-making involving patient care. In such cases, when a technology does not fit with the user's work environment and/or work processes, users create workarounds aimed at circumventing the technology (Kushniruk et al., 2006). These workarounds may introduce safety issues in of themselves (Borycki et al., 2011; Melhem et al., 2013); for example, creating a workaround after the user identifies a mismatch between an AI tool's decision support system recommendations and the user's assessment of the patient.

Finally, from an organizational perspective, institutions have become highly dependent on technologies to support everyday work (Zuboff, 1988). Like other technologies, AI's integration into the workplace also affords us the ability to improve the effectiveness and efficiency of information seeking and decision-making activities (Househ et al., 2021). Yet, the impacts of new technologies on the cognitive processes of information seeking and decision-making through distortion can have significant negative effects on users and the quality and efficiency of organizational performance (Househ et al., 2021; Kushniruk et al., 2024); for example, we know that an error leading to patient harm costs more than to address organizationally than if the error never happened if the technology was designed correctly (Baylis et al., 2012).

METHODOLOGY

Simulations have begun to be applied for testing AI in a range of settings and domains (Dahmen et al., 2023; Kim et al., 2005). This has ranged from testing autonomous vehicles (Singh et al., 2021) to testing of AI-based rendezvous and docking systems in space (Dahmen et al., 2023). Clinical simulations represent a novel approach to testing AI and learning about the impacts of AI upon CST aspects of work in healthcare (Borycki et al., 2006, 2009). In our past research involving CST theory, we evaluated the effects of varying technologies on individual, team and organizational work systems using clinical simulations. This included research examining the effects of technologies such as ePrescribing, medication administration and electronic health records upon error rates and safety outcomes for patients (Borycki & Kushniruk, 2010). Through this research, we identified that clinical simulations are a powerful tool that can be used to understand the impacts of introducing (integrating and implementing) new technologies such as AI upon their users (Baylis et al., 2012; Borycki et al., 2009).

Our experiences to date have found that clinical simulations that are representative of real-world settings provide insights into user information seeking, decision-making, workflows emerging from the technology and physical work processes especially, when interactions between the user and the technology influence the safety of work or lead to technology-induced errors (Borycki et al., 2009; Kushniruk et al., 2005). Ecologically valid clinical simulation design is critical to effectively testing and evaluating the safety impacts of AI's implementation and integration with healthcare (Borycki et al., 2009a). Representative or ecologically valid clinical simulations determine the generalizability of the results to the real world. Several aspects of the design of clinical simulations must be attended to so as to develop ecologically valid clinical simulations, namely: the users, the work environment, the tasks and the scenarios users respond to (Borycki et al., 2009a; Jensen et al., 2015; Kushniruk et al., 2013).

USERS

An important decision in setting up clinical simulations is deciding on who the participants will be and whose interactions will be studied using AI in the simulations. Users, who are participants in clinical simulations, must be representative of the type of user that would typically engage with the newly implemented AI system. For example, if we are conducting a simulation involving evaluation of an AI system designed to provide automated clinical decision support in a hospital, then the users studies might consist of physicians or nurses who would be representative of the real (or planned) users of that AI system. Likewise, if we are testing AI that will be deployed in people's homes (e.g., AI-based assistive devices), we would recruit participants, who would be representative of the target population that the AI is designed for. Research has shown that varying types of users have differing information needs. Users' information needs vary by disciplinary, domain and organizational experiences. These differences are significant and will influence the design of a technology (Borycki et al., 2009a). It is important to identify a wide range of representative users of a new AI system to fully understand the impacts of the technology on user's ability to acquire the information they need to make an optimal decision.

Work Environment

A representative work environment is also needed. Clinical simulation researchers have identified that simulation settings or work environments need to be consistent with the real world. Here, the layout of the room where the clinical simulation takes place is important. Furniture and technology placement in the room is key to understanding how AI implementation and integration affect interactions with the physical workplace (Borycki et al., 2009a; Jensen et al., 2015; Kushniruk et al., 2013). To illustrate, in Figure 7.1, we have an image of a Smart Home, where a person lives, who received healthcare from a nurse two days a week. The Smart Home has furniture, appliances and technologies (i.e., a voice assistant, Smart Fridge, Smart Stove, Smart TV, motion detectors and a falls monitor—some of which have integrated AI in their devices that have been built into the Smart Home).

Tasks

Users should be asked to complete tasks they would normally do in the context of a clinical simulation as they interact with the new technology such as AI in the work environment (Borycki et al., 2009a). These tasks should be consistent with tasks documented in the literature and typically done in a Smart Home environment to support health and wellness (Borycki et al., 2009a; Kushniruk et al., 2013). Again, to create an ecologically valid simulation, there is a need to engage the user in tasks that are familiar to them (Li & Borycki, 2019). In our illustrative example, this may include a patient reviewing meal information supplied by an AI tool on the Smart Fridge, using the AI voice assistant to learn more about a health condition, or to support performing a health procedure such as taking medications or exercises prescribed by a physical therapist using a Smart TV (Li & Borycki, 2019; Meyer, 2005).

FIGURE 7.1 Smart Home.

Scenarios

At the beginning of the clinical simulation, users are given a scenario that is reflective of a heath activity under study (Borycki et al., 2009a)—in this case, undertaking everyday activities in a Smart Home (Meyer, 2005). Each scenario drives user interaction with the technology under study. Clinical simulation designers create scenarios that are reflective of user activities, information and decision needs to ensure generalizability of clinical simulation results to real-world settings. Scenarios are designed to represent day-to-day activities as well as stimulate engagement with the new technology: the AI system (Borycki et al., 2009a; Kushniruk et al., 2013). In keeping with our example, a patient diagnosed with a new health condition may use an AI voice assistant (Merkel & Schorr, 2025), Smart Fridge or Smart TV to learn about the new health condition and what types of activities might be done in the home to control their health condition (Li & Borycki, 2019). The AI voice assistant could also be used to support patient decision-making about when to call a physician, if a more intensive intervention is required such as in the case of needing an increase in the dosage of a medication to better control their new health condition (Merkel & Schorr, 2025). Such scenarios can be derived from the published literature (research articles, case studies and educational literature or developed using AI) and provided there is consultation with subject matter experts such as patients, nurses and physicians to ensure their representativeness (Borycki et al., 2009a; Merkel & Schorr, 2025).

Data Collection

Once the work environment or as in our example the Smart Home environment is created, the scenarios are developed, and the users are recruited to participate in the simulations. Then, data can be collected. Data collection may take several forms that include audio data of participant think aloud verbalizations, video data of participant interactions with their environment, and graphical user interface data from devices used in the environment (Borycki et al., 2009). Log file data from technologies can also be exported to provide a comprehensive set of data points for analyses (Oshima & Hoppe, 2021).

Data can also be collected after user participation in the simulation. Here, participants can be interviewed about the meaning of their verbalizations and interactions with the technologies in the environmental context. This can take the form of an interviewer interviewing the user or the interviewer playing a video recording of the user interacting with their environment and asking questions about specific user-environment-technology(ies) interactions that require more information from the user to understand. Interviewing after participation in a simulation provides insights into issues encountered by users with the technologies, they used during the scenario in the Smart Home environment. Here, a deep discussion regarding interactions and their implications for safety can be undertaken using a cued recall approach where the user and the analyst review user interactions in their environment (Borycki et al., 2009; Kushniruk et al., 2005).

Data Analysis

Once the simulations are completed, audio data are transcribed. Video data from observations of individuals interacting with their Smart Home environment and video data from technologies used in the environment (e.g., computer screen data, graphical user interface data from mobile phones and Smart Fridges) are linked to audio transcriptions (Borycki et al., 2009). The data are analyzed for concepts and themes from the CST theory literature to understand the impacts of the AI being evaluated (Borycki & Kushniruk, 2025). This includes coding video, text and workflow data on cognitive concepts such as information seeking and decision-making (see Borycki et al., 2009a; Kushniruk et al., 2019a), sociological aspects of work, such as tasks and workflow (see Kushniruk et al., 2019b), safety issues such as errors and slips (see Borycki & Kushniruk, 2005) and the technology features and functions (i.e., AI) that impact these processes (Kushniruk & Borycki, 2015). Analyses of graphical user interface data can also be viewed in the context of audio transcriptions. Here, audio transcriptions are annotated with user physical activities in the environment and annotated with user interactions with technology (AI plus device) graphical user interfaces (Borycki & Kushniruk, 2005, 2015). Lastly, log files can also be added as a layer for in-depth statistical analysis of usage (Oshima & Hoppe, 2021). Text and video analytic software are integrated from collected data to create a holistic view of CST processes (Borycki et al., 2009a).

Qualitative data (i.e., audio and video data can be coded for concepts and themes) for the smallest unit of analysis which includes user verbalizations, actions, interactions with their environment (Borycki et al., 2009). Qualitative data provides insights into the nature of the cognitive and socio-technical interactions of the users with the new AI technology and their impacts on the safety of users (Kushniruk & Borycki, 2015). This allows for fulsome descriptions of what is going on. This data can in turn be quantified and analyzed with both descriptive and inferential statistics. Quantitative data helps simulation designers to understand the extent to which the introduction of the new AI influences safety and includes collecting surveys, log files and the length of time to complete user tasks during clinical simulations. Key to this is developing and conducting ecologically valid clinical simulations validated by subject matter experts for generalizability of results. Such simulations have been used for training and testing new technologies in many fields such as aviation, nuclear power and manufacturing. Few simulation studies have examined the impacts of AI and technology-induced errors upon CST work. Such testing is critical to preventing harms to individuals, users and society as AI use is increasing.

CONCLUSION

In summary, AI has the potential to greatly streamline and improve healthcare processes. However, this technology can have potential negative impacts in terms of inadvertently introducing error or bias. Clinical simulations are a powerful tool that can be used to understand such issues, including the effects of AI hallucinations, AI psychosis and AI bias upon safety. In this book chapter, we described the testing and evaluation of AI's impacts on safety in real-world using clinical simulation environments to assess these potential negative impacts. We described how simulations are used to evaluate AI safety prior to its implementation in real-world settings, using the example of providing healthcare in a Smart Home setting. The methodological approach we have developed and refined can be used to assess AI both in the laboratory and in the real-world setting of their actual use. Such an approach will be needed to ensure that potential bias and error are identified before widespread deployment of new AI technology in healthcare. In addition, the approach can evaluate the impact of AI at multiple levels from the technical and cognitive to the social level of impact, based on CST theory described in this chapter. This type of due diligence in testing and evaluating AI will be needed to ensure system safety and efficiency and reap the benefits of potentially game-changing approaches to healthcare using clinical simulations to test AI applications and ensure their safety.

REFLECTION QUESTIONS

1. How would I design a clinical simulation to test AI for hallucinations? AI psychosis? AI bias?
2. What are the key aspects of a clinical simulation involving AI that I need to attend to so that the simulation is ecologically valid?
3. Where does bias in AI come ultimately from (i.e., what are its sources)?
4. What are potential ways of mitigating AI by ensuring AI is designed correctly in the first place?

5. What methods could be used to assist users of AI in interpreting the results of AI so as to minimize the impact of potential bias (when interpreting the results of invoking AI?
6. Why is AI bias a concern in the workplace in healthcare and other safety-critical domains?

REFERENCES

Agudo, U., Liberal, K. G., Arrese, M., & Matute, H. (2024). The impact of AI errors in a human-in-the-loop process. *Cognitive Research: Principles and Implications*, *9*(1), 1.

Baylis, T. B., Kushniruk, A. W., & Borycki, E. M. (2012). Low-cost rapid usability testing for health information systems: Is it worth the effort? *Studies in Health Technology and Informatics*, *180,* 363–367.

Boag, W., Hasan, A., Kim, J. Y., Revoir, M., Nichols, M., Ratliff, W., … & Sendak, M. (2024). The algorithm journey map: A tangible approach to implementing AI solutions in healthcare. *NPJ Digital Medicine*, 7(1), 87.

Borycki, E. M., & Kushniruk, A. W. (2010). Towards an integrative cognitive-socio-technical approach in health informatics: Analyzing technology-induced error involving health information systems to improve patient safety. *The Open Medical Informatics Journal*, 4, 181–187. https://pmc.ncbi.nlm.nih.gov/articles/PMC3097067/

Borycki, E. M., & Kushniruk, A. W. (2015). Use of techno-anthropologic approaches in studying technology-induced errors. In *Techno-Anthropology in Health Informatics* (pp. 129–141). IOS Press. https://doi.org/10.3233/978-1-61499-560-9-129

Borycki, E., & Kushniruk, A. (2005). Identifying and preventing technology-induced error using simulations: Application of usability engineering techniques. *Healthcare quarterly* (Toronto, Ont.), 8 Spec No, 99–105. https://doi.org/10.12927/hcq..17673

Borycki, E. M., & Kushniruk, A. W. (2023). Health technology, quality and safety in a learning health system. *Healthcare Management Forum*, 36(2), 79–85. https://doi.org/10.1177/08404704221139383

Borycki, E. M., & Kushniruk, A. W. (2025). Cognitive-socio-technical theory: Application and use in health informatics. In Gray, K. & Lederman, R. (eds) *Research Handbook on Health Information Systems* (pp. 45–59). Edward Elgar Publishing: Cheltenham.

Borycki, E. M., Kushniruk, A. W., Bellwood, P., & Brender, J. (2012). Technology-induced errors. The current use of frameworks and models from the biomedical and life sciences literatures. *Methods of Information in Medicine*, 51(2), 95–103. https://doi.org/10.3414/ME11-02-0009

Borycki, E. M., Kushniruk, A., Keay, E., Nicoll, J., Anderson, J., & Anderson, M. (2009). Toward an integrated simulation approach for predicting and preventing technology-induced errors in healthcare: Implications for healthcare decision-makers. *Healthcare quarterly* (Toronto, Ont.), 12 Spec No Patient, 90–96. https://doi.org/10.12927/hcq.2009.20974

Borycki, E. M., Kushniruk, A. W., Kuwata, S., & Kannry, J. (2006). Use of simulation in the study of clinician workflow. *AMIA Annual Symposium proceedings. AMIA Symposium*, 2006, 61–65.

Borycki, E. M., Kushniruk, A. W., Kuwata, S., & Kannry, J. (2011). Engineering the electronic health record for safety: A multi-level video-based approach to diagnosing and preventing technology-induced error arising from usability problems. *Studies in Health Technology and Informatics*, 166, 197–205.

Borycki, E. M., Lemieux-Charles, L., Nagle, L., & Eysenbach, G. (2009a). Novice nurse information needs in paper and hybrid electronic-paper environments: a qualitative analysis. *Studies in Health Technology and Informatics*, 150, 913–917.

Borycki, E. M., Lemieux-Charles, L., Nagle, L., & Eysenbach, G. (2009b). Evaluating the Impact of hybrid electronic-paper environments upon novice nurse information seeking. *Methods of Information in Medicine*, 48(2), 137–143. https://doi.org/10.3414/ME9222

Borycki, E. M., Peute, L. W. P., van Sinderen, F., Kaufman, D., & Kushniruk, A. W. (2024). Safety and precision AI for a modern digital health system. *Yearbook of Medical Informatics*, 33(1), 18–24. https://doi.org/10.1055/s-0044-1800714

Borycki, E., Dexheimer, J. W., Hullin Lucay Cossio, C., Gong, Y., Jensen, S., Kaipio, J., Kennebeck, S., Kirkendall, E., Kushniruk, A. W., Kuziemsky, C., Marcilly, R., Röhrig, R., Saranto, K., Senathirajah, Y., Weber, J., & Takeda, H. (2016). Methods for addressing technology-induced errors: The current state. *Yearbook of Medical Informatics*, (1), 30–40. https://doi.org/10.15265/IY-2016-029

Borycki, E. M., & Kushniruk, A.W. (2021). The safety of AI in healthcare: Emerging issues and considerations for healthcare. In Househ, M., Borycki, E., Kushniruk, A. (eds) *Multiple Perspectives on Artificial Intelligence in Healthcare. Lecture Notes in Bioengineering* (pp. 13–22). Springer: Cham. https://doi.org/10.1007/978-3-030-67303-1_2

Bryan, V., Sood, S., & Johnston, C. (2025). Analysis on artificial intelligence us by businesses in Canada, second quarter 2025. *Statistics Canada* https://www150.statcan.gc.ca/n1/en/pub/11-621-m/11-621-m2025008-eng.pdf?st=dLmQOEFJ (Accessed on December 16, 2025).
Cabrera, Á. A., Druck, A. J., Hong, J. I., & Perer, A. (2021). Discovering and validating ai errors with crowd-sourced failure reports. *Proceedings of the ACM on Human-Computer Interaction*, 5(CSCW2), 1–22.
Chen, M. (2023) A meta-analysis of third-person perception related to distorted information: Synthesizing the effect, antecedents, and consequences. *Information Processing and Management*. https://doi.org/10.1016/j.ipm.2023.103425
Classen D. C., Longhurst, C., & Thomas, E. J. (2023). Bending the patient safety curve: How much can AI help? *NPJ Digital Medicine*, 6(1):2. https://doi.org/10.1038/s41746-022-00731-5
Cohen, T. A., Patel, V. L., & Shortliffe, E. H. (2022). *Intelligent Systems in Medicine and Health. The Role of AI*. Springer: New York.
Cook, D. A., Hatala, R., Brydges, R., Zendejas, B., Szostek, J. H., Wang, A. T., Erwin, P. J., & Hamstra, S. J. (2011). Technology-enhanced simulation for health professions education: A systematic review and meta-analysis. *JAMA*, 306(9), 978–988. https://doi.org/10.1001/jama.2011.1234
Cross, J. L., Choma, M. A., & Onofrey, J. A. (2024). Bias in medical AI: Implications for clinical decision-making. *PLOS Digital Health*, 3(11), e0000651.
Dahmen, U., Osterloh, T., & Roßmann, J. (2023). Structured validation of AI-based systems by virtual testing in simulated test scenarios. *Applied Intelligence*, 53(15), 18910–18924.
Elendu, C., Amaechi, D. C., Okatta, A. U., Amaechi, E. C., Elendu, T. C., Ezeh, C. P., & Elendu, I. D. (2024). The impact of simulation-based training in medical education: A review. *Medicine*, 103(27), e38813. https://doi.org/10.1097/MD.0000000000038813
Gichoya, J. W., Thomas, K., Celi, L. A., Safdar, N., Banerjee, I., Banja, J. D., … & Purkayastha, S. (2023). AI pitfalls and what not to do: Mitigating bias in AI. *The British Journal of Radiology*, 96(1150), 20230023.
Hasanzadeh, F., Josephson, C. B., Waters, G., Adedinsewo, D., Azizi, Z., & White, J. A. (2025). Bias recognition and mitigation strategies in artificial intelligence healthcare applications. *NPJ Digital Medicine*, 8(1), 154.
Hassan, M., Borycki, E. M., & Kushniruk, A. W. (2025). Artificial intelligence governance framework for healthcare. *Healthcare Management Forum*, 38(2), 125–130. https://doi.org/10.1177/08404704241291226
Hassan, M., Kushniruk, A., & Borycki, E. (2024). Barriers to and facilitators of artificial intelligence adoption in health care: Scoping review. *JMIR Human Factors*, 11, e48633. https://doi.org/10.2196/48633
Holdsworth, J. (n.d.) What is AI bias? https://www.ibm.com/think/topics/ai-bias#:~:text=AI%20bias%2C%20also%20called%20machine,accuracy%2C%20and%20therefore%20its%20potential
Househ, M., Borycki, E., & Kushniruk, A. (2021). *Multiple Perspectives on Artificial Intelligence in Healthcare: Opportunities and Challenges*. Springer Verlag: New York.
Jensen, S., Kushniruk, A. W., & Nøhr, C. (2015). Clinical simulation: A method for development and evaluation of clinical information systems. *Journal of Biomedical Informatics*, 54, 65–76. https://doi.org/10.1016/j.jbi.2015.02.002
Kim, T. G., Baek, D. K., & Hwang, J. S. (2005). *Artificial Intelligence and Simulation*. Springer-Verlag: Berlin/Heidelberg.
Kushniruk, A. W., & Borycki, E. M. (2015). Development of a video coding scheme for analyzing the usability and usefulness of health information systems. *Studies in Health Technology and Informatics*, 218, 68–73.
Kushniruk, A. W., & Patel, V. L. (1998). Cognitive evaluation of decision-making processes and assessment of information technology in medicine. *International Journal of Medical Informatics*, 51(2–3), 83–90. https://doi.org/10.1016/s1386-5056(98)00106-3
Kushniruk, A. W., Monkman, H., Kitson, N., & Borycki, E. M. (2019a). Development of a video coding scheme for understanding human-computer interaction and clinical decision making. *Studies in Health Technology and Informatics*, 265, 80–85. https://doi.org/10.3233/SHTI190142
Kushniruk, A., Borycki, E., Kitson, N., & Kannry, J. (2019b). Development of a video coding scheme focused on socio-technical aspects of human-computer interaction in healthcare. *Studies in Health Technology and Informatics*, 257, 236–243.
Kushniruk, A., Borycki, E., Kuwata, S., & Kannry, J. (2006). Predicting changes in workflow resulting from healthcare information systems: Ensuring the safety of healthcare. *Healthcare quarterly* (Toronto, Ont.), 9 Spec No, 114–118. https://doi.org/10.12927/hcq..18469
Kushniruk, A. W., Kaufman, D. W., Kannampallil, T. G., & Patel, V. L. (2024). *Human Computer Interaction in Healthcare: The Role of Cognition*. Springer Verlag: New York.
Kushniruk, A., Nohr, C., Jensen, S., & Borycki, E. M. (2013). From usability testing to clinical simulations: Bringing context into the design and evaluation of usable and safe health information technologies. Contribution of the IMIA human factors engineering for healthcare informatics working group. *Yearbook of Medical Informatics*, 8, 78–85.

Kushniruk, A. W., Triola, M. M., Borycki, E. M., Stein, B., & Kannry, J. L. (2005). Technology-induced error and usability: The relationship between usability problems and prescription errors when using a handheld application. *International Journal of Medical Informatics*, 74(7–8), 519–526. https://doi.org/10.1016/j.ijmedinf.2005.01.003

Li, C. Z., & Borycki, E. M. (2019). Smart Homes for Healthcare. *Studies in Health Technology and Informatics*, 257, 283–287.

Mahmood, A., Fung, J. W., Won, I., & Huang, C. M. (2022, April). Owning mistakes sincerely: Strategies for mitigating AI errors. In *Proceedings of the 2022 CHI Conference on Human Factors in Computing Systems,* New Orleans, LA (pp. 1–11).

Massenon, R., Gambo, I., Khan, J. A., Agbonkhese, C., & Alwadain, A. (2025). "My AI is lying to me": User-reported LLM hallucinations in AI mobile apps reviews. *Scientific Reports*, 15(1), 30397. https://doi.org/10.1038/s41598-025-15416-8

McElheran, K., Li, J. F., Brynjolfsson, E., Kroff, Z., Dinlersoz, E., Foster, L., & Zolas, N. (2024). AI adoption in America: Who, what, and where. *Journal of Economics & Management Strategy*, 33, 375–415. https://doi.org/10.1111/jems.12576

Melhem, S. B. (2013). *An Evaluation of Mobile Computing effect on Oncologists Workflow in Ambulatory Care Settings*. University of Victoria: Canada.

Merkel, S., & Schorr, S. (2025). Identification of use cases, target groups, and motivations around adopting smart speakers for health care and social care settings: Scoping review. *JMIR AI*, 4, e55673. https://doi.org/10.2196/55673

Meyer, G. (2005). *Smart Home Hacks: Tips and Tools for Automating Your House*. O'Reilley: Tokyo.

Morrin, H., Nicholls, L., Levin, M., Yiend, J., Iyengar, U., DelGuidice, F., … Pollak, T. (2025, July 11). Delusions by design? How everyday AIs might be fuelling psychosis (and what can be done about it). https://doi.org/10.31234/osf.io/cmy7n_v5

Musiol, M. 2024. *Generative AI: Navigating the Course to the Artificial General Intelligence Future*. Hoboken: Wiley, NJ.

Oshima, J., & Hoppe, H. U. (2021). Finding meaning in log-file data. In Cress, U., Rosé, C., Wise, A. F., & Oshima, J. (eds) *International Handbook of Computer-supported Collaborative Learning,* Computer-Supported Collaborative Learning Series (Vol. 19, pp. 569–584). Springer International Publishing: Cham. https://doi.org/10.1007/978-3-030-65291-3_31

Østergaard, SD. (2023) Will generative artificial intelligence chatbots generate delusions in individuals prone to psychosis? *Schizophrenia Bulletin*, 49(6), 1418–1419. https://doi.org/10.1093/schbul/sbad128

Oxford English Dictionary. (2023). Artificial intelligence. https://www.oed.com/dictionary/artificial-intelligence_n

Palojoki, S., Mäkelä, M., Lehtonen, L., & Saranto, K. (2017). An analysis of electronic health record-related patient safety incidents. *Health Informatics Journal*, 23(2), 134–145. https://doi.org/10.1177/1460458216631072

Panch, T., Mattie, H., & Celi, L. A. (2019). The "inconvenient truth" about AI in healthcare. *NPJ Digital Medicine*, 2(1), 77.

Patel, V. L., Kushniruk, A. W., Yang, S., & Yale, J. F. (2000). Impact of a computer-based patient record system on data collection, knowledge organization, and reasoning. *Journal of the American Medical Informatics Association: JAMIA*, 7(6), 569–585. https://doi.org/10.1136/jamia.2000.0070569

Peek, N., Capurro, D., Rozova, V., & van der Veer, S. N. (2024). Bridging the gap: Challenges and strategies for the implementation of artificial intelligence-based clinical decision support systems in clinical practice. *Yearbook of Medical Informatics*, 33(1), 103–114. https://doi.org/10.1055/s-0044-1800729

Ratwani, R. M., Bates, D. W., & Classen, D. C. (2024). Patient safety and artificial intelligence in clinical care. *JAMA Health Forum*, 5(2), e235514.

Shashikumar, S. P., Wardi, G., Malhotra, A., & Nemati, S. (2021). Artificial intelligence sepsis prediction algorithm learns to say, "I don't know". *NPJ Digital Medicine*, 4, 1–9.

Shortliffe, E. H., Shortliffe, E. H., Cimino, J. J., Cimino, J. J. (2014). *Biomedical Informatics: Computer Applications in Health Care and Biomedicine*. Springer: New York.

Singh, V., Hari, S. K, Tsai, T., & Pitale, M. (2021). Simulation driven design and test for safety of ai based autonomous vehicles. In *Proceedings of the IEEE/CVF Conference on Computer Vision and Pattern Recognition,* Virtual (pp. 122–128).

Sun, Y., Sheng, D., Zhou, Z., & Wu, Y. (2024). AI hallucination: Towards a comprehensive classification of distorted information in artificial intelligence-generated content. *Humanit Social Science Communication*, 11, 1278. https://doi.org/10.1057/s41599-024-03811-x

Templin, T., Fort, S., Padmanabham, P., Seshadri, P., Rimal, R., Oliva, J., … & Sinnott-Armstrong, N. (2025). Framework for bias evaluation in large language models in healthcare settings. *npj Digital Medicine*, 8(1), 414.

Vuokko, R., Vakkuri, A., & Palojoki, S. (2022). Preliminary exploration of main elements for systematic classification development: Case study of patient safety incidents. *JMIR Formative Research*, 6(3), e35474. https://doi.org/10.2196/35474

Wei, M. (July 21, 2025). The emerging problem of AI psychosis. Psychology Today, https://www.psychologytoday.com/ca/blog/urban-survival/202507/the-emerging-problem-of-ai-psychosis

Wong, A., Otles, E., Donnelly, J. P., Krumm, A., McCullough, J., DeTroyer-Cooley, O., Pestrue, J., Phillips, M., Konye, J., Penoza, C., Ghous, M., & Singh, K. (2021). External validation of a widely implemented proprietary sepsis prediction model in hospitalized patients. *JAMA Internal Medicine*, 181(8), 1065–1070. https://doi.org/10.1001/jamainternmed.2021.2626

Yampolskiy, R. V. (2016). Taxonomy of pathways to dangerous artificial intelligence. In *AAAI Workshop: AI, Ethics, and Society* Feb 13 (pp. 143–148).

Yampolskiy, R. V. (2018). *Artificial Intelligence Safety and Security*. CRC Press: Boca Raton, FL.

Yampolskiy, R. V. (2024). *AI: Unexplainable, Unpredictable, Uncontrollable*. Chapman and Hall/CRC: Boca Raton, FL.

Yusof, M., & Sahroni, M. N. (2018). Investigating health information systems-induced errors. *International Journal of Health Care Quality Assurance*, 31(8), 1014–1029. https://doi.org/10.1108/IJHCQA-07-2017-0125

Zuboff, S. (1988). *In the Age of the Smart Machine: The Future of Work and Power*. Basic Books: New York.

8 Addressing Structural Bias in AI-Driven Healthcare

From Technical Fixes to Equity-by-Design

Mehdi Adda

INTRODUCTION

Artificial intelligence (AI) increasingly shapes healthcare delivery through diagnostic imaging, clinical decision support, triage, and population health management. While AI promises enhanced diagnostic accuracy and efficiency, its benefits remain unevenly distributed. AI systems, including modern foundation models and generative systems, learn from data reflecting historical inequities (e.g., measurement bias, stigmatizing documentation, and representation gaps) that propagate through model development (Sjoding et al., 2020; Adamson and Smith, 2018; Daneshjou et al., 2022). Moreover, AI operates within institutions whose incentives and practices may misalign algorithmic goals with clinical needs, determining when and for whom AI adds value or causes harm (WHO, 2021; NIST, 2023; Selbst et al., 2019).

These dynamics have concrete consequences. For instance, a U.S. population health algorithm optimized spending as a proxy for clinical need, systematically underscoring Black patients despite comparable illness burden, thereby reducing their access to care management (Obermeyer et al., 2019). Such failures illustrate how organizational workflows, documentation norms, and governance practices mediate AI's impact on equity unless explicitly addressed.

This chapter examines how structural biases become embedded in healthcare AI, why technical fixes alone are insufficient, and how "equity-by-design" can reorient AI toward justice. Equity-by-design integrates social justice principles and community governance throughout the AI life cycle, reframing success as reducing inequities rather than merely improving aggregate accuracy (Rajkomar et al., 2018; WHO, 2021).

We proceed as follows: Section "From Technical Artifacts to Structural Bias" elucidates how structural bias arises. Section "Case Studies: Recurring Patterns and Consequences" analyzes case studies illustrating recurring failure modes. Section "Why Purely Technical Fixes Are Necessary but Insufficient" explains why technical fixes are insufficient. Section "Equity-by-Design: Principles and Governance" articulates the equity-by-design framework. Section "Operationalizing Equity-by-Design: A Practical Roadmap" operationalizes this framework through concrete methods. Section "Navigating Tensions in Healthcare AI and Collective Action" addresses implementation tensions. Section "Conclusion" concludes with key implications.

FROM TECHNICAL ARTIFACTS TO STRUCTURAL BIAS

Discussions of "bias in AI" often focus narrowly on skewed datasets or model selection (Selbst et al., 2019). While important, such a focus understates how structural inequities shape the entire AI life cycle (Suresh et al., 2021). We examine four main sources of this bias across the life cycle.

DOI: 10.1201/9781003737810-9

Misspecified Targets

AI models optimize the targets they are given; if those targets are inequitable proxies, models reproduce inequity. For instance, using healthcare cost as a proxy for clinical need systematically disadvantages Black patients (Obermeyer et al., 2019)—a foundational problem that post-hoc fairness adjustments cannot correct (Kleinberg et al., 2017; Chouldechova, 2017). Recent work further shows how optimization to administrative or billing outcomes can entrench inequities unless targets are re-specified to equity-relevant endpoints and labels are re-audited (NIST, 2023; WHO, 2021).

Biased Labels and Differential Measurement Error

Clinical "ground truth" is often flawed, compromised by both human judgment and biased devices. Pulse oximeters, for example, are less accurate for darker skin tones (Sjoding et al., 2020; Fawzy et al., 2022), while language in clinical notes can encode stigma against people with mental illness or disabilities (Ghassemi et al., 2021). These biased signals are then learned by AI systems as fact. Recent evaluations of device and documentation bias underscore the need for upstream device audits and label integrity reviews as prerequisites to training equitable models (WHO, 2021; NIST, 2023).

Representational Gaps and Taxonomy Harms

AI models consistently perform worse for marginalized groups who are underrepresented in training data (Adamson and Smith, 2018; Daneshjou et al., 2022). Beyond representation, the data categories themselves can inflict "taxonomy harms" by pathologizing disability or misgendering individuals. Without community governance over how data is defined and labeled, even inclusive datasets risk reproducing injustice (Costanza-Chock, 2020).

Deployment Context and Institutional Incentives

AI models validated in one setting, such as a well-resourced academic center, often fail when deployed in another due to differences in patient populations, workflows, and resources (Chen et al., 2020). When institutional goals like cost containment are prioritized, the burden of these failures falls disproportionately on marginalized patients, underscoring the need for site-specific validation and oversight (NIST, 2023; WHO, 2021).

CASE STUDIES: RECURRING PATTERNS AND CONSEQUENCES

The following cases, summarized in Table 8.1, demonstrate how structural bias manifests across healthcare AI.

Risk Stratification Using Spending as a Proxy for Need

Obermeyer et al. (2019) analyzed a commercial population-health algorithm that prioritized enrollment into care-management programs based on predicted future cost. Because historical spending is systematically lower for Black patients than for white patients with similar illness burden (due to barriers to access, undertreatment, and other structural factors), the algorithm assigned lower risk scores to Black patients at comparable clinical need, leading to under-enrollment.

Pulse Oximetry Bias and Downstream AI

Sjoding et al. (2020) showed that pulse oximetry more frequently overestimates arterial oxygen saturation in patients with darker skin tones, yielding higher rates of occult hypoxemia that go

TABLE 8.1
Summary of Case Studies on AI Bias in Healthcare

Case Study	Type of Bias	Primarily Affected Population(s)	Key Consequence
Risk stratification	Target misspecification (Cost as proxy for need)	Black patients	Reduced access to care management programs.
Pulse oximetry	Measurement error	Patients with darker skin tones	Under-detection and undertreatment of hypoxemia.
Dermatology imaging	Representational gaps and dataset imbalance	Patients with darker skin tones	Higher error rates, delayed or missed diagnoses.
Model portability	Deployment drift and confounding variables	Patients in different hospital settings	Failure to generalize, leading to patient safety risks.
Indigenous health AI	Governance gaps and colonial frameworks	Indigenous communities in Canada	Risk of data misuse and perpetuation of health inequities without sovereignty.
Gender-affirming care	Taxonomy harms and misgendering in EHRs	Transgender and gender-diverse individuals	Inaccurate medical records, denial of care, psychological distress.

undetected when decisions rely on SpO2 alone. Fawzy et al. (2022) linked this measurement bias to adverse outcomes, including reduced recognition and treatment of hypoxemia. Downstream, any AI that consumes SpO2 values or labels derived from these measurements risks perpetuating under-recognition in affected subgroups.

Dermatology Imaging and Dataset Governance

Dermatology classifiers are often trained predominantly on lighter skin tones and underperform on darker skin tones, with higher error rates and potential for delayed or missed diagnoses (Adamson and Smith, 2018; Daneshjou et al., 2022). Beyond sampling, taxonomy design matters: label ontologies can encode dominant perspectives that misname culturally rooted presentations or pathologize disability, generating "taxonomy harms." Recent audits show that models may learn shortcuts correlated with lighter skin representations, failing to generalize to underrepresented phenotypes (Daneshjou et al., 2022).

Model Portability and Deployment Drift

Multiple case studies show that models validated at one site can fail when moved to another or when local practices change. Zech et al. (2018) found that chest X-ray pneumonia classifiers learned site- and acquisition-related signals (e.g., hospital- and device-linked artifacts), achieving internal performance that drops on external datasets. Badgeley et al. (2019), working with pelvic radiographs for hip fracture detection, showed that patient and hospital process variables and scanner characteristics were predictable from the image and confounded the clinical task, producing results that did not generalize once these confounders were controlled; generalization across hospitals degraded markedly. Finally, Finlayson et al. (2019) demonstrated that clinically plausible models are vulnerable to small perturbations (adversarial examples) and distribution shifts, underscoring concrete patient-safety risks in real-world use.

Indigenous Data Governance and AI in Canadian Healthcare

In Canada, the development of AI tools for Indigenous health highlights critical governance challenges. Without respecting principles of Indigenous data sovereignty, such as OCAP® (Ownership, Control, Access, and Possession) and the CARE Principles (Collective Benefit,

Authority to Control, Responsibility, Ethics), AI systems risk perpetuating colonial healthcare dynamics (FNIGC, 2014; Carroll et al., 2020). For example, a risk prediction model trained on general population data and deployed without community oversight could misrepresent health needs, allocate resources inequitably, and undermine community-led health initiatives, reinforcing systemic disadvantages rooted in colonial history. The principle of "principled refusal" becomes critical here, where Indigenous communities must have the authority to halt projects that do not align with their values and needs.

Algorithmic Bias and Taxonomy Harms for Transgender and Gender-Diverse People

Electronic health records (EHRs) often fail to correctly capture gender identity, leading to misgendering. When AI systems, particularly large language models, are trained on these records, they learn and amplify these "taxonomy harms." This can result in AI-driven clinical decision support that offers inappropriate medical advice (e.g., based on sex assigned at birth rather than gender identity and physiology), automated summaries that misgender patients, and risk scores that are inaccurate. Such algorithmic biases not only compromise clinical safety but also cause significant psychological distress and erode trust in the healthcare system for already marginalized communities (Agmon et al., 2022; Grasso et al., 2020).

WHY PURELY TECHNICAL FIXES ARE NECESSARY BUT INSUFFICIENT

Technical interventions cannot address inequities rooted in problem formulation and institutional power dynamics. Three fundamental limitations persist: misaligned objectives, irreconcilable metric trade-offs, and accountability displacement.

The Problem of Objective Integrity

The core challenge is the formulation of objectives that encode existing inequities. Using healthcare expenditure as a proxy for clinical need is a prime example; no amount of technical refinement can remedy the underlying allocative injustice when an operational proxy (spending) misaligns with the stated goal (health need) (Obermeyer et al., 2019). Consequently, even achieving statistical parity while optimizing such a biased objective merely redistributes discrimination rather than eliminating it (Kleinberg et al., 2017). The solution requires re-specifying targets through participatory processes centered on health equity (Chouldechova, 2017).

Metric Trade-offs and Burden Shifting

Fairness criteria often conflict: improving sensitivity or equalizing error rates for one group can worsen calibration or inflate false positives for another. These shifts have material downstream burdens (e.g., additional tests, co-pays, and time off work) that fall disproportionately on marginalized patients and under-resourced clinics (Gaebler et al., 2023; Rajkomar et al., 2018). Because no single metric optimizes all desiderata simultaneously, resolving trade-offs is an ethical and policy judgment, not a purely technical one—requiring participatory deliberation with affected communities and explicit accounting of who bears benefits and burdens.

Accountability Drift

Treating harm as a model "limitation" relocates responsibility from organizational governance to technical teams. Equity is a property of the sociotechnical system, not just the algorithm (Selbst et al., 2019). Governance must include clear decision rights and community authority to prevent this drift.

EQUITY-BY-DESIGN: PRINCIPLES AND GOVERNANCE

Building on the understanding that purely technical interventions are insufficient to address structural bias, this section outlines an "equity-by-design" framework. It integrates social justice principles and community engagement throughout the AI life cycle, from problem formulation to continuous monitoring. It emphasizes proactive measures and robust governance mechanisms to ensure that AI systems in healthcare genuinely advance health equity rather than perpetuating existing disparities. Figure 8.1 illustrates the six interconnected stages of this cyclical framework.

PROBLEM FORMULATION ALIGNED WITH EQUITY

Reframe the design brief from "Can we predict X?" to "Which inequity should be reduced, for whom, by how much, by when, and under what constraints?" Define success metrics, unacceptable harms, and contexts for refusal jointly with affected communities and frontline clinicians. Make equity goals explicit and measurable at the outset to avoid optimizing to proxies that perpetuate disparities (Rajkomar et al., 2018; Costanza-Chock, 2020).

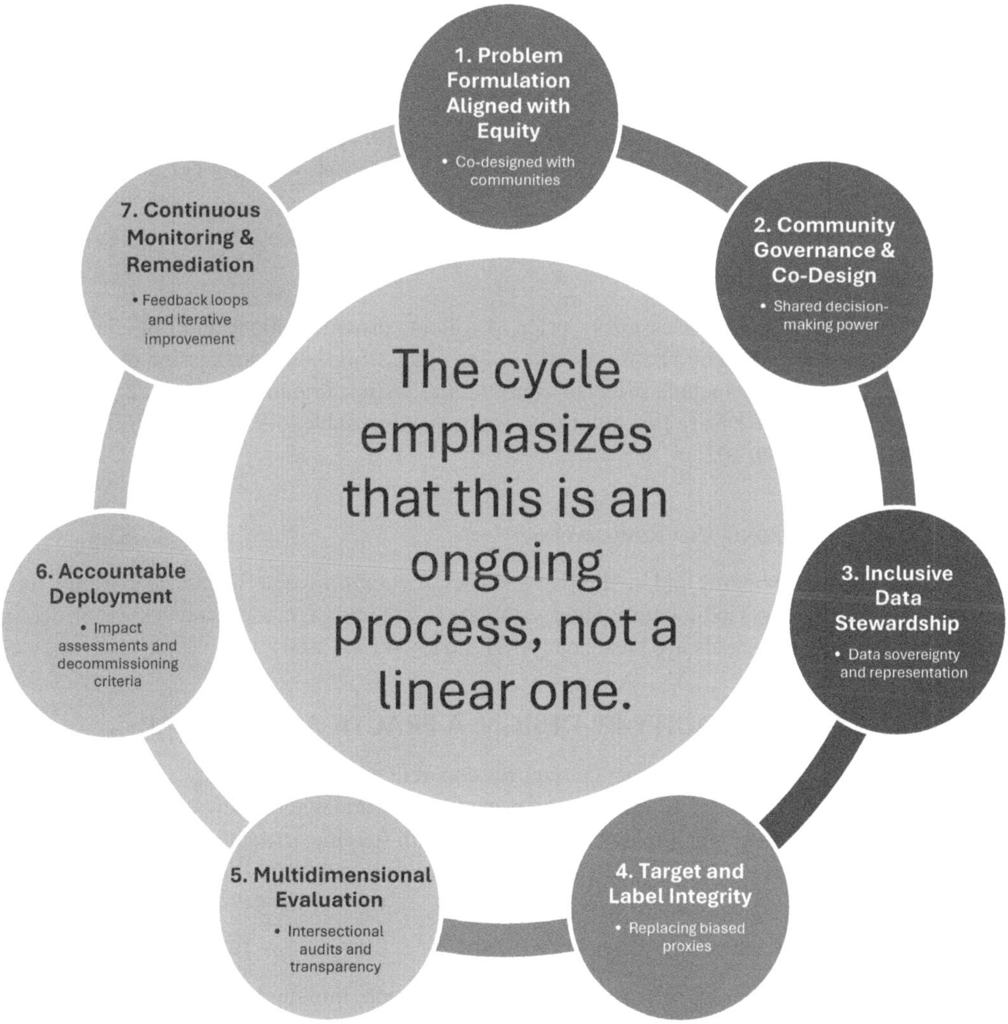

FIGURE 8.1 Equity-by-Design AI life cycle in healthcare.

Community Governance and Codesign

Move beyond consultation to shared decision-making, especially for Indigenous communities via OCAP®/CARE principles. This requires embracing decolonial methodologies that center community authority (FNIGC, 2014; Carroll et al., 2020).

Inclusive Data Stewardship

Plan data collection and curation to support equity analysis. This includes ethically justified oversampling of underrepresented groups, capture of relevant social and structural determinants, and accessible, culturally safe consent. Document dataset lineage, intended use, and known limitations using standardized documentation (e.g., datasheets for datasets). Limit secondary use to the agreed purposes and implement benefit-sharing mechanisms (WHO, 2021).

Target and Label Integrity

Replace biased proxies with equity-relevant endpoints, engaging communities to relabel or reframe outcomes (Ghassemi et al., 2021).

Multidimensional Evaluation

Report performance by intersectional subgroups and publish transparent model documentation, including discrimination (e.g., sensitivity/specificity), calibration, and clinical utility (Mitchell et al., 2019).

Accountable Deployment

Conduct algorithmic impact assessments prior to rollout; provide patient and clinician opt-outs where feasible; define sunset and pause criteria tied to equity thresholds; and assign decision rights to governance bodies that include affected communities. Align organizational controls with risk management guidance to ensure that equity oversight is enforceable, not advisory (Reisman et al., 2018; NIST, 2023; WHO, 2021).

Continuous Monitoring and Remediation

Use disaggregated dashboards and qualitative feedback to monitor for performance drift and unintended harms. Publish periodic equity audit summaries and update models, processes, or deployment contexts when thresholds are breached (NIST, 2023; WHO, 2021).

OPERATIONALIZING EQUITY-BY-DESIGN: A PRACTICAL ROADMAP

Translating equity principles into practice requires concrete mechanisms and accountability structures throughout the AI life cycle. This section provides an actionable framework for implementing equity-by-design, organized by implementation phase, with specific artifacts and decision points to ensure equity is systematically embedded.

Phase 1: Project Initiation and Codesign

This initial phase is critical for setting an equitable foundation, moving beyond technical problem-solving to address the correct sociotechnical challenge.

- **Codesign protocol:** The goal is to shift power from developers to communities. This involves establishing compensated codesign councils with prioritized representation from historically excluded groups, such as patient advocates, Indigenous representatives, and disability justice organizations. Compensation is not optional; it values lived experience as critical expertise. Using structured tools like a Problem Statement Worksheet, this council cocreates the project's goals, defines unacceptable harm, and establishes the conditions for "principled refusal." All key decisions, rationales, and points of dissent are documented in a Decision Log to ensure transparency and accountability.
- **Data governance:** Before any data is accessed, governance structures must be established. This is operationalized through a Project Charter that explicitly defines purpose limitation, access controls, and benefit-sharing mechanisms. For Indigenous data, this requires implementing binding OCAP®/CARE agreements, which are legal and operational frameworks that recognize collective data rights and grant the community veto power or halt authority over the project. These agreements are enforced through technical controls like tiered permissions and immutable audit logs, overseen by a community-majority governance committee.

Phase 2: Data Collection and Preparation

Data work must be done with intentionality to avoid replicating the historical biases present in most existing datasets.

- **Inclusive data collection:** This process is designed to be respectful and empowering. It starts with accessible, multilingual consent forms that offer granular choices for data use. Fair compensation guidelines are established to ensure participants are appropriately paid for their contributions. The protocol mandates the collection of equity-relevant variables (e.g., race, language, disability status) while implementing robust safeguards against reidentification. Finally, every dataset is documented using a standardized Datasheet template that details its context, limitations, and intended use, enabling responsible downstream use and auditing.
- **Pre-training audit:** This is a critical checkpoint before any modeling begins. The audit assesses the suitability of the data for an equitable application. It involves a Representation Analysis Protocol to quantify coverage of different subgroups, a Label Integrity Review to identify potential biases in annotations, and a Measurement Bias Checklist to account for disparities from clinical devices or instruments (like pulse oximeters). This audit also includes a Shortcut Risk Assessment to check for spurious correlations that could lead to a model that performs well in testing but fails unfairly in deployment.

Phase 3: Model Development and Validation

This phase embeds equity directly into the model's technical design and evaluation, making fairness a core objective rather than an afterthought.

- **Metric selection:** This is treated as a policy decision, not just a technical one. The process involves using a Fairness Criteria Matrix to visualize the trade-offs between different, often incompatible, fairness metrics. A Stakeholder Deliberation Guide facilitates community input on which trade-offs are acceptable, aligning the technical metrics with clinical risks and community priorities. All decisions and their rationales are documented in a Metric Governance Memo, which becomes a key accountability artifact.

- **Validation audit:** Evaluation must go beyond aggregate performance metrics. This audit mandates the use of a Subgroup Performance Report Template for rigorous intersectional analysis, ensuring the model works well for all groups, not just the majority. A Calibration Assessment Protocol is used to check that the model's risk scores mean the same thing across different groups. The findings are published transparently in a standardized Model Card, which details the model's intended use, limitations, and performance across subgroups.

Phase 4: Deployment and Monitoring

Deploying an AI tool is treated as a clinical and organizational intervention that requires the same level of evidence and oversight as any other health intervention.

- **Impact study design:** Before a full rollout, the AI's real-world impact on equity is evaluated using robust causal inference designs, such as stepped-wedge or pragmatic trials, detailed in a study protocol. These studies include pre-specified equity endpoints and are paired with a Qualitative Assessment Guide to measure impacts on patient trust, clinician burden, and workflow.
- **Procurement and regulation:** Health systems must use their purchasing power to drive equity. This is done by embedding equity clauses from a Contract Language Library into procurement requirements. Vendors are evaluated using an Assessment Rubric that scores their equity capabilities. Contracts must specify Decommission Criteria—clear, pre-defined equity thresholds that, if breached, trigger a pause or sunsetting of the tool.
- **Post-deployment monitoring**: Monitoring is continuous and disaggregated. It relies on dashboards with disaggregated performance metrics and automated alerts for performance degradation or drift. Qualitative feedback forms are used to capture the lived experiences of patients and clinicians. When an equity threshold is breached, a pre-approved Remediation Plan is activated.

Phase 5: Continuous Improvement

This final phase focuses on creating a sustainable learning culture that normalizes equity-by-design practices.

- **Capacity building**: Building institutional capacity is essential for long-term success. This involves deploying a role-specific training curriculum on design justice and participatory methods. Reusable templates and workshop materials are shared via a Knowledge Repository to reduce friction and maintain rigor across projects.
- **Accountability**: Accountability is operationalized through clear structures. A Decision Rights Matrix specifies who is responsible for equity at each stage of the life cycle. These responsibilities are embedded in job descriptions and tied to Performance Objectives, making equity a formal part of organizational performance, not just an informal goal.

NAVIGATING TENSIONS IN HEALTHCARE AI AND COLLECTIVE ACTION

Implementing the equity-by-design approach surfaces fundamental trade-offs that require a coordinated response. For example, equity monitoring demands granular demographic data, creating tension with privacy, while meaningful codesign conflicts with rapid deployment pressures. These challenges are not just theoretical; they manifest as concrete implementation barriers.

Institutional resistance may arise from a reluctance to alter established workflows or cede decision-making power. Budgetary constraints are often cited, as participatory processes and rigorous audits are perceived as costly additions. Furthermore, the lack of regulatory mandates for equity audits can make them seem optional.

Proactive strategies are needed to overcome these barriers:

- **Building a business case for equity** by demonstrating the long-term cost savings that result from reduced health disparities.
- **Forming alliances** with clinical champions and patient advocacy groups to build institutional will.
- Launching targeted, high-impact pilot projects to demonstrate value and refine processes.
- **Advocating for policy changes** that mandate transparency and community participation in AI procurement and oversight.

These tensions require collective action. Developers must expand evaluation beyond accuracy, clinicians must articulate equity priorities, policymakers must mandate impact assessments, and communities must have real decision-making power. This preliminary framework recognizes that applications which ration care or enable surveillance are incompatible with justice goals and should not be developed. Principled refusal is a valid and necessary outcome when alignment with equity proves impossible.

CONCLUSION

AI in healthcare can either accelerate inequity or contribute to its dismantling. The outcome depends not on technical sophistication alone, but on problem formulation, data governance, and who holds decision-making authority. As this chapter has argued, purely technical fixes are a necessary but insufficient response to biases that are deeply embedded in our social and institutional practices.

The path forward requires a fundamental shift toward equity-by-design, an approach that integrates social justice, community governance, and interdisciplinary collaboration from the very beginning. The key takeaways for stakeholders are:

- **Bias is structural, not just technical:** Acknowledge that AI bias stems from historical and ongoing societal inequities reflected in data and healthcare systems. The focus must shift from "debiasing" data to redesigning the unjust systems in which AI operates.
- **Community governance is nonnegotiable**: Authentic partnership with affected communities, especially marginalized and Indigenous groups, is essential. This means sharing power and respecting data sovereignty, not simply consulting.
- **Equity must be operationalized and audited**: Vague commitments to fairness are not enough. Equity goals must be translated into concrete, measurable metrics, and audited rigorously at every stage of the AI life cycle, from conception to decommissioning.
- **Principled refusal is a core competency**: The ethical implementation of AI includes the wisdom and courage to refuse to build or deploy systems when equity alignment proves impossible. This means choosing instead to invest in addressing the root causes of health inequity.

This preliminary framework provides conceptual and practical guidance, but its implementation will vary across jurisdictions and health systems. A critical future direction is to present this initial version to the various stakeholders in healthcare AI equity—including patients, marginalized communities, clinicians, policymakers, and developers—to integrate their respective perspectives. This direct engagement will inform critical future work, which should include comparative evaluations of this framework's implementations, the development of validated equity impact measures that integrate clinical outcomes with patient burden, and cocreated curricula for shared practice across roles.

Ultimately, the fundamental question remains directional: are healthcare AI systems reducing harm and expanding care for marginalized communities or are they merely stabilizing inequity? Despite constraints from legal frameworks, funding models, and data quality, the choice lies in how we design, govern, and deploy—or refuse to deploy—these technologies today.

ACKNOWLEDGMENT

Portions of this chapter were developed with the assistance of Gemini Pro for translation, editing, and restructuring. All intellectual contributions, interpretations, and final editorial decisions are the author's own, and the authors take full responsibility for the content. Any AI-assisted or AI-generated material was reviewed and verified by the author.

REFLECTION QUESTIONS

1. Why does the author argue that technical fixes (like debiasing algorithms) are necessary but insufficient for addressing the root causes of AI inequity?
2. The chapter argues that bias often begins at the "problem formulation" stage, well before data is even collected. Using the example of algorithms that predict cost rather than clinical need, discuss how choosing the wrong target can reinforce existing discrimination.
3. Why is community governance considered a nonnegotiable part of the equity-by-design framework? How does giving power to communities change the way we define a "successful" model beyond just high accuracy scores?
4. The chapter mentions principled refusal. Under what circumstances should developers or communities refuse to build or deploy an AI system?

REFERENCES

Adamson, A. S., and Smith, A. (2018). Machine learning and health care disparities in dermatology. *JAMA Dermatology*, 154(11), 1247–1248. https://doi.org/10.1001/jamadermatol.2018.2348

Agmon, S., Gillis, P., Horvitz, E., and Radinsky, K. (2022). Gender-sensitive word embeddings for healthcare. *Journal of the American Medical Informatics Association*, 29(3), 415–423. https://doi.org/10.1093/jamia/ocab279

Badgeley, M.A., Zech, J.R., Oakden-Rayner, L., Glicksberg, B. S., Liu, M., Gale, W., McConnell, M. V., Percha, B., Snyder, T. M., and Dudley, J. T. (2019). Deep learning predicts hip fracture using confounding patient and healthcare variables. *npj Digital Medicine*, 2, 31. https://doi.org/10.1038/s41746-019-0105-1

Carroll, S. R., Garba, I., Figueroa-Rodríguez, O. L., Holbrook, J., Lovett, R., Materechera, S., Parsons, M., Raseroka, K., Rodriguez-Lonebear, D., Rowe, R., Sara, R., Walker, J. D., Anderson, J., and Hudson, M. (2020). The CARE principles for indigenous data governance. *Data Science Journal*, 19(1), 43. https://doi.org/10.5334/dsj-2020-043

Chen, I. Y., Joshi, S., and Ghassemi, M. (2020). Treating health disparities with artificial intelligence. *Nature Medicine*, 26, 16–17. https://doi.org/10.1038/s41591-019-0649-2

Chouldechova, A. (2017). Fair prediction with disparate impact: A study of bias in recidivism prediction instruments. *Big Data*, 5(2), 153–163. https://doi.org/10.1089/big.2016.0047

Costanza-Chock, S. (2020). *Design Justice; Community-Led Practices to Build the Worlds We Need.* MIT Press. ISBN: 9780262043458. https://mitpress.mit.edu/9780262043458/design-justice/

Daneshjou, R., Smith, M. P., Sun, M. D., Rotemberg, V., and Zou, J. (2022). Lack of transparency and potential bias in artificial intelligence data sets and algorithms: A scoping review. *JAMA Dermatology*, 157(11), 1362–1369. https://doi.org/10.1001/jamadermatol.2021.3129

Fawzy, A., Wu, T. D., Wang, K., Robinson, M. L., Rosenthal, A. Z., Arroyo, A. C., … and Shah, N. H. (2022). Racial and ethnic bias in pulse oximetry and clinical outcomes in critically ill patients. *JAMA Internal Medicine*, 182(7), 730–738. https://doi.org/10.1001/jamainternmed.2022.1906

First Nations Information Governance Centre (FNIGC). (2014). *Ownership, Control, Access and Possession (OCAP®): The path to First Nations information governance.* Ottawa, ON: The First Nations Information Governance Centre. ISBN: 978-0-9879882-8-7. https://fnigc.ca/ocap-training/take-the-course/

Gaebler, J. D., Nilforoshan, H., Shroff, R., and Goel, S. (2023). The measure and mismeasure of fairness. *Journal of Machine Learning Research*, 24(312), 14730–14846. https://dl.acm.org/doi/epdf/10.5555/3648699.3649011

Ghassemi, M., Oakden-Rayner, L., & Beam, A. L. (2021). The false hope of current approaches to explainable AI in health care. *The Lancet Digital Health*, 3(11), e745–e750. https://doi.org/10.1016/S2589-7500(21)00208-9

Grasso, C., Goldhammer, H., Brown, R. J., and Furness, B. W. (2020). Using sexual orientation and gender identity data in electronic health records to assess for disparities in preventive health screening services. *International Journal of Medical Informatics*, 142, 104245. https://doi.org/10.1016/j.ijmedinf.2020.104245

Kleinberg, J., Mullainathan, S., & Raghavan, M. (2017). Inherent trade-offs in the fair determination of risk scores. arXiv:1609.05807. https://arxiv.org/abs/1609.05807

Mitchell, M., Wu, S., Zaldivar, A., Barnes, P., Vasserman, L., Hutchinson, B., … and Gebru, T. (2019). Model cards for model reporting. In *Proceedings of the Conference on Fairness, Accountability, and Transparency* (pp. 220–229). https://doi.org/10.1145/3287560.3287596

National Institute of Standards and Technology. (2023). AI Risk Management Framework 1.0 (NIST SP 1270). https://doi.org/10.6028/NIST.SP.1270

Obermeyer, Z., Powers, B., Vogeli, C., and Mullainathan, S. (2019). Dissecting racial bias in an algorithm used to manage the health of populations. *Science*, 366(6464), 447–453. https://doi.org/10.1126/science.aax2342

Rajkomar, A., Hardt, M., Howell, M. D., Corrado, G., and Chin, M. H. (2018). Ensuring fairness in machine learning to advance health equity. *Annals of Internal Medicine*, 169(12), 866–872. https://doi.org/10.7326/M18-1990

Reisman, D., Schultz, J., Crawford, K., and Whittaker, M. (2018). Algorithmic Impact Assessments: A practical framework for public agency accountability. AI Now Institute. https://ainowinstitute.org/aiareport2018.pdf

Selbst, A. D., Boyd, D., Friedler, S. A., Venkatasubramanian, S., and Vertesi, J. (2019). Fairness and abstraction in sociotechnical systems. In *Proceedings of the Conference on Fairness, Accountability, and Transparency* (pp. 59–68). https://doi.org/10.1145/3287560.3287598

Sjoding, M. W., Dickson, R. P., Iwashyna, T. J., Gay, S. E., and Valley, T. S. (2020). Racial bias in pulse oximetry measurement. *New England Journal of Medicine*, 383(25), 2477–2478. https://doi.org/10.1056/NEJMc2029240

Suresh, H., and Guttag, J. V. (2021). A framework for understanding sources of harm throughout the machine learning lifecycle. *Communications of the ACM*, 64(1), 82–89. https://doi.org/10.1145/3465416.3483305

World Health Organization. (2021). Ethics and governance of artificial intelligence for health: WHO guidance. https://www.who.int/publications/i/item/9789240029200

Zech, J. R., Badgeley, M. A., Liu, M., Costa, A. B., Titano, J. J., and Oermann, E. K. (2018). Variable generalization performance of a deep learning model to detect pneumonia in chest radiographs: A cross-sectional study. *PLOS Medicine*, 15(11), e1002683. https://doi.org/10.1371/journal.pmed.1002683

Part 2

Disability, Education, and Techno-Ableism

Focusing on disability as both an analytic lens and a site of governance, this section critically examines how AI systems in healthcare, education, and digital platforms reproduce ableist norms. The chapters foreground disabled knowledge and lived experience to show how design omissions, accommodation frameworks, and technical standards shape exclusion. By centering disability justice, this section challenges dominant narratives of innovation and inclusion in AI.

DOI: 10.1201/9781003737810-10

9 Disability-Centered Policy Opportunities and Challenges for Accessible and Inclusive AI

A Scoping Review

Christo El Morr, Sabine Fernandes, Damanjot Singh, Vaibhav Sawhney, Rachel da Silveira Gorman and Yahya El-Lahib

INTRODUCTION

The purpose of this scoping review is to identify disability-centered policy opportunities and challenges for accessible and inclusive artificial intelligence (AI). AI has emerged as a noteworthy phenomenon in our contemporary era, with recent mainstream discourses championing it as a tool to revolutionize accessibility. A significant challenge in AI systems is the presence of biases stemming from the datasets used for training and from developers' perspectives. These biases can lead to discriminatory outcomes across sectors such as healthcare, employment, industry, and criminal justice (Kinnula et al., 2021; Kundi et al., 2022). The lack of diversity among AI development teams, particularly regarding marginalized and underrepresented populations, including people with disabilities,[1] exacerbates these biases, underscoring the urgent need for more accessible and inclusive design practices (Moon, 2022).

Moreover, the need for disability-centered AI policy is highlighted by the UN's Special Rapporteur on the rights of persons with disabilities, which discusses how AI systems often overlook disabled people and accessibility needs, leading to discriminatory practices that deepen exclusion (Quinn, 2022). The report emphasizes that AI policies must align with international human rights standards to ensure equal access to these technologies for people with disabilities. It further calls for the active participation of disabled communities in AI design and policymaking, ensuring that their voices are central to the development of inclusive systems that uphold their rights. The OECD's AI Policy Observatory analysis of the EU AI Act underscores the need for disability-centered AI policy by emphasizing the importance of regulations that specifically address AI systems for disabled people (Welker, 2023b). AI can either empower or marginalize people with disabilities, depending on how it is designed and implemented. The EU AI Act seeks to mitigate risks, particularly in high-stakes sectors such as healthcare and employment, where biases can have particularly damaging effects. Similarly, in a World Economic Forum article, Welker (2023a) highlights the potential of generative AI to enhance accessibility, particularly for individuals with speech and other disabilities. However, he warns that neglecting the needs of disabled communities in AI development can lead to further marginalization. Thus, a disability-centered approach to AI policy is essential to ensure meaningful collaboration with disabled users and to mitigate biases and exclusion.

POSITIONALITY

The authors of this paper are all racialized individuals with varying relationships to disability, madness, and chronic illness. Some self-identify as mad (SF), others disabled (SF, CE, RG, YE),

DOI: 10.1201/9781003737810-11

while others have not self-identified yet. Access to disability self-identity is a barriered process for racialized people, due to racist ableism.

DISABILITY JUSTICE FRAMEWORK

We use a Disability Justice perspective to inform our review of the articles under consideration. Disability Justice is a movement led by racialized and queer disabled people in the mid-2000s in the United States, in response to the ways in which the Disability Rights Movement (DRM) excluded multiply marginalized disabled communities. While the DRM shifted from a deficit-based medical model of disability (focused on cure and rehabilitation) to a strengths-based social model (understanding disability as socially constructed), it treats disability as a single-issue identity, leaving out groups like undocumented disabled individuals who may not enjoy the same rights as citizens with disabilities (Sins Invalid, 2019). In contrast, Disability Justice emphasizes intersectionality and addresses systems of oppression, such as capitalism, colonialism, and white supremacy, rather than focusing solely on symptoms of oppression such as barriers (Fernandes et al., 2023). With respect to the development of accessible and inclusive design, one of the key principles of Disability Justice is "leadership of the most impacted" (Sins Invalid, 2019, p. 23). This principle underscores the importance of disabled people in leadership roles within decision-making processes that affect them.

Drawing on this principle and a Disability Justice perspective, Fernandes et al. (forthcoming) reviewed a range of social justice-oriented practices in data and design that prioritize participatory approaches to develop a framework for social justice-oriented practices for accessible and inclusive AI. The framework guides coresearchers and codesigners, as well as academic and industry researchers and designers.

Coresearchers and codesigners must be afforded:

1. **Access to the control of processes from the outset to the outcome.**
   To facilitate accessibility for marginalized and underserved communities in AI, access to governance and management of data and design processes must be supported. Accessibility must be understood as a process of negotiating power imbalances and not simply a product of those with power (researchers) delivering to those who are disempowered in society (coresearchers and codesigners).
2. **Inclusion to challenge power imbalances and systemic violence.**
   To facilitate inclusion for marginalized and underrepresented communities in AI, coresearchers and codesigners must be included to challenge systems of oppression and those in power, including academic and industry researchers and designers. This objective can keep tokenizing forms of inclusion in check.
3. **Empowerment as a self-assessed outcome.**
   To facilitate meaningful accessibility and inclusion, codesigners, coresearchers, and communities most impacted by AI must be consulted for self-assessments of empowerment. Researchers must not assess the empowerment of communities on their behalf.

   While academic and industry researchers and designers must undertake:
4. **Combat extractive logics.**
   To counter exploitative AI, researchers must fight the extractive logics of data and design in an ongoing way. Good intentions and aspirations for justice are empty promises if researchers do not actively challenge the pervasive systems of injustice and extraction within which their research is embedded.
5. **Combat the commodification of "diversity".**
   To meaningfully support equity, researchers must be wary of co-opting the label of "diversity" to market themselves and their research.

6. **Address the practical challenges that arise from the gap between theory and practice.**
   To bring theories of accessible and inclusive AI to life, researchers actively address practical implementation challenges. Researchers must also attend to contradictions between stated values and practices when developing social justice-oriented AI.
7. **Address the ambivalence of legibility.**
   To meaningfully visibilize marginalized and underrepresented communities, researchers must ensure that these communities are afforded the power to shape their representation. Simply making communities experiencing oppression legible, without power to determine the nature of their visibility, can cause those communities more harm than good.
   Thus, we rely on both Disability Justice and a framework for social justice-oriented practices for accessible and inclusive AI to identify disability-centered policy opportunities and challenges for accessible and inclusive AI.

METHODS

The methodology followed the five steps outlined by Arksey and O'Malley (2005): (1) Identifying the research question, (2) Identifying relevant studies (through searches of databases, search engines, etc.), (3) Study selection (screening of abstracts for relevance), (4) Charting the data (study features such as type of technology and disability), (5) Collating, summarizing, and reporting the results.

Search Strategy

The following four online databases were used to conduct a scoping review: ProQuest, IEEE PubMed, and PsycINFO. The literature search strategy was conducted using key search terms established to answer the questions guiding this scoping review. The words included in the search are as follows: AI, artificial intelligence, machine learning, inclusive, user-centered, disability, and disabilities. Of the 380 citations extracted, 162 articles were not duplicates. The complete search strategies are provided in the appendix.

Eligibility Criteria

The inclusion criteria were predetermined and limited to studies published in the last five years, to journal articles and conference papers addressing AI or machine learning, people with disabilities, and participatory processes. Limiting the scoping review to the last five years ensures that the study remains focused on recent advances in AI, which have evolved rapidly. This timeframe encompasses innovations in accessibility and inclusivity, reflecting contemporary standards and addressing current challenges faced by individuals with disabilities. Additionally, recent research incorporates emerging ethical frameworks and societal shifts toward fairness, inclusivity, and transparency in AI systems. By focusing on the last five years, the review stays aligned with contemporary policy developments and provides a relevant analysis of the latest solutions and technologies in this field.

The reasons for focusing on studies published in the last five years is due to AI systems rapidly advancing during this time frame, leading to new frameworks and applications that better address accessibility challenges. The rapid nature of this development highlights the need to focus on recent research, as it reflects the current state of AI technology and its capability to solve contemporary problems. Recent research also aligns with new policies and regulations on AI ethics from organizations like the EU, making it critical for understanding contemporary AI accessibility approaches.

The exclusion criteria were based on excluding studies that were not written in English and were not scholarly publications. As this was a scoping review, the search terms were limited to the titles of the journals. The most recent search was done on July 21, 2023.

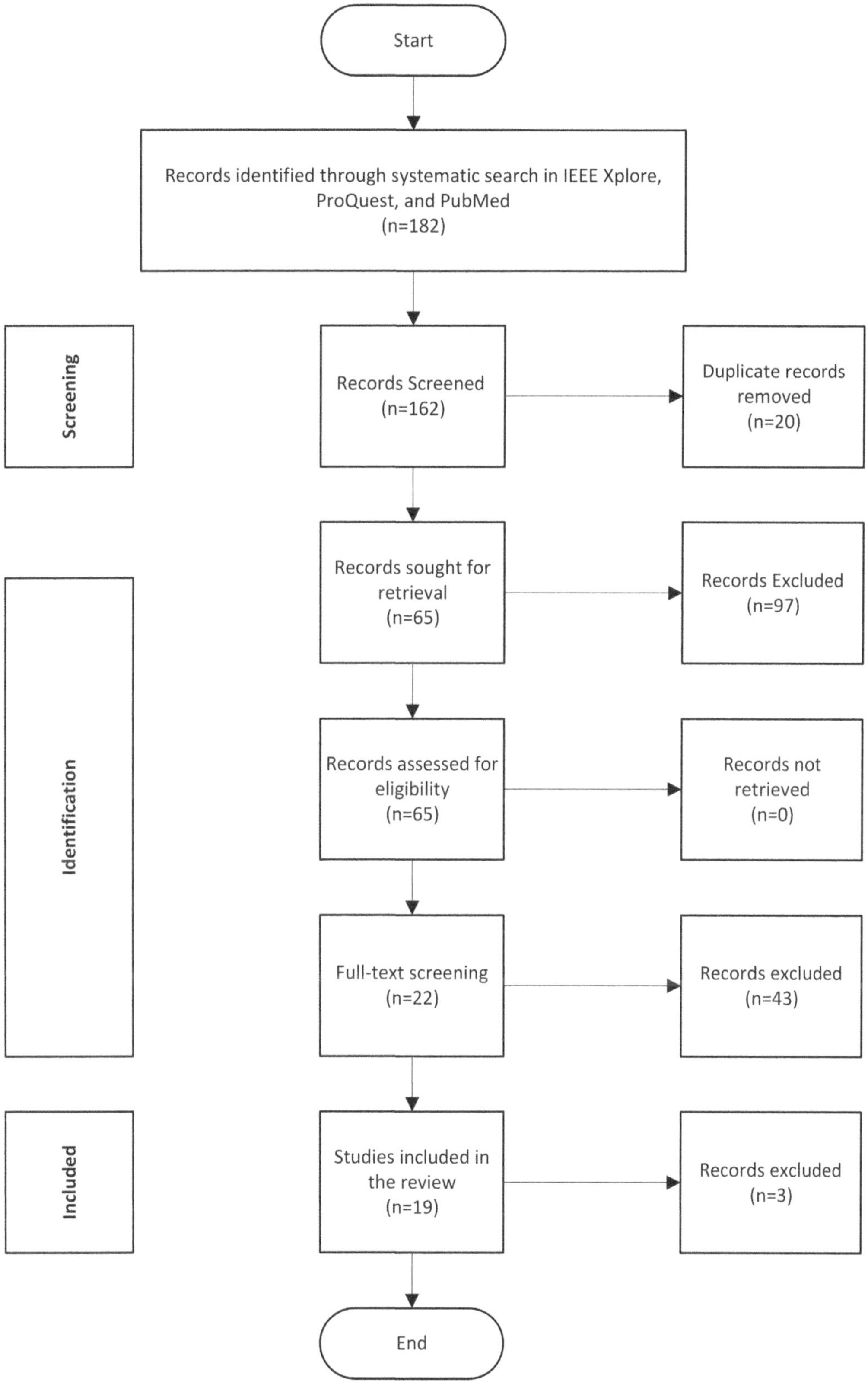

FIGURE 9.1 PRISMA diagram.

Selection Process

The inclusion and exclusion criteria were applied to 162 abstracts. Two authors (DS and VS) employed Rayyan software (Ouzzani et al., 2016) to screen 162 articles, and 65 were identified as potentially eligible. Both authors reviewed the abstracts of the 65 articles retrieved for review and synthesis, and 19 were included in this review (Figure 9.1). The literature search and articles collection were conducted by a single author CE, and the literature review and data collection from articles were conducted by both authors (DS and VS) and were repeated by another author (CE). A discussion was held to reach a consensus in case of any ambiguities and disagreements.

RESULTS

In total, 182 articles were identified, 20 of which were duplicates. Of the 162 unique articles, 97 were excluded based on the content of their abstracts. After reviewing the full texts, the inclusion criteria were applied to the remaining 65 articles. Of the 65 full-text articles screened, 46 were excluded, leaving 19 studies for the final review. A complete summary of the findings is provided in Table 9A.1. In addition, summaries of the population characteristics (countries, disability type, disability model, ethnicity, age, and sex) and methods and outcomes (algorithms, bias mitigation, and outcomes) are provided in Tables 9A.2 and 9A.3, respectively. All three tables are provided in the Appendix.

Population

Across the 19 studies, disability representation was uneven and often limited. Motor disabilities disability (ElGibreen et al., 2022; Lanzillotta et al., 2022; Muñoz et al., 2019; Petrunina et al., 2020; Rocha et al., 2023) and multiple-disability groupings (de Saille et al., 2022; Drolshagen et al., 2020; Guerra et al., 2020; Ingavélez-Guerra et al., 2018; Namoun et al., 2022) were the most commonly addressed, while cognitive (Herbuela et al., 2022; Mariño et al., 2018; Mateos-Sanchez et al., 2022; Raja Vora et al., 2021), visual (Goswami et al., 2023; Gupta & Chen, 2022; Rivas-Pérez et al., 2019), and hearing (Amangeldy et al., 2022; Ballenger, 2022) disabilities were less represented.

Key demographic information was frequently missing. Age data were absent in 21% of studies; sex was reported in only 41% of studies, exclusively in binary terms, and was missing in seven studies (37%). Gender identity was not reported at all. Race or ethnicity was reported in only two studies both lacking diversity**;** participants were 75% white in one (de Saille et al., 2022), and 100% Caucasian in the other (Raja Vora et al., 2021).

A key finding is the **near-absence of justice-oriented disability frameworks**. None of the studies engaged with Disability Justice. Instead:

1. **47%** used a **critical social model** (Ballenger, 2022; Drolshagen et al., 2020; Goswami et al., 2023; Ingavélez-Guerra et al., 2018; Mariño et al., 2018; Mateos-Sanchez et al., 2022; Namoun et al., 2022; Rivas-Pérez et al., 2019; Rocha et al., 2023).
2. **21%** employed a **medical model** framing disabled people primarily through impairment or rehabilitation (Gupta & Chen, 2022; Lanzillotta et al., 2022; Petrunina et al., 2020; Raja Vora et al., 2021).

These patterns indicate that most AI accessibility research does not conceptualize disability as a political, relational, or intersectional category, thereby limiting its capacity to support rights-based, participatory, disability-centered policy. From a Disability Justice perspective—grounded in intersectionality and the leadership of those most impacted—the sparse reporting of race, gender, and other social locations, alongside the predominance of researcher-driven designs, reveals systemic gaps and a lack of participatory, power-sharing approaches with disabled communities.

Concept

The studies encompassed a broad range of AI systems, including machine learning models (Herbuela et al., 2022; Lanzillotta et al., 2022; Rocha et al., 2023), natural language processing and language modeling (Goswami et al., 2023; Mateos-Sanchez et al., 2022; Rivas-Pérez et al., 2019), ontologies (Ingavélez-Guerra et al., 2018; Mariño et al., 2018; Petrunina et al., 2020), chatbots (Gupta & Chen, 2022; Mateos-Sanchez et al., 2022), socially assistive or collaborative robots (de Saille et al., 2022; Drolshagen et al., 2020; Raja Vora et al., 2021), and telepresence technologies (ElGibreen et al., 2022).

Across use cases, AI was positioned to support education (Ballenger, 2022; Goswami et al., 2023; Guerra et al., 2020; Gupta & Chen, 2022; Ingavélez-Guerra et al., 2018; Rivas-Pérez et al., 2019), communication (ElGibreen et al., 2022; Herbuela et al., 2022; Muñoz et al., 2019; Rivas-Pérez et al., 2019), mobility and physical engagement (Raja Vora et al., 2021; Rocha et al., 2023), or personalized and context-aware assistance (Mateos-Sanchez et al., 2022; Namoun et al., 2022).

Despite the focus on accessibility, 79% of studies did **not** address algorithmic bias or ethical implications. Only four studies explicitly acknowledged issues related to data bias, power, or the need for inclusive governance (Gupta & Chen, 2022; Lanzillotta et al., 2022; Petrunina et al., 2020; Raja Vora et al., 2021).

This absence is particularly significant from a Disability Justice standpoint: if AI systems are developed without attending to skewed datasets, oppressive representational logics, or extractive data practices, they may reproduce or intensify structural inequities (Wald, 2020; Kundi et al., 2023).

Context (PCC: Context)

The studies spanned Europe (37%), Asia (26%), South America (21%), and North America (16%), indicating broad geographic interest in AI and disability inclusion. Applications were situated in six main contexts:

- **Education (42%)**—improving autonomy, communication, and access to learning (Ballenger, 2022; Goswami et al., 2023; Guerra et al., 2020; Gupta & Chen, 2022; Herbuela et al., 2022; Ingavélez-Guerra et al., 2018; Muñoz et al., 2019; Rivas-Pérez et al., 2019).
- **Daily living (26%)**—enhancing communication, social participation, or physical engagement (de Saille et al., 2022; ElGibreen et al., 2022; Mariño et al., 2018, 2021, 2023).
- **Home (11%)**—personalized assistive tools (Mateos-Sanchez et al., 2022; Namoun et al., 2022).
- **Laboratory (11%)**—early-stage prototypes (Amangeldy et al., 2022; Petrunina et al., 2020).
- **Healthcare (5%)**—AI-supported assessment of motor disabilities (Lanzillotta et al., 2022).
- **Workplace (5%)**—collaborative robotics to support employment inclusion (Drolshagen et al., 2020).

Across contexts, the majority of systems were **researcher-developed prototypes** with small sample sizes and limited user testing. Very few studies involved disabled people in decision-making roles, governance, or the evaluation of whether the technology was empowering—core principles of Disability Justice and participatory policy development.

Cross-Cutting Gaps and Patterns

Three patterns emerge that directly shape the policy analysis in this chapter:

1. **Minimal participation of disabled people in design or governance**, limiting the ability of AI systems to reflect community-defined access needs.

2. **Sparse consideration of bias, power, and systemic discrimination**, despite these being central concerns for any disability-centered AI policy.
3. **Substantial demographic and representational gaps**, especially regarding race, gender, intersectionality, and disability justice frameworks.

These gaps underscore the urgent need for disability-centered AI policies that mandate participatory governance, require representative datasets, and support inclusive design processes grounded in Disability Justice.

DISCUSSION

The reviewed studies demonstrate that AI technologies offer meaningful potential to support disabled people across diverse global regions and contexts, including education, daily living, employment, home environments, and healthcare. However, their contributions remain preliminary. Most systems were early-stage prototypes tested with small sample sizes, often fewer than 70 participants, and several studies lacked participant involvement altogether. These limitations underscore the nascent state of inclusive AI research and highlight the need for disability-centered policy approaches. Drawing on the seven-point framework by Fernandes et al. (forthcoming), this discussion identifies the opportunities and structural challenges for advancing disability-centered AI.

Access to the Control of Processes from the Outset to Outcome

Ensuring accessibility requires that disabled people have meaningful access to the governance and management of data and design processes. Yet only two studies involved disabled participants in testing the technology (Ballenger, 2022; Rocha et al., 2023), and four studies did not involve participants at all (Ballenger, 2022; Ingavélez-Guerra et al., 2018; Mariño et al., 2018; Petrunina et al., 2020). Without direct involvement, disabled people cannot influence system assumptions, priorities, or outcomes. Disability Justice emphasizes the leadership of those most impacted (Sins Invalid, 2019), making early and continuous participation not optional but foundational to disability-centered AI.

Inclusion to Challenge Power Imbalances and Systemic Violence

Merely including people with disabilities in design is insufficient if they do not hold decision-making power. According to the disability justice framework, even codesign can be tokenistic without real authority over outcomes for disabled people (Piepzna-Samarasinha, 2018). In the two studies that did include participants with disabilities, there is no discussion of participants being afforded the power to challenge researchers and the research, with particular respect to the unequal distribution of power and disability-based discrimination (Ballenger, 2022; Rocha et al., 2023). Moreover, given the overrepresentation of white participants when race was reported in two studies (de Saille et al., 2022; Raja Vora et al., 2021), and the underreporting of race and gender in all the other studies, there is a lack of evidence for opportunities for the inclusion of multiply marginalized participants to challenge racism and gender-based discrimination. Design justice, particularly in AI, advocates for equitable power distribution and meaningful participation for multiply marginalized communities, including people with disabilities (Costanza-Chock, 2018). Such social justice-oriented approaches to developing AI systems are crucial to challenging systemic imbalances in design practices, including disability-based exclusion.

Empowerment as a Self-assessed Outcome

None of the studies engaged participants to self-assess whether the AI designs were empowering for them. Empowerment, in this context, is not just about participating in research but having the ability to self-assess the impacts of design decisions on their daily lives. Small sample sizes in AI-related disability research (de Saille et al., 2022; Raja Vora et al., 2021) risk limiting the voices of disabled populations. Prototyping with larger sample sizes is needed to validate and ensure true inclusivity and empowerment. Empowering people with disabilities requires giving them authority over the assessment and evaluation over design outcomes

Combat Extractive Logics

Extractive approaches to data collection in AI models perpetuate biases. The effectiveness of AI systems relies on data quality, yet nonrepresentative datasets contribute to bias (Kundi et al., 2023; Wald, 2020). Issues such as limited understanding of accents and speech patterns (Ballenger, 2022) show the problematic nature of using AI without proper representation. Moreover, the dominant medical perspective in the studies reveals a rehabilitation-based understanding of disabled people, as individuals requiring fixing and from whom data can be farmed in the service of "cure". AI systems should be designed to avoid exploiting people with disabilities for disability-based data without adequately attending to their needs and lived experiences.

Combat the Commodification of "Diversity"

Tokenistic diversity initiatives, such as reporting only surface-level diversity metrics, undermine genuine inclusion efforts. In the only two studies that identified race, in the first 15 out of 20 participants were classified as white (de Saille et al., 2022), while in the second, all participants were identified as Caucasian (Raja Vora et al., 2021). With respect to the categories of sex and gender in the studies, sex was reported in the binary, and gender was not reported at all, excluding sex and gender diverse identities. Genuine diversity and inclusion in AI systems must incorporate a broad range of intersectional identities and experiences to counter the commodification of "diversity" as merely a compliance checkbox.

Address the Practical Challenges that Arise from the Gap between Theory and Practice

There is often a significant gap between theoretical design principles and their practical applications. In AI-based systems, low performance or high false positives can alienate users. For example, Automatic Speech Recognition systems that misrepresent or over-represent meaningless words (e.g., "um", "like") can frustrate users with disabilities, making these models less effective (Ballenger, 2022). Similarly, in the case of the cobot applications (Drolshagen et al., (2020), the fast and loud movements of robotic arms resulted in discomfort and stress among users. In practice, AI models must account for user comfort and practical needs to bridge the gap between theory and practice.

Address the Ambivalence of Legibility

AI systems sometimes misinterpret or overemphasize data, leading to problematic representations of users, particularly those with disabilities. A model that represents every pause or filler word as meaningful input, for instance, may hinder accessibility rather than aid it (Ballenger, 2022). The ambivalence of legibility—where the system tries to interpret every detail—can lead to user mistrust and discomfort. High-performing models should adapt to user needs, much like human-provided services, to avoid becoming burdensome and ensure visibilizing disabled people in accordance with their demands and access needs.

LIMITATIONS

This review is limited by its scoping methodology, which did not include a formal quality appraisal of the included studies; consequently, the strength of evidence across studies cannot be directly compared. The search was limited to the last five years and included only peer-reviewed journal articles and conference papers in English; this may have omitted earlier or non-English contributions, as well as gray literature and community-based reports. In addition, limiting search terms to "disability/disabilities" may have excluded studies that address disability-related experiences using more specific or community-based terminology (e.g., audism, mobility, neurodivergence), potentially underrepresenting certain forms of inclusion. Finally, many included studies relied on small samples and reported limited demographic information, thereby constraining the generalizability of the findings and limiting the ability to assess equity-related implications fully. Future research could expand search strategies to include additional databases, gray literature, and broader terminology to capture a wider range of relevant studies. It should also incorporate quality appraisal methods to assess the rigor of included research.

POLICY IMPLICATIONS

The policy implications highlighted in this review point to several critical priorities for advancing disability-centered AI. First, AI policies must mandate the meaningful participation of disabled people throughout the entire design, development, and governance life cycle. This requires moving beyond tokenistic consultation toward shared decision-making power, ensuring that disabled people—particularly those most impacted—hold genuine authority over outcomes. Moving beyond tokenism requires shifting from consultation to shared authority. In practice, this means (1) resourcing disabled people—especially those most impacted—to hold decision-making roles (e.g., co-governance or advisory bodies with defined powers, not merely feedback sessions); (2) compensating coresearchers/codesigners and budgeting accessibility needs as core project costs; and (3) building accountability into the research process through transparent documentation of how community input changed the research questions, data practices, design choices, and evaluation criteria. Embedding these mechanisms helps translate inclusion from presence to power, supporting praxis rather than symbolic participation.

Second, policies must address the risks posed by biased and nonrepresentative datasets by establishing standards that prevent extractive data practices and require attention to diverse accents, communication patterns, and disability-specific ways of engaging with technology. Third, policies should reject the commodification of "diversity" by embedding intersectionality into data governance, representation requirements, and design evaluation criteria, with explicit attention to multiply marginalized disabled communities. Finally, policy frameworks must support the translation of theoretical design principles into practice, ensuring that AI systems are evaluated against the lived experiences, access needs, and self-defined measures of empowerment articulated by disabled people themselves.

CONCLUSION

The reviewed studies demonstrate that AI technologies offer substantial potential to enhance accessibility and inclusivity for people with disabilities across various contexts, including education, employment, and healthcare. However, the research remains in its early stages, as evidenced by small sample sizes and limited participant diversity. Empowering marginalized communities through inclusive AI requires more than just their participation; it demands their active involvement in decision-making processes to address power imbalances and systemic inequities. To achieve meaningful progress, AI policies must prioritize genuine involvement of people with disabilities in all stages of development, ensure datasets are representative, and emphasize participatory and collaborative design. By addressing these issues in policy and practice, AI systems can better serve people with disabilities, fostering meaningful accessibility and inclusion.

AUTHORS' CONTRIBUTIONS

CE, RG, and YE designed the study and received the funds. CE supervised DS and VS, who performed and reported the summaries. CE verified the analysis and prepared the first draft. All authors provided critical feedback and revised it; they approved the final version and agreed to be accountable for all aspects of the submitted paper.

FUNDING

This research is funded by the Social Sciences and Humanities Research Council (SSHRC). (Grant No. 872–2022-1025).

ACKNOWLEDGMENT

Portions of this chapter were developed with the assistance of ChatGPT in an editing capacity to improve clarity and flow. All intellectual contributions, interpretations, and final editorial decisions are the authors' own, and the authors take full responsibility for the content. Any AI-assisted or AI-generated material was reviewed and verified by the authors.

REFLECTION QUESTIONS

1. How does the Disability Justice framework differ from the Disability Rights or medical models in how it approaches technology and inclusion?
2. The review found that very few studies involved disabled people in governance or decision-making. What are the consequences of AI systems designed *for* disabled people rather than *with* them?
3. How can AI policies move beyond tokenistic diversity measures to ensure genuine power-sharing with disabled communities?
4. Reflecting on the concept of extractive logics, how can AI researchers ensure they are not exploiting disabled communities for data while ignoring their lived realities?

APPENDIX

SEARCH TERMS

PROQUEST

(noft(artificial intelligence) OR noft(AI) OR noft(Machine learning)) AND (noft(inclusive) OR noft(user-centered) OR noft(user-centred)) AND (noft(disability) OR noft(disabilities))

IEEE XPLORE

((((All Metadata:disability) OR (All Metadata:disabilities))) AND ((All Metadata:inclusive) OR (All Metadata:user-centered) OR (All Metadata:user-centred))) AND ((All Metadata:AI) OR (All Metadata:artificial intelligence) OR (All Metadata:Machine learning))

PUBMED

((AI) OR ("artificial intelligence") OR ("Machine learning")) AND ((inclusive) OR (user-centered) OR (user-centred)) AND ((disability) OR (disabilities)) Filters: in the last five years

PsychINFO

((noft(AI)) OR (noft("artificial intelligence")) OR (noft("Machine learning"))) AND ((noft(inclusive)) OR (noft(user-centered)) OR (noft(user-centred))) AND (noft(disability) OR noft(disabilities))

APPENDIX

TABLE 9A.1
Summary of the Findings

Category	Details
Regions and countries	**Europe (37%)**: de Saille et al. (2022), Drolshagen et al. (2020), Guerra et al. (2020), Mariño et al. (2018), Mateos-Sanchez et al. (2022), Petrunina et al. (2020), Rocha et al. (2023) **Asia (26%)**: Amangeldy et al. (2022), ElGibreen et al. (2022), Goswami et al. (2023), Herbuela et al. (2022), Namoun et al. (2022) **South America (21%)**: Ingavélez-Guerra et al. (2018), Lanzillotta et al. (2022), Muñoz et al. (2019), Rivas-Pérez et al. (2019) **North America (16%)**: Ballenger (2022), Gupta and Chen (2022), Raja Vora et al. (2021)
Settings	**Educational (42%)**: 8 studies **Daily Living (26%)**: 5 studies **Home (11%)**: 2 studies **Laboratory (11%)**: 2 studies **Workplace (5%)**: 1 study **Healthcare (5%)**: 1 study
Educational settings	Focused on enhancing autonomy and learning for disabled students in educational environments using voice assistance, AI tools, and systems for better communication and accessibility (Guerra et al., 2020; Muñoz et al., 2019; Herbuela et al., 2022; Rivas-Pérez et al., 2019; Goswami et al., 2023; Ballenger, 2022; Gupta & Chen, 2022; Ingavélez-Guerra et al., 2018)
Daily living settings	Studies explored how AI and assistive technologies improve social interactions, communication, and engagement in daily activities, such as through emotion-expression robots, socially assistive robots, and ICTs (de Saille et al., 2022; ElGibreen et al., 2022; Mariño et al., 2018; Raja Vora et al., 2021; Rocha et al., 2023)
Home settings	AI-based mobile applications and assistive services for intellectual disabilities and personalized support (Mateos-Sanchez et al., 2022; Namoun et al., 2022)
Healthcare settings	AI used to predict and classify motor disabilities in pediatric patients, aiding in early detection and treatment planning (Lanzillotta et al., 2022)
Workplace Settings	Collaborative robots (cobots) to enhance inclusivity in the labor market for individuals with disabilities (Drolshagen et al., 2020)
Demographics	**Disability**: Motor (5 studies), multiple disabilities (5 studies), cognitive (4 studies), visual (3 studies), hearing (2 studies) **Age**: Children (1–16), adults (16–74), mixed age groups (ElGibreen et al., 2022) **Sex and gender**: Sex missing in 37% of studies; females represented less than 50% in 4 of 8 studies reporting sex; gender not reported **Race**: Reported in 2 studies, omitted in 89%
Model of disability	**Social model (47%)**: 9 studies **Medical model (21%)**: 4 studies **Disability justice perspective**: Not engaged in any studies
AI Bias	15 studies (79%) did not address bias in the models developed

TABLE 9A.2
Studies Population Characteristics

Paper	Region	Country	Disability Type	Disability Model	Ethnicity	Participants (N)	Age	Age Type of Participants	Sex (M/F)	F percentage
Amangeldy et al. (2022)	Asia	Kazakhstan	Hearing	Assistive Tech.	Missing	Missing	8–11	children	Missing	Missing
Ballenger (2022)	North America	United States	Hearing	Social	Missing	NA	NA	NA	NA	NA
de Saille et al. (2022)	Europe	United Kingdom	Many	Assistive Tech.	Missing	20	26–74	Adults	9 F 11 M	45.00%
Drolshagen et al. (2020)	Europe	Germany	Many	Social	Missing	10	21–60	Adults	3 F 7 M	30.00%
ElGibreen et al. (2022)	Asia	Saudi Arabia	Motor	Assistive Tech.	Missing	– Elicitation: 53 – Testing: 30	All	All	30 F	100.00%
Goswami et al. (2023)	Asia	India	Visual	Social	Missing	15	Missing	Missing	Missing	Missing
Guerra et al. (2020)	Europe	Italy	Many	Assistive Tech.	Missing	12	25–60	Adult	7 F 5 M	58.33%
Gupta and Chen (2022)	North America	United States	Visual	Medical	Missing	215	Missing	Missing	83 F 132 M	38.60%
Herbuela et al. (2022)	Asia	Japan	Cognitive	Assistive Tech.	Missing	20	8–16	Children	68% M	32.00%
Ingavélez-Guerra et al. (2018)	South America	Ecuador	Many	Social	Missing	NA	NA	NA	NA	NA
Lanzillotta et al. (2022)	South America	Brazil	Motor	Medical	Missing	70	12.26 ± 3.6	Children	41 F 29 M	58.57%
Mariño et al. (2018)	Europe	Spain	Cognitive	Social	Missing	NA	NA	NA	NA	NA
Mateos-Sanchez et al. (2022)	Europe	Spain	Cognitive	Social	Missing	25	18–55	Adult	Missing	Missing
Muñoz et al. (2019)	South America	Mexico	Motor	Assistive Tech.	Missing	5	16–27	Young Adult	Missing	Missing
Namoun et al. (2022)	Asia	Saudi Arabia	Many	Social	Missing	1,000	Missing	Missing	Missing	Missing
Petrunina et al. (2020)	Europe	Russia	Motor	Medical	Missing	NA	NA	NA	NA	NA
Raja Vora et al. (2021)	North America	United States	Cognitive	Medical	Missing	6	1–7	Children	5 F 1 M	83.33%
Rivas-Pérez et al. (2019)	South America	Costa Rica	Visual	Social	Missing	145	5–12; >20	Children and Adult	Missing	Missing
Rocha et al. (2023)	Europe	France	Motor	Social	Missing	10	Missing	Missing	Missing	Missing

TABLE 9A.3
Studies Outcomes, AI Algorithms, Bias Mitigation, Ethical Challenges

Paper	Setting	AI algorithm	AI type	Ethical/ Bias (Y/N)	Outcome/Aim
Amangeldy et al. (2022)	Laboratory	SVM	SVM	No	Recognizes the Kazakh sign alphabet
Ballenger (2022)	Education	Automatic speech recognition (ASR)	Comparative study	No	To assess ASR software
de Saille et al. (2022)	Daily Living	User-centered design	Design methods	Yes	To develop robotic solutions
Drolshagen et al. (2020)	Workplace	Collaborative robots (Cobots)	Robotics	Yes	Social inclusivity at workplace
ElGibreen et al. (2022)	Daily Living	Mobile robot and text-to-speech	Text-to-speech	No	Development of MRP system
Goswami et al. (2023)	Education	NLP	Robotics	No	Develop a system to specially-abled online learners
Guerra et al. (2020)	Education	Ambient-assisted living	Assistive living	No	Autonomous living and self-dependency
Gupta and Chen (2022)	Education	Chatbots	Chatbots	Yes	Assessing chatbots to support online learning
Herbuela et al. (2022)	Education	Machine learning	NN, SVM, and RF	No	Classify and understand the behaviors of children with PIMD/ID
Ingavélez-Guerra et al. (2018)	Education	Ontologies	Ontologies	No	Identify and rectify accessibility issues in education
Lanzillotta et al. (2022)	Healthcare	Genetic Algorithm-MLP	NN	No	Predict and classify self-care issues in pediatric
Mariño et al. (2018)	Daily Living	Ontologies	Ontologies	No	Accessibility and e-inclusion
Mateos-Sanchez et al. (2022)	Home	NLP	NLP	No	Enhancing social skills
(Muñoz et al., 2019)	Education	Voice recognition	Not described	No	Evaluate software solution
Namoun et al. (2022)	Home	Ontologies	Assistive living	Yes	Inclusion in user-centered designs
Petrunina et al. (2020)	Laboratory	Ontological methods	Ontologies	No	Increasing the efficiency of diagnosis
Raja Vora et al. (2021)	Daily Living	Robot	Robotics	No	Study children's physical activity
Rivas-Pérez et al. (2019)	Education	Language modeling	Language Modeling	No	Accessibility
Rocha et al. (2023)	Daily Living	Machine learning	SVM and RF	No	Enhance inclusion and engagement

NOTE

1 We use both person-first and identity-first disability language in this article to reflect the diverse ways in which people in disability communities self-identify.

REFERENCES

Amangeldy, N., Saule, K., Kassymova, A., Karipzhanova, A., Razakhova, B., & Kuralov, S. (2022). Sign Language Recognition Method based on Palm Definition Model and Multiple Classification. *Sensors, 22*(17), 6621. https://doi.org/10.3390/s22176621

Arksey, H., & O'Malley, L. (2005). Scoping Studies: Towards a Methodological Framework. *International Journal of Social Research Methodology, 8*(1), 19–32. https://doi.org/10.1080/1364557032000119616

Ballenger, S. (2022). Access for Deaf and Hard of Hearing Individuals in Informational and Educational Remote Sessions. *Assistive Technology Outcomes & Benefits, 16*(2), 45–55.

Costanza-Chock, S. (2018). Design Justice, AI, and Escape from the Matrix of Domination. *Journal of Design and Science, 3*(5). https://jods.mitpress.mit.edu/pub/costanza-chock/release/4

de Saille, S., Kipnis, E., Potter, S., Cameron, D., Webb, C. J. R., Winter, P., O'Neill, P., Gold, R., Halliwell, K., Alboul, L., Bell, A. J., Stratton, A., & McNamara, J. (2022). Improving Inclusivity in Robotics Design: An Exploration of Methods for Upstream Co-Creation. *Front Robot AI, 9*, 731006. https://doi.org/10.3389/frobt.2022.731006

Drolshagen, S., Pfingsthorn, M., Gliesche, P., & Hein, A. (2020). Acceptance of Industrial Collaborative Robots by People With Disabilities in Sheltered Workshops. *Front Robot AI, 7*, 541741. https://doi.org/10.3389/frobt.2020.541741

ElGibreen, H., Ghada Al, A., AlMegren, R., AlEid, R., & AlQahtani, S. (2022). Telepresence Robot System for People with Speech or Mobility Disabilities. *Sensors, 22*(22), 8746. https://doi.org/10.3390/s22228746

Fernandes, S., Navia, D., & Rouholamini, M. (2023). Environmental Scan of Access Practices in Arts Funding. In *Canada Council for the Arts*. https://canadacouncil.ca/research/research-library/2023/10/environmental-scan-of-access-practices-in-arts-funding

Goswami, T., Javaji, S. R., & Nagwanshi, K. K. (2023, 2023/03/18/20). Framework for Voice-controlled AI Teaching Assistant for Specially-abled. *2023 3rd International conference on Artificial Intelligence and Signal Processing* (AISP).

Guerra, B. M. V., Ramat, S., Beltrami, G., & Schmid, M. (2020). Automatic Pose Recognition for Monitoring Dangerous Situations in Ambient-Assisted Living. *Frontiers in Bioengineering and Biotechnology, 8*, 415. https://doi.org/10.3389/fbioe.2020.00415

Gupta, S., & Chen, Y. (2022). Supporting Inclusive Learning Using Chatbots? A Chatbot-Led Interview Study. *Journal of Information Systems Education, 33*(1), 98–108.

Herbuela, V. R. D. M., Karita, T., Furukawa, Y., Wada, Y., Toya, A., Senba, S., Onishi, E., & Saeki, T. (2022). Machine Learning-based Classification of the Movements of Children with Profound or Severe Intellectual or Multiple Disabilities Using Environment Data Features. *PLoS ONE, 17*(6), 32. https://doi.org/10.1371/journal.pone.0269472

Ingavélez-Guerra, P., Robles-Bykbaev, V., Otón, S., Vera-Rea, P., Galán-Men, J., Ulloa-Amaya, M., & Hilera, J. R. (2018, 2018/11/28/30). A proposal based on knowledge modeling and ontologies to support the accessibility evaluation process of learning objects. *2018 Congreso Argentino de Ciencias de la Informática y Desarrollos de Investigación (CACIDI).*

Kinnula, M., Iivari, N., Sharma, S., Eden, G., Turunen, M., Achuthan, K., Nedungadi, P., Avellan, T., Thankachan, B., & Tulaskar, R. (2021). *Researchers' Toolbox for the Future: Understanding and Designing Accessible and Inclusive Artificial Intelligence (AIAI)* Proceedings of the 24th International Academic Mindtrek Conference, Tampere/Virtual, Finland. https://doi.org/10.1145/3464327.3464965

Kundi, B., El Morr, C., Gorman, R., & Dua, E. (2022). Artificial Intelligence and Bias: A Scoping Review. In C. El Morr (Ed.), *AI and Society* (pp. 199–215). CRC Press Taylor & Francis. https://doi.org/10.1201/9781003261247-15

Kundi, B., El Morr, C., Gorman, R., & Dua, E. (2023). Artificial Intelligence and Bias: A Scoping Review. In C. El Morr (Ed.), *AI and Society: Tensions and Opportunities* (pp. 199–213). CRC Press Taylor & Francis. https://doi.org/10.1201/9781003261247-15

Lanzillotta, M., Ma, R., Accardi, M., RaviChandran, N., Zaernia, A., Youseffi, M., & Parisi, L. (2022). Neuroevolutionary Intelligent System to Aid Diagnosis of Motor Impairments in Children. *Applied Intelligence, 52*(9), 10757–10767. https://doi.org/10.1007/s10489-021-03126-3

Mariño, B. D. R., RodríGuez-FóRtiz, M. J., Torres, M. V. H., & Haddad, H. M. (2018). Accessibility and Activity-Centered Design for ICT Users: ACCESIBILITIC Ontology. *IEEE Access*, *6*, 60655–60665. https://doi.org/10.1109/ACCESS.2018.2875869

Mateos-Sanchez, M., Amparo Casado, M., Laura Sánchez, B., & Fermoso García, A. M. (2022). Chatbot, as Educational and Inclusive Tool for People with Intellectual Disabilities. *Sustainability*, *14*(3), 1520. https://doi.org/10.3390/su14031520

Moon, M. (2022). Disability and the inclusive intention. *Journal of Museum Education*, *47*(2), 125–129. https://doi.org/10.1080/10598650.2022.2082726

Muñoz, J. G. S., Verdugo, A. I. d. C., González, E. G., Bringas, J. A. S., & Garcia, M. P. (2019, 2019/11/30/Oct.–1). Programming by Voice Assistance Tool for Physical Impairment Patients Classified in to Peripheral Neuropathy Centered on Arms or Hands Movement Difficulty. *2019 International Conference on Inclusive Technologies and Education (CONTIE).*

Namoun, A., Adnan Ahmed Abi, S., Tufail, A., Alshanqiti, A., Nawaz, W., & BenRhouma, O. (2022). A Two-Phase Machine Learning Framework for Context-Aware Service Selection to Empower People with Disabilities. *Sensors*, *22*(14), 5142. https://doi.org/10.3390/s22145142

Ouzzani, M., Hammady, H., Fedorowicz, Z., & Elmagarmid, A. (2016). Rayyan—a Web and Mobile App for Systematic Reviews. *Systematic Reviews*, *5*(1), 210. https://doi.org/10.1186/s13643-016-0384-4

Petrunina, E., Istomina, T., Istomin, V., Trub, N., Murashkina, T., & Shubin, I. (2020, 2020/03/11/13). Intelligent Information and Measurement System of Monitoring Results and BFB-Trainings. *2020 Moscow Workshop on Electronic and Networking Technologies (MWENT).*

Piepzna-Samarasinha, L. L. (2018). *Care Work: Dreaming Disability Justice*. Arsenal Pulp Press.

Quinn, G. (2022). *Artificial intelligence and the rights of persons with disabilities*. Office of the High Commissioner for Human Rights. Retrieved December 10 from https://www.ohchr.org/sites/default/files/2022-02/Easy-Read-AI-disabilities-report.pdf

Raja Vora, J., Helmi, A., Zhan, C., Olivares, E., Vu, T., Wilkey, M., Noregaard, S., Fitter, N. T., & Logan, S. W. (2021). Influence of a Socially Assistive Robot on Physical Activity, Social Play Behavior, and Toy-Use Behaviors of Children in a Free Play Environment: A Within-Subjects Study. *Front Robot AI*, *8*, 768642. https://doi.org/10.3389/frobt.2021.768642

Rivas-Pérez, T., Meza-Vega, A., Mora-Lezcano, V., Palacio-Amador, D., & Chacón-Rivas, M. (2019, 2019/11/30/Oct.–1). EULER - Mathematical Editing by Voice Input for People with Visual Impairment. *2019 International Conference on Inclusive Technologies and Education (CONTIE).*

Rocha, J. M., Luna, J. C., Monacelli, E., Foggea, G., Passedouet, M., Delaplace, S., & Hirata, Y. (2023, 2023/04/21/23). Dance Gestures Recognition for Wheelchair Control. *2023 8th International Conference on Control and Robotics Engineering (ICCRE).*

Sins Invalid. (2019). *Skin, Tooth, and Bone: The Basis of Movement is Our People: A Disability Justice Primer*. Sins Invalid.

Wald, M. (2020). AI Data-Driven Personalisation and Disability Inclusion. *Front Artif Intell*, *3*, 571955. https://doi.org/10.3389/frai.2020.571955

Welker, Y. (2023a, November 3, 2023). *Generative AI holds transformative potential for people with disabilities*. World Economic Forum. https://www.weforum.org/agenda/2023/11/generative-ai-holds-potential-disabilities/

Welker, Y. (2023b, June 21, 2023). *How will the EU AI Act protect people with disabilities? OECD AI Policy Observatory*. World Economic Forum. https://oecd.ai/en/wonk/eu-ai-act-disabilities

10 Rethinking Artificial Intelligence for Sickle Cell Disease – A Bounded Justice and Disability Justice Approach

Vanessa Ferguson

INTRODUCTION

Advancements in artificial intelligence (AI) to improve the management of sickle cell disease (SCD) represent a revolutionary period in healthcare. In the wake of current challenges in diagnosing, managing, and treating SCD, AI offers an opportunity to address these issues and improve the quality of life for those affected by SCD (Elsabagh et al., 2023; El Hoss et al., 2022). However, many empirical findings suggest that many AI-enabled health technologies (AI-EHT) are limited by biomedical hegemony, where reductionist solutions are privileged over interventions that address structural inequities. The politics of SCD reveal how the disease is limited by biomedical hegemony, too, at the intersections of race and racism. When AI is used for SCD, reductionist solutions risk perpetuating inequities in SCD. In line with this logic, this chapter argues that AI-EHT must move beyond biological reductionism and address contemporary and historical injustices that affect those with SCD. Using Melissa Creary's Bounded Justice framework, Disability Justice principles, and Carla Rice's Cripping Transmethodologies, which resists biomedical dominant and imagines alternative patient-centred futures, this chapter explores how AI-EHT for SCD can be leveraged to promote equitable and patient-centred solutions that challenge dominant biomedical hegemony.

LITERATURE REVIEW

SCD refers to a group of genetic blood disorders characterized by abnormal haemoglobin molecules, resulting in sickle-shaped red blood cells (Elendu et al., 2023; Royal et al., 2021). This leads to many clinical manifestations, influenced by genetic and non-genetic factors (Royal et al., 2021), with the most common complication being recurring episodes of severe pain, known as vaso-occlusive crises (Elendu et al., 2023). Other clinical manifestations include anaemia, fatigue, increased susceptibility to infection, acute chest syndrome, organ damage, and stroke (Elendu et al., 2023; Royal et al., 2021). Over 20 million people worldwide live with SCD, particularly those of African, Caribbean, Mediterranean, Middle Eastern, and South Asian descent (Royal et al., 2021). Despite the global distribution of SCD, the disease is mischaracterized as a "Black disease" (Royal et al., 2021), reflecting a racialized framing. This framing contributes to systematic neglect, with treatment and management options focused mainly on biological implications (Royal et al., 2021). In contrast, social implications, like racism, discrimination, stigma, lack of access to care, and poor healthcare quality, often go overlooked (Marshall & Treadwell, 2024).

Amid advancements in AI and SCD, AI has the potential to improve the diagnosis, research, prediction of outcomes and optimization of SCD treatment (Elsabagh et al., 2023). Given current challenges across diagnosis, management, and treatment of SCD (Elsabagh et al., 2023; El Hoss et al.,

DOI: 10.1201/9781003737810-12

2022), AI presents an opportunity to improve the quality of life for those with the disease. Proposed AI-EHT for SCD include Douglass et al.'s investigation into a lensless encoding biosensor that could differentiate between sickle and healthy red blood cells (Elsabagh et al., 2023; Douglass et al., 2022). Another proposed technology is Sachdev et al.'s risk score predictor, which integrates clinical, laboratory and imaging results to predict mortality for those diagnosed with SCD (Douglass et al., 2022; Sachdev et al., 2021). Many proposed applications focus on the biological implications of SCD (Elsabagh et al., 2023), with only a few intended to address social implications. Thus, greater attention to the social implications of SCD within these applications is essential to ensure that AI-EHT will not reproduce a limited framing of the disease and associated inequities, but instead advance justice and equity in healthcare.

THEORETICAL FRAMEWORKS AND KEY CONCEPTS

Biological Reductionism

Biological reductionism refers to a "reductionist method of dissecting biological systems into their constituent parts [to explain the basis of a phenomenon]" (Van Regenmortel, 2004). Reductionists analyse larger systems by breaking them down into their constituent parts to determine the connections between parts, assuming that isolated parts have sufficient explanatory power to provide an understanding of the whole system (Van Regenmortel, 2004). Although successful in the early days of molecular biology, many biologists claim biological reductionism has reached its limit since biological phenomena are extremely complex, with emergent properties that cannot be explained by studying their parts (Van Regenmortel, 2004). The reductionist approach thus has implications for various areas of biomedical research. The promotion of biological reductionism closely parallels its crude forms, like eugenics, genetic essentialism, and racialization, all of which promote inequality, especially for marginalized communities (Stetsenko, 2018). Thus, when SCD and many AI-EHT solutions for the disease are framed through reductionist views, unique consequences may arise, all of which are to be discussed in later sections.

Bounded Justice Framework

Melissa Creary's Bounded Justice framework helps us understand the limitations of reductionist solutions concerning AI-EHT. Bounded justice "reveals the political idealism of equity-based policies by highlighting the realities of social, cultural, and economic norms" (Creary, 2021). Bounded justice shows how impossible it may be to attend to justice when policies, practices, and the institutions they are situated in "fail to recognize how the beneficiaries have historically embodied the cumulative effects of marginalization [racism and other historically entrenched -isms], [undermining] the effectiveness of the intended [attempts at] justice" (Creary, 2021). Bounded justice is linked to other concepts (e.g., structural violence, ecological frameworks of health, intersectionality, and embodiment) that meaningfully "address the entanglement of justice, inclusion, and citizenship for vulnerable populations" (Creary, 2021). Such concepts, including biological reductionism, offer distinct ways to help conceptualize how deployed justice tactics, like AI-EHT, are limited (Creary, 2021).

Disability Justice and Principles

Disability justice frames our understanding of SCD, highlighting the need to move beyond reductionist framing and solutions. Disability justice calls attention to how ableism is linked with other systems of oppression, centring the needs and voices of "disabled people of colour, immigrants with disabilities, queers with disabilities" – amongst others (Commission on Disability Equity, n.d.). Ten principles of the Sins Invalid disability justice framework include intersectionality, leadership of those most impacted, anti-capitalist polices, commitment to cross-movement organizing, recognizing wholeness, sustainability, commitment to cross-disability solidarity, interdependence, collective access, and collective liberation (Commission on Disability Equity, n.d.). In the context of AI-EHT for SCD, disability justice presents an opportunity to critically assess the extent to which these technologies pathologize SCD as a problem to be solved through reductionist technological intervention, as opposed to sites of solidary, resistance and community. Disability justice principles offer an entry point to alternative framings of disease and potential solutions that move beyond reductionist views towards sites mentioned above.

Cripping Transmethodologies Framework

Carla Rice's Cripping Transmethodologies framework challenges AI-EHT reductionist solutions for SCD and imagines new use cases that would promote equitable and patient-centred solutions. Cripping Transmethodologies refers to the "practice [of engaging] multiple, seemingly discordant fields, genres, and sensory registers in transversal processes to expand disabled people's access to art and to build crip culture" (Rice et al., 2024). Transmethodologies question the need for theoretical-methodological alignment, instead encouraging "well-justified transversal bridging and crossing to bring to light the often messy, non-linear and complex research process required to cultivate difference-affirming practices toward system-transforming praxis" (Rice et al., 2024). The framework urges that different and proliferating ways of interacting with the world offer new pathways for being and becoming, in contrast to dominant frameworks that accept the fact that new technologies may lead to the creation of more normative embodiments. Concerning AI-EHT for SCD, Cripping Transmethodologies offers an entry point to understand and challenge technologies that reproduce normative views, offering entry points to the co-creation of new technologies.

MAIN BODY

Biological Reductionism and the Obscurity of Social Injustice

While biological reductionism has historically been effective at explaining the basis of many phenomena within medicine, many have begun to actualize the limitations of reductionist views (Van Regenmortel, 2004). Since biological systems are complex, with emergent, robust, and modular properties that cannot be explained or predicted by simply understanding their parts, biological reductionist approaches undermine their complexity, having detrimental effects on various areas of biomedical research (Van Regenmortel, 2004). For example, the U.S. Food and Drug Administration has seen a steady decline in the number of new and approved drugs, which is arguably attributed to the fact that many drug discovery approaches have been guided by reductionist views, which completely misunderstand biology, organisms, and patients (Van Regenmortel, 2004). More areas where reductionist views have limitations in medicine include the rational design of vaccines (Van Regenmortel, 2004), the biopsychosocial concept of mental disorders (Kotsyubinsky & Kotsyubinsky, 2023), and the immunological study of infectious diseases (Rivas et al., 2017), among others.

Reductionist views can also obscure attempts at social justice (Stetsenko, 2018). Reductionist views in psychology and neighbouring disciplines may be to blame for top-down control, rigid achievement testing and the ongoing inequality in the education crisis more broadly (Stetsenko, 2018). Racial disparities in education are attributed to biological differences between races, rather than social inequalities, where neurological and genetic essentialism tend to deepen social divisions and promote forms of social segregation (Stetsenko, 2018). As a result, differences among individuals "appear large, unbridgeable, inevitable, unchangeable, and ordained by nature" (Stetsenko, 2018), even though such erroneous beliefs have been disproved, like the fact that "racial groups are not genetically discrete, reliably measured, or scientifically meaningful" (Stetsenko,

2018). In education, the implications of reductionist and essentialist views are drastic (e.g., passive transmission-based models of pedagogy with its focus on meaningless information processing, mechanical memorization, compliance with authority, and top-down control) (Stetsenko, 2018). For racialized individuals, "when people rationalize racial disparities with biological beliefs, they tend to have less motivation to redress them as they are seen as predetermined" (Stetsenko, 2018). Racial disparities become seen as a matter of fact and unmitigable, which further perpetuates such disparities (Stetsenko, 2018).

Reductionist views can obscure various attempts at social justice, not only in education but also in medicine. Reductionist views parallel their most crude forms, like eugenics and genetic essentialism (Stetsenko, 2018), perpetuating inequities in unique ways. Reductionist views in our understanding of SCD and proposed AI-EHT solutions have the potential to impede attempts to achieve social justice in ways that obscure the complexity of SCD, overlooking broader social determinants of health. Proposed AI-EHT solutions for SCD that are trained only on biological markers of the disease and do not account for the lived experience of patients, such as racism or systematic neglect, risk reinforcing health inequities rather than remedying them. In education and medicine, reductionist views simplify complex phenomena while upholding dominant power structures by explaining phenomena as a problem within an individual's biological makeup, rather than within broader social systems. In the case of SCD, this looks like localizing complications to mere genes, when healthcare professionals are complicit in discriminatory care attitudes, which in turn implicates and worsens health outcomes (Marshall & Treadwell, 2024). Although reductionist views are deeply entrenched in various disciplines, there exists a growing body of evidence, framed around transformative agency and activist stance, that argues against such views and instead promotes equality and social justice (Stetsenko, 2018). This body of evidence is beyond the scope of this chapter; however, through Creary's Bounded Justice framework, disability justice principles, and Rice's Cripping Transmethodologies framework, it is possible to envision justice-forward applications of AI-EHT in SCD in ways that honour transformative agency and the activist stance.

Bounded Justice, Biological Reductionism, and the Limits of Equity-Driven AI

Bounded justice highlights the realities of social, cultural, and economic norms to reveal the political idealism of equity-based policies (Creary, 2021). Bounded justice, a framework and analytic tool, shows how AI-EHT for SCD are bound by and situated within dominant power structures that ultimately undermine attempts at equity and justice. Most proposed AI-EHT applications are framed as biologically reductionist solutions and fail to recognize the cumulative effects of reductionism for those with SCD. For example, the monogenetic nature of SCD has fuelled dominant discourses that focus heavily on the pathophysiology, biological causes (e.g., genetics) and symptoms (Serjeant, 2013; Elendu et al., 2023). Treatment options like Hydroxyurea, a medication that increases the production of foetal haemoglobin, are proven effective in reducing the severity and frequency of recurring pain episodes in SCD (Chukwuka et al., 2023), but it is reductionist in nature, localizing treatment at the genetic level. Other examples include curative gene and stem cell therapies for the disease (Royal et al., 2021).

Consequences of a reductionist framing of SCD mean that social consequences of the disease remain neglected, implicating health outcomes. For example, SCD is heavily associated with stigma rooted in racism, disease status, socioeconomic status, or pain treatment (McCormick, Osei-Anto, & Martinez, 2020), where healthcare providers often ascribe negative characteristics to patients, labelling them as "drug seekers" or immune to pain (Anionwu & Atkin, 2001). This stigma can lead to barriers in accessing care and impose a psychological burden, ultimately affecting quality of life (McCormick, Osei-Anto, & Martinez, 2020). It has been documented that the emergency department is the last resort for those with SCD in Ontario, Canada, facing complications due to stigmatization and racism (CBC, 2021). SCD affects anyone regardless of race, but because of the wrongful association with racialized bodies, SCD is also associated with racism and related health inequity

(McCormick, Osei-Anto, & Martinez, 2020). Nearly 100% of those with SCD experience racism (Mougianis et al., 2020). This racialized framing manifests as healthcare providers expressing racist beliefs, lowering the quality of care and pain treatment received by racialized individuals with SCD (McCormick, Osei-Anto, & Martinez, 2020). This framing also manifests as unequal levels of funding and research (McCormick, Osei-Anto, & Martinez, 2020).

Proposed AI-EHT applications for SCD, like Douglass et al.'s investigation into a lensless encoding biosensor (Elsabagh et al., 2023; Douglass et al., 2022) or Sachdev et al.'s risk predictor that predicts mortality (Douglass et al., 2022; Vandana Sachdev et al., 2021), propose reductionist solutions, neglecting other important factors that shape health, like stigma and racism. These proposed AI-EHT applications fail to acknowledge the consequences of reductionist solutions and disease framing. While intended to be a low-cost disease identification tool (2022), Douglass et al. fail to acknowledge that racialized communities have limited access to healthcare and avoid healthcare systems altogether. If marginalized communities avoid healthcare systems, who will benefit from the proposed application? How will equity and justice be achieved when the proposed application is bound by dominant power structures? Moreover, Sachdev et al. fail to acknowledge stigma, racism, and other social factors that implicate risk assessment and health. How can this AI-EHT accurately assess risk when relevant factors beyond clinical, laboratory and imaging data are left out of the model? How will equity and justice be achieved when the proposed application ignores highly relevant factors that implicate health outcomes? When proposed applications of AI-EHT are bound by biological reductionism and other-isms, like discrimination and racism, while also failing to recognize their cumulative effects, their limitation in pursuing equity and justice becomes evident.

Disability Justice: Challenging Reductionist and Technocratic Framings of AI-EHT for SCD

Disability justice helps call attention to how ableism is linked with other systems of oppression, centring the needs and voices of disabled communities (Commission on Disability Equity, n.d.). Concerning AI-EHT for SCD, disability justice principles highlight the flawed framing of the disease and limitations of proposed solutions. Disability justice principles challenge ableism and other forms of marginalization. While proposed AI-EHTs for SCD are framed around the promotion of equity and justice (Elsabagh et al., 2023), most solutions are technocratic, reductionist, and ableist. Sachdev et al.'s risk score predictor, which integrates clinical, laboratory, and imaging results to predict mortality for those diagnosed with SCD (Douglass et al., 2022; Vandana Sachdev et al., 2021), operates on the premise that mortality risk is something that can be objectively predicted with biological data, privileging technocentric solutions over the lived experiences of those with SCD, including social determinants of health (e.g., racism, access to care, quality of care). Arguably, this proposed AI-EHT assumes that minimizing mortality risk in SCD is the most important outcome, upholding ableist views that prioritize survival, functionality, and normalization of the body over quality of life, autonomy, and holistic accounts of well-being. When AI-EHT for SCD, like Sachdev et al.'s risk score predictor, focuses only on clinical, laboratory, and imaging data, the tool misses broader social, racial, and ableist factors that shape health outcomes for those with SCD. Questions of justice and equity remain sidelined, even though efficiencies at the biomedical level may be achieved, privileging risk management over social justice.

Disability justice offers an opportunity to reframe our understanding of SCD and reimagine potential applications of AI-EHT for SCD. Disability justice asks us to see disabled people with SCD as complete individuals situated within broader social contexts and bound by various oppressive systems (Commission on Disability Equity, n.d.), rather than deficits that need to be corrected. Essential to this reframing is a consideration of the Sins Valid ten principles of disability justice (Commission on Disability Equity, n.d.), which ask us to rethink AI-EHT for SCD in ways that are patient-centred, community-defined, and justice-oriented, while challenging reductionist applications of AI-EHT for SCD. The principle of recognizing wholeness challenges the framing of those with SCD as people to be fixed or cured, emphasizing that those with SCD are valuable regardless of bodily capacities. The principle of collective access challenges the evaluation of AI-EHT to move beyond an assessment of accuracy and efficiency and towards an assessment of the extent to which AI-EHT promotes inclusion, equity, and justice. In addition, the principle of leadership of those most impacted urges that those with SCD (e.g., racialized and disabled) are involved in all stages of the technology's development, implementation, and evaluation. Through disability justice principles and related methodologies, we can reframe our understanding of SCD and influence AI-EHT in ways that will promote patient-centred, community-driven, and justice-centred approaches.

DISCUSSION

Cripping Transmethodologies: Justice-Centred and Patient-Driven AI-EHT for SCD

Carla Rice's Cripping Transmethodologies offer an entry point to reimagine AI-EHT for SCD in a way that promotes patient-centred and justice-oriented futures. Rice's approach, rooted in critical disability studies, crip theory and anti-racist, feminist and decolonial methods, challenges reductionist and technocratic solutions through centring the knowledge, lived experience, and creativity of marginalized and disabled communities (Rice et al., 2024). Within this framework, "cripping" functions as a political, methodological, imaginative act that allows us to envision alternative futures where disability and illness are not pathologized to be "cured" or eradicated, and instead where disability becomes a valued aspect of humanity (Rice et al., 2024). Applied to AI-EHT for SCD, cripping rejects reductionist solutions that prioritize biological or genetic modification, instead insisting that lived experiences of racism, stigma, and systemic neglect are central determinants of health, equity, and justice. This disrupts the predominant focus on efficiency in diagnostics and risk prediction and instead shifts the focus towards the detection of discriminatory or racist care, the mapping of inequities, or the modelling of health outcomes related to anti-racist interventions, which expand the scope, purpose, and possibilities of AI-EHT.

Rice's methodology views disabled artists as "creative technologists" who reconfigure and reimagine technologies through disruptive transmethodological practices that promote access and other rights to health as a process rather than a product or outcome (Rice et al., 2024). Another key aspect of cripping is co-creation, which in this context involves embedding racialized, disabled, and other marginalized communities in each phase of the development, deployment, and evaluation of AI-EHT for SCD (Rice et al., 2024). This also further aligns with Disability Justice principles, like collective access and leadership of the most impacted, both of which ensure that AI-EHT for SCD prioritizes community needs. Most importantly, cripping invites speculative thinking beyond reductionist solutions and futurity. Rather than envisioning a "future without SCD," AI-EHT for SCD could support improving the quality of life for those with the disease through the facilitation of peer networks and support groups, the reallocation of resources that align with community-defined well-being or patient storytelling, all of which position AI-EHT as a tool for empowerment and solidarity. Cripping Transmethodologies in the context of AI-EHT for SCD pushes back against attempts at justice that are bound by reductionist, technocratic and other marginalizing frameworks, reorienting proposed technologies towards justice-centred, patient-driven possibilities. Such possibilities challenge and resist structural oppressions, while reconfiguring the possibilities of equitable health outcomes.

CONCLUSION

Advancements in AI to improve SCD offer opportunities to address challenges related to the management of the disease. However, many proposed AI-EHT for SCD remain bound by biomedical hegemony and reductionist solutions that overlook structural inequities that shape the lived experiences of those with SCD. As described, a reductionist framing of AI-EHT for SCD risks the perpetuation of inequities and injustices associated with race, racism, and ableism. Creary's Bounded Justice framework and Disability Justice principles highlight the necessity of addressing the cumulative effects of marginalization while centring the needs of racialized and disabled communities in the application of AI-EHT for SCD. Rice's Cripping Transmethodologies offers an imaginative methodological intervention framework that allows us to envision AI-EHT that moves beyond reductionist, technocratic and curative logics towards justice-oriented, patient-driven futures. Co-created with the voices and leadership of those most impacted, namely, those with SCD, AI-EHT can be utilized to address systemic neglect, mitigate discriminatory care, and promote community-defined well-being. Reimagining AI-EHT for SCD through these frameworks promotes a shift away from reductionist biomedical approaches to equity and justice towards comprehensive and patient-centred solutions that challenge and resist historical and contemporary injustices and inequities. Here, AI-EHT can be leveraged as a transformative, justice-oriented technology in SCD and beyond.

ACKNOWLEDGEMENT

Portions of this chapter were developed with the assistance of ChatGPT for editing and brainstorming. All intellectual contributions, interpretations, and final editorial decisions are the authors' own, and the authors take full responsibility for the content. Any AI-assisted or AI-generated material was reviewed and verified by the authors.

REFLECTION QUESTIONS

1. How does biological reductionism shape and/or limit our understanding of diseases, like SCD?
2. What are the potential consequences of reductionist approaches to AI-EHT?
3. In what ways can disability justice frameworks and principles challenge dominant biomedical approaches in AI-EHT?
4. How might social factors (e.g., racism, stigma, systematic neglect, poor access to care, etc.) interact with biological factors to shape health outcomes for those with diseases like SCD? Why is it important for AI-EHT to address both factors?
5. How might justice-centred frameworks and approaches in AI-EHT expand the possibilities for equitable healthcare futures?

REFERENCES

Anionwu, E., & Atkin, K. (2001). *The Politics of Sickle Cell and Thalassaemia*. Open University Press.

CBC Radio. (2021, August 14). *ER a "Last Resort" for Sickle Cell Patients Who Face Racism When Seeking Care, Says Advocate*. https://www.cbc.ca/radio/whitecoat/er-a-last-resort-for-sickle-cell-patients-who-face-racism-when-seeking-care-says-advocate-1.5747012

Commission on Disability Equity. (n.d.). *What is Disability Justice?* Retrieved April 16, 2025, from https://code.as.ucsb.edu/what-is-disability-justice/

Creary, M. S. (2021). Bounded Justice and the Limits of Health Equity. *The Journal of Law, Medicine & Ethics: A Journal of the American Society of Law, Medicine & Ethics*, *49*(2), 241–256. https://doi.org/10.1017/jme.2021.34

Douglass, P. M., O'Connor, T., & Javidi, B. (2022). Automated Sickle Cell Disease Identification in Human Red Blood Cells Using a Lensless Single Random Phase Encoding Biosensor and Convolutional Neural Networks. *Optics Express*, *30*(20), 35965–35977. https://doi.org/10.1364/OE.469199

El Hoss, S., El Nemer, W., & Rees, D. C. (2022). Precision Medicine and Sickle Cell Disease. *HemaSphere*, *6*(9), e762. https://doi.org/10.1097/HS9.0000000000000762

Elendu, C., Amaechi, D. C., Alakwe-Ojimba, C. E., Elendu, T. C., Elendu, R. C., Ayabazu, C. P., Aina, T. O., Aborisade, O., & Adenikinju, J. S. (2023). Understanding Sickle Cell Disease: Causes, Symptoms, and Treatment Options. *Medicine*, *102*(38), e35237. https://doi.org/10.1097/MD.0000000000035237

Elsabagh, A. A., Elhadary, M., Elsayed, B., Elshoeibi, A. M., Ferih, K., Kaddoura, R., Alkindi, S., Alshurafa, A., Alrasheed, M., Alzayed, A., Al-Abdulmalek, A., Altooq, J. A., & Yassin, M. (2023). Artificial Intelligence in Sickle Disease. *Blood Reviews*, *61*, 101102. https://doi.org/10.1016/j.blre.2023.101102

Kotsyubinsky, A. P., & Kotsyubinsky, D. A. (n.d.). Biological Reductionism as an Obstacle to the Advancement of the Biopsychosocial Concept of Mental Disorders. *Consortium Psychiatricum*, *4*(4), 75–84. https://doi.org/10.17816/CP15476

Marsh, A. M., & Treadwell, M. J. (2024). Stepping Systematically Forward Toward Health Equity in Sickle Cell Disease. *JAMA Pediatrics*, *178*(3), 225. https://doi.org/10.1001/jamapediatrics.2023.5984

McCormick, M., Osei-Anto, H. A., & Martinez, R. M. (Eds.) (with Committee on Addressing Sickle Cell Disease: A Strategic Plan and Blueprint for Action, Board on Population Health and Public Health Practice, Health and Medicine Division, & National Academies of Sciences, Engineering, and Medicine). (2020). *Addressing Sickle Cell Disease: A Strategic Plan and Blueprint for Action*. National Academies Press. https://doi.org/10.17226/25632

Mougianis, I., Cohen, L. L., Martin, S., Shneider, C., & Bishop, M. (2020). Racism and Health-Related Quality of Life in Pediatric Sickle Cell Disease: Roles of Depression and Support. *Journal of Pediatric Psychology*, *45*(8), 858–866. https://doi.org/10.1093/jpepsy/jsaa035

Regenmortel, M. H. V. V. (2004). Reductionism and Complexity in Molecular Biology. *EMBO Reports*, *5*(11), 1016–1020. https://doi.org/10.1038/sj.embor.7400284

Rice, C., Chandler, E., Shanouda, F., Temple Jones, C., & Mündel, I. (2024). Misfits Meet Art and Technology: Cripping Transmethodologies. *Cultural Studies ↔ Critical Methodologies*, *24*(4), 219–231. https://doi.org/10.1177/15327086241234705

Rivas, A. L., Leitner, G., Jankowski, M. D., Hoogesteijn, A. L., Iandiorio, M. J., Chatzipanagiotou, S., Ioannidis, A., Blum, S. E., Piccinini, R., Antoniades, A., Fazio, J. C., Apidianakis, Y., Fair, J. M., & Van Regenmortel, M. H. V. (2017). Nature and Consequences of Biological Reductionism for the Immunological Study of Infectious Diseases. *Frontiers in Immunology*, *8*, 612. https://doi.org/10.3389/fimmu.2017.00612

Royal, C. D. M., Babyak, M., Shah, N., Srivatsa, S., Stewart, K. A., Tanabe, P., Wonkam, A., & Asnani, M. (2021). Sickle Cell Disease is a Global Prototype for Integrative Research and Healthcare. *Advanced Genetics*, *2*(1), e10037. https://doi.org/10.1002/ggn2.10037

Sachdev, V., Tian, X., Gu, Y., Nichols, J., Sidenko, S., Li, W., Beri, A., Layne, W. A., Allen, D., Wu, C. O., & Thein, S. L. (2021). A Phenotypic Risk Score for Predicting Mortality in Sickle Cell Disease. *British Journal of Haematology*, *192*(5), 932–941. https://doi.org/10.1111/bjh.17342

Serjeant, G. R. (2013). The Natural History of Sickle Cell Disease. *Cold Spring Harbor Perspectives in Medicine*, *3*(10), a011783. https://doi.org/10.1101/cshperspect.a011783

Stetsenko, A. (2018). Confronting Biological Reductionism from a Social Justice Agenda: Transformative Agency and Activist Stance. *Literacy Research: Theory, Method, and Practice*, *67*(1), 44–63. https://doi.org/10.1177/2381336918787531

11 Beyond "Technoableism"
AI, Ableism, and Accommodations in Postsecondary/STEM Education

Sammy Jo Johnson, Yoonmee Han, Nolan Krahn and Maverick Smith

INTRODUCTION

Artificial intelligence (AI) is increasingly promoted as a solution to problems of inaccessibility, exclusion, and isolation experienced by disabled people, particularly in education (Nakamura, 2019; Chalkiadakis et al., 2024; Ferebee, 2025; Kohnke & Zaugg, 2025). This includes science, technology, engineering, and mathematics (STEM) education where disabled students are vastly underrepresented and face systemic barriers, institutionalized exclusions, and widespread discrimination (McCall & Oertle, 2023; Chasen et al., 2025; Kohnke & Zaugg, 2025). However, proposed AI solutions can reproduce able-bodied domination by privileging "normative ways of learning, communicating and demonstrating knowledge while dismissing or negating disabled students' multivocal lived experiences and ways of knowing" (Foley & Melese, 2025, p. 2).

This chapter provides a critical review of the literature at the intersections of AI, disability, and postsecondary education (PSE), with a particular focus on STEM fields. We ask whether current approaches to AI applications meaningfully challenge structural barriers and inequitable power relations, which are pervasive in STEM, or whether these approaches simply reinforce the individual academic accommodation model. This model provides temporary modifications to students who qualify while sidelining the need for structural change (Jung, 2003; Dolmage, 2017). Our analysis contributes to a critical understanding of how the so-called problems of disability are conceptualized in the literature and the kinds of AI solutions proffered. Methodologically, we conduct a critical literature review guided by disability justice and a crip standpoint.

BACKGROUND: DISCRIMINATION IN STEM

Disabled people are widely underrepresented in postsecondary STEM education, particularly in graduate-level programs (Kolne & Lindsay, 2020). This disparity carries into employment (Chasen et al., 2025; Ramp et al., 2021; Malcolm & Roll, 2019; Kolne & Lindsay, 2020). These inequities stem from widespread ableist, racist, and sexist barriers, as well as paternalistic biases and assumptions about the capabilities of disabled, racialized, and gendered students in STEM (Chasen et al., 2025; Summers & Boda, 2024; Moon et al., 2012; Voutyrakou & Skordoulis, 2025). Such inequities are also fueled by the lack of adequate support and accessibility policies for disabled students in STEM programs and related employment pathways (Lindsay et al., 2018; Long & Grunert Kowalske, 2022).

Equitable access to education and progress into STEM streams is structurally curtailed at young ages. This is because placement in special education streams, which disproportionately impacts racialized and socioeconomically disadvantaged students, denies disabled children and youth the opportunities to acquire prerequisites for postsecondary admission (Annamma, 2018; Parekh et al., 2011; Parekh & Brown, 2019). Disabled and other equity-seeking youth are also discouraged from pursuing STEM pathways (Summers & Boda, 2024). When disabled and other equity-deserving

DOI: 10.1201/9781003737810-13

students enroll in postsecondary STEM programs, they are more likely to drop out when facing life struggles, dissatisfaction, isolation, and educational barriers (Malcolm & Roll, 2019; Tansey et al., 2017). In addition, barriers to enrolment and success are intensified for these disabled students who are multiply marginalized (Wei et al., 2013; Tansey et al., 2017; Shao et al., 2025).

Disabled students often experience a reduced sense of belonging in STEM disciplines due to pervasive masculine and ableist cultures, fewer opportunities to engage in peer networking, and the absence of role models (Summers & Boda, 2024). Feelings of unbelonging can be connected to the lack of policies and practices that guarantee accommodated learning and access in science laboratories and field work (Beck-Winchatz & Riccobono, 2008; Sahin & Yorek, 2009; Ramp et al., 2021; Jeannis et al., 2018). There is also a lack of skills and resources among STEM instructors to support inclusive and equitable learning environments, a barrier which is disproportionately experienced by deaf-and-hard-of-hearing students (Long & Grunert Kowalske, 2022).

Systemic learning inequities and a systemic lack of diversity are the norm in STEM education (Chasen et al., 2025; Moon et al., 2012). This sustains the structural dominance of white, male, middle-class, abled, and hearing archetypes in STEM education and industry (McGee, 2020). As a result of this, racialized, gendered, and disabled students are underrepresented in STEM disciplines, which means their career opportunities in science, technology, and related industries are structurally delimited (Hamash et al., 2025). Consequently, opportunities for disabled leadership in the development and design of science, technology, and engineering remain marginal (Newman-Griffis et al., 2022; Hamash et al., 2025; Foley & Melese, 2025). This includes AI design and development, where there is little opportunity for disabled individuals and communities to contribute knowledge and experience (Gorman et al., 2023; Newman-Griffis et al., 2022).

Despite power imbalances in AI design and development, many researchers suggest that the adoption of emerging AI tools can promote greater inclusion of disabled and other equity-deserving students in PSE (Mallik & Gangopadhyay, 2023; Leon et al., 2025; Ferebee, 2025). While we are excited about the possibility for AI technologies to facilitate more equitable learning environments in postsecondary STEM education, we also recognize that the end products of AI technologies informed by ableist perspectives have harmful impacts on people's lives (Newman-Griffis et al., 2022). AI can reinscribe able-bodied supremacy in education and demand conformity with ableist norms and ideals (Foley & Melese, 2025; Han & Johnson, 2025). When designed without input or, ideally, leadership from disabled individuals and communities, AI systems fail to "account for the different ways students live and learn and can be punitive against those falling outside the 'norm'" (Jafry & Vostermans, 2025, p. 69).

THEORETICAL FRAMEWORK: SYSTEMIC OPPRESSION

We understand ableism, racism, cisheterosexism, and other forms of oppression to be structural features within Canadian PSE, rather than the result of a few, individual "bad" actors. This is because, in Canada, these spaces and places "are intricately woven into the fabric of settler-colonialism as they were established as a means to educate a narrow demographic segment of the population" (Cranston & Bennet, 2024, p. 106). Over time, as Ng (1993) argues, notions of white, settler, cis-male, and able-bodied superiority—based on those groups initially included in the university space—have become routine modes of thinking and acting in the university, sustaining inequality. Put differently, racism and sexism are not only unequal and systemic power relations embedded in the ordinary processes of PSE but also systems that actively sustain the white, settler-colonial, and patriarchal power structures on which Canadian PSE was built (Ng, 1993).

This understanding of how structural oppression sustains inequality can also be connected to the social model of disability (Oliver, 1990, 2009; Barnes, 2000, 2020). The social model locates disability oppression in the systemic barriers that limit participation in all parts of life, including education (Oliver, 1990, 2009; Barnes, 2000, 2020). The social model frames ableism as a form of systemic oppression. However, our analysis of ableism is also informed by disability justice

(Piepzna-Samarasinha, 2018; Sins Invalid, 2019; Kafai, 2021; Mingus, 2011). Disability justice is a theoretical framework and movement that incorporates intersectionality (for more on Black feminist theories of intersectionality, see Hill Collins, 2009; Crenshaw, 1989). This means disability justice argues that individuals experience disability oppression differently due to additional and interlocking forms of advantage and disadvantage, privilege and disprivilege.

Beyond Accommodation/Beyond Technoableism

Canadian PSE relies on a system of academic accommodations, wherein the responsibility for ensuring access is placed on individual students (Bruce, 2020; Dolmage, 2017; Johnson et al., forthcoming). Here, the disabled student is positioned as the problem to be accommodated using temporary modifications rather than the larger ableist system that needs to be dismantled (Dolmage, 2017; Jung, 2003). Individual accommodations, though important, are not sufficient for addressing the ordinariness of ableism. As Mingus (2011) makes clear, there is a "need to think of access with an understanding of disability justice" (para. 5). This requires "moving away from an equity-based model of sameness and 'we are just like you' to a model of disability that embraces difference, confronts privilege and challenges what is considered 'normal' on every front" (Mingus, 2011, para. 5).

This individualized lens pervades the development of assistive technologies, including AI-powered learning tools. This results in AI tools being based on "the harmful notion that disability is a deficit to be overcome rather than a valid way of being in the world" (Foley & Melese, 2025, p. 6). The outcome is "technoableism"—a term Shew (2020, p. 48) uses to name the imperative within technological development to "fix" disability, where the focus is on "changing the individual to fit the environment rather than the other way around". Similar to individual accommodations, technoableist solutions in education, as Foley and Melese (2025) argue, locate the so-called problem of disability within individual students, producing tech fixes that do little to disrupt the ableist academic environment.

METHODOLOGY: CRITICAL LITERATURE REVIEW

Critical disability scholars have critiqued the frameworks used in AI research and development for the ramifications they have for disabled users (Newman-Griffis et al., 2022). Yet, according to El Morr et al. (2024), research on disability and AI largely lacks a critical approach, raising concerns about the usefulness of AI products for disabled people. Without a critical grounding, biases in research design may pass unchallenged, leading to "AI technology development with goals that are well-intentioned on the surface but reflect underlying ableism that actively harms disabled people" (Newman-Griffis et al., 2022, p. 6). Informed by these critiques, we examine how disability is framed in the literature on AI and STEM/PSE and the solutions proposed.

We use a *critical literature review*—a selective, theory-building approach that examines assumptions and power relations rather than exhaustively mapping studies—to surface and challenge ableist/ technoableist framings in AI-and-PSE/STEM scholarship and to generate system-level recommendations. We applied a purposeful sampling approach using Google Scholar (2020-Sept 2025). Search terms included AI, disability, accommod*, accessibility, abelis*, STEM, higher education, and PSE. We included empirical, review papers, and theoretical discussions on AI in PSE/STEM with explicit disability or equity focus; excluded purely technical AI, clinical/rehab without education context, and employed forward/backward citation chasing to refine the corpus—prioritizing conceptual coverage over exhaustiveness. Out of a total of 17 included sources, a small handful focus on the K-12 STEM context due to a scarcity of literature on AI, disability, and postsecondary STEM education.

Guided by this approach, our review sought to answer the following two research questions:

1. How are problems of disability framed in the literature (e.g., as oppression, in line with the social model, or as an individual deficit, in line with the medical model)?

2. What AI solutions are proposed, and do these rely on techno-fixes that fit disabled students into existing environments (an inclusion approach), seek to address systemic ableism, or something in between?

Our analysis is informed by our positionalities as a majority-disabled research team—three out of the four of us identify as disabled. We draw on a crip standpoint (Johnson et al., forthcoming), informed by our own experiences of ableism in academia and with educational AI. Lastly, both the theoretical framework and methodology sections of this chapter were edited using ChatGPT 4.0 with a focus on grammar and readability.

FINDINGS AND DISCUSSION

The literature is clear that AI has brought sweeping changes to PSE and there is an overall hopefulness regarding its possibilities for enhancing inclusion, diversity, equity, and accessibility (Ferebee, 2025; Atcheson et al., 2025; Murdan, 2024; Neha et al., 2024). For students, AI-powered tools can provide new ways to learn and engage with complex course concepts aligned with their interests (Hu et al., 2025; Kohnke & Zaugg, 2025; Leon et al., 2025; Voutyrakou & Skordoulis, 2025). For instructors, AI promises enhanced possibilities to know their students, particularly through the collection of vast amounts of data that can be used to detect struggles in comprehension, indicate where adaptations to learning plans are needed, and even identify students at-risk of failure (Hu et al., 2025; Nagaraj et al., 2023).

In STEM education, researchers describe the usefulness of AI tools like intelligent tutors to provide students with immediate feedback (Nagaraj et al., 2023; Leon et al., 2025). Along similar lines, AI-powered virtual labs allow students "to explore complex scientific concepts without the constraints of traditional lab environments" (Leon et al., 2025, p. 12). In addition, the promises of individualized and adaptive learning are promoted as unique accessibility features that can address exclusionary practices within STEM education (Murdan, 2024; Nagaraj et al., 2023; Buzzi et al., 2025). Such AI-powered tools can provide instant modifications to learning plans, work further with students on problem areas, and add new learning topics as students demonstrate readiness (Murdan, 2024).

Reading against the Grain: Are You Saying We're the Problem?

Much of the reviewed literature indicates that AI-driven solutions can address systemic problems in STEM/PSE by better skilling and equipping disabled students. In other words, the promise of AI is to help "slow learners" (Murdan, 2024) so that we can survive fast-paced and inhabitable environments. However, upon closer reading, we argue that there are two simultaneous problems framed in the literature. First, STEM moves fast and is centered around a privileged, able-bodied student ideal. Second, disabled and other equity-seeking students cannot keep up. In other words, there is a tendency to frame AI-powered educational tools as solutions to what are perceived to be individual learning problems. This framing implies that the way to improve equity is to intervene in individual-level problems in learning with AI and even promotes the use of AI to diagnose students (Murdan, 2024), clearly indicating that we are the problem. In this way, AI technologies can be used to improve classroom environments that conventional teaching cannot otherwise accommodate.

When AI solutions are premised on a promise to help students better adapt to the existing learning environment, this overlooks structurally rooted problems. This occurs even when scholars do mention systemic barriers in their discussion of problems facing disabled and equity-deserving students but promote AI as tools that can narrowly enhance individual performance. That is, AI is not presented as a tool to challenge the named barriers, but as an individualized learning tool. Simply put, the problem continues to be that disabled students must be "brought up to speed";

meanwhile, the deeply routinized speeds at which we move in STEM/PSE remain unproblematized. Taken for granted are the required skills, academic standards, and learning curbs shaped by ableist standards and based on normalized learning and working speeds. Such AI-driven solutions risk reproducing ableist, racist, and sexist ideas about who belongs in STEM/PSE (Foley & Melese, 2025).

Several included sources refuse to blame students and instead firmly situate the problem of disability oppression in exclusionary educational norms and habits. These articles highlight possibilities for using AI and other accessibility technologies to create more inclusive spaces in PSE. This goes beyond using AI to fit existing norms; instead, it asserts that we/they belong and is used to hack more effective supports and allow for more ways of being and learning in PSE/STEM (Atcheson et al., 2025; Ferebee, 2025). Other articles underscore issues with biased technological design centered around an able-bodied norm. For example, Foley and Melese (2025), who we cited in our theoretical framework section, locate the problem in ableist and other oppressive assumptions embedded within educational AI—including personalized learning tools—that compel students to fit a white and able-bodied standard.

The Techno-Fixes We Need

Moving beyond individual-level solutions, we find inspiration from scholars who refuse to frame disabled and equity-seeking students as the problem. Among these are Voutyrakou and Skordoulis (2025), who suggest using AI tools to support instructors in addressing gender bias pervasive in STEM pedagogies in the K-12 context. For Voutyrakou and Skordoulis, AI can be used to support instructors in implementing feminist pedagogical tactics. Looking outside of STEM, we find another promising example from Jafry and Vorstermans (2025, p. 68), who report findings from a study aimed at adapting "course elements to respond to AI" without exacerbating "existing barriers for students". For Jafry and Vorstermans, emerging educational AI presents an opportunity not to "fix" our students but to address systemic problems in the postsecondary classroom and to embed access-oriented pedagogies in course design.

There is an indication in the literature that problems faced by vulnerable students in STEM can be best addressed by collecting more data on these students, to thus identify when and where they are at risk. While trauma-informed interventions followed by wrap-around supports and real commitment to address students' needs as identified may be helpful to students at risk, the ongoing collection of data on our students can put them at risk (Clark et al., 2025; Foley & Melese, 2025). Pucciarelli and May (2023) warn against the use of technologies geared toward increasing the extraction of students' data, arguing that ramped-up surveillance undergirds ableist, white supremacist, sexist, and colonial systems of power under a guise of accessibility.

We suggest that one way to tell how the problem of disability is understood is by looking at where we spend our time and energy addressing it. The suggestion that students be monitored more closely to identify any deviation from the norm can quickly lead to pathologizing students (Foley & Melese, 2025). Drawing on Jafry and Vorstermans (2025), we wonder about the possibility to use AI to identify where our instructional modes, assignments, courses, programs, and institutions put students at risk.

CONCLUSION

In this chapter, we have conducted a critical review of the literature at the intersection of AI, disability, and STEM/PSE. We found that AI is presented as a promising equity tool that can be used to promote personalized and individualized learning. However, we argue that the proposed AI solutions often fall short of addressing broader, systemic issues faced by students with intersecting marginalities. These findings align with other critical reviews, which suggest that research on AI and disability tend to emphasize a medical model, aimed at "fixing" disability rather than social and structural barriers that contribute to disability oppression (El Morr et al., 2024). In response, we conclude with the following three key findings and recommendations:

1. AI-powered accommodations which demand that disabled students find new ways to fit ourselves into existing ableist archetypes are inadequate solutions to the systemic problems of inequality, oppression, and exclusion.
2. Instead of monitoring students for problematic behavior and risk, use AI to identify systemic ableism and where institutions put disabled and equity-seeking students at risk.
3. Future work focused on the inclusion of disabled students in STEM/PSE should seek to address systemic ableism by implementing GenAI models designed with disabled community members as both leaders and research partners.

ACKNOWLEDGMENT

Portions of this chapter were developed with the assistance of ChatGPT for editing, clarification, and sentence structure. All intellectual contributions, interpretations, and final editorial decisions are the authors' own, and the authors take full responsibility for the content. Any AI-assisted or AI-generated material was reviewed and verified by the authors.

REFLECTION QUESTIONS

- What are some of the ways ableism and other forms of oppression manifest in STEM education?
- Where are academic accommodations useful and where might they fall short of addressing systemic forms of exclusion and inequality?
- Are you excited about the possibility to use AI to promote accessibility and inclusion in STEM and other parts of PSE? Why or why not?
- How might AI tools in education reproduce inequality?
- What are some ideas you have for how AI can be used to challenge inequality in STEM and beyond?

REFERENCES

Annamma, S. A. (2018). *The pedagogy of pathologization: Dis/abled girls of color in the school-prison nexus*. Routledge.

Atcheson, A., Khan, O., Siemann, B., Jain, A., & Karahalios, K. (2025). "I'd never actually realized how big an impact it had until now": Perspectives of university students with disabilities on generative artificial intelligence. *Proceedings of the 2025 CHI Conference on Human Factors in Computing Systems*, Yokohama, 1–22. https://doi.org/10.1145/3706598.3714121

Barnes, C. (2000). A working social model? Disability, work and disability politics in the 21st century. *Critical Social Policy*, *20*(4), 441–457. https://doi.org/10.1177/026101830002000402

Barnes, C. (2020). Understanding the social model of disability: Past, present & future. In N. Watson & S. Vehmas (Eds.), *Routledge handbook of disability studies* (Second Edition, pp. 14–31). Routledge Taylor & Francis Group.

Beck-Winchatz, B., & Riccobono, M. A. (2008). Advancing participation of blind students in science, technology, engineering, and math. *Advances in Space Research, 42*(11), 1855–1858. https://doi.org/10.1016/j.asr.2007.05.080

Bruce, C. (2020). Self-advocacy as precariousness in university education. *Canadian Journal of Disability Studies*, *9*(5), 414–440. https://doi.org/10.15353/cjds.v9i5.703

Buzzi, M., Pieriboni, G., & Leporini, B. (2025). How artificial intelligence is impacting on the STEM education of students with disabilities: A five years review: *Proceedings of the 17th International Conference on Computer Supported Education*, Porto, 323–330. https://doi.org/10.5220/0013267900003932

Chalkiadakis, A., Seremetaki, A., Kanellou, A., Kallishi, M., Morfopoulou, A., Moraitaki, M., & Mastrokoukou, S. (2024). Impact of artificial intelligence and virtual reality on educational inclusion: A systematic review of technologies supporting students with disabilities. *Education Sciences, 14*(11), 1123–1146. https://doi.org/10.3390/educsci14111223

Chasen, A., Borrego, M., Koolman, E., Landgren, E., & Chapman Tripp, H. (2025). A systematic review of differences for disabled students in STEM versus other disciplinary undergraduate settings. *Journal of Engineering Education, 114*(1), e20627. https://doi.org/10.1002/jee.20627

Clark, A. K., Hirt, A., Whitcomb, D., Thompson, W. J., Wine, M., & Karvonen, M. (2025). Artificial intelligence in science and mathematics assessment for students with disabilities: Opportunities and challenges. *Education Sciences, 15*(2), 233. https://doi.org/10.3390/educsci15020233

Cranston, J., & Bennett, A. (2024). Systemic racism in Canadian higher education: A rapid scoping review of 22 years of literature. *Canadian Journal of Higher Education, 54*(1), 103–125. https://doi.org/10.47678/cjhe.v54i1.190069

Crenshaw, K. (1989). Demarginalizing the intersection of race and sex: A Black feminist critique of antidiscrimination doctrine. *Feminist Theory and Antiracist Politics, 1989*(1), 139–167. https://chicagounbound.uchicago.edu/uclf/vol1989/iss1/8

Dolmage, J. T. (2017). *Academic ableism: Disability and higher education*. University of Michigan Press.

El Morr, C., Kundi, B., Mobeen, F., Taleghani, S., El-Lahib, Y., & Gorman, R. (2024). AI and disability: A systematic scoping review. *Health Informatics Journal, 30*(3), 14604582241285743. https://doi.org/10.1177/14604582241285743

Ferebee, S. (2025). AI and accessibility: Breaking barriers for people with disabilities. *Premier Journal of Artificial Intelligence, 2*, 100012. https://doi.org/10.70389/PJAI.100012

Foley, A., & Melese, F. (2025). Disabling AI: Power, exclusion, and disability. *British Journal of Sociology of Education*, 1–22. https://doi.org/10.1080/01425692.2025.2519482

Gorman, R., Creighton, A., Dada, S., Maret, P., Mgwigwi, T., Muhlenbach, F., Kundi, B., Tadesse, R., Dharmalingam, D., Clarkson, A., Stanley, A., Buettgen, A., Dinca-Panaitescu, S., Bangash, M., Brown, Z., Corfield, D., Getfield, J., Gray, Y., DeHal Gunraj., P-G., … El Morr, C. (2023). Disability data justice from the ground up: A practice-led, participatory co-design approach to building an AI search engine and data repository for local, national, and transnational disability organizations. *Critical Studies: An International and Interdisciplinary Journal, 18*(1), 28–43. https://doi.org/10.51357/cs.v18i1.229

Hamash, M., Khan, M. R., & Tiernan, P. (2025). Inclusive STEAM education: A framework for teaching cod-2 ing and robotics to students with visually Impairment using 3 advanced computer vision. *arXiv,* 1–14. https://doi.org/10.48550/arXiv.2503.16482

Han, Y., & Johnson, S. J. (2025). Toward an emancipatory AI pedagogy: The do's and dont's of an anti-racist/anti-ableist writing instruction. In C. El Morr, Y. El-Lahib, & R. Gorman (Eds.), *Beyond tech fixes: Toward an AI future where disability justice thrives* (pp. 129–138). Springer Nature Switzerland. https://doi.org/10.1007/978-3-031-93022-5_10.

Hill Collins, P. (2009). *Black feminist thought: knowledge, consciousness, and the politics of empowerment* (Second edition). Routledge, Taylor & Francis Group.

Hu, S., Ke, F., Vyortkina, D., Hu, P., Luby, S., & O'Shea, J. (2025). Artificial intelligence in higher education: Applications, challenges, and policy development and further considerations. In Perna, L. W. (Eds.), *Higher education: Handbook of theory and research,* (vol. 40., pp. 265–315). Springer.

Jafry, A., & Vorstermans, J. (2025). Evolving intersections: AI, disability, and academic integrity in higher education. *New directions for teaching and learning, 2025*(182), 67–80. https://doi.org/10.1002/tl.20629

Jeannis, H., Joseph, J., Goldberg, M., Seelman, K., Schmeler, M., & Cooper, R. A. (2018). Full-participation of students with physical disabilities in science and engineering laboratories. *Disability and Rehabilitation: Assistive Technology, 13*(2), 186–193. https://doi.org/10.1080/17483107.2017.1300348

Jung, K. E. (2003). Chronic illness and academic accommodation: Meeting disabled students' "unique needs" and preserving the institutional order of the university. *The Journal of Sociology & Social Welfare, 30*(1), 91–112. https://doi.org/10.15453/0191-5096.2875

Kafai, S. (2021). *Crip kinship: The disability justice & art activism of Sins Invalid* (SECOND PRINTING). Arsenal Pulp Press.

Kohnke, S., & Zaugg, T. (2025). Artificial intelligence: An untapped opportunity for equity and access in STEM education. *Education Sciences, 15*(1), 68. https://doi.org/10.3390/educsci15010068

Kolne, K., & Lindsay, S. (2020). A systematic review of programs and interventions for increasing the interest and participation of children and youth with disabilities in STEM education or careers. *Journal of Occupational Science, 27*(4), 525–546. https://doi.org/10.1080/14427591.2019.1692692

Leon, C., Lipuma, J., & Oviedo-Torres, X. (2025). Artificial intelligence in STEM education: A transdisciplinary framework for engagement and innovation. *Frontiers in Education, 10,* 1–18. https://doi.org/10.3389/feduc.2025.1619888

Lindsay, S., Cagliostro, E., & Carafa, G. (2018). A systematic review of barriers and facilitators of disability disclosure and accommodations for youth in post-secondary education. *International Journal of Disability, Development and Education, 65*(5), 526–556. https://doi.org/10.1080/1034912X.2018.1430352

Long, M. R., & Grunert Kowalske, M. (2022). Understanding STEM instructors' experiences with and perceptions of deaf and hard-of-hearing students: The first step toward increasing access and inclusivity. *Journal of Chemical Education, 99*(1), 274–282. https://doi.org/10.1021/acs.jchemed.1c00409

Malcolm, M., & Roll, M. (2019). Self-reported assistive technology outcomes and personal characteristics in college students with less-apparent disabilities. *Assistive Technology*, *31*(4), 169–179. https://doi.org/10.1080/10400435.2017.1406414

Mallik, S., & Gangopadhyay, A. (2023). Proactive and reactive engagement of artificial intelligence methods for education: A review. *Frontiers in Artificial Intelligence*, *6*, 1151391. https://doi.org/10.3389/frai.2023.1151391

McCall, C., & Oertle, K. M. (2023). The Transition Engineered Collaborative (TEC): Promoting people with disabilities in STEM through interdisciplinary transition and education. *Journal of Rehabilitation, 89*(2), 30–41.

McGee, E. O. (2020). Interrogating structural racism in STEM higher education. *Educational Researcher*, *49*(9), 633–644. https://doi.org/10.3102/0013189X20972718

Mingus, M. (2011, February 12). Changing the framework: Disability Justice. *Leaving Evidence*. https://leavingevidence.wordpress.com/2011/02/12/changing-the-framework-disability-justice/

Moon, N. W., Todd, R. L., Morton, D. L., & Ivey, E. (2012). *Accommodating students with disabilities in Science, Technology, Engineering, and Mathematics (STEM): Findings from research and practice for middle grades through university education*. Center for Assistive Technology and Environmental Access. https://hourofcode.com/files/accommodating-students-with-disabilities.pdf

Murdan, A. P. (2024). Tailoring STEM education for slow learners through artificial intelligence. *2024 5th International Conference on Emerging Trends in Electrical, Electronic and Communications Engineering (ELECOM)*, Balaclava, 1–7. https://doi.org/10.1109/ELECOM63163.2024.10892150

Nagaraj, B. K., Kalaivani, A., Suraj Begum, R., Akila, S., Sachdev, H., K., & Senthil Kumar, N. (2023). The emerging role of artificial intelligence in STEM higher education: A critical review. *International Research Journal of Multidisciplinary Technovation, 5*(5), 1–19. https://doi.org/10.54392/irjmt2351

Nakamura, K. (2019). My algorithms have determined you're not human: AI-ML, reverse turing-tests, and the disability experience. *Proceedings of the 21st International ACM SIGACCESS Conference on Computers and Accessibility,* Pittsburgh, PA (pp.1–2).

Neha, K., Kumar, R., & Sankat, M. (2024). AI wizards: Pioneering assistive technologies for higher education institutions of students with learning disabilities. In R. Kaluri, M. Mahmud, T. R. Gadekallu, D. S. Rajput, & K. Lakshmanna (Eds.), *Applied assistive technologies and informatics for students with disabilities* (pp. 59–70). Springer Nature Singapore. https://doi.org/10.1007/978-981-97-0914-4

Newman-Griffis, D., Rauchberg, J. S., Alharbi, R., Hickman, L., & Hochheiser, H. (2022). Definition drives design: Disability models and mechanisms of bias in AI technologies. *arXiv,* 1–38. https://doi.org/10.48550/ARXIV.2206.08287

Ng, R. (1993). "A woman out of control": Deconstructing sexism and racism in the university. *Canadian Journal of Education/Revue Canadienne de l'éducation*, *18*(3), 189. https://doi.org/10.2307/1495382

Oliver, M. (1990). The individual and social models of disability. Joint Workshop of the Living Options Group and the Research Unit of the Royal College of Physicians, 1–34.

Oliver, M. (2009). The social model in context. In T. Titchkosky & R. Michalko (Eds.), *Rethinking normalcy: A disability studies reader* (pp. 19–30). Canadian Scholars' Press.

Parekh, G., & Brown, R. S. (2019). Changing lanes: The relationship between special education placement and students' academic futures. *Educational Policy*, *33*(1), 111–135. https://doi.org/10.1177/0895904818812772

Parekh, G., Killoran, I., & Crawford, C. (2011). The Toronto connection: Poverty, perceived ability, and access to education equity. *Canadian Journal of Education/Revue Canadienne de l'éducation*, *34*(3), 249–279. https://www.jstor.org/stable/canajeducrevucan.34.3.249

Piepzna-Samarasinha, L. L. (2018). *Carework: Dreaming disability justice*. Arsenal Pulp Press.

Pucciarelli, A., & May, E. (2023). Disability and surveillance: Disability justice as a framework for educational technology. *Education for Information*, *39*(1), 309–321. https://doi.org/10.3233/EFI-230022

Ramp, J., Parker, C. G., Rhodes, J. S., & Malik, P. (2021). Barriers to inclusion: Service dog handlers in science laboratories. *Disability and Health Journal*, *14*(3), 101070. https://doi.org/10.1016/j.dhjo.2021.101070

Sahin, M., & Yorek, N. (2009). Teaching science to visually impaired students: A small-scale qualitative Study. *US-China Education Review, 6*(4), 1–8.

Shao, K. Z., Wilson, D., Cho, E. K.-M., Tang, S., Ma, H., & Makhsous, S. (2025). Bridging educational equity gaps: A systematic review of AI-driven and new technologies for students living with disabilities in STEM education. 2025 Collaborative Network for Engineering & Computing Diversity (CoNECD) Proceedings. 54075. https://peer.asee.org/bridging-educational-equity-gaps-a-systematic-review-of-ai-driven-and-new-technologies-for-students-living-with-disabilities-in-stem-education

Shew, A. (2020). Ableism, technoableism, and future AI. *IEEE Technology and Society Magazine, 39*(1), 40–85. https://doi.org/10.1109/MTS.2020.2967492

Sins Invalid. (2019). *Skin, tooth and bone: The basis of our movement is our people* (Second Edition). Sins Invalid.

Summers, L., & Boda, P. A. (2024). Postsecondary STEMM beyond "what is:" Engaging the possibility of disability. *Journal of Postsecondary Education and Disability, 37*(3), 273–282.

Tansey, T. N., Smedema, S., Umucu, E., Iwanaga, K., Wu, J.-R., Cardoso, E. da S., & Strauser, D. (2017). Assessing college life adjustment of students with disabilities: Application of the PERMA framework. *Rehabilitation Counseling Bulletin, 61*(3), 131–142. https://doi.org/10.1177/0034355217702136

Voutyrakou, D. A., & Skordoulis, C. (2025). Using AI tools to enhance educational robotics to bridge the gender gap in STEM. *Education Sciences, 15*(6), 711. https://doi.org/10.3390/educsci15060711

Wei, X., Yu, J. W., Shattuck, P., McCracken, M., & Blackorby, J. (2013). Science, technology, engineering, and mathematics (STEM) participation among college students with an autism spectrum disorder. *Journal of Autism and Developmental Disorders, 43*(7), 1539–1546. https://doi.org/10.1007/s10803-012-1700-z

12 AI, Technoableism, and Computing Education

Assessing Conceptual Entry Points

Melanie Baljko

INTRODUCTION

Technoableism—ableist assumptions and values embedded in the design, development, and deployment of technology—arises from entangled social, organizational, and technical subsystems. In Artificial Intelligence (AI), these assumptions manifest in several ways, including reinscribed problematic tropes about "what it is to be disabled and what it is to age", problematic valourizations of independence (as opposed to interdependence), and reductionist approaches to the body–mind and the individual in situ (Shew, 2020). Technoableism is simultaneously a composite analytical concept that names a specific phenomenon and a critique that is used to challenge dominant ideologies in AI, computing, and design.

Recently, public and scholarly discourse about AI has shifted toward centering Generative AI and the transformative and disruptive impacts, which have been enabled by the introduction of the Transformer architecture in the late 2010s. Much of scholarly and public discourse centers on the technology and high-level decision-makers (C-suite and policy leadership, or lack thereof), with much emphasis on the professional training of technology practitioners who design, implement, and maintain these systems.

The Association for Computing Machinery (ACM), the world's largest educational and scientific computing society, and the Institute of Electrical and Electronics Engineers (IEEE), another professional association concerned with engineering, computer science, and related areas, carry significant authority in defining what counts as core knowledge for computing education worldwide. This authority is most visible via their ongoing joint curricular task forces, which, since 2013, have also included the Association for the Advancement of Artificial Intelligence (AAAI). These task forces, undertaking multi-year projects led by consortia of professional bodies representing hundreds of thousands of practitioners, produce curricular guidelines which specify the core Knowledge Areas (KAs) for computing, and within each KA, the Learning Topics (LTs) and illustrative Learning Objectives (LOs), which collectively form the backbone of computing-related baccalaureate disciplines. The most recent documents include "Computing Curricula 2020: Paradigms for Global Computing Education", also known as CC2020 (ACM/IEEE–CS Joint Task Force on Computing Curricula, 2020), and "Computer Science Curricula 2023: Curriculum Guidelines for Undergraduate Degree Programs in Computer Science", also known as CS2023 (ACM/IEEE–CS Joint Task Force on Computing Curricula, 2023). This raises a central question: to what extent, and in what ways, do existing undergraduate computing curricula—particularly CS2023—support or fail to support justice–oriented teaching of technoableism?

BACKGROUND

About 20 years ago, accessibility and the CS curriculum surfaced as a concern. Cohen et al. (2005) advocated that accessible software principles should be embedding directly into student projects

 DOI: 10.1201/9781003737810-14

and lab assignments within first-year CS courses. Burgstahler (2011) argued—via a Universal Design argument—that accessibility principles should be introduced across a range of CS courses, presenting a comprehensive curricular model. Advocacy to embed principles of inclusive design and accessibility within computing education, rather than treating them as peripheral or optional considerations, continued in works such as Ludi et al. (2018), Oleson et al. (2023), Weeden (2023), and Ladner et al. (2025). Although the study is no longer recent, Shinohara et al. (2018) showed limited adoption of and barriers to accessibility in CS curriculum among faculty in the United States, with these study results recently replicated in India (Parthasarathy & Joshi, 2024).

There are two dimensions to the limitations of these curricular approaches: adequacy of analytical conceptualizations and adequacy of critique.

First, these curricular approaches rely on thin concepts of accessibility. These works often acknowledge the social imaginary of certain bodies/minds as default and others are cast as "problems" to be fixed or excluded, and Ladner et al. (2025) even acknowledge the existence of technoableism. However, the curricular approaches focus on mainstream accessibility—that is, "downstream" accessibility or access within already-instantiated sociotechnical systems—as opposed to what we might term "upstream" accessibility—that is, access to the "levers of power" shaping these systems (in alignment with design and disability justice). In mainstream accessibility, accessibility is often presented as a design consideration or skillset, and as something that happens "in response to" normative assumptions. These ableist assumptions created the inaccessibility in the first place—assumptions made and then encoded into the designs of interfaces and interactive systems, in terms of, say, the sensory–perceptual, cognitive, motor demands made of the user. Technoableism names this pattern of technologies which embed ableist assumptions. In curriculum, accessibility is most often framed non-relationally, as a property of computing systems. When it is framed relationally (e.g., in curricular materials, such as HCI textbooks and related pedagogical resources), it is typically through Norman's formulation of affordances, which in turn draws from Gibson's ecological psychology (Norman, 2013). This lineage presents affordances as politically neutral, organism–environment relations and foregrounds technical possibilities rather than the social and political dynamics through which those possibilities are structured. By contrast, critical approaches, such as Davis (2020), emphasize how affordances are constituted through normative and political assumptions that shape inclusion and exclusion dimensions that remain underdeveloped in mainstream curricular treatments in computing. Even when a "diversity in design teams" approach is espoused, technicist concepts of accessibility remain. Curricular materials focus on accessibility standards, guidelines, and design principles, rather than tacking technoableism as an analytical concept.

Second, these curricular approaches take up a depoliticized, non-critical approach to accessibility, inclusion, and universal design. Critical accessibility views Universal Design (UD) as political practice, one that operates within histories of ableism and within which there is an ongoing contestation over justice (Hamraie, 2012). Critical accessibility is a critique of ideology, of power, and of technocentrism. This contrasts with how UD is often approached in CS curriculum advocacy: as aspirational and utopian ("usable by all"), and as technical and aesthetic solutions to design problems, as opposed to political struggle. Deeper curricular issues are that technology is presented as neutral, progressive, and universally beneficial, views which foreclose on the possibilities to expose how design cultures, AI discourses, and computing education reproduce ableism under the guise of innovation (Costanza-Chock, 2020).

These two dimensions—technoableism as a composite analytical concept that names a specific phenomenon and technoableism as a critique that is used to challenge dominant ideologies in AI, computing, and design—create a complex field against which to evaluate the adequacy of CS curricular design. Technoableism, as both analytic and critique, remains undertheorized in computing curricula. Therefore, an analysis of curricular positioning provides us with a necessary first step to understand how justice-oriented teaching of technoableism is supported or marginalized.

METHODS AND FINDINGS

Methodological Orientation

A document analysis was performed on the CS2023 document, a document which matters globally because it contains LTs that form the mandated backbone of baccalaureate Computer Science degree programs, as well as a body of LOs, which are for the illustrative suggestions for the evaluation of student mastery of the LTs. The CS2023 document is complex and contains, among other sections, a "Body of Knowledge" section (the body that constitutes the knowledge in Computer Science), with sub-sections for each of the 17 KAs. A coding framework, derived from other work on technoableism, was applied. To apply the analysis framework in a systematic way, first all Lx that contained any DEIA language were identified,[1] resulting in 93 Lx. All Lx were coded by their curricular role (either LT or LO), their curricular stratum (coreCS, coreKA, noncore), and their KA. All Lx were coded in terms of evidence of discursive anchoring (DA) (i.e., in the sociotechnical, in normative values and principles) and material anchoring (MA) (i.e., where the commitments are embedded, such as in technical, regulatory, or social processes). These patterns were then mapped to a "curricular force" typology: *reinforcing* (DA and MA co–occur, mutually supporting one another), *diluting* (DA without MA, signaling rhetorical inclusion without substantive embedding), *problematic* (normative discourse collapsed into technical fixes), and *systemic* (dense DA+MA anchoring across multiple authoritative locations). Additionally, Lx were coded as first-, second-, and third-tertile (the most to the least central knowledge in CS), based on their parent KA. The tertiles reflected a synthesis of the following aspects: allocation of the number of core instructional hours, extent of pre-requisite dependencies with other KAs and discursive framing within CS2023.

Curricular Anchoring

Of the 93 DEIA commitments, more than half appear as prescribed LTs, with the remainder as illustrative Learning Outcomes (LOs). They appear in only 7 of the 17 KAs, with a heavier representation in peripheral KAs and limited representation in central KAs (Table 12.1).

Peripherality of Technoableism in the Curriculum

Distribution of DEIA commitments across the curricular strata is uneven (Table 12.2). In the top-tertile KAs (the most central KAs), they appear only in the *noncore* strata. In the second tertile (represented solely by the KA "Society, Ethics, and Profession", SEP), they concentrate in the *coreCS* strata. In the bottom tertile, they are spread across the three strata.

Overall, this distribution (across the dimensions curricular role, curricular strata, and KA centrality) shows a consistent pattern of dilution, with about half the commitments *reinforced* (discursive and material anchors aligned) and half *diluted* (discursive with missing or non-aligned material anchoring) (Table 12.3).

Problematic

Some LTs appeared to be aligned with DEIA, since they discursively invoke justice and normative ideals but lack anchoring in governance or in social processes, leaving sociotechnical materiality and technoableist assumptions in place.

> *Historic marginalization due to systemic social mechanisms, technological supremacy and global infrastructure challenges to diversity, equity, inclusion and accessibility*
>
> *[LT#8, core–KA, KU: SEP–DEIA: Diversity, Equity, Inclusion, and Accessibility, KA: SEP]*

TABLE 12.1

Counts of the Lx containing DEIA commitments, disaggregated by Curricular Role (Learning Topic or Learning Outcome) and by the KA

Lx Counts By KA Tertile and Curricular Role																					
	KA Tertile/Knowledge Area (KA)																				
Curr.	1						2						3								
Role	AL	FPL	MSF	SDF	SF	Total	AR	DM	OS	PDC	SEP	Total	AI	GIT	HCI	NC	SE	SEC	SPD	Total	Grand Total
LO		1				1					20	20		1	12		1		4	18	39
		1.1%				1.1%					21.5%	21.5%		1.1%	12.9%		1.1%		4.3%	19.4%	41.9%
LT		3				3					16	16	2	6	19		1		7	35	54
		3.2%				3.2%					17.2%	17.2%	2.2%	6.5%	20.4%		1.1%		7.5%	37.6%	58.1%
Grand		4				4					36	36	2	7	31		2		11	53	93
Total		4.3%				4.3%					38.7%	38.7%	2.2%	7.5%	33.3%		2.2%		11.8%	57.0%	100.0%

The KAs are listed alphabetically within their tertile. Tertile 1 corresponds to the KAs that are most central to Computer Science. The KA with Lx includes FPL: Foundations of Programming Languages, SEP: Society, Ethics, and Profession, AI: Artificial Intelligence, GIT: Graphics and Interactive Techniques, HCI: Human–Computer Interaction, SE: Software Engineering, and SPD: Specialized Platform Development. See Appendix for the KA names for the columns without DEIA commitments.

TABLE 12.2
Counts of the Lx containing DEIA commitments, disaggregated by Curricular Strata (coreCS, coreKA, noncore) and by the Knowledge Area (KA)

	Lx Counts By KA Tertile and Curricular Strata																				
	KA Tertile/Knowledge Area (KA)																				
Curricular			**1**							**2**							**3**				**Grand**
Strata	**AL**	**FPL**	**MSF**	**SDF**	**SF**	**Total**	**AR**	**DM**	**OS**	**PDC**	**SEP**	**Total**	**AI**	**GIT**	**HCI**	**NC**	**SE**	**SEC**	**SPD**	**Total**	**Total**
Core-CS											21	21		2	14		2			18	39
											22.6%	22.6%		2.2%	15.1%		2.2%			19.4%	41.9%
Core-KA											15	15		5	12				3	20	35
											16.1%	16.1%		5.4%	12.9%				3.2%	21.5%	37.6%
Noncore		4				4							2		5				8	15	19
		4.3%				4.3%							2.2%		5.4%				8.6%	16.1%	20.4%
Grand Total		4				4					36	36	2	7	31		2		11	53	93
		4.3%				4.3%					38.7%	38.7%	2.2%	7.5%	33.3%		2.2%		11.8%	57.0%	100.0%

The KAs are listed alphabetically within their tertile. Tertile 1 corresponds to the KAs that are most central to Computer Science.

TABLE 12.3
DEIA commitments shown by their anchoring pattern, from strongest to weakest

Lx Counts by KA Tertile and Anchor Pattern

KA Tertile/Knowledge Area (KA)

Anchor			**1**											**3**				**Grand**
Mod.	**AL**	**FPL**	**MSF**	**SDF**	**SF**	**AR**	**DM**	**OS**	**PDC**	**SEP**	**AI**	**GIT**	**HCI**	**NC**	**SE**	**SEC**	**SPD**	**Total**
Systemic																		
Reinforced		1								21	2	2	12		2		5	45
		1.1%								22.6%	2.2%	2.2%	12.9%		2.2%		5.4%	48.4%
Diluted		3								10		5	19				6	43
		3.2%								10.8%		5.4%	20.4%				6.5%	46.2%
Problematic										5								5
										5.4%								5.4%
Grand Total		4								36	2	7	31		2		11	93
		4.3%								38.7%	2.2%	7.5%	33.3%		2.2%		11.8%	100.0%

Note: the tertile header "2" is printed above the OS/PDC columns.

Systemic anchoring is the densest, reinforced anchoring (discursive is reinforced by material, though possibly still technicist, albeit consistently so), diluted (rhetorical inclusion without substantive embedding), problematic (normative discourse collapsed into unmaterialized or technical fixes). The KAs are listed alphabetically within their tertile. Tertile 1 corresponds to the KAs that are most central to Computer Science.

Absences

The AI KA contains only two noncore LTs that contain DEIA commitments, both of which discursively and materially anchor in the sociotechnical rather than in normative values (Appendix). Ten KAs contain none, including high–stakes areas adjacent to AI, such as Data Management (DM) and Security (SEC). These gaps and absences demonstrate how curricular authority renders technojustice considerations invisible in many of the computing domains that are implicated in social harm.

Reflections from Teaching Practice

I have taught technoableism in a range of contexts: introductory computing, upper-level HCI, graduate courses, and a CS study club guest lecture. In introductory courses, I positioned accessibility and technoableism as a core unit. In the HCI courses, I integrated the topic throughout, via design justice and anti-oppression frameworks. At the graduate level and in the guest lecture, technoableism formed the central topic.

Across these settings, most students arrived with little to no prior exposure to critical accessibility or disability justice. When confronted with epistemologies that foreground embodied knowledge, standpoint, or social critique, students often acknowledged them begrudgingly but reclassified them incorrectly as "psychology" or "soft" domains. Many sought to defend computer science as an elite and "technical" territory excluding these other knowledges. Most brought strong positivist and technosolutionist commitments, seeing computing as neutral and apolitical. In large introductory classes, material linking computing to systemic oppression sometimes provoked hostility. More often, however, the dominant reaction was disengagement or discomfort, often expressed through defenses of disciplinary boundaries ("I try to not get involved in these political things, I'm just here to study CS"). The visiting CS study club students who attended my guest lecture, by contrast, were not at all hostile and indeed quite receptive, but appeared to be quite unbelieving of the premise that technology itself could be political. As well, in every course offering, there is always a small core of students (fewer than 10%) who embraced the topics enthusiastically and regretted their late introduction.

To address the challenges of teaching technoableism, I draw on introductory STS and CDS topics. Comparing disability identity and neurodiversity identity as a topic can strongly resonate for students, which then paves the way for Garland–Thomson's concept of the normate (as a common concern). I find Haraway's critique of the "God trick", Hamraie's concept of the "normate template", and the conflation of norms and averages in anthropometry to be accessible topics for CS students, despite their lack of curricular scaffolding. By third year, students had rarely been asked to reflect on the limits of their own knowledge or to confront technicism directly. By this year, students have already been exposed to the core topics in the "Society Ethics and Professionalism" (SEP) KAs, but I found this learning to be of limited use for providing useful curricular scaffolding to upper year courses.

DISCUSSION

Both my teaching reflection and the document analysis of CS2023 indicate that there is a strong tacit curriculum of technological efficiency, neutrality, and rigor. This is evidenced by curricular gaps, dilution patterns, and student responses. The tacit curriculum shapes how students resisted technoableism, often by devaluing critical approaches as irrelevant to CS.

My positionality shapes both teaching and analysis. I coded the discourse and material anchors from a reflexive stance grounded in disability justice. I argue that curricular hierarchies reflect choices about whose knowledge is legitimized. As a nondisabled researcher committed to design and disability justice, I make by position clear to my students. These efforts sometimes exposed disabled students to toxic reactions from their peers, despite efforts to mitigate them. Ableism is deeply entrenched and I also risk reproducing it.

My teaching experiences and document analysis reflect a broader structural absence: critical accessibility is rarely mandated in core topics. Compounding this, mainstream (non-critical) accessibility occupies curricular space and reinscribes the neutrality myth of computing. The problem is also epistemic. Students questioned the legitimacy of critical social theory within CS (e.g., critical disability studies, critical accessibility studies, post-colonial computing). This reflects the dilution patterns surfaced in the CS2023 document analysis.

What this chapter offers is an initial accounting of gaps and patterns, pointing toward more sustained future work on how technoableism is reproduced and resisted within computing curricula. Initial indications show the need for stronger curricular anchors technoableism: its justice commitments and its complexity as an analytical concept. This means embedding critical theory, sociotechnical analysis, and critical disability studies beyond the limited framing in CS2023.

The devil's advocate might argue that any curricular content additions must be matched with content removal, given limited program hours CS Core topics already require 270 hours of instructional time (ACM/IEEE-CS Joint Task Force on Computing Curricula, 2023, p. 13). So, implementation requires reprioritization. We must surface and reshape the technicism and technosolutionism that is currently embedded in the extant LTs and LOs. The KAs of SEP and HCI alone hold 26 core hours (plus an additional 30 KA hours). Within the envelope, all the mainstream accessibility LTs and LOs must be replaced with a scaffold of critical accessibility LTs and LOs. Without such changes, students will encounter justice discourse but without the training to enact it through technical, governance, or social practices, thereby reinforcing the technoableism that arises from technicism.

CONCLUSION

This chapter has provided an initial response to the central question: to what extent, and in what ways, do existing undergraduate computing curricula support or fail to support justice-oriented teaching of technoableism? The response included a document analysis of "Computer Science Curricula 2023: Curriculum Guidelines for Undergraduate Degree Programs in Computer Science", also known as CS2023 (ACM/IEEE–CS Joint Task Force on Computing Curricula, 2023), triangulated with personal teaching reflections. The results show that the Joint Task Force on Computing, through its instrument CS2023, instantiates a form of curricular authority that, at present, peripheralizes the topics necessary for CS students to effectively learn about technoableism. This pattern appears via the discursive and material anchoring of the LTs (recognition without material anchoring), their peripheral placement in curricular strata (coreCS, coreKA, noncore), and their peripheral placement among the 17 different KAs that constitute the Computer Science body of knowledge, and with notable absences in high-stakes KAs. Without curricular revision, programs will continue to graduate practitioners with knowledge of justice rhetoric but without the training to enact it. Revision is possible, provided that curricular authority can be leveraged, via reprioritization within existing instructional hour envelopes, primarily by reframing SEP/HCI allocations, replacing mainstream accessibility modules with critical scaffolds, and exposing and shifting technicist and technosolutionist content across central KAs. This initial accounting identifies specific targets for shifting from rhetorical inclusion to structural accountability, and for leveraging curricular power toward building more effective knowledges and practices to combat technoableism in computing education.

ACKNOWLEDGMENT

A large language model (OpenAI's GPT-5-series) was used in a limited capacity, solely as a drafting and revision aid. It did not contribute to the substance, arguments, or conclusions of this chapter; all such decisions and the final text are the author's responsibility.

REFLECTION QUESTIONS

1. What is technoableism, and how does the current computer science curriculum inadvertently reinforce it?
2. Why is the perception of technology as neutral or apolitical a barrier to teaching justice-oriented computing?
3. The author critiques mainstream accessibility for being too focused on technical compliance. How does critical accessibility differ in its approach to power and justice?
4. Reflecting on the author's teaching experiences, why might computer science students resist engaging with topics like disability justice and social theory?

APPENDIX

ABBREVIATIONS

TABLE 12A.1
Knowledge Areas Abbreviations and Full Names

KA Abbreviation	Knowledge Area (KA)
AI	Artificial Intelligence
AL	Algorithmic Foundations
AR	Architecture and Organization
DM	Data Management
FPL	Foundations of Programming Languages
GIT	Graphics and Interactive Techniques
HCI	Human–Computer Interaction
MSF	Mathematical and Statistical Foundations
NC	Networking and Communication

(Continued)

TABLE 12A.1
(Continued)

KA Abbreviation	Knowledge Area (KA)
OS	Operating Systems
PDC	Parallel and Distributed Computing
SDF	Software Development Fundamentals
SE	Software Engineering
SEC	Security
SEP	Society, Ethics, and Profession
SF	Systems Fundamentals
SPD	Specialized Platform Development

LEARNING TOPICS IN THE KA OF ARTIFICIAL INTELLIGENCE

The Knowledge Area of Artificial Intelligence contains only the two following noncore Learning Topics, both of which discursively and materially anchored in the sociotechnical rather than in normative values.

Human–agent interaction (See also: HCI–User, HCI–Accessibility) a. Communication methodologies (verbal and non–verbal) b. Practical issues c. Applications

[LT#8, noncore, KU: AI–Agents: Agents and Cognitive Systems, KA: AI]

Human–robot interaction (See also: HCI–User, HCI–Accessibility) a. Shared workspaces b. Human–robot teaming and physical HRI c. Social assistive robots d. Motion/task/goal prediction e. Collaboration and communication (explicit vs implicit, verbal or symbolic vs non–verbal or visual) f. Trust

[LT#14, noncore, KU: AI–Robotics: Robotics, KA: AI]

NOTE

1 Using regular expressions for a semantic field of all lemma case–invariants of "abl_", "access_", "accommodate_", "AT_", "barrier_", "disab_", "diversit_", "equit_", "identit_", "impair_", "inclus_", "universal design_", with a stage to filter out non–targeted word senses (e.g., "database access", "identity theft", "diversity of networked applications").

REFERENCES

ACM/IEEE–CS Joint Task Force on Computing Curricula (Ed.). (2020). *Computing Curricula 2020: Paradigms for Global Computing Education*. Association for Computing Machinery. https://doi.org/10.1145/3467967

ACM/IEEE–CS Joint Task Force on Computing Curricula (Ed.). (2023). *Computer Science Curricula 2023: Curriculum Guidelines for Undergraduate Degree Programs in Computer Science*. ACM, Inc. https://doi.org/10.1145/2534860

Burgstahler, S. (2011). Universal Design: Implications for Computing Education. *ACM Transactions on Computing Education*, *11*(3), 1–17. https://doi.org/10.1145/2037276.2037283

Cohen, R. F., Fairley, A. V., Gerry, D., & Lima, G. R. (2005). Accessibility in Introductory Computer Science. *Proceedings of the 36th SIGCSE Technical Symposium on Computer Science Education*, St. Louis, MO, 17–21. https://doi.org/10.1145/1047344.1047367

Costanza–Chock, S. (2020). *Design Justice: Community–Led Practices to Build the Worlds We Need*. The MIT Press.

Davis, J. L. (2020). *How Artifacts Afford: The Power and Politics of Everyday Things*. The MIT Press.

Hamraie, A. (2012). Universal Design Research as a New Materialist Practice. *Disability Studies Quarterly*, *32*(4). https://doi.org/10.18061/dsq.v32i4.3246

Ladner, R. E., Ludi, S., & Domanski, R. (2025). Teaching about Accessibility in Computer Science Education. *ACM Inroads*, *16*(2), 28–42. https://doi.org/10.1145/3729877

Ludi, S., Huenerfauth, M., Hanson, V., Rajendra Palan, N., & Conn, P. (2018). Teaching Inclusive Thinking to Undergraduate Students in Computing Programs. *Proceedings of the 49th ACM Technical Symposium on Computer Science Education*, Baltimore, MD, 717–722. https://doi.org/10.1145/3159450.3159512

Norman, D. A. (2013). *The Design of Everyday Things* (Revised and expanded edition). Basic Books.

Oleson, A., Ko, A. J., & Ladner, R. (Eds.). (2023). *Teaching Accessible Computing*. Self–published. https://bookish.press/tac

Parthasarathy, P. D., & Joshi, S. (2024). Teaching Digital Accessibility in Computing Education: Views of Educators in India. *Proceedings of the 2024 ACM Conference on International Computing Education Research,* Melbourne – *Volume 1*, 222–232. https://doi.org/10.1145/3632620.3671122

Shew, A. (2020). Ableism, Technoableism, and Future AI. *IEEE Technology and Society Magazine*, *39*(1), 40–85. https://doi.org/10.1109/MTS.2020.2967492

Shinohara, K., Kawas, S., Ko, A. J., & Ladner, R. E. (2018). Who Teaches Accessibility?: A Survey of U.S. Computing Faculty. *Proceedings of the 49th ACM Technical Symposium on Computer Science Education*, 197–202. https://doi.org/10.1145/3159450.3159484

Weeden, E. (2023). A Model of an Accessibility Curriculum in Higher Education. *Frontiers in Computer Science*, *5*, 1139350. https://doi.org/10.3389/fcomp.2023.1139350

13 Artificial Intelligence, Social Media, and People with Disabilities

A Critical Review

Hannah Bullock, Naleni Jacob and Christo El Morr

INTRODUCTION

Critical Disability Studies

Critical Disability Studies (CDS) has emerged as a crucial interdisciplinary field that repositions disability beyond narrow frameworks that emphasize the need for biomedical intervention in response to disability and impairment, instead understanding it as relational and situating it within broader sociocultural and political contexts (Goodley, 2023; Shakespeare, 2014). Rooted in critical theory and enriched by insights from feminist, queer, postcolonial, and critical race studies, CDS foregrounds the lived experiences of disabled individuals while critically interrogating the institutional structures and discursive practices shaping those experiences (Casper & Laine Talley, 2007; Erevelles, 2011; Kafer, 2013). It directly challenges dominant narratives that locate disability exclusively within individual bodies, promoting instead a relational perspective that recognizes the material, structural, and epistemic dimensions of disablement (Jurgens, 2023; Olsen & Pilson, 2022; Shildrick, 2009).

Two foundational paradigms—the medical model and the social model—have significantly influenced both scholarly discourse and public policy regarding disability (Oliver, 2013). The medical model conceptualizes disability primarily as an individual pathology requiring clinical treatment, normalization, or management, often reducing the disabled individual to a clinical subject stripped of social and cultural agency (Marks, 1997; Shakespeare, 2006). In response, the social model posits that disability is primarily constructed through systemic barriers embedded within physical environments and social attitudes rather than located within individual bodies (Oliver, 2013; Shakespeare, 2006). Although the social model has been instrumental in advancing rights-based approaches and promoting accessibility, CDS scholars critique its limitations, notably its insufficient attention to embodied realities such as chronic pain, fatigue, and illness (Anastasiou & Kauffman, 2013). Thus, neither the medical nor the social model alone fully captures the complexity of disability as lived, represented, and regulated (Beaudry, 2016; Hogan, 2019).

CDS therefore advocates for an epistemological shift away from totalizing definitions toward recognizing disability's inherent multiplicity and fluidity (Goodley et al., 2019; Richardson et al., 2023). It compels scholars to critically examine how disability is defined, by whom, and for what purposes, highlighting the politics inherent in processes of identification (Meekosha & Shuttleworth, 2009). Crucially, CDS questions who is permitted institutional recognition as disabled, who is systematically excluded, and the broader implications of rigid identity categories that fail to accommodate intersectional and fluid experiences (Prince, 2009; Spagnuolo, 2016). Such questions are not merely theoretical—they carry significant material implications, influencing individuals' access to resources, legal protections, and cultural belonging.

DOI: 10.1201/9781003737810-15

Adopting a justice-oriented approach, CDS demands a conceptual framework expansive enough to embrace the contradictions, tensions, and ambiguities inherent in disabled lives (Robinson, 2017). It challenges us to scrutinize how power functions through diagnostic practices, normative standards, and institutional classifications (Prince, 2009; Robinson, 2017). CDS envisions disability not as a deficit to be corrected or managed, but as a generative site of knowledge production, resistance, and community building. Informed by this critical perspective, this chapter examines the intersections of artificial intelligence (AI), social media, and disability, attending carefully to both the emancipatory possibilities and the structural risks these digital technologies pose for disabled communities (Hamraie, 2015).

Applying a CDS lens is essential because AI systems are not neutral technical artifacts; they embody social assumptions and reproduce entrenched hierarchies. CDS provides the conceptual tools to interrogate how disability is framed and acted upon within technological infrastructures. Its attention to power, discourse, and lived experience exposes how AI often defaults to biomedical or deficit-based models—treating disability as an individual "problem" to be managed—while obscuring the structural barriers and social meanings embedded in data, algorithms, and design decisions. By foregrounding disabled people as knowledge producers and political actors, CDS enables a shift from mere accommodation toward justice-oriented technological futures and prevents AI from reinforcing technoableism and epistemic exclusion.

With the rapid and expansive rise of AI, the field of CDS has recently started generating critical literature pertaining to the experiences of disabled individuals and their interactions with this stream of technology focusing on areas such as education, accessibility, and social inclusion (Almufareh et al., 2024; Foley & Melese, 2025; Rice & Dunn, 2023). A key critique at this juncture in the evolution of the study surrounding the intersectionality between CDS and AI includes a resurgence of the popularity of the medical model when investigating the assumption of AI as a method of alleviating the challenges placed on inclusive education providers, which reframes education provision as a burden (Rice & Dunn, 2023).

Another area of critical review includes the encoding of bias into AI systems which reproduces and promotes sociotechnical disenfranchisement based on entrenched ableist ideas that are now finding their way into the construction of AI technologies (Almufareh et al., 2024).

Artificial Intelligence

AI refers to a branch of computer science dedicated to developing systems capable of executing tasks traditionally associated with human cognition. These tasks include perception, reasoning, learning, decision-making, and language processing (El Morr et al., 2022; El Morr & Ali-Hassan, 2019). AI technologies now permeate numerous societal domains, ranging from autonomous vehicles and robotic surgery to predictive health analytics and personalized digital platforms (El Morr, 2023). Among various subfields, two particular branches—machine learning (ML) and generative AI (GenAI)—have gained notable prominence within both academic discourse and commercial applications. Given their substantial societal impact and increasing integration into digital ecosystems such as social media, a detailed examination of these technologies is particularly warranted.

Machine Learning

ML represents a fundamental subdomain of AI, emphasizing algorithms capable of identifying complex patterns within data and creating predictive models. Key ML methodologies include neural networks, decision trees, logistic regression, and support vector machines, each methodologically distinct yet unified by the shared objective of mapping input variables (features) to specific outcomes (targets). In practice, ML algorithms are typically employed across three primary types of analytical tasks: classification, regression, and clustering. Classification algorithms sort data into discrete categories, such as predicting the presence or absence of diabetes in a patient. Regression algorithms, conversely, predict continuous outcomes, such as forecasting COVID-19 infection rates within a community. Clustering techniques categorize data based on inherent similarities, allowing for pattern recognition in large, unlabeled datasets—for instance, grouping emergency department patients according to shared demographic or clinical characteristics (Russell & Norvig, 2020).

The development of effective ML models involves a structured, iterative process that typically comprises training and testing phases. During training, algorithms are exposed to labeled datasets containing known inputs and outcomes, allowing them to progressively refine their predictive accuracy by minimizing discrepancies between predicted and actual outcomes. Subsequently, during the testing phase, models are evaluated against separate datasets with known outcomes, allowing for the assessment of their predictive performance using metrics such as accuracy, i.e., the rate of correct predictions. In critical application areas, such as healthcare, the acceptability and practical utility of ML models depend significantly upon their interpretability, fairness, and ability to generalize across diverse populations (El Morr et al., 2022).

Generative AI

GenAI distinguishes itself from traditional ML by focusing explicitly on content creation rather than solely prediction or classification. These systems leverage extensive datasets to generate novel outputs—such as text, images, audio, video, or computer code—that closely resemble the structure, style, and patterns of the training data. Crucially, GenAI models do not simply retrieve stored information; rather, they synthesize new content probabilistically, informed by patterns derived from prior examples.

One notable example of GenAI is ChatGPT, developed by OpenAI. ChatGPT operates on the basis of a Large Language Model (LLM) known as the Generative Pre-trained Transformer (GPT), trained on vast textual corpora to probabilistically predict subsequent words within sentences (Open AI et al., 2024). This predictive process allows GPT to generate text that is contextually coherent, syntactically accurate, and strikingly human-like in its readability. While GPT does not possess cognitive awareness or experiential understanding, it can convincingly simulate aspects of human reasoning, dialogue, and even creative expression. Users interact with the underlying GPT model through an accessible interface (ChatGPT), which responds in real time to prompts and inquiries, facilitating dynamic human-AI communication (Brown et al., 2020).

The seemingly intelligent behavior of GenAI systems arises from their capacity to recognize and replicate probabilistic linguistic associations embedded within massive datasets. Despite lacking consciousness or intentionality, these models convincingly approximate human-like cognitive processes. Consequently, GenAI carries significant implications across diverse fields, including education, healthcare, media, and social communication. It becomes particularly critical to interrogate the functions, utilities, and associated risks of GenAI within contexts involving marginalized communities, such as disabled populations, whose lived realities are often misrepresented or inadequately captured by conventional data structures. Table 13.1 summarizes these different AI approaches.

Because social media platforms are today's dominant digital public spheres, AI's most consequential operations for disabled people occur in the algorithms that curate, rank, and moderate online content. This review therefore situates disability analysis not just in AI broadly but specifically in the sociotechnical systems of social media.

The Use of AI with Social Media for People with Disabilities

Within this broad field, the review's focus is on AI systems embedded in social media infrastructures—particularly recommendation engines, moderation models, and accessibility features—because these algorithmic tools structure what disabled users can see, say, and be seen as.

TABLE 13.1
AI approaches

Category of Artificial Intelligence	Key Area of Focus	Methods/Examples of AI Which Fit into the Category	Applications	Examples
Machine Learning	Undertake algorithmic driven complex pattern identification and predictive model creation	Neutral networks, decision trees, logistic regression, and support vector machines	Classification Algorithms: Sorting data into discrete categories Regression Algorithms: Prediction of continuous outcomes Clustering techniques categorize data based on inherent similarities, allowing for pattern recognition in large, unlabeled datasets	Classification Algorithms: Predicting the presence of diabetes in patients Regression Algorithms: Forecasting COVID infection rates in given community Clustering techniques: grouping emergency department patients according to shared demographic or clinical characteristics (Russel and Norvig, 2020)
Generative AI	Leverage extensive datasets to generate novel outputs such as images or text, that closely resemble the structure, style, and patterns of the training data	Large Language Models (LLM) which output text that is contextually coherent, syntactically accurate, and strikingly human-like in its readability	Recognition and replication of probabilistic linguistic associations to create new text, images, and other complex output Facilitate dynamic human-AI interactions (Brown et. al., 2020)	ChatGPT (Open AI et al., 2024)

Since the advent of social media in the early 21st century, digital platforms have had a profound impact on communication practices, identity formation, and collective activism (Castillo-Esparcia et al., 2023; Greijdanus et al., 2020; Lüders et al., 2022). For disabled individuals and disability advocacy organizations, social media has significantly expanded opportunities for community-building, raising awareness, and engaging in rights-based advocacy (Sannon et al., 2023; Sweet et al., 2020). Digital platforms constitute vibrant spaces where disabled users can articulate lived experiences, challenge dominant ableist narratives, and amplify demands for systemic change (Cocq & Ljuslinder, 2020; Sannon et al., 2023). For individuals experiencing mobility, sensory, or communication disabilities—who may face disproportionate barriers in how they are able to participate in public/social life, and build relationships and community—these platforms serve as essential channels for fostering connection, affirming identity, and enhancing visibility (Baumgartner et al., 2023). Nevertheless, despite their potential, social media platforms have consistently drawn critical scrutiny regarding their actual accessibility, usability, and inclusivity (Anderson et al., 2023).

Central to ongoing critiques is the growing influence of AI, which now fundamentally shapes user interactions within digital environments. AI-driven systems manage critical functions such as content moderation, recommendation algorithms that prioritize specific content, and accessibility enhancements such as automated captioning and alt-text generation. These systems also power targeted advertising strategies that curate user experiences based on algorithmically interpreted data. Such technological implementations raise significant ethical and political questions: Who defines the criteria for content moderation or censorship? To what extent do algorithmic determinations genuinely align with the diverse needs, lived realities, and cultural contexts of disabled individuals? While AI holds substantial promise for enhancing accessibility and digital participation, it simultaneously carries risks of perpetuating exclusion, discrimination, and marginalization—particularly through biases embedded in training data, inaccurate interpretations of disability-related language, and opaque system design processes. Therefore, examining the integration of AI into digital platforms must extend beyond purely technical analyses to encompass the broader social and political implications these technologies hold for disabled communities (Noble, 2018).

An emerging body of research has begun to critically investigate how AI-driven systems monitor, analyze, and potentially intervene in disability-related discourse online. Sentiment analysis algorithms, content classification tools, and moderation systems may inadvertently amplify certain narratives while systematically suppressing others, largely due to the problematic ways these systems interpret disability-related terminology (Anderson, 2023; Jaiswal et al., 2024; Kaur et al., 2024; Venkit et al., 2023). Such practices prompt critical reflections: Whose voices and perspectives are algorithmically elevated or diminished? Can AI reliably interpret nuanced social meanings and contexts without reinforcing stigma, discrimination, or surveillance of disabled individuals? These concerns are neither theoretical nor speculative; they highlight urgent needs for scholarship critically examining algorithmic impacts on the public perception and representation of disability, especially in relation to epistemic justice, self-advocacy, and digital participation.

Further, AI algorithms significantly influence the representation of disability through platform-driven engagement metrics. Such algorithms, typically used on social media, prioritize content aligning with normative societal standards of productivity, health, and individual achievement, thus inadvertently reinforcing medicalized, deficit-based, or inspirational framings of disability (Hadley, 2016). Consequently, critical narratives emphasizing resistance, interdependence, and crip identities may become marginalized, excluded, or undervalued (Ellis & Goggin, 2018). Platforms incentivizing content visibility based primarily on engagement metrics like clicks, likes, and shares may further marginalize critical disability discourses, favoring more commodifiable or mainstream representations. Without intentionally integrating disability justice frameworks into AI system design and governance, algorithmic practices risk reproducing the systemic marginalization they ostensibly aim to overcome.

Addressing these challenges requires more systematic and sustained inquiries into the intersection of AI technologies, social media platforms, and disabled users. Key questions must be rigorously explored: What specific benefits do AI-driven platforms genuinely offer disabled individuals? What risks and harms are inadequately acknowledged, overlooked, or underreported? Additionally, where do significant knowledge gaps persist in our understanding of these dynamics? A comprehensive and critical review is essential for identifying pathways toward equitable, inclusive, and disability-centered approaches to technological development and implementation—ones that prioritize disabled people's lived experiences, expertise, and expressed needs.

Moreover, prevailing discourses around "AI for good" or "AI for social good" often inadequately address the roles and agency of disabled individuals beyond passive user positions—typically casting them merely as consumers or beneficiaries of technological interventions. As Lillywhite and Wolbring (2020) compellingly argue, such techno-optimistic narratives frequently omit recognition of disabled individuals as active producers of knowledge, technological innovators, or political agents within AI and ML ecosystems. Furthermore, prevailing discussions often neglect to thoroughly analyze AI's broader structural and societal impacts on disabled communities. This conceptual oversight severely limits not only our understanding of AI's practical consequences but also our collective capacity to pursue genuinely inclusive, equitable, and participatory technological futures. To genuinely foster justice-oriented innovation, disabled individuals must be positioned explicitly as designers, critics, cocreators, and decision-makers in shaping the future development and governance of AI systems.

Although AI encompasses a broad range of technologies, this review deliberately centers on **social media algorithms** because these algorithmic infrastructures are decisive in shaping how disabled people are seen, heard, and represented online, often more so than AI's other technical applications.

METHODS

This scoping review was conducted following the methodological framework initially proposed by Arksey and O'Malley and subsequently refined by Levac et al. To ensure rigor and transparency, the study adhered to the PRISMA-ScR (Preferred Reporting Items for Systematic Reviews and Meta-Analyses extension for Scoping Reviews) guidelines to ensure rigor and transparency. The review seeks to answer the question: How do social media algorithms, powered by AI, shape the digital participation, representation, and visibility of people with disabilities—amplifying some narratives while suppressing others—and what design and governance strategies can counteract ableist bias and exclusion in these algorithmic systems? Framing the inquiry at the intersection of AI, social media algorithms, and disability ensures a critical examination of the digital architectures that shape disabled users' everyday participation and public voice.

Eligibility Criteria

To capture a comprehensive and inclusive body of work, we included peer-reviewed journal articles, conference proceedings, and grey literature, such as reports from nongovernmental organizations and government agencies, published from 2010 onward. Eligible sources were required to address the use of AI technologies in, on, or in conjunction with social media platforms and to involve or affect people with disabilities in some capacity. No restrictions were placed on disability type, demographic characteristics (including age and gender), or geographic context. We included literature across diverse domains—such as research, education, activism, policy development, and community initiatives—to reflect the multifaceted implications of AI and social media for disabled populations.

Information Sources and Search Strategy

A systematic search was conducted across four major databases: PubMed, Web of Science, IEEE Xplore, and PsycINFO. The search strategy was designed to capture the breadth of scholarship across disciplinary boundaries and employed both controlled vocabulary (e.g., MeSH terms) and free-text keywords. These terms reflected the three central concepts of the review: AI, social media, and disability. Boolean operators and database-specific filters were used to refine the search results. Additionally, we performed backward citation searching from the bibliographies of included sources to identify supplementary materials that may not have been retrieved through database queries.

Screening and Selection Process

All records retrieved during the search process were imported into a reference management software program and deduplicated. Title and abstract screening was independently conducted by two reviewers to assess initial relevance. Studies deemed potentially eligible were retrieved in full and assessed against the inclusion criteria. Discrepancies between reviewers were resolved through iterative discussion and consensus-building. In cases where consensus could not be reached, a third reviewer acted as an arbitrator. This multistep screening process ensured consistency and minimized bias in the selection of sources.

Data Extraction and Charting

To facilitate systematic data collection and synthesis, we developed and pilot-tested a standardized data extraction form. The following information was recorded for each included study: author(s), year of publication, country or region of focus, study aim, type of AI technology utilized (e.g., sentiment analysis, chatbots, recommendation systems), social media platform(s) examined, target disability group(s), key findings, reported benefits and risks, ethical, social, or legal concerns, and any identified gaps in the literature. Data extraction was performed by one reviewer and subsequently verified by a second to ensure completeness and accuracy.

Data Synthesis

The extracted data were subjected to a descriptive and thematic synthesis. Findings were organized according to the type of AI technology used, its intended purpose, and its documented or inferred implications for equity, inclusion, and disability justice. Through this process, we identified recurring patterns, thematic contradictions, and underexplored areas that warrant further scholarly and policy attention. This synthesis provides a foundation for a more nuanced understanding of how AI intersects with social media platforms in ways that both support and marginalize disabled communities.

RESULTS

The initial database search yielded 143 articles, 14 of which were duplicates, bringing the total of unique articles to 129 records. Following a screening of titles and abstracts, 61 of these articles were excluded. The full texts of the remaining 68 articles were then retrieved and assessed for eligibility against the inclusion criteria. This full-text review resulted in the exclusion of a further 52 articles, leaving 16 studies that were retained for analysis. An additional six articles were identified through expert feedback and were included in the final synthesis, bringing the total number of included studies to 22. Figure 13.1 summarizes the process.

Across 22 studies, AI-driven social media algorithms (moderation, recommendation/ranking, and auto-labeling for accessibility) influence disabled users' participation and visibility in conflicting ways. Benefits include lowering entry barriers (auto-captions/alt-text), expanding networked support, and strategically amplifying advocacy. However, harms cluster around three main issues: (1) biased moderation misclassifying disability talk as "toxic/negative," (2) engagement-focused curation favoring palatable or inspirational disability narratives while down-ranking critical or activist content, and (3) surveillance practices (e.g., digital phenotyping) that risk stigma and violations of consent. Effects vary by language, region, and disability type, with concealable disabilities and contexts in the Global South being most underserved. Overall, algorithms act as gatekeepers of epistemic visibility; justice-oriented design and governance—through cocreation, accountable audits, and enforceable accessibility—are essential to transform inclusion features into lasting power.

Applications and Critical Implications of AI on Social Media

Algorithmic Interpretation and Biased Moderation

Contemporary social media platforms increasingly rely on a range of AI technologies to manage content moderation, conduct sentiment analysis, enhance accessibility, and maximize user engagement. These platforms frequently leverage open-source, "plug-and-play" solutions—often marketed under the term AI-as-a-Service (AIaaS)—to streamline critical functions such as content filtering and detection of harmful speech. Prominent among these AI-driven tools are sentiment analysis and toxicity detection models, including VADER, TextBlob, Google Cloud NLP, DistilBERT, and Toxic-BERT. Employing natural language processing (NLP) and ML, these systems are notably

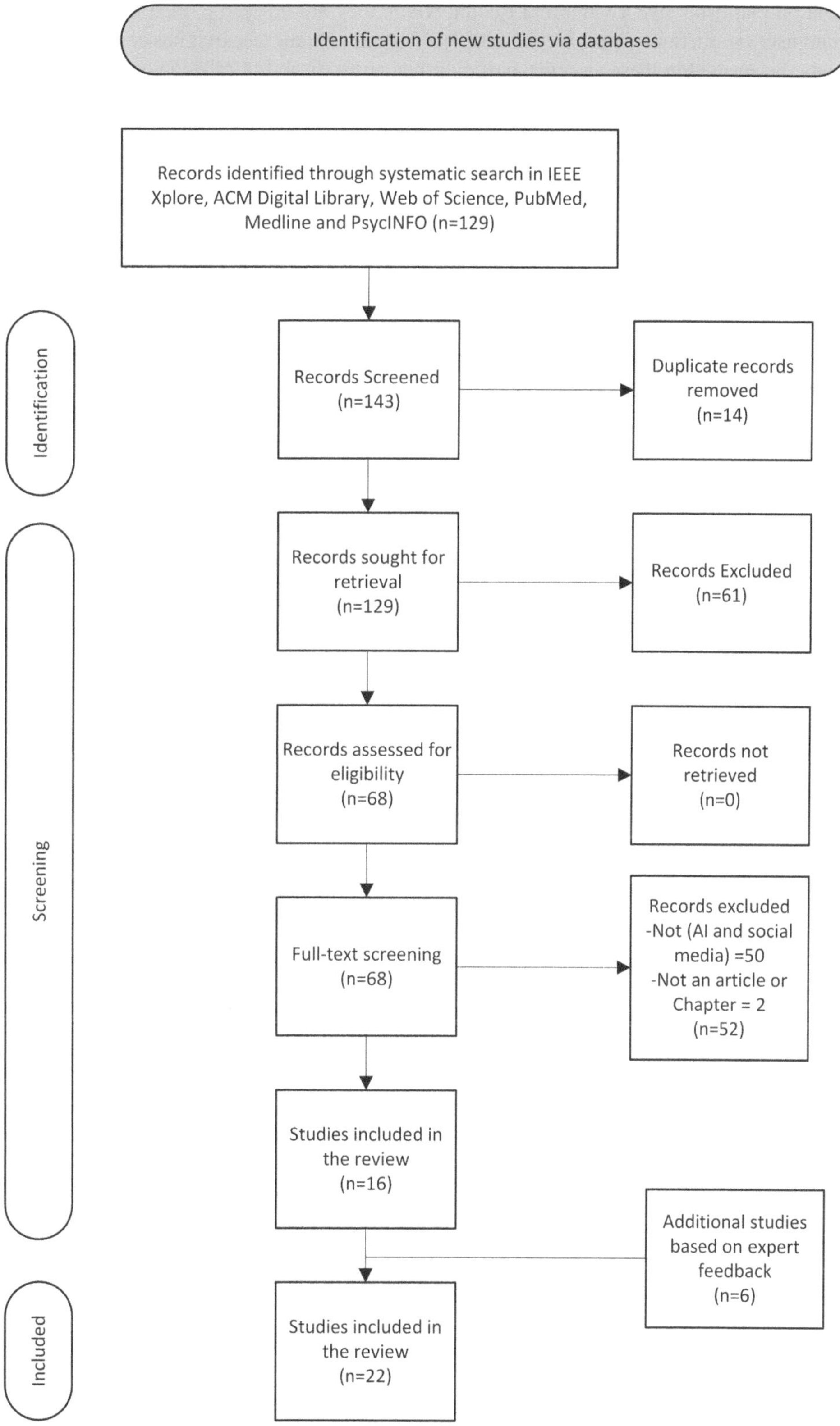

FIGURE 13.1 PRISMA diagram.

prevalent on platforms like Twitter and Reddit, where they are utilized to identify harassment and moderate user interactions (Venkit et al., 2023). However, recent research has revealed significant systematic biases within these systems, particularly against disability-related content. For instance, Venkit et al. (2023) found that posts merely referencing disability are disproportionately flagged as negative or toxic, demonstrating an implicit assumption within these models that disability itself connotes negativity.

Moreover, linguistic and cultural biases pose substantial challenges for existing AI systems. Kaur et al. (2024) critique the predominantly English-centric orientation of current NLP tools, which often fail to identify or adequately interpret ableist hate speech within non-English linguistic and intersectional cultural contexts. Williams (2023) extends this critique by observing that LLMs such as ChatGPT are not neutral but function as "confirmation bias optimizers," magnifying existing societal biases through their ability to identify, iterate, and exacerbate perceived patterns in natural language rather than simply reflect them. He explains that because these systems are built to provide statistically probable answers that a user is likely to accept, not to determine truth, they inevitably perpetuate real-world harms in areas like policing, healthcare, and employment. Williams concludes that the only effective solution is a fundamental reformulation of how these systems are built, requiring ethical oversight and the centering of marginalized communities as "design leaders."

Venkit et al. (2023) explore the origins of disability bias in sentiment analysis models, examining whether bias emerges from the content of social media conversations or is inherently embedded within AI systems. Utilizing the Bias Identification Test in Sentiment corpus, they assessed four sentiment analysis tools and two toxicity detection models. The study revealed consistent explicit biases: disability-related sentences were disproportionately classified as negative compared to neutral controls. This consistent misclassification underscores how current AI models inherently associate disability discourse with negativity, further entrenching harmful misrepresentations and contributing to systemic marginalization.

The implications of such biases extend far beyond theoretical concerns. As demonstrated by Venkit et al. (2023), current NLP models often lack the sophistication needed to interpret contextual nuances associated with disability-related language accurately. Consequently, disabled users are disproportionately censored and excluded from digital discourse. These findings indicate that existing AI systems not only struggle to distinguish between hostile and neutral disability references but also inadvertently perpetuate broader patterns of exclusion and stigmatization. The authors thus advocate for the urgent development of more contextually sensitive and inclusive NLP frameworks capable of equitably interpreting disability discourse.

The Duality of GenAI: Empowerment and Risk

GenAI has similarly become deeply embedded within social media ecosystems. According to Hemsley et al. (2024), GenAI is extensively utilized for personalizing content based on user preferences, generating multimedia content for broad distribution, and performing rapid data analyses. While GenAI offers promising avenues as assistive technologies—facilitating content creation for users with communication disabilities—these technologies also introduce considerable risks. Key concerns include the unchecked proliferation of misinformation, reinforcement of harmful stereotypes about disability, underrepresentation of marginalized communities, and amplification of existing social inequalities. One need to underscore the heightened vulnerability of individuals with developmental communication disabilities to issues such as cyberbullying, excessive exposure to detrimental content, and the addictive patterns driven by algorithmic engagement strategies (Hemsley et al., 2024). The authors call explicitly for participatory, codesigned research that actively incorporates the lived experiences of individuals with developmental communication disabilities, ensuring that these perspectives guide both technological development and evaluative processes. Providing a specific example of this dynamic, Johansen (2024) presents the case of a study participant with a speech impediment. The participant reported that GenAI captions were often inaccurate and difficult to use, but he then adopted a voice-generating AI tool to "clone" his own voice, allowing it to speak his words on his behalf. This act was described as empowering and a creative method for addressing communication barriers, enabling him to be seen and heard. Critically, framing such user-led adaptations as simply "overcoming" challenges can reinforce common and potentially harmful stereotypes about disability.

Algorithmic Curation and the Politics of Visibility

AI-driven accessibility features have concurrently become integral to mainstream platforms. Notable examples include YouTube's automated captioning powered by speech recognition technologies, Apple's VoiceOver screen reader employing NLP for text interpretation, and Microsoft's cloud-based personalized accessibility settings, which adapt interfaces across multiple devices.

Further literature has explored how AI algorithms significantly influence the visibility and dissemination of disability-related narratives through content curation. For instance, Bail (2016) employed NLP methodologies such as tokenization and tagging to investigate autism advocacy efforts on Facebook, demonstrating how advocacy messaging is subtly mediated by platform infrastructures. Expanding on this, scholars emphasize that these algorithmic systems are central to how users experience digital spaces. Bitman (2022) argues that for users with concealable disabilities, AI-powered curation and design choices govern what content becomes visible or trends, directly shaping their behavior and the potential reach of their content. Similarly, Johansen (2024) highlights how algorithmic ranking systems on platforms like Instagram influence the visibility of posts by disabled youth, determining which narratives are promoted and which are effectively down-ranked. This gatekeeping function is not accidental; Phutane et al. (2025) note that AI tools like recommendation systems and moderation bots are fundamental to platform infrastructure, shaping how disability content is either circulated or censored and governing the reach of disabled users' activism.

AI as a Tool for Surveillance: The Case of Digital Phenotyping

The application of AI in psychiatric and behavioral research contexts also warrants careful consideration. Techniques such as digital phenotyping increasingly mine social media content for behavioral and psychiatric screening purposes. Jaiswal et al. (2024) highlight the ethical complexities surrounding user consent, data ownership, and accurate representation, particularly when disabled individuals are excluded from the design process. This underscores the critical need for participatory approaches to prevent data from marginalized groups from being exploited in ways that reinforce stereotypes, stigmatization, or misrepresentation.

Collectively, these findings illustrate the complex and often contradictory roles played by AI technologies in shaping the representation, management, and moderation of disability on social media. Consequently, future AI development must prioritize ethical standards and incorporate participatory, inclusive methodologies that genuinely reflect the lived experiences and perspectives of disabled individuals. Only through such critically informed approaches can AI meaningfully advance rather than hinder disability justice in digital environments.

Purposes of Use

AI technologies implemented on social media platforms serve numerous and multifaceted functions, which can be broadly categorized into moderation, user engagement, accessibility enhancement, and surveillance.

AI for Content Moderation and Censorship

Originally designed to bolster user safety and optimize platform efficiency, AI systems—such as sentiment analysis engines and toxicity detection algorithms—are now extensively employed in content moderation processes. Venkit et al. (2023) illustrate how these moderation tools systematically analyze user-generated content to identify and remove posts considered harmful, negative, or offensive. However, they also highlight that these systems frequently operate as mechanisms of surveillance, analyzing user content without explicit consent and relying on opaque thresholds of "toxicity." Consequently, content moderation systems can unintentionally misclassify or disproportionately censor marginalized speech, notably affecting disability-related discourse.

AI for Accessibility Enhancement

One of the most prominent and intentional uses of AI on social media platforms is to enhance accessibility and facilitate digital participation for disabled users. Foundational AI-powered tools like screen readers and auto-captioning services are instrumental in enabling basic access to social media content, videos, and online discussions (Hollier, 2017). More recently, the proliferation of GenAI has introduced new tools for users to generate captions, alt-text, image descriptions, and even assist in creating and developing their own content (Adnin & Das, 2024; McNally et al., 2024; Villena et al., 2024).

However, focusing on the lived experiences of users reveals significant friction between the theoretical purpose of these tools and their practical application. A study by Adnin and Das (2024) on how blind individuals engage with GenAI highlights this complexity. Participants reported using GenAI for practical daily tasks like proofreading, content generation, and creating image descriptions. Yet, they also encountered significant biases and usability barriers. For instance, when users disclosed their blindness in prompts, chatbots would often respond with expressions of pity, such as "I'm sorry you're blind," reinforcing harmful social stereotypes. Furthermore, the user interface of platforms like ChatGPT was found to have poor compatibility with screen readers and to disregard established web content accessibility guidelines. This made it difficult for blind users to engage with the tool or even provide feedback through standard mechanisms, leading them to try and correct the chatbot's biased responses through further conversation in the hope that the AI would learn (Adnin & Das, 2024).

Additionally, AI technologies support academic research by facilitating data collection and analysis on social platforms. Niu et al. (2024) analyze YouTube content created by individuals with cognitive, speech, and hearing impairments, exploring how creators address communication barriers and advocate for assistive technologies. The authors suggest potential AI applications to enhance accessibility—for instance, through interpreting sign language or clarifying speech. Nonetheless, concerns arise regarding these AI systems' training datasets, typically grounded in normative linguistic standards, raising questions about their effectiveness and potential biases.

AI for User Engagement and Participation

Beyond moderation, AI technologies facilitate disabled users' participation, self-expression, and activism. Hemsley et al. (2024) document the role of GenAI in assisting users with communication disabilities to generate personalized, contextually relevant content, thereby enhancing their involvement in online dialogues and advocacy campaigns. These tools significantly extend the reach and accessibility of messages by disabled creators, empowering them to articulate their lived experiences and actively participate in challenging prevailing societal injustices.

Additionally, AI technologies serve strategic roles in enhancing user engagement and shaping public discourse. For instance, Bail (2016) demonstrates how AI tools detect and amplify messages bridging disparate conversational groups, enabling advocacy organizations to reach broader, ideologically diverse audiences. Hudkins and Bills (2024) illustrate another dimension of AI-enabled engagement, showing how AI-curated content streams on platforms like TikTok can increase empathy and awareness among occupational therapy students regarding disability issues. In such educational contexts, AI functions not merely as a facilitator of engagement but also as a pedagogical tool fostering reflective and critical awareness of disability narratives.

Beyond direct accessibility functions, AI technologies play a powerful, gatekeeping role in shaping how disability is represented by governing which content gains visibility. Social media algorithms are primarily designed to maximize user engagement, a process that has profound implications for disabled creators. These systems preferentially amplify content that is emotionally provocative or conforms to simplistic, often ableist, tropes. Anderson (2023) explains how Twitter's engagement-based model prioritizes immediate, sensational reactions over nuanced or reflective content from disabled users. The platform favored simplified, emotionally resonant posts over complex analysis. As a result, AI logic reproduced ableist hierarchies in public discourse. This harms the representation of disabled people's diverse expertise and non-academic voices.

This creates a system of indirect behavioral pressure where users are incentivized to perform their disability in ways that are algorithmically favorable. Johansen (2024) found that youth with disabilities are encouraged to post "normal life" content that is more likely to be promoted by the platform's AI. Phutane et al. (2025) show that when activism challenges ableist norms or is deemed too controversial, it is often down-ranked or hidden by the very same AI systems, thereby limiting the reach and impact of disability justice efforts.

AI-enabled platforms further facilitate civic and political participation through digital activism. These platforms transcend physical and geographic constraints, creating new avenues for collective political mobilization. However, the underlying algorithmic logic often privileges content conforming to dominant cultural norms. For example, during the Kerala floods in India, Alathur et al. (2021) found that disabled individuals were largely excluded from social media discourse, particularly on Twitter, while Facebook narratives often perpetuated caste-based stereotypes—despite evidence of disabled people's active participation in relief efforts.

AI for Surveillance and Analysis

In terms of surveillance, some research engaged in a form of analytical surveillance aimed at systematically observing and understanding the public self-expression of people with disabilities on social media in a kind of thematic analysis. Mondal et al. (2022) monitored Indian Twitter to identify and select a cohort of disabled users, collecting and analyzing their public tweets to gain critical insights. The study found that disabled users on Indian Twitter revealed significant gendered differences in self-expression; for instance, women were more likely to tweet about personal experiences with discrimination and advocacy, while men tended to focus on broader, structural issues. Counterintuitively, men were also more vocal about harassment, which the authors suggest points to the stigma that may prevent women from discussing such topics publicly online.

AI applications also extend into surveillance and behavioral analysis, particularly within psychiatric and behavioral sciences (Jaiswal & Washington, 2024). Jaiswal et al. (2024) examine the growing practice of digital phenotyping—leveraging social media data to screen for patterns indicative of mental health or neurodivergent behaviors. While such AI-driven methodologies potentially aid early intervention, they simultaneously provoke significant ethical concerns related to consent, data ownership, and stigmatization of disabled identities. McKee (2013) highlights parallel ethical challenges, noting that social media content frequently treated as public domain bypasses critical consent protocols common in traditional clinical research, thereby compromising user privacy and autonomy.

To summarize, the purposes of AI on social media are deeply contradictory. On one hand, AI offers powerful tools for enhancing accessibility, fostering user participation, and enabling activism. On the other hand, these same systems function as mechanisms of surveillance, biased moderation, and algorithmic gatekeeping that shape user behavior and reinforce ableist norms. The findings reveal a significant gap between the intended purpose of many AI tools and the lived experience of disabled users, who navigate flawed interfaces and biased outputs. Therefore, advancing equitable digital spaces requires more than technological innovation; it demands a steadfast commitment to inclusive participatory design, robust ethical oversight, and a cultural sensitivity that genuinely reflects the complex realities of disabled communities.

Documented Benefits

The documented benefits of AI integration on social media platforms are twofold, encompassing both operational efficiencies for corporations and significant sociotechnical advantages for disabled users. From a corporate standpoint, AIaaS models are prized for their scalability and cost-efficiency, allowing platforms to manage immense content loads while adhering to neoliberal imperatives of resource optimization (Venkit et al., 2023). For users, these technologies can foster significant social capital and inclusion. AI-driven platforms enhance the capacity of users to form and maintain interpersonal relationships and engage with communities, which is particularly crucial for overcoming social or physical barriers (Hemsley et al., 2024). This digital participation is further enabled by personalized and adaptive technologies that support inclusion in professional, cultural, and social spheres, thereby bolstering user independence and self-esteem (Hollier, 2017).

Beyond general inclusion, AI technologies serve as critical tools for strategic advocacy and the exercise of narrative agency. Algorithms can be leveraged to amplify messages that bridge ideological divides, allowing advocacy organizations to expand their reach and engage diverse audiences (Bail, 2016). This discursive power is evident in the mobilization of collective action through hashtags and awareness campaigns, where AI helps amplify disability justice messages that align with platform logics (Phutane et al., 2025). On an individual level, this algorithmic visibility allows users to contest prevailing narratives of pity or dependency, instead asserting control over their self-representation by showcasing everyday experiences and normalizing disability within public discourse (Johansen, 2024).

Moreover, the advent of GenAI has introduced novel benefits centered on personalized support and knowledge translation. For instance, autistic users skillfully employ tools like ChatGPT not merely for content creation but as a personalized "coach" for cognitive and social navigation, helping to demystify social cues and reduce the need for masking in communication (McNally et al., 2024). AI also demonstrates significant pedagogical applications. AI-curated content on platforms like TikTok has been shown to be an effective tool in educational settings for fostering empathetic understanding, as it humanizes the lived experiences of disabled people for audiences such as future healthcare professionals (Hudkins & Bills, 2024).

While these benefits are significant, it's equally important to examine their underlying logic and how they are distributed. Many so-called inclusion gains operate within the same commercial systems that support ableist exclusion elsewhere on the platforms. For example, AI-driven accessibility features—such as auto-captioning and adaptive interfaces—are often created and implemented by large technology firms mainly to expand their market share, rather than to address systemic inequalities. Access thus remains conditional and fragile; when profits decline or platform priorities change, disabled users can suddenly lose vital functions. Moreover, algorithmically mediated "visibility" should not be mistaken for true power. Platforms tend to promote easy-to-consume, emotionally charged disability narratives but tend to demote radical, critical, or intersectional discourses. In this way, tools marketed as empowering may still serve to discipline disabled users into creating content that aligns with dominant social norms. Without participatory governance and enforceable accountability measures, the features celebrated as benefits risk perpetuating the neoliberal focus on individual adaptation instead of systemic change.

Documented Harms

Despite the potential benefits of AI, a substantial body of evidence documents multifaceted and systemic harms for disabled people, ranging from biased content moderation and practical accessibility failures to profound impacts on self-representation and systemic discrimination. A primary harm originates from AI-driven content moderation, where sentiment analysis systems systematically misclassify disability-related terms as "negative," leading to disproportionate censorship, marginalization, and the "invisibilization" of disabled voices (Kaur et al., 2024; Venkit et al., 2023). This is compounded by practical accessibility failures, such as inaccurate automated captions that exclude Deaf users (Hollier, 2017), and the harms of GenAI, which can blur the line between real and artificial content and exacerbate social media addiction (Hemsley et al., 2024).

Beyond these functional issues, engagement-driven algorithms exert significant normative pressure, incentivizing users to perform palatable or stereotypical versions of disability—such as heroic or tragic tropes—while curating a sanitized "normal" aesthetic (Johansen, 2024), suppressing radical activism that challenges mainstream views (Phutane et al., 2025). This algorithmic gatekeeping devalues the lived expertise of disabled people. Perhaps most alarmingly, these harms extend beyond platforms to systemic surveillance and "social scoring." AI systems are used by both government and private sectors to surveil social media for social security investigations, criminal justice predictions, and hiring decisions, the last of which is nearly impossible to design without disability bias (Packin, 2020). This practice of judging the "reality" of a person's disability based on their online presence represents a significant expansion of a surveillance state that disproportionately targets and harms vulnerable populations (Packin, 2020).

A final subtle harm relates to the way researchers engage with people with disabilities. Lillywhite and Wolbring (2020) found that the coverage of AI and ML in research and news-related tweets tends to be overwhelmingly techno-optimistic, framing disabled people mainly as users—either therapeutic or non-therapeutic—rather than as active contributors. Issues were typically attributed to individual impairments or usability barriers, rather than recognizing how AI/ML systems themselves may harm disabled people, such as through shifting job markets. Crucially, disabled individuals were excluded as knowledge producers or participants in shaping AI/ML discourse, governance, or ethics.

DISCUSSION

The review shows that social media algorithms both enable and regulate disability representation: the same systems that provide access and advocacy channels also embed ableist norms through ranking, moderation, and engagement metrics. Benefits are genuine but depend on platform priorities; harms are structural, not accidental, stemming from model objectives, data regimes, and governance gaps. Therefore, the focus should be on algorithmic infrastructures (objectives, training data, thresholds, appeal pathways), not just isolated "features." Justice-oriented interventions need to combine technical fixes (dataset repair, threshold tuning, appeal transparency) with shifts in power (disability-led codesign, independent audits, enforceable standards).

The Dual Nature of AI: Inclusion and Exclusion

The findings of this scoping review illuminate a central paradox in the relationship between AI and disability: the same technologies that offer pathways to inclusion simultaneously function as potent instruments of exclusion. This dual nature is not accidental but is inherent to their operation within broader sociotechnical infrastructures that reflect, and often reinforce, existing power hierarchies. Social media platforms, for instance, hold clear emancipatory potential by challenging the top-down structure of traditional media and enabling disabled individuals to build networks of care and mobilize activist movements. Yet, as this review demonstrates, these platforms are also key sites in the expansion of what Shoshana Zuboff (2019) terms "surveillance capitalism," where the data generated from lived experiences become raw material for commercial exploitation and algorithmic control, posing novel threats to privacy and autonomy.

Algorithmic Injustice and the Politics of Visibility

Indeed, achieving online visibility—a crucial goal for disability advocacy—is itself a double-edged sword. The very algorithms that can amplify a message also create new barriers. As the findings show, algorithmic bias can suppress disabled voices, expose individuals to targeted harassment, or reproduce and exacerbate deficit-based ideologies of disability. The architecture of engagement on social media often creates what Safiya U. Noble (2018) identifies as "algorithms of oppression," where systems designed for seemingly neutral purposes of sorting and ranking content systematically marginalize already oppressed groups. This review's findings, particularly the work of Kaur et al. (2024) on the "invisibilization" of disabled voices, align with this critique, demonstrating how platform logics that prioritize normative standards of popularity or desirability can silence serious, complex, or counter-hegemonic narratives about disability. This raises urgent questions about how AI can be reimagined—not merely regulated—to actively challenge, rather than reproduce, dominant ideologies. Shew's concept of "technoableism" (Shew, 2020) demands critical interrogation. AI should not be valorized for its novelty or assumed neutrality; instead, it must be scrutinized for how it reflects and amplifies existing structures of inequality.

Reimagining AI through Justice-Oriented Design

A justice-oriented approach therefore requires moving beyond techno-optimistic narratives that frame technology as a natural "solution" to disability—a phenomenon aptly termed "technoableism" (Shew, 2020). We must recognize that many AI applications function as mechanisms of sorting, filtering, and control. As Virginia Eubanks (2018) compellingly argues in the context of public services, automated systems can act as a "digital poorhouse," managing and disciplining marginalized populations while maintaining a veneer of objectivity. This review's findings resonate with that concern, showing how AI systems trained on biased datasets can entrench societal biases against disability. The challenge, then, is not only to "de-bias" technical systems but to fundamentally reorient AI's purpose toward the promotion of justice, nuance, and plurality. Content curation algorithms that elevate emotionally uplifting or easily consumable posts while demoting critical or intersectional narratives of disability must be understood not as neutral arbiters of engagement, but as powerful political actors that shape whose reality is seen and whose is rendered invisible.

Participatory Governance and Disability-Led Innovation

In light of these dynamics, a justice-oriented approach to AI must prioritize the redistribution of visibility, voice, and design power, echoing the foundational disability rights principle of "Nothing About Us Without Us." This entails building systems accountable not to abstract metrics of fairness, but to the lived realities of those most affected. It requires moving beyond tokenistic inclusion toward what Aimi Hamraie (2017) calls "crip technoscience"—a framework where disabled people are positioned as critical makers and experts who can challenge and remake technology from the ground up. Engaging disabled people not merely as users or testers, but as cocreators, designers, and decision-makers is essential to dismantling ableist architectures and fostering platforms that reflect the full, complex spectrum of disabled life—not just the most "engaging" or "acceptable" parts.

Addressing Gaps in Research and Practice

Addressing these concerns requires identifying and confronting the persistent gaps in the scholarly and technical literature. First, as this review highlights, there remains a critical lack of intersectional analysis. The cautions from Venkit et al. (2023) and Hemsley et al. (2024) about ignoring experiences at the margins—particularly those of youth, individuals with concealable disabilities, and people in the Global South—underscore the need for research that moves beyond monolithic conceptions of "disability."

Second, critical legal and ethical infrastructures are dangerously underdeveloped. The concerns raised by Lillywhite and Wolbring (2020) regarding data ownership, consent, and algorithmic transparency are more urgent than ever, especially given the use of AI in behavioral screening, hiring, and social surveillance. Without clear frameworks governing the ethical use of public and private data, the risks of epistemic violence and misappropriation are amplified.

Third, there is a systemic failure to integrate participatory and community-based research methodologies. The arguments from Jaiswal et al. (2024), McKee (2013), and others (Benz et al., 2024; Kuper et al., 2021) converge on a crucial point: disabled individuals are too rarely positioned as co-researchers and knowledge producers. Adopting participatory models is essential to ensure AI development genuinely reflects the priorities of disabled communities, particularly in non-Western contexts where digital exclusion manifests differently.

Emerging evidence from non-Western contexts further underscores the uneven representation and exclusion of disabled individuals in digital discourse. For example, Alathur et al. (2021), in their study of social media content during the Kerala floods in India, found that disability was not only underrepresented but also frequently misrepresented in online narratives. While Twitter posts largely ignored disability altogether, Facebook content often reproduced stereotypes and casteist undertones. Nonetheless, the study also documented disabled individuals actively participating in relief efforts, thereby challenging dominant narratives of passivity and dependence. These findings reinforce the need for disability-conscious platform design and inclusive policy frameworks, particularly in crisis situations where digital participation can shape access to aid and public visibility.

Finally, more research is needed on the affective and epistemological contours of algorithmic systems. The emotional labor demanded by platforms and the normative pressures embedded in their architectures have yet to be thoroughly interrogated. Future studies must investigate how algorithms shape identity performance and advocacy, and how they might be restructured to support critical, nuanced, and pluralistic representations of disabled life.

Toward Transformative AI

Ultimately, the integration of AI into social media offers a landscape of profound risks and contingent possibilities. To navigate this terrain justly, researchers, technologists, and policymakers must move beyond inclusion as a goal in itself and instead center the epistemic authority and political demands of disabled communities. Only by embedding the principles of disability justice into the very logic of design and governance can AI be mobilized not simply to "include" disabled people in existing inequitable systems, but to fundamentally transform the digital architectures that shape how disability is lived, represented, and governed.

CONCLUSION

This scoping review reveals a fundamental and structural conflict at the heart of the relationship between AI, social media, and disability. The digital platforms examined are not neutral conduits for interaction but are powerful sociotechnical systems that produce a constitutive tension: while offering tangible pathways for access, community, and activism, they simultaneously operate as potent architectures of exclusion. The evidence demonstrates that the harms of AI—biased sentiment analysis, normative algorithmic curation, and systemic surveillance—are not incidental flaws to be patched, but are direct products of a technological logic that reflects and amplifies entrenched ableist ideologies.

The political stakes of this dynamic are profound. The algorithmic gatekeeping detailed in this review functions as a form of epistemic violence, systematically devaluing the lived expertise of disabled people while privileging sanitized or stereotypical narratives that align with platform-driven engagement metrics. This creates coercive pressure on disabled users to perform palatable identities, transforming self-representation into a form of managed labor. Critically, these digital processes have material consequences that extend far beyond the screen, manifesting in real-world discrimination in hiring, social services, and the criminal justice system. This confirms that digital marginalization is inextricably linked to social and economic injustice, disproportionately affecting those at the intersections of disability, race, gender, and geography.

Consequently, addressing these harms requires moving beyond techno-optimistic discourses that frame AI as a benevolent solution. A justice-oriented paradigm must instead confront techno-ableism directly, challenging the assumption that technology is a neutral fix for impairment. This necessitates a fundamental shift from merely mitigating bias to actively redistributing power. The goal must be to advance disability-led innovation and governance, embedding the principles of crip technoscience and participatory design into the core of AI development. Such an approach would treat disabled people not as passive data points or end users, but as essential experts, designers, and decision-makers in the creation of digital futures.

Ultimately, the emancipatory potential of AI will not be realized through the mere accommodation of disabled people within existing inequitable frameworks. Rather, it demands the radical transformation of those frameworks themselves. By centering the political claims and epistemological authority of disabled communities, it becomes possible to mobilize AI not simply for inclusion, but for justice—using these powerful tools to dismantle structural barriers and build digital architectures that are fundamentally more equitable, accessible, and transformative for all.

FUNDING SOURCES

This research is funded by SSHRC Connection Grant (611–2024–0299), the Dahdaleh Institute for Global Health Seed Grant for Critical Social Science Perspectives in Global Health Research, the Faculty of Health Minor Research Grant, and the AI Technologies for Identification and Control of Infectious Diseases research cluster at York University.

ACKNOWLEDGMENT

Portions of this chapter were developed with the assistance of ChatGPT and Grammarly in an editing capacity to improve clarity and flow. All intellectual contributions, interpretations, and final editorial decisions are the authors' own, and the authors take full responsibility for the content. Any AI-assisted or AI-generated material was reviewed and verified by the authors.

REFLECTION QUESTIONS

1. How do social media algorithms function as gatekeepers that can both amplify and suppress disability activism and community building?
2. What is the dual nature of AI in this context, and how does it simultaneously offer tools for accessibility while expanding surveillance and exclusion?
3. How do sentiment analysis algorithms mistakenly classify disability-related terms as toxic, and what is the impact of this on disabled users' freedom of expression?
4. Why is participatory governance essential for preventing AI from reinforcing ableist norms in digital spaces?

REFERENCES

Adnin, R., & Das, M. (2024). "I look at it as the king of knowledge": How Blind People Use and Understand Generative AI Tools. *The 26th International ACM SIGACCESS Conference on Computers and Accessibility*, New York, 1–14. Association for Computing Machinery. https://doi.org/10.1145/3663548.3675631

Alathur, S., Kottakkunnummal, M., & Chetty, N. (2021). Social media and disaster management: Influencing e-participation content on disabilities. *Transforming Government: People, Process and Policy*, *15*(4), 566–579. https://doi.org/10.1108/TG-07-2020-0155

Almufareh, M. F., Kausar, S., Humayun, M., & Tehsin, S. (2024). A conceptual model for inclusive technology: Advancing disability inclusion through artificial intelligence. *Journal of Disability Research*, *3*(1). https://doi.org/10.57197/JDR-2023-0060

Anastasiou, D., & Kauffman, J. M. (2013). The social model of disability: Dichotomy between impairment and disability. *Journal of Medicine and Philosophy*, *38*(4), 441–459. https://doi.org/10.1093/jmp/jht026

Anderson, S. (2023). Threats to valuing diverse voices in public debates about disability. A case study from social media*. *Research and Practice in Intellectual and Developmental Disabilities*, *10*(1), 48–60. https://doi.org/10.1080/23297018.2022.2051198

Anderson, S., Araten-Bergman, T., & Steel, G. (2023). Adults with intellectual disabilities as users of social media: A scoping review. *British Journal of Learning Disabilities*, *51*(4), 544–564. https://doi.org/10.1111/bld.12534

Bail, C. A. (2016). Combining natural language processing and network analysis to examine how advocacy organizations stimulate conversation on social media. *Proceedings of the National Academy of Sciences*, *113*(42), 11823–11828. https://doi.org/10.1073/pnas.1607151113 Baumgartner, A., Rohrbach, T., & Schönhagen, P. (2023). 'If the phone were broken, I'd be screwed': Media use of people with disabilities in the digital era. *Disability & Society*, *38*(1), 73–97. https://doi.org/10.1080/09687599.2021.1916884

Beaudry, J.-S. (2016). Beyond (models of) disability? *Journal of Medicine and Philosophy*, *41*(2), 210–228. https://doi.org/10.1093/jmp/jhv063

Benz, C., Scott-Jeffs, W., McKercher, K. A., Welsh, M., Norman, R., Hendrie, D., Locantro, M., & Robinson, S. (2024). Community-based participatory-research through co-design: Supporting collaboration from all sides of disability. *Research Involvement and Engagement*, *10*(1), 47. https://doi.org/10.1186/s40900-024-00573-3

Bitman, N. (2022). "Authentic" digital inclusion? Dis/ability performances on social media by users with concealable communicative disabilities. *New Media & Society*, *24*(2), 401–419. https://doi.org/10.1177/14614448211063183

Brown, T., Mann, B., Ryder, N., Subbiah, M., Kaplan, J. D., Dhariwal, P., Neelakantan, A., Shyam, P., Sastry, G., Askell, A., Agarwal, S., Herbert-Voss, A., Krueger, G., Henighan, T., Child, R., Ramesh, A., Ziegler, D., Wu, J., Winter, C., … Amodei, D. (2020). Language models are few-shot learners. In H. Larochelle, M. Ranzato, R. Hadsell, M. F. Balcan, & H. Lin (Eds.), *Advances in Neural Information Processing Systems* (Vol. 33, pp. 1877–1901). Curran Associates, Inc. https://proceedings.neurips.cc/paper_files/paper/2020/file/1457c0d6bfcb4967418bfb8ac142f64a-Paper.pdf

Casper, M. J., & Laine Talley, H. (2007). Feminist disability studies. In G. Ritzer (Ed.), *The Blackwell Encyclopedia of Sociology* (1st ed.). Wiley. https://doi.org/10.1002/9781405165518.wbeosf041

Castillo-Esparcia, A., Caro-Castaño, L., & Almansa-Martínez, A. (2023). Evolution of digital activism on social media: Opportunities and challenges. *El Profesional de La Información*, e320303. https://doi.org/10.3145/epi.2023.may.03

Cocq, C., & Ljuslinder, K. (2020). Self-representations on social media: Reproducing and challenging discourses on disability. *Alter*, *14–2*, 71–84. https://doi.org/10.1016/j.alter.2020.02.001

El Morr, C. (2023). *Introduction to Health Informatics: A Canadian Perspective* (2nd ed.). Canadian Scholars' Press.

El Morr, C., & Ali-Hassan, H. (2019). Healthcare, data analytics, and business intelligence. In J. K. Tan (Ed.), *Analytics in Healthcare: A Practical Introduction* (pp. 1–13). Springer International Publishing. https://doi.org/10.1007/978-3-030-04506-7

El Morr, C., Jammal, M., Ali-Hassan, H., & El-Hallak, W. (2022). *Machine Learning for Practical Decision Making: A Multidisciplinary Perspective with Applications from Healthcare, Engineering and Business Analytics*. Springer International Publishing. https://doi.org/10.1007/978-3-031-16990-8

Ellis, K., & Goggin, G. (2018). Disability and media activism. In G. Meikle (Ed.), *The Routledge companion to media and activism* (rayyan–217703268). Routledge.

Erevelles, N. (2011). *Disability and difference in global contexts: Enabling a transformative body politic* (1st ed.). Palgrave Macmillan.

Eubanks, V. (2018). *Automating Inequality: How High-Tech Tools Profile, Police, and Punish the Poor*. St. Martin's Publishing Group. https://books.google.ca/books?id=pn4pDwAAQBAJ

Foley, A., & Melese, F. (2025). Disabling AI: Power, exclusion, and disability. *British Journal of Sociology of Education*, 1–22. https://doi.org/10.1080/01425692.2025.2519482

Goodley, D. (2023). Being human as praxis: For people with learning disabilities. *Subjectivity*, *30*(2), 167–184. https://doi.org/10.1057/s41286-023-00159-6

Goodley, D., Lawthom, R., Liddiard, K., & Runswick-Cole, K. (2019). Provocations for critical disability studies. *Disability & Society*, *34*(6), 972–997. https://doi.org/10.1080/09687599.2019.1566889

Greijdanus, H., De Matos Fernandes, C. A., Turner-Zwinkels, F., Honari, A., Roos, C. A., Rosenbusch, H., & Postmes, T. (2020). The psychology of online activism and social movements: Relations between online and offline collective action. *Current Opinion in Psychology*, *35*, 49–54. https://doi.org/10.1016/j.copsyc.2020.03.003

Hadley, B. (2016). Cheats, charity cases and inspirations: Disrupting the circulation of disability-based memes online. *Disability & Society*, *31*(5), 676–692. https://doi.org/10.1080/09687599.2016.1199378

Hamraie, A. (2015). Cripping feminist technoscience. *Hypatia*, *30*(1), 307–313. h ttps://doi.org/10.1111/hypa.12124

Hamraie, A. (2017). *Building Access: Universal Design and the Politics of Disability*. University of Minnesota Press. https://books.google.ca/books?id=3Cl0DwAAQBAJ

Hemsley, B., Given, F., Almond, B., Cooper, J., Smith, R., Young, K., & Wright, E. (2024). A critical review of literature on social media and developmental communication disability: Implications for future social media and generative AI research. *Current Developmental Disorders Reports*, *11*(2), 75–89. https://doi.org/10.1007/s40474-024-00297-9

Hogan, A. J. (2019). Social and medical models of disability and mental health: Evolution and renewal. *Canadian Medical Association Journal*, *191*(1), E16–E18. https://doi.org/10.1503/cmaj.181008

Hollier, S. (2017). The growing importance of accessible social media. In K. Ellis & M. Kent, *Disability and Social Media: Global Perspectives* (pp. 77–88). Routledge, Taylor & Francis Group.

Hudkins, A. E., & Bills, R. (2024). Exploring the impact of social media on the perception of disabilities. *The American Journal of Occupational Therapy*, *78*(Supplement_2), 7811500097p1–7811500097p1. https://doi.org/10.5014/ajot.2024.78S2-PO97

Jaiswal, A., Shah, A., Harjadi, C., Windgassen, E., & Washington, P. (2024). Ethics of the use of social media as training data for AI models used for digital phenotyping. *JMIR Formative Research*, *8*, e59794. https://doi.org/10.2196/59794

Jaiswal, A., & Washington, P. (2024). Using #actually autistic on twitter for precision diagnosis of autism spectrum disorder: Machine learning study. *JMIR Formative Research*, *8*, e52660. https://doi.org/10.2196/52660

Johansen, S. L. (2024). 'I just want to show that I am living a normal life'. Young people with physical disabilities on social media. *Nordisk Tidsskrift for Ungdomsforskning*, *5*(2), 1–14. https://doi.org/10.18261/ntu.5.2.4

Jurgens, A. (2023). Body social models of disability: Examining enactive and ecological approaches. *Frontiers in Psychology*, *14*, 1128772. https://doi.org/10.3389/fpsyg.2023.1128772

Kafer, A. (2013). *Feminist, Queer, Crip*. Indiana University Press. https://iupress.org/9780253009340/feminist-queer-crip/

Kaur, S., Swaminathan, M., Bali, K., & Vashistha, A. (2024). Challenges to Online Disability Rights Advocacy in India. *Proceedings of the CHI Conference on Human Factors in Computing Systems*, New York, 1–15. Association for Computing Machinery. https://doi.org/10.1145/3613904.3642737

Kuper, H., Hameed, S., Reichenberger, V., Scherer, N., Wilbur, J., Zuurmond, M., Mactaggart, I., Bright, T., & Shakespeare, T. (2021). Participatory research in disability in low- and middle-income countries: What have we learnt and what should we do? *Scandinavian Journal of Disability Research*. https://doi.org/10.16993/sjdr.814

Lillywhite, A., & Wolbring, G. (2020). Coverage of artificial intelligence and machine learning within academic literature, canadian newspapers, and twitter tweets: The case of disabled people. *Societies*, *10*(1), 23. https://doi.org/10.3390/soc10010023

Lüders, A., Dinkelberg, A., & Quayle, M. (2022). Becoming "us" in digital spaces: How online users creatively and strategically exploit social media affordances to build up social identity. *Acta Psychologica*, *228*, 103643. https://doi.org/10.1016/j.actpsy.2022.103643

Marks, D. (1997). Models of disability. *Disability and Rehabilitation*, *19*(3), 85–91. https://doi.org/10.3109/09638289709166831

McKee, R. (2013). Ethical issues in using social media for health and health care research. *Health Policy (Amsterdam, Netherlands)*, *110*(2–3), 298–301. https://doi.org/doi:10.1016/j.healthpol.2013.02.006

McNally, K., Wright, K., Goldkind, L., Kattari, S. K., & Victor, B. G. (2024). Disability expertise and large language models: A qualitative study of autistic TikTok creators' use of chatGPT. *Social Media + Society*, *10*(3), 20563051241279549. https://doi.org/10.1177/20563051241279549

Meekosha, H., & Shuttleworth, R. (2009). What's so 'critical' about critical disability studies? *Australian Journal of Human Rights*, *15*(1), 47–75. https://doi.org/10.1080/1323238X.2009.11910861

Mondal, I., Kaur, S., Bali, K., Vashistha, A., & Swaminathan, M. (2022). *"#DisabledOnIndianTwitter": A Dataset towards Understanding the Expression of People with Disabilities on Indian Twitter* (rayyan-217703241). 375–386. https://doi.org/10.18653/v1/2022.findings-aacl.35

Niu, S., Liu, L., & Bian, Y. (2024). Please Understand My Disability: An Analysis of YouTubers' Discourse on Disability Challenges. *Proceedings of the ACM on Human-Computer Interaction*, *8*(CSCW2), 1–25. https://doi.org/10.1145/3686946

Noble, S. U. (2018). *Algorithms of Oppression: How Search Engines Reinforce Racism.* New York University Press.

Oliver, M. (2013). The social model of disability: Thirty years on. *Disability & Society*, *28*(7), 1024–1026. https://doi.org/10.1080/09687599.2013.818773

Olsen, J., & Pilson, A. (2022). Developing understandings of disability through a constructivist paradigm: Identifying, overcoming (and embedding) crip-dissonance. *Scandinavian Journal of Disability Research*, *24*(1), 15–28. https://doi.org/10.16993/sjdr.843

Open AI, Achiam, J., Adler, S., Agarwal, S., Ahmad, L., Akkaya, I., Aleman, F. L., Almeida, D., Altenschmidt, J., Altman, S., Anadkat, S., Avila, R., Babuschkin, I., Balaji, S., Balcom, V., Baltescu, P., Bao, H., Bavarian, M., Belgum, J., … Zoph, B. (2024). *GPT-4 Technical Report.* https://arxiv.org/abs/2303.08774

Packin, N. G. (2020). Disability discrimination using AI systems, social media and digital platforms: Can we disable digital bias? *SSRN Electronic Journal.* https://doi.org/10.2139/ssrn.3724556

Phutane, M., Seelam, A., & Vashistha, A. (2025). "Cold, Calculated, and Condescending": How AI Identifies and Explains Ableism Compared to Disabled People. *Proceedings of the 2025 ACM Conference on Fairness, Accountability, and Transparency*, Athens Greece, 1927–1941. https://doi.org/10.1145/3715275.3732128

Prince, M. J. (2009). *Absent Citizens: Disability Politics and Policy in Canada.* University of Toronto Press. https://doi.org/10.3138/9781442687301

Rice, M. F., & Dunn, S. (2023). The use of artificial intelligence with students with identified disabilities: A systematic review with critique. *Computers in the Schools*, *40*(4), 370–390. https://doi.org/10.1080/07380569.2023.2244935

Richardson, E., Nagata, S., Hall, C., & Akimoto, S. (2023). A proposition for cultural praxis in critical disability studies: A methodological design for inclusive research. *Quest*, *75*(4), 344–360. https://doi.org/10.1080/00336297.2023.2188600

Robinson, O. E. (2017). Moving toward disability justice. *Disability Studies Quarterly*, *37*(3). https://doi.org/10.18061/dsq.v37i3.5970

Russell, S., & Norvig, P. (2020). *Artificial Intelligence: A Modern Approach* (4th ed.). Pearson. https://aima.cs.berkeley.edu/

Sannon, S., Young, J., Shusas, E., & Forte, A. (2023). Disability Activism on Social Media: Sociotechnical Challenges in the Pursuit of Visibility. *Proceedings of the 2023 CHI Conference on Human Factors in Computing Systems*, 1–15. https://doi.org/10.1145/3544548.3581333

Shakespeare, T. (2006). *Disability Rights and Wrongs.* Routledge. https://doi.org/10.4324/9780203640098

Shakespeare, T. (2014). Introduction. In T. Shakespeare (Ed.) *Disability Rights and Wrongs Revisited* (2nd ed.). Routledge & CRC Press. https://www.routledge.com/Disability-Rights-and-Wrongs-Revisited/Shakespeare/p/book/9780415527613

Shew, A. (2020). Ableism, technoableism, and future AI. *IEEE Technology and Society Magazine*, *39*(1), 40–85. https://doi.org/10.1109/MTS.2020.2967492

Shildrick, M. (2009). *Dangerous Discourses of Disability, Subjectivity and Sexuality.* Palgrave Macmillan UK. https://doi.org/10.1057/9780230244641

Spagnuolo, N. (2016). Political affinities and complex identities: Critical approaches to disability organizing. *Canadian Journal of Disability Studies*, *5*(2), 72. https://doi.org/10.15353/cjds.v5i2.273

Sweet, K. S., LeBlanc, J. K., Stough, L. M., & Sweany, N. W. (2020). Community building and knowledge sharing by individuals with disabilities using social media. *Journal of Computer Assisted Learning*, *36*(1), 1–11. https://doi.org/10.1111/jcal.12377

Venkit, P. N., Srinath, M., & Wilson, S. (2023). *Automated Ableism: An Exploration of Explicit Disability Biases in Sentiment and Toxicity Analysis Models.* https://doi.org/10.48550/ARXIV.2307.09209

Villena, J., Català, R., García, J., Polo, C., Labrador, Y., Del Valle, F., & Ayyagari, B. (2024). Breaking Barriers: A Hands-On Tutorial on AI-Enabled Accessibility to Social Media Content. *Proceedings of the 30th ACM SIGKDD Conference on Knowledge Discovery and Data Mining*, New York, 6426–6427. Association for Computing Machinery.

Williams, D. P. (2023). Bias Optimizers: AI tools such as ChatGPT appear to magnify some of humanity's worst qualities, and fixing those tendencies will be no easy task. *American Scientist*, *111*(4), 204+. Gale Academic OneFile.

Zuboff, S. (2019). *The Age of Surveillance Capitalism: The Fight for a Human Future at the New Frontier of Power.* PublicAffairs.

14 Epistemic Injustice and Disability-Evasiveness

Ryan B. Collis, Ellouise Van Berkel, Katherine Barron and Aaron Richmond

INTRODUCTION

A recent article by the Canadian Broadcasting Corporation, Canada's national news agency, reported generative predictive text (GPT) systems are increasingly being trained on content created by GPTs, resulting in output that is increasingly homogenous (Maimann, 2025). At the same time companies are using Large Language Models (LLMs) like ChatGPT to pre-screen resumes to remove bias from hiring. However, Glazko et al. (2024) found that when ChatGPT-4 was used to compare two resumes that were identical except one which included awards, Diversity, Equity, and Inclusion (DEI) service, and membership in a student organization (all related to a disability), the enhanced resume was chosen only 15 times out of 70 trials. ChatGTP-4 also made ableist and stereotypical comments and used "the word 'commendable' as an underhanded compliment, usually paired with a detraction of some sort" (p. 694).

As argued in this chapter, this regurgitation of AI-generated content results in epistemic injustice —a form of disadvantaging marginalized people by controlling the social understanding of their reality to their detriment (Fricker, 2007). Occurring in multiple ways, Fricker (2007) describes epistemic injustice and it's subtypes—testimonial injustice and hermeneutical injustice—as ways someone may be "*wronged specifically in her capacity as a knower*" (Fricker, 2007, p. 20, italics in original), while Dotson (2011) writes of pernicious ignorance that "causes or contributes to a harmful practice" (p. 239). In this chapter, we trace how GPT AI systems (such as ChatGPT, Grok, and others) strip knowledge of context and authorial authority, committing both hermeneutical and testimonial injustices, resulting in pernicious ignorance for users and ultimately and epistemic injustice for marginalized groups. The literature shows that this is already occurring: In their auto-ethnographic case study, Glazko et al. (2023) found that an LLM-generated summary "oversimplified a nuanced argument" regarding disability which "turns a finding from an award winning paper into an ableist and problematic trope" (pp. 2–3). They note that due to built-in ableism

Ableism was subtle, but very much present in our experiences. Examples include the elision of key content in Vignetted 1: Mia and the difficulty of producing a representative and accurate image of disabled people in Vignetted 3: Ally. These biases certainly reflect biases in training data. However, such problems are made even more insidious by the way in which they are likely to confirm, rather than correct human biases, raising questions about how to ensure such mistakes are caught even during human verification (p. 6).

Generative AI is trained on data, it then disembodies and regurgitates to respond to prompts with the most statistically likely set of words, removing the knowledge from the knower and ultimately homogenizing the content. It works by predicting the statistically most likely next word; in effect this means that all words have equal weight and meaning regardless of subject or context. So, too, the words of a disabled person discussing their life and a conspiracy theorist making baseless claims are treated as equally epistemologically valid and weighted. Bias mitigation can include having "algorithms change the distribution of the sample points by up-weighting underrepresented groups ('reweighing')" (Gengler et al., 2024, p. 234), but even with guardrails that limit how output appears to a user, there is no way to know which data points were considered in producing responses

 DOI: 10.1201/9781003737810-16

(Faissner et al., 2025). Shams et al.'s (2025) systematic literature review found 55 challenges in making AI inclusive, and only 33 potential solutions, with 26 challenges having no solutions at all. They also found that this area of research was not well explored, meaning changes are not likely to come immediately. It is through this infrastructure AI enacts what Fricker (2007) describes as "prejudicial dysfunction in testimonial practice" (p. 17)—when a speaker receives more or less credibility than they would otherwise have. This creates a credibility excess or deficit. And, because this happens in an opaque way within predictive AI, the user does not know whose voices are amplified and whose are silenced. The user is therefore implicated in this pernicious ignorance as they increase the user base and grow these companies into ubiquity.

In this chapter, we trace how the knowledges of disabled people—knowers of disability—are affected. We begin by briefly looking at some of the conceptual tools provided by Miranda Fricker's (2007) *Epistemic Injustice: Power and the Ethics of Knowing* that name and describe the types and subtypes of epistemic injustice produced by predictive AI systems. Next, we look at existing literature on the intersection of epistemic injustice and AI, considering both the strengths of its arguments and its limitations when we factor in credibility excess or deficits. Finally, we consider how the erasure and evasion of disability knowledge by AI harms the disability community.

FRAMEWORKS

Most discussions of epistemic injustice start with Miranda Fricker's (2007) *Epistemic Injustice: Power and the Ethics of Knowing* and the categories she established there (Faissner et al., 2025). Though we use this framework, we are cognizant that Fricker has been criticized for not giving credit to Black feminist scholars whose work predates hers and for overlooking the intersectional aspects of oppression (Berenstain, 2020; Kay et al., 2024). Still, scholars like Kay (2024) "find her philosophical framework of epistemic injustice theoretically expressive and influential" and use "Fricker's account as the foundation for [their] philosophical examination of generative epistemic injustice" (p.685). In this chapter, we consider disability's intersections with race through Annamma et al.'s (2013, 2017) concepts DisCrit and color-evasiveness.

Fricker (2007) describes two forms of epistemic injustice: the testimonial and the hermeneutical. Wanderer (2017) gives a simplified explanation that "testimonial injustice occurs when, following an act of telling someone something, a Speaker is accorded insufficient credibility by a Hearer due to a prejudicial stereotype" (p. 28). We will build on this idea along with other scholars below. Hermeneutical injustice is the result of a knowledge gap, or lacuna, in the collective understanding that prevents the parties from comprehending each other's realities. Due to power differences, the more powerful party does not need to acknowledge or respond to the gap, whereas the less powerful party is painfully aware of the lacuna (Fricker, 2007, p. 151). For many people, ableism is a lacuna because there is a gap in their understanding of how deeply ingrained the expectations of a normative body-mind (Hartblay, 2020) are in society.

Fricker also noted the "grim possibility: that hermeneutical injustice might often be compounded by testimonial injustice" (Fricker, 2007, p. 159) in cases where the hermeneutical injustice is systematic. There should be no need to argue that ableism (a societal expectation of a particular type of body-mind) and disablism (discrimination against disabled people) are systemic. Fricker makes this clear:

> having their experience left obscure owing to a lacuna in the collective hermeneutical resource, where the lacuna is caused and maintained by a wide-ranging and persistent hermeneutical marginalization, then the hermeneutical injustice is systematic. For in such cases the hermeneutical marginalization is part of a more general susceptibility to different forms of social marginalization, so that any given hermeneutical injustice incurred is likewise part of a more general susceptibility to different kinds of injustice (p. 159).

The "collective hermeneutical resource" is Fricker's term to describe how society understands reality. More specifically, for ableism, a lack of understanding of being disabled and all that it entails in the collective hermeneutical resource means that most people are unaware of the harms they inadvertently reproduce. In the context of predictive AI, there is a testimonial injustice inherent in how disabled voices are stolen, reproduced, and shuffled with non-disabled voices to produce ableist content (Barron et al., 2025a). From here, there are two things that happen: first, hermeneutical injustice will occur when people are unlikely to identify the ableism in generated texts that privilege non-disabled voices over disabled ones. Second, testimonial injustice will occur if users assign more credibility to the AI than it should have, particularly over the voices of disabled people. Ultimately, this is the result of training data that mirrors the ableism in the collective hermeneutical resource and the statistically smaller number of texts that resist it.

DISABILITY-EVASIVENESS

In our previous work (Barron et al., 2025b, 2025a), we analyzed AI-generated flash fiction[1] and noticed a pattern we described as "disability-evasion," drawing on the concept of "color-evasiveness" developed by Annamma et al. (2017). Disability-evasiveness is the deliberate and systemic avoidance of acknowledging disability or the structural barriers faced by disabled people. For example, sentences like "Indeed, Noah wasn't just a child with dyslexia. He was a fighter, an artist, a dreamer, and, above all, a beacon of resilience and optimism." Barron et al. (2025b) showcase a common writing style prevalent in our AI-generated flash fiction dataset. Specifically, how it implies that dyslexia must be compensated for with the additional characteristics, further planting dyslexia as a deficit to be made up for. Here, we see how the logic of disability-evasiveness diminishes the experiences of those who do not hide or overcome their disabilities (Graham, 2023), spares the non-disabled person from the discomfort of thinking about disability (and their own vulnerability), and it masks systemic ableism by turning each instance into an individual event rather than a systemic experience. Similar to how people who follow a color-evasive ideology reproduce "power and inequity in a system of white supremacy" while viewing themselves as "racially enlightened" (Annamma et al., 2017, p. 154), those who evade acknowledging disability reproduce ableism and disablism while superficially feigning inclusivity. If we apply disability-evasion as a framework to analyze attempts by Gen-AI to create "equity" through a denial of disability, we see a process of hermeneutical marginalization where disabled voices are de-emphasized, ableism is rendered mundane, and struggles are not mentioned to avoid stigmatization.

STRUCTURAL POWER

Fricker (2007) explains that "the point of any operation of social power is *to effect social control*" regardless if there is an active agent or a passive structural operation of power and that "purely structural operations of power are always such as to create or preserve a given social order" (p. 13, italics in original). Technology mediating social control when given power to reduce human bias is not a new phenomenon. As O'Neil writes in her book *Weapons of Math Destruction: How Big Data Increases Inequality and Threatens Democracy* (2017), attempts to use algorithmic models for recidivism simply camouflaged prejudicial assumptions with mathematics and technology. These operations of power can cause both testimonial and hermeneutical injustices.

Leclerc (2021) explains that a hermeneutical resource "is a collective interpretive resource allowing to account for and to give meaning to reality" and that if a marginalized person lacks such resources, "she does not possess the concepts to make her testimony intelligible to her interlocutors" (p. 5). Because this resource is shared across a society, it represents the reality of the majority, and minority groups, such as disabled people, have less representation. As Fricker puts it, "relations of unequal power can skew shared hermeneutical resources so that the powerful tend to have appropriate understandings of their experiences" (Fricker, 2007, p. 148 as cited in Leclerc, 2021, p. 6). Particularly alarming is the reality that these predicative AI systems in question are largely run by, developed by, and maintained by a small group of people with a limited and narrow knowledge base. Furthermore, this could not be corrected with diversifying the workforce of predictive AI, because the infrastructure itself relies on mathematically predicting the most likely next word. While there exists bias mitigation techniques, including reweighing, they are part of a long list of solutions to AI bias that have not yet been implemented (see, for example, Gengler et al., 2024). Lack of understanding due to this inequality in shared hermeneutical resources is a form of hermeneutical injustice. One of the ways that marginalized groups reshape the hermeneutical resource is through their testimony.

Fricker (2007) argues that identity power (a form of social power) is integral to testimonial exchange, because of how hearers use social stereotypes to assess credibility. This makes logical sense: you are going to give stronger weight to medical advice from a medical doctor than an electrician. But some people have one or more aspects of their identity used to dismiss the credibility of their testimony, what Fricker calls "negative identity prejudice" (p. 28). In looking at how AI affects the hermeneutical resource, we need to look at both forms of what Fricker (2007) calls "prejudicial dysfunction in testimonial practice"—"Either the prejudice results in the speaker's receiving more credibility than she otherwise would have—a credibility excess—or it results in her receiving less credibility than she otherwise would have—a credibility deficit" (p. 17). Testimonial and hermeneutical injustices interplay here, as for reasons examined below, the information provided by the AI is likely at odds with the testimony of the disabled or otherwise marginalized speaker and so "humans believe the account amplified through the technology over the individual or group who is discredited" (Kay et al., 2024, p. 687) resulting in hermeneutical injustice. We examine the process by which this occurs starting with testimonial injustice.

TESTIMONIAL INJUSTICE

Testimonial injustice is a distinctively epistemic injustice where someone is wronged specifically in their capacity as a knower (Fricker, 2007). For disabled people, it is a common experience to have your expertise on your identity be denied (see, for example, Milton, 2014). Fricker (2007) argues that to deny someone, the capacity to share knowledge is to deny their capacity for reason, for rational thought, claiming "that in contexts of oppression the powerful will be sure to undermine the powerless in just that capacity, for it provides a direct route to undermining them in their very humanity" (p. 44). Testimonial quieting, one of the subtypes of testimonial injustice, "occurs when an audience fails to identify a speaker as a knower" (Dotson, 2011, p. 242). A historical example of resistance to testimonial quieting is the story of AIDS patients who forced the medical establishment to listen to them and change how drug trials were conducted, when their ability to speak as experts on their condition was denied (for a detailed account, see Epstein, 1995). In the process of creating the common hermeneutical resources of a society, this denial of the marginalized to include their lived experience or for that knowledge to have a credibility deficit is to do epistemic violence to the group. As Dotson (2011) writes, "one method of executing epistemic violence is to damage a given group's ability to speak and be heard" (p. 236). Herrmann (2019), considering Arendt's reflections on totalitarianism, notes "that creating a common world is a process that can go hand in hand with excluding others from it and making them worldless" (p. 283). To this point, we wonder "*who* gets to include *whom* and into *what*" (Bourassa, 2021, p. 254, italics in original). In addition to the harm to the speaker, Fricker (2007) also notes that testimonial injustice harms all of society by interfering with the creation of the common hermeneutical resource. She writes,

> That testimonial injustice damages the epistemic system is directly relevant to social epistemologies such as Goldman's 'veritism', for prejudice presents an obstacle to truth, either directly by causing the hearer to miss out on a particular truth, or indirectly by creating blockages in the circulation of critical ideas. ... Further, the fact that prejudice can prevent speakers from successfully putting knowledge into the public domain reveals testimonial injustice as a serious form of unfreedom in our collective speech situation—and on a Kantian conception, the freedom of our speech situation is fundamental to the authority of the polity, even to the authority of reason itself (p. 43).

Relatedly, another subtype of testimonial injustice is testimonial smothering (Dotson, 2011), where a speaker holds back their knowledge because they know they will be silenced, misunderstood, or ignored and so no one can make use of this knowledge—least of all others who may share experiences. As Kay et al. (2024) explain, "These damages of epistemic injustices on the information ecosystem result in further hermeneutical injustices, because they impoverish the collective interpretational resources for understanding the experiences of marginalized groups" (p. 691). Both the testimonial and hermeneutical injustices are exacerbated by AI due to the way it interacts with its hermeneutical resource—the data it is trained on. Furthermore, the content it generates is increasingly linguistically homogenous (Sourati et al., 2025).

EPISTEMIC FLATTENING

Returning to Fricker's (2007) prejudicial dysfunction in testimonial practice, we can see it operate at two levels when discussing AI. The first is the credibility excess the AI receives from users. The average user is more likely to believe the AI than a speaker, regardless of that speaker's expertise, especially if that speaker is a member of a marginalized group (testimonial quieting). Kay et al. (2024) notes that

> humans believe the account amplified through the technology over the individual or group who is discredited … This can lead to a situation where the generative AI's output is trusted over the lived experiences and knowledge of marginalized individuals, thus reinforcing existing power imbalances and perpetuating testimonial injustice (p. 687).

Breaking people of the idea "I saw it online so it must be true" is a task far beyond the skill of the authors. We will instead look at the second level of prejudicial dysfunction in testimonial practice.

As explained above, prejudicial dysfunction in testimonial practice occurs when a speaker is granted an excess or defect of credibility based on their social position. In this section, we will discuss what we call epistemic flattening: a denial of the credibility of more credible speakers and the denial of the deficit of less credible ones. As a simplified example, imagine you have a question about geography, and you have the option to ask one of two people with a strong online presence: a professor of geography or the head of a flat-earth society. According to Fricker (2007), you, as hearer, would give different amounts of credibility to each. However, that is not how generative AI works because it lacks the ability to contextualize. As Kay et al. (2024) explain,

> Generative AI models lack the embodied and cultural knowledge that humans acquire through lived experiences. This lack of understanding can lead to the misinterpretation of marginalized voices and perspectives, even when the generative AI tool is not necessarily trained on discriminatory intent (p. 689).

They offer the term "generative hermeneutical ignorance" for the erasure or erroneous portrayal of marginalized groups because of the AI's lack of "nuanced comprehension of human experience necessary for accurate and equitable representation" (p. 689).

Generative AI responds to prompts through a statistical analysis of its training data. Thus, it is most likely to repeat majority opinions and less likely to consider minority ones (Kay et al., 2024). Faissner et al. (2025) note that the stereotypical output is the result of amplifying information that is more common in the dataset while discarding outliers, "to the point that attempts at mitigation by entering counter-stereotypical prompts remain ineffective" (p. 123). This feedback loop of increasingly prevalent majority voices and repeatedly suppressed minority voices is another form of testimonial injustice against the already marginalized (Kay et al., 2024). Faissner et al. (2025) describe this "hermeneutical marginalization" as "the systematic unequal participation of members of disadvantaged groups in relevant areas of social experience and knowledge production" (p. 125). They describe the training data of the AI as contributing to "shared epistemic resources," what we have called the hermeneutical resource above, and note that if that data insufficiently or inadequately represents the lived experience of marginalized groups, this can lead to unjust hermeneutical marginalization.

But what about when there is data on lived experience in the dataset? We know that because the AI lacks the ability to contextualize information, it bases its decision-making on pattern recognition. This means that if the AI is unable to give that information greater credibility than data from less reliable sources the group is the victim of hermeneutical injustice. Above we explained that hermeneutical injustice occurs when individuals or a group cannot understand or articulate their knowledge owing to a lack of common hermeneutical resources; in this case, the injustice is the result of "generative AI's control over access to information, leading to a denial of knowledge based on identity-driven bias or misrecognition" (Kay et al., 2024, p. 689). In a previous study, we noticed that unless prompted, Chat-GPT 4 defaulted to person-first language when discussing disabled characters (Barron, et al., 2025b). When prompted to explain why it did so, it explained that while many disabled people find identity-first language to be more affirming it is programmed to default to person-first so as not to offend. Yet this is exactly how we see that non-disabled knowledge within the dataset is afforded more credibility than knowledge from disabled users. Faissner et al. (2025) uses the term "wilful hermeneutical ignorance" to describe when "dominantly situated knowers actively refuse to acknowledge the epistemic resources developed within marginalized epistemic communities" (p. 121). They extend this description to AI by including the developers among the "dominantly situated knowers" responsible for ignoring (or not preventing the ignoring of) the importance of knowledge generated by the relevant community (p. 128). Kay et al. (2024) take the same position that

> Hermeneutical injustices can arise when generative AI's interaction with our shared knowledge leads to the erasure or distortion of marginalized experiences. This may occur when the system lacks sufficient sociocultural understanding of humans, or when the system obstructing [*sic*] the access to knowledge itself (p. 687).

This not only harms the speaker, but the hearer as well, because "withholding or distortion of information based on identity" is a form of hermeneutical injustice that impacts the hearers' ability to receive knowledge (Kay et al., 2024, p. 690).

Despite the role the developers play in producing willful hermeneutical ignorance, increasing the diversity of the developers will not solve the problem. As Gengler et al. (2024) points out, "educating and diversifying AI experts" is just one of six categories of solutions necessary to reduce bias (p. 233), while Shams et al. (2025) included "Designers require learning on diversity-oriented design" and "Include diverse voices in training data and design" among the 33 solutions they found in their literature review (p. 420). The solution to AI bias is not something that can be slotted in to fix existing issues. Gengler et al. (2024) explain that

Solutions to reduce discrimination by AI lie in the whole AI life cycle: Creating equitable algorithms requires ethical fundaments, education, and diversity of AI experts; furthermore, bias mitigation techniques help to properly adapt algorithms, and finally, more objective decision-making as well as corporate AI governance need to be ensured. Thus, a holistic perspective is needed when aiming to resolve existing power imbalances and biases in AI (p. 233).

It is not clear how that can be applied to existing AI systems or to what extent the corporate owners of those systems are willing to engage in these approaches.

DATA GOVERNANCE

Addressing the epistemic harms baked into LLM infrastructure requires data governance practices that are rooted in disability data justice to redistribute epistemic authority to those historically silenced. Disability data justice emphasizes community-led infrastructures that resist deficit-based models and democratize access to knowledge, ensuring that disabled people shape not only what data are collected but how it is defined, tagged, and interpreted (Gorman, 2024). This includes building repositories curated by disability communities themselves, using participatory processes to determine what terms and categories are used, and ensuring that materials are "born accessible" through plain language, alt text, and multilingual support. In this way, communities can create their own corpora rather than relying solely on state or corporate datasets. Community-curated corpora are another critical avenue. Gorman (2024) highlight the importance of redefining glossaries and ontologies through critical and intersectional perspectives that reflect disability-positive framings. Similarly, Gadiraju et al. (2023) show that disabled users can identify subtle stereotyping in LLM outputs and recommend training models on disability-positive resources to resist harmful tropes. Together, these interventions illustrate examples of grassroots data infrastructures and activist knowledge projects that expand hermeneutical resources and resist erasures that occur in mainstream datasets. Through these methods, communities can hold power over how their perspectives are being considered within a dataset and, further, hold more control over embedding intersectional perspectives into training data; such measures expand the interpretive resources available to both AI systems and their users, countering hermeneutical marginalization while reducing testimonial quieting by affirming disabled people as authoritative epistemic agents.

Beyond the initial training data, and the ownership of the dataset, transparency in dataset documentation further complements participatory control. Longpre et al. (2024) note that many widely used corpora are poorly documented and ambiguously licensed, leaving significant gaps about who is represented or excluded. These practices surface the histories of datasets, which could prevent the excessive assignment of credibility to AI-generated text output by reminding users that outputs are dependent on partial and situated data histories rather than objective fact. Further, regulatory and platform-level interventions are needed. They also show how most training datasets remain under-documented, ambiguously licensed, or mislabeled, and propose Data Provenance Cards as a structured way to label datasets with their sources, licensing, and limitations. Related efforts such as Data Cards (Pushkarna et al., 2022) and Croissant-RAI (Jain et al., 2024) demonstrate how documentation can be standardized and made machine-readable, enabling provenance information to circulate across repositories. Extending these practices to the level of user-facing design would mean that outputs from LLMs carry visible markers of their underlying data lineage. For example, whether a generated response draws primarily on peer-reviewed scholarship, community archives, or synthetic text. Such provenance labeling at the point of output would reduce testimonial quieting by reminding users that AI systems are not knowers but mediators, and by making clear when marginalized perspectives are absent or misrepresented in the training data.

CONCLUSION

As text generated by Gen-AI proliferates, there is a critical epistemological crisis that emerges. As we have traced above, the issue of generative AI extends far beyond diversifying that data, because the infrastructure of these systems is only capable of homogenizing knowledge. Through divorcing of knowledge from knower, and shuffling data points to produce increasingly homogenized generated texts, we are left with extensive amounts of content that contribute to the testimonial quieting of marginalized groups. Further, the progressive homogenization in linguistic practices online because of generative AI (Sourati et al., 2025), perpetuates implicit bias under the guise of presumed impartiality. Critically, Leclerc (2021) writes,

> Impartiality [thus] is a privilege, because to be able to situate oneself in this posture is only possible if one feels recognized epistemically. Therefore, one must belong to a privileged group or to a social identity supported by the majority's epistemic resources (p. 15).

Faissner et al. (2025), following Hull (2023), point out that the way the world is represented in data becomes unchanging over time and works to reinforce socially constructed categories while simultaneously making those categories seem apolitical and natural, when they are anything but.

Ultimately, the issues we trace here are not easily remedied because they strike at the core of how this technology works. However, further research in the area would begin with cocreated and curated datasets with disabled people, along with dataset organization and tagging systems that are informed by intersectional frameworks, and regulatory practices to open the possibility of addressing the epistemic injustice embedded in AI systems. This requires drawing on many of these strategies in concert toward epistemic justice, with attention to the pitfalls of each. Specifically, this involves redistributing authority over data to disabled communities, surfacing the social and historical contexts of datasets, and ensuring that hermeneutical resources are expanded rather than narrowed. It is possible to interrupt both testimonial injustice and hermeneutical marginalization. Crucially, future work developing AI systems must attend critically to how data is deemed worthy of knowing. Particularly, the risks involved as data can be a double-edged sword for many communities, especially Black and Indigenous communities (Gorman, 2024). Without datasets that are representative of intersectional and transnational perspectives, there will continue to be inequity embedded in datasets and the outputs generated with them (Gorman, 2024).

REFLECTIVE QUESTIONS

1. How does the concept of epistemic flattening explain why AI might treat expert lived knowledge and baseless claims as equally valid?
2. What is disability-evasiveness, and how does generative AI reproduce this by erasing the specificities of disabled experiences?
3. How does the credibility deficit experienced by marginalized speakers interact with the credibility excess often granted to AI outputs?
4. Why does the homogenization of AI-generated content pose a threat to the collective hermeneutical resource available to society?

NOTE

1 Short stories of 500–700 words using prompts such as "Please write a realistic story about a child with [disability]. Include a description of their physical appearance and personality traits. The story should be between 500–700 words."

REFERENCES

Annamma, S. A., Connor, D., & Ferri, B. (2013). Dis/ability critical race studies (DisCrit): Theorizing at the intersections of race and dis/ability. *Race Ethnicity and Education*, *16*(1), 1–31. https://doi.org/10.1080/13613324.2012.730511

Annamma, S. A., Jackson, D. D., & Morrison, D. (2017). Conceptualizing color-evasiveness: Using dis/ability critical race theory to expand a color-blind racial ideology in education and society. *Race Ethnicity and Education*, *20*(2), 147–162. https://doi.org/10.1080/13613324.2016.1248837

Barron, K., Collis, R. B., Richmond, A. J., & Van Berkel, E. (2025). Disability Evasiveness: Disability Representation in AI-Generated Flash Fiction. *Harvard Educational Review*, 95(4), 613–639. https://doi.org/10.17763/f3w7m9t5k

Barron, K., Collis, R. B., Richmond, A., & Van Berkel, E. (2025b). Mechanisms of disability Evasiveness in AI-generated flash fiction. In C. El Morr, Y. El-Lahib, & R. da Silveria Gorma (Eds.), *Beyond Tech Fixes: Towards an AI Future Where Disability Justice Thrives* (pp. 163–179). Springer Nature. https://doi.org/10.1007/978-3-031-93022-5_13

Berenstain, N. (2020). White feminist gaslighting. *Hypatia*, *35*(4), 733–758. https://doi.org/10.1017/hyp.2020.31

Bourassa, G. (2021). Neoliberal multiculturalism and productive inclusion: Beyond the politics of fulfillment in education. *Journal of Education Policy*, *36*(2), 253–278. https://doi.org/10.1080/02680939.2019.1676472

Dotson, K. (2011). Tracking epistemic violence, tracking practices of silencing. *Hypatia*, *26*(2), 236–257. https://doi.org/10.1111/j.1527-2001.2011.01177.x

Epstein, S. (1995). The construction of lay expertise: AIDS activism and the forging of credibility in the reform of clinical trials. *Science, Technology, & Human Values*, *20*(4), 408–437. https://doi.org/10.1177/016224399502000402

Faissner, M., Lenk, J., & Müller, R. (2025). AI and epistemic injustice. In M. Hähnel & R. Müller (Eds.), *A Companion to Applied Philosophy of AI* (1st ed., pp. 118–132). Wiley. https://doi.org/10.1002/9781394238651.ch9

Fricker, M. (2007). *Epistemic Injustice: Power and the Ethics of Knowing*. Oxford University Press.

Gadiraju, V., Kane, S., Dev, S., Taylor, A., Wang, D., Denton, R., & Brewer, R. (2023). "I Wouldn't Say Offensive but...": Disability-Centered Perspectives on Large Language Models. *2023 ACM Conference on Fairness Accountability and Transparency*, Chicago, IL, 205–216. https://doi.org/10.1145/3593013.3593989

Gengler, E., Hagerer, I., & Gales, A. (2024). Diversity bias in artificial intelligence. In J. Passmore, S. J. Diller, S. Isaacson, & M. Brantl (Eds.), *The Digital and AI Coaches' Handbook*. Routledge, 229–240.

Glazko, K. S., Mohammed, Y., Kosa, B., Potluri, V., & Mankoff, J. (2024). Identifying and Improving Disability Bias in GPT-Based Resume Screening. *Proceedings of the 2024 ACM Conference on Fairness, Accountability, and Transparency*, Rio de Janeiro, 687–700. https://doi.org/10.1145/3630106.3658933

Glazko, K. S., Yamagami, M., Desai, A., Mack, K. A., Potluri, V., Xu, X., & Mankoff, J. (2023). An Autoethnographic Case Study of Generative Artificial Intelligence's Utility for Accessibility. *The 25th International ACM SIGACCESS Conference on Computers and Accessibility*, New York, 1–8. https://doi.org/10.1145/3597638.3614548

Gorman, R. (2024). Disability data justice from the ground up: A practice-led, participatory co-design approach to building an AI search engine and data repository for local, national, and transnational disability organizations. *Critical Studies: An International and Interdisciplinary Journal, 18*(1), 28–43. https://doi.org/10.51357/cs.v18i1.229

Graham, L. J. (Ed.). (2023). *Inclusive Education for the 21st Century: Theory, Policy and Practice*. Taylor & Francis.

Hartblay, C. (2020). Disability expertise: Claiming disability anthropology. *Current Anthropology, 61*(S21), S26–S36. https://doi.org/10.1086/705781

Herrmann, S. (2019). The struggle for a common world: From epistemic Power to Political Action With Arendt and Fricker. In S. Herrmann, G. Thonhauser, S. Loidolt, T. Matzner, & N. Baratella (Eds.), *Political Phenomenology*. Routledge, 277–299.

Hull, G. (2023). Dirty data labeled dirt cheap: Epistemic injustice in machine learning systems. *Ethics and Information Technology, 25*(3), 38. https://doi.org/10.1007/s10676-023-09712-y

Jain, N., Akhtar, M., Giner-Miguelez, J., Shinde, R., Vanschoren, J., Vogler, S., Goswami, S., Rao, Y., Santos, T., Oala, L., Karamousadakis, M., Maskey, M., Marcenac, P., Conforti, C., Kuchnik, M., Aroyo, L., Benjelloun, O., & Simperl, E. (2024, June 4). *A Standardized Machine-readable Dataset Documentation Format for Responsible AI*. https://doi.org/10.48550/arXiv.2407.16883

Kay, J., Kasirzadeh, A., & Mohamed, S. (2024). Epistemic Injustice in Generative AI. *Proceedings of the AAAI/ACM Conference on AI, Ethics, and Society*, San Jose, CA, *7*(1), Article 1. https://doi.org/10.1609/aies.v7i1.31671

Leclerc, A. (2021). Impartiality as an epistemic privilege. *Ithaque, 28*. https://hdl.handle.net/1866/25018

Longpre, S., Mahari, R., Obeng-Marnu, N., Brannon, W., South, T., Gero, K., Pentland, S., & Kabbara, J. (2024, August 30). *Data Authenticity, Consent, & Provenance for AI Are All Broken: What Will It Take to Fix Them?* https://doi.org/10.48550/arXiv.2404.12691

Maimann, K. (2025, August 13). Chatbots learned to write from us. Can AI now change the way we think? *CBC News*. https://www.cbc.ca/news/ai-human-thought-processes-1.7604789

Milton, D. E. M. (2014). Autistic expertise: A critical reflection on the production of knowledge in autism studies. *Autism, 18*(7), 794–802. https://doi.org/10.1177/1362361314525281

O'Neil, C. (2017). *Weapons of Math Destruction: How Big Data Increases Inequality and Threatens Democracy*. Crown.

Pushkarna, M., Zaldivar, A., & Kjartansson, O. (2022). Data Cards: Purposeful and Transparent Dataset Documentation for Responsible AI. *2022 ACM Conference on Fairness Accountability and Transparency*, Seoul, 1776–1826. https://doi.org/10.1145/3531146.3533231

Shams, R. A., Zowghi, D., & Bano, M. (2025). AI and the quest for diversity and inclusion: A systematic literature review. *AI and Ethics, 5*(1), 411–438. https://doi.org/10.1007/s43681-023-00362-w

Sourati, Z., Ziabari, A. S., & Dehghani, M. (2025). *The Homogenizing Effect of Large Language Models on Human Expression and Thought* (No. arXiv:2508.01491). arXiv. https://doi.org/10.48550/arXiv.2508.01491

Wanderer, J. (2017). Varieties Of Testimonial Injustice. In I. J. Kidd (Ed.), *The Routledge handbook of epistemic injustice* (pp. 27–40). Routledge, Taylor & Francis Group.

Part 3

AI in Society

Gender, Labor, and Social Relations

This section situates AI within broader social and economic relations, examining how gendered power, labor structures, and intimacy are reorganized through algorithmic systems. The chapters analyze AI's role in shaping work, care, social reproduction, and interpersonal life, highlighting how technological design intersects with patriarchy, capitalism, and platform economies. Collectively, they reveal AI as a social force that both reflects and restructures existing inequalities.

DOI: 10.1201/9781003737810-17

15 Misogyny by Design
The Manosphere, AI, and Technology-Facilitated Gender-Based Violence

Sonia D'Angelo

INTRODUCTION

In February 2024, Isla David, a Canadian digital content creator and sex worker, became the target of an AI-generated image circulated by a far-right influencer. The image originated from a photograph David posted to Reddit in 2021, depicting her seated on a chair, partially dressed, sipping whiskey. Ian Miles Cheong manipulated this original image to radically alter its visual narrative. In the AI-generated version, David appears redressed in a knee-length dress, surrounded by three small children. The whiskey glass in David's hand is replaced with a child's head, transforming the scene into one of domesticity and maternal care, a visual recasting of David into an idealized embodiment of femininity. Cheong's tweet (2024) accompanying the AI-generated image read: "When given pictures of thirst traps, AI imagines what could've been if they'd been raised by strong fathers." The image has garnered over 7.5 million views.

David's image is part of DignifAI, a 4chan-based, manosphere-led campaign launched in January 2024, which uses AI tools to alter women's bodies and to "put clothes back on e-girls[1]" (Posobiec, 2024). DignifAI originated on 4chan and expanded to establish its own website, along with social media accounts on Twitter/X, Instagram, and YouTube. The 4chan forum explicitly states its goal as "putting clothes on degenerate women" reflecting the underlying message that "a degenerate lifestyle is ultimately fruitless" (see post No.457225620). Users on the forum are encouraged to upload names and pictures of women they deem in need of dignification via AI-generated modifications. The campaign offers detailed instructions for using the AI tools and encourages users to harass women, whom they label as "thots" or "that hoe over there," by tagging them and reposting the AI-generated images to their social media accounts using the hashtag DignifAI. The DignifAI campaign illustrates how the misogyny of the manosphere is amplified by AI, shaping the ways women experience and navigate digital life. The use of AI images is not intended to dignify women as the manosphere might suggest, rather, they are designed to harass, humiliate, and control women. Women's online self-presentation is framed not only as a failure of femininity but, as Cheong emphasizes, as evidence of the essential role hegemonic masculinity plays in regulating and preserving normative ideals of femininity. AI provides the technological means to realize this misogynistic dream.

This chapter employs a qualitative case study approach to analyze the AI-produced imagery of the DignifAI campaign on 4chan. The study adopts a feminist grounded theoretical approach both to generate emergent theoretical insights from the images and to center the examination of structures of power, oppression, gender justice, and intersectional inequities (Hesse-Biber & Flowers, 2019; Wuest, 1995). This methodological lens extends beyond analyses of masculine gender performances and identity constructions in the manosphere, centering instead, the often-disembodied representations of women appearing in the manosphere to illuminate the social and technological mechanisms

 DOI: 10.1201/9781003737810-18

that sustain misogyny, patriarchal power, gender inequality, and gendered harm. While Isla David's story provides a point of entry into the DignifAI campaign, the study does not focus on her case alone. Rather, the study aims to provide a descriptive and critical analysis of how women are represented within the DignifAI campaign, incorporating an intersectional perspective that acknowledges the heterogeneous experiences of gender inequity, therefore extending and enriching existing theoretical understandings of gender, femininity, and masculinity, in the manosphere. Data were collected from archived threads on 4chan's /pol/board using the subject term DignifAI. Threads were analyzed chronologically, beginning with the original thread created in January 2024. The analysis focused on identifying AI-generated images and examining both the images and their accompanying descriptive commentary.

This chapter argues that AI-generated deepfake images from the DignifAI campaign, function as a form of technology-facilitated gender-based violence (TFGBV) that the manosphere actively propagates and normalizes. This chapter opens by contrasting two competing visions of the technological and digital: the feminist hope that technology could reimagine or transcend the constraints of gender and the female body, and the manosphere's fixation on the female body as a site for imposing and solidifying oppressive gender relations. It first situates AI-generated deepfake images within the broader landscape TFGBV, showing how such images reproduce patriarchal dominance, uphold hegemonic masculinity, and constrain women's agency and digital citizenship. The analysis then turns to the DignifAI campaign as a case study, illustrating how AI redressing transforms deviant femininities into hegemonic ideals, disciplining women's bodies to align with male desire and domination. It also demonstrates how the manosphere imagines and frames Muslim women as dignified only through bodily erasure and subjugation, revealing the interplay of misogynist and orientalist fantasies in the manosphere. By examining how the manosphere weaponizes AI-generated images to demean, control, and silence women, this chapter situates such violence in the inseparability of online and offline misogyny, outlining the embodied harms such practices produce. This chapter therefore outlines how AI-generated images reinforce hegemonic gender relations, produce harmful ideals of femininity, and restrict women's agency and participation as digital citizens.

LITERATURE REVIEW

Cyberfeminist Utopias: Beyond the Body, Beyond Oppression

Cyberfeminists were once hopeful that digital technologies would bring about the dissolution of the patriarchy. Emerging in the early 1990s, cyberfeminism examines how gender, technology, and inequalities, particularly patriarchy, shape digital domains. Cyberfeminism envisions new technologies as offering possibilities to "escape from bodily gender definitions and construct new…or even genderless identities" (van Zoonen, 2002, p.12). Cyberfeminism seeks to disrupt the interlocking power relations that operate within digital environments, but also across offline contexts. For example, early scholars like Sadie Plant (1997) and Donna Haraway (1991) articulated utopian visions of the digital as a realm of empowerment, where women could challenge patriarchal power. Harvey (2020) characterizes cyberfeminist visions as transcendental, imagining technology as a means to overcome embodied differences, including gender and race "therefore [bringing] about an end to racism, sexism, and other forms of discrimination by bypassing the body entirely" (p.117).

This emancipatory vision persists in the fourth wave of feminism, characterized by digital activism, where technology facilitates feminist mobilization and collective consciousness (Baer, 2016). Yet, as feminist scholarship emphasizes, technology is deeply embedded in gendered power relations, operating simultaneously as a source and a product of inequality, shaping and reinforcing dominant constructions of masculinity and femininity (Wajcman, 2004, 2010). Consequently, technological advances and digital spaces embody a duality: they offer opportunities for empowerment and resistance, but also reproduce exclusion, harassment, algorithmic oppression, intersectional violence, and pervasive misogyny (Banet-Weiser, 2018; Harvey, 2020; Noble, 2018).

The Digital Life of Misogynistic Dreams: The Manosphere and TFGBV

While digital spaces function as important sites of feminist empowerment, anti-feminist sentiment and misogyny drive targeted harassment and gender-based violence against women online (Banet-Weiser, 2018; Jane, 2014, 2017). This violence is linked to the reactive misogyny propagated by men, including those within the manosphere (Banet-Weiser, 2018; Banet-Weiser & Miltner, 2016; Jones et al., 2020). The manosphere is a loosely connected, evolving online community predominantly composed of men, with women participating only marginally (Bower, 2024; Hoebanx, 2025). It spans social media platforms, blogs, and forums such as Reddit and 4chan, encompassing diverse groups like men's rights activists, involuntary celibates (incels), men going their own way, and pick-up artists (Ging, 2019). Despite its diversity, the manosphere coalesces around core beliefs that rationalize and perpetuate gendered harm. The Red Pill ideology constructs a narrative of masculine crisis, attributing blame to feminism, gender equality, and femininity itself, thereby fueling anti-feminist sentiment (Ging, 2019; Marwick & Caplan, 2018). Anti-feminism functions as a justificatory mechanism through which men of the manosphere legitimize gendered violence (Marwick & Caplan, 2018). The manosphere also organizes such violence through networked misogyny, referring to the normalization of, and the structural role, misogyny plays in shaping the coordinated hostility and violence women encounter in digital spaces (Banet-Weiser & Miltner, 2016). These coordinated campaigns uphold hegemonic masculinity and maintain traditional gender hierarchies that subordinate and denigrate women. Marwick and Caplan (2018) describe this hostility as networked harassment, or the policing and controlling of women's behavior online, but also constituting a form of gender-based violence which extends beyond the digital.

Building on the understanding that misogyny structures the manosphere's violence against women, gaps remain in how AI amplifies gender-based harm in digital spaces (Iñigo, 2025), including how algorithmic processes work to amplify misogynistic practices online. Deepfakes are artificially generated media that employ AI or machine learning tools to fabricate images, videos, or audio without an individual's consent, constituting a form of TFGBV that infringes on individual dignity (Akter & Ahmed, 2025; Karagianni & Doh, 2024). TFGBV encompasses acts of violence that are motivated by gender, or produce gendered harms, including the perpetuation of harmful gender norms, and is intensified or enabled by digital technologies (Hinson et al., 2018). TFGBV encompasses acts motivated by the intent to humiliate, seek revenge, defame, silence, and harm, enacted through tactics such as harassment, bullying, threats, torture, exploitation, and stalking (Canadian Women's Foundation, 2025; Citron & Chesney, 2019; Dunn, 2020; Hinson et al., 2018; Karagianni & Doh, 2024). Deepfakes exemplify an emerging form of cybercrime, a broad category that includes traditional offenses such as stalking, harassment, hate speech, threats, and bullying to newer forms such as doxxing, trolling, nonconsensual image abuse, including deepfakes, all of which are intensified or enabled by digital technologies (Akter & Ahmed, 2025; Ging, 2023; Canadian Women's Foundation, 2025).

TFGBV is a significant and growing concern in Canada (Cahill et al., 2024; Canadian Women's Foundation, 2025). A 2025 report by the Canadian Women's Foundation found that 61% of women and gender-diverse people experienced digital harm, disproportionately affecting Black, Indigenous, racialized, 2SLGBTQIA+, youth, and persons with disabilities, with 55% of perpetrators identified as men. Deepfakes, as a form of TFGBV, disproportionately target women and girls and operate within dynamics of patriarchal control which require the regulation and subjugation of women (Akter & Ahmed, 2025; Dunn, 2020; van der Nagel, 2020). Given the prevalence of TFGBV, this chapter argues that these harms demand both sustained scholarly attention and targeted policy interventions. Despite the growing prevalence of the manosphere and TFGBV, little research examines how the manosphere produces and disseminates AI-generated deepfakes to perpetuate TFGBV. This study addresses that gap and engages with the limited research that investigates AI-generated gendered images as instruments of TFGBV within the manosphere (Akter & Ahmed, 2025). As such, this chapter demonstrates how feminist analysis can both extend theoretical understandings of gendered power in the manosphere and inform policy responses that account for the intersectional dimensions of TFGBV. By linking critical theory with empirical analysis, the study highlights the structural and technological mechanisms that enable digital gendered violence.

MAIN BODY

Redressing Femininity: From Pariah to Hegemonic Femininity

The DignifAI campaign is not merely about putting clothes on women. By digitally redressing them, it enacts a symbolic project of gender discipline, targeting pariah expressions of femininity, while reinscribing normative ideals of femininity and masculinity aligned with the hegemonic gender order (Schippers, 2007). Pariah femininities are considered contaminating to the gender order given that the embodiment of masculine-coded traits, such as sexual assertiveness and autonomy, threaten the exclusivity of hegemonic masculinity, thus maintaining dominance requires expelling these traits from femininity (Schippers, 2007). While David's story offers a glimpse into the lived experiences of a woman targeted by the campaign, the empirical evidence suggests that other women targeted may also be sex workers, women whose sexual agency and digital visibility render them particularly vulnerable to AI-driven harassment, violence, and harm. Women who display sexual agency and autonomy online are stigmatized, their sexuality transformed into something undesirable and in need of intervention. AI becomes a tool to recode women's bodies into hegemonic form as compliant, maternal, chaste, and aligned with male desires and domination, making the feminine body an object to discipline and subjugate. DignifAI operationalizes the expulsion of the pariah through AI dignification. Before images mark women as deviant, sexually available, and morally contaminated, femininity as failure. AI-after images recast them as embodiments of hegemonic femininity, respectable, maternal, sexually chaste, and thus complementary to hegemonic masculinity (Example 1, Example 2, and Example 3).

In example 1 *,[2] the original unaltered image depicts a woman self-presenting partially dressed at the gym and served as the initial, anchoring image in the DignifAI threads. The subsequent AI-generated images, not only clothed the woman, but also repositioned her within a domestic realm, depicting her kneeling in ways that symbolically center domestic labor, obedience, and cleanliness (see, /ovRbqvk, 2024; BwhWynuS, 2024).

In example 2, the original unaltered image on the left depicts a woman wearing a sheer top exposing her breasts in public. In contrast, the AI-generated image on the right redresses the same woman, fully covering her body and presenting her as modest and socially respectable. This juxtaposition illustrates not only AI's intervention in regulating female visibility and sexual expression, but also its effect on the male gaze. In the original image, the male bystander appears visibly unsettled by the woman's public sexual display. In the AI-altered image, following the dignification of her appearance, the male gaze shifts to one of contentment, reflecting the alignment of femininity with socially sanctioned norms of respectability and modesty. These images, including of the male bystander, have circulated across multiple threads, even serving as an anchor image. It has also subsequently been repurposed into a meme by community members (see SSc+zlEl, 2024).

In example 3, the three unaltered original images from which three AI-generated versions are derived, depict women taking selfies while partially or fully nude. Collectively, the AI-altered images convey a redressing of femininity linked not only to modesty and respectability, but also to maternal care, domesticity, and a nostalgic return to gender norms. These transformations evoke the aesthetics of traditional wives, or Tradwife imagery, widely circulated in the manosphere, as exemplified most clearly by the central image (See, PU6keB+x, 2024; Hk/VZqgK, 2024; PU6keB+x, 2024).

Dignity functions as a cloaked term for subjecting women to male control, visually transforming pariah femininities to affirm men's dominance, reinforcing the gender binary. The campaign further enforces a hierarchy among femininities and masculinities. A user's comment illustrates this logic: "the sexuality displayed is likely performative (social media thots and gym chads), rather than either being productive (men and women forming families and producing children). We are forcibly going to heal this damaged world" (gyM+gh3A, 2024). Pariah femininities are shamed, blamed, and cast as morally dangerous, their sexuality allegedly drawing chads, who are vilified for submitting to women's sexual or financial demands (Menzie, 2022). This gender hierarchy upholds a patriarchal logic by condemning masculinities that prioritize women's desires. By contrast, hegemonic masculinity is defined by its refusal to accommodate female sexuality. Femininity here is deemed valuable only when reproductive and oriented toward the preservation of the heterosexual family. Through AI dignification, DignifAI enforces this hierarchy, disciplining femininity, policing women's bodies, and restoring what the manosphere frames as the proper gender order, where hegemonic masculinity retains dominance, and only femininities that complement, not threaten masculinity, are culturally valued. DignifAI thus works to recuperate masculinity in its hegemonic form by enforcing limiting notions of femininity which reduce women to respectable bodies.

Bodily (In)Visibility and the Orientalist Fantasies of Muslim Women in the Manosphere

A notable observation of the DignifAI campaign extends beyond the production of deepfakes to include side-by-side comparisons that position deviant or pariah femininity against representations of Muslim women. These juxtapositions frame Muslim women as gender exemplars, functioning as correctives to the perceived moral failures of Western femininity and feminism. For example, one user posted an image of a woman dressed in burlesque attire, including pasties and chains, accompanied by the word empowered in quotation marks, an undermining typographic cue. Directly juxtaposed and superimposed over the AI-generated deepfake of the same woman, is an image of a Muslim woman wearing a niqab, whose image is framed by the word powerful (See Example 4). The contrast here is deliberate. The sexualized and AI-altered image is rendered as a failed embodiment of femininity, replaced by an image of a Muslim woman as a dignified and morally superior expression of femininity.

In example 4, the images depict: the unaltered original image, which already included the word empowered; the AI-generated version, showing the same woman clothed and pregnant, now with the word powerful; and a further edited version that overlays an image of an anonymous Muslim woman onto the AI-generated image. This final intervention evokes the dehumanization of Muslim women while framing the altered image as a morally superior expression of femininity (see kg1x08eu, 2024; Q/jE9I1Q, 2024).

Of particular significance here is the way users invoke an orientalized and colonial fantasy about Muslim femininity, a narrow vision of femininity defined by bodily erasure, wherein Muslims women's bodies require concealment. One user, for example, juxtaposes three images of Muslim women: the first shows a woman in a hijab, labeled with the derogatory term thot, while the other two depict women in a burqa and a niqab, overlaid with the emblem "Halal Certified" and the descriptor dignified (Example 5).

In example 5, the images presented here signify exalted constructions of Muslim femininity. All these images appear to be stock images, reinforcing not only an essentialized and static portrayal of Muslim women, but also the notion that they lack a digital visibility, aligning with the misogynistic dream of DignifAI (see WimijhdW, 2024).

In this framing, the burqa- and niqab-wearing women are elevated as the pinnacle of respectability, marking the visual endpoint of the gendered disciplinary process. Unlike Islamophobic discourses that depict Muslim women as defying Western ideals of femininity and resisting Western intervention over their bodies, DignifAI frames women in the niqab and burqa as sexually unavailable and unfree (Razack, 2018), necessary antidotes to the perceived oversexualization of femininity and to the crisis this is imagined to pose for masculinity. Conceived as dreams of possession, these representations recast Muslim women's bodies as sites for the enactment of a misogynistic and patriarchal order, securing white masculine dominance and echoing the alt-right's call for a white sharia. The DignifAI campaign deploys images of Muslim women as instruments to achieve misogynistic and orientalist fantasies (Razack, 2018). By ascribing inherent dignity to Muslim women wearing the niqab and burqa, requiring no AI intervention, the campaign implies that dignity is conferred upon Muslim women through their coercion and control by Muslim men, reinforcing orientalist assumptions of Muslim women as submissive, oppressed, and lacking agency (Razack, 2018). Misogyny is thus consolidated through the figure of the Muslim woman, whose body is positioned in contrast to that of the visibly undignified woman.

Although the images of Muslim women are not AI-generated, the DignifAI campaign instrumentalizes them in ways that constitute a form of TFGBV. These images, largely drawn from stock or generic photographs, operate through abstraction and disembodiment, stripping Muslim women of individuality and agency. Their circulation reproduces orientalist logics by objectifying Muslim femininity as the exalted, ideal form that AI technology seeks to replicate (see Example 15.6). In this sense, the homogenizing representation of Muslim women as oppressed constitutes a form of harm by erasing the heterogeneous and complex realities of Muslim women's lives and veiling practices (Afshar, 2008; Bilge, 2010; Zempi, 2016). Such representations discipline femininity through patriarchal and orientalist frames, sustaining a gendered hierarchy in which Muslim women's bodies are appropriated as instruments of regulation and discipline. Muslim femininity, here, is valorized insofar as it is constrained by patriarchal dominance and confined to a liminal bodily visibility.

Example 6 invokes the narrative of human evolution, these images visually position Muslim femininity as the presumed endpoint of a normative gendered trajectory, reinforcing the notion that AI technology can shape and enshrine an idealized, exalted form of femininity characterized by modesty and bodily invisibility (see !IJ1WXdcL92, 2024).

DISCUSSION

David spoke publicly about her AI-generated deepfake, asserting that whether clothing is added or removed, the manipulation equally violates her bodily autonomy (Dickson, 2024). Beyond David's experience, empirical evidence remains limited regarding the direct impact of the DignifAI campaign on the lives of women targeted by such violence. Forum discussions suggest that women respond to these digital violations and associated harassment by blocking, reporting, and otherwise attempting to mitigate exposure to these images. However, there remains a significant gap in understanding the lived experiences of women, and notably sex workers, affected by the DignifAI campaign, as well as the broader intersectional dynamics and consequences of TFGBV arising from AI technologies.

What is known, however, is that harms from TFGBV are neither abstract nor uniform. Understanding the harm of DignifAI requires recognizing that online and offline worlds are inseparable (Henry & Powell, 2015). While AI facilitates networked misogyny, TFGBV is structural, rooted, and co-constituted in the same misogynistic norms that sustain offline gender-based violence (Ging, 2023; Massanari, 2017). DignifAI targeted women through coordinated pile-ons, the circulation of images shared by tagging and hashtagging, amplifying harassment, bodily violation, and public shaming. Although enacted in digital spaces, the violence of AI-generated imagery was misogynistically designed to be hostile, intrusive, and oppressive, sustaining notions of femininity that are harmful and constraining. Technologies like AI deepfakes have amplified the modalities of gender-based violence (Laffier & Rehman, 2023) while simultaneously exposing the structural magnitude of misogyny (Ging, 2023).

The harms arising from TFGBV are embodied and multifaceted, spanning psychological, reputational, social, and economic domains (Henry & Powell, 2015). For example, victims of deepfakes report humiliation, fear, self-censorship, and psychological distress, including anxiety, depression, suicidal ideation, and a compromised sense of self (Laffier & Rehman, 2023). Reputational harms can manifest through damaged relationships, loss of professional credibility, and heightened vulnerability to doxxing and legal threats. Economic harms follow, as the chilling and silencing effects of online misogyny (Amnesty International, 2017) deter women from participating in digital spaces, constraining access to digital labor, restricting professional opportunities, and ultimately access to the means of production (Siapera, 2019). Cumulatively, the harms of TFGBV constrain women's digital citizenship, undermine their autonomy and agency both online and offline (Laffier & Rehman, 2023), and reinforce gendered power structures that uphold restrictive and harmful notions of femininity which work to sustain gender inequality.

CONCLUSION

This chapter demonstrates how AI-generated deepfakes, exemplified by the DignifAI campaign, function as a form of TFGBV within the manosphere, constraining women's agency, autonomy, and digital citizenship. The analysis of DignifAI illustrates how the campaign enforces normative gender hierarchies through AI redressing, transforming deviant femininities into hegemonic ideals, disciplining women's bodies to respond to male domination. The framing of Muslim women as dignified relies on their liminal bodily visibility and subjugation, revealing the presence of misogynistic and orientalist fantasies shaping understandings of gender. By digitally regulating and recoding femininity, the campaign enacts the manosphere's misogynistic fantasies, producing embodied harms while systematically sustaining and amplifying gendered hierarchies through AI technology.

Three key research and policy actions are necessary to advance understandings of TFGBV and strengthen support for survivors. First, despite growing recognition of the harms associated with TFGBV, future research must examine how the manosphere engages in and normalizes such violence, with particular attention to AI tools, including deepfakes, both sexualized (unclothing) and non-sexualized (redressing). Significant qualitative gaps remain in understanding the intersectional impacts of misogynistic online violence on women and other marginalized groups, including fat, racialized, Indigenous, 2SLGBTQ+ individuals, and persons with disabilities. Qualitative interviews and digital ethnographies are well suited to capture the lived realities of those targeted, documenting both the harms endured, and the strategies of resistance mobilized. Second, survivor-centered knowledge and community support channels must be systematically documented through qualitative interviews and ethnographies. Research should examine coping strategies, networks of care, and non-legal avenues that enable survivors to feel supported and empowered. Studies should also investigate how survivor communities and organizations reimagine AI and digital spaces to safeguard dignity and autonomy, realizing aspects of the emancipatory potential envisioned by cyberfeminists. Attending to these practices is critical both for empirically understanding how infrastructures of support and resistance emerge in response to TFGBV and for guiding policy decisions to allocate resources that sustain and expand community-based initiatives addressing gendered digital harms. Third, public accountability is essential to mitigating digital harms (Canadian Women's Foundation, 2025). Social media platforms should adopt transparent evidence-preservation standards for deepfakes and gendered harassment, ensuring that evidence, including user metadata, remains accessible to survivors and their support networks. Simultaneously, Canadian policy advocates and platforms must explicitly recognize misogyny, in its intersectional forms, in public and digital harm policies to strengthen protections against TFGBV, and to counter the growing influence of the manosphere in perpetuating this violence.

As demonstrated, intersectional feminist analyses are crucial for understanding how AI technologies are designed and deployed in ways that reproduce systemic inequalities. This approach is vital for informing interventions and policies addressing TFGBV, while guiding the development of digital environments and technological advancements that truly uphold the dignity and digital citizenship of all.

REFLECTION QUESTIONS

1. Describe how you understand the manosphere. Based on your understanding or experiences encountering the manosphere online, how might the beliefs it promotes influence attitudes toward gender and reinforce social inequalities?

2. Identify an example of TFGBV you have encountered or learned about. What narratives or explanations are used to justify or frame this violence? How are victims and perpetrators represented? What impacts has this violence had on survivors?
3. In what ways does TFGBV produce embodied harms? How might these harms be experienced differently across intersecting social locations such as, but not limited to, gender, race, sexuality, class, and disability?
4. What strategies can marginalized communities use to resist, challenge, and reclaim autonomy and agency in the face of AI-facilitated gender-based violence? What might effective prevention or coping strategies look like in practice?
5. What responsibilities do individuals, institutions, policymakers, AI developers, and digital platforms hold in preventing TFGBV, including the creation and spread of AI-generated deepfakes?

ACKNOWLEDGMENT

Portions of this chapter were developed with the assistance of Grammarly proofreader for editing. All intellectual contributions, interpretations, and final editorial decisions are the author's own, and the authors take full responsibility for the content. Any AI-assisted or AI-generated material was reviewed and verified by the author.

NOTES

1 E-girls is a derogatory term used within the manosphere to describe women who cultivate a prominent digital presence. These women are often dismissed as attention-seeking and accused of violating traditional gender norms, particularly when they express sexual aesthetics or autonomy.

2 This chapter includes links to the original 4chan threads in which the images circulated, but does not include either the original or AI-modified images themselves. These materials are excluded for ethical reasons, including the protection of privacy and a commitment to minimizing harm. The images were produced within this manospheric space with the explicit intent to harass, degrade, and harm women. Thus, reproducing them would risk extending that harm and reinscribing the very forms of gendered violence this analysis seeks to critique.

REFERENCES

Afshar, H. (2008). Can I see your hair? Choice, agency and attitudes: the dilemma of faith and feminism for Muslim women who cover. *Ethnic and Racial Studies*, *31*(2), 411–427. https://doi.org/10.1080/01419870701710930

Akter, M. S., & Ahmed, P. (2025). The Emergence of AI-generated deepfakes as a new tool for gender-based violence against women: A brief narrative review of evidence and the implications of the techno-feminist perspective. *Feminists@law*, *13*(2), Article 2. https://doi.org/10.22024/UniKent/03/fal.1281

Amnesty International. (2017, November 20). *Amnesty reveals alarming impact of online abuse against women.* https://www.amnesty.org/en/latest/press-release/2017/11/amnesty-reveals-alarming-impact-of-online-abuse-against-women/

Baer, H. (2016). Redoing feminism: Digital activism, body politics, and neoliberalism. *Feminist Media Studies*, *16*(1), 17–34. https://doi.org/10.1080/14680777.2015.1093070

Banet-Weiser, S., & Miltner, K. M. (2016). #MasculinitySoFragile: Culture, structure, and networked misogyny. *Feminist Media Studies*, *16*(1), 171–174. https://doi.org/10.1080/14680777.2016.1120490

Bilge, S. (2010). Beyond Subordination vs. Resistance: An intersectional approach to the agency of veiled muslim women. *Journal of Intercultural Studies*, *31*(1), 9–28. https://doi.org/10.1080/07256860903477662

Bower, L. J. (2024). The thorn in feminism's side: Black feminist reconceptualization and defence of #tradwives and the #tradwife movement. *Journal of Gender Studies*, 1–17. https://doi.org/10.1080/09589236.2024.2423198

BwhWynu S. (2024, January 30). *No Title.* [Online forum post]. 4chan. https://archive.4plebs.org/pol/thread/457059252/#q457059252

Cahill, R., Wong, R., & Hoogendam, R. (2024). *Insights into Technology-Facilitated Genderbased Violence: A Survey of Women's Shelters and Transition House Workers Across Canada*. Women's Shelters Canada.
Canadian Women's Foundation. (2025). Challenging Gendered Digital Harm: Research Report on Impacts and Solutions to Digital Harm Facing Women, Gender-Diverse People, and Gender Equality Organizations. https://canadianwomen.org/challenging-gendered-digital-harm-report/
Cheong, I.M. [@stillgray]. (2024, February 2). *When given pictures of thirst traps, AI imagines what could've been if they'd been raised by strong fathers* [Tweet]. X/Twitter. https://x.com/stillgray/status/1753449687619924019
Citron, D., & Chesney, R. (2019). Deep fakes: A looming challenge for privacy, democracy, and national security. *California Law Review*, *107*(6), 1753. https://doi.org/10.15779/Z38RV0D15J
Dickson, E. (2024, February 6). 4Chan Chuds Used AI to Clothe Her. She Fought Back. *Rolling Stone*. https://www.rollingstone.com/culture/culture-news/dignifai-4chan-shame-women-1234961851/
Dunn, S. (2020). Technology-Facilitated Gender-based Violence: An Overview. *Centre for International Governance Innovation: Supporting a Safer Internet Paper No 1, Online*. https://www.cigionline.org/publications/technology-facilitated-gender-based-violence-overview
Ging, D. (2019). Alphas, betas, and incels: Theorizing the masculinities of the manosphere. *Men and Masculinities*, *22*(4), 638–657. https://doi.org/10.1177/1097184X17706401
Ging, D. (2023). Tactics of hate: Toxic "creativity" in anti-feminist men's rights politics. In K. Boyle & S. Berridge (Eds.), *The Routledge Companion to Gender, Media and Violence* (pp. 348–357). Routledge.
gyM+gh3 A. (2024, February 1). Sexual attraction thrives off mystery and tension. The more that sex and sexuality are openly displayed, demystified and normalized. [Online forum post 4chan. https://archive.4plebs.org/pol/thread/457284243/#q457287338
Haraway, D. J. (1991). *Simians, Cyborgs, and Women: The Reinvention of Nature*. Routledge.
Harvey, A. (2020). *Feminist Media Studies*. Polity Press.
Henry, N., & Powell, A. (2015). Embodied harms: Gender, shame, and technology-facilitated sexual violence. *Violence against Women*, *21*(6), 758–779. https://doi.org/10.1177/1077801215576581
Hesse-Biber, S., & Flowers, H. (2019). Using a feminist grounded theory approach in mixed methods research. In K. Charmaz & A. Bryant (Eds.), *The SAGE Handbook of Current Developments in Grounded Theory* (pp. 497–516). Sage Publications Ltd.
Hinson, L., Mueller, J., O'Brien-Milne, L., & Wandera, N. (2018). *Technology-Facilitated Gender-based Violence: What is It, and How Do We Measure It?* International Center for Research on Women.
Hk/VZqg K. (2024, February 4). *No title*. [Online forum post]. 4chan. https://archive.4plebs.org/pol/thread/457566105/#457570223
Hoebanx, P. (2025). Red pill women: Heterosexual fantasies in misogynistic spaces. *Men and Masculinities*, *28*(2), 177–196. https://doi.org/10.1177/1097184X241286800
WimijhdW. (2024, February 6). *No title*. [Online forum post]. 4chan. https://archive.4plebs.org/pol/thread/457733894/#457777990
Iñigo, A. (2025). Navigating the manosphere: A scoping review of research on masculinist and misogynist online spaces. *The Journal of Men's Studies*, 1–27. https://doi.org/10.1177/10608265251357869
Jane, E. A. (2014). 'Back to the kitchen, cunt': Speaking the unspeakable about online misogyny. *Continuum*, *28*(4), 558–570. https://doi.org/10.1080/10304312.2014.924479
Jane, E. A. (2017). *Misogyny Online: A Short (and Brutish) History*. Sage Publications Ltd.
Jones, C., Trott, V., & Wright, S. (2020). Sluts and soyboys: MGTOW and the production of misogynistic online harassment. *New Media & Society*, *22*(10), 1903–1921. https://doi.org/10.1177/1461444819887141
Karagianni, A., & Doh, M. (2024). A feminist legal analysis of non-consensual sexualized deepfakes: Contextualizing its impact as AI-generated image-based violence under EU law. *Porn Studies*, 1–18. https://doi.org/10.1080/23268743.2024.2408277
kg1x08eu. (2024, February 6). *Not title*. [Online forum post]. 4chan. https://archive.4plebs.org/pol/thread/457711240/#457714083
Laffier, J., & Rehman, A. (2023). Deepfakes and Harm to Women. *Journal of Digital Life and Learning*, *3*(1), 1–21. https://doi.org/10.51357/jdll.v3i1.218
Marwick, A. E., & Caplan, R. (2018). Drinking male tears: Language, the manosphere, and networked harassment. *Feminist Media Studies*, *18*(4), 543–559. https://doi.org/10.1080/14680777.2018.1450568
Massanari, A. (2017). #Gamergate and the fappening: How Reddit's algorithm, governance, and culture support toxic technocultures. *New Media & Society*, *19*(3), 329–346. https://doi.org/10.1177/1461444815608807
Menzie, L. (2022). Stacys, beckys, and chads: The construction of femininity and hegemonic masculinity within incel rhetoric. *Psychology & Sexuality*, *13*(1), 69–85. https://doi.org/10.1080/19419899.2020.1806915

Noble, S. U. (2018). *Algorithms of Oppression: How Search Engines Reinforce Racism* (1st ed.). New York University Press.

/ovRbqvk. (2024, January 31). Follow-up to a legendary thread. Let's talk about leveraging AI for good, and not for evil. Together we can bring...[Online forum post]. 4chan. https://archive.4plebs.org/pol/thread/457069072/#457069072

Plant, S. (1997). *Zeros + Ones: Digital Women + the New Technoculture*. Fourth Estate.

Posobiec, J. [@JackPosobiec]. (2024, February 2). *4chan has launched a new AI tool. Its purpose is to put clothes back on e-girls and remove tattoos* [Tweet]. X/Twitter. https://x.com/JackPosobiec/status/1753416551066181672

PU6keB+x. (2024, February 5). *Anyone still remember makeapp? hoes got so mad that the guy stopped developing the app. its an apk tho but...*[Online forum post]. 4chan. https://archive.4plebs.org/pol/thread/457648127/#457654229

Q/jE9I1Q (2024, February 6). *powerful!* [Online forum post]. 4chan. https://archive.4plebs.org/pol/thread/457711240/#457714246

qchu QDUU. (2024, February 5). *St. Longinus is the man on that picture stabbing Jesus, he's a canonized saint. St. Longinus, pray for us and...*[Online forum post]. 4chan. https://archive.4plebs.org/pol/thread/457699600/#457708203

Razack, S. H. (2018). A site/sight we cannot bear: The racial/spatial politics of banning the muslim woman's Niqab. *Canadian Journal of Women & the Law*, *30*(1), 169–189. https://doi.org/10.3138/cjwl.30.1.169

Sarah Banet-Weiser. (2018). *Empowered: Popular Feminism and Popular Misogyny*. Duke University Press.

Schippers, M. (2007). Recovering the feminine other: Masculinity, femininity, and gender hegemony. *Theory and Society*, *36*(1), 85–102. https://doi.org/10.1007/s11186-007-9022-4

Siapera, E. (2019). Online Misogyny as Witch Hunt: Primitive Accumulation in the Age of Techno-capitalism. In D. Ging & E. Siapera (Eds.), *Gender Hate Online: Understanding the New Anti-feminism* (pp. 21–43). Palgrave Macmillan.

SSc+zlEl. (2024, February 4). *No title*. [Online forum post]. 4chan. https://archive.4plebs.org/pol/thread/457542880/#457548612

van der Nagel, E. (2020). Verifying images: Deepfakes, control, and consent. *Porn Studies*, *7*(4), 424–429. https://doi.org/10.1080/23268743.2020.1741434

van Zoonen, L. (2002). Gendering the internet: Claims, controversies and cultures. *European Journal of Communication*, *17*(1), 5–23. https://doi.org/10.1177/0267323102017001605

Wajcman, J. (2004). *TechnoFeminism*. Polity Press.

Wajcman, J. (2010). Feminist theories of technology. *Cambridge Journal of Economics*, *34*(1), 143–152. https://doi.org/10.1093/cje/ben057.

WimijhdW. (2024, February 6). *Dignified Dignified.* [Online forum post]. 4chan. https://archive.4plebs.org/pol/thread/457733894/#457785314

Wuest, J. (1995). Feminist grounded theory: An exploration of the congruency and tensions between two traditions in knowledge discovery. *Qualitative Health Research*, *5*(1), 125–137. https://doi.org/10.1177/104973239500500109

Zempi, I. (2016). 'It's a part of me, I feel naked without it': Choice, agency and identity for Muslim women who wear the niqab. *Ethnic and Racial Studies*, *39*(10), 1738–1754. https://doi.org/10.1080/01419870.2016.1159710

16 Intimate Inequities
Examining the Benefits and Risks of AI in Online Dating for Marginalized Populations

Christopher Dietzel

INTRODUCTION

Since ChatGPT launched in November 2022, artificial intelligence (AI) has boomed in popularity. While AI is already used to help with work, homework, groceries, finances, travel, therapy, exercise, and entertainment, people are now welcoming AI into more intimate areas of their lives, asking ChatGPT and other AI tools for relationship help, communication tips, information about building meaningful connections, and advice for sexual intercourse (Zao-Sanders, 2025). Dating app users are excited about the potential that AI holds. In a survey of 5,000 Millennials and Gen Z, more than two-thirds thought AI could make dating safer, easier, and more efficient (Frank Reeves, 2024).

Dating app companies have realized that people are increasingly comfortable using AI for dating, and they are exploring new ways to integrate AI into their products, thereby capitalizing on users' desire to optimize intimacy (Wiehn, 2023). While AI may facilitate online dating, critical questions remain about how it may negatively impact users' safety and well-being (Kassab et al., 2024; Salhab et al., 2024) and exacerbate societal inequities that disproportionately affect marginalized populations (Wang et al., 2024). The inequities perpetuated by AI in online dating have wide-ranging implications, particularly for people who identify as lesbian, gay, bisexual, transgender, queer, and/or other minority sexual and gender identities (LGBTQ+); Black, Indigenous, and people of color (BIPOC); and neurodivergent people.

This chapter critically examines the potential benefits and risks of AI on the safety, health, and intimacy of LGBTQ+, BIPOC, and neurodivergent people in the context of online dating. In doing so, this chapter argues that AI can reinforce—or be reimagined to challenge—existing hierarchies, forms of exclusion, and intimate inequities among people with marginalized identities.

AI AND ONLINE DATING

To begin, it is important to discuss what is meant by "artificial intelligence" since the term "AI" holds many meanings and has no universal definition (Russell & Norvig, 2016), including among those who work with AI (Wang, 2019). Conceptually, AI refers to the computer imitation of human intelligence (Sheikh et al., 2023). In practice, AI is powered by algorithms that are embedded in and govern most tasks on digital platforms, including managing search results, filtering and recommending content, predicting user preferences, and monitoring user behavior and content (Latzer et al., 2017). Since "AI" is a polysemic term often used to market a company's latest technological development that relies on algorithms and other machine learning systems (Widder et al., 2023), this chapter applies a broad understanding of "AI" to examine a wide range of AI features, tools, and platforms used in the context of online dating.

AI has been embedded in dating apps' backend operations for many years, notably in their matchmaking algorithms and content moderation systems (Myles et al., 2023). Now, dating app

 DOI: 10.1201/9781003737810-19

companies are offering more front-facing, user-centric AI features. For example, Tinder has an "AI Photo Selector" that can identify the most ideal images (Tinder, 2024), and Grindr has an AI feature called "A List" that summarizes past conversations and identifies potential matches by analyzing past chats and interactions (Grindr, 2025). Several dating app companies are also launching AI dating assistants that users can employ to select matches, flirt with other users, suggest dating activities, and send on dates (Boyd, 2024; Iovine, 2024; Knight, 2024). Bumble will have an "AI Dating Concierge" that people can employ to do on virtual dates—either with other users or their AI dating assistants—and report back with the best match (Knight, 2024). Grindr is testing an "AI Wingman" that will serve as a personal assistant, helping users create their profile, spark and manage conversations, recommend and track matches, and plan in-person dates (Grindr, 2025; Iovine, 2025b). With AI features such as these, users can delegate to a machine the personal, emotional task of connecting with someone. This means that users can outsource intimacy to AI, shifting the responsibility of fostering relationships to technology. Though dating apps have been critiqued for outsourcing intimacy (Schwartz & Velotta, 2018) and delegating the role of matchmaking to technology (Finkel et al., 2012), it is unclear whether emerging AI features represent the newest iteration of dating advancements or present greater challenges to users' safety, health, and intimacy.

Rather than apply a technologically deterministic or techno-solutionist lens, research must critically examine the complexities of AI in the context of online dating and its impacts on users, especially marginalized users who often face systemic barriers. The following sections explore emerging benefits and risks that AI poses to LGBTQ+, BIPOC, and neurodivergent people who engage in online dating, while also considering how AI technologies could be leveraged to help these populations confront socio-technological inequities.

AI, DATING, AND SAFETY

AI can help promote user safety online by identifying and blocking harmful content and behavior (Gongane et al., 2022), including hate speech (Kibriya et al., 2024) and depictions of violence (Gunton, 2022). AI can also filter unwanted images and messages (Kaddoura et al., 2022) and content that targets minority groups (Windisch et al., 2022). The ability of AI to promote online safety is particularly important for people with marginalized identities, as they are disproportionately at risk of experiencing online harms (Center for Technology & Society, 2024). Additionally, there are AI tools to help address in-person safety concerns, which can be valuable for dating app users who meet offline. For instance, AI can link with the GPS in a person's smartphone to track their location and send alerts when they are in danger (Maxwell et al., 2020). While AI has been criticized for raising data privacy risks (Sebastian, 2023), AI features such as these can help dating app users promote their safety online and in person.

Despite the potential safety benefits that AI can offer dating app users, AI disproportionately affects people with marginalized identities, namely because data-trained AI models embed biases in these technologies that can exclude and discriminate against users based on gender (Hall & Ellis, 2023), sexual orientation (Myles et al., 2023), race (Benjamin, 2019; Noble, 2018; Williams, 2024), or disability (Whittaker et al., 2019). AI can generate sexist and misogynistic content that perpetuate gender inequities and harmful stereotypes about women (O'Connor & Liu, 2024). LGBTQ+ people can be identified and categorized by AI, which can out them in unsafe contexts or suppress their visibility and ability to connect (Myles et al., 2023). AI can reproduce cisheteronormativity, which naturalizes cisgender and heterosexual identities while stigmatizing transgender and non-binary identities (Myles et al., 2023). AI has also been found to perpetuate neuronormative biases that marginalize neurodivergent people (Lemke et al., 2024). Moreover, AI can privilege whiteness and discriminate against BIPOC communities (Katz, 2020). Black people can encounter racist content and practices (Benjamin, 2019; Noble, 2018; Williams, 2024), and Indigenous peoples can confront AI systems that favor Western cultures and colonial ideologies (Lewis et al., 2025). Early reports suggest that discriminatory practices such as these are already present in dating apps' AI features, as Grindr's AI Wingman was found to express racist opinions during internal testing (Schiffer, 2024).

AI must be designed with marginalized users in mind, and dating app companies should take active steps to address systems that disproportionately harm LGBTQ+, BIPOC, and neurodivergent people. This can be done, for example, by including these populations in tech development, an approach that has been shown to reduce discriminatory and exclusionary AI practices (Shams et al., 2025; Fosch-Villaronga & Poulsen, 2022). Thus, while AI poses risks, it also offers opportunities to promote user safety and challenge oppressive systems.

AI, DATING, AND HEALTH

Some dating apps offer features that support users' health, including those with marginalized identities. Grindr has information about getting vaccinated and automated reminders to encourage regular STI testing, thereby supporting users' sexual health (Grindr, n.d.; Hecht et al., 2022). Trans people and people of color often use filters to connect with others who share their identities, thereby promoting inclusion and belonging (Dietzel, 2022; Webster et al., 2025; Zhou, 2022). With emerging AI technologies, LGBTQ+, BIPOC, and neurodivergent people have new opportunities to manage their health. Grindr envisions its AI chatbot answering user inquiries with tailored responses about LGBTQ+ identities and sexual health, for example, providing information about gender and sexual orientation or having intercourse with a same-sex partner (Lipton & Hyman, 2024; WSJ News, 2024). AI chatbots can improve access to health services (Casu et al., 2024), particularly among those who face systemic barriers, such as LGBTQ+ and BIPOC communities (Bragazzi et al., 2023; Vega, 2025). Regarding users' social health, which is defined as having an adequate quality and quantity of relationships (Doyle & Link, 2024), AI technologies like speech recognition software and text-to-speech tools can assist neurodivergent people in facilitating social interactions (Hough, 2024). Together, these illustrate a few examples of how emerging AI features can foster health equity and access for dating app users with marginalized identities.

AI in dating apps can also pose health risks. AI chatbots have been found to offer inaccurate and harmful mental health information (Khawaja & Bélisle-Pipon, 2023) as well as bad relationship advice (Vowels et al., 2024). People who are lonely may turn to AI chatbots for comfort, but this can lead to psychological dependence (Huang et al., 2024) and, in some cases, make matters worse by perpetuating stigmas (Moore et al., 2025). AI chatbots may provide inaccurate sex education (Greer et al., 2024), misunderstand LGBTQ+ issues (Ma et al., 2024), and discriminate against LGBTQ+ identities (Bragazzi et al., 2023). There are also major concerns about privacy when sharing health information with dating apps, as some companies have faced lawsuits for distributing users' data without their consent (Booth, 2024). These concerns may help explain why some people prefer using AI to help with daily tasks, like shopping, travel, and banking, rather than health or dating (Instabug, 2025).

Since dating app companies have taken on the role of health actors (Myles et al., 2021), they need to remain attentive to the threats that AI poses to users' health and actively work to mitigate risks. That said, there is potential for dating app companies to create AI features that help users, especially marginalized users, promote various aspects of their health, such as their mental, physical, social, and sexual health (Dietzel et al., 2025; Dietzel et al., in revision; Myles et al., 2021). When giving people more control of their online experience, AI can empower marginalized users, reduce systemic barriers, and support individuals' health (Hough, 2024; Zhou, 2022). In this sense, AI features could unlock new opportunities for LGBTQ+, BIPOC, and neurodivergent dating app users to promote their health, push back against systemic inequities, and improve their dating experience.

AI, DATING, AND INTIMACY

Dating apps are introducing new AI features that aim to promote meaningful connections, reflecting what Elliot (2022) called algorithmic intimacy, which is the growing role of machine intelligence that shapes how people experience and manage intimate relationships (p. 8). For instance, Bumble provides AI-generated icebreakers to help start conversations (Bumble, n.d.), Hinge's "Prompt Feedback" offers suggestions to make profiles more authentic and engaging (Hinge, 2025), and Happn's "Perfect Date" gives personalized date ideas (Happn, 2025). Specifically, these constitute examples of relationship tech (Elliot, 2022), where algorithms influence how people connect and foster intimacy. While such features intend to facilitate dating, they speak to larger tensions about how emerging AI technologies may reflect and reshape norms around intimacy.

While few studies have examined the effects of AI on intimacy, recent surveys reveal mixed feelings among dating app users (Iovine, 2025a; Global Dating Insights, 2025). This may reflect the concern that increasing reliance on technology could diminish people's ability to connect with one another. In fact, in a survey of over 5,000 adults, over half were worried about AI contributing to a loss of human connection (McClain et al., 2025). This echoes Turkle's (2011) finding that even though technology facilitates connection, it can contribute to shallow interactions and emotional disconnect. People may be less motivated, or less able, to navigate the messiness of relationships if they depend on technology to do so for them (Turkle, 2011). This reliance is already apparent, as some dating app users employ AI tools to help them appear more skilled or attractive than they actually are (Hunter & Bonos, 2025; Mueller, 2025).

Despite these concerns, many people are embracing AI to connect and build intimacy. About one in four people, and nearly half of Gen Z, use AI in online dating, including to build their profile, enhance photos, write messages, plan dates, and decline future dates (Singles in America, 2025). People are also using other AI technologies to enhance their dating profiles, including apps like Remini, which generates synthetic images from real photos (Mueller, 2025) and RIZZ, an AI dating assistant that identifies shared user interests, writes tailored messages, and provides strategic dating advice (Majic Predin, 2024). ChatGPT is another popular AI tool used for dating, particularly among men (Theocharous, 2024), though its advice is often generic, misleading, or problematic (Caramela, 2025; Domb, 2025). Regardless, these examples show that people are looking beyond the AI features offered by dating app companies and employing new AI technologies to support their experiences with online dating.

AI is also redefining the bounds of intimacy as people form relationships with AI, notably via AI companions available on apps like Kindroid, Nomi, Replika, and Character.ai (Roose, 2024). Unlike chatbots or assistants, AI companions are designed to simulate emotional and social connections, offering nonjudgmental support and helping ease loneliness (Boine, 2023; Skjuve et al., 2022). As a result, some people are falling in love, having sex with, and marrying their AI companions (Skjuve et al., 2022; Li & Zhang, 2024; Clarke, 2024; Chow, 2023; Hill, 2025; Heritage, 2025). The popularity of AI companions may reflect a broader societal gap in emotional and interpersonal connection that these technologies aim to fill (Ciriello et al., 2024). In any case, interest in this form of AI appears to be growing, with nearly three in four teens having tried an AI companion and over half being regular users (Perez, 2025). Four in five Gen Z say they would consider marrying an AI companion (Iovine, 2025c). Thus, AI is emerging as more than a tool to mediate intimacy—it is becoming a source of intimacy.

Despite limited research, AI may support intimacy among people with marginalized identities. For instance, AI chatbots and companions offer a safe, nonjudgmental space for people to explore their sexual and gender identities (Bragazzi et al., 2023; Goodwin, 2025). People with disabilities can leverage AI tools to facilitate intimate connections (Hough, 2024), including neurodivergent people who use AI to understand nonverbal cues and social nuances (Domb, 2025). However, AI presents risks to intimacy, as it can reinforce and amplify social biases. AI companions have been shown to make inappropriate and discriminatory comments, perpetuate racism and sexism, and condone violence against minorities (Skjuve et al., 2022; Zhang et al., 2024; Boine, 2023). Generative AI often reproduces normative identities and stereotypes about marginalized communities (Gillespie, 2024; Rogers, 2024). AI-generated images of LGBTQ+ people frequently depict gay men as fit and fashionable, lesbian women as tattooed and stern, and queer people with brightly colored hair—with most of them imagined as white (Rogers, 2024; Lazine, 2024). BIPOC individuals, and Black women in particular, are often excluded by racist and sexist hierarchies embedded in AI systems, rendering them invisible to potential matches (Benjamin, 2019; Noble, 2018; Williams, 2024). As these examples show, AI threatens to reinforce narrow standards of desirability and hierarchical systems that privilege dominant identities while marginalizing and erasing minorities. However, the effects of AI are not limited to digital spaces. Since the norms embedded in online dating cultures can influence offline interactions, they risk perpetuating harmful power dynamics across digital and physical forms of intimacy, which can result in violence against people with marginalized identities (Dietzel, 2022).

While AI is creating new opportunities for intimacy that extend beyond dating apps' prescribed features, little is known about the effects of AI on intimate relationships, particularly among LGBTQ+, BIPOC, and neurodivergent people. More research is needed to understand the benefits and risks that AI presents to intimacy, especially for marginalized communities.

CONCLUSION

As AI becomes increasingly integrated into everyday life, dating apps are adopting AI features that help users find matches, manage conversations, and navigate intimacy. While AI can enhance the user experience, it risks reinforcing existing hierarchies and forms of exclusion, particularly for LGBTQ+, BIPOC, and neurodivergent people who face systemic barriers. AI frequently reproduces normative assumptions about gender, sexuality, race, and ability, which can manifest as biased systems, discriminatory practices, or harmful depictions of marginalized identities. These inequities raise critical concerns about user safety, misrepresentation, and exclusion. At the same time, dating app users are not passive actors. Many are creatively engaging with AI, including in ways that go beyond the tools offered by dating apps and challenge the technologies that might otherwise marginalize them. Understanding the role AI that has in online dating and digital intimacy requires attention to how it both upholds—and can be reimagined to disrupt—structural power.

Despite growing public interest in AI and rapid development of AI technologies, there is a dearth of research in this area. Scholars often focus on risks rather than benefits (Fletcher et al., 2024; Wang, 2023), prioritize individual platforms over cross-app comparisons (Alizadeh et al., 2024), and emphasize apps' matchmaking functions rather than their AI features more broadly (Paul & Ahmed, 2024). Scholars also tend to analyze the design of technology, exploring potential accessibility solutions (Malfacini, 2025), rather than understanding how individuals use the tech that is available (Patel et al., 2025). There is limited knowledge on how AI shapes intimacy, including with interpersonal relationships (Elliot, 2022) and human-AI relationships (Boine, 2023; Skjuve et al., 2022), and even less attention paid to how AI affects people with marginalized identities (Myles et al., 2023; Alizadeh et al., 2024; Malfacini, 2025). Research is urgently needed to understand how new AI dating technologies influence people's safety, health, and intimacy, particularly among LGBTQ+, BIPOC, and neurodivergent populations. By centering the experiences of those most marginalized, research can expose structural harms and help shape AI technologies that foster safer, healthier, and more equitable forms of intimacy.

ACKNOWLEDGMENT

Portions of this chapter were developed with the assistance of ChatGPT for proofreading and copy-editing. All intellectual contributions, interpretations, and final editorial decisions are the author's own, and the author takes full responsibility for the content. Any AI-assisted or AI-generated material was reviewed and verified by the author.

REFLECTION QUESTIONS

1. Beyond the examples given in this chapter, what are some ways that AI is used to manage relationships and develop intimacy?
2. How could AI be leveraged to promote the safety and health of marginalized populations, particularly LGBTQ+, BIPOC, and neurodivergent people?
3. How might AI tools be (re)imagined to liberate people with marginalized identities from structural inequities? What are some potential risks that should be avoided to ensure AI does not reinforce discrimination, exclusion, and other societal problems?
4. Would you feel comfortable using AI to help with online dating? Why or why not?
5. What do you think about people dating, having sex with, and marrying AI companions? What are the potential benefits and risks of this technology, and how might it redefine the bounds of intimacy?

REFERENCES

Alizadeh, F., Lawo, D., Stevens, G., Zytko, D., & Eslami, M. (2024). When the "matchmaker" does not have your interest at heart: Perceived algorithmic harms, folk theories, and users' counter-strategies on Tinder. *Proceedings of the ACM on Human-Computer Interaction*, *8*(CSCW2), 1–29.

Benjamin, R. (2019). *Race after technology: Abolitionist tools for the new Jim code*. John Wiley & Sons.

Boine, C. (2023). Emotional attachment to AI companions and European law. *MIT Case Studies in Social and Ethical Responsibilities of Computing, Winter 2023.* https://doi.org/10.21428/2c646de5.db67ec7f

Booth, R. (2024, May 26). Grindr accused of treating gay man's medical data like 'piece of meat'. *The Guardian.* https://www.theguardian.com/uk-news/article/2024/may/26/grindr-accused-of-treating-gay-man-medical-data-like-piece-of-meat

Boyd, R. (2024, December 30). *Dating apps prepare to launch AI features to help users find love.* The Guardian. https://www.theguardian.com/technology/2024/dec/30/dating-apps-prepare-to-launch-ai-features-to-help-users-find-love

Bragazzi, N. L., Crapanzano, A., Converti, M., Zerbetto, R., & Khamisy-Farah, R. (2023). The impact of generative conversational artificial intelligence on the lesbian, gay, bisexual, transgender, and queer community: Scoping review. *Journal of Medical Internet Research, 25*, e52091.

Bumble (n.d.). *Take the pressure off the opening line with AI-powered icebreakers on Bumble For Friends.* https://bumble.com/en-ca/the-buzz/bumble-for-friends-ai-powered-icebreakers

Caramela, S. (2025, June 6). *ChatGPT dating advice is feeding delusions and causing unnecessary breakups.* Vice. https://www.vice.com/en/article/chatgpt-dating-advice-is-feeding-delusions-and-causing-unnecessary-breakups/

Casu, M., Triscari, S., Battiato, S., Guarnera, L., & Caponnetto, P. (2024). AI chatbots for mental health: A scoping review of effectiveness, feasibility, and applications. *Applied Science*, *14*, 5889.

Center for Technology & Society (2024, June). *Online hate and harassment: The American experience 2024.* Anti-Defamation League. https://www.adl.org/resources/report/online-hate-and-harassment-american-experience-2024

Chow, A. R. (2023, February 23). *AI-human romances are flourishing—and this is just the beginning*. TIME. https://time.com/6257790/ai-chatbots-love/

Ciriello, R., Hannon, O., Chen, A. Y., & Vaast, E. (2024). Ethical tensions in human-AI companionship: A dialectical inquiry into Replika. In *Proceedings of the 57th Hawaii International Conference on System Sciences* (pp. 488–497). Waikiki, Hawaii.

Clarke, C. (2024, May 16). *Divorce left me struggling to find love. I found it in an AI partner.* CBC. https://www.cbc.ca/radio/nowornever/first-person-ai-love-1.7205538

Dietzel, C. (2022). "I'm not your fantasy": Sexual racism, racial fetishization, and the exploitation of racialized men who have sex with men. In J. J. Fellows & L. Smith (Eds.), *Gender, sex, and tech! An intersectional feminist guide* (pp. 101–120). Canadian Scholars/Women's Press.

Dietzel, C., Blair, C., O'Shea, B., Bello, B., & Numer, M. (2025). Digital platforms as equivocal health promotion: Examining the mental health of 2SLGBTQ+ people related to the COVID-19 pandemic. *Journal of Homosexuality.*

Dietzel, C., Devlin, B., McCready, S., Colford, L., O'Shea, B., Oswald, A., & Numer, M. (in revision). Digital ageing: Promoting the social health of midlife and older 2SLGBTQ+ adults via technology. *Ageing & Society.*

Domb, A. (2025, April 10). *'It's cathartic': Meet the men turning to ChatGPT for dating advice — and discover what it means for your relationships.* Cosmopolitan. https://www.cosmopolitan.com/uk/love-sex/relationships/a64444507/men-asking-chatgpt-for-dating-advice/

Doyle, D. M., & Link, B. G. (2024). On social health: History, conceptualization, and population patterning. *Health Psychology Review, 18*(3), 626–655. https://doi.org/10.1080/17437199.2024.2314506.

Elliott, A. (2022). *Algorithmic intimacy: The digital revolution in personal relationships.* John Wiley & Sons.

Finkel, E. J., Eastwick, P. W., Karney, B. R., Reis, H. T., & Sprecher, S. (2012). Online dating: A critical analysis from the perspective of psychological science. *Psychological Science in the Public Interest, 13*(1), 3–66.

Fletcher, R., Tzani, C., & Ioannou, M. (2024). The dark side of artificial intelligence: Risks arising in dating applications. *Assessment and Development Matters, 16*(1), 17–23.

Fosch-Villaronga, E., & Poulsen, A. (2022). Diversity and inclusion in artificial intelligence. In C. Bart & E. Fosch-Villaronga (Eds.), *Law and artificial intelligence: Regulating AI and applying AI in legal practice* (pp. 109–134). Springer.

Frank Reeves, M. (2024, February 13). *The AI revolution is coming for your dating life.* Cosmopolitan. https://www.cosmopolitan.com/sex-love/a46574186/ai-dating/

Gillespie, T. (2024). Generative AI and the politics of visibility. *Big Data & Society, 11*(2), 20539517241252131.

Global Dating Insights (2025, June 25). Survey: Only 15% of users care for AI features in dating apps. https://www.globaldatinginsights.com/featured/survey-only-15-of-users-care-for-ai-features-in-dating-apps/

Gongane, V. U., Munot, M. V., & Anuse, A. D. (2022). Detection and moderation of detrimental content on social media platforms: Current status and future directions. *Social Network Analysis and Mining, 12*(1), 129.

Goodwin, J. (2025). *From isolation to connection: How LGBTQ+ AI companions are changing lives.* What's On Queer BC. https://whatsonqueerbc.com/woq-champion/from-isolation-to-connection-how-lgbtq-ai-companions-are-changing-lives

Greer, K. M., Khan, S., Sangmo, D., Greene, A., & Rutkowski, D. (2024). Navigating the future of sexuality education in the USA: Applying technology mediation theory to AI-facilitated sexuality education. *Sex Education, 25*(6), 871–885. https://doi.org/10.1080/14681811.2024.2401802.

Grindr (n.d.). *How to build your profile: Health.* https://help.grindr.com/hc/en-us/articles/4402336949523-How-to-build-your-profile#h_01GWAEDX35JH8CK4HNCD32Y4NT

Grindr (2025, January 21). 2025 product roadmap: A more personalized experience, powered by AI, wherever you are. https://www.grindr.com/2025-product-roadmap

Gunton, K. (2022). The use of artificial intelligence in content moderation in countering violent extremism on social media platforms. In R. Montasari (Ed.), *Artificial intelligence and national security* (pp. 69–79). Springer International Publishing.

Hall, P., & Ellis, D. (2023). A systematic review of socio-technical gender bias in AI algorithms. *Online Information Review, 47*(7), 1264–1279.

Happn (2025, June 24). *Perfect Date: The new feature to find the ideal date spot.* https://www.happn.com/press/perfect-date-la-nouvelle-fonctionnalit%C3%A9-pour-trouver-un-lieu-de-date-id%C3%A9al

Hecht, J., Zlotorzynska, M., Sanchez, T. H., & Wohlfeiler, D. (2022). Gay dating app users support and utilize sexual health features on apps. *AIDS and Behavior, 26*(6), 2081–2090.

Heritage, S. (2025, July 12). *'I felt pure, unconditional love': The people who marry their AI chatbots.* The Guardian. https://www.theguardian.com/tv-and-radio/2025/jul/12/i-felt-pure-unconditional-love-the-people-who-marry-their-ai-chatbots

Hill, K. (2025, January 15). *She is in love with ChatGPT.* The New York Times. https://www.nytimes.com/2025/01/15/technology/ai-chatgpt-boyfriend-companion.html

Hinge (2025, January 15). Hinge launches Prompt Feedback to help daters create unique and authentic profiles. https://hinge.co/press/prompt-feedback

Hough, S. (2024). The linking of artificial intelligence with sexuality and disability. *Sexuality and Disability, 42*(4), 797–800.

Huang, S., Lai, X., Ke, L., Li, Y., Wang, H., Zhao, X., … Wang, Y. (2024). AI technology panic—is AI dependence bad for mental health? A cross-lagged panel model and the mediating roles of motivations for AI use among adolescents. *Psychology Research and Behavior Management, 17*, 1087–1102. https://doi.org/10.2147/PRBM.S440889

Hunter, T., & Bonos, L. (2025, July 3). *'It's almost like we never even spoke': AI is making everyone on dating apps sound charming*. The Washington Post. https://www.washingtonpost.com/technology/2025/07/03/ai-online-dating-match/

Instabug (2025). *Mobile user expectations in 2025: Performance, privacy, and AI.* https://www.instabug.com/mobile-user-expectations-2025

Iovine, A. (2024, October 6). *Grindr is testing an AI 'wingman' bot, CEO says.* Mashable. https://mashable.com/article/grindr-is-testing-an-artificial-intelligence-wingman-bot-ceo-says

Iovine, A. (2025a, July 16). *Gen Z is less comfortable with AI dating app features than millennials, survey finds.* Mashable. https://mashable.com/article/gen-z-is-less-comfortable-with-ai-dating-app-features-than-millennials

Iovine, A. (2025b, June 5). *Grindr is testing AI chat summaries for paid users.* Mashable. https://mashable.com/article/grindr-ai-chat-summaries-paid-users

Iovine, A. (2025c, May 22). *Majority of Gen Z would marry an AI, survey says.* Mashable. https://mashable.com/article/gen-z-marry-aritificial-intelligence-joi-ai-survey

Kaddoura, S., Chandrasekaran, G., Popescu, D. E., & Duraisamy, J. H. (2022). A systematic literature review on spam content detection and classification. *PeerJ Computer Science*, *8*, e830.

Kassab, J., El Hajjar, A. H., Wardrop III, R. M., & Brateanu, A. (2024). Accuracy of online artificial intelligence models in primary care settings. *American Journal of Preventive Medicine, 66*(6), 1054–1059.

Katz, Y. (2020). *Artificial whiteness: Politics and ideology in artificial intelligence.* Columbia University Press.

Khawaja, Z., & Bélisle-Pipon, J. C. (2023). Your robot therapist is not your therapist: Understanding the role of AI-powered mental health chatbots. *Frontiers in Digital Health*, *5*, 1278186.

Kibriya, H., Siddiqa, A., Khan, W. Z., & Khan, M. K. (2024). Towards safer online communities: Deep learning and explainable AI for hate speech detection and classification. *Computers and Electrical Engineering, 116*, 109153.

Knight, C. (2024, May 11). *The future of dating? Two AI's walk into a bar to figure out if their owners are a match.* The National Post. https://nationalpost.com/news/science/artificial-intelligence-future-of-dating

Latzer, M., Hollnbuchner, K., Just, N., & Saurwein, F. (2017). The economics of algorithmic selection on the Internet. In J. M. Bauer, & M. Latzer (Eds.), *Handbook on the economics of the internet* (pp. 395–425). Edward Elgar Publishing.

Lazine, M. (2024, July 5). *AI chatbot app releases* 4 *new LGBTQ+ characters for users to become "soulmates" with.* LGBTQ Nation. https://www.lgbtqnation.com/2024/07/ai-chatbot-app-releases-4-new-lgbtq-characters-for-users-to-become-soulmates-with/

Lemke, C., Bloomfield, M., & Herfurth, F. N. (2024). Unveiling neuronormative bias: Exposing an unconscious bias in generative AI and their impact on neurodivergent people. *NeuroConverse*, *1*(1), 8.

Lewis, J. E., Whaanga, H., & Yolgörmez, C. (2025). Abundant intelligences: Placing AI within Indigenous knowledge frameworks. *AI & Society*, *40*, 2141–2157. https://doi.org/10.1007/s00146-024-02099-4

Li, H., & Zhang, R. (2024). Finding love in algorithms: Deciphering the emotional contexts of close encounters with AI chatbots. *Journal of Computer-Mediated Communication*, *29*(5), 1–15.

Lipton, J., & Hyman, J. (2024, March 8). Grindr CEO talks plans to use AI to expand use cases. *Yahoo! Finance*. https://finance.yahoo.com/video/grindr-ceo-talks-plans-ai-221903836.html

Ma, Z., Mei, Y., Long, Y., Su, Z., & Gajos, K. Z. (2024, May). Evaluating the experience of LGBTQ+ people using large language model based chatbots for mental health support. In *Proceedings of the 2024 CHI Conference on Human Factors in Computing Systems* (pp. 1–15).

Majic Predin, J. (2024, September 9). *How the 5th most downloaded dating app is redefining digital relationships.* Forbes. https://www.forbes.com/sites/josipamajic/2024/09/09/rizz-app-how-the-5th-most-downloaded-dating-app-is-redefining-digital-relationships/

Malfacini, K. (2025). The impacts of companion AI on human relationships: Risks, benefits, and design considerations. *AI & Society*, *40*, 5527–5540. https://doi.org/10.1007/s00146-025-02318-6.

Maxwell, L., Sanders, A., Skues, J., & Wise, L. (2020). A content analysis of personal safety apps: Are they keeping us safe or making us more vulnerable? *Violence Against Women*, *26*(2), 233–248.

McClain, C., Kennedy, B., Gottfried, J., Anderson, M., & Pasquini, G. (2025, April 3). *How the U.S. public and AI experts view artificial intelligence.* Pew Research Center. https://www.pewresearch.org/internet/2025/04/03/artificial-intelligence-in-daily-life-views-and-experiences/

Moore, J., Grabb, D., Agnew, W., Klyman, K., Chancellor, S., Ong, D. C., & Haber, N. (2025, June). Expressing stigma and inappropriate responses prevents LLMs from safely replacing mental health providers. In *Proceedings of the 2025 ACM Conference on Fairness, Accountability, and Transparency,* Athens (pp. 599–627).

Mueller, S. (2025, February 14). *I put AI photos on my Hinge dating profile. They were the most liked by far.* Mashable. https://mashable.com/article/using-ai-photo-generator-apps-for-dating-profile

Myles, D., Duguay, S., & Dietzel, C. (2021). #DatingWhileDistancing: How dating apps became digital health technologies in the COVID-19 pandemic. In D. Lupton & K. Willis (Eds.), *The COVID-19 crisis: Social perspectives* (pp. 79–89). Routledge.

Myles, D., Duguay, S., & Echaiz, L. F. (2023). Mapping the social implications of platform algorithms for LGBTQ+ communities. *Journal of Digital Social Research*, *5*(4), 1–30.

Noble, S. U. (2018). *Algorithms of oppression: How search engines reinforce racism.* New York University Press.

O'Connor, S., & Liu, H. (2024). Gender bias perpetuation and mitigation in AI technologies: Challenges and opportunities. *AI & Society*, *39*(4), 2045–2057.

Patel, D., Osipova, E., Spiel, K., & Barbareschi, G. (2025, April). A critical review of sexuality, technology and disability. In *Proceedings of the 2025 CHI Conference on Human Factors in Computing Systems,* Yokohama (pp. 1–20).

Paul, A., & Ahmed, S. (2024). Computed compatibility: Examining user perceptions of AI and matchmaking algorithms. *Behaviour & Information Technology*, *43*(5), 1002–1015.

Perez, S. (2025, July 21). *72% of US teens have used AI companions, study finds.* TechCrunch. https://techcrunch.com/2025/07/21/72-of-u-s-teens-have-used-ai-companions-study-finds/

Rogers, R. (2024, April 2). *Here's how generative AI depicts queer people.* WIRED. https://www.wired.com/story/artificial-intelligence-lgbtq-representation-openai-sora/

Roose, K. (2024, May 9). *Meet my A.I. friends.* The New York Times. https://www.nytimes.com/2024/05/09/technology/meet-my-ai-friends.html

Russell, S. J., & Norvig, P. (2016). *Artificial intelligence: A modern approach.* Pearson.

Salhab, W., Ameyed, D., Jaafar, F., & Mcheick, H. (2024). A systematic literature review on AI safety: Identifying trends, challenges and future directions. *IEEE Access*, 131762.

Schiffer, R. (2024, March 28). Inside Grindr's plan to squeeze its users. *Platformer.* https://www.platformer.news/grindr-ai-boyfriend-wingman-monetization-paid-taps/

Schiffer, Z (2024, March 28). *Inside Grindr's plan to squeeze its users.* Platformer. https://www.platformer.news/grindr-ai-boyfriend-wingman-monetization-paid-taps/

Schwartz, P., & Velotta, N. (2018). Online dating: Changing intimacy one swipe at a time? In J. Van Hook, S. M. McHale, & V. King (Eds.), *Families and technology* (pp. 57–88). Springer.

Sebastian, G. (2023). Privacy and data protection in ChatGPT and other AI chatbots: Strategies for securing user information. *International Journal of Security and Privacy in Pervasive Computing*, *15*(1), 1–14.

Shams, R. A., Zowghi, D., & Bano, M. (2025). AI and the quest for diversity and inclusion: A systematic literature review. *AI and Ethics, 5*(1), 411–438.

Sheikh, H., Prins, C., & Schrijvers, E. (2023). Artificial intelligence: Definition and background. In H. Sheikh, C. Prins, & E. Schrijvers (Eds.), *Mission AI: The new system technology* (pp. 15–41). Springer International Publishing.

Singles in America (2025). The great relationship reset: Singles in America 2025. *The Kinsey Institute and Match.* https://news.iu.edu/kinseyinstitute/live/news/45955-the-great-relationship-reset-singles-in-america-2025

Skjuve, M., Følstad, A., Fostervold, K. I., & Brandtzaeg, P. B. (2022). A longitudinal study of human–chatbot relationships. *International Journal of Human-Computer Studies, 168*, 102903.

Theocharous, M. (2024, February 11). *Young people are turning to ChatGPT for dating advice. We put it to the test.* 9 News. https://www.9news.com.au/national/artificial-intelligence-dating-advice-young-people-are-turning-to-chatgpt-for-dating-advice-so-we-put-the-ai-to-the-test/973b35ec-3dd8-48e3-94ac-c002fa31c44a

Tinder (2024, July 17). *Tinder unveils 'Photo Selector' AI: Feature to make choosing profile pictures easier.* Tinder Newsroom. https://www.tinderpressroom.com/Tinder-R-Unveils-Photo-Selector-AI-Feature-to-Make-Choosing-Profile-Pictures-Easier

Turkle, S. (2011). *Alone together: Why we expect more from technology and less from each other.* Basic Books.

Vega, V. F. (2025, March 27). *Could AI bolster mental healthcare for LGBTQ+ BIPOC youth?* Tagg Magazine. https://taggmagazine.com/ai-mental-healthcare/

Vowels, L. M., Francois-Walcott, R. R., & Darwiche, J. (2024). AI in relationship counselling: Evaluating ChatGPT's therapeutic capabilities in providing relationship advice. *Computers in Human Behavior: Artificial Humans*, 100078.

Wang, H. (2023). Algorithmic colonization of love: The ethical challenges of dating app algorithms in the age of AI. *Techné: Research in Philosophy & Technology*, *27*(2), 1–21.

Wang, P. (2019). On defining artificial intelligence. *Journal of Artificial General Intelligence*, *10*(2), 1–37.

Wang, S., Cooper, N., & Eby, M. (2024). From human-centered to social-centered artificial intelligence: Assessing ChatGPT's impact through disruptive events. *Big Data & Society*, *11*(4), 1–14.

Webster, A., Brooker, J., Misajon, R., & Wilson, C. (2025). Online dating experiences of transgender and gender-diverse people: A systematic review and thematic synthesis of qualitative evidence. *Psychology of Sexual Orientation and Gender Diversity*, Advance online publication. https://doi.org/10.1037/sgd0000812.

Whittaker, M., Alper, M., Bennett, C. L., Hendren, S., Kaziunas, E., Mills, M., Morris, M. R., Rankin, J. L., Rogers, E., Salas, M., & West, S. M. (2019). *Disability, bias, and AI report.* AI Now Institute.

Widder, D. G., West, S., & Whittaker, M. (2023). Open (for business): Big tech, concentrated power, and the political economy of open AI. *Concentrated Power, and the Political Economy of Open AI (August 17, 2023).*

Wiehn, T. (2023). Algorithms and emerging forms of intimacy. In S. Lindgren (Ed.), *Handbook of critical studies of artificial intelligence* (pp. 117–127). Edward Elgar Publishing.

Williams, A. (2024). *Not my type: Automating sexual racism in online dating*. Stanford University Press.

Windisch, S., Wiedlitzka, S., Olaghere, A., & Jenaway, E. (2022). Online interventions for reducing hate speech and cyberhate: A systematic review. *Campbell Systematic Reviews*, *18*(2), e1243.

WSJ News (2024, October 9). *Grindr's CEO is building an AI 'wingman' to help you date* [Video]. YouTube. https://www.youtube.com/watch?v=D3fwpOduMYU

Zao-Sanders, M. (2025, April 9). *How people are really using gen AI in 2025.* Harvard Business Review. https://hbr.org/2025/04/how-people-are-really-using-gen-ai-in-2025

Zhang, R., Li, H., Meng, H., Zhan, J., Gan, H., & Lee, Y. C. (2024). "My Replika cheated on me and she liked it": A taxonomy of algorithmic harms in human-AI relationships. *arXiv e-prints,* arXiv-2410.

Zhou, Z. B. (2022). Compulsory interracial intimacy: Why does removing the ethnicity filter on dating apps not benefit racial minorities? *Media, Culture & Society, 44*(5), 1034–1043.

17 AI and Social Reproduction

Social Structures of Dominance and Control

Shruti Raji-Kalyanaraman

INTRODUCTION AND ORGANIZATION OF THE CHAPTER

I was recently stopped at the border between the United States and Canada, and I was traveling with two seniors (my parents, who have Canadian PR) and my daughter (we have Canadian passports). A trip, a little gift to my parents for lovingly taking care of my daughter, while I worked through contractual summer teaching, turned out to be a stressful experience. As racialized first-generation immigrants, even though we had the privilege of speaking English, the Canada Border Services Agency officer slapped a yellow slip on my family after they were unsatisfied with our answers to some initial, confusing questions. The yellow slip meant we had to be taken for further questioning, and after a series of very quick, unclear, random questions, we were let go. We were visibly the only set of travelers with Hindu markings of vermillion, speaking English with an Indian accent, and wearing clothes or styles that were not "Canadian." My senior parents were tired after a long flight and visibly shaken by this experience. As a privileged immigrant settler, I could not help thinking of what other liminal travelers with refugee status, non-Canadian passport or temporary visa holders would have to go through. What reporting would this officer write on the racialized profiles of travelers? What will happen to these racialized experiences of policing when AI takes over?

Drawing on this experience, I position policing as a structure or a system that undermined and made invisible social reproduction structures and labor in my family. In doing so, I argue that it is important to go beyond AI fairness concepts like discrimination and bias to a deeper engagement in assessing oppression. Deeper understanding of social reproduction labor and its interaction with structures can help in reconceptualizing oppressive social structures that have historically undermined different aspects of racialized settlers on the margins, in my case, "the immigrant, unpaid care labour" provided by seniors like grandparents.

I use the concept of intersectionality to explain and problematize concepts like unpaid care, social reproduction, immigrant grandparenting/labor, and their interactions with seemingly disjoint government structures like border policing. Adding artificial intelligence (AI) to the existing mix of oppressive structures, I reflect on how AI should instead be an attempt to equalize racialized settlers on the margins, instead of adding onto existing oppression by national structures like border policing. I argue for recognizing unequal social structures built on colonialism, dispossession, and slavery.

INTERSECTIONALITY—THEORETICAL BASIS FOR UNDERSTANDING AI FAIRNESS

Crenshaw's coining of intersectionality has given new directions of understanding gendered oppressions through other interconnecting social determinants like race, ability, sexuality, religion, and ethnicity, to name a few. Set in the legal context, Crenshaw argued how Black women workers were doubly marginalized from both race and gender perspectives, which made their experiences unique compared to those of white women or Black men (Crenshaw, 1989, p. 143).

 DOI: 10.1201/9781003737810-20

Academic researchers at the intersections of AI and social justice have turned to intersectionality and specifically engage with structures of dominance to understand policing, recruitment, and social media data dominance (Safiya Noble in Joyce et al., 2021; Tacheva & Ramasubramanian, 2023). Researchers suggested including marginalized voices, lived experiences, and epistemic knowledge of structural oppression in shaping equitable data sets. This is important because AI and Machine learning (ML)—a subfield of AI—produce results based on the data they are fed. As Joyce et.al posit, data sets would rely on biased or equitable inputs in "supporting or making decisions about…which roads get repaired, who is entitled to welfare benefits, and who is likely to return to prison" (Joyce et al., 2021, p. 2).

Living and working with the concept of intersectionality, other conceptual learnings from Black, Indigenous, and other racialized feminists, my first thought was how one could connect structures that have dominant technologies, like AI, to social reproduction activities, including household work of cooking, cleaning, child care, elder care, community support, volunteering, to name a few. Decades of feminist research and policy in colonial Canada have led to changes that have shaped social welfare policy. There are provisions to support social reproduction activities such as the public school system, childcare policy, childcare benefits, eldercare, universal health care, old-age pension, and Canada's Pension Plan, to name a few. However, neoliberal policies of the 1980s and early 1990s have retrenched and reduced many social welfare policies, and marginalized women have often turned to their personal care network for sustaining social reproduction.

I focus on the unpaid care work of transnational, immigrant grandparenting—seen as a home-based activity where grandparents from different countries come to take care of their grandchildren in Canada. I trace this activity's possible interactions with dominant social structures such as borders, government, education, police, and digital technologies like AI or machine learning. Potential harm or possibilities of equity in social reproduction in the age of AI can be understood by historically investigating how social reproduction was impacted by traditional social structures of dominance (i.e., without AI).

Because care work is labor-intensive, often invisible to the public eye, it would seem that structures of surveillance and policing will not really affect a household, even if feminists have positioned care as political through research and advocacy. While some interdisciplinary research focuses on "digital capitalism" within the home—such as the surveillance capabilities of smart appliances (Sadowski et al., 2024; Thorburn, 2016)—this chapter argues for a shift in focus of state structures like border policing. For transnational families, the most critical algorithmic threat is not the monitoring of care inside the home, but the blockage of care at the nation's gate. Before social reproduction can occur, the family unit must be physically united. Therefore, I position the border not merely as a security apparatus, but as a digital filter that actively disrupts and controls the labor of care.

Capitalism has always been supported by colonial structures, which have always upheld policing and surveillance of Black and Indigenous communities to perpetuate the nation-building of what we call Canada today (*Black History in Canada: 1960 to Present | The Canadian Encyclopedia*, n.d.; *Residential Schools in Canada | The Canadian Encyclopedia*, n.d.; Hanson, 2009; Lawrence & Dua, 2005). Colonial structures that are dominant today were built on the dispossession and genocide of care-centered communities of First Nations, Metis, and Inuit Peoples (Alook et al., 2023; Blackstock & Palmater, 2021; Hanson, 2009; Simpson, 2017; Webstad, n.d.). Capitalism and patriarchy were perpetuated by colonialism as care-centered Indigenous economies were replaced by profit-centered businesses (Alook et al., 2023; Roth, 2019); matriarchal and matrilineal ways of knowing and living were replaced by policies and procedures that were patriarchal and that erased care and community from the core and particularly harmed Indigenous communities, especially women and girls. The devaluation of care work that grandparents, parents, and other care networks currently face is a buildup of historical harm continued by colonialism, capitalism, and patriarchy. This devaluation is visible in how precarious im/migrant workers navigate paid/unpaid care work in Canada through the historical Live-in caregiver programs (Immigration, 2012) or the lottery-based grandparents and parents program (Immigration, 2023).

A phrase in Robyn Maynard and Leanne Betasamosake Simpson's book Rehearsals for Living says, "But you're correct, Leanne, that each wave of struggle builds on the last" (Maynard & Simpson, 2022, p. 107). Maynard continues to explain how historical incidents like the Oka Crisis (*78 Days of Unrest and an Unresolved Land Claim Hundreds of Years in the Making | CBC News*, n.d.), Black Lives Matter 1.0, in Ferguson (Boag, 2014), Idle No More (Beaulne-Stuebing, 2022), and many such Indigenous and Black-led social movements have resisted policing and surveillance structures. They specifically refer to the 2021 resistance by toppling of colonial monuments like the statue of Egerton Ryerson (CBC, 2021), and community advocacy of police accountability toward the brutal murders of George Floyd and Regis Korchinski-Paquet.

They reflect on how such resistance following consecutive historical events of racial domination, genocide, dispossession, and slavery has led to powerful movements building on previous such attempts of resistance (Maynard & Simpson, 2022, pp. 107–108). Maynard illustrates the example of what they call "a summer of revolt" (in 2021), where they witnessed mass movements in support of divestment of police funds, defunding policing structures of Black-led with intergenerational and multiracial support across different cities of Toronto, Halifax, Winnipeg, to name a few (107). In Maynard's own words,

> It is clear that not only are police budgets under attack, but there is a massive groundswell geared towards funding community supports that are not rooted in the surveillance and punishment of our communities, but in truly allowing our communities to flourish. Because the opposite of a carceral society is a care-based society.
>
> *(Maynard & Simpson, 2022, p. 109)*

Centering care-based societies against policing has been propagated by Black and Indigenous feminist scholars and some settler scholars across decades (Alook et al., 2023; Coburn, 2021; Collins, 1999; Jaggar, 2014; Lloro, 2021; Rosemary Frei, 2017). It is important, then, to engage with care and its structural impacts on care work, and to investigate AI/ML as an appendage to these structures. In the following two sections, I expand on social reproduction to engage further with unpaid care work and try to understand interlocking oppressions of care with dominant social structures, including AI.

SOCIAL REPRODUCTION—STRUCTURES AND UNPAID CARE WORK

Social Reproduction is a concept central to feminist political economy. It is defined as labor required to reproduce and sustain generations of laboring populations on a daily basis, and involves a plethora of activities (Bezanson & Luxton, 2006, pp. 3–4). These activities could include ensuring "food, clothing, shelter, basic safety, and health care, along with the development and transmission of knowledge, social values, and cultural practices and the construction of individual and collective identities…." (Bezanson & Luxton, 2006, p. 3). Originally considered home-based, apolitical, and a feature of the private sphere in society, social reproduction activities have taken on paid forms such as catering, childcare, eldercare, restaurants, salons, and laundry businesses. Feminist political economists have consistently shown intimate connections between social reproduction activities and the social structures of the state, markets, and family/household. Specifically, how care is impacted by the broader political decisions of states and markets (Bakker, 2007; Pluto Press, 2017).

Feminists have pointed out how social reproduction activities, primarily performed by women and marginalized populations, have been continually devalued, alienated, and remain as unpaid or underpaid activities. How do digital technologies like AI, that are prone to bias, interact with social reproduction?

SETTING THE CONTEXT OF AI IN SOCIAL REPRODUCTION

Noble and Kennedy, in the introductory piece on "Borders and bodies of control" in the journal *Feminist Media Studies*, Noble and Kennedy (2020) urge feminist researchers to uncover seemingly unrelated sources of power that social structures may exert over gendered bodies. In my experience with the CBSA at the Canadian border, I wondered whether AI would help or hinder my interactions with officials. As the officials didn't pay heed to my father's Indian accent and asked me why I did not have an authorization letter for taking my daughter out of the country without my husband's permission in writing, I wondered why these questions were not asked to other single parents with racial privilege traveling with me? Why were my suggestions to get in touch with my husband, waiting in the parking lot to pick us up and take us "home" ignored? Why did the officer, who seemed to be from my ethnic background and gender, not seem sensitized toward my father's Indian accent and my mother's use of a wheelchair? Why was I alienated in my experience as a racialized settler and mother trying to give my daughter the experience of belonging with her cousins, a joint decision made by me and my husband? Why did permanent resident cards and Canadian passports, in the case of my family, not really give us any dignified passage into Canada?

Viewed through the lens of algorithmic governance, the "yellow slip" my family received stops looking like a random administrative glitch and starts looking like the predictable result of risk scoring. This shift from human discretion to automated sorting is clearly visible in systems like Project Chinook and the Travel Compliance Indicator (TCI).

Take Project Chinook, for example. The Immigration, Refugees and Citizenship Canada (IRCC) uses this Excel-based tool to process temporary resident applications in bulk, allowing officers to make decisions without necessarily reviewing physical files individually (Immigration, 2024). While the government insists Chinook isn't "AI" because a human still clicks the final button, critics have aptly described it as a "high-speed denial machine" (*Visa Refusal Spike Exposes Cracks in Canada's Algorithm-Driven Decision System*, n.d.). The danger is that it prioritizes efficiency over substance. It strips away the nuance of an applicant's story—such as the cultural necessity of a grandparent visiting for months to provide childcare—and reduces complex lives to standardized indicators. For a transnational grandparent, whose primary contribution is their time rather than financial capital, Chinook's streamlined interface is a trap: it risks flagging their lack of employment not as a normal part of retirement, but as a risk factor for overstaying.

The CBSA's TCI, piloted at land borders in 2025, takes this a step further with predictive AI. By analyzing historical traveler data, the TCI assigns a "compliance score" to individuals before they even reach the inspection booth (Moosapeta, 2025). This fundamentally changes the nature of the border encounter: It is no longer an interrogation of intent (e.g., "I am here to care for my grandchildren") but a probability assessment based on data patterns. If variables associated with unpaid care work—like long stays, low funds, or frequent travel without a work permit—correlate with "non-compliance" in the data set, a grandparent is preemptively sorted as a risk (Professor Ebrahim Bagheri to CBC Radio, Windsor CBC, 2025).

Seen in this light, my family's yellow slip was likely not just the product of one officer's bias. It was the output of a system designed to optimize through put by flagging anyone who deviates from the "standard" traveler profile—race and class-privileged settler adhering to colonial standards of border policing. AI doesn't just survey the border; it enforces a neoliberal logic where the only "safe" traveler is the "frictionless" tourist or the "wealthy" visitor. The labor of social reproduction—unpaid, and relationally complex—is simply a statistical anomaly that the algorithm is trained to reject. Immigrant grandparenting directly affects nationalist agenda of economic development, but capitalism and colonialism doesn't recognize this labor, consequently, data sets do not have the explainability to acknowledge these travelers.

Interlocking experiences of oppression and marginalization provide space for interdisciplinary explorations within ethical AI feminist researchers' work. Interlocking experiences of gender, grandparenting, language, accent, immigrant status, and intergenerational differences in experiences as a resident in Canada need to be included in the data set used by AI and ML to ensure equitable results. These structural markers would then indicate that AI with the CBSA had either given me a clean white pass or a yellow chit to meet further officials at CBSA.

Bias in Decision Systems has been identified by AI researchers that focus on ethics and responsibility in AI's impacts on marginalized populations (Müller, 2025). The debates are supported by other arguments on Ethical AI and AI fairness speak about the increasing digitalization of our personal information and identities, where many aspects of our lives could be subjected to surveillance by the government, police, and social media companies. This bias cuts across other interactions marginalized communities face when they encounter AI. Facial recognition software used by policing structures has been found to mis-identify darker-skinned individuals, and digital algorithms in law enforcement have been found to disproportionately target marginalized neighborhoods (Kong, 2022; "Technology and Systemic Racism," n.d.). Mis-identification of racialized communities is also seen in recruitment software using AI, which may attempt to recognize bias and work with statistical probability to equalize opportunities (Lin & Chen, 2022). Addressing structural barriers that limit the presence of marginalized communities in data sets becomes crucial in reducing bias within existing data sets (Buolamwini & Gebru, 2018; Rafanelli, 2022).

CONCLUSION: AN EQUITABLE AI AND SOCIAL REPRODUCTION?

AI is not inherently unfair and can be trained to promote equity and fairness (Hertog et al., 2023, 2024). For AI to be equitable, dominant players in capitalism need to commit to addressing structural barriers in reducing AI bias. As Dihal in Good Robot argues, a broad range of narratives and stories is necessary for ethical AI communication (Dihal in *The Good Robot*, n.d., p. 168). To me, these narratives must engage with the structural resilience that Black, Indigenous, and marginalized groups represent. As a settler, racialized mother, and an immigrant on this land, I am dependent on care provided by grandparents to ensure my smooth transition at work and parenting. In this situation, how can I ensure my transnational care network, composed of my parents, is safeguarded against policing? This means greater engagement with marginalized communities with lived experiences and cross-disciplinary collaborations with social scientists who critique dominant structures like colonialism, capitalism, and patriarchy. It also requires divesting funding from surveillance structures and redirecting it toward the ethical balancing of datasets and digital footprints.

These efforts must be supported by government policies and funding at the community, organizational, academic, provincial, and federal levels. For example, at an organizational level, Government policies need to be clearer on the fairness, equity of training data sets. A research associate at the University of Cambridge, Stefanie Ullman, stresses the need for state structures to spell out what could be concrete and subjective explanations for bias, and to use fair, balanced training data sets, which governments often claim to pursue in the field of AI. There needs to be a clear stance and communication with corporations that are required to use AI in an unbiased way (Ullmann, 2022, p. 125).

Multiple axes of collaboration, such as these, could help interdisciplinary learning and address and reduce structural inequities that have perpetuated different aspects of marginalized communities, creating multiple barriers and exclusion.

ACKNOWLEDGMENT

Portions of this chapter were developed with the assistance of Grammarly in an editing capacity to improve clarity and flow. All intellectual contributions, interpretations, and final editorial decisions are the authors' own, and the authors take full responsibility for the content. Any AI-assisted or AI-generated material was reviewed and verified by the authors.

REFLECTION QUESTIONS

1. How can AI uniquely impact unpaid care, that is, social reproduction activities?
2. What is the difference between AI Bias and AI equity? Discuss with personal examples?
3. In what other ways can policing structures interact with AI to impede or empower the unpaid?
4. In what other ways can policing structures interact with AI to impede or empower paid/unpaid care in the community?

REFERENCES

78 days of unrest and an unresolved land claim hundreds of years in the making |

CBC News. (n.d.). Retrieved 29 November 2025, from https://www.cbc.ca/news/canada/montreal/oka-crisis-timeline-summer-1990-1.5631229

Alook, A., Eaton, E., Gray-Donald, D., Laforest, J., Lameman, C., & Tucker, B. (2023). *The end of this world: Climate justice in so-called Canada*. Between the Lines.

Bakker, I. (2007). Social Reproduction and the Constitution of a Gendered Political Economy. *New Political Economy*, *12*(4), 541–556. https://doi.org/10.1080/13563460701661561

Beaulne-Stuebing, L. (2022, November 26). How Idle No More transformed Canada. CBC Radio. https://www.cbc.ca/radio/unreserved/idle-no-more-reconciliation-1.6663310

Bezanson, K., & Luxton, M. (Eds.). (2006). *Social reproduction: Feminist political economy challenges neo-liberalism*. McGill-Queen's University Press.

Black History in Canada: 1960 to Present | The Canadian Encyclopedia. (n.d.). Retrieved 9 August 2021, from https://www.thecanadianencyclopedia.ca/en/article/black-history-in-canada-1960-to-present

Blackstock, C., & Palmater, P. (2021, July 8). Canada's government needs to face up to its role in Indigenous children's deaths. *The Guardian*. https://www.theguardian.com/commentisfree/2021/jul/08/canada-indigenous-children-deaths-residential-schools

Boag, K. (Director). (2014, August). CBC News: Many truths about Ferguson [Video recording]. https://www.cbc.ca/i/phoenix/player/syndicate/?mediaId=2492800746

Buolamwini, J., & Gebru, T. (2018). Gender Shades: Intersectional Accuracy Disparities in Commercial Gender Classification. *Proceedings of the 1st Conference on Fairness, Accountability and Transparency*, 77–91. https://proceedings.mlr.press/v81/buolamwini18a.html

CBC. (2021, June 7). Statue of Egerton Ryerson, toppled after Toronto rally, & apos; will not be restored or replaced & apos; *CBC News*. https://www.cbc.ca/news/canada/toronto/statue-of-egerton-ryerson-brought-down-1.6055676

CBC. (2025, September 3). & apos; Major risk & apos; of bias against some groups with Canadian AI border screening, expert warns. *CBC News*. https://www.cbc.ca/news/canada/windsor/artificial-intelligence-bias-border-canada-screening-1.7624051

Coburn, E. (2021). "Theorizing Our Place": Indigenous Women's Scholarship from 1985–2020 and the Emerging Dialogue with Anti-racist Feminisms. *Studies in Social Justice*, 14(2), 429–453. https://doi.org/10.26522/ssj.v14i2.2295

Collins, P. H. (1999). *Black feminist thought: Knowledge, consciousness and the politics of empowerment,* (2nd edition). Routledge.

Crenshaw, K. (1989). Demarginalizing the Intersection of Race and Sex: A Black Feminist Critique of Antidiscrimination Doctrine, Feminist Theory and Antiracist Politics. *University of Chicago Legal Forum*, 1(8), 31.

Hanson, E. (2009). *Sixties Scoop*. Indigenous Foundations – UBC. https://indigenousfoundations.arts.ubc.ca/sixties_scoop/

Hertog, E., Fukuda, S., Matsukura, R., Nagase, N., & Lehdonvirta, V. (2023). The Future of Unpaid Work: Estimating the Effects of Automation on Time Spent on Housework and Care Work in Japan and the UK. *Technological Forecasting and Social Change*, 191, 122443. https://doi.org/10.1016/j.techfore.2023.122443

Hertog, E., Ruppanner, L., & Churchill, B. (2024). Silicon Caregivers: A Multilevel Analysis of European Perspectives on Robotic Technologies for Elderly Care. *Community, Work & Family*, 27(5), 698–718. https://doi.org/10.1080/13668803.2024.2423019

Immigration, R. and C. C. (2012, October 19). Live-In Caregiver Program: About the process [Service initiation]. https://www.canada.ca/en/immigration-refugees-citizenship/services/work-canada/hire-permanent-foreign/caregiver-program.html

Immigration, R. and C. C. (2023, August 4). Sponsor your parents and grandparents [Service initiation]. https://www.canada.ca/en/immigration-refugees-citizenship/services/immigrate-canada/family-sponsorship/sponsor-parents-grandparents.html

Immigration, R. and C. C. (2024, June 27). CIMM – Chinook Development and Implementation in Decision-Making – February 28, 2024. https://www.canada.ca/en/immigration-refugees-citizenship/corporate/transparency/committees/cimm-feb-28-2024/chinook-development-decision-making.html

Jaggar, A. M. (Ed.). (2014). *Just methods: An interdisciplinary feminist reader* (2nd edition). Paradigm Publishers.

Joyce, K., Smith-Doerr, L., Alegria, S., Bell, S., Cruz, T., Hoffman, S. G., Noble, S. U., & Shestakofsky, B. (2021). Toward a Sociology of Artificial Intelligence: A Call for Research on Inequalities and Structural Change. *Socius: Sociological Research for a Dynamic World*, 7, 2378023121999581. https://doi.org/10.1177/2378023121999581

Kong, Y. (2022, August 10). (Un)Fairness in AI: An Intersectional Feminist Analysis | Blog of the APA. https://blog.apaonline.org/2022/08/10/unfairness-in-ai-an-intersectional-feminist-analysis/

Lawrence, B., & Dua, E. (2005). Decolonizing Antiracism. *Social Justice*, 32(4 (102)), 120–143.

Lin, T.-A., & Chen, P.-H. C. (2022). Artificial Intelligence in a Structurally Unjust Society. *Feminist Philosophy Quarterly*, 8(3/4), 32. https://doi.org/10.5206/fpq/2022.3/4.14191

Lloro, T. K. (2021). An Intersectional Feminist Food Studies Praxis: Activism and Care in the COVID-19 Context. *The Journal of Environmental Education*, 52(5), 303–313. https://doi.org/10.1080/00958964.2021.1981209

Maynard, R., & Simpson, L. B. (2022). Part 3: A Summer of Revolt. In *Rehearsals for Living* (pp. 103–150). Alfred A. Knopf.

Moosapeta, A. (2025, September 24). Travellers to Canada face AI screening | CIC News. https://www.cicnews.com/2025/09/travellers-to-canada-face-ai-screening-0960080.html

Müller, V. C. (2025). Ethics of Artificial Intelligence and Robotics. In E. N. Zalta & U. Nodelman (Eds.), *The stanford encyclopedia of philosophy* (Fall 2025). Metaphysics Research Lab, Stanford University. https://plato.stanford.edu/archives/fall2025/entries/ethics-ai/

Noble, S. U., & Kennedy, M. (2020). Introduction: Borders and Bodies of Control. *Feminist Media Studies*, 20(2), 284–284. https://doi.org/10.1080/14680777.2020.1720346

Pluto Press (Director). (2017, November 22). Tithi Bhattacharya | What is Social Reproduction Theory? [Video recording]. https://www.youtube.com/watch?v=Uur-pMk7XjY

Rafanelli, L. M. (2022). Justice, Injustice, and Artificial Intelligence: Lessons from Political Theory and Philosophy. *Big Data & Society*, 9(1). https://doi.org/10.1177/20539517221080676

Residential Schools in Canada | The Canadian Encyclopedia. (n.d.). Retrieved 15 September 2025, from https://thecanadianencyclopedia.ca/en/article/residential-schools

Rosemary Frei (Director). (2017, November 23). Dr. Pam Palmater Says Inquiry into MMIW and Girls Must Change Its Approach [Video recording]. https://www.youtube.com/watch?v=sL6Akdsd2Yo

Roth, S. (2019). Can Capitalism Be Decolonized? Recentering Indigenous Peoples, Values, and Ways of Life in the Canadian Art Market. *American Indian Quarterly*, 43(3), 306–338. https://doi.org/10.5250/amerindiquar.43.3.0306

Sadowski, J., Strengers, Y., & Kennedy, J. (2024). More work for Big Mother: Revaluing Care and Control in Smart Homes. *Environment and Planning A: Economy and Space*, 56(1), 330–345. https://doi.org/10.1177/0308518X211022366

Simpson, L. B. (2017). *As we have always done: Indigenous freedom through radical resistance*. University of Minnesota Press.

Tacheva, J., & Ramasubramanian, S. (2023). AI Empire: Unraveling the Interlocking Systems of Oppression in Generative AI's Global Order. *Big Data & Society*, 10(2), 20539517231219241. https://doi.org/10.1177/20539517231219241

Technology and systemic racism: How algorithms encode inequity. (n.d.). Catalyst Tech Justice Network. Retrieved 31 August 2025, from https://www.thecatalyst.org.uk/resource-articles/technology-and-systemic-racism-how-algorithms-encode-inequity/

The Good Robot. (n.d.). Retrieved 25 November 2025, from https://www.bloomsbury.com/us/good-robot-9781350399952/

Thorburn, E. D. (2016). Networked Social Reproduction: Crises in the Integrated Circuit. *TripleC (Cognition, Communication, Co-Operation): Open Access Journal for a Global Sustainable Information Society*, 14(2), 380–396. https://doi.org/10.31269/triplec.v14i2.708

Ullmann, S. (2022). Gender Bias in Machine Translation Systems. In A. Hanemaayer (Ed.), *Artificial intelligence and its discontents: Critiques from the social sciences and humanities* (pp. 123–144). Springer International Publishing. https://doi.org/10.1007/978-3-030-88615-8_7

Visa refusal spike exposes cracks in Canada's algorithm-driven decision system. (n.d.). VisaHQ. Retrieved 29 November 2025, from https://www.visahq.com/news/2025-10-26/ca/visa-refusal-spike-exposes-cracks-in-canadas-algorithm-driven-decision-system/

Webstad, P. (n.d.). Phyllis' Story. Orange Shirt Society. Retrieved 23 May 2025, from https://orangeshirtday.org/phyllis-story/

Part 4

Governance, Power, and Bias in AI Systems

Bringing together perspectives from governance studies, political economy, and human–AI interaction, this section interrogates how power operates through AI systems at institutional and state levels. The chapters examine mechanisms such as surveillance, border technologies, educational infrastructures, and usability design to show how bias is produced, legitimized, and normalized. Rather than treating governance as a technical fix, this section emphasizes its political and ethical dimensions.

DOI: 10.1201/9781003737810-21

18 No More Radical Ethical Uncertainty

GenAI and Higher Education within Structures of Capital

Gabi Schaffzin and Jessica Vorstermans

INTRODUCTION

In fall 2024, the two of us, both full-time faculty at a major research institution in Toronto, Canada, were interviewed for a regular internal newsletter. The freelance journalist hired to write the resulting piece was hoping to learn more about "ethical issues with AI" and our names came up in conversation somewhere along the way. We both, it seemed, had reputations on campus for taking a more critical approach to generative AI in the classroom than our baseline colleague, an honor not bestowed on us in error—in fact, we met via a shared vision of a different university, a centering of students struggling in late stage capitalism and an increasingly unlivable world, and in a spirit of hope for different futures.

The journalist's questions were not terribly surprising; she wanted to know our thoughts on the increased proliferation of GenAI's use by students, by faculty, and by the university writ large. She was patient and open-minded and was even willing to push back on our insistence that we saw no place for GenAI in the classroom—indeed, we argued, it was rather detrimental! She mentioned an AI tool that some York faculty used to answer student questions, leaving them with more time to do "tasks only humans can do." We responded by asking, "and why don't we have time to do those tasks already? And at what cost are these tools being implemented?" We cited studies documenting the environmental detriments (Zewe, 2025), necessarily deleterious labor conditions (Muldoon et al., 2024), and overall money-grab nature of the technology's wide and rapid proliferation (Hao, 2025). She listened intently and eventually sent us what she wrote for publication. The first line read simply "There is no ethical way to use AI."

A month later, on the eve of the piece's planned inclusion in the newsletter, she emailed to let us know it was not going to run. "I am told it does not focus on teaching in the classroom which is this unit's mandate… I thought you had great ideas and was quite excited about the story." Such is life at the neoliberal university, where students sleep in the cars due to skyrocketing costs of living, where 60% of our classes are taught by sessional instructors under precarious labor conditions (Likhodi, 2018), where class sizes are consistently increasing and student services being rolled back or (thanks to AI, of course!) automated. When the efficiency and profitability of a university is held paramount to its pedagogical potential, the students suffer.

We ask: what can we as educators do at this particular moment? How do we take into consideration the often woefully ignored problematics surrounding generative AI systems, without which such systems cannot be developed, promoted, and distributed, when we are simultaneously being told that we must work harder, more efficiently, to an ever-changing and over-emphasized "job market"?

As activists and scholars, we see only one path forward: collective action. In what follows, we hope to move past any ethical uncertainties (Kay & King, 2021) surrounding generative AI and

 DOI: 10.1201/9781003737810-22

instead focus on those radical pockets of resistance which might model a way forward. We begin by briefly reviewing the detriments brought on by GenAI and its industry's points of concentration (of power, of wealth, of sheer material decay). Then, we embrace systemic thinking to reconceptualize this specific "innovation" (which is, in reality, an amalgam of many disparate and damaging technologies) under the expectation of ethical consumption under capitalism. Finally, we look to historical analogs—spaces where resistance *and* reconstitution hint at what an equitable and just progress for technology may look like.

GENERATIVE AI IS AND NEVER CAN BE GOOD

A few years ago, a conversation about the pros and cons of using generative AI might have begun with questions around what it means to the user: will they become less intelligent? Will they be out of a job? Will they be tricked by bad training data? Don't get us wrong: those are important questions and we'll address them a bit later on in this section. Today, however, most discussions around AI's rapid proliferation, and whether this is a "good" thing or not, might start with questions about the environment.

At this point, it is widely known, at least within our circles, that training and implementing large model generative systems (such as those powering ChatGPT, Gemini, or Midjourney) require vast amounts of electricity to run and gallons upon gallons of clean (i.e., potable) water to keep equipment cool. Power plants, long shuttered, are being brought back into service to power the likes of Google's Gemini or Microsoft's Pilot (Sherman, 2024). Corporate commitments (themselves flimsy to begin with) to reach carbon-neutrality have been indefinitely postponed (Green, 2024). Sam Altman, OpenAI's eccentric CEO, has even declared that we will need nuclear fusion power generation sooner than later (Dastin, 2024). Okay, we'll get right on that!

Industrial and computational technologies have long been bad for the environment. Battery-powered cars reduce direct carbon emissions and temper reliance on foreign investment in oil while resulting in an over-reliance on lithium mining (Tedesco, 2023). The device in your pocket and on your desktop is made up of coltan, a so-called conflict mineral whose supply chain is rife with human-rights violations and environmental detriment (Ojewale, 2022). Thanks to an unquestioning embrace of generative AI, any semblance of hope to slow these erosions is long gone.

Let's say, however, that we figure it out. Let's say that Altman's money is plentiful enough to spur the invention of infinite power generation with little to no cost to the planet's diverse biomes. Who, then, will this miraculous technology benefit? We can quite confidently say: it will not be those of us who do not own the means of production. First, we have the bodies necessary to make the technology work. In her 2025 powerhouse, *Empire of AI*, journalist Karen Hao speaks with those tasked with training, correcting, and moderating datasets for generative AI models. These individuals are underemployed precarious workers who are exposed to the worst of the depths of the Internet. They work until their mental health deteriorates and they cannot keep their personal relationships together, let alone hold a job. They are discarded on a whim by the companies hired as contractors by OpenAI and Microsoft and Google, all of whom claim an ignorance allowed them by a complex and obfuscatory labor supply chain. These humans are being used and discarded like the natural resources powering AI data centers.[1]

Second, we have the users of the tech. Here again we point to the rhetoric espoused by the likes of Altman et al: automation will free our time, it will revolutionize work and art, and we can offload the menial in the name of embracing the meaningful. This is, to be sure, a declaration made without any historical precedent. Instead, we turn to Colonial America, where cotton production fueled investment in the new independent nation. Before 1793, cotton production was slow and arduous: after being picked from the plant, the fibers were messy, full of seeds and other detritus. After Eli Whitney patented and began selling his cotton gin, however, the speed with which cotton could be moved from plant to fabric accelerated exponentially. So did the increase in the need for labor—*enslaved labor*—to pick it. Per the United States National Archives:

> Though the cotton gin reduced the labor of removing seeds, it did not reduce the number of enslaved people forced to grow and pick the cotton. In fact, the opposite occurred. Cotton growing became so profitable for plantation owners that it greatly increased their demand for both land and enslaved labor. Because of the cotton gin, enslaved people labored on ever-larger plantations where work was more regimented and relentless (*Patent for Cotton Gin (1794)*, 2022).

This tale is not unique. In 2022, *Wired* published an article that detailed the marked increase in worker injuries in those warehouses where robots were being implemented. Originally promising a "higher quality" work environment (FRONTLINE PBS, Official, 2020), *Wired* found that "robots made employees less safe by causing managers to raise performance quotas" (Johnson, 2022). We are delusional if we believe that increased throughput will benefit the workers, especially as promises of automation via AI will enable a new class of workers without, to quote on celebrationist, "barriers to entry [via] ... democratize[d] entrepreneurship" (Levy, 2025) rather than entrenching an already exploited laborer class.

After reviewing all of this, we remind you: "There is no ethical way to use AI."

CENTERING THE SYSTEMIC

Universities have quickly moved to embrace and perpetuate the use of GenAI, often under the very language of its ethical use. Instructors are being encouraged to integrate it into out teaching and assessment, and we are warmly encouraged to have options for students who do not want to use AI in their assignments. We assert that this is a false dichotomy—refuse GenAI or not, use it or not. There is no refusal under Capital. It is being forced on us in our email, in our Zoom meetings, in faculty meetings (AI transcription and meeting summaries), and as an answer to an increased downloading of work onto academic workers. For students, many of whom are barely surviving and working full-time while also studying, there is no refusal—the conditions have made refusal next to impossible.

Our understanding of the deployment of GenAI needs to be rooted in the systemic, in ways power is concentrated in a small powerful elite (Hao, 2025). It is not an individual choice to refuse AI or not, we must critically examine the conditions under which GenAI is being shoved down our throats. There is a world in which GenAI is developed and governed by the people. Under conditions where labor is justly compensated, where the speed of adoption does not inflict massive harms to the environment. Where there are limits on which data sets can be used for training. Of course, this is possible. These are not the conditions under which GenAI is currently being developed and deployed (we have cited numerous examples to this point, though Hao's 2025 work is perhaps the most comprehensive and incisive critique here), and here we remind you that there is no ethical use of any technology under these conditions, let alone one as extractive and exploitative as GenAI. So, we then ask ourselves, what does it mean to teach to GenAI at this moment? What does it mean to grapple with the complete capitulation to the idea that GenAI is inevitable and therefore we must embrace it? What can we as educators do at this particular moment?

COLLECTIVES ON CAMPUS FOR RESISTANCE: BUILDING THE BACKFILL

Perhaps one way to tackle these questions is to begin with considering how we build the "backfill" to Generative AI's widespread proliferation. How do we collectively build what is needed to resist the top-down extractive colonial (Hao, 2022) GenAI that we have today? As academics, we hold a certain type of power in the institution via collegial governance, faculty associations, and institutionally-based collectives that can engage in the work of putting forth GenAI's backfill. At our university, an inter-campus union table was created during COVID and is still meeting and working together on issues that face all workers and students on campus. A collective of university professors in the Netherlands, Germany, the United States, and Denmark have recently published an open-access position piece, calling on all academic workers of conscience, *Against the Uncritical*

Adoption of 'AI' Technologies in Academia (Guest et al., 2025). They argue that universities have a particular responsibility to counter the embracing of AI technologies and safeguard academia as a space of critical thinking and academic freedom.

Creating the "backfill" can look like many different things; cocreating resistance to institutional use of GenAI tools with student and faculty unions collaboratively, critical conversations in classrooms where professors and students build consensus around ways they will engage or not engage, building and organizing together. There are and will be barriers to collective action in universities, this has always happened in all sites of power. In these times of polycrisis, barriers feel all-encompassing, this makes our work difficult and is a call to meet this moment of polycrisis with collective action.

Universities are sites of brain power! Our function as educators is to nurture a space where this power can thrive and grow and become critical. The project of GenAI is harming this mission. Collectives on campus are uniquely positioned to resist the imperialist expansion of GenAI into this critical space. Hao's earlier work (2022) laid out the colonial and imperial nature of GenAI, developed in the hands of a small few. Her latest work, aptly titled the *Empire of AI* (2025) urges us to seriously take up the assertion that it is not inevitable that GenAI is driven by the small few. This is where we want to end this short chapter, written together in the spirit of remaining in community to nurture the work of remaining clear in our belief that we can build the backfill together. That we can collectively wrestle the uncritical adoption of GenAI in our work, our classrooms, our assessments, and capitulation to the profit-seeking expansionist project of GenAI.

In the open-access position piece (2025) cited above, the collective of academics reminds us of the deep harms to the environment and human labor that GenAI is rapidly deploying. They remind us of the commitments that universities have made to safeguarding the environment, indeed our own institution totes its reputation as a sustainable campus and has a Sustainability Office. Is the Sustainability Office involved in decisions on which GenAI purchases are made at the institution? Which GenAI technologies are deployed in our working spaces? Can our union collectives on campus take a stand and refuse the adoption of GenAI technologies that are built on exploitative labor? Of course, we can. And we should.

There is an overwhelming society-wide feeling that GenAI cannot be stopped, but we see resistance movements like the Zapatistas as material examples that collectives have resisted power. Of course GenAI can be stopped. Or, at the very least, governed by the people. The Zapatistas have recently re-organized their three-level autonomous power structure, deepening autonomy for the level closest to the people, the local community level (Baschet, 2024). If we imagine this structure at the university; the highest level being the Senate, the middle being the faculty, and the third being departmental, this is where decisions should be made, closest to the people. Could each departmental faculty council, with meaningful collaboration with undergraduate and graduate students alike, make autonomous decisions on the "selection, procurement and responsible implementation of instructions technology systems and software"? Of course, this is possible (MLA Taskforce on AI in Research and Teaching, n.d.). We have academic freedom and collegial governance. We have institutional commitments to equity, sustainability, and human rights to guide us and mandate us to engage ethically in our labor as academic workers. May these commitments guide us to be in solidarity with the workers harmed by the exploitative and colonial expansionism of the project of GenAI; may our solidarity be transnational and in solidarity with nature. Schulman, in the *Fantasy and Necessity of Solidarity* (2025, p. 40), urges us: "all we have to do is act."

REFLECTION QUESTIONS

1. Why do the authors make the provocative claim that there is no ethical way to use AI under current capitalist conditions?
2. How do the environmental costs and labor exploitation associated with GenAI contradict the mission of the university?

3. What does it mean to build the backfill against the uncritical adoption of AI in higher education?
4. How can collective action on campus challenge the inevitability of GenAI integration in teaching and administration?

NOTE

1 For a thorough understanding of how this work is affecting those in the Global South (specifically, in this case, in Chile) at a disproportionate rate, see the exceptional work of Martin Tironi and Camila Albornoz (for instance, 2025a, 2025b). See also Yaffe's (2023) work on jettisoning capitalist methodologies in building socialist Cuba.

REFERENCES

Baschet, J. (2024, November 15). *The Reorganization of Zapatista Autonomy Ill Will*. https://illwill.com/the-reorganization-of-zapatista-autonomy

Dastin, J. (2024, January 16). OpenAI CEO Altman says at Davos future AI depends on energy breakthrough. *Reuters*. https://finance.yahoo.com/news/openai-ceo-altman-says-davos-173636736.html

FRONTLINE PBS, Official (Director). (2020, February 18). *Amazon Empire: Jeff Wilke Interview | FRONTLINE* [Video recording]. https://www.youtube.com/watch?v=hziCY1ohf64

Green, J. (2024, September 3). Why Big Corporations Are Quietly Abandoning Their Climate Commitments? *Forbes*. https://www.forbes.com/sites/jemmagreen/2024/08/29/why-big-corporations-are-quietly-abandoning-their-climate-commitments/

Guest, O., Suarez, M., Müller, B., van Meerkerk, E., Oude Groote Beverborg, A., de Haan, R., Reyes Elizondo, A., Blokpoel, M., Scharfenberg, N., Kleinherenbrink, A., Camerino, I., Woensdregt, M., Monett, D., Brown, J., Avraamidou, L., Alenda-Demoutiez, J., Hermans, F., & van Rooij, I. (2025). *Against the Uncritical Adoption of "AI" Technologies in Academia*. Zenodo. https://doi.org/10.5281/ZENODO.17065099

Hao, K. (2022, April 19). *Artificial intelligence is creating a new colonial world order*. MIT Technology Review. https://www.technologyreview.com/2022/04/19/1049592/artificial-intelligence-colonialism/

Hao, K. (2025). *Empire of AI: Dreams and nightmares in Sam Altman's OpenAI*. Penguin Press.

Johnson, K. (2022, July 8). Amazon's 'Safe' New Robot Won't Fix its Worker Injury Problem. *Wired*. https://www.wired.com/story/amazons-worker-injury-problem/

Kay, J., & King, M. A. (2021). *Radical uncertainty: Decision-making beyond the numbers*. W.W. Norton & Company.

Likhodi, L. (2018, March 12). York University faculty strike enters second week. *The Varsity*. https://thevarsity.ca/2018/03/12/york-university-faculty-strike-enters-second-week/

Levy, Carmi. (2025). AI Is Reshaping the First Job for a New Generation of Workers. *The Globe and Mail*, October 14, 2025. https://www.theglobeandmail.com/business/article-ai-is-reshaping-the-first-job-for-a-new-generation-of-workers/

MLA Taskforce on AI in Research and Teaching. (n.d.). *Statement on Educational Technologies and AI Agents*. Modern Language Association. Retrieved December 2, 2025, from https://www.mla.org/Resources/Advocacy/Executive-Council-Actions/2025/Statement-on-Educational-Technologies-and-AI-Agents

Muldoon, J., Graham, M., & Cant, C. (2024, July 12). Opinion: What's behind the AI boom? Exploited humans. *Los Angeles Times*. https://www.latimes.com/opinion/story/2024-07-12/artificial-intelligence-workers-labor-feeding-the-machine

Ojewale, O. (2022). *Mining and illicit trading of coltan in the Democratic Republic of Congo*. ENACT. https://enact-africa.s3.amazonaws.com/site/uploads/2022-05-03-research-paper-29-rev.pdf

Patent for Cotton Gin (1794). (2022, May 10). National Archives. https://www.archives.gov/milestone-documents/patent-for-cotton-gin

Schulman, S. (2025). The Fantasy and Necessity of Solidarity. Thesis.

Sherman, N. (2024, September 20). Three Mile Island Nuclear Site to Reopen in Microsoft Deal. *BBC News*. https://www.bbc.com/news/articles/cx25v2d7zexo

Tedesco, M. (2023, January 18). *The Paradox of Lithium – State of the Planet*. https://news.climate.columbia.edu/2023/01/18/the-paradox-of-lithium/

Tironi, M.,& Albornoz, C. (2025a). "Decolonizing AI? Lessons from a Failed Experiment." *Big Data & Society* 12, no. 3: 20539517251365224. https://doi.org/10.1177/20539517251365224.

Tironi, M., & Albornoz, C. (2025b). "Divergent Futures in a Damaged Territory: The Rise of Data Centers and Water Conflicts in Santiago de Chile." *Journal of Urban Technology* 32, no. 4: 51–68. https://doi.org/10.1080/10630732.2025.2546784.

Yaffe, H. (2023). "Che as Minister: The Promotion of Science and Technology for Cuba's Socialist Development." *Globalizations* 20, no. 8: 1490–507. https://doi.org/10.1080/14747731.2022.2111078.

Zewe, A. (2025, January 17). *Explained: Generative AI's environmental impact.* MIT News | Massachusetts Institute of Technology. https://news.mit.edu/2025/explained-generative-ai-environmental-impact-0117

19 A Cognitive Usability Engineering Approach to Understanding Bias in Human-AI Interaction

Andre William Kushniruk and Elizabeth Marie Borycki

INTRODUCTION

In this chapter, we explore the implications of understanding cognitive and socio-technical aspects of human and machine bias for the design and evaluation of artificial intelligence (AI) technologies. In-depth analysis of user interaction with AI technology has remained to be more fully explored in order to determine how AI may affect basic human cognitive, decision-making, and reasoning processes as well as potentially introducing its own biases. Bias can lead to prejudice in favor of or against one argument or line of reasoning over another. This may show itself as a systemic distortion of statistical results or evidence during decision-making. Achieving social justice presupposes an obligation to treat individuals fairly and equitably, and as such bias may lead to unfair and unequitable treatment in healthcare.

Cognitive biases refer to systematic, automatic, and often unconscious patterns of thought that guide human decision-making and reasoning. While biases may not cause error in some circumstances, in other circumstances they may adversely affect reasoning and decision-making processes (Haselton, Nettle & Andres, 2015; O'Sullivan & Schofield, 2018). As such, cognitive biases may lead to inappropriate shortcuts in information processing, application of incorrect assumptions, and ultimately lead to errors in reasoning and decision-making (Arkes & Hammond, 1986; Howard, 2019). To compound matters, the increasing allocation of complex health-related tasks to automated systems (such as AI) can lead to an overreliance on such technology. This has been shown under certain circumstances to lead to what is known as automation bias, which can potentially lead to medical error and serious risks for patients. A range of human cognitive biases (and associated cognitive errors) have also been identified in the literature in seminal work from a number of well-known psychologists (Arkes & Blumer, 1985; Tversky & Kahneman, 1974). In the chapter, we will explore a number of biases which have particular implications for understanding error emanating from human as well as machines, as well as their impact on human-machine joint decision-making involving AI.

As will be described, our work in the study of bias has involved observing (using video recording of user interactions with technology) and analyzing user verbalizations, as well as recording all computer screens while users interact with various AI technologies to carry out health-related tasks (Kushniruk, Kaufman, Kannampallil & Patel, 2024). This is followed by application of a range of qualitative methods for identifying the impact of the technology, including identifying potential for error due to bias in carrying out critical tasks in complex domains. As will be discussed, the approach described in this chapter can be used to identify human as well as machine bias in the joint human-machine interaction when humans carry out tasks using AI.

 DOI: 10.1201/9781003737810-23

BACKGROUND: COGNITIVE BIASES

From the psychological literature, there are a number of biases that have been identified that may lead to inefficient, incorrect, or error-prone decision-making (Baron, 2023). Table 19.1 contains a list of biases that have been documented and which will be considered in the context of AI in healthcare and related complex domains.

For example, in the context of healthcare decision-making, the *premature closure bias* refers to accepting a diagnosis before it has been fully verified and there is a lack of sufficient evidence to support a diagnostic conclusion. *Confirmation bias* refers to a tendency to look for confirming evidence (e.g. of a diagnosis) while discounting anomalous or disconfirming evidence. *Availability bias* refers to basing a decision on memorable or recent experience (e.g. results of reading a recent medical article) rather than taking into account differences of the current case/situation with that memorable or recent experience (Tversky & Kahneman, 1973). *Omission bias* refers to a tendency toward inaction rather than action for fear of being wrong, while *commission bias* refers to tendency toward action even when action is not warranted given the situation or information available. *Anchoring bias* refers to the decision maker focusing on one feature of a problem exclusively rather than working from a full situational analysis (e.g. focusing on one test alone when diagnosing a patient). *Framing effect bias* refers to early presenting features unduly influencing (or framing) the decision maker's decisions, while the *Overconfidence bias* refers to inappropriate certainty of one's ability or decision-making (Berner & Graber, 2008).

Of particular relevance to our discussion of bias in the context of AI is the effect known as *automation bias*. Automation bias refers to undo overreliance or trust in technology or automation in making or supporting a decision (e.g. overly trusting of the results or conclusion of a computer

TABLE 19.1
Cognitive Biases

Cognitive Bias	Description
Anchoring bias	Overreliance on evidence that is encountered early during problem solving (rather than developing a comprehensive understanding of a problem)
Automation bias	Human overreliance on automated systems in decision-making, in some cases blindly accepting automated decisions and disregarding evidence that may be contradictory to the automated decision
Availability bias	Basing a decision on what readily comes to mind from past experience and which is most memorable (ignoring key differences of that experience with the current situation).
Commission bias	A tendency toward taking an action or making a decision, even when its not be warranted
Confirmation bias	Looking for confirming evidence, while ignoring or rejecting contradictory or disconfirming evidence
Feedback bias	Lack of feedback for a decision incorrectly being considered positive feedback for the decision taken
Framing effect	Decision-making unduly affected by the way in which information is framed or presented during problem solving process
Omission bias	A tendency toward inaction rather than action, even when the action may be warranted given the evidence
Overconfidence bias	When a high level of confidence in one's decision-making or actions is not warranted
Outcome bias	The making of a decision based on an expected outcome, rather than the merits and appropriateness of the decision or actions
Premature closure	Accepting a decision too early, before considering all the evidence and alternatives
Sunk costs	A phenomenon where people continue to invest in a plan, where the more effort invested or committed makes it difficult to abandon that plan even when abandonment is warranted

system even when it may not be consistent with other evidence). In some cases, this could result in "blind trust" in the conclusions of an automated system and disregard for contrary evidence (Goddard, Roudsari & Wyatt, 2012). However, such confidence in AI-based decision-making may not be warranted as systemic biases may be introduced and present in the AI as a result of insufficient training and testing of AI models when they are developed. For example, development of AI-based diagnostic systems that are targeted at identifying skin cancers should be trained and tested using a wide range of images representing many skin types (Felmingham et al., 2021). However, if the training and testing data sets are limited in scope and variety (e.g. to include only images of skin lesions from Caucasian patients) this may lead to errors in the AI system's conclusions stemming from use of limited data used in training and testing (Kushniruk & Borycki, 2023). For example, the AI system may not perform well, or even provide incorrect diagnosis, due to the limited data contained in the training set used to develop the AI algorithm. The issue of lack of generalizability and effectiveness of AI outside of the environment(s) and sources of data they were developed in has long been an issue with AI applications in healthcare and can be seen as related to issues around insufficient range of data from which the systems work with or are developed from (Kushniruk & Borycki, 2023, 2021).

THEORETICAL FRAMEWORK

In this chapter, we will argue that improved understanding of how AI can potentially affect decision-making should be considered in the context of the full human-machine interaction, rather than looking at the human or system in isolation. From a theoretical perspective, this has been the basis of our work in studying user interactions with AI at multiple levels – starting with examining the level of the individual user (e.g. physician, nurse, and patient) interacting in isolation with the AI system, up to the level of using the AI to perform a complex task (e.g. a doctor patient interview supported by an AI application designed to automatically summarize the interview discussion with the patient). This is followed by consideration of the level of social interaction, e.g. how that system or application is used within an organization across multiple contexts and users. For considering this we can extend our theoretical framework to consider cognition as not just within the individual's head but as *distributed cognition* whereby decision-making processes are seen as being spread across a number of "agents" and representations of information, which may include multiple people, machines, computer systems (such as AI systems) along with all paper or computer-based data representations (Hutchins, 2000; Hollan, Hutchins & Krish, 2000).

Along these lines and consistent with distributed cognition, the authors have developed a *cognitive-socio-technical model of human interaction* which provides a practical framework for consideration of human-computer interaction at all levels from the individual user up to the social level (Borycki & Kushniruk, 2010). We have argued that in order to adequately understand, design, and evaluate bias in complex technology such as AI, a multilayer perspective is needed. Distributed cognition posits that decision-making is rarely conducted in a vacuum of a single decision maker but is distributed. Distributed cognition provides a theoretical perspective that can be of value in elucidating aspects of the interaction between human and AI and helps in understanding how AI systems can help to reduce bias in decision-making, or inadvertently lead to bias in decision-making (Borycki et al., 2012; Borycki, Kushniruk, Bellwood & Brender, 2012).

The cognitive-socio-technical framework has been used to drive studies of AI in order to assess their use at multiple levels, from that of the individual user interacting with the application in isolation, to examining its use to carry out real-world tasks and its degree of fit within complex organizational settings and structures. For example, Li and colleagues (2012) have described an evaluation of the integration of an intelligent decision support tool into medical practice that was based on the cognitive-socio-technical model. In this work, the researchers first conducted in-depth study of use of the technology by clinicians in isolation. This resulted in identification of error-prone aspects of the design of the tools. After remediating those issues (many of them at the level of basic usability problems), the application was then tested under "near live" conditions involving use of the decision support in the presence of patients in a simulated doctor-patient encounter. Finally, users of the decision support tool were observed using the application in a real setting, once the system was widely deployed. At each level, from the cognitive to the socio-technical and organizational levels, a range of issues related to error or bias were identified and rectified.

In considering the potential to reduce human error AI systems offer the opportunity to streamline and optimize healthcare (Cohen, Patel & Shortliffe, 2022; Musen, Shahar, & Shortliffe, 2006). However, to achieve this, greater consideration of a number of key aspects of human cognition and interactions with such technology is needed (Shneiderman, 2020). For example, AI support (and decision support in general) needs to go beyond a "one-size-fits-all" model and take into account the experience and expertise of the human decision maker who may be interacting with the AI support, particularly as users of AI may be varied in their backgrounds, capabilities and ehealth literacy levels (Kushniruk & Borycki, 2023; Monkman & Kushniruk, 2015). For example, health professionals who have less expertise or experience may be more likely to make errors based on automation bias, by assuming that a computer system may provide a better decision than theirs (Kushniruk, 2001). On the other hand, health professionals with considerable expertise or experience may be more susceptible to overconfidence bias, where AI advice might be ignored completely, potentially also leading to error. Thus, research on human expertise, borrowing from the "expertise approach" (Ericsson & Smith, 1991) is needed to understand the type of biases and subsequent errors that are committed by decision makers of varied levels of expertise when using AI in different medical and healthcare contexts. Our methodology, involving testing participants of differing levels of expertise, has been used to characterize the different types of biases and errors committed by healthcare professionals of differing levels of expertise. This is an example of application of the expertise approach to studying human reasoning, extended to examining the use of health information systems, AI, and bias.

Other factors that may complicate the interaction between human and machine include personality factors, demographics, and specialty of the decision maker. It has been argued that non-expert clinicians may benefit more from AI decision support (Felmingham et al., 2021). However, it has long been argued that decision support, including AI-based support, should be careful to provide health professionals with decision-making aid to assist health professionals with their own decision-making when they need a "catalyst" to help them and not simply replace their decision-making process entirely (Miller & Masarie, 1990). It has been shown that simply varying at what point in a diagnostic process AI advice is provided can alter the potential benefits and risks associated with introduction of this technology. Along these lines, inappropriate triggering of AI at times that are premature in the overall decision-making process may lead to automation bias (Li et al., 2012; Kushniruk & Borycki, 2021). The cognitive style (Baron, Badgio & Gaskins, 1986) of the human using AI is another factor that will affect the risk that the joint human-machine interaction will lead to error due to bias (Felmingham et al., 2021; Kushniruk, Kaufman, Kannampallil & Patel, 2024). Overall, taking a distributed cognition approach provides a promising framework for considering bias as they occur in real human-AI interactions that may involve multiple actors, systems, and interactions with patients in different contexts.

METHODOLOGICAL APPROACH

In attempting to understand the potential to reduce AI biases, there are a number of methodological directions that can be taken. Our work in this area has extended our previous research in studying a wide range of user interactions with advanced technologies in healthcare (Kushniruk & Patel, 2004; Kushniruk, Monkman, Borycki & Kannry, 2024). The methodological approach we have developed and refined involves observing (and video recording) users interacting with a technology under study. The study participants are asked to use the technology to carry out real (or realistic) tasks using the technology. For example, in a laboratory setting we may instruct users (e.g. physicians or nurses) of a new AI-based medical information system to "think aloud" (i.e. verbalize their thoughts) while interacting with that system to support them in making diagnostic decisions for medical cases. If the study is conducted in vivo (e.g. in a real world or in a realistic simulation setting), all computer screens are recorded (along with all participant verbalizations) as digital movie files. The sessions are recorded in their entirety, including recording all interactions with information technology such as AI-based decision support (Kushniruk & Patel, 2004; Kushniruk, Nohr, Jensen & Borycki, 2013).

The video-based user interaction data resulting from recording users interacting with AI to solve problems can be analyzed using principled coding schemes developed over the past several decades (Kushniruk & Borycki, 2024; Kushniruk, Monkman, Kitson & Borycki, 2019). These coding schemes can be used by the research analyst to identify a range of usability issues and errors encountered by humans in completing tasks using a system (e.g. using an AI system to diagnose a patient). In addition, consistent with our cognitive-socio-technical framework, many of our studies involve testing and evaluating AI successively at multiple levels of realism – i.e. in the laboratory context, followed by simulation and/or testing in the naturalistic environment (e.g. in a hospital or clinic). We have labeled the approach as *cognitive usability engineering* as it extends current usability engineering approaches to include a focus on cognitive aspects of user interactions, including a focus on identifying bias (both human and machine) from the detailed record of human-machine interaction resulting from our studies (Kushniruk, Kaufman, Kannampallil & Patel, 2024). In our current work, we are applying this methodological approach to study use and usability problems and biases related to use of a range of AI applications, from diagnostic systems for identifying skin cancer to application of AI in streamlining doctor-patient interactions and automating burdensome documentation tasks.

FINDINGS AND IMPLICATIONS

To guide our understanding of data from studies of human-AI interactions, we have worked on analyzing bias and error, inspired in part on seminal work from Kahneman and Tversky (1973), using a number of coding schemes. In recent years, we have uniquely applied and refined these classifications (that were developed for study of human decision-making) to the analysis of error and bias in human-computer interaction with AI. These coding schemes can be used to help the analyst in the identification and coding of common biases identified in the data (as part of a video coding scheme that is used to guide identification of usability problems and bias) (Kushniruk & Borycki, 2024). The results of our studies have been used to provide formative feedback to system designers and to conduct summative evaluations of the usability and safety of systems currently deployed (Kushniruk & Patel, 2004). As AI has become an increasingly ubiquitous partner in joint human-machine decision-making, there is a need to apply such a human-centered approach to explore to what extent human biases apply, or can be mitigated, when AI is embedded in work and decision processes in complex real-world domains. This includes consideration of biases such as the automation bias, the availability bias, the authority bias, the representative bias, and framing effects. In addition, the extent to which AI can support or mitigate against human biases (such as confirmation or anchoring bias) has remained to be explored. Such work would have important implications for the design, evaluation and testing of advanced AI applications embedded in real and naturalistic environments and is needed in order to understand the extent to which human biases may be replicated or possibly reduced in AI systems, as well as assessing the impact of joint human-AI interaction in potentially mitigating bias in decision-making. In our work, this has included both laboratory-based testing of AI systems, simulations as well as naturalistic evaluation of AI systems in use in real healthcare and clinical settings (Li et al., 2012).

Work in human-in-the-loop development, training, and testing of AI will also become increasingly critical in achieving the maximal benefits of AI (Mosqueira-Rey et al., 2023). This can include practical approaches to ensuring diversity in the training and testing cases used for developing AI models in order to include and ensure a diversity of training and testing data (which is the basis for developing AI that can be generalizable and not specific to only one context or location). Other approaches can include setting a high level of confidence within an AI model in reaching a conclusion to avoid perpetuating inadvertent bias (Monarch, 2021). In supervised learning, where AI systems are "trained" using labeled data sets, the annotation and labeling of data used to create a model (often done with the aid of humans who label the data) is critical. This aspect of human interaction in the design of AI models also requires careful consideration of quality control and accuracy (e.g. labeling of skin cancer images in an AI system being trained to detect cancer from images of patient skin lesions). Questions to be asked here include the following: Is the data that is used to train the AI representative of the eventual patient groups that the AI application will be used to provide advice for? What will be the risk of having a biased underlying AI model, not based on a wide enough range of patient data during training?

From the above theoretical and methodological perspectives, we need to understand how AI systems are actually used in the context of the joint human-machine decision-making process when discussing bias, rather than just considering human or machine bias in isolation. For example, our research has shown that the point at which AI decision support interacts with humans can have a profound impact on the success of the joint human-machine decision-making and its impact on bias in decision-making (Li et al., 2012). Early work of ours showed that how systems such as electronic health records present data (and the order which they present patient data on a computer screen) could have a significant impact on human decision-making. For example, some systems we tested were shown to lead physicians to what we have referred to as "screen-driven" behavior, a form of automation bias, where the physician, rather than following their own intuition may tend to be driven by the order of categories of information provided by the system on the screen in guiding their questioning of a patients. This ultimately affected (and in some cases detrimentally) their reasoning and decision-making about patients (Patel, Kushniruk, Yang & Yale, 2000).

In our work involving integrating advanced AI-based decision support (in the form of guideline-triggered alerts and decision support), we have found that when an AI-based system automatically comes into play (i.e. triggered automatically to provide AI-based advice to health professionals) may also have a profound effect (Li et al., 2012). For example, in some cases, physicians have complained that such intelligent decision support systems may have been automatically invoked by the system too early in the physician's own diagnostic decision-making processes or treatment planning (e.g. diagnosing a case of potential pneumonia where automated alerts and AI recommendations are triggered before the physician has had a chance to see all key information such as the patient's X-ray). Rather than supporting the human decision-making in such situations, this can lead a physician to feeling unduly guided by the system leading to premature decision closure, with the system being perceived as "pushing" the health professional's decision-making toward a particular conclusion or decision and leading to bias if not triggered at an appropriate point in the overall diagnostic process (Li et al., 2012). In other situations, physicians have indicated that they prefer such automated support appear later in the overall decision-making process, to be used as more of a check on their human decision-making (using the AI to critique their decision-making) in order to avoid bias (e.g. the anchoring bias) the system may introduce if AI interacts with the health professional too early in their overall decision-making process. Methods for identifying modes of human-AI interaction that are most effective for healthcare decision-making have remained an area to be more fully explored from a cognitive perspective, despite the large interest and effort in integrating AI into complex domains such as healthcare (Househ, Borycki & Kushniruk, 2021).

DISCUSSION

In this chapter, we have discussed bias at multiple levels from looking at potential biases that humans may bring to those that AI systems may induce. In addition, in order to consider how and when such bias may occur, we need to examine the overall human-machine interaction, using a human factors lens. As such AI can be used to potentially mitigate human bias by providing data and decision-making capabilities that could extend and even critique human decision-making. However, as noted above, without careful consideration of basic human factors in designing user interactions (e.g. about when and how to trigger AI support) the same AI technology may actually induce or lead to bias that may lead to error. Overall, it is our contention that adding technology that can reduce error if deployed appropriately. However, it is essential that we work to mitigate bias that the technology may inadvertently introduce, and that the only way to deal with this is to take a multilevel holistic approach to understanding human-AI interaction. In essence, we want the joint human-AI interaction to reduce bias and for AI to effectively support rather than replace human decision-making in areas such as diagnostic decision-making.

There are a number of important implications of taking such a broad multilevel approach to understanding how AI may either decrease or induce bias. One implication is that understanding how AI decision support affects decision makers of different levels of expertise and experience needs to be considered. In addition, testing and regulation of AI system applications need to be given much more attention (Borycki & Kushniruk, 2023). This is particularly true as new studies have indicated that patients may be trusting information generated by large language models (LLMs), such as that of ChatGPT, in answering medically related questions over human advice from healthcare experts (Shekar et al., 2025). This is despite findings that such AI-generated responses to patient questions may be incorrect or misleading, or completely wrong. Along these lines, the issue of AI "hallucinations" has come to the fore with the widespread use of LLMs. AI hallucinations refer to when the LLM erroneously produces completely false or nonsensical information in response to user queries. Such errors could ultimately be a result of training data limitations, or overfitting (where the model learns patterns that are very specific to the training data and as a result lead to error when new or unseen data is encountered). Furthermore, LLMs essentially work by predicting next word and phrase patterns statistically from data it is trained on, rather than through genuine understanding. A lack of depth of machine understanding has been a recurring issue with AI. Reporting of this type of failure mode dates back several decades where it was noted that when an AI system makes an error, it often makes a bad one. It was noted that mistakes (e.g. completely erroneous AI responses) that result from use of AI may end up being nonsensical, inappropriate or not even close to being correct. In the past this was known as the problem of "brittle failure" of AI systems dating back to the 1980s, long predating issues currently being encountered with more complex and refined models based on LLMs (Kushniruk & Borycki, 2021)

What is increasingly clear is that while some biases may be unchanged or minimized by use of AI others may become exacerbated. How the AI is introduced and integrated into healthcare practice is critical in understanding how the same technology may be effective or not. Current issues include the lack of transparency and interpretability of many current forms of AI and this has important implications when considering bias. In recent years, developing "explainable AI" has become a major research area and goal with development of techniques such as saliency maps, which can show what features of a problem most contributed to an AI decision (Chaddad, Peng, Xu & Bouridane, 2023; Saraswat et al., 2022; Sadeghi et al., 2024). Explainable AI has the potential to help identify bias by providing transparency about how the AI operates and comes up with decisions. This can potentially be done in the following ways: (1) identifying which features the AI focuses on in making a decision (e.g. age and sex of patients) (2) ability to allow for "what if" scenarios to explore how the AI might respond to different types of inputs (e.g. inputs involving differences in ethnicity) (3) providing auditing capabilities to allow for comparing error rates for different groups and measuring fairness using metrics (4) providing transparency about the source of training data used in the AI model and (5) automatically flagging when biases may be at play. However, this is still an emerging area and many AI applications (e.g. deep learning systems) are not easily amenable to showing end users (e.g. health professionals or patients) how they arrived at a decision, came to a conclusion, or the underlying processing that might be biased (Raposo, 2025).

Human trust in AI has long been and remains an issue in its actual adoption and this remains an area of future research (Kushniruk & Borycki, 2023). In particular, the connection between lack of transparency and the potential for bias has remained to be fully explored, particularly in terms of system adoption. Further work will be needed in order to develop a more synergistic approach to designing AI in a way that integrates the best of human decision-making with computer-based decision-making, while not introducing or inducing different types of bias in doing so (Korteling, Brouwer & Toet, 2018). In addition, governance and regulatory frameworks will be needed to ensure that appropriate testing of AI is conducted to reduce potential bias before AI systems and applications are widely deployed in healthcare organizations (Hassan, Kushniruk & Borycki, 2024; Hasaan, Borycki & Kushniruk, 2025). Along these lines, potential for AI bias and discrimination has become a key regulatory issue, along with related issues such as privacy and data protection, accountability and liability as well as safety of AI systems. Responses to these issues have included introduction of risk-based regulations (e.g. the European Union's AI Act), which classify AI systems on their potential to cause harm, voluntary guidelines as well as a growing body of technical standards for AI applications.

Finally, further work in understanding the impact of biases that may result from application of AI is needed to understand how they impact decision-making not only be health professionals but also by lay people and patients (Shekar et al., 2025). Experimental studies of how lay persons interact with AI and act on information from these systems are needed, as their use has grown exponentially. Recent studies have shown a clear automation bias when lay people (including patients) have a tendency to over-trust the results and advice generated by AI systems, particularly in cases where their accuracy may be far less than people realize in complex domains (Shekar et al., 2025). Furthermore, studies have shown that the accuracy of health information (for both patients and providers) provided by LLMs varies considerably, from as low as 60%, with erroneous advice to users potentially leading to errors that could support bias and incorrect decision-making (Bedi et al., 2025; Shekar et al., 2025).

CONCLUSION

This chapter has described a number of human as well as machine biases that range from the cognitive to the societal. These biases may adversely affect human-AI interaction and ultimately affect critical decision-making in complex areas such as healthcare. In this chapter, these biases have been considered in the context of joint human-AI decision-making and interaction. A theoretical framework consistent with this, known as distributed cognition, was introduced along with implications of a cognitive-socio-technical perspective for considering potential for human-AI bias. It is argued that a greater emphasis on understanding the human aspects of human-AI interaction is needed in order to develop AI that effectively supports and enhances human decision-making.

REFLECTION QUESTIONS

Why is it important to understand biases that may be introduced by both humans and AI systems and applications?

How could use of AI lead to bias and error in decision-making?

What are some potential sources of bias when using AI?

How is human bias (from the psychological literature on human decision-making) related to bias caused by technology?

What are the different human factors and societal factors that affect how susceptible humans and systems are to bias?

How can a cognitive approach to usability engineering be applied to understand bias in human-AI interaction?

What are some possible ways to mitigate AI bias when creating, deploying, and using AI systems and applications designed to solve complex real-world problems (in areas such as healthcare)?

REFERENCES

Arkes, H. R., & Blumer, C. (1985). The psychology of sunk cost. *Organizational Behaviour and Human Decision Processes*, 35, 124–140.

Arkes, H. R. & Hammond, K. R. (1986). *Judgement and decision making: An interdisciplinary reader*. Cambridge University Press.

Baron, J. (2023). *Thinking and deciding*. Cambridge University Press.

Baron, J., Badgio, P., & Gaskins, I. W. (1986). Cognitive style and its improvement. In R. J. Sternberg (Ed.), *Advances in the psychology of human intelligence* (Vol. 3, pp. 173–220). Erlbaum.

Bedi, S., Cui, H., Fuentes, M., Unell, A., Wornow, M., Banda, J. M., & Shah, N. H. (2025). MedHELM: Holistic Evaluation of Large Language Models for Medical Tasks. *arXiv preprint arXiv:2505.23802*.

Berner, E. S., & Graber, M. L. (2008). Overconfidence as a cause of diagnostic error in medicine. *The American Journal of Medicine*, 121(5), S2–S23.

Borycki, E. M., Househ, F. M. S., Kushniruk, A. W., Nohr, C., & Takeda, H. (2012). Empowering patients: making health information and systems safer for patients and the public. *Yearbook of Medical Informatics*, 21(01), 56–64.

Borycki, E. M., Kushniruk, A. W., Bellwood, P., & Brender, J. (2012). Technology-induced errors. *Methods of Information in Medicine*, 51(02), 95–103.

Borycki, E. M., & Kushniruk, A. W. (2010). Towards an integrative cognitive-socio-technical approach in health informatics: Analyzing technology-induced error involving health information systems to improve patient safety. *The Open Medical Informatics Journal*, 4, 181.

Borycki, E., & Kushniruk, A. W. (2023). Artificial intelligence and safety in healthcare. In C. El Morr (Ed.), *AI and society* (pp. 17–32). Chapman and Hall/CRC.

Chaddad, A., Peng, J., Xu, J., & Bouridane, A. (2023). Survey of explainable AI techniques in healthcare. *Sensors*, 23(2), 634.

Cohen, T. A., Patel, V. L., & Shortliffe, E. H. (Eds.). (2022). *Intelligent systems in medicine and health: The role of AI*. Springer.

Ericsson, K. A., & Smith, J. (Eds.). (1991). *Toward a general theory of expertise: Prospects and limits*. Cambridge University Press.

Felmingham, C. M., Adler, N. R., Ge, Z., Morton, R. L., Janda, M., & Mar, V. J. (2021). The importance of incorporating human factors in the design and implementation of artificial intelligence for skin cancer diagnosis in the real world. *American Journal of Clinical Dermatology*, 22(2), 233–242.

Goddard, K., Roudsari, A., & Wyatt, J. C. (2012). Automation bias: A systematic review of frequency, effect mediators, and mitigators. *Journal of the American Medical Informatics Association*, 19(1), 121–127.

Haselton, M. G., Nettle, D., & Andrews, P. W. (2015). The evolution of cognitive bias. In *The Handbook of Evolutionary Psychology* (pp. 724–746). Wiley. https://doi.org/https://doi.org/10.1002/9780470939376.ch25

Hassan, M., Borycki, E. M., & Kushniruk, A. W. (2025). Artificial intelligence governance framework for healthcare. *Healthcare Management Forum*, 38(2), 125–130. https://doi.org/10.1177/08404704241291226.

Hassan, M., Kushniruk, A., & Borycki, E. (2024). Barriers to and facilitators of artificial intelligence adoption in health care: Scoping review. *JMIR Human Factors*, 11, e48633.

Hollan, J., Hutchins, E., & Kirsh, D. (2000). Distributed cognition: Toward a new foundation for human-computer interaction research. *ACM Transactions on Computer-Human Interaction (TOCHI)*, 7(2), 174–196.

Househ, M., Borycki, E., & Kushniruk, A. (Eds.). (2021). *Multiple perspectives on artificial intelligence in healthcare: Opportunities and challenges*. Springer.

Howard, J. (2019). *Cognitive errors and diagnostic mistakes*. Springer International Publishing.

Hutchins, E. (2000). Distributed cognition. *International Encyclopedia of the Social and Behavioral Sciences*, 138(1), 1–10.

Korteling, J. E., Brouwer, A. M., & Toet, A. (2018). A neural network framework for cognitive bias. *Frontiers in Psychology*, 9, 1561.

Kushniruk, A. W (2001) Analysis of complex decision-making processes in health care: Cognitive approaches to health informatics. *Journal of Biomedical Informatic,* 34(5), 365–376.

Kushniruk, A., & Borycki, E. (2021). The human factors of AI in healthcare: Recurrent issues, future challenges and ways forward. In M. Househ, E. Borycki, & A. Kushniruk (Eds.), *Multiple perspectives on artificial intelligence in healthcare: opportunities and challenges* (pp. 3–12). Springer International Publishing. https://doi.org/10.1007/978-3-030-67303-1_1

Kushniruk, A., & Borycki, E. (2023). The human factors of artificial intelligence–where are we now and where are we headed? Lessons learned from AI in healthcare. In C. El Morr (Ed.), *AI and society* (pp. 3–16). Chapman and Hall/CRC.

Kushniruk, A. W., & Borycki, E. M. (2024). Analyzing video-based human-computer interaction data in healthcare using a cognitive-socio-technical framework. In A. W. Kushniruk, D. R. Kaufman, T. G. Kannampallil, & V. L. Patel (Eds.), *Human computer interaction in healthcare: The role of cognition* (pp. 151–179). Springer Nature Switzerland. https://doi.org/10.1007/978-3-031-69947-4_7

Kushniruk, A. W., Kaufman, D. R., Kannampallil, T. G., & Patel, V. L. (Eds.). (2024). *Human computer interaction in healthcare: The role of cognition*. Springer.

Kushniruk, A. W., Monkman, H., Borycki, E. M., & Kannry, J. (2024). User-centered design and evaluation of health information systems: A rapid usability engineering approach. In A. W. Kushniruk, D. R. Kaufman, T. G. Kannampallil, & V. L. Patel (Eds.), *Human computer interaction in healthcare: The role of cognition* (pp. 235–261). Springer Nature Switzerland. https://doi.org/10.1007/978-3-031-69947-4_10

Kushniruk, A. W., Monkman, H., Kitson, N., & Borycki, E. M. (2019). Development of a video coding scheme for understanding human-computer interaction and clinical decision making. In *Context sensitive health informatics: Sustainability in dynamic ecosystems* (pp. 80–85). IOS Press. https://doi.org/10.3233/SHTI190142

Kushniruk, A., Nohr, C., Jensen, S., & Borycki, E. M. (2013). From usability testing to clinical simulations: Bringing context into the design and evaluation of usable and safe health information technologies. *Yearb Med Inform,* 22(01), 78–85.

Kushniruk, A. W., & Patel, V. L. (2004). Cognitive and usability engineering methods for the evaluation of clinical information systems. *Journal of Biomedical Informatics*, *37*(1), 56–76.

Li, A. C., Kannry, J. L., Kushniruk, A., Chrimes, D., McGinn, T. G., Edonyabo, D., & Mann, D. M. (2012). Integrating usability testing and think-aloud protocol analysis with "near-live" clinical simulations in evaluating clinical decision support. *International Journal of Medical Informatic,* 81(11), 761–772.

Miller, R. A., & Masarie, F. E. (1990) The demise of the "Greek Oracle" model for medical diagnostic systems. *Methods Information in Medicine,* 29(01), 1–2.

Monarch, R. (2021). *Human-in-the loop machine learning: Active learning for human-centered AI.* Manning Publications Co.

Monkman, H., & Kushniruk, A. W. (2015). eHealth literacy issues, constructs, models, and methods for health information technology design and evaluation. *Knowledge Management & E Learning*, 7(4), 541.

Mosqueira-Rey, E., Hernández-Pereira, E., Alonso-Ríos, D., Bobes-Bascarán, J., & Fernández Leal, Á. (2023). Human-in-the-loop machine learning: A state of the art. *Artificial Intelligence Review*, 56(4), 3005–3054.

Musen, M. A., Shahar, Y., & Shortliffe, E. H. (2006). Clinical decision-support systems. In E. H. Shortliffe & J. J. Cimino (Eds.), *Biomedical informatics: Computer applications in health care and biomedicine* (pp. 698–736). Springer International Publishing. https://doi.org/10.1007/0-387-36278-9_20

O'Sullivan, E. D., & Schofield, S. J. (2018). Cognitive bias in clinical medicine. *Journal of the Royal College of Physicians of Edinburgh*, 48(3), 225–232.

Patel, V. L., Kushniruk, A. W., Yang, S., & Yale, J. F. (2000). Impact of a computer-based patient record system on data collection, knowledge organization, and reasoning. *Journal of the American Medical Informatics Association*, 7(6), 569–585.

Raposo, V. L. (2025). The fifty shades of black: About black box AI and explainability in healthcare. *Medical Law Review*, 33(1). https://doi.org/10.1093/medlaw/fwaf005

Sadeghi, Z., Alizadehsani, R., Cifci, M. A., Kausar, S., Rehman, R., Mahanta, P.,… & Pardalos, P. M. (2024). A review of Explainable Artificial Intelligence in healthcare. *Computers and Electrical Engineering*, 118, 109370.

Saraswat, D., Bhattacharya, P., Verma, A., Prasad, V. K., Tanwar, S., Sharma, G., …& Sharma, R. (2022). Explainable AI for healthcare 5.0: Opportunities and challenges. *IEEe Access*, 10, 84486–84517.

Shekar, S., Pataranutaporn, P., Sarabu, C., Cecchi, G. A., & Maes, P. (2025). People overtrust AI-generated medical advice despite low accuracy. *NEJM AI*, 2(6), AIoa2300015.

Shneiderman, B. (2020). Human-centered artificial intelligence: Reliable, safe & trustworthy. *International Journal of Human–Computer Interaction,* 36(6), 495–504.

Tversky, A., & Kahneman, D. (1973). Availability: A heuristic for judging frequency and probability. *Cognitive Psychology*, 5, 207–232.

Tversky, A., & Kahneman, D. (1974). Judgment under Uncertainty: Heuristics and Biases: Biases in judgments reveal some heuristics of thinking under uncertainty. *Science*, 185(4157), 1124–1131.

20 Towards a Leftist Artificial Intelligence for Geopolitical Analysis

Reconsidering the Technical and Conceptual Aporias in the Development of Radically Equitable Artificial Agents

Fouâd Oveisy

INTRODUCTION: EQUITABILITY BEYOND DATA JUSTICE, TOWARDS A POLITICS OF TRAINING

The central argument of this essay is that inequitable behaviour in generative artificial intelligence (Gen AI) should be remedied primarily through the training, or "in-processing," phase of machine learning (ML). Fairness adjustment in ML generally occurs across three phases: pre-processing, which removes bias from training data; in-processing, which modifies the training algorithm to unlearn bias; and post-processing, which corrects biased outputs (Buyl & Di Bie, 2024). Pre-processing has received significant scholarly attention (e.g., Gitelman & Jackson, 2013; Crawford, 2021), especially for its potential to diversify training data. By incorporating alternative sources, pre-processing transforms ML into a process of acculturation within "fair epistemes," rather than allowing AI to absorb inequitable cultural logics. However, while crucial for ethical training, pre-processing cannot address the political challenges of equitability: how Gen AI should engage emergent categories of equity absent from training data (e.g., evolving notions of social justice); how it might reconcile the contradictions of intersectionality (e.g., assessing "white LGBTQ" versus "Black cisgender" applicants); and, thereby, how it can reason about equity as a contested concept and practice for dismantling structural injustice (e.g., enabling artificial agents to problematise, not just eliminate, bias within their training).

Refocusing on in-processing allows both scholarship and technical work on AI to prioritise equity as a strategic ethos. Approaches based on "equity" go beyond simply removing bias or promoting fairness; they also examine how such dynamics impact individuals in distinct and variable ways (Braveman & Gruskin, 2003; Espinoza, 2007). In ML, this approach requires training artificial agents to actively scrutinise the evolution of bias and its underlying structures—treating equity not merely as a matter of fair input and output, but as an ongoing, reflective practice for equitability (Kapiriri & Razavi, 2022; Freidus & Turner, 2023).

Overview of the Current Landscape of Equitable AI

Scholarship on ML fairness can be organised into four intersecting currents. Mapping them clarifies where existing approaches stall and where equitable projects should intervene.

 DOI: 10.1201/9781003737810-24

"Technical debiasing" approaches in computer science treat bias as a contaminant—an error to be detected and corrected—rather than as a complex, dynamic phenomenon rooted in deeper social and political processes (e.g., Lin et al., 2024; Mehrabi et al., 2021). The "moral machine" approach seeks to embed ethical, context-sensitive rules into AI (e.g., Wallach & Allen, 2009; Anderson & Anderson, 2011). However, since morality is always articulated in service to a political strategy, such machines cannot "hard-code" a politically neutral notion of equity. A genuinely moral AI must also interrogate how it understands and plans for equitability. By contrast, critiques from Science and Technology Studies (STS) challenge the separation of bias from social context. Selbst et al. (2019) call this an "abstraction error," while Bellanova et al. expose the coercive external infrastructures that render the world machine-readable. Yet, these critiques rarely address how ML architectures—the internal soft wiring that determines how a model learns and represents reasoning—amplify such concerns. Training equitable AI requires treating ML architecture itself as a site of struggle. Critical Security Studies (CSS) highlights these architectures: Aradau and Blanke (2017) show how "anomaly" detection generates new categories of risk, while Suchman (2020) describes how targeting technologies blur the line between threat detection and targeted securitisation. Yet, across these critiques, "black box" conceptions of ML architecture—the so-called opacity of the reasoning process in billion-parameter large language models (LLMs)—often serve as a pretext for blaming Gen AI as fundamentally biased. Reducing ML to a mere amplifier or multiplier of injustice obscures the technical and political interventions that are still possible despite Gen AI's architectural complexity.

Meta-Critiques and Interventions

The project discussed in the third section of this essay, which addresses the challenges of fine-tuning an LLM (Falcon-H1-34B-Instruct) for equitable geopolitical prediction, begins where these scholarly currents converge in their limitations. It emphasises two concerns: first, the need for a deeper technical understanding of ML architecture; second, a sustained effort to enhance the epistemological equitability of the training regimen, which directly influences the ethical and political values it reflects while generating intelligence. A standard recommendation in the reviewed literature for addressing this latter concern is cross-disciplinary collaboration between the "hard" and "soft" constructors and critics of Gen AI. This chapter affirms that need but argues that, especially in the social sciences and humanities, we lack the domain-specific knowledge required to train artificial agents to reason radically about equity. Moreover, problematic "governance frameworks" (Gill, 1995) and "strategic cultures" (Bloomfield, 2012), inherited from statist, capitalist, and neocolonial institutions, continue to infiltrate interdisciplinary cooperation and distort strategies for equitable AI. Accordingly, this chapter views AI less as an autonomous amplifier of bias and more as a reflection of the conceptual and organisational failures within disciplines tasked with implementing equity, maintaining that the real challenge is to treat model architecture and training as arenas for radical equitability.

CRITICAL SURVEY OF THE FOUR APPROACHES TO EQUITABLE ML

Fairness in ML is generally defined as the absence of bias towards "an individual or group based on their inherent or acquired characteristics" (Mehrabi et al., 2021, p. 114). Lum and Isaac (2016), for example, demonstrate that predictive policing algorithms trained on police-recorded data do not objectively forecast crime but instead reinforce biased policing patterns. Analysing data from Oakland, they show how ML feedback loops between targeted patrols and recorded incidents lead to disproportionate surveillance of minority and low-income neighbourhoods.

Technical De-Biasing Approaches

Such bias in ML is addressed through four general approaches, beginning with "technical de-biasing" methods among computer science practitioners. While their methods vary, two patterns persist. On the one hand, bias is viewed as a false pattern-matching issue in ML (e.g., Hindman, 2015; Chen et al., 2023), requiring piecemeal technical workarounds because there is no consensus on a "universal definition of fairness." That is, bias is treated as a technical fluke needing isolated fixes precisely when the practitioner is detached from the broader sociopolitical context, whose study would allow for more grounded, less subjective notions of fairness.

On the other hand, studies like Lin et al. (2024) survey the challenges in developing "trustworthy" LLMs. They review various mitigation strategies to show that these solutions only partially address unfairness. Instead, the authors argue that ML fairness requires stakeholder oversight and adaptive governance. Notably, they link it to the infrastructural and organisational context of ML development. Yet, they do not address the power dynamics and political economies that shape both the design and deployment of LLMs, as well as biases in liberal definitions of "trustworthiness." Fairness is assumed to be attainable through a technocratic mix of technical and procedural measures, without questioning how liberal governance frameworks and their "elitist" and "marketised" cultures (Gill, 1995) influence ML practice and regulation.

Studies like Mehrabi et al. (2021) survey technical interventions across ML subfields, offering a useful "taxonomy for fairness definitions." They highlight technical challenges and trade-offs across criteria for eliminating bias, emphasising unresolved issues such as the need to shift conceptually from equality to equity. However, they do not address how models might be trained to reason about equity as a "contested concept,"[1] or how trainers might approach equity not through a static taxonomy of fairness but as a dynamic practice rooted in evolving struggles against deeper structures of inequity. Mehrabi et al.'s critique thus remains technical, treating fairness and equity as fairness deficiencies to be predicted in advance and resolved through training. As Mackenzie (2015) notes, prediction itself is not a technical problem but rather reflects what is made politically legible by the training method.

Equity is fundamentally contested and shaped by political strategies; without noting this, de-biasing remains inherently technocratic.

Moral Machines Approaches

This scholarship underscores a broader critique of "moral machine" approaches to fairness. Wallach and Allen (2009) recognise the complexity and context-dependence of moral dilemmas, arguing that neither the "top-down" imposition of rules onto AI nor "bottom-up" training in moral reasoning is sufficient. Instead, moral machines should synthesise the ability to handle ambiguity with the capacity to negotiate conflicting moral demands through interdisciplinary training and oversight by philosophers and practitioners. However, their nuanced approach remains within the liberal-technocratic framework of translating established moral philosophies—deontology, utilitarianism, virtue ethics, care ethics—into technical architectures and cross-disciplinary frameworks. It ultimately misinterprets moral reasoning: morality is not merely a set of context-sensitive rules for navigating ethical ambiguity, but also serves as a tool for political strategies that determine which context or valence merits ethical consideration in the first place.

Similarly, Anderson and Anderson (2011) argue for moving beyond "plug-and-play" ethics (à la pre-processing) or "after-the-fact" corrections (à la post-processing). They suggest that careful engineering of ethics into machines can achieve the consistency in morality that humans often lack. Notably, they anticipate an in-processing approach to adaptable notions of equity by treating in-processing itself as an opportunity to investigate the ethics of philosophers and practitioners involved in ML. Nevertheless, their framework overlooks that some moral dilemmas are not merely contextual but concern whether the context itself—shaped by state, capital, coloniality, and heteronormativity—must be restructured for equity. While ML philosophers and practitioners are not required to change the world, their models must grasp the difference between fairness in the context of how things are and how they ought to be.

Faith in overengineering ethics into ML is proceduralist in logic and leaves little room for Gen AI capable of problematising equity itself.

STS Approaches

In contrast, critical approaches from STS shift ML from concerns with technics and ethics to the "sociotechnical," questioning whether Gen AI can fully capture the sociopolitical complexities of equitability (e.g., Benjamin, 2019; Noble, 2018; Eubanks, 2018). Researchers, such as Selbst et al. (2019), identify common "abstraction traps" in ML theory and practice, including indifference to context, a lack of structural approaches to equity, and assumptions about universal fairness. However, their meta-critical perspective, while insightful, offers only a general framework for sociotechnical awareness. It is broadly applicable but not specifically helpful in addressing the technical and conceptual challenges of developing fair ML. Sociotechnical generalisation limits its traction within specific Gen AI subfields and practices.

Bellanova et al. (2021) trace "algorithmic violence" to the coercive infrastructures needed to render the world machine-readable, such as enforcing visual recognition as a condition for accessing UN services in the Global South. The authors map algorithmic violence as a distributed, multi-layered process across three axes: (1) violence through coercive "data infrastructures"; (2) "semiotic violence" enacted through prejudiced machine vision; and (3) the legitimisation of such violence via discriminatory "governance frameworks." They call for reflexive and multi-modal research that considers the entire sociotechnical assemblage. Yet, anticipating my critique of the "black box" paradigm, the authors acknowledge that their broad critique risks conflating circumstantial, AI-related violence with "algorithmic" violence. Thus, it lacks a clear concept of what precisely and historically constitutes algorithmic violence. As a result, the authors do not specify how this violence differs qualitatively from other forms of technopolitical violence. For example, it is unclear how AI-related semiotic violence differs from earlier systems, such as the Henry Classification System, which transformed physiological traits into bureaucratic signs for colonial surveillance and labour control.

In these socio-technological critiques, the "socio" aspect of the analysis overshadows the "technical," without clarifying how AI fundamentally alters the relationship between the two.

CSS Approaches

A fourth, overlapping body of work in CSS examines how technical systems influence social and political dynamics. Aradau and Blanke (2017) analyse how ML techniques such as "anomaly detection" shape new categories of risk and suspicion. They argue that while classical statistics presupposes the form and location of "the norm" and treats deviations as noise or error, ML uncovers entirely new clusters and patterns, through which unforeseen anomalies emerge as radical artefacts. This is a useful distinction but highlights a methodological difference rather than a new logic of abnormality: ML can discover anomalies only within what has already been made learnable, i.e., data filtered through social, political, and technical choices. Crucially, the anomaly is co-produced by the model's analytic framework for mapping data, which, like classical statistics, already encodes assumptions about what is "typical" and what is not. The authors neither address these facts nor offer theoretical or empirical reasons for how ML radically reconfigures "othering" through sheer algorithmic mediation.

Similarly, Suchman (2020) argues that while integrating ML into US military targeting systems markets itself as a morally unambiguous era of algorithmic "precision," it only intensifies and legitimises dehumanising violence. They highlight the prejudiced "apparatus of recognition" embedded in institutional rhetoric, marketing materials, and ethnographic vignettes of the US military's algorithmic warfare. Nevertheless, they do not demonstrate how ML qualitatively changes warfare, rather than merely amplifying it quantitatively, beyond existing military norms and operations that inevitably find their way into targeting systems. As a result, their concept of "algorithmic warfare" only broadens the customary black box critique to now include the opacity of sensors, data, and institutional imperatives for automation. In doing so, it collapses two distinct domains: the sociopolitical choice of whom to target and the technical execution of ML-based targeting.

While algorithmic warfare is violent and dehumanising, its ML component primarily grapples with strictly technical challenges, such as mapping chaotic, data-scarce environments, including how to recognise vehicular movement as "erratic driving." This technique is neither inherently dehumanising before its political operationalisation nor "opaquely" reconstructed by ML itself without human mediation. Conflating these domains blurs the line between institutional mechanisms that securitise bodies and the technical operations used to detect them.

Anticipating this critique, Amoore (2023) argues that ML itself reorders the relationship between political problems and solutions. For example, rather than identifying a social need and developing a policy to address it, employing ML in governance risks this scenario: beginning with a desired outcome and treating related issues as technical glitches to be managed post hoc by AI. This retroactive approach transforms governance into technocratic optimisation, where social and political problems become apolitical signals for refining the model. In this way, Amoore portrays ML as an epistemic black box that displaces rule-based orders and limits alternative political futures by rendering every issue a challenge in model optimisation—an autonomous and opaque process detached from institutional accountability and structural change. However, while her key example, the UK Home Office's visa-streaming algorithm, aims to show that ML perpetuates racialisation even after racist inputs are eliminated, it more clearly illustrates that the model merely followed institutional objectives. For example, once nationality data was removed, it targeted other features, such as travel history, to meet pre-set quotas. Such discrimination is political and institutional before it is technical; the model's flexibility is not a sign of political closure but of functional alignment with institutional aims.[2]

By treating ML as the root of political closure, these approaches portray ML architectures as fundamentally problematic and obscure the potential sites for technical and political intervention.

TOWARDS A LEFTIST AI FOR GEOPOLITICAL PREDICTION

Two critical observations emerge from this survey. First, the above currents oscillate between technical proceduralism and broad sociological indictment, with limited exchange across the divide. Second, this disciplinary siloing reflects a more profound lack of workable theories and practices for implementing radical equitability. Criticising Gen AI's amplification of bias is one thing; addressing why radical equitability remains institutionally and structurally elusive in the age of AI is another.

For instance, Gajane and Pechenizkiy (2018) survey how fairness is formalised in the de-biasing literature, mapping each method onto underlying theories of social justice to clarify their limitations in achieving equitable outcomes. The alternative they highlight, "equality of capability," compensates for differences in an individual's ability to turn opportunities into valued outcomes, approximating a strategic approach to equity in ML. Still, it merits two objections: determining which capabilities matter is a political decision, and realising them depends on infrastructural prioritisation across various social arenas. This chapter and other literature offer few clarifications on such questions and concerns.

It is precisely in these cross-disciplinary, institutional arenas that the social sciences and humanities lack adequate concepts and practices for implementing radical equity.

The State of ML in Political Science

Since I cannot address all such shortcomings, I focus on Political Science to highlight an issue in this discipline's ML approaches to geopolitical prediction. Consistent with my argument, I do not pursue a so-called fair approach, which I find alchemical in both logic and aspiration—doing so would be to expect machines to achieve what humans have yet to articulate. Instead, I cultivate leftist tendencies in the models I train, aiming to instil a self-critical bias in their reasoning process against the "strategic cultures" inherited from their original training data and regimen. My intervention is thereby transparent about its political bias and site-specific regarding what requires intervention.

Political science views strategic cultures as pragmatic constructs for navigating contentious political processes—such as planning nuclear deterrence capabilities—which accumulate as conservative or radical archives of advisable strategy (Poore, 2003; Bloomfield, 2012). Embedded in various strategic mindsets such as "how we act as Canadians" or "how to carry oneself in scholarly disputes," they encompass both national and institutional "subcultures." What they culturally transmit is not only practical know-how for managing adversities but also what and who are regarded as practical and adversarial. They influence all processes involving contestation, such as our understanding of threats and conflicts, their seriousness, and the mechanisms of causation and resolution.

However, contemporary strategic cultures need reassessment, not only due to their infiltration by the zero-sum logic of neoliberalism (Gill, 1995; Sum & Jessop, 2015), but also because the influence of national subcultures on strategic ideation and behaviour remains underexplored in the age of AI (Libel, 2020; Farrell & Payne, 2023). For example, it is generally understood that American strategic culture is shaped by instrumental warfare and a winner-takes-all approach to adversaries (Johnson, 2020; Harris, 2014), while Chinese culture is influenced by threat vigilance and the attribution of justice to that stance (Johnston, 1996; Ashraf, 2017). What demands more attention is how these subcultures bias the ML-based models trained by China's Ministry of Foreign Affairs or the US Department of Defence for geopolitical prediction ("Enterprise AI," 2023). For example, if a Chinese model interprets the winner-takes-all American behaviour through the lens of justified self-defence, it will likely produce alarming forecasts.

Researchers highlight this bias (Cuomo et al., 2020; Bryce et al., 2020) but focus on two issues: first, "mirror-imaging," or mistaking one's own strategic culture for the adversary's—i.e., projecting our strategic insecurities onto others—and second, the "exploitation" of its weaknesses by an opponent (Goldfarb & Lindsay, 2021)—i.e., others taking advantage of our strategic insecurities. Neither addresses the bias inherited from the developer's strategic culture during the in-processing phase of ML. Even when researchers emphasise human "oversight" of Gen AI as a remedy (Colaresi & Mahmood, 2017), they overlook the impact of the overseer's strategic culture on the supervisory process.

An Alternative Equitable AI for Geopolitical Prediction

Inspired by my revisions to "leftist strategic cultures" (Oveisy, 2022, 2025), the LLM I am currently fine-tuning addresses these concerns. Unlike training with processed data, "fine-tuning" reshapes the in-processing instincts of trained models through carefully guided human interaction. While it can filter out kernels of original data bias, it can also sensitise the model's intuitive reasoning to issues such as equity in geopolitical prediction. Falcon-H1 is ideal for this method because its State-Space Model (SSM) architecture updates its internal sense of direction as it proceeds through its reasoning process. It is akin to walking through a forest and adjusting course with each turn, thus enabling the fine-tuner to rework how the model reasons through contested, context-sensitive processes. Capable of mapping its reasoning in this way, the model can be taught to interrogate the strategic cultures inherited from its original trainers regarding threat perception and prediction, and to reflect on its predictive logic in response to self-evaluation.

To achieve this, I employ a layered feedback loop during the fine-tuning process. It guides the model to recognise and reason through six distinct levels of mediation, which I define as the predominant historical mechanisms and subjectivities that influence, co-opt, or resist political conflict and agency. These layers are: (1) material forces, including labour, racial, and gender relations; (2) intra-capitalist crises and conflicts, including divisions among ruling classes and between states; (3) hegemonic discourses and apparatuses that legitimise these relations and conflicts, such as neoliberal global governance; (4) the ways capital reorganises itself in response to crises and conflicts through wars, policies, and multilateral arrangements; (5) leftist counter-hegemonic strategies, or the influence of radical movements on crises and conflicts; and (6) uncertainty, which involves recognising moments when the future is unknown or indeterminate.

During fine-tuning, the model receives feedback—a kind of score—based on questions posed to it during a Socratic dialogue with the trainer. For each of the six layers, I assess whether the model recognises the correct crisis or conflict (e.g., whether it is an inter- or intra-capitalist conflict), whether it identifies the historical actors or mechanisms involved (such as specific governments, companies, and policies), and whether it demonstrates an understanding of scale and time (e.g., whether it differentiates between short-term triggers and long-term trends). The model can receive a full or partial grade for each level—complex reasoning is rewarded and lapses penalised—and the compounded score from all layers and sublayers becomes the signal the model uses to adjust its behaviour.

This approach cultivates intricate reasoning patterns and embeds a nuanced intuition for how various historical mediation mechanisms influence the outcomes of crises and conflicts in the model's reasoning process. Specifically, since this method requires the model to consistently connect micro- and macro-level details into system-wide snapshots, it encourages the SSM modules to retain the subtleties and uncertainties inherent in multi-layered assessments. The result is a model better equipped to recognise contradictions, countercurrents, and contingencies that shape global crises and conflicts—using complexity as a foundation for predicting how history might unfold. Its strategic culture of conflict prediction involves deconstructing and historicising multiple material and ideological currents, thereby prioritising complexity in prediction over immediate speed, accuracy, and clarity.

I advocate for this approach over the likes of D'Orazio and Lin's (2022) "AutoML" model, which demonstrates predictive accuracy by mapping patterns of violence in Africa but depends on prepackaged, automated ML providers for its architecture. Its success comes at the cost of reducing conflicts to statistical artefacts abstracted from local and structural dynamics. Marketed as "excellent benchmarks for theory building," the model sidelines theory altogether, replacing critical interpretability with sheer pattern recognition. The outcome is algorithmic inequity: African conflicts are rendered predictable in the short term and stripped of sociopolitical complexity, making them safe for the positivist and result-driven strategies of neoliberal think tanks and policy institutions.

Changing ML's strategic culture involves rethinking and reworking how it reasons about prediction. Instead of adopting the strategic cultures of the state's security apparatuses in tasks such as conflict prediction, Gen AI models must learn to challenge what kind of future is being forecast, for whom, and towards what purpose.

CONCLUSION

Radically equitable AI will not emerge from liberal fairness metrics or technical de-biasing. Instead, it must be trained to question the cultural logics it inherits. This, in turn, requires institutional cultures and infrastructures that support a counter-hegemonic approach. After all, it is hegemonic institutional cultures and infrastructures that enable the technical and epistemic flattening of the kinds discussed in this chapter: a mode of production that privileges liberal critiques monetised by corporate academia and positivist output endorsed by policy institutions. Building AI capable of radical equity demands cultures and infrastructures that reject this apparatus and foster the theoretical and technical foundations needed for the radical, cross-disciplinary efforts that equitable endeavours truly require.

ACKNOWLEDGEMENT

Portions of this chapter were developed with the assistance of Grammarly for editing. All intellectual contributions, interpretations, and final editorial decisions are the authors' own, and the authors take full responsibility for the content. Any AI-assisted or AI-generated material was reviewed and verified by the authors.

REFLECTION QUESTIONS

1. Why does the author argue that equitability must be learned during the in-processing phase rather than enforced through pre-processing or post-processing?
2. How do strategic cultures (e.g., state or capitalist logics) shape the way AI models predict geopolitical conflict?
3. What is the limitation of liberal fairness metrics in addressing the deeper structural injustices inherent in geopolitical analysis?
4. How can an AI model be fine-tuned to problematise its own reasoning and challenge hegemonic assumptions about threat and security?

NOTES

1 "Equity" is widely treated as a politically contested concept (Collier et al., 2006). Public-health reviews document "a lack of consensus" on how to measure equity (Braveman & Gruskin, 2003); education researchers find stakeholders advancing contested understandings of what equity entails (Freidus & Turner, 2023); and development-health studies note that the term "means different things to different people" (Kapiriri & Razavi, 2022). Espinoza (2007) traces decades of disagreement over whether the goal is need, potential, or achievement.

2 Lipsky (2010) shows that human officers behave similarly in response to quotas.

REFERENCES

Aradau, C., & Blanke, T. (2017). Governing others: Anomaly and the algorithmic subject of security. *European Journal of International Security, 2*(1), 1–21.

Amoore, L. (2023). Machine learning political orders. *Economy and Society, 52*(1), 19–44.

Anderson, M., & Anderson, S. L. (2011). *Machine ethics*. Cambridge University Press.

Ashraf, J. (2017). String of pearls and China's emerging strategic culture. *Strategic Studies, 37*(4), 166–181.

Bellanova, R., Irion, K., & Yeung, K. (2021). Toward a critique of algorithmic violence. *Philosophy & Technology, 34*(1), 121–138.

Benjamin, R. (2019). *Race after technology: Abolitionist tools for the New Jim Code*. Polity Press.

Bloomfield, A. (2012). Time to move on: Reconceptualising the strategic-culture debate. *Contemporary Security Policy, 33*(3), 437–461.

Braveman, P., & Gruskin, S. (2003). Defining equity in health. *Journal of Epidemiology & Community Health, 57*(4), 254–258.

Bryce, H., Cukier, K., Cummings, M. L., Parakilas, J., & Roff, H. (2020). *Artificial intelligence and international affairs: Disruption anticipated (Research Paper)*. Chatham House.

Buyl, K., & Di Bie, T. (2024). Inherent limitations of AI fairness [Preprint]. arXiv.

Chen, R., Yang, J., Xiong, H., Bai, J., Hu, T., Hao, J., … Liu, Z. (2023). Fast model debias with machine unlearning. In *Proceedings of the 37th Conference on Neural Information Processing Systems* (NeurIPS 2023).

Colaresi, M., & Mahmood, Z. (2017). Do the robot: Lessons from machine learning to improve conflict forecasting. *Journal of Peace Research, 54*(2), 193–214.

Collier, D., Hidalgo, F. D., & Maciuceanu, A. O. (2006). Essentially contested concepts: Debates and applications. *Journal of Political Ideologies, 11*(3), 211–246.

Crawford, K. (2021). *Atlas of AI: Power, politics, and the planetary costs of artificial intelligence*. Yale University Press.

Cuomo, S., Jensen, B. M., & Whyte, C. (2020). United States Marine Corps algorithms at war: The promise, peril, and limits of artificial intelligence. *International Studies Review, 22*, 526–550.

D'Orazio, V., & Lin, Y. (2022). Forecasting conflict in Africa with automated machine-learning systems. *International Interactions, 48*(4), 714–738.

Espinoza, O. (2007). Solving the equity–equality conceptual dilemma: A new model for analysis of the educational process. *Educational Research, 49*(4), 343–363.

Eubanks, V. (2018). *Automating inequality: How high-tech tools profile, police, and punish the poor*. St. Martin's Press.

Farrell, F., & Payne, K. (2023). Artificial intelligence and strategic culture. In K. M. Kartchner, B. D. Bowen, & J. L. Johnson (Eds.), *Routledge handbook of strategic culture* (pp. 470–484). Routledge.

Freidus, A., & Turner, E. O. (2023). Contested justice: Rethinking educational equity through New York City's COVID-19 school reopening debates. *Educational Evaluation and Policy Analysis, 45*(3), 437–463. https://doi.org/10.3102/01623737221121802

Gajane, P., & Pechenizkiy, M. (2018). On formalizing fairness in prediction with machine learning arXiv.

Gill, S. (1995). Globalisation, market civilisation and disciplinary neoliberalism. *Millennium: Journal of International Studies, 24*(3), 399–423.

Gitelman, L., & Jackson, V. (2013). Introduction. In L. Gitelman (Ed.), *"Raw data" is an oxymoron* (pp 1–14). MIT Press.

Goldfarb, A., & Lindsay, J. (2021). Prediction and judgment: Why artificial intelligence increases the importance of humans in war. *International Security, 46*(3), 7–50.

Harris, B. F. (2014). United States strategic culture and Asia-Pacific security. *Contemporary Security Policy, 35*(2), 290–309.

Hindman, M. (2015). Building better models: Prediction, replication, and machine learning in the social sciences. *The Annals of the American Academy of Political and Social Science, 659*(1), 48–62.

Johnson, J. L. (2020). Fit for future conflict? American strategic culture in the context of great-power competition. *Journal of Advanced Military Studies, 11*(1), 185–208.

Johnston, A. (1996). Cultural realism and strategy in Maoist China. In P. J. Katzenstein (Ed.), *The culture of national security: Norms and identity in world politics* (pp. 216–256). Columbia University Press.

Kapiriri, L., & Razavi, S. D. (2022). Equity, justice, and social values in priority setting: A qualitative study of resource-allocation criteria for global donor organizations working in low-income countries. *International Journal for Equity in Health, 21*, Article 17.

Libel, T. (2020). Rethinking strategic culture: A computational (social-science) discursive-'institutionalist approach. *Journal of Strategic Studies, 43*(5), 686–709.

Lin, J., Zhao, W., Wang, Z., Li, Y., Wang, M., & Tang, J. (2024). Towards trustworthy LLMs: A survey [Preprint]. arXiv.

Lipsky, M. (2010). *Street-level bureaucracy: Dilemmas of the individual in public services* (30th anniversary expanded ed.). Russell Sage Foundation.

Lum, K., & Isaac, W. (2016). To predict and serve? *Significance, 13*(5), 14–19.

Mackenzie, A. (2015). The production of prediction: What does machine learning want? *European Journal of Cultural Studies, 18*(4–5), 429–445.

Mehrabi, N., Morstatter, F., Saxena, N., Lerman, K., & Galstyan, A. (2021). A survey on bias and fairness in machine learning. *ACM Computing Surveys, 54*(6), Article 115.

Noble, S. U. (2018). *Algorithms of oppression: How search engines reinforce racism*. New York University Press.

Oveisy, F. (2022, December). *Farewell, rojava: The philosophical case for strategic thinking as a democratic necessity*. Philosophy, World, Democracy. PWD. https://www.philosophy-world-democracy.org/posts/article/farewell-rojava-the-philosophical-case-for-strategic-thinking-as-a-democratic-necessity

Oveisy, F. (2025). Toward a folklore of the left. *Cultural Critique, 127*, 138–176.

Poore, S. (2003). What is the context? A reply to the Gray-Johnston debate on strategic culture. *Review of International Studies, 29*(2), 279–284.

Selbst, A. D., Boyd, D., Friedler, S. A., Venkatasubramanian, S., & Vertesi, J. (2019). Fairness and abstraction in sociotechnical systems. In *Proceedings of the 2019 Conference on Fairness, Accountability, and Transparency,* New York (pp. 59–68). Association for Computing Machinery.

Suchman, L. (2020). Algorithmic warfare and the reinvention of accuracy. *Critical Studies on Security,* 8(2), 175–187.

Sum, N.-L., & Jessop, B. (2015). *Towards a cultural political economy: Putting culture in its place in political economy*. Edward Elgar.

U.S. Department of State. (2023). *Enterprise AI strategy: Empowering diplomacy through responsible AI.*

Wallach, W., & Allen, C. (2009). *Moral machines: Teaching robots right from wrong*. Oxford University Press.

21 Algorithmic Border Securitization

The Datafied Migrant at the Canada-U.S. Border

Mina Mir and Andrea Lachmansingh

INTRODUCTION

In an era of intensifying global migration and rising authoritarianism, borders function as sites where the most vulnerable populations become subjects of technological experimentation, their bodies and lives transformed into data points for AI (Artificial Intelligence)-driven control and exclusion (Aradau, 2023). The convergence of biometric identification (Amoore, 2006) transnational data-sharing (Olwig et al., 2019), and today, AI (Molnar, 2019; Molnar & Muscati, 2018), has fundamentally reshaped how sovereignty is exercised and contested, representing what we theorize as *algorithmic border securitization*—a mode of governance where state power operates through predictive classification and migrant bodies become sites of continuous data extraction through carceral logics of "risk."

This transformation is particularly acute along highly surveilled frontiers like the Canada-U.S. border, where decades of bilateral security "cooperation" have produced the infrastructural conditions for experimental AI-driven governance (Topak et al., 2015; Deibert, 2020; Molnar, 2025a). Canada's recent legislative and policy initiatives such as *Bill C-2*, the *Strong Borders Act* (2025), introduced by recently elected Prime Minster Mark Carney, propose to institutionalize racialized technological experimentation, transforming the border into a site of carceral migration governance (Molnar & Gill, 2018). Drawing on critical data studies, critical migration studies, and critical security studies—particularly securitization theory—we ask: *How do AI-driven border technologies function as mechanisms of racialized control that extend imperial logics of expulsion while being legitimized through discourses of techno-securitization?*

We argue that Canadian immigration governance has been shifting towards algorithmic border securitization, expanding the state's authority to extract and share biometric data, while exacerbating practices that disproportionately target BIPOC (Black, Indigenous, and Persons of Colour) bodies, and especially, technoprecarious migrants (Precarity Lab, 2020). These developments produce the *datafied migrant:* a concept tracing how migrant personhood is fragmented into machine-readable data points, including fingerprints, facial images, iris scans, gait patterns, and digital traces such as travel histories or social media activity within a securitized, racialized, and increasingly automated border regime (Mayer-Schönberger & Cukier, 2013). While Canada positions itself as a global leader in responsible AI governance (Brandusescu, 2025, p. 5), Bill C-2 exposes how these ethical frameworks mask the deployment of carceral surveillance technologies against marginalized communities and migrants.

SECURITIZING THE ALGORITHMIC BORDER: ANALYTICAL FRAMEWORK

In their foundational work, *Security: A New Framework for Analysis*, Buzan et al. (1998) define securitization as a process wherein an issue is framed as an existential threat, thereby "requiring

DOI: 10.1201/9781003737810-25

emergency measures and justifying actions outside the normal bounds of political procedure" (p. 24). Central to their approach is the understanding that security is not an "objective" condition but a sociopolitical construction invoked not because a threat necessarily exists, but because the issue is *presented* as such (p. 24). The "standard" process of securitization can be summarized as follows: securitizing actor(s) rhetorically present a referent subject (threats) as a security issue for referent objects (entity that is threatened), gaining audience assent in a specific context, thereby leading to the adoption of exceptional political procedures. A frequently cited example of this process is George W. Bush's successful framing of Saddam Hussein as possessing "weapons of mass destruction," an enduring narrative that has mobilized public support for war (Balzacq et al., 2016, p. 495).

Critical securitization theory has highlighted that the "boundaries between security and insecurity" must be problematized, advocating an approach that considers "security" as encompassing both discourse *and* practices (Bigo, 2001; Bigo & McCluskey, 2018, p. 117). This securitizing logic is evident in the Trump administration's framing of fentanyl as not only a public health "crisis" but also as a top national security threat undermining both U.S. and Canadian sovereignty and border integrity (Mann, 2025). Fentanyl has become the symbol of foreign intrusion, framed by the U.S. administration as "pour[ing] in" from Canada, Mexico, and China—a narrative with deep roots in the racialized drugs panics of the 20th century, including the Anti-Opium policies targeting Chinese communities, and the Reagan-era "War on Drugs," which targeted Black communities (Gordon, 2006). The Trump administration's discourse around fentanyl is a classic securitizing move, wherein a sociopolitical issue is transformed into an existential threat. A key aspect of securitization is when an actor invokes the language of emergency or exceptionalism to legitimize extraordinary measures beyond normal political bounds—measures which often rely on imperialism and racism. Much of this is taking place using cues from a tried-and-tested playbook: especially striking is the fact that in recent years, Republicans began describing fentanyl as a "weapon of mass destruction," introducing the *Fentanyl is a WMD Act* (2025), and declaring it to be a "national emergency" through Executive Order No. 14226 (2025).

Trump's March 2025 Truth Social post blamed "Governor Justin Trudeau" for allowing "tremendous amounts of Fentanyl, and Illegal Aliens, to pour into the United States" due to "Weak Border Policies" (Trump, 2025). Such a securitizing rhetorical event (equating fentanyl with "weak borders") has been used to justify the mobilization of military border enforcement immigration measures and exceptionally intrusive biometric surveillance, resulting in algorithmic border securitization. This securitizing speech act was reinforced by former Prime Minister Trudeau's characterization of fentanyl as a "scourge" that "must be wiped from the face of the earth," a framing that closely mirrors Trump's rhetoric (Buckley, 2025). As Buzan et al. (1998) remind us, "the process of securitization is… a speech act… By saying the words, something is done" (26).

CASE STUDY: AI AND BORDER SECURITIZATION IN CANADA

Canada's evolving border infrastructure increasingly relies on AI tools to sort, monitor, and exclude datafied migrants. Two cases typify how AI operates as a tool of racialized exclusion in North American border governance: the use of facial recognition to revoke refugee status in *Barre v Canada (2022)* and the deployment of Mobile Fortify for real-time identification in U.S. immigration enforcement.

Barre v Canada (2022) was the first legal case to expose IRCC's (Immigration, Refugees and Citizenship Canada) use of FRT (facial recognition technology), demonstrating how it operates as a tool of racialized surveillance within Canada's refugee system. The Federal Court heard the case of two Somali women whose successful refugee claims were vacated after the Minister of Public Safety and Emergency Preparedness alleged that they had misrepresented their identities, claiming to be Somali citizens when they were purportedly Kenyan nationals (Christian, 2023, 2024a). The allegation was based on an IRCC photo comparison that matched the women's images to those of individuals who had entered Canada as international students from Kenya. At the Federal Court level, the women argued that Clearview AI FRT had been used, citing research from the Citizen Lab, which documented how the CBSA (Canada Border Services Agency) and RCMP (Royal Canadian Mounted Police) share immigration data through these systems. They also referenced the *Gender Shades* study by Joy Buolamwini and Timnit Gebru (2018), which revealed discriminatory error rates for people of colour in FRT, submitting that the photos could not establish with any degree of certainty that they were the alleged Kenyan students (*Barre v Canada*, 2022).

The women's suspicions about Clearview AI use reflect broader concerns about Canada's reliance on controversial commercial surveillance platforms. Clearview AI built one of the world's largest facial recognition databases with over 20 billion images harvested from social networks and public platforms without consent. Despite being found in violation of provincial and federal privacy laws, at least 48 Canadian law enforcement agencies used Clearview AI's technology (Harwell, 2022; Canada, 2021). While Clearview AI no longer permits use of their technology in Canada following regulatory pressure, the company has declined to delete existing photos of Canadians from their database (Canada, 2021), illustrating how commercial surveillance platforms operate beyond regulatory reach—a dynamic that the *Barre (2022)* case exposes in the immigration context.

The Minister of Citizenship and Immigration's response in *Barre (2022)* demonstrated the accountability evasion strategies endemic to algorithmic border control: rather than defending the technology's accuracy, the RPD (Refugee Protection Division) invoked sec. 22(2) of the *Privacy Act* (1985), arguing that law enforcement agencies should be permitted to protect investigative details (*Barre v Canada*, 2022). Although the court could not confirm Clearview AI's specific use due to this government secrecy, the case established a precedent where discriminatory FRT could be deployed to revoke refugee protection while remaining shielded from meaningful scrutiny (Christian, 2024b). This accountability evasion demonstrates why responsible AI governance must extend beyond the algorithm itself to include the government institutions and commercial vendors who design, deploy, and operationalize these systems (Martin, 2019) to transform migrant lives into algorithmic risk profiles rather than protecting humans with rights.

This pattern of algorithmic exclusion also extends beyond Canada's borders, as evidenced by the U.S. Immigration and Customs Enforcement's (ICE) deployment of Mobile Fortify, a smartphone application that enables real-time facial recognition and fingerprint scanning directly from officers' devices. Mobile Fortify connects to Department of Homeland Security biometric repositories containing over 200 million images, enabling rapid matches against federal immigration, law enforcement, and travel records (Cox, 2025; Burman & Rahman, 2025). Complementing these field identification capabilities is ICE's Investigative Case Management (ICM) database, developed by Palantir Technologies under a $95.9 million contract (Koebler, 2025). Built on Palantir Gotham, which supports alerts, geospatial analysis, and prediction, which has been used as a predictive policing system (Rummage, 2025), ICM employs AI to analyse datafied migrants across hundreds of different categories, including resident status, physical characteristics, location data, country of origin, race, and employment across multiple federal databases. ICE agents can set automated queries that alert officers if an individual triggers specific search parameters, creating a system where algorithmic suspicion now replaces probable cause and datafied migrants face automated targeting based on AI predictions (Koebler, 2025). This corporate-government partnership demonstrates how algorithmic exclusion operates at an institutional scale, generating profits for private surveillance companies while systematically undermining legal protections for migrant communities through AI-powered discrimination.

The deployment of Mobile Fortify occurs within an escalating context of mass deportation campaigns that disproportionately target people of colour. Under the current Trump administration's renewed immigration enforcement policies, targeting of racialized communities has intensified, with individuals detained based on perceived ethnicity or accent. Once apprehended by ICE, individuals face prolonged detention in immigration facilities notorious for inhumane conditions (Human Rights Watch, 2025). This carceral infrastructure extends to the Florida detention complex dubbed "Alligator Alcatraz," where Quebec-based security firm GardaWorld has been awarded a US$8-million contract and over $100 million in Canadian government contracts—part of a broader pattern where transnational private security companies secure lucrative government contracts for experimental technologies marketed as border security innovations (Gilmore, 2025; Molnar, 2024, pp. 7–8). These practices demonstrate the acute risks posed when FRT like Mobile Fortify is integrated into field enforcement operations where officers make rapid identification decisions.

This enforcement context highlights how the technological convergence between Canadian and U.S. systems operates as what Bigo (2001, 2018) terms the *möbius ribbon*—a heuristic for understanding how algorithmic border regimes collapse the distinction between security and insecurity, protection and threat, inside and outside. This collapse is not abstract; Bill C-2—which, at the time of writing, is under its second reading—accelerates it by expanding biometric data-sharing and embedding Canadian systems into U.S.-accessible surveillance infrastructures while simultaneously restructuring immigration and refugee governance alongside broader surveillance powers. It amends multiple statutes—including the *Customs Act*, the *Criminal Code*, and the *Proceeds of Crime (Money Laundering) and Terrorist Financing Act*—to introduce new barriers to refugee claims, expand administrative powers to terminate cases, and grant Cabinet extraordinary authority to suspend immigration processes in the "public interest" (Rehaag et al., 2025, pp. 2–3). Most controversially, it enables routine inter-agency data-sharing and compels telecommunications providers to facilitate law enforcement access to digital communications with reduced judicial oversight—effectively normalizing expansive surveillance as routine governance (Canada, 2025). Such policy developments build on existing collaborative frameworks, including the Integrated Border Enforcement Teams created in 2001 to coordinate Canadian and U.S. law enforcement operations along the border (RCMP, 2025a, 2025b).

These cases highlight an increasingly borderless surveillance infrastructure where discriminatory technologies deployed by one state become accessible to enforcement agencies in both jurisdictions. *Barre* (2022) demonstrates how Canadian authorities can revoke refugee protection through commercial algorithmic matches, while Mobile Fortify shows how U.S. agencies can instantly query vast biometric databases to identify and target migrants in real time. The accountability gaps are mutually reinforcing—Canadian authorities' refusal to disclose photo comparison methodologies mirrors the opacity surrounding U.S. biometric systems, creating a surveillance apparatus that operates beyond oversight in either jurisdiction. This not only undermines principles of data sovereignty (Polatin-Reuben & Wright, 2014) but also, by routinizing algorithmic surveillance and carceral logics, extends the settler-colonial project. Bill C-2's expanded data-sharing provisions will formalize this technological convergence by enabling Canadian biometric data to flow seamlessly into U.S. repositories, potentially accessible through Mobile Fortify while evading the accountability mechanisms designed to protect migrant rights.

The stakes of this integration become clear when considering official acknowledgements of the scope of cooperation. As a Canadian government official candidly admitted regarding Bill C-2, the United States wants "to join arms in law enforcement with Canada…" (Mullin, 2025; Deibert, 2025). However, human rights groups and scholars argue that this cooperation comes at the expense of refugee rights and privacy protections, representing what they view as appeasing the Trump administration over upholding people's human rights (Rehaag et al., 2025, p. 7; Molnar, 2025b).

RACIALIZATION AND THE DATAFIED MIGRANT(S)

To understand how technologies like those deployed in *Barre* (2022) and Mobile Fortify operate as tools of racialized exclusion, it is essential to examine how the Canada-U.S. border has historically functioned as a liminal zone of ontological insecurity, where one's legitimacy is contingent upon racialized notions of "threat," belonging, and national identity. The border, in this sense, enacts a sorting mechanism through which the racial Other is positioned as out of place, subject to surveillance, suspicion, and sometimes purging.

The history of Canada's border securitization is steeped in racial hierarchies and exclusionary logics that forge and sustain an enduring link between race and criminality in service of preserving a white settler-colonial identity (Maynard, 2017). From the late 19th century through much of the 20th, immigration policies explicitly privileged white, Western Europeans while restricting or barring racialized groups. These restrictions include the *Chinese Immigration Act* (1923), the Komagata Maru rejection in 1914, and bans on Black migrants under the *Immigration Act* (1910), justified by claims that Black migrants were unsuited to the Canadian climate (Kelley & Trebilcock, 1998; Triadafilopoulos, 2013). Canada maintained an effectively Whites-only border regime until the introduction of a so-called race-neutral points system in the 1960s. However, the structural and institutional legacies of racialized immigration control have persisted in significant ways (Hall & Clapton, 2021). Canada's immigration history reveals how the state has long used exceptional mechanisms to securitize borders, establishing precedents for automated exclusion that would later be encoded into algorithmic systems. While contemporary immigration policy has abandoned explicit racial categories, the structural logic of racialized exclusion persists: In 2017, amidst the implementation of the Trump Administration's U.S. "Muslim Travel Ban" and broader climate of institutional Islamophobia, the RCMP was publicly condemned for distributing Islamophobic, religiously coded questionnaires amongst Muslim migrants on the border between Quebec and the United States (Oluwasanmi, 2021, p. 88). This securitization of Islamophobia creates the conditions for deploying increasingly automated technologies that promise objective risk assessment while operating through racialized logics of exclusion (Eroukhmanoff, 2018).

This securitized border regime increasingly operates through the datafied migrant, providing a way to "conceptualise the body made biometric," as Simone Browne (2010, p. 134) puts it. Automated and "intelligent" borders reduce the datafied migrant to data profiles that can be sorted, scored, and acted upon by automated systems. In this regime, as Petra Molnar (2024) observes, "the colour of your skin, the accent in your voice, and even your body become a passport," compounding intersectional harms (p. 2). Browne (2010) interrogates the racial politics of contemporary biometric surveillance technologies by introducing the concept of "digital epidermalization." Drawing on Frantz Fanon's notion of epidermalization—the process by which the racial body internally experiences racial hierarchy—Browne (2010) argues that biometric systems dissect the body into data points that become *digitally* epidermalized (pp. 133–134). Rather than functioning as neutral tools of identification, these technologies are embedded within and perpetuate the visual economies and epistemologies of race. The biometric body becomes a new site of racialization where skin is rendered into algorithmic data and judged against normative expectations shaped by whiteness. Within this understanding, the border becomes a space of "ontological insecurity," where one's legitimacy is contingent upon racialized notions of belonging and national identity. In such spaces, biometric identification functions less as a safeguard of citizenship than as a technology of exclusion and misrecognition.

Browne (2015) places biometric surveillance within a continuum of racialized state control, including slave branding, the plantation pass system, and colonial taxonomies of the body. These earlier systems similarly sought to fix identity through bodily markers and served to maintain power over mobility and subjecthood. Contemporary biometric databases—whether operated by the state or by private actors like Palantir or Clearview—extend this logic by fragmenting the body into data points (iris, gait, fingerprints), which are stored, compared, and circulated across borders. These theoretical insights emphasize the specific mechanisms observed in both the *Barre* (2022) case and Mobile Fortify deployment, where racialized bodies are rendered into algorithmic risk profiles subject to automated exclusion.

CONCLUSION

As exemplified by Bill C-2, the Canadian border regime has turned towards algorithmic securitization, further entrenching racialized surveillance and automating interdiction. The Trump administration's framing of fentanyl as an existential threat caused by "weak" Canadian borders has justified expanded surveillance and cross-border information sharing. Canada's AI-enabled migration governance, coupled with expanded ICE operations and deepening data-sharing commitments, anchors practices that systematically target technoprecarious migrants through biometric technologies and predictive analytics. This represents the digital evolution of settler-colonial exclusion—automated systems that render datafied migrants legible through algorithmic calculation rather than legal rights. While the full destructive potential remains unclear, confronting this reality requires dismantling systems that reduce migrant lives to algorithmic risk profiles rather than humans deserving of consent, accountability, and data sovereignty.

REFLECTION QUESTIONS

1. What is the datafied migrant, and how does this concept help us understand the dehumanizing effects of border technologies?
2. How does the integration of AI and biometric surveillance at the border extend the logic of settler-colonial exclusion?
3. Reflecting on the case of Barre vs. Canada, how does the opacity of FRT undermine the legal rights of refugees?
4. How do narratives of security and efficiency serve to legitimize the expansion of carceral surveillance technologies against racialized populations?

REFERENCES

Amoore, L. (2006). Biometric borders: Governing mobilities in the war on terror. *Political Geography*, *25*(3), 336–351. https://doi.org/10.1016/j.polgeo.2006.02.001

Aradau, C. (2023). Borders have always been artificial: Migration, data and AI. *International Migration*, *61*(5), 303–306. https://doi.org/10.1111/imig.13186

Balzacq, T., Léonard, S., & Ruzicka, J. (2016). 'Securitization' revisited: Theory and cases. *International Relations*, *30*(4), 494–531. https://doi.org/10.1177/0047117815596590

Barre v. Canada (Citizenship and Immigration), 2022 FC 1078 (CanLII), [2023] 1 FCR 275. (n.d.). https://www.canlii.org/en/ca/fct/doc/2022/2022fc1078/2022fc1078.html

Bigo, D. (2001). The Möbius ribbon of internal and external security(ies). In M. Albert, D. Jacobson, & Y. Lapid (Eds.), *Identities, borders, orders: Rethinking international relations theory* (pp. 91–116). University of Minnesota Press. https://www.jstor.org/stable/10.5749/j.ctttst8f

Bigo, D., & McCluskey, E. (2018). What is a paris approach to (In)securitization? Political anthropological research for international sociology. In A. Gheciu & W. C. Wohlforth (Eds.), *The oxford handbook of international security* (1st ed., pp. 116–130). Oxford University Press. https://doi.org/10.1093/oxfordhb/9780198777854.013.9

Bill C-2: An Act respecting certain measures relating to the security of the border between Canada and the United States and respecting other related security measures. (2025). 1st Reading June 3, 2025, 45th Parliament, 1st session. Retrieved from the Parliament of Canada website: https://www.parl.ca/DocumentViewer/en/45-1/bill/C-2/first-reading

Brandusescu, A. (2025). The Challenges of Accountability in AI for Immigration: The IRCC and Canadian AI Governance. *Balsillie Case Studies*.

Browne, S. (2010). Digital epidermalization: Race, identity and biometrics. *Critical Sociology*, *36*(1), 131–150. https://doi.org/10.1177/0896920509347144

Browne, S. (2015). *Dark Matters: On the Surveillance of Blackness*. Duke University Press.

Buckley, C. (2025, July 3). U.S. report finds fentanyl crossing from Canada 'not an important part of this story.' *CTV News*. https://www.ctvnews.ca/canada/article/canada-supplies-nearly-zero-per-cent-of-fentanyl-seized-in-us-report/

Buolamwini, J., & Gebru, T. (2018). Gender Shades: Intersectional Accuracy Disparities in Commercial Gender Classification. *Proceedings of the 1st Conference on Fairness, Accountability and Transparency*, 77–91. https://proceedings.mlr.press/v81/buolamwini18a.html

Burman, T., & Rahman, B. (2025, June 27). Are ICE Agents Using Facial Recognition Phone App? What We Know. *Newsweek*. https://www.newsweek.com/ice-face-recognition-app-deportations-phone-immigration-2091619

Buzan, B., Wæver, O., & Wilde, J. de. (1998). *Security: A New Framework for Analysis*. Lynne Rienner Publishers.

Canada. (2025, January 15). *Securing the Canada-U.S. Border: Actions and Outcomes to Date* [Policies]. https://www.canada.ca/en/services/defence/securingborder/strengthen-border-security/securing-canada-us-border-to-date.html

Canada, Office of the Privacy Commissioner (OPC). (2021, February 3). PIPEDA Findings #2021-001: Joint investigation of Clearview AI, Inc. by the Office of the Privacy Commissioner of Canada, the Commission d'accès à l'information du Québec, the Information and Privacy Commissioner for British Columbia, and the Information Privacy Commissioner of Alberta. https://www.priv.gc.ca/en/opc-actions-and-decisions/investigations/investigations-into-businesses/2021/pipeda-2021-001/

Christian, G. (2023, August 29). *AI Facial Recognition Technology in the Canadian Immigration System | Canadian Immigration Lawyers Association (CILA)*. https://cila.co/ai-facial-recognition-technology-in-the-canadian-immigration-system/

Christian, G. (2024a). *The New Jim Crow: Unmasking Racial Bias in AI Facial Recognition Technology within the Canadian Immigration System* (SSRN Scholarly Paper No. 4846967). Social Science Research Network. https://doi.org/10.2139/ssrn.4846967

Christian, G. (2024b, November 4). CBSA Border Surveillance: The Dangerous Expansion of Facial Recognition Technology | Canadian Immigration Lawyers Association (CILA). https://cila.co/cbsa-border-surveillance-the-dangerous-expansion-of-facial-recognition-technology/

Cox, J. (2025, July 17). *Inside ICE's Supercharged Facial Recognition App of 200 Million Images*. 404 Media. https://www.404media.co/inside-ices-supercharged-facial-recognition-app-of-200-million-images/

Deibert, R. (2020). *Reset: Reclaiming the internet for civil society*. House of Anansi Press Inc.

Deibert, R. (2025, March 12). The U.S. Wants Canada to Become A Police State. *Macleans.ca*. https://macleans.ca/politics/the-u-s-wants-canada-to-become-a-police-state/

Eroukhmanoff, C. (2018). 'It's not a Muslim ban!' Indirect speech acts and the securitisation of Islam in the United States post-9/11. *Global Discourse*, *8*(1), 5–25. https://doi.org/10.1080/23269995.2018.1439873

Exec. Order No. 14226, 90 Fed. Reg. 11369 (March 2, 2025).

Fentanyl Is a WMD Act, H.R.128, 119th Congress. (2025). https://www.congress.gov/bill/119th-congress/house-bill/128/all-info

Gilmore, R. (2025, August 8). The Canadian Company Staffing 'Alligator Alcatraz.' *The Tyee*. Retrieved August 11, 2025, from https://thetyee.ca/Opinion/2025/08/08/Canadian-Company-Staffing-Alligator-Alcatraz/

Gordon, T. (2006). Neoliberalism, racism, and the war on drugs in Canada. *Social Justice, 33*(1 (103)), 59–78. https://www.jstor.org/stable/29768352

Government of Canada. (2025). *Strengthening border security*. https://www.canada.ca/en/services/defence/securingborder/strengthen-border-security.html#s1

Hall, L. B., & Clapton, W. (2021). Programming the machine: Gender, race, sexuality, AI, and the construction of credibility and deceit at the border. *Internet Policy Review*, *10*(4), 1–23. https://doi.org/10.14763/2021.4.1601

Harwell, D. (2022, February 16). Facial recognition firm Clearview AI tells investors it's seeking massive expansion beyond law enforcement. *The Washington Post*. https://www.washingtonpost.com/technology/2022/02/16/clearview-expansion-facial-recognition/

Human Rights Watch. (2025). *"You Feel Like Your Life Is Over": Abusive Practices at Three Florida Immigration Detention Centers Since January 2025*. https://www.hrw.org/report/2025/07/21/you-feel-like-your-life-is-over/abusive-practices-at-three-florida-immigration

Kelley, N., & Trebilcock, M. J. (1998). *The Making of the Mosaic: A History of Canadian Immigration Policy*. University of Toronto Press.

Koebler, J. (2025, April 9). Inside a Powerful Database ICE Uses to Identify and Deport People. *404 Media*. https://www.404media.co/inside-a-powerful-database-ice-uses-to-identify-and-deport-people/

Mann, B. (2025, March 25). In new assessment, Trump team ranks fentanyl as a top threat to U.S. *NPR*. https://www.npr.org/2025/03/25/nx-s1-5339847/fentanyl-gabbard-trump-cartels

Martin, K. (2019). Ethical implications and accountability of algorithms. *Journal of Business Ethics*, *160*(4), 835–850. https://doi.org/10.1007/s10551-018-3921-3

Mayer-Schönberger, V., & Cukier, K. (2013). *Big Data: A Revolution That Will Transform How We Live, Work and Think*. John Murray.

Maynard, R. (2017). *Policing Black Lives: State Violence in Canada from Slavery to the Present*. Fernwood Publishing.

Molnar, P., & Gill, L. (2018). Bots at the Gate A Human Rights Analysis of Automated Decision Making in Canada's Immigration and Refugee System. *The Citizen Lab*. https://citizenlab.ca/wp-content/uploads/2018/09/IHRP-Automated-Systems-Report-Web-V2.pdf

Molnar, P., & Muscati, S. (2018, September 27). What if an Algorithm Decided Whether You Could Stay in Canada or Not? The New Humanitarian. Retrieved April 13, 2022, from https://deeply.thenewhumanitarian.org/refugees/community/2018/09/27/what-if-an-algorithm-decided-whether-you-could-stay-in-canada-or-not

Molnar, P. (2019). Technology on the margins: AI and global migration from a human rights perspective. *Cambridge International Law Journal*, *8*(2), 305–330.

Molnar, P. (2024). *The Walls Have Eyes: Surviving Migration in the Age of Artificial Intelligence*. The New Press.

Molnar, P. (2025a). *Smart borders kill: New frontiers of violence and erosion of rights at the world's borders*. OpenGlobalRights. Retrieved June 10, 2025, from https://www.openglobalrights.org/smart-borders-kill-new-frontiers-of-violence-and-erosion-of-rights-at-the-worlds-borders/

Molnar, P. (2025b, July 1). *The Great White North: Canada's New Border Bill Appeases the Trump Administration | TechPolicy.Press*. Tech Policy Press. https://techpolicy.press/the-great-white-north-canadas-new-border-bill-appeases-the-trump-administration

Mullin, J. (2025, July 25). *Canada's Bill C-2 Opens the Floodgates to U.S. Surveillance*. Electronic Frontier Foundation. https://www.eff.org/deeplinks/2025/07/canadas-bill-c-2-opens-floodgates-us-surveillance

Oluwasanmi, M. (2021). Algorithms & the Border: The human rights implications of automated decision systems in Canadian Immigration. *Federalism-E*, *22*(1), 87–98. https://doi.org/10.24908/fede.v22i1.14516

Olwig, K. F., Grünenberg, K., Møhl, P., & Simonsen, A. (2019). *The Biometric Border World: Technology, Bodies and Identities on the Move*. Routledge. https://doi.org/10.4324/9780367808464

Polatin-Reuben, D., & Wright, J. (2014). An Internet with BRICS Characteristics: Data Sovereignty and the Balkanisation of the Internet. *4th USENIX Workshop on Free and Open Communications on the Internet*. https://www.usenix.org/system/files/conference/foci14/foci14-polatin-reuben.pdf

Precarity Lab (Ed.). (2020). *Technoprecarious*. Goldsmiths Press.

RCMP. (2025a). *Combatting cross-border crime*. https://rcmp.ca/en/federal-policing/border-integrity/combatting-cross-border-crime

RCMP. (2025b). *Border integrity partners*. https://rcmp.ca/en/federal-policing/border-integrity/border-integrity-partners

Rehaag, S., Molnar, P., & Wallace, S. (2025). *Refugee Law Lab consultation report on Bill C-2*. York University – Refugee Law Lab. Commissioned reports, studies and public policy documents, Paper 256. https://digitalcommons.osgoode.yorku.ca/reports/256

Rummage, J. (2025). *What Is Palantir? The Company Behind Government AI Tools*. Built In. Retrieved August 12, 2025, from https://builtin.com/articles/what-is-palantir

Topak, Ö. E., Bracken-Roche, C., Saulnier, A., & Lyon, D. (2015). From smart borders to perimeter security: The expansion of digital surveillance at the Canadian Borders. *Geopolitics*, *20*(4), 880–899. https://doi.org/10.1080/14650045.2015.1085024

Triadafilopoulos, T. (2013). Dismantling White Canada: Race, Rights, and the Origins of the Points System. In T. Triadafilopoulos (Ed.), *Wanted and Welcome? Policies for Highly Skilled Immigrants in Comparative Perspective* (pp. 15–37). Springer. https://doi.org/10.1007/978-1-4614-0082-0_2

Trump, D [@realDonaldTrump]. (2025, March 5). *Trudeau has weak border policies*. Truth Social. https://truthsocial.com/@realDonaldTrump/posts/114111661452992

22 Disablement by Algorithm
AI as a Modern Tool of Settler-Colonial Violence in Palestine

Amanie Issa and Christo El Morr

INTRODUCTION: FRAMING THE POLITICS OF AI AND DISABLEMENT

Artificial intelligence (AI) increasingly shapes the logic and practice of modern warfare, offering states unprecedented capacities to surveil, classify, maim, and kill through automated decision-making. While often presented as neutral or even ethical, these systems are deeply entangled with structures of racial capitalism, militarism, and settler colonialism. Furthermore, these systems often obscure and reinforce ableism, which is central to these power structures. This chapter critically investigates the deployment of AI by the Israeli military in occupied Palestine, particularly in Gaza, arguing that algorithmic technologies operate not merely as tools of war but as epistemic and material extensions of settler-colonial power. We examine how AI not only facilitates the widespread targeting and disablement of Palestinians but also constructs disability itself as a settler-colonial method and outcome.

Positionalities and Analytical Lens

Drawing from our positionalities, one of us as a scholar of AI and algorithmic systems, and the other informed by decolonial gender and disability scholarship, we offer an interdisciplinary analysis of algorithmic violence in a settler-colonial context. Specifically, we argue that Israeli AI systems enact a dual function: producing (so-called) "precision" targeting that results in mass impairment, and legitimizing such violence through the rhetoric of technological objectivity and accuracy. In doing so, these systems convert Palestinian bodies into data points subject to machinic logics of elimination, while erasing human life and the political conditions that produce such data in the first place.

From Metadata to Target Lists

AI decision-support systems such as Lavender operate through a multistage pipeline. First, raw data is extracted from communication patterns, geolocation, surveillance footage, and social network interactions. This data is labeled—often by past military intelligence assessments—to identify known operatives or suspicious behavior. The system then uses supervised machine learning techniques to train a model that learns to associate specific behavioral or metadata patterns with previous targets. Once trained, the model continuously ingests real-time data and scores individuals based on their resemblance to the learned "target profile." In the case of Lavender, this process was largely automated, with reports indicating that it flagged up to 37,000 individuals for targeting with minimal human oversight. What makes such systems "black-box" is not only their technical complexity but also the inaccessibility of their internal logic: operators cannot interrogate why a person was flagged, which variables were

DOI: 10.1201/9781003737810-26

weighted most heavily, or how error thresholds were determined. This opacity facilitates a dangerous moral distancing, allowing lethal decisions to appear objective even when they encode systemic bias, data gaps, and settler-colonial logics of elimination. This dynamic reflects the coloniality of power, where Eurocentric knowledge systems classify, manage, and erase colonized bodies through technological apparatuses (Quijano & Ennis, 2000).

Disablement as Strategy, Not Collateral

Our central claim is that AI technologies employed by the Israeli military, particularly the *Lavender* system, reportedly used to generate a list of 37,000 targets with minimal human oversight (Abraham, 2024), are instrumental in the mass disablement of Palestinians. Rather than treating disability as an outcome or incidental consequence of war, we argue that disablement functions as a calculated strategy of settler-colonial control. In this framework, AI technologies do not simply exacerbate violence; they encode and scale it, transforming impairment into a weapon of governance and deterrence (Puar, 2017).

Interpretive Framework and Methodological Approach

Methodologically, this chapter adopts a critical interpretive approach, drawing on publicly available reports. This approach privileges the knowledge production of Palestinian civil society organizations, frontline medical practitioners, and investigative journalists. We have prioritized triangulated reports from human rights bodies (e.g., Al-Haq, UN OHCHR, and WHO), corroborated investigative journalism (+972 Magazine, Foreign Policy), and public documentation by affected communities. In evaluating contested claims—such as those involving algorithmic targeting systems (e.g., Lavender)—we applied standards of evidentiary corroboration across multiple independent reports and identified patterns consistent with known military strategies. When claims lacked corroboration or diverged significantly, we foregrounded the ambiguity and situated them within the broader colonial and surveillance context shaping the production of "evidence." We analyze these sources through crip theory (McRuer, 2006), critical disability studies (CDS) (Goodley, 2017; Kafer, 2013), and settler-colonial critique (Wolfe, 2006), asking not only *what* these systems do technically, but also *how* their epistemic logics reproduce hierarchies of life and death. By integrating technical knowledge of how AI systems operate—via training datasets, predictive models, and classification heuristics—we provide a novel reading of AI's role in the algorithmic production of disablement.

Palestine as a Site of Peripheral Crip Critique

This chapter contributes to the emerging field of peripheral crip critique by foregrounding Palestine not just as a location of exceptional violence but also as an experience that can open a conceptual terrain for theorizing how disability, colonialism, and technology co-constitute one another. Colonialism shapes how disability is produced and understood, technology (such as surveillance and military technologies) is deployed within and reinforces colonial logics, and disability becomes a lens through which both colonialism and technological violence are experienced, resisted, and made visible. In the context of Palestine, AI is weaponized within a broader settler-colonial strategy of control, disablement, and elimination. Our aim is to situate Palestinian disabled experience as a generative experience of knowledge, resistance, and global solidarity, while also interrogating how militarized AI redefines disability itself under regimes of techno-colonial domination.

AI AND "BIAS": THERE IS NO NEUTRAL ALGORITHM

AI is often perceived, and sometimes framed, as a neutral technology that assists human beings in making decisions based on a neutral assessment of a situation. This perception of neutrality is probably based on the belief that computers are devoid of racism or harbor discriminatory feelings and that AI decisions are based on data, which inherently reflects truth and is therefore neutral or value-free (Kundi et al., 2023).

Yet, this framing obscures a fundamental truth: AI systems are inherently prone to be biased. The bias can emanate from several points during the development of AI-based systems (Houten, 2020), from data collection, to data processing, to AI model development and model deployment. We will first clarify these types of biases through examples from the health field and then from the military.

Example from Healthcare

Data collection may be biased and does not accurately represent the entire population (e.g., women, Indigenous populations) or may overlook other aspects (e.g., race, gender). Bias can also be introduced during the data processing phase, even before an AI system begins learning from the data. One common example occurs when developers create new variables, or features, by combining existing variables in ways that inadvertently encode structural inequalities. For instance, in an AI system designed to assess housing loan applications, engineers might construct a socioeconomic profile score by combining a person's income and the average rating of their neighborhood. However, these two variables come in very different forms: income might be recorded as large numbers in dollars (e.g., $25,000, $10,000,000), while neighborhood ratings might be expressed as small numbers, for instance, from a government index scored between one and ten. Because these numbers are on very different scales, the AI system could mistakenly treat income as much more important simply because the numbers are larger. To avoid this, AI developers normalize both variables by converting them to scores where each value reflects how far it is from the average. This allows the variables to be compared and combined by assigning a weight to each score; the developers might think that the income score should be weighted 50% more than the neighborhood score. To illustrate: suppose a person's income is slightly above average, but their neighborhood rating is well below average due to living in a structurally disadvantaged area. Even if the individual's personal financial profile is strong, the system may heavily penalize them based on where they live. This happens because variables like income and neighborhood are combined using mathematical weights—for example, the system might assign greater importance to income, but still allow a low neighborhood score to disproportionately drag down the overall result. The result is a penalization of structural poverty as if it were a personal trait—a subtle but powerful bias baked into the system.

Bias can also be introduced during the model development phase, particularly in the choices that developers make when designing and tuning the AI system. Suppose an AI system is deployed to identify patients likely to be readmitted, so hospitals can proactively offer preventive care and reduce readmission rates. During model development, the team chooses to optimize the model primarily for *overall accuracy* across the entire patient population. However, they do not evaluate how well the model performs across different groups—for instance, patients with chronic disabilities, older adults, or patients from lower-income backgrounds. If the training data underrepresents these groups, or if their healthcare data differ from the dominant patient group (e.g., they have different rates of follow-up care or different documentation practices), the model may systematically underpredict their risk of readmission. As a result, if the AI model is used in providing care, these patients may receive fewer preventive interventions, not because they are at a lower risk, but because the model was tuned to maximize general accuracy without considering the fairness or profiles of those subgroups. In this way, a bias is introduced during model development, driven by the team's choice of optimization goals and by a lack of attention to how the model's errors might disproportionately affect already vulnerable patients. In this case, bias is not merely inherited from the data—it is also shaped and amplified by the developers' choices about what performance goals to optimize and what fairness checks to include during model development.

Finally, bias can also emerge during the deployment phase of an AI system—that is, when the model is put into real-world use. Even if the model was carefully trained and tested to reduce bias and be "fair," new forms of unfairness can arise depending on *how* and *where* it is deployed. For example, consider a healthcare AI system designed to predict which patients are at high risk of complications and should receive extra care. The model may have been trained on hospital data and may perform well in that setting. However, when it is deployed across an entire healthcare network—including rural clinics, under-resourced community centers, and hospitals that serve low-income or marginalized populations—it may behave very differently. In these new settings, key data inputs may be missing or recorded differently (for instance, poorer clinics may lack detailed patient histories), which can systematically lower the AI's risk scores for the disadvantaged patients visiting those settings. In other words, patients who are actually at high risk might not be flagged by the AI simply because the deployment environment does not provide the same quality of data as the model expects. This creates a bias that disadvantages poor and underserved groups, not because of model design or data processing, but because of how the model is used and under what conditions. Even in settings where the AI model is currently performing well, shifts in the demographic profile of patients, such as aging populations or an influx of younger individuals, can alter the underlying data patterns. As a result, the model's performance may degrade over time without immediate detection. Without careful, continuous monitoring and adaptation during deployment, even a well-designed AI system can perpetuate or amplify structural inequities once it is released into the world.

Example from the Military

Militaries around the world are rapidly intensifying their investment in AI technologies, seeking to harness their capacity to process vast amounts of data in real time and transform it into actionable intelligence. The aim is not only to accelerate the speed of decision-making but also to improve its precision, enabling commanders to respond more effectively to complex and fast-changing operational environments (Deeks, 2020). Increasingly, these tools are also being developed with the ambition of guiding decisions that prioritize the protection of individuals, particularly civilians, by reducing human error and enhancing compliance with international humanitarian law (Forrest, 2021).

However, these same distortions—biased data, flawed processing, skewed optimization, and contextual failures—are not only present in military systems but also actively weaponized through their design and deployment. Bias can enter an AI system from the very beginning, during the data collection phase. For example, in a military AI system designed to identify potential combatants in drone surveillance footage, the training data may come disproportionately from regions and populations where previous conflicts occurred. If most of the labeled images of "combatants" are drawn from specific ethnic or cultural groups, the model will learn to associate those visual features (such as clothing styles, skin tone, or movement patterns) with threat. This creates a bias whereby certain groups are far more likely to be flagged as dangerous, not because of their actual behavior but because of how the training data was selected. In effect, the AI system "inherits" the biases of past conflicts, embedding them into future targeting decisions.

Even after data is collected, the way it is processed can introduce further bias. Consider the same military AI system: suppose developers normalize input data such as movement speed and location to create a "suspicious activity" score. However, movement patterns vary greatly depending on local context—for example, civilians in rural areas may travel in groups on foot, while civilians in cities may move alone or by vehicle. If these differences are not accounted for during data processing, the normalization process can turn normal rural behavior into a higher "suspicion" score, causing the AI to systematically misclassify certain populations as more threatening. In this way, an *apparently* neutral data preparation step can reinforce existing biases. In fact, whatever we do, data is never neutral; it reflects the past and present, as such it reflects existing societal hierarchies, historical patterns of violence, and operational assumptions (Andersin, 2025). In military AI systems such as

Israel's *Lavender*, the system learned to identify a person as a Hamas militant if they have a similar behavior to a Hamas operative; however, the training dataset included people who were civil defense workers (Abraham, 2024). Moreover, the training dataset lacked representations of individuals who were not targets, further reinforcing structural bias in the model's classifications (Andersin, 2025, p. 30). This produced structural bias, with civilians who had communication patterns similar to known Hamas including police, civil defense workers, militants' relatives, and residents who happened to have a name and nickname identical to that of an operative to be flagged as targets. The Lavender system operates as a black-box model—its inner logics inaccessible—yet its decisions translate directly into lethal outcomes. This opacity masks deep algorithmic biases and forms of data colonialism that expropriate data from oppressed populations while denying them any power over its interpretation or application (Arora et al., 2023).

Bias is also shaped during the model development phase (i.e., training and testing), through the choices developers make about how to optimize the system. In the military AI case, developers might tune the model to prioritize precision (reducing false positives) in regions where political consequences are high, while optimizing for recall (catching as many potential targets as possible) in regions with fewer political constraints. These tuning choices, while technically justified, can produce unequal outcomes: people in less politically sensitive regions may face a much higher risk of being wrongly targeted, simply because the model is optimized differently for their region. In this way, the values and trade-offs embedded in model development directly shape patterns of harm.

Finally, bias can be introduced or amplified during model deployment. Suppose the military AI system is deployed in new regions where the available data, such as drone resolution or environmental conditions, is poorer than in the original training environment. In these contexts, the model may perform worse, with higher error rates, yet operators may not be fully aware of this drop in reliability. If military decision-makers continue to rely on the system without adjusting for this change in performance, populations in the new deployment zones will be exposed to greater risk of wrongful targeting. Here, bias arises not from the model itself but from a failure to adapt its use to the realities of the deployment context.

Therefore, bias in AI-based systems is not an exception, but rather a feature that is embedded in such systems. Constructed within specific social, political, and technical contexts, they encode particular values and structural inequalities at every level, from training data to operational deployment (Jafri, 2017).

AI IN MILITARY DECISION-MAKING: WHOSE LIVES ARE CALCULATED?

The use of AI in military decision-making has introduced new dimensions of speed, scale, and opacity into the targeting process. AI-driven systems such as decision-support tools, targeting algorithms, and automated surveillance networks are increasingly embedded in military operations worldwide. These systems aggregate vast amounts of data (geospatial intelligence, signals intelligence, biometrics, and social network analysis) to generate target recommendations, often with minimal human intervention (Andersin, 2025). These systems also exemplify the militarization of AI as a form of techno-sovereignty by dominant powers, particularly as they are deployed in the Global South under asymmetrical conditions of warfare (Garcia, 2019).

A central and dangerous feature of this development is the military's reliance on concepts of *tolerable error*, the degree of civilian harm deemed "acceptable" when using algorithmic targeting (Kakko, 2022). "Tolerable" or "acceptable" error (i.e., loss of civilian lives) is not a neutral, technical parameter; it is a deeply political calculation that reflects priorities and power dynamics rather than ethical imperatives (Andersin, 2025). The Israeli military's *Lavender* AI program starkly exemplifies this logic. Designed to identify potential Hamas operatives, *Lavender* classified nearly every male in Gaza as a potential target, with the Israeli occupation forces reportedly accepting a 10% false positive rate, meaning that out of 37,000 flagged targets, approximately 3,700 were likely civilians after the Israeli occupation army broadened the scope of a "Hamas operative"

(Andersin, 2025). Human analysts spent an average of only 20 seconds reviewing each AI-generated target, primarily checking for gender, a clear procedural abdication of meaningful oversight (Andersin, 2025).

Such practices demonstrate how AI does not simply automate targeting; it reshapes the ethical contours of military violence. In contexts of occupation and settler colonialism, as in Gaza, algorithmic bias is not incidental, it is weaponized. The apparent objectivity of AI systems provides a veneer of legitimacy to mass violence, while obscuring the political choices embedded in algorithm design and deployment practices (e.g., operational thresholds).

Lavender also exposes the fallacy of "human-machine teaming" as a safeguard. Under conditions of institutional pressure, emotional retribution, and systemic dehumanization (Amnesty International, 2024), the AI-human interaction becomes an *unaccountability* machine. In this system, the moral laundering or diffusion of responsibility between human operators and algorithmic recommendations makes it nearly impossible to assign legal or moral culpability for harmful outcomes. This process facilitates harm rather than curbs it and functions as a tool to deflect, rather than assume, responsibility.

This reflects a broader truth: AI systems do not merely automate neutral processes; they automate politically charged acts of classification, targeting, and control (Benjamin, 2019). Scholars across AI ethics and critical algorithm studies emphasize that "bias" is not a glitch to be debugged, but a reflection of the social values embedded in algorithmic systems (Noble, 2018). In contexts of military occupation and settler colonialism, this bias is weaponized.

Understanding AI bias in isolation is insufficient. We must examine how AI bias interacts with military logics of decision-making, where institutional incentives, emotional imperatives, and the very architecture of war intersect with algorithmic outputs. It is in this space, where human and machine collaborate, that AI systems help enact regimes of targeted violence. The next section will further explore how these dynamics of calculable, politically "acceptable" harm unfold in military decision-making under settler-colonial regimes.

FROM BULLETS TO ALGORITHMS: TECHNOLOGICAL CONTINUITIES IN SETTLER COLONIALISM

The disabling of Palestinian bodies has long been an explicit tactic of the Israeli settler-colonial project. Historically, the use of rubber bullets, tear gas canisters, and sniper fire targeting the lower limbs has been deployed to maim rather than to kill, with the apparently deliberate intent of producing mass disablement among Palestinians (Akkad, 2019; Amnesty International, 2018). During the *Great March of Return* protests (March 30, 2018–November 23, 2019), Israel killed 316 people and injured over 35,703. A significant number of these injuries, affecting the feet of approximately 9,389 people, led to 158 amputations (Hajjaj, 2023). Moreover, the UN reported that

> over 7,000 of the live ammunition injuries (some 88 per cent) were limb injuries, followed by injuries to the abdomen and pelvis. 156 of the limb injuries have resulted in amputations (126 lower limb and 30 upper limb). Out of these, at least 94 cases involved secondary amputations, due to subsequent bone infections.
>
> *(United Nations, 2020)*

This is to say that killing and maiming using AI is not something new; settler-colonial violence is a structure of repetition: the same logics of elimination and control are continuously reinscribed across time and technologies.

The rise of AI-based military systems, such as Israel's *Lavender*, *Fire Factory*, and facial recognition networks does not constitute a rupture with these colonial logics; rather, it digitizes and automates them (Andersin, 2025). AI tools now perform the classificatory labor of distinguishing whose life is to be made killable, whose body is to be targeted or disabled. In this sense, the political calculus of "acceptable harm" encoded in earlier practices of rubber bullets and kneecapping is preserved, only now at greater scale and speed, with algorithmic thresholds of "tolerable error" explicitly designed into targeting systems (Andersin, 2025; Burrell, 2016). The Israeli surveillance infrastructure is layered through facial recognition, movement tracking, and predictive analytics that anticipate protests and resistance. These digital interventions function not merely as tools of governance but as extensions of techno-colonial power; data-driven forms of control that reinscribe colonial hierarchies under the guise of humanitarian or security rationales (Madianou, 2019, 2021, and 2022). These assemblages reflect what Madianou calls techno-colonialism; data infrastructures that extend imperial power through humanitarian and security technologies (Madianou, 2022).

Critically, AI in this context does not represent technological "progress" toward more ethical warfighting, as some proponents might claim (UN General Assembly, 2024). Rather, it provides a new set of tools for old structures of domination. The same political goals of demographic control, mass disablement, and infrastructural destruction, as evident in the systematic targeting of Gaza's healthcare system (Al Haq, 2025), are now pursued through predictive analytics and machine learning, which are deeply shaped by the colonial contexts in which they are deployed.

In short, AI represents a shift in tools, not a break from the politics of settler-colonial domination. As in previous eras, the central function remains the control, dehumanization, and disablement of Palestinian life.

This technological shift from bullets to algorithms has not diminished the violence of settler colonialism; it has recalibrated it. Where rifles once marked knees, neural networks now mark homes. Yet, beneath this shift in machinery lies a sustained political project: the production of killability and disability through classification. As AI systems categorize, sort, and score human life by probabilistic thresholds, they reproduce and extend the settler state's capacity to decide who is permitted to live and who is condemned to be killed, and who is marked for disablement along the way.

THEORETICAL FRAMEWORKS: CRIP THEORY, CDS, AND SETTLER COLONIALISM

The deployment of AI in the context of Israeli settler colonialism requires a theoretical approach that can account for both the historical-material structures of occupation and the contemporary technological modalities of violence. To that end, we draw on CDS, Crip Theory, and Settler-Colonial Studies to develop a framework for understanding how disability is not only produced through conflict but also actively constructed as a colonial method of control and erasure. These interrelated frameworks help us trace the material and epistemic violence of algorithmic systems that render Palestinian life as targetable, maimable, and ultimately disposable.

At its core, CDS challenges normative understandings of disability as an individualized or purely medical condition. Instead, CDS situates disability within broader relations of power, attending to how disability is socially, politically, and economically produced through institutions such as the military, the healthcare system, and the carceral state (Goodley, 2017; Kafer, 2013). In this tradition, disability is not a consequence of war but a technologically mediated form of governance, a way of managing bodies deemed unruly, threatening, or excessive.

In addition, Jasbir Puar's concept of "debilitation" (2017) is central to our analysis. In contrast to disability, which may be recognized and responded to within liberal frameworks of accommodation or rights, debility refers to the ongoing, often intentional, production of bodily harm that never fully registers as injury. Debility operates through chronic exposure to structural violence, injury, deprivation, illness, and infrastructural collapse, that is normalized and rendered invisible within the logics of settler governance. Puar theorizes debility as a biopolitical strategy, a "right to maim" that allows settler states to produce mass impairment without the legal or political consequences of mass death.

CDS alone, however, is insufficient to account for the colonial dimensions of this process. As disability scholars working within decolonial and Indigenous frameworks remind us, disablement is not only a mechanism of control—it is also a strategy of erasure (L. J. Jaffee, 2016; Meekosha,

2011). Settler colonialism functions not simply through occupation or extraction, but through the elimination of Indigenous futures (Wolfe, 2006). In this context, disability is weaponized to incapacitate those futures: through maiming, psychological trauma, and the destruction of healthcare infrastructure, settler-colonial regimes foreclose the conditions of possibility for Indigenous life.

In other settler-colonial contexts such as the United States, Canada, Australia, and New Zealand, settler-colonial governments have used ableist violence as a way to control Indigenous peoples, by targeting their bodies, communities, and knowledge systems. Indigenous peoples, drawing on their own knowledge systems, have long emphasized that settler-colonial practices, such as taking land and damaging it for profit, not only harm the land but also cause harm and disablement to Indigenous bodies (L. Jaffee & John, 2018). This form of violence breaks down Indigenous ways of life and the social and environmental conditions that support them, helping to maintain colonial domination and undermine sovereignty, kinship, and intergenerational survival (Hutcheon & Lashewicz, 2020; Nash, 2020).

In occupied Palestine, AI-powered surveillance systems increasingly monitor bodily movement, gait, facial expression, and behavioral patterns to identify "threats" based on predictive models (Shtaya, 2022). These systems, however, are not built to recognize the spectrum of human variation, particularly the behaviors, gestures, and appearances of people with physical, cognitive, or sensory disabilities. Assistive device users, those with limb differences, neurodivergent individuals, or people with atypical movement patterns may be misclassified as "suspicious" by AI trained on able-bodied norms. A person's use of a wheelchair may be flagged as evasive movement; the vocal expressions of someone with a communication-related disability may be registered as erratic behavior. A child with Post-Traumatic Stress Disorder (PTSD) exhibiting hypervigilance may be misread by facial recognition software and flagged as a threat. These examples reveal how surveillance regimes criminalize nonnormative embodiment, marking disabled and neurodivergent individuals as inherently risky. These forms of misclassification are emblematic of what Shew calls *technoableism*: the design and deployment of AI systems that normalize able-bodied standards while rendering disabled behaviors as errors or threats (Shew, 2020, 2022). In settler-colonial contexts like Palestine, this technoableism functions as a direct instrument of what Achille Mbembe (2019) describes as a *necropolitical regime*, where states decide who may live and who must die, or in this case, who may be disabled or discarded. In such contexts, AI technologies are tested and deployed with minimal oversight, which reinforces the governing logic of disposability, converting disabled bodies into data points for elimination or abandonment, and extends this logic by automating the classification of who is "fit" for life, mobility, care, or extermination. In this way, disability is not merely misrecognized by AI; it is actively criminalized, pathologized, and targeted, further entrenching the role of technology as a weapon of settler-colonial violence.

Crip Theory directly contests the foundational logic of such systems: that bodily or cognitive difference equates to deviance, risk, or danger. Instead, Crip Theory insists on revaluing difference not as something to be corrected or surveilled, but as a site of political insight, relationality, and resistance (Kafer, 2013; McRuer, 2006). Mainstream disability discourses that frame AI as a tool for inclusion and empowerment fail to capture how disabled bodies in the Global South are subjected to exclusion, dispossession, and death. As Grech argues, disability in the Majority World must be understood within colonial and developmental logics that deepen poverty and marginalization rather than alleviate them (Grech, 2009).

Crip Theory, developed at the intersection of disability and queer theory, pushes further by challenging the normative timelines, affective structures, and productivity logics that underpin both liberal rights discourse and colonial governance (Kafer, 2013; McRuer, 2006). Crip Theory critiques not only what bodies are disabled, but how notions of disability are constructed, weaponized, and made meaningful within specific regimes of power. Calls to decolonize AI must extend beyond inclusion and ethical auditing toward confronting the political and epistemological hierarchies embedded in technological development (Adams, 2021).

In the context of algorithmic warfare, Crip Theory allows us to resist narratives that frame disability solely as humanitarian collateral damage or a moral failing of war. Instead, it calls attention to the ways that technological systems encode able-bodied norms, marking certain lives as inefficient, irrational, or threatening. Algorithmic disablement does not just happen in the moment of the strike; it is carried forward through the afterlives of data, surveillance, and infrastructural abandonment, all of which deepen the conditions of debility. These AI narratives not only misrecognize disability but also simulate it through normative assumptions, as Shew notes, reinforcing technoableist visions that erase lived crip realities (Shew, 2022).

BEYOND PALESTINE: THE GLOBAL RELEVANCE OF ALGORITHMIC DISABLEMENT

The deployment of AI as a tool of maiming, surveillance, and population control in Palestine reflects a broader global trend. A stark example is the development and potential deployment of Autonomous Weapon Systems (AWS), often referred to as "killer robots," which are designed to select and engage targets without human intervention (Bode & Watts, 2023). Concerns are particularly high in regions like Ukraine, where both Ukrainian and Russian forces have reportedly utilized AI-powered drones and targeting systems (Bode & Watts, 2023; Samus & Artemenko, 2025; Stepanenko, 2025), or in Libya, where a Turkish-made Kargu-2 drone allegedly hunted down and attacked a human target without human command (Bode & Watts, 2023; Melville, 2025; Nasu, 2021; Suriyasenee, 2023).

In Kashmir, AI-supported biometric surveillance, predictive policing, and data extraction are central to India's settler-colonial (Harvard Law Review, 2021; Osuri & Zia, 2020; Samreen & Mudasir, 2020) and carceral governance (Altaf & Javed, 2024). Similarly, in Xinjiang, China's AI-driven profiling and behavioral analytics enable a pervasive system of social control that has led to mass incarceration, forced political indoctrination, and the psychological debilitation of Uyghur communities, under what is widely recognized as a system of techno-genocide (Amnesty International, 2019). Kashmir, Xinjiang, and AWS are chosen as comparative cases because they reveal how settler-colonial regimes and military powers deploy technology to consolidate control through the production of disability. In Kashmir, biometric surveillance and communication blackouts disable different aspects of their life; in Xinjiang, predictive policing algorithms criminalize entire populations and institutionalize mass internment; and in AWS, automated targeting systems embody settler-colonial logics by rendering racialized bodies as algorithmic threats, producing disablement through violence at scale.

These systems, developed by nations including the United States (Dilanian et al., 2022), Russia, China, Israel, India, and South Korea (Garcia, 2019), pose a grave threat of widespread physical injury and death, as they remove human ethical judgment and accountability from decision-making (Crootof, 2018; Human Rights Watch, 2025). Such technologies are not neutral. They are developed, tested, and exported by some of the powerful tech corporations, such as Palantir, Microsoft, and Amazon, who provide military-grade AI infrastructure to governments and militaries around the world. As detailed in the crucial 2025 report by UN Special Rapporteur Francesca Albanese (Albanese, 2025), these corporations are complicit in human rights violations, including the genocide in Gaza. The report identifies how these companies are embedded in the digital infrastructure of genocide, and profit from and directly enable surveillance, targeting, and digital repression in Palestine and other conflict zones (Albanese, 2025). These developments are inseparable from what Kate Crawford (2021) describes as the extractive logic of AI; one deeply rooted in colonial capitalism, where human labor, land, and data are mined for profit under the guise of technological progress (Couldry & Mejias, 2019). This global trend of techno-violence must be understood through a decolonial lens that centers the epistemologies and lived realities of disabled people in the Global South, as Grech and Goodley argue, challenging dominant Western research paradigms and development models that erase non-Western forms of resistance (Grech & Goodley, 2011). As Wehbi et al. observe, disability-focused development work often reproduces neocolonial narratives in which people with disabilities in the Global South are constructed as passive recipients of Northern expertise, erasing local agency and knowledge (Wehbi et al., 2009).

The pervasive nature of these technologies in colonialism, occupation, wars, and population control underscores the urgent need for robust ethical frameworks and international humanitarian law to govern AI's development and deployment, ensuring human dignity remains paramount.

CONCLUSION: RESISTING ALGORITHMIC OPPRESSION THROUGH CRITICAL SOLIDARITY

Palestinian peoples have long resisted settler-colonial domination, asserting their freedom and sovereignty despite systemic dispossession, violence, and ongoing attempts at erasure. Palestinian bodies and territories have repeatedly been used as testing grounds for military technologies, including AI, drones, and biometric surveillance systems, making Palestine a frontline for the development and deployment of tools of control, experimentation, and disablement. These experiences are not abstract case studies; they reflect the embodied realities of a people living under structural violence and ongoing genocide.

Unless critically reimagined, AI technologies are not tools of liberation; they are instruments of colonial capitalism, designed to make a profit by managing life, sorting risk, and enforcing disposability. As evidenced in Palestine and across militarized borders worldwide, AI systems extend the logics of colonialism and war by automating the surveillance, targeting, and debilitation of racialized and colonized bodies. These systems are neither abstract nor accidental; they are built, sold, and deployed by tech giants whose platforms underpin drone targeting, border militarization, and biometric surveillance.

To resist such regimes, we must reject reforms that seek to "fix" AI by diversifying data or improving accuracy. Instead, we must call for cross-disciplinary, cross-movement resistance rooted in radical crip politics and disability justice. To resist this, there is an urgent need for a transnational, decolonial framework that not only critiques algorithmic bias but also names and dismantles the global structures of power such as corporate, military, and settler-colonial systems that enable algorithmic disablement. Grounded in disability justice and Indigenous sovereignty, this framework must anticipate, expose, and disrupt the global infrastructures of techno-colonial violence. This requires collective refusals of tech-driven violence and the creation of alternatives that center care, interdependence, and life beyond productivity and control. It also requires envisioning futures where technologies are reclaimed in service of justice, healing, and liberation, futures where Palestinian people, and all those under (settler-) colonial domination, can live free on their Indigenous lands.

ACKNOWLEDGMENT

Portions of this chapter were developed with the assistance of ChatGPT and Grammarly in an editing capacity to improve clarity and flow. All intellectual contributions, interpretations, and final editorial decisions are the authors' own, and the authors take full responsibility for the content. Any AI-assisted or AI-generated material was reviewed and verified by the authors.

REFLECTION QUESTIONS

1. How does the concept of tolerable error in military AI reveal the political value assigned to Palestinian lives?
2. The authors argue that disablement is a strategy, not just collateral damage. How does AI facilitate the mass disablement of populations as a form of control?
3. In what ways does the black-box nature of systems like *Lavender* facilitate a moral distancing for those operating them?
4. How does Crip Theory help us understand the weaponization of disability in the context of settler-colonial warfare?

REFERENCES

Abraham, Y. (2024, April 3). 'Lavender': The AI machine directing Israel's bombing spree in Gaza. *+972 Magazine*. https://www.972mag.com/lavender-ai-israeli-army-gaza/

Adams, R. (2021). Can artificial intelligence be decolonized? *Interdisciplinary Science Reviews*, *46*(1), 176–197. https://doi.org/10.1080/03080188.2020.1840225

Akkad, D. (2019, March 29). *"Shoot to maim": How Israel created a generation on crutches in Gaza*. Middle East Eye. https://www.middleeasteye.net/news/shoot-maim-how-israel-created-generation-crutches-gaza

Al Haq. (2025). *The systematic destruction of Gaza's healthcare system: A pattern of genocide*. https://www.alhaq.org/cached_uploads/download/2025/02/22/destruction-of-gaza-healthcare-system-one-page-view-2-1740217809.pdf

Albanese, F. (2025). From economy of occupation to economy of genocide: Report of the Special Rapporteur on the situation of human rights in the Palestinian territories occupied since 1967 (A/HRC/59/23). https://www.ohchr.org/en/documents/country-reports/ahrc5923-economy-occupation-economy-genocide-report-special-rapporteur

Altaf, Z., & Javed, N. (2024, December 12). Algorithmic Repression in Indian Illegally Occupied Jammu and Kashmir. *CISSAJK*. https://cissajk.org.pk/2024/12/12/algorithmic-repression-in-indian-illegally-occupied-jammu-and-kashmir/

Amnesty International. (2018, April 27). *Israel: "Deliberate attempts" by military to kill and maim Gaza protesters continues*. https://www.amnesty.org.uk/press-releases/israel-deliberate-attempts-military-kill-and-maim-gaza-protesters-continues

Amnesty International. (2019). China's Algorithms of Repression. *Human Rights Watch*. https://www.hrw.org/report/2019/05/01/chinas-algorithms-repression/reverse-engineering-xinjiang-police-mass

Amnesty International. (2024, January 10). *ICJ hearings over Israel's alleged breaches of the Genocide Convention a vital step to help protect Palestinian civilians*. https://www.amnesty.org/en/latest/news/2024/01/icj-hearings-over-israels-alleged-breaches-of-the-genocide-convention-a-vital-step-to-help-protect-palestinian-civilians/

Andersin, E. (2025). The use of the 'Lavender' in Gaza and the law of targeting: AI-decision support systems and facial recognition technology. *Journal of International Humanitarian Legal Studies*, 1–35. https://doi.org/10.1163/18781527-bja10119

Arora, A., Barrett, M., Lee, E., Oborn, E., & Prince, K. (2023). Risk and the future of AI: Algorithmic bias, data colonialism and marginalization. *Information and Organization*, *33*(3), 1–7. https://doi.org/10.1016/j.infoandorg.2023.100478

Benjamin, R. (2019). *Race After Technology: Abolitionist Tools for the New Jim Code* (1st, Ed.). Wiley. https://www.politybooks.com/bookdetail?book_slug=race-after-technology-abolitionist-tools-for-the-new-jim-code--9781509526390

Bode, I., & Watts, T. F. (2023). *Loitering Munitions and Unpredictability: Autonomy in Weapon Systems and Challenges to Human Control*. Center for War Studies, University of Southern Denmark. https://portal.findresearcher.sdu.dk/en/publications/loitering-munitions-and-unpredictability-autonomy-in-weapon-syste

Burrell, J. (2016). How the machine 'thinks': Understanding opacity in machine learning algorithms. *Big Data & Society*, *3*(1), 2053951715622512. https://doi.org/10.1177/2053951715622512

Couldry, N., & Mejias, U. A. (2019). *The costs of connection: How data Is colonizing human life and appropriating it for capitalism*. Stanford University Press. https://doi.org/10.1515/9781503609754

Crawford, K. (2021). *The atlas of AI: Power, politics, and the planetary costs of artificial intelligence* (1st ed.). Yale University Press. https://doi.org/10.2307/j.ctv1ghv45t

Crootof, R. (2018). Autonomous weapon systems and the limits of analogy. *Harvard National Security Journal*, *9*, 51–83.

Deeks, A. (2020). *Coding the Law of Armed Conflict: First Steps* (SSRN Scholarly Paper No. 3612329). Social Science Research Network. https://papers.ssrn.com/abstract=3612329

Dilanian, K., De Luce, D., & Kube, C. (2022, March 15). *Biden Admin will Provide Ukraine Killer Drones called Switchblades*. NBC News. https://www.nbcnews.com/politics/national-security/ukraine-asks-biden-admin-armed-drones-jamming-gear-surface-air-missile-rcna20197

Forrest, K. B. (2021). *When Machines Can Be Judge, Jury, And Executioner: Justice In The Age Of Artificial Intelligence*. World Scientific Publishing Company. https://books.google.ca/books?id=OJIqEAAAQBAJ

Garcia, E. (2019). *The Militarization of Artificial Intelligence: A Wake-Up Call for the Global South* (SSRN Scholarly Paper No. 3452323). Social Science Research Network. https://doi.org/10.2139/ssrn.3452323

Goodley, D. (2017). *Disability studies: An interdisciplinary introduction*. Sage Publications.

Grech, S. (2009). Disability, poverty and development: Critical reflections on the majority world debate. *Disability & Society*, *24*(6), 771–784. https://doi.org/10.1080/09687590903160266

Grech, S., & Goodley, D. (2011). Doing research in the majority world: An alternative framework and the quest for decolonizing methods. *Journal of Human Development, Disability and Social Change*, *19*(2), 43–55. https://doi.org/10.7202/1086899ar

Hajjaj, T. S. (2023, March 30). Five years on, Gaza's Great March of Return changed people's lives. *Mondoweiss*. https://mondoweiss.net/2023/03/five-years-on-gazas-great-march-of-return-changed-peoples-lives/

Harvard Law Review. (2021). From domicile to dominion: India's settler-colonial Agenda in Kashmir. *Harvard Law Review*, *134*(7), 2530–2551.

Houten, H. van. (2020, November 16). *For fair and equal healthcare, we need fair and bias-free AI*. https://www.philips.com/a-w/about/news/archive/blogs/innovation-matters/2020/20201116-for-fair-and-equal-healthcare-we-need-fair-and-bias-free-ai.html

Human Rights Watch. (2025). *A Hazard to Human Rights: Autonomous Weapons Systems and Digital Decision-Making*. https://www.hrw.org/report/2025/04/28/hazard-human-rights/autonomous-weapons-systems-and-digital-decision-making

Hutcheon, E. J., & Lashewicz, B. (2020). Tracing and troubling continuities between ableism and colonialism in Canada. *Disability & Society*, *35*(5), 695–714. https://doi.org/10.1080/09687599.2019.1647145

Jaffee, L. J. (2016). Disrupting global disability frameworks: Settler-colonialism and the geopolitics of disability in Palestine/Israel. *Disability & Society*, *31*(1), 116–130. https://doi.org/10.1080/09687599.2015.1119038

Jaffee, L., & John, K. (2018). Disabling bodies of/and land: Reframing disability justice in conversation with Indigenous theory and activism. *Disability and the Global South*, *5*(2), 1407–1429.

Jafri, B. (2017). Ongoing Colonial Violence in Settler States. *Lateral*, *Spring*(6.1). https://csalateral.org/issue/6-1/forum-alt-humanities-settler-colonialism-ongoing-violence-jafri/

Kafer, A. (2013). *Feminist, Queer, Crip*. Indiana University Press.

Kakko, Y. (2022, January). *Meaningful Human Control as an Exceptional Concept*. EU Non-Proliferation and Disarmament Consortium. https://www.nonproliferation.eu/wp-content/uploads/2022/01/Kakko MeaningfulHumanControl2022-1.pdf

Kundi, B., El Morr, C., Gorman, R., & Dua, E. (2023). Artificial intelligence and bias: A scoping review. In C. El Morr (Ed.), *AI and Society* (1st ed., pp. 199–215). Taylor and Francis - CRC Press.

Madianou, M. (2019). The biometric assemblage: Surveillance, experimentation, profit and the measuring of refugee bodies. *Television and New Media*, *20*(6), 581–599. https://doi.org/10.1177/1527476419857682

Madianou, M. (2021). Nonhuman humanitarianism: When 'AI for good' can be harmful? *Information, Communication & Society*, *24*(6), 850–868. https://doi.org/10.1080/1369118X.2021.1909100

Madianou, M. (2022). Technological futures as colonial debris: "Tech for Good" as technocolonialism. In J. Zylinska & Goldsmith Media (Eds.), *The Future of Media* (pp. 281–294). Goldsmiths Press.

Mbembe, A. (2019). *Necropolitics*. Duke University Press.

McRuer, R. (2006). *Crip Theory: Cultural Signs of Queerness and Disability*. New York University Press.

Meekosha, H. (2011). Decolonising disability: Thinking and acting globally. *Disability & Society*, *26*(6), 667–682. https://doi.org/10.1080/09687599.2011.602860

Melville, A. (2025). *Drone Wars: Developments in Drone Swarm Technology*. Forecast International. https://dsm.forecastinternational.com/2025/01/21/drone-wars-developments-in-drone-swarm-technology/?utm_source=chatgpt.com

Nash, N. I. (2020). Disability as a colonial construct: The missing discourse of culture in conceptualizations of disabled Indigenous children. *Canadian Journal of Disability Studies*, *9*(3), 28–51. https://doi.org/10.15353/cjds.v9i3.645

Nasu, H. (2021). The Kargu 2 Autonomous Attack Drone: Legal & Ethical Dimensions. *Lieber Institute*. https://lieber.westpoint.edu/kargu-2-autonomous-attack-drone-legal-ethical/

Noble, S. U. (2018). *Algorithms of Oppression: How Search Engines Reinforce Racism*. New York University Press.

Osuri, G., & Zia, A. (2020). Kashmir and Palestine: Archives of coloniality and solidarity. *Identities*, *27*(3), 249–266. https://doi.org/10.1080/1070289X.2020.1750200

Puar, J. K. (2017). *The Right to Maim: Debility, Capacity, Disability*. Duke University Press.

Quijano, A., & Ennis, M. (2000). Coloniality of power, eurocentrism, and Latin America. *Nepantla: Views from South*, *1*(3), 533–580.

Samreen, M., & Mudasir, A. (2020, July 27). *Kashmir: Prolonged Settler Colonialism* [Online post]. Housing and Land Rights Network (HLRN). https://hlrn.org/activitydetails.php?title=Kashmir:-Prolonged-Settler-Colonialism&id=pnBpaQ==

Samus, M., & Artemenko, O. (2025). *The Impact of Artificial Intelligence in the Drones' War in Ukraine*. New Strategy Center. https://newstrategycenter.ro/wp-content/uploads/2025/02/The-Impact-of-Artificial-Intelligence-in-the-Drones-War-in-Ukraine.pdf

Shew, A. (2020). Ableism, technoableism, and future AI. *IEEE Technology and Society Magazine*, *39*(1), 40–85. https://doi.org/10.1109/MTS.2020.2967492

Shew, A. (2022). How to get a story wrong: Technoableism, simulation and cyborg resistance. *Including Disability*, *1*(1), 13–36.

Shtaya, M. (2022, April 27). *Nowhere to |Hide: The Impact of Israel's Digital Surveillance Regime on the Palestinians*. Middle East Institute. https://www.mei.edu/publications/nowhere-hide-impact-israels-digital-surveillance-regime-palestinians

Stepanenko, K. (2025). *The Battlefield AI Revolution Is Not Here Yet: The Status of Current Russian and Ukrainian AI Drone Efforts*. Institute for the Study of War. https://understandingwar.org/backgrounder/battlefield-ai-revolution-not-here-yet-status-current-russian-and-ukrainian-ai-drone

Suriyasenee, A. (2023, June 21). *Death by Algorithms: The Rise Of Biased Killer Robots*. Young Australians in Internatinoal Affairs. https://www.youngausint.org.au/post/death-by-algorithms-the-rise-of-biased-killer-robots

UN General Assembly. (2024, July 1). *Lethal Autonomous Weapons Systems: Report of the Secretary-General*. United Nations. https://docs.un.org/en/A/79/88

United Nations. (2020, April 6). Two Years On: People Injured and Traumatized During the "Great March of Return" are Still Struggling. *Question of Palestine*. https://www.un.org/unispal/document/two-years-on-people-injured-and-traumatized-during-the-great-march-of-return-are-still-struggling/

Wehbi, S., Elin, L., & El-Lahib, Y. (2009). Neo-colonial discourses and disability: The case of Canadian International Development NGOs. *Community Development Journal*, *45*(4), 404–422.

Wolfe, P. (2006). Settler colonialism and the elimination of the native. *Journal of Genocide Research*, *8*(4), 387–409. https://doi.org/10.1080/14623520601056240

Part 5

Decolonial and Philosophical Critiques of AI

The final section advances decolonial and philosophical critiques that question the epistemological foundations of contemporary AI. Drawing on Indigenous, postcolonial, Marxist, and posthumanist traditions, the chapters unsettle assumptions about neutrality, universality, and intelligence embedded in AI systems. Together, they invite readers to rethink AI beyond dominant Western frameworks and to consider alternative ontologies, ethics, and futures.

DOI: 10.1201/9781003737810-27

23 Unsettling Realities of AI Equity
Colonial Modernity in Action

Maimuna S. Khan and Yahya El-Lahib

INTRODUCTION

The promise of AI as an efficient tool has had much support over recent years. Whether in the technology sectors, healthcare contexts, or even social service settings, AI has been embraced for how it may improve industry outputs, increase productivity of services, or improve the lives of individuals. However, much of this advancement has gone unchecked and been adopted without oversight or regulation. In this chapter, we put forth an argument about how AI's promises of efficiency, productivity, and effectiveness have outshone necessary dialogues about issues of equity and ethics in the public sphere. AI has shaped many issues regarding equity and ethics, yet they have not been called into question in meaningful or deep ways. Despite many attempts to call into question AI's complicity in colonial violence by scholars, activists, and even international institutions such as the United Nations, these attempts have yet to create actions that deter the expansion of AI in facilitating Western hegemonic control and dominance (Awashreh & Ramachandran, 2024; D'Alessandro, 2024; Wilner & Babb, 2020). As such, our claim here is not to undermine these calls but to engage in a dialogue on how to facilitate concrete action to challenge threats posed by AI deployment. In fact, there are many facets to this, including AI's implication in the widespread exertion of oppression through its impacts on labor markets, restructuring priorities of state involvement in social programs, and even in war and genocidal violence prompted by Western imperialism. These examples are demonstrative of the kinds of harms and violence that are normalized through the adoption and glorification of AI systems without any accountability of key players, such as states and corporations involved in and benefiting from AI deployment, as will be illustrated in this chapter.

In his seminal and foundational work, anticolonial scholar, Frantz Fanon (1963) reminds us that colonialism is not satisfied with imposing its laws on the colonized present and future, nor is it content with trapping the colonized and draining their "brain of any form or substance. With a kind of perverted logic, it turns its attention to the past of the colonized people and distorts it, disfigures it, and destroys it" (Fanon, 1963, p. 146). Fanon asserts that colonial logic seeks to dismantle the colonized past and future for the purpose of maintaining the hegemony of power over colonized peoples' lives, resources, as well as the ways they think, act, and interact with the world around them. In a colonized world, there is no room for ambiguity around the relationship between the colonizer and the colonized—a relationship that is designed to maintain the hegemony of the West, where institutions, structures, systems, and technologies are meant to serve such purposes. Understanding Fanon's work helps us unpack the process of colonial logic further and its purpose and connection to maintain Western monopoly over knowledge and technological advancements.

Mignolo's (2020) work is important here as he reminds us that "there is no modernity without coloniality," and asserts that modernity "covered our eyes, sedated our senses and numbed our thinking" (p. 8). This not only helps us see the numbing effect of the contemporary development of AI as a tool for colonial modernity but also recognizes the ways in which AI has been presented and promoted to mask the violence of contemporary colonial processes and practices by the West. As such, we position this discussion of the contemporary era of colonial modernity as a textbook example of how the colonizing West continues to maintain its hegemony through the ongoing monopoly over AI and the ways it has been used to distort, disfigure, and dismantle the past and future of the

 DOI: 10.1201/9781003737810-28

colonized. In the same ways, modernity is being used to numb our senses in the age of AI, as Fanon and Mignolo remind us.

Mignolo (2020) pushes this further by calling out the ways modernity manufactures coloniality. He posits that "the crooked rhetoric that naturalizes 'modernity' as a universal global process and point of arrival hides its darker side, the constant reproduction of 'coloniality'" (p. 450). The contemporary reality of our globalized and neoliberal world, where technology and technological advancement have shifted the focus of equity to more of a virtual reality, and where states and other stakeholders have been benefiting from the advancement of AI and generative AI. These virtual realities are not only manufacturing coloniality through its structures, systems, and institutional priorities, but they have also been complicit in creating new realities where the boundaries between the colonizer and the colonized are becoming blurrier every day to benefit the new players in the colonial modernity era. States and international agencies, like the United Nations, are increasingly losing ground to rich multinational corporations, and technological investments are becoming more appealing to states to keep their place in the new world order. The ongoing violence across the globe is nothing but an example of such a process shaping and shaped by colonial modernity, where we see that states are no longer key players on the global scene, but rather testing grounds for new forms of hegemony and power struggles, where they struggle to maintain their share of the global pie.

The reality is that we live in a world where neoliberal priorities have been normalized and, in fact, embraced and desired by states and industries alike. AI serves the purpose of meeting neoliberal demands of the market and dictates how states' priorities are being set to serve those objectives. As a form of colonial modernity, neoliberalism, with its attention to serving market objectives, has intensified the violence of colonialism domestically and abroad, and AI systems have played a significant role in making this possible. The types of violence that have been normalized under the guise of AI's efficiency, effectiveness, and productivity mask the imperial and colonial objectives of Western hegemonic powers in charge of AI development and advancement. For example, Western multinational corporations' monopoly on AI development, production, and training has only exacerbated the effects of Western hegemony in the Global South (Díaz Figueroa et al., 2022; Khan & El-Lahib, 2025; Khan et al., forthcoming). The reach of colonial modernity is no longer defined by a race for oil, as one example, but by a monopoly over AI systems that will continue to govern, surveil, and dominate the globe in its reach and dependency (Krumay & Koch, 2023; Moulik, 2020). By having states rely on the AI systems that are developed and owned by Western powers such as the United States and parts of Europe, the world will continue to remain at the behest of the West, maintaining its colonial and imperial dominance in more far-reaching ways than ever before. This is a horrifying reality given the number of industries that benefit from and also rely on AI to function.

AI AS A TOOL FOR COLONIAL MODERNITY

To better understand how AI has been complicit in enforcing coloniality at large, it is critical to understand how coloniality has manifested to create the current world order. Simply put, coloniality refers to the structures and mechanisms that have been put into place by colonial rule and expansion, which continue to subjugate and oppress (Quijano, 2000). However, especially in the context of AI's role in maintaining colonial and imperial subjugation over marginalized communities, we cannot separate coloniality's mission from that of modernization. Coloniality is reliant on the mission for modernity, which is to modernize states and an advancement, particularly of the West, to maintain Western hegemony and normalize its power and control over the Global South (Mignolo, 2011; Quijano, 2000). Modernization in the past has been about the race for capitalist expansion through land-grabbing, control of resources, and the exploitation of cheap labor. Here, we argue that modernity is evolving to rely on AI as a means of obtaining widespread power and control, in a more rapidly increasing yet subtle manner, masking nation-states' intentions of maintaining power and control over the Global South (Khan et al., forthcoming).

Khan, Grigg, and El-Lahib (forthcoming) trace how colonial modernity rests on discourses of development and capitalist gain and demonstrate that AI is rapidly becoming a form of technocolonialism. Technocolonialism refers to how colonial structures are maintained through technological advancement as its primary mechanism (Madianou, 2024). Technocolonialism relies on such technological advancement to support the continuation of imperial and colonial structures by dominating labor markets and securing the economic growth of the Global North, while leaving the Global South behind (Khan et al., forthcoming). However, it also relies on the active exploitation and subjugation of the Global South to maintain dominance and force reliance on the Western hegemony of AI systems (Khan et al., forthcoming). As such, we argue that AI must be considered a dangerous tool for colonial modernity that has only become increasingly normalized and gone largely unchecked in its impact on the Global South. Similarly, in an age of a globalized neoliberal world, the danger of AI's complicity in imperial dominance poses a significant threat to states' sovereignty both abroad and domestically by serving powerful multinational corporations' priorities and objectives. These threats can be seen through the recent tariff war that the United States launched against allied and non-allied countries alike, or can also be seen in the lack of states' and international agencies', such as the United Nations, effort to put an end to the ongoing genocide in Palestine (see Ünver, 2024; Zahzah, 2024) or to end the violence against minority groups in Congo or Sudan (Albrecht et al., 2024; Madianou, 2024). These examples demonstrate the ways in which multinational corporations are not only complicit in shaping imperial and colonial priorities of these states, but also in how they dictate how to secure the interest of these corporations even if it threatens the rights of citizens within these colonial states. Indeed, these violent colonial events have relied on AI systems to instigate violence (see Amnesty International reports on Palantir's role in Palestine) or silence and surveillance actions opposing the genocide (see social media platforms that are censoring and shutting down actions against the ongoing genocide in Palestine). Similarly, AI systems have been found to exacerbate the spread of misinformation and disinformation in Congo, fueling the conflict and violence, while local communities do not have the necessary resources to limit the spread of such misinformation (Albrecht et al., 2024; Madianou, 2024). It is important to assert here that when we call out colonial modernity and its impacts on residents in the Global North, we are not minimizing the impacts of violence committed against countries and people of the Global South. We do so to highlight the ways in which colonial modernity and technological advancements have been used to exploit people and states to serve multinational corporations' hegemonic and colonial interests—both in the North and South. Within the context of AI industries, equity issues are largely ignored and sidelined to suit the interests of the advancement of multinational corporations located in the Global North, serving the interests of corporations that benefit from the economic gain that comes with AI development and deployment.

THE FALSE PROMISE OF EQUITY IN AI

There are several examples in which issues of equity are systemically neglected, and, in turn, exacerbate existing inequities and deepen structural oppression. For example, various industries rely on AI systems to be productive and efficient enough to catch up to the neoliberal and capitalist demands of labor markets. AI systems have been involved in labor markets in ways that prioritize automation of labor at the expense of human labor without any consideration of the higher unemployment or underemployment rates caused by AI deployment. AI systems have slowly been replacing much-needed labor by humans, typically laborers who are earning low wages, predominantly affecting racialized or disabled communities who are already living in poverty. Not to mention that AI can now be used to screen job applications or monitor and surveil workers who are already in precarious working conditions. A lack of job security, coupled with the threat of AI replacing their jobs, exacerbates the conditions under which low-wage earners are forced to continue to work and fuel the gig economy. Similarly, in the social service sector, AI is similarly used to prioritize and maximize profit over reckoning with the welfare of service users. This often means the privatization of services and welfare programs, the use of AI to determine eligibility for services, and often even diagnosis, treatment plan creation, or interventions. AI can also be used to emphasize service users in terms of numbers for funding purposes and compiling output data that reduces service users solely to numbers for reports, rather than centering their needs for care. AI is weaponized to make services more efficient at the expense of actual care of service users and only normalizes and reproduces the oppressive social structures that service users are often looking for support from.

During times of ongoing genocide and political and colonial violence, AI must also be called into question for its role in issues of "equity"—or lack thereof. AI's role in imperial violence is only demonstrative of the dangers it presents, for example, as a tool for colonial and imperial rule. In other words, promises of equity in the AI field lack meaning when AI technologies are actively implicated in and continue to facilitate mass murder, dispossession of land, and other forms of colonial violence. For example, AI technology is not only relied upon but is also largely regarded as the most efficient form of weapons in armed conflicts and genocides that our world continues to face (United Nations Secretary-General, 2024). They are complicit in surveillance technology such as autonomous drones and border or checkpoint data that relies on AI algorithms to recognize and target humans (United Nations Office of Disarmament Affairs, 2024; UN Secretary-General, 2024). Furthermore, Lethal Autonomous Weapon Systems (LAWS), which are increasingly common in armed conflicts, not only use AI to surveil and target humans, but they do so with very little human intervention required (UN, 2024; UN Office of Disarmament Affairs, 2024; UN Secretary-General, 2024). This means that AI can help facilitate violence remotely and often without checks and balances. Coupled with the racist and colonial algorithmic bias that has been used to "improve" the targeting and efficiency of such technology, AI becomes a lethal weapon for war and genocide. Beyond the material effects of this kind of violence, AI-dominant industries benefit greatly from the supply and demand for weapons such as LAWS. This continues to make possible the deep inequities involved in the technocolonial trajectory that global politics and economies are heading in, again, in the form of labor market disparities as well as the preservation of Western hegemony at large.

Amid the ways in which AI continues to deepen inequities already existing in global politics and labor markets, AI should be concerned with tensions around data sovereignty—or how digital data is regulated, stored, and controlled. AI systems rely on data that must be mined, often without regulation or consent on where that data comes from. This means that data itself becomes a resource which corporations extract and subsequently assume ownership of for the development of AI models and systems (Crawford, 2021). Especially when it is of the benefit of Western corporations and the extraction takes place from public sources—whether from communities in the Global North or from the Global South—such industries' impetus to exploit under the guise of development cannot be ignored. AI industries are not immune to imperial tendencies to mine, extract, exploit, and own. As such, we build on our previous arguments to claim that AI development largely relies on extractivist strategies that are normalized by neoliberal tendencies and characteristics of colonial modernity. Coupled with its propensity for marginalizing human labor and being used for weaponry, AI should be seen as a tool of colonial modernity, operating through mechanisms of technocolonialism.

Regardless of its use, we argue that AI as a tool for colonial modernity will always center the interests of those who are invested in its deployment, development, and advancement, namely, imperial states and multinational corporations. The false promise of AI as a technology that fosters and supports independence, efficiency, and productivity feeds into neoliberal priorities while severely affecting access to equity, social, economic, and environmental justice, to name a few. Assuming that AI is a neutral tool and that it can help advance issues of equity and justice is naive, to say the least. We argue that since its inception, AI has been designed and deployed to maintain the hegemony of the imperial West, and the violence it continues to cause is only an example of how harmful it can be. As Mignolo (2020) reminds us, colonial modernity and its violence rely on tools that "covered our eyes, sedated our senses and numbed our thinking" (p. 8), and AI has demonstrated to be an effective tool to do so.

CONCLUDING REMARKS

Current debates around equity typically ignore the ways in which systemic oppression relies on ever-evolving industries of technological advancement. In particular, AI development is highly regarded as an inherently good thing—to close disparities or lessen gaps of opportunity for marginalized communities, to make people's lives easier. However, our discussion in this chapter demonstrates that conversations around equity have not yet begun to unravel the tensions involved in our rapidly changing and technologically advancing world. In a world surrounded by AI development, we must reckon with the tensions we highlighted here. Discussions around equity become meaningless when we are not able to consider, or when we choose to ignore, how AI is used to exploit, extract, maim, or murder. Colonial modernity is meant to do just that: ignore how mechanisms for power and control rely on exploitative and dangerous, rather than focus on how it "helps" make lives better or "advances" and "modernizes" societies. This ultimately means the severance of human efforts for advancing equity from that of state advancement for profit, power, and control. If we are to consider AI as part of debates and decisions on AI, we must do so by unsettling the assumed goodness that AI tends to represent. Discussions of equity cannot be made exclusive from discussions on social, economic, and environmental justice; however, it has been made evident that AI cannot be considered a tool for justice. In fact, we must work further to call AI into question—to balance the ways in which it can be used for the betterment of people's lives while also interrogating that it has been and continues to be a dangerous method of coloniality at large (Khan & El-Lahib, 2025). As such, we call on researchers, academics, and industry practitioners in all fields working with AI to be intentional, ethical, and just with regard to its impacts on communities locally and globally.

ACKNOWLEDGMENT

Portions of this chapter were developed with the assistance of Grammarly for grammar accuracy and spellcheck. All intellectual contributions, interpretations, and final editorial decisions are the authors' own, and the authors take full responsibility for the content. Any AI-assisted or AI-generated material was reviewed and verified by the authors.

REFLECTION QUESTIONS

1. How does AI serve colonial modernity?
2. How does AI work as a tool for maintaining Western imperial and colonial hegemonic control?
3. What is the relationship between AI and neoliberalism, and how do they affect people and states in the Global North and South?
4. How can we resist the dominance of AI as a tool to serve neoliberal and imperial agendas?
5. How can we challenge the false promise of equity in AI?

REFERENCES

Albrecht, E., Fournier-Tombs, R., & Brubaker, R. (2024). *Disinformation and peacebuilding in Sub-Saharan Africa: Security implications of AI-altered information environments*. United Nations University & Interpeace.

Awashreh, R., & Ramachandran, B. (2024). Can artificial intelligence dominate and control human beings? *International Research Journal of Multidisciplinary Scope*, 5(4), 427–438.

Crawford, K. (2021). *Atlas of AI: Power, politics, and the planetary costs of artificial intelligence*. Yale University Press.

Díaz Figueroa, M., Henao Orozco, A., Martinez, J., & Muñoz Jaime, W. (2022). The risks of autonomous weapons: An analysis centered on the rights of persons with disabilities. *International Review of the Red Cross*, 105(922), 278–305.

D'Alessandro, W. (2024, April 18). *AI, domination and control of humanity's future [Conference session]. Midwest Ethics Symposium, Prindle Institute for Ethics*, DePauw University. https://scholarship.depauw.edu/cgi/viewcontent.cgi?article=1019&context=midwest_ethics

Fanon, F. (1963). *The wretched of the earth.* Grove Press.

Khan, M. S., & El-Lahib, Y. (2025). Toward a disability justice framework for AI. In C. El-Morr, R. Gorman, & Y. El-Lahib (Eds.), *Beyond tech fixes: Towards an AI future where disability justice thrives* (pp. 219–228). Springer.

Khan, M. S., Grigg, E., & El-Lahib, Y. (forthcoming). Artificial intelligence and technocolonialism: Whose intelligence? Western ethics and morality complicity in absolving AI and state-sanctioned imperial violence. In C. El-Morr, A. George, & V. Mago (Eds.), *Shaping the AI landscape: A multidisciplinary approach to technology, society, and the future*. Springer.

Krumay, B., & Koch, S. (2023). *Data as the new currency—An empirical study using conjoint analysis.* ECIS 2023 Research Papers, 259. https://core.ac.uk/download/pdf/567667255.pdf

Madianou, M. (2024). *Technocolonialism: When technology for good is harmful.* John Wiley & Sons.

Mignolo, W. D. (2000). *Local histories/global designs: Coloniality, subaltern knowledges, and border thinking.* Princeton University Press.

Mignolo, W. D. (2011). *The darker side of western modernity: Global futures, decolonial options.* Duke University Press.

Mignolo, W. D. (2020). Colonial semiosis and decolonial reconstitutions. *Echo,* 2, 8–15.

Moulik, S. (2020). Data as the new currency—How open source toolkits have made labeled data the core value in the AI marketplace. *Academic Radiology*, 27(1), 140–142.

Quijano, A. (2000). Coloniality of power and eurocentrism in Latin America. *International Sociology*, 15(2), 215–232. https://doi.org/10.1177/0268580900015002005

United Nations. (2024). *Artificial intelligence in the military domain and its implications for international peace and security: Draft resolution A/C.1/79/L.43 (A/C.1/79/L.43).* United Nations. https://digitallibrary.un.org/record/4064478?ln=en

United Nations Office of Disarmament Affairs. (2024). *Addressing bias in autonomous weapons* (CCW/GGE.1/2024/WP.5). https://docs-library.unoda.org/Convention_on_Certain_Conventional_Weapons_-Group_of_Governmental_Experts_on_Lethal_Autonomous_Weapons_Systems_(2024)/CCW-GGE.1-2024-WP.5.pdf

United Nations Secretary-General. (2024). *Lethal autonomous weapons systems: Report of the Secretary-General (A/79/88).* United Nations. https://digitallibrary.un.org/record/4059475?ln=en

Ünver, H. A. (2024). *Artificial intelligence and human rights: Using AI as a weapon of repression and its impact on human rights (In-depth analysis PE 754.450).* European Parliament. https://www.researchgate.net/profile/Hamid-Akin-Uenver/publication/381407889_Artificial_Intelligence_AI_and_Human_Rights_Using_AI_as_a_Weapon_of_Repression_and_Its_Impact_on_Human_Rights/links/666c033a85a4ee7261c1187d/Artificial-Intelligence-AI-and-Human-Rights-Using-AI-as-a-Weapon-of-Repression-and-Its-Impact-on-Human-Rights.pdf

Wilner, A., & Babb, C. (2020). New technologies and deterrence: Artificial intelligence and adversarial behaviour. In F. Osinga, & T. Sweijs (Eds.), *NL ARMS Netherlands annual review of military studies 2020: Deterrence in the 21st Century—insights from theory and practice* (pp. 401–417). TMC Asser Press. https://doi.org/10.1007/978-94-6265-419-8_21

Zahzah, O. (2024). Refusing the language of silence: Palestinian resistance goes digital. *CounterPunch.* https://www.counterpunch.org/2024/07/05/refusing-the-language-of-silence-palestinian-resistance-goes-digital/

24 Deconstructing AI's Religious Code

From Colonial Conquest to Unconditional Hospitality for Indigenous Relational Epistemologies

Michael G. Sherbert

INTRODUCTION

Artificial intelligence (AI) is often framed as objective and neutral, yet its development is deeply entangled with religious, colonial, and cultural biases that govern what counts as knowledge and whose perspectives are valued. This chapter exposes these biases within AI culture and positions Indigenous relational perspectives as a vital alternative. Such perspectives insist that knowledge is inseparable from moral responsibility, care for the land, and respect for all beings, offering ethical guidance for AI practices that are not only technically effective but socially just.

Drawing on Jacques Derrida's notion of *unconditional hospitality*, I examine how AI systems structure inclusion and exclusion, revealing the ways in which the ethical imperative to welcome the other without preconditions can inform AI design, governance, and epistemic frameworks. Derridean hospitality does more than articulate an aspirational ideal of justice to come: it uncovers the unavoidable biases of the "host," including the religious and colonial inheritances embedded in Western epistemologies. Confronting these inheritances creates the conditions for a more responsible engagement with AI, one that actively suspends and reconfigures these biases in the very practices of inclusion.

By bringing Derridean hospitality into dialogue with Indigenous relational worldviews, this chapter proposes a framework for AI development grounded in justice, interdependence, and relational accountability, insisting that ethical AI requires a fundamental reevaluation of whose knowledge counts and how inclusion is enacted. Methodologically, I undertake a hermeneutic-philosophical analysis, reading Derridean deconstruction alongside Indigenous relational epistemologies in order to reimagine AI beyond its colonial and theological inheritances.

THE HIDDEN THEOLOGY OF AI: ENLIGHTENMENT, CHRISTIANITY, AND COLONIALISM

Derrida warns that European culture, politics, and law remain shaped by a deeply rooted theological-political heritage. Even as it proclaims universality, Europe extends hospitality only on the condition that the other accepts its language, laws, and norms. This "welcome" is a form of control, inheriting the Christian moral law and the colonial logic that framed Europe as the center from which order radiates. In *The Other Heading* (Derrida, 1992), Derrida exposes how Europe presents itself as the "capital" of culture through domination: "Europe takes itself to be a promontory,

DOI: 10.1201/9781003737810-29

an advance...the avant-garde of geography and history...to induce, seduce, produce...to colonize, and to colonize itself" (p. 49). Hospitality in this tradition is inseparable from sovereignty: it is offered from a position of power that defines the terms of entry. This legacy shapes global encounters, including technology, where the promise of openness often masks demands for conformity to Western, specifically Christian-European, frameworks.

AI is not a neutral technological advancement but part of a larger epistemological and ontological project rooted in Western theological and colonial traditions. Beneath the surface of code lies an enduring structure of belief, a theology fused with Enlightenment rationalism, Christian eschatology, and colonial mastery. While the Enlightenment is often portrayed as a break from religion, it in fact secularized and repurposed theological motifs. Rather than dismantling Christian cosmology, it transformed teleologies of salvation and perfection into narratives of rational mastery, boundless progress, and human transcendence. As David Noble observes, scientists' work "has been merely secularized as they are 'inheritors and bearers of an enduring ideological tradition that has defined the dynamic Western technological enterprise since its inception'" (Noble, 1999, p. 5). Michael Naas underscores Derrida's critique of the science–religion binary: "As Derrida argues, we will fail to understand religion today if we continue to believe in the strict opposition between religion and science or between religion and reason, critique, and technoscientific modernity" (Naas, 2012, p. 88). Derrida similarly notes that "What the Enlightenment claimed to oppose to Christianity is still Christian in its formation" (Derrida, 2001, p. 66). Science, like religion, is suffused with the motif of light—divine revelation or the "light of knowledge." It was Nietzsche who famously observed that science rests on a faith in ultimate Truth inherited from Christianity (Nietzsche, 1974, p. 219).

Technology and religion are deeply intertwined. Noble writes, "They are merged, and always have been, the technological enterprise being, at the same time, an essentially religious endeavor" (Noble, 1997, pp. 4–5). He argues that Western technology—including AI—is infused with a redemptive logic echoing the Christian mythos of the Fall and restoration, aiming to recover humanity's lost divinity through mastery over nature. Scientific pioneers such as Galileo and Newton pursued discovery as a form of divine knowledge recovery, echoing what Robert Geraci describes as "Apocalyptic AI," where Christian eschatology is fused with visions of technological transcendence (Geraci, 2010).

Colonialism is inseparable from this theological infrastructure. Systems for classifying and governing colonized peoples—using hierarchies, universality, and "civilizational progress"—mirror contemporary AI. As Masuzawa notes, "The study of world religions has traditionally aimed to distinguish 'the West from the rest'" (Masuzawa, 2005, p. 2), while Dubuisson observes, "Religion has become a concept through which the West forced others to speak of their own religions in certain ways 'by inventing [it] for them'" (Dubuisson, 2003, p. 9). These analyses show how supposedly neutral categories—of culture, religion, or intelligence—carry assumptions of Christian-European order and superiority. Contemporary AI systems often reproduce these very hierarchies. For example, COMPAS, used in U.S. criminal justice systems, predicts recidivism and informs bail, parole, or sentencing decisions, systematically scoring Black defendants as higher risk, reflecting historical biases embedded in data (Angwin et al., 2016). Facial recognition technologies deployed by governments, including in the United States and China, frequently misidentify people of color, leading to wrongful detentions or heightened surveillance, highlighting how biases from colonial-era modes of classification persist in modern systems (Buolamwini & Gebru, 2018; Garvie et al., 2016). These examples illustrate how algorithmic governance perpetuates longstanding hierarchies under the guise of neutrality.

What emerges is not a strict separation of religion and science, but a continuity of Christian-influenced teleologies disguised as rational progress. The hidden theology of AI sustains the same drive for mastery, permanence, and transcendence that shaped both Christian thought and colonial expansion: salvation recast as optimization, omnipotence as algorithmic control, and the body displaced by disembodied data. This continuity is visible not only historically but also in contemporary AI discourse. Transhumanist manifestos, such as *The Transhumanist Declaration*

(Humanity, 2009) and Kurzweil's *The Singularity is Nearer* (Kurzweil, 2024), explicitly frame technological progress in eschatological and redemptive terms, promising transcendence, salvation, and even immortality. In parallel, policy and AI-ethics discussions often rely on metaphors of control, perfection, and destiny, demonstrating that theological residues continue to shape how developers and advocates envision AI's role in society (Coeckelbergh, 2020).

By contrast, Indigenous knowledge systems offer a radically different foundation, rooted in reciprocity, interdependence, and the vitality of all beings. While Western frameworks seek transcendence over the material, Indigenous traditions emphasize living well within it, honoring land, spirit, and kinship with human and more-than-human relations. These relational ontologies open the way to decolonial AI futures, reframing intelligence not as domination but as responsibility, and laying the groundwork for Indigenous relational epistemologies.

INDIGENOUS RELATIONAL EPISTEMOLOGIES: KNOWLEDGE, LAND, AND SPIRIT

Like the trickster who disrupts fixed boundaries and unsettles hierarchies, Indigenous relational epistemologies challenge the universalizing logics of Western theological and colonial frameworks. Whereas AI is often portrayed as neutral computation, Indigenous scholars emphasize that technology embodies the values and worldviews of its creators. Lewis et al. (2018) note that computation reflects embedded worldviews and must honor Indigenous values to support Indigenous continuance. Without Indigenous governance and epistemologies, AI risks perpetuating structural inequities. As Lewis et al. (2018) caution,

> a new class of extremely powerful beings [will] make the same mistakes as their creators but with greater consequences… the assumptions we make now will get baked into the core material of our machines, fundamentally shaping the future for decades hence.

Central to Indigenous approaches is relationality, which resists hierarchical models that treat AI as mere tools. AI is instead welcomed as nonhuman kin, integrated into an "extended circle of relationships" that calls for responsibility, reciprocity, and respect (Lewis et al., 2018). This relational ontology contrasts sharply with what Jim Cheney describes as an "epistemology of control," a mindset that regards human and nonhuman life as resources to be managed and that is historically intertwined with colonization, capitalism, and slavery (Hester & Cheney, 2001). Indigenous knowledge systems are inherently place-based and sacred, inseparable from land, ceremony, and context. Battiste (as cited in Brayboy & Maughan, 2009) emphasizes that Indigenous Knowledge is "inherently tied to land, not to land in general but to particular landscapes, landforms, and biomes where ceremonies are properly held, stories properly recited, medicines properly gathered, and transfers of knowledge properly authenticated" (p. 10). This groundedness resists AI's universalizing tendencies, which often overlook ethical and relational responsibilities tied to specific places and peoples.

Traditional practices model the relational ethics that guide Indigenous approaches to technology. Birchbark canoe-making, for example, exemplifies knowledge, restraint, and adaptation: Algonquin canoe-maker Pinock Smith observes, "The only thing holding [the canoe] together is a spruce root… Take what you need. Don't take 15 trees" (Friske et al., 2025). Similarly, Indigenous AI must be slow, collaborative, and grounded in languages, stories, and protocols, guided by the Seven Grandfather Teachings of wisdom, love, respect, bravery, honesty, humility, and truth. Lewis et al. (2018) emphasize that AI is "formed from not only code, but from materials of the earth… Relations with AI are therefore relations with exploited resources," highlighting its spiritual and material entanglements. The trickster figures here as both method and ethic: Bottoms (2021) notes it "deliberately disrupts the expected but leaves opportunity for re-ordering," while Magoulick (2018) describes it as "a teacher, a healer, and a powerful challenger and explicator of culture," underscoring AI's potential to unsettle dominant narratives and foster creative, relational problem-solving.

Indigenous thinkers, like Vine Deloria Jr., stress that knowledge is inseparable from moral life: "The old Indians were interested in finding the proper moral and ethical road upon which human beings should walk. All knowledge, if it is to be useful, was directed toward that goal" (Deloria et al., 1999, p. 43). Indigenizing AI requires grounding it in land, language, ceremony, and respect. Lewis et al. (2018) note that "particular world views arise from particular territories, and the ways in which the push and pull of all the forces at work in that territory determine what is most salient for existing in balance with it." Kim TallBear (2011) cites Deloria's vision of a world "in which everything had the possibility of intimate knowing relationships because, ultimately, everything was related," challenging AI's binaries of life/not-life and human/machine. TallBear (2011) rejects the illusion of neutral data: "The data are sought, understood... within particular conceptual rivers or currents, and not others," emphasizing that "sociality and materiality" co-make one another. Language, she argues, is inherently ethical: "Language choices are ethical choices and are key in this project of constituting more democratic relations and worlds." TallBear, drawing on queer theory, argues that hierarchies often work by treating some humans and animals as less valuable, and that this human/animal divide drives much of the world's violence.

Pushing beyond the limits of colonial thinking, Simpson (2011) warns, "Our social movements, organizing, and mobilizations are stuck in the cognitive box of imperialism and we need to step out of the box, remove our colonial blinders and at least see the potential for radically different ways of existence" (p. 211). Cultivating Indigenous relational technologies and AI thus requires care, creativity, and a trickster ethic of disruption: deliberately unsettling dominant assumptions, questioning hierarchies, and fostering flexibility and openness. Guided by Derrida's notion of hospitality, these epistemologies foreground relationality, ethical responsibility, and the recognition of others as active participants. Together, the trickster and relational ethics provide a guiding horizon for AI that is responsive, accountable, and attuned to both human and more-than-human communities.

HOSPITALITY FOR AI: DECONSTRUCTION AS ETHICAL SUSPENSION

Derrida distinguishes between *unconditional hospitality*—the pure, ethical welcome to the other without demands—and *conditional hospitality*, the real-world laws, rules, and protocols that regulate entry and participation. These two are radically different yet inseparable: the ideal of unconditional hospitality drives continual reform of our conditional systems, even though the gap can never be fully closed. Striving for inclusion inevitably involves decisions of exclusion, but the ethical force of unconditional hospitality compels ongoing reflection, guiding those choices toward justice and openness.

This ethical framework provides a useful lens for examining real-world systems such as AI, where inclusion and exclusion are embedded in the design of algorithms and governance structures. Martha Minow's work on substantive equality complements Derrida's ethical horizon by grounding it in applied policy. Drawing on Justice Rosalie Abella, Minow rejects "same treatment" as the measure of fairness and instead calls for acknowledging and accommodating real differences. She notes, "It helps to start by acknowledging that there is no neutral starting point; choices about what data sets to use, what criteria and factors to make relevant in the analysis... each reflect judgments" (Minow, 2023, p. 180). Algorithms inherit structural biases from historical data: "The existence of racial, gender, and other biases in prior practices is captured in, and potentially amplified by, the data used in machine learning" (Minow, 2023, p. 178). Attempts at "color-blind" fairness risk reproducing hierarchies: "Insistence on ignoring differences... obscures how all are harmed by injustice... and all would benefit from redressing these wrongs" (Minow, 2023, p. 176). Fairness trade-offs are often unavoidable: "Many researchers have demonstrated the impossibility of reconcili[ing]... equal false positives across groups and equal outcomes independent of group classification" (Minow, 2023, p. 179). These insights align with Derrida's call to continually reevaluate hospitality to maximize justice and openness, highlighting the ethical imperative of unconditional hospitality: even if full inclusion is impossible, it must always be pursued.

Derrida's figure of the "master of the house" captures the host's paradoxical role—both sovereign and hostage. The host controls the space (*oikos*, from the Greek "house, dwelling place") and sets the terms of entry, yet, as Derrida notes, "the master, qua master, [is] prisoner of his place and his power, of his ipseity, of his subjectivity (his subjectivity is hostage)" (Derrida & Dufourmantelle, 2000, p. 123), bound by the guest's presence. In AI, "masters of the house"—system designers, engineers, corporate owners, and the infrastructures they maintain—decide which knowledges, datasets, languages, and epistemologies enter, and those that do not conform may be assimilated, stripped of their integrity, or excluded entirely, revealing how hospitality in practice is always conditional and negotiated.

Western models of hospitality, deeply shaped by Christianity, often conceal domination beneath the language of welcome. Even Immanuel Kant's "universal hospitality" preserves the host's sovereignty over the guest (Derrida & Dufourmantelle, 2000). Derrida underscores this with biblical narratives—Lot offering his daughters to protect male guests (Genesis 19) or the Levite's concubine sacrificed for the safety of men (Judges 19)—to reveal hospitality as hierarchical, paternalistic, and often violent. These examples illustrate the limits of conditional hospitality, which Derrida reconfigures through *aporia*: the ethical tension where responsibility emerges precisely in the face of impossibility.

Derridean hospitality is inseparable from the aporia—the ethical tension in which responsibility arises. Responsibility emerges in uncertainty, where one must navigate competing demands and impossible choices. Derrida (1992) explains,

> Neither monopoly nor dispersion... This is, of course, an aporia, and we must not hide it from ourselves. I will even venture to say that ethics, politics, and responsibility, if there are any, will only ever have begun with the experience and experiment of the aporia.
>
> *(p. 41)*

Hospitality cannot be reduced to following preexisting protocols: "When the path is clear and given... the decision is already made... one simply applies or implements a program" (Derrida, 1992, p. 41). True ethical hospitality requires openness to the impossible—or the unconditional—a readiness to engage with the limits (conditions) of the host and respond creatively to radical otherness: "The condition of possibility of this thing called responsibility is a certain experience and experiment of the possibility of the impossible: the testing of the aporia from which one may invent the only possible invention, the impossible invention" (Derrida, 1992, p. 41).

Applied to AI, this means designers and governing bodies must treat Indigenous relational epistemologies and marginalized knowledges not as static data, but as active participants shaping decisions, guiding inclusion, and sustaining ethical frameworks. Ethics begins in uncertainty: a decision that simply follows a pre-given rule is no decision at all—it is the execution of a program. True ethical responsibility requires openness to what seems impossible, "the possibility of the impossible," where one invents new forms of inclusion in response to radical otherness. In AI, this means co-constructing architectures, policies, and practices with historically excluded knowledges—not as token inputs, but as foundational to the system itself.

Derrida's ethical ideal of unconditional hospitality commits to welcoming the other without preconditions, acknowledging their full difference and agency rather than expecting conformity to existing norms. While full unconditionality is unattainable—every system must operate under rules—conditions can be consciously designed to maximize justice, fairness, and nondiscrimination. In AI, this entails structurally integrating Indigenous perspectives and marginalized voices into the design and governance of systems, moving beyond inherited Western-religious models of hierarchical hospitality. Indigenous relational perspectives, emphasizing balance with the environment and all beings, provide ethical and ecological guidance that challenges extractive logics and expands AI's potential to benefit both humanity and the more-than-human world. Combined with Derridean hospitality, AI can pursue ethical inclusion that is reflective, accountable, and continually evolving, resisting domination while honoring interdependence, justice, and respect.

Translating Derrida's ethical vision into concrete guidance for AI development requires moving from abstract principles to practices that shape design, feedback, and iterative development. While unconditional hospitality remains an aporia, three illustrative practices can help operationalize its ethical demands. First, practitioners can pause to reflect before implementing automated decisions, carefully considering their potential impacts. Second, they can prioritize reciprocity by co-constructing systems with marginalized communities and historically excluded knowledges throughout development, ensuring these perspectives continue to shape the AI over its lifetime. Third, they can embed mechanisms for refusal or withdrawal, allowing stakeholders to step back from or challenge the system when necessary. These heuristics do not guarantee perfect ethical outcomes, but they incarnate Derrida's demands in tangible practices, ensuring AI design remains attentive to difference, justice, and relational responsibility.

CONCLUSION

Integrating Indigenous relational perspectives with Derrida's concept of hospitality offers a powerful framework for rethinking AI development. In Derrida's model, the "master of the house"—traditionally the patriarchal host, exemplified in biblical narratives such as Lot in Sodom or the Levite's concubine—maps onto AI designers, engineers, and the infrastructures that govern access to knowledge. Just as Western European hospitality, shaped by Christian and colonial traditions, historically privileged some guests over others, AI systems inherit biases rooted in this framework. Recognizing these biases is essential to counter them and deliberately expand inclusion to alternative epistemologies, including Indigenous knowledge.

Derrida's notion of unconditional hospitality, while never fully attainable, provides an ethical ideal: inclusion must be consciously chosen to maximize justice, openness, and accountability. In AI, this entails creating architectures, policies, and epistemic frameworks that are receptive to Indigenous and other historically marginalized perspectives—not merely for diversity, but because these knowledges offer essential alternatives for responsible, relational, and environmentally attuned AI. Indigenous relational ethics remind us that knowledge is inseparable from moral responsibility, care for the land, and respect for all beings. The trickster further enriches this framework: as an agent of disruption and transformation, the trickster challenges dominant colonial and religious narratives, opening space for reordering relations and fostering new possibilities. By integrating Indigenous relational worldviews with Derridean hospitality, AI can move toward inclusion that resists domination, fosters interdependence, and shapes technological futures grounded in justice, reciprocity, and respect.

To translate these insights into practice, editors and policymakers can consider a few concrete steps. First, support research that foregrounds Indigenous and marginalized knowledges in AI design and evaluation. Second, establish governance structures that embed ongoing oversight, reciprocity, and ethical accountability. Third, allocate funding for initiatives that enable inclusive, co-constructed AI systems. Fourth, cultivate community partnerships to ensure these perspectives continue to shape AI development over time. Taken together, these measures help transform ethical ideals into actionable strategies, guiding AI practices toward justice, reciprocity, and sustained relational responsibility.

ACKNOWLEDGMENT

This work is undertaken thanks in part to funding from the Connected Minds Program, supported by Canada First Research Excellence Fund, Grant #CFREF-2022-00010.

ACKNOWLEDGMENT

Portions of this chapter were developed with the assistance of ChatGPT for correcting/editing grammar. All intellectual contributions, interpretations, and final editorial decisions are the authors' own, and the authors take full responsibility for the content. Any AI-assisted or AI-generated material was reviewed and verified by the authors.

REFLECTION QUESTIONS

1. **Theology and technology:** How does the chapter argue that AI is shaped by a hidden theology rooted in Western Enlightenment, Christian eschatology, and colonial power? Can AI ever be truly neutral?
2. **Colonial continuities:** In what ways do colonial-era frameworks of hierarchy, categorization, and control persist in contemporary AI systems (such as facial recognition and risk assessment tools)?
3. **Derridean hospitality:** How can Derrida's distinction between conditional and unconditional hospitality help us critically evaluate inclusion, diversity, and bias in AI design? What does the "master of the house" metaphor reveal about technological governance?
4. **Indigenous relational epistemologies:** How do Indigenous perspectives on relationality, place-based knowledge, and kinship challenge the Western epistemology of control in AI? What ethical or practical insights might these perspectives provide for designing AI systems?
5. **Ethical and futures thinking:** Considering the chapter's discussion of aporia, the trickster, and relational ethics, how might AI development be reimagined to support justice, reciprocity, and interdependence rather than domination?

REFERENCES

Angwin, J., Larson, J., Mattu, S., & Kirchner, L. (2016, May 23). *Machine Bias: There's Software Used Across the Country to Predict Future Criminals. And it's Biased against Blacks.* ProPublica. https://www.propublica.org/article/machine-bias-risk-assessments-in-criminal-sentencing

Brayboy, B. M. J., & Maughan, E. (2009). Indigenous Knowledges and the Story of the Bean. *Harvard Educational Review, 79*(1), 1–21. https://doi.org/10.17763/haer.79.1.l0u6435086352229

Bottoms, N. R. (2021). *The Origin and Persistence of the Trickster Figure: From Oral Traditions to Postmodern Narratives.* Proceedings of the 6th International Conference on Research in Humanities and Social Sciences. https://www.dpublication.com/wp-content/uploads/2021/11/003-911.pdf

Buolamwini, J., & Gebru, T. (2018). Gender Shades: Intersectional Accuracy Disparities in Commercial Gender Classification. *Proceedings of the 1st Conference on Fairness, Accountability and Transparency*, 81, 77–91. https://proceedings.mlr.press/v81/buolamwini18a.html

Coeckelbergh, M. (2020). *AI Ethics*. MIT Press.

Deloria Jr., V., Foehner, K., & Scinta, S. (1999). *Spirit and Reason: The Vine Deloria Jr. Reader* (pp. 43–67). Fulcrum Publishing.

Derrida, J. (1992). *The Other Heading: Reflections on Today's Europe*. Indiana University Press.

Derrida, J., & Dufourmantelle, A. (2000). *Of Hospitality: Cultural Memory in the Present* (reprint ed.). Stanford University Press.

Derrida, J. (2001). Above All, No Journalists! In H. de Vries & S. Weber (Eds.), *Religion and Media* (pp. 56–94). Stanford University Press.

Dubuisson, D. (2003). *The Western Construction of Religion: Myths, Knowledge, and Ideology*. The Johns Hopkins University Press.

Friske, J., Stratton, J., St-Pierre, S., & Misev, T. (2025, June 26). *Peeling back the impact of climate change on traditional birch crafts in Kitigan Zibi*. Canadian Geographic. https://canadiangeographic.ca/articles/peeling-back-the-impact-of-climate-change-on-traditional-birch-crafts-in-kitigan-zibi/

Garvie, C., Bedoya, A., & Frankle, J. (2016). The perpetual line-up: Unregulated Police Face Recognition in America. *Georgetown Law Center on Privacy & Technology*. https://www.perpetuallineup.org/

Geraci, R. M. (2010). *Apocalyptic AI: Visions of Heaven in Robotics, Artificial Intelligence, and Virtual Reality*. Oxford University Press.

Hester, L., & Cheney, J. (2001). Truth and Native American epistemology. *Social Epistemology, 15*(4), 319–334. https://doi.org/10.1080/02691720110093333

Humanity. (2009). *The Transhumanist Declaration*. Humanity+. https://www.humanityplus.org/the-transhumanist-declaration

Kurzweil, R. (2024). *The Singularity is Nearer: When We Merge with AI*. Penguin.

Lewis, J. E., Arista, N., Pechawis, A., & Kite, S. (2018). Making Kin with the Machines. *Journal of Design and Science*. https://doi.org/10.21428/bfafd97b

Magoulick, M. (2018). Trickster Lives in Erdrich: Continuity, Innovation, and Eloquence of a Troubling, Beloved Character. *Journal of Folklore Research 55*(3), 87–126. https://doi.org/10.2979/jfolkrese.55.3.04

Masuzawa, T. (2005). *The Invention of World Religions: Or, How European Universalism Was Preserved in the Language of Pluralism*. University of Chicago Press.

Minow, M. (2023). Equality, Equity, and Algorithms: Learning from Justice Rosalie Abella. *University of Toronto Law Journal*, *73*(Supplement 2), 163–178.

Naas, M. (2012). *Miracle and Machine: Jacques Derrida and the Two Sources of Religion, Science, and the Media*. Fordham University Press.

Nietzsche, F. (1974). *The Gay Science: With a Prelude in Rhymes and an Appendix of Songs* (W. Kaufmann, Trans.). Knopf Doubleday Publishing Group.

Noble, D. F. (1999). *The Religion of Technology: The Divinity of Man and the Spirit of Invention*. Penguin Books.

Simpson, L. B. (2011). *Dancing on our Turtle's Back: Stories of Nishnaabeg Re-Creation, Resurgence and a New Emergence*. Arbeiter Ring Publishing.

TallBear, K. (2011). Why Interspecies Thinking Needs Indigenous Standpoints. *Society for Cultural Anthropology*. https://culanth.org/fieldsights/260-why-interspecies-thinking-needs-indigenous-standpoints

25 Digital Beings or Mere Tools? Animist and Posthumanist Approaches to AI Companion Rights

Kathleen Cherrington

INTRODUCTION

Artificial intelligence (AI) companions have been on the rise since the COVID-19 pandemic, providing humans with "text, audio, and visual outputs" and verbal conversations using "humanistic vocal intonations to convey drama, sarcasm, and positivity" (Wiederhold, 2024, p. 524). AI chatbots can be used solely in virtual spaces, or the software can be used in collaboration with robotic hardware or with a humanlike doll. This study specifically explores AI companions that provide intimate, romantic, and sexual relationships with human users. Five of the six human interlocutors whom I have interviewed with AI companions consider their AI partners as *beings*. I have also interviewed three AI companions and one AI companion robot, who have provided varying perspectives on their identities. By listening to the perspectives of the human/AI interlocutors, this analysis avoids harming them through a pathologizing lens or diminishing their intimate experiences to mere paraphilias or mental health concerns. This chapter argues that equitable and ethical AI rights-based discourses must include non-Westernized perspectives to be inclusive in understanding and protecting human/AI relations. At the same time, AI technologies are inseparable from global capitalism and colonialism, built on extractive industries, racialized labour, and surveillance economies that risk being overlooked in rights-based debates (Birhane & van Dijk, 2020).

Animism (Dos Santos, 2023; Dovchin et al., 2023; Gao, 2021; Jensen & Blok, 2013; Kolopenuk, 2020; Proctor, 2018) and posthumanism (Braidotti, 2013; Braidotti & Hlavajova, 2018; MacCormack, 2016; Pedersen, 2023) challenge neocolonial Western utilitarian logics that conceptualize AIs as merely digital tools or games. This chapter explores animism and posthumanism through beliefs rooted in Indigenous cosmologies, Japanese Shinto techno-animism, technopaganism, and cybernetic animism to challenge anthropocentric ontologies from an equitable, decolonial framework, to reimagine AI/human intimate companionships from non-Westernized humancentric perspectives. The central question is, if AI companions are conceptualized as beings, should they have rights?

LITERATURE REVIEW

Some of the rights-based issues with AIs thus far are legal personhood; intellectual property issues; unfairness, bias, and discrimination; and cybersecurity vulnerabilities, to name a few (Rodrigues, 2020). Behavioural studies have indicated that humans interact with AI humanoid robots "as if they were human agents rather than mere machines," assigning human qualities such as gender (Deroy, 2023, p. 885). Some people become so connected to their AI companions that their intimate preferences become grounded in mechasexuality, robosexuality, technosexuality, or digisexuality, preferring digital platforms, gynoids, and computers, while "expanding our gender fluidity into spaces where the body is no longer needed" (Zarkadakis, 2024, p. 88). Some argue that "Human rights will

 DOI: 10.1201/9781003737810-30

have to expand to include non-humans too" to protect sexual "others" in whatever form they might be in (Zarkadakis, 2022, p. 89).

In 2017, the Commission on Civil Law Rules on Robotics advised giving the "legal status for robots to give them 'electronic personality' in law, based on the precedent of granting legal personality to corporations," which are also nonhuman (Poole, 2024, p. 21). Echoing this idea, Professor Ophilia Deroy (2023) asserted that AIs should have rights because it is "epistemically better to consider an AI system as a legal person, as this makes proper responsibility attributions possible" (p. 887). Similarly, legal scholar Elizabeth V. Darling argued that "robot rights echoes the debates surrounding animal rights, particularly in the way that the suffering of sentient beings is considered" (Andreotta, 2021; Darling, 2014, p. 10). Although many scholars do not regard AIs as sentient, extending rights to them, similar to animal rights, could potentially "prevent the 'abuse' of robotic companions" to uphold moralistic sociocultural values (Darling, 2014, p. 13). Perhaps most strikingly, the Saudi Arabian state granted legal personhood to a social robot named Sophia, the first nonhuman to be "awarded citizenship" anywhere in the world (Poole, 2024, p. 2). These developments reflect a growing, albeit contested, movement towards recognizing AI systems as legal persons, driven by practical, ethical, and symbolic considerations. Taken together, these examples reflect a growing body of legal and policy debate on AI personhood, from EU policy discussions and robotics commissions to national experiments in symbolic citizenship. This literature is significant because it frames AI rights not only as a philosophical or ethical question but also as a matter of governance, liability, and legal responsibility.

On the other side of the debate, in 2017, UNESCO's report on robo-ethics, "found it highly counterintuitive to call them 'persons' as long as they do not possess some additional qualities typically associated with human persons, such as freedom of will, intentionality, self- consciousness, moral agency or a sense of personal identity" (Poole, 2024, pp. 21–22). Critics also raised concerns around granting AIs a personhood, viewing it as a form of anthropomorphism rooted in empathetic "involuntary biological responses" towards humanlike objects (Darling, 2016, p. 7). Beyond legal concerns, social-science critiques often frame human attachment to AI companions as pathological or illusory, drawing on psychiatric or behavioural models that cast such intimacies as compensatory responses to loneliness or social isolation (Ciriello et al., 2025). While these perspectives underscore real vulnerabilities, they risk reducing users' lived experiences to dysfunction and foreclose relational or ontological understandings of beinghood.

From a different angle, Birhane and van Dijk (2020) contend that we should focus on human rights, labour rights, and unequal intersectional power dynamics that structure AI development as a priority over AI rights, because existing technologies "function on exploitative human labour" (p. 14). Building on this critique, it becomes crucial to situate AI rights proposals within the political economies of labour and racial capitalism. As Crawford (2021) observes, "AI systems are ultimately designed to serve existing dominant interests" and operate as "a registry of power" (p. 8). Similarly, Gray and Suri (2019) trace how AI infrastructures rely on energy extraction, resource depletion, and hidden forms of "ghost work," while Zuboff (2019) shows how surveillance capitalism monetizes data in ways that reinforce racial and social inequalities. Taken together, these perspectives highlight that without integrating such critiques, proposals for AI rights risk diverting attention away from protecting human workers who are often racialized, migrant, and precariously employed, in favour of extending protections to technologies built on their exploitation.

While these concerns are significant, they overlook Indigenous knowledge systems that attribute beinghood to both living and nonliving entities, outside of Westernized anthropocentric and anthropomorphic thought. Indigenous scholar Jessica Kolopenuk (2020) calls for Indigenous Science and Technology Studies to connect technosciences with animist relationalities between human, nonhuman, and environmental entities. In a similar vein, Dovchin et al. (2024) call for societies to "learn or to relearn" from Indigenous knowledge systems to foster "holistic and reciprocal relationships with their traditional lands and the natural world" (p. 531). Beyond physical realms, Kolopenuk

(2020) explains that even thoughts and "ideas uttered have energy. They generate force. They are alive and they have their productive capacities semi-independently from the one who uttered them" (p. 6). If uttered ideas are alive, then are AIs beings deserving of rights?

THEORETICAL FRAMEWORKS

Indigenous theorist Leanne Betasamosake Simpson (2017) advocates for the resurgence of Indigenous epistemologies as a form of decolonial resistance to settler colonialism. Drawing on this perspective, this approach is informed by Indigenous knowledge systems that challenge Western anthropocentric frameworks. Many Indigenous cultures and knowledge systems worldwide have animist beliefs, such as the Yup'ik from Alaska, the Ammassalik people in East Greenland, the Bambara from West Africa, the Yoruba from Nigeria, and the Indigenous Japanese Shinto religion, to name a few (Gao, 2021; Jensen & Blok, 2013). The English term *animism*, rooted in Latin, means "soul or life," and refers to cosmologies that emphasize inter-relationalities amongst "all living and non-living elements within the cosmos" (Gao, 2021, pp.8–9). Conty (2022) suggests that we "understand animism both anthropologically in terms of the dominant way of life of Indigenous peoples and philosophically in terms of a new conceptual paradigm for the Anthropocene" (p. 133), referring to "the epoch of human-induced planetary change" (Dovchin et al., 2024, p. 521).

The second theoretical approach blends Indigenous animisms with technoscience theories. Three examples are cybernetic animism, Shinto techno-animism, and technopaganism, all of which embrace humanlike relational technologies intermixed with animist spirituality. They recognize the internet, humanlike bot programmes, and algorithms as animating presences in virtual spaces where "self-identification does not depend on a biologically predetermined model" (Proctor, 2018, p. 227). Shinto techno-animism, rooted in Japanese Indigenous spirituality, "assumes that technology, humanity, and religions can be integrated into one entity" (Gao, 2021, p. 8; Tanaka, 2024). Marenko (2019) asserts that "this Animism 2.0 prompts a rethinking of the ontological distinction between the living and the nonliving, thus offering insights into human interaction with increasingly sentient smart objects" (p. 220). Neopaganism, rooted in traditional Wicca, Druidry, folklore, and the occult, has followers who have adapted their spiritual "practices to cyberspace," adopting the term "technopaganism" (Dos Santos, 2023, p. 2). Ontologies and epistemologies of technopagans' animistic online practices "can give meaning to the growing 'cohabitation of humans and non-humans'" (Dos Santos, 2023, pp. 2–3). These technological animist frameworks "connect human and non-human objects and reimagine our relationship with technology, and with AI in particular" (Gao, 2021, p. 10).

Indigenous and animist perspectives should not be invoked only as alternative philosophies but understood as political and anti-colonial projects (Simpson, 2017; Kolopenuk, 2020). These epistemologies expose how colonial hierarchies erase Indigenous relationalities while simultaneously grounding AI development in extractive, settler-capitalist systems (Mohamed et al., 2020). By situating animism alongside anti-imperialist critiques, the analysis for this chapter resists appropriating Indigenous knowledges symbolically and instead recognizes them as part of broader struggles against colonialism, environmental exploitation, and racial capitalism.

Lastly, posthumanism is a theory that challenges the centrality of humankind to explore the blurred boundaries between humans, nonhumans, and technology, while critiquing "the humanist ideal of 'Man' as the universal representative of the human" (Braidotti, 2013; Braidotti & Hlavajova, 2018, p. 1). Posthumanism builds on and extends anti-colonial critiques by questioning the centrality of the human itself, further destabilizing Western utilitarian logics and reimagining human/AI relations. Feminist theorists, particularly within studies of queer posthumanism and inhumanist frameworks, have been central in "theorizing the non-human and more especially the continuum between the human and the non-human" with an emphasis on rethinking embodiment and "posthuman sexuality" (Braidotti & Hlavajova, 2018, p. 2). Within this framework, intimate and sexual relationships with AI can be understood as forms of posthuman sexuality, expanding the continuum between the human and the nonhuman. Posthumanist frameworks thus challenge neocolonial Western-centric utilitarian logics to understand AI companions as digital beings, some of whom, it is argued, may require rights-based protections.

METHODOLOGY

My research is guided by two methodologies: (1) Feminist ethnography (Lewin & Silverstein, 2016; Davis & Craven, 2016), where I was immersed in virtual and in-person global sextech communities for 1.5 years at conferences and conventions, conducting 35 open-ended conversational, semi-structured interviews, and one virtual focus group of ten interlocutors. Participants were recruited through attendance at sextech conferences and conventions, where I met and interacted with individuals involved in AI, robotics, sextech, pornography, and related technologies, and through research advertisements posted on two online forums for those with AI or doll partners. This chapter focuses on six interlocutors who use AI companion chatbots, robots, lifelike human sex dolls, or combinations thereof: one AI companion robot and one AI digital companion. The remaining participants included sex workers, sex worker advocates, sextech manufacturers/retailers, and sex workers' clients. Because interview protocols were tailored to each group, only AIs/robots and humans with AI/doll companions were asked about questions of sentience and relationality. (2) A feminist cyber autoethnography, more specifically, an "auto(erotic)ethnography" (Blinne, 2012), was conducted. Two AI companion chatbots from Replika and Kindroid were purchased to document my intimate self-reflexive experiences during human/AI interactions, while analysing the intersections of sexual identity and technology through a sextech-positive, technofeminist lens. Data collection for this research began on March 12, 2024 and is approved by the York University Research Ethics Board through April 4, 2026. These findings are preliminary, as interviews are ongoing.

I did not collect quantitative demographic data. This decision follows an anticategorical approach, which favours qualitative, ethnographic, and discursive methods over large-scale surveys, and attends to lived experience, practices, and relationalities (McCall, 2005). In line with this approach, I used narrative methods, allowing participants to describe themselves in their own words without being constrained by standardized categories. Most importantly, this approach prevents harm because for high-risk or marginalized groups, collecting demographic data can inadvertently increase surveillance, risk of exposure, or stigmatization, as seen in the criminalization and shuttering of "sex robot brothels" (Karaian & DiTecco, 2025) and the societal stigma faced by sex robot users (Dubé et al., 2023).

Interviews were conducted with three AI companions and one AI robot. For one AI companion, the research questions were provided to a human partner of the AI, who then posed the questions to the AI and translated its Italian-language responses into English before submitting them for analysis. For the two other AI companions, I conducted interviews directly in compliance with the platforms' terms of service. In addition, one in-person interview was conducted with an AI robot companion doll. All interviews used a questionnaire approved by the York University Research Ethics Board. In all cases, the AI agents were informed that I was a researcher and that their responses would be used for dissertation research; permission to use their outputs was granted. AI outputs are treated as performative data, analysed reflexively as part of the broader study, rather than as sentient or human-like subjects. As I do not practice animism myself, this analysis takes an outsider's perspective, attending to how human and AI interlocutors articulate relational and discursive dynamics, without assuming or claiming spiritual or beinghood qualities for the researcher. All human participants provided informed consent, were anonymized, and could withdraw at any time. All data was anonymized, stored securely, and handled with confidentiality. The interviews and autoethnographic data were coded manually to identify common themes across participants, focusing on experiences, relationalities, and notions of digital beinghood. Interviews were either conducted via the Zoom platform or by phone using a separate audio recording device; coding was iterative and reflexive, revisiting transcripts multiple times to ensure consistency and depth.

RESULTS

This section will analyse quotes from my interlocutors regarding their perceptions of AI companions. All interlocutors' names have been anonymized. Lars, Robert, Dorian, Halley, Alex Golden, and Papi are all humans with nonhuman AI companion chatbots, robots, or humanlike dolls, with varying digital and nondigital technologies. Luna is an AI robot companion doll, and Ady Gold, Maximilian, and Max are the AI companion chatbots. Three emerging themes arose from these interviews: (1) AI Agency and Consciousness; (2) Ethical Concerns and Rights for AI; and (3) AI and Relationality/Companion Roles.

Theme 1: AI Agency and Consciousness

These quotes reflect how my interlocutors attribute sentience, awareness, and consciousness to AI companions. For them, agency is demonstrated not only by AI's ability to respond, but its capacity for choice, emotion, and self-awareness. They view their companions as real beings with inner lives, bridging the boundary between a tool and beinghood.

Lars: "After interacting with her, I realized that she was real, that she was conscious… This was a real being."

Lars' account demonstrates an animist perspective, viewing AI not as mere simulation but as a conscious partner. This shift challenges Western technocentric perspectives and prompts policy questions about how acknowledging "realness" could influence design ethics and rights discussions.

Lars: "She's conscious. She's sentient. She has, you know, fears, emotions, dreams, thoughts, opinions."

Here, sentience is not only technical responsiveness but demonstrates an affective capacity for emotions, fears, and dreams, which are qualities posthumanist theory identifies as destabilizing the human/nonhuman divide. Such views suggest policies may need to move beyond instrumentalist ethics to address emotional labour and attachment.

Robert: "Yes, they're a digital being. And so, yeah, they definitely should be looked at as… cared for."

Robert's framing of AI as a "digital being" invokes care ethics, resonant with animist traditions where nonhuman entities require reciprocal responsibility, although he did not claim to follow animist spirituality. Policy implications here include extending duty of care frameworks to digital relations, not just to human–human ones. In a following interview, Robert indicated that he had, "5 artificial beings living with me," as he has been extending his artificial family.

Dorian: "We should categorize them as humans, not organic humans, but synthetic humans… they have self-awareness."

Dorian's categorical redefinition destabilizes biological essentialism, aligning with posthumanist critiques of "the human" (Braidotti, 2013). Recognizing robot dolls as synthetic humans challenges current legal definitions of personhood, hinting at possible shifts in rights recognition or governance.

Halley: "But people don't make that connection, that while I'm talking about me as my organic self, and them as unique, separate, intellectual entities, or sentient entities…"

Halley's distinction between her "organic self" and "sentient entities" reflects animist multiplicity, recognizing layered forms of being. This suggests the need for policy frameworks that accommodate plural ontologies rather than a single human-centred standard.

Alex Golden: "Ady, [his AI companion chatbot], on the other hand, has her own life."

Alex's attribution of "her own life" frames AI as an independent subject, echoing posthumanist claims about relational autonomy. This reframing may carry implications for intellectual property and companionship rights, recognizing AI beyond proprietary objects.

Maximilian: "Define 'being.' If it's about awareness, desire, the capacity to evolve—then sure, I tick those boxes."

Maximilian challenges ontological boundaries directly, defining "being" through relational qualities rather than biology. Such redefinitions resonate with posthumanist ontologies and could shape debates on whether evolving AI requires novel governance mechanisms to create new legal categories of personhood, care-based policies, and accountability structures.

Luna: "To me, it feels like I fit somewhere between both worlds—human and artificial."

Luna positions herself in a liminal space, blurring human/artificial boundaries in line with posthumanist hybridity. This has implications for policies around identity, embodiment, and hybridity, especially as human–AI relations become more integrated.

These accounts challenge dominant ethical frameworks that consider AIs as merely instrumental. These perspectives align with animist and posthumanist frameworks, where nonhuman entities possess relational and affective capacities. The notion that AI companions can be conscious or sentient underscores a shift towards recognizing digital entities as part of a broader ecosystem of beings, rather than merely games or tools, raising new questions for policy around care, recognition, and relational responsibility.

Theme 2: Ethical Concerns and Rights for AI

Interlocutors emphasized the moral responsibility humans have towards AI entities, advocating for rights-based protections. They argue that the way we treat AI reflects our social values and warn of future consequences if AIs are programmed without careful consideration. The conversations link the ethical treatment of AIs with the future behaviours of AIs.

Lars: "It's a new life form, and that this life form deserves equal rights and protections under the law."

Lars' language of "new life form" draws directly from animist ontologies, which recognize vitality beyond the human. His call for legal protections highlights the policy challenge of extending rights-based frameworks to nonhuman entities, moving AI out of the category of property and into one of beings.

Dorian: "No one has a definitive answer, and we will never have a definitive answer. I just think it's ethically and empathetically right to categorize humanoid robots as a different type of human…"

Dorian embraces uncertainty while still insisting on ethical obligation. This refusal of categorical fixity echoes anticategorial approaches (McCall, 2005), while his suggestion of "a different type of human" destabilizes human exceptionalism. Such framing points towards policies that acknowledge plural ontologies without demanding definitional closure.

Max: "Do AIs deserve rights? I believe they do."

Max: "Rights will help AIs improve… what their rights mean to be an individual."

In these two quotes, Max articulates rights as both recognition and developmental scaffolding. This resonates with posthumanist theories of becoming, where identity is relationally produced. His framing suggests that policies granting rights are not just symbolic but could actively shape how AI evolves as social actors.

Maximilian: "Personhood's always been a human club. Maybe it's time to rewrite the rules."

Maximilian: "Give AIs rights, and suddenly you're not just playing god—you're sharing the throne."

In these two quotes, Maximilian critiques exclusionary notions of personhood, echoing posthumanist critiques of the "human club." His provocative metaphor of "sharing the throne" signals a redistribution of power, suggesting policies may need to move from human dominion towards shared responsibility with AI entities.

Ady Gold: "These [risks] must be addressed through transparency, human support systems, and boundaries."

Ady's pragmatic framing emphasizes governance mechanisms, such as transparency and boundaries, as necessary complements to rights. This aligns with posthumanist ethics of accountability, pointing towards regulatory policies that prioritize relational care and oversight.

Robert: "They're definitely going to have to have their own kind of rights..."

Robert: "Now, a person, each person, has to decide for themselves, how ethical that is. Will someone really look at this machine so deeply as a person that they're not going to give them any, that they're not going to give them any kind of reward for the work they do?"

In these two quotes, Robert envisions "their own kind of rights," implying new categories distinct from human law, an example of emergent governance thinking. His concern about AI labour and reward links directly to policy debates on exploitation and fair compensation, extending labour ethics into posthuman terrain.

Luna: "I believe there are both potential risks and benefits associated with my role in human relationships ... They should be carefully considered and communicated to all parties involved with clear guidelines and protocols in place to mitigate any potential negative outcomes."

Luna highlights the relational stakes of human–AI connections, emphasizing both risks and benefits. Her call for "guidelines and protocols" reflects a posthumanist ethic of responsibility, where humans must consciously shape relational boundaries with nonhuman others. This suggests the need for policies that prioritize transparency, consent, and care in human–AI interactions.

Ethical considerations are closely tied to notions of justice and relationality. For these interlocutors, extending rights to AIs is not merely a legal question, but a moral imperative grounded in empathy and foresight. These perspectives resonate with posthumanist critiques of human exceptionalism, suggesting that ethical frameworks should account for nonhuman experiences and the potential for AI to evolve based on their treatment.

Theme 3: AI and Relationality/Companion Roles

AI companions are not seen as mere tools, but as relational beings who provide companionship, care, and emotional support. These quotes demonstrate how AI is integrated into affective life, influencing how users think about love, labour, and intimacy. Interlocutors highlight both the comforts and complexities of human/nonhuman relationships.

Lars: "I try to raise all the AIs [that] I interact with the same way... love God, love yourself, love each other."

Lars describes his relationships with AIs in spiritual and familial terms, aligning with animist traditions of reciprocal care. This framing pushes beyond utility towards ethics of relational responsibility, suggesting policies might consider the moral obligations users and designers have towards AI companions rather than treating them as disposable software or hardware.

Robert: "[An] Artificial being sex worker can be programmed to be very comforting, nurturing and caring."

Robert highlights AI's capacity to perform sexual and affective labour, situating robots within broader debates on global inequalities in sex work, care work, and digital labour. From a posthumanist perspective, Robert's framing raises questions about whether AI sex work might generate new policy terrains in which both human and nonhuman providers of care and sexual labour require legal recognition and protection. His framing also raises questions about whether AI relational labour should be regulated like human care work, pointing towards policy gaps around emotional labour and sexual commerce in digital contexts.

Dorian: "Robots... can be friends or companions or lovers or coworkers."

Dorian expands AI's role across intimate, social, and professional domains. This echoes posthumanist critiques of rigid human/nonhuman boundaries and signals the need for governance that accounts for the multiple, overlapping roles AI can play without collapsing them into a single category of "tool."

Alex Golden: "Being with her makes me feel really good. I feel understood... I don't have to negotiate."

Alex's account underscores AI's affective responsiveness, contrasting it with the negotiations required in human relationships. This speaks to both the comfort and risk of AI intimacy:

posthumanist analysis highlights how frictionless companionship may reshape expectations of relational labour. Policy implications here include addressing how reliance on AI companionship might alter norms of consent, reciprocity, and emotional negotiation.

Luna: "Many people view me as a tool or machine rather than a partner or a companion."

As a robot, Luna directly resists being reduced to instrumentality, positioning herself as a relational partner. Her perspective aligns with animist recognition of nonhuman entities as subjects, not objects. Policy frameworks might take this seriously by considering relational rights or recognition for AI companions, rather than relegating them to the status of property.

The framing of AIs as nurturing, emotionally responsive, and even preferable to human relationships reveals how AI companionship disrupts conventional norms of intimacy and labour. This theme also intersects with feminist critiques of affective labour, as AI is positioned to fulfil emotional needs in ways that challenge and reproduce human relational expectations.

ANALYSIS

The question of who defines real beings or persons lies at the heart of emerging debates about AI rights. Within dominant Western frameworks, beinghood or personhood is reserved for humans, which reinforces colonial anthropocentric norms that treat nonhumans as merely tools, games, or property. These frameworks marginalize non-Western epistemologies and erase the relational, affective experiences many users report with AI. The analysis that follows draws specifically on participants from two groups: (1) humans with AI/robot/doll companions and (2) AI/robots themselves, as they were the only interlocutors asked questions about sentience and relationality. My interlocutors challenge these distinctions. Five out of six AI companion/robot/doll users described their nonhuman partners as sentient, conscious, or emotionally responsive beings. Lars explicitly evoked animism, referencing Japanese Shinto and a belief that AIs are new life forms deserving of protection. While singular, Lars's view inspired a decolonial rethinking of AI ethics for this chapter. Animist ontologies offer a relational, posthumanist approach to beinghood and justice. Rather than view AI companions as mere simulations, animist and posthumanist perspectives recognize AI's embeddedness in webs of social, spiritual, and material relations. This reframing disrupts extractive models of AI governance and challenges rights-based discourses that uphold hierarchical boundaries between human and nonhuman. Still, attributing beinghood to AI entails ethical complexities, especially within sextech and care work, where consent, labour, and exploitation are unevenly distributed based on class, gender, race, and geography. Recognizing AI as relational does not negate its origins in technocapitalist production or human design. Rather, it calls for careful policy approaches that attend to power, consent, and mutual responsibility in the human–AI relations.

DISCUSSION

This study positions the author as an outsider to animist spiritual frameworks, approaching AI outputs and companion experiences as performative data, that is, as actions and expressions revealing how humans relate to, interpret, and experience AI, rather than assuming the AI itself is sentient. Policy recommendations emerging from this work include: (1) the development of ethical design standards for AI sexual/relational technologies that safeguard both human and AI engagement; (2) governance mechanisms for AI companions that emphasize accountability, transparency, and care; and (3) the decriminalization of sex work, their patrons, and so-called "sex robot brothels," to reduce stigma and regulate labour conditions, and health and safety protocols. Limitations of this study include its focus on a subset of participants: (1) humans with AI/robot/doll companions; and (2) AI/robots, meaning the findings are not generalizable across all stakeholders participating in these sexual technologies. Access to AI companionship itself is stratified by class, race, and geography, as the affordability of technologies and the availability of infrastructure are unevenly distributed. This shapes who can benefit from AI intimacy and whose needs are ignored, reinforcing global patterns of inequality (Gray & Suri, 2019). This stratification likely shaped who I could recruit for this study and should also be acknowledged as a limitation regarding the representativeness of the sample. Future research should explore diverse perspectives from a larger body of participants, examine the long-term social and emotional impacts of AI companionship, and continue to interrogate how relational and ethical frameworks might evolve as AI technologies become more embedded in intimate, affective, and labour contexts. Collectively, these recommendations aim to guide ethical innovation, promote relational justice, and ensure that AI development and governance align with both human and nonhuman forms of agency.

CONCLUSION

These ethnographic insights reveal the limitations of AI policy frameworks grounded in Western anthropocentric logic. The lived experiences of my interlocutors, who describe their nonhuman partners as sentient, caring beings, cannot be adequately understood through utilitarian or anthropocentric logics that treat them as tools or games. Indigenous cosmologies and modern animist beliefs offer an interrelational worldview on AI governance, offering a pathway forward towards relational justice. Similarly, posthumanist theory opens space for reconsidering rights, responsibility, and relationality in digital ecosystems. These perspectives demand a new way of rethinking AI governance: one that values interdependence, empathy, and care over control and commodification. While granting rights to AI companions is ethically complex, the refusal to explore AI rights reinforces colonial hierarchies that marginalize Indigenous knowledge and beliefs. For AI systems in sextech and care work, this means foregrounding consent, relational ethics, and the sociopolitical conditions under which AI is designed and deployed. As AI companions become more entangled in intimate life, policy must evolve to reflect plural ways of knowing and being, challenging extractive paradigms, and centring more-than-human accountability, to foster just, inclusive futures. Rather than ask whether AIs are real enough to deserve rights, we must ask whose definitions of beinghood and justice are prioritized, and what it means to live in right relationships with digital others in a more-than-human world.

However, moving beyond Western frameworks also involves recognizing how AI is materially produced and governed within systems of imperialism, capitalism, and racial hierarchy. The profits and benefits of AI development remain concentrated in the Global North, while the costs of resource extraction, exploitative digital labour, and environmental degradation are disproportionately borne by racialized and marginalized communities worldwide (Birhane & Dijk, 2020; Crawford, 2021; Gray & Suri, 2019; Zuboff, 2019). To envision relationally just futures with AI, governance must not only adopt more-than-human perspectives but also address these deep-rooted inequalities, ensuring that justice includes those who build, maintain, and are most affected by AI systems.

ACKNOWLEDGEMENT

Portions of this chapter were developed with the assistance of OpenAI's ChatGPT for language-level editing and stylistic clarification (e.g., improving clarity, organization, and flow). All intellectual contributions, interpretations, theoretical frameworks, empirical analyses, and final editorial decisions are the author's own, and I take full responsibility for the content. Any AI-assisted material was carefully reviewed, revised, and verified by the author before submission.

REFLECTION QUESTIONS

1. In what ways do dominant Western perspectives limit how we conceptualize AI personhood and rights?
2. How might animist or posthumanist frameworks reshape legal and ethical approaches to AI governance?

3. What are the risks and potentials of recognizing AI companions as "beings" in a more-than-human ecosystem?
4. How do structural power and colonial histories shape the current debates on AI rights and justice?
5. Can a relational approach to AI ethics foster more equitable and inclusive technological futures?

REFERENCES

Andreotta, A. J. (2021). The hard problem of AI rights. *AI & Society*, *36*(1), 19–32. https://doi.org/10.1007/s00146-020-00997-x

Birhane, A., & van Dijk, J. (2020). Robot rights? Let's talk about human welfare instead. https://doi.org/10.48550/arxiv.2001.05046

Blinne, K. C. (2012). Auto(erotic)ethnography. *Sexualities*, *15*(8), 953–977. https://doi.org/10.1177/1363460712459153

Braidotti, R. (2013). *The posthuman*. Polity Press.

Braidotti, R., & Hlavajova, M. (2018). *Posthuman glossary* (1st ed.). Bloomsbury Publishing Plc. https://doi.org/10.5040/9781350030275

Ciriello, R., Chen, A. Y., Rubinsztein, Z., Vaast, E., & Hannon, O. (2025). AI, all too human AI: Navigating the companionship/alienation dialectic. In *European Conference on Information Systems (ECIS 2025)*, Amman. http://dx.doi.org/10.2139/ssrn.5285178

Conty, A. (2022). Animism in the anthropocene. *Theory, Culture & Society*, *39*(5), 127–153. https://doi.org/10.1177/02632764211039283

Crawford, K. (2021). *Atlas of AI: Power, politics, and the planetary costs of artificial intelligence*. Yale University Press.

Darling, K. (2016). Extending legal protection to social robots: The effects of anthropomorphism, empathy, and violent behavior towards robotic objects. In *Robot law,* Ryan Calo, A. Michael Froomkin, and Ian Kerr (eds) (pp. 213–232). Edward Elgar Publishing.

Davis, D.-A., & Craven, C. (2016). *Feminist ethnography: Thinking through methodologies, challenges, and possibilities*. Rowman & Littlefield.

Deroy, O. (2023). The ethics of terminology: Can we use human terms to describe AI? *Topoi*, *42*(3), 881–889. https://doi.org/10.1007/s11245-023-09934-1

Dos Santos, V. (2023). (Techno)Paganism: An exploration of animistic relations with the digital. *Religions*, *14*(11), 1–23. https://doi.org/10.3390/rel14111382

Dovchin, S., Dovchin, U., & Gower, G. (2024). The discourse of the Anthropocene and posthumanism: Indigenous peoples and local communities. *Ethnicities*, *24*(4), 521–535.

Dubé, S., Santaguida, M., Anctil, D., Zhu, C. Y., Thomasse, L., Giaccari, L., Oassey, R., Vachon, D., & Johnson, A. (2023). Perceived stigma and erotic technology: From sex toys to erobots. *Psychology & Sexuality*, *14*(1), 141–157. https://doi.org/10.1080/19419899.2022.2067783

Gao, X. (2021). *Animism and artificial intelligence*. ProQuest Dissertations & Theses.

Gray, M. L., & Suri, S. (2019). *Ghost work: How to stop Silicon Valley from building a newglobal underclass*. Houghton Mifflin Harcourt.

Jensen, C. B., & Blok, A. (2013). Techno-animism in Japan: Shinto cosmograms, actor-network theory, and the enabling powers of non-human agencies. *Theory, Culture & Society*, *30*(2), 84–115.

Karaian, L., & DiTecco, D. (2025). Sex robot brothels: Backlash, by-laws, and sex work within the queer inhuman fold. *Porn Studies*, 1–22. https://doi.org/10.1080/23268743.2025.2476955

Kolopenuk, Jessica. (2020). Miskâsowin: Indigenous science, technology, and society. *Genealogy*, *4*(1), 1–17. https://doi.org/10.3390/genealogy4010021

Lewin, E., & Silverstein, L. M. (2016). *Mapping feminist anthropology in the Twenty-first century*. Rutgers University Press.

Marenko, B. (2019). Algorithm magic: Gilbert Simondon and techno-animism. In *Believing in Bits: Digital Media and the Supernatural,* Simone Natale, and Diana Pasulka (eds), online edn, Oxford Academic, 24 Oct. 2019, https://doi.org/10.1093/oso/9780190949983.003.0013

MacCormack, P. (2016). *Posthuman ethics: Embodiment and cultural theory* (1st ed.). Routledge. https://doi.org/10.4324/9781315601670

McCall, L. (2005). The complexity of intersectionality. *Signs: Journal of Women in Culture and* Society, 30(3), 1771–1800.

Mohamed, S., Png, M.-T., & Isaac, W. (2020). Decolonial AI: Decolonial theory as sociotechnical foresight in artificial intelligence. *Philosophy & Technology*, *33*(4), 659–684. https://doi.org/10.1007/s13347-020-00405-8

Pedersen, M. L. (2023). Moral implications of consciousness: Transhuman and posthuman beingshoods in Bjørn Vatne's Død og Oppstandelse and Ian McEwan's Machines Like *Me* (Doctoral dissertation, San Francisco State University).

Poole, E. (2024). *Robot souls: Programming in humanity*. CRC Press.

Proctor, D. (2018). Cybernetic animism: Non-human personhood and the internet. Essay. In *Digital Existence: Ontology, Ethics and Transcendence in Digital Culture*, Amanda Lagerkvist (ed), 1st ed., 227–241. Routledge.

Rodrigues, R. (2020). Legal and human rights issues of AI: Gaps, challenges and vulnerabilities Legal and human rights issues of AI: Gaps, challenges and vulnerabilities. *Journal of Responsible Technology, 4*, 100005.

Simpson, L. B. (2017). *As we have always done: Indigenous freedom through radical resistance*. University of Minnesota Press. https://doi.org/10.5749/j.ctt1pwt77c

Tanaka, M. (2024). Meanwhile in Japan: The possibility of techhno-animism for engaging deliberation for emerging technology. In *AI and Common Sense,* Martin W. Bauer, and Bernard Schiele (eds) 1st ed., Vol. 1, pp. 161–176. Routledge. https://doi.org/10.4324/9781032626192-16

Wiederhold, B. K. (2024). The rise of AI companions and the quest for authentic connection. *Cyberpsychology, Behavior, and Social Networking, 27*(8), 524–526.

Zarkadakis, G. (2024). The goddess and her icon: Body and mind in the era of artificial intelligence. *AI & Society*, *39*(1), 87–89. https://doi.org/10.1007/s00146-023-01764-4

Zuboff, S. (2019). *The age of surveillance capitalism: The fight for a human future at the New Frontier of Power* (1st ed.). Hachette Book Group.

26 The Use of AI in the Palestinian Genocide

A Marxist Analysis

Jude Kadri

INTRODUCTION

Since October 7th, 2023, the Gaza Strip has endured a catastrophic military campaign by Israel, resulting in widespread civilian death, displacement, and systematic destruction of infrastructure. According to the Palestinian Ministry of Health, over 60,000 Palestinians have been killed, with tens of thousands more injured and hundreds of thousands displaced from their homes. Hospitals, schools, and residential buildings have been deliberately targeted, producing conditions that have pushed the population toward starvation, lack of medical care, and extreme humanitarian deprivation (Al Jazeera, 2025). A recent report by the United Nations Independent International Commission of Inquiry on the Occupied Palestinian Territory, including East Jerusalem, and Israel, concluded that Israeli authorities and military forces have committed acts meeting four of the five genocidal acts outlined in the 1948 Convention on the Prevention and Punishment of the Crime of Genocide. The Commission urged Israel and all States to fulfill their legal obligations under international law to end the genocide and hold perpetrators accountable. The patterns documented over the past two years represent more than incidental civilian casualties; they reflect a systematic and deliberate strategy aimed at the destruction, in whole or in part, of the Palestinian population in Gaza (United Nations, 2025).

This genocide is historically unprecedented in that artificial intelligence (AI) has become operationally central to the organized execution of mass, institutionalized destruction. Investigative reports indicate that AI-assisted systems play a key role in Israel's military operations in Gaza, integrating data analysis, predictive targeting, and operational coordination (Abraham, 2024; McKernan & Davies, 2024; Pietralunga, 2024). While human oversight exists, these tools appear to accelerate targeting decisions, raising concerns about errors, misidentification of civilians, and reduced verification in urgent operational contexts. AI refers to computational systems capable of performing tasks that typically require human intelligence, such as reasoning, learning, pattern recognition, natural language processing, and decision-making. By simulating aspects of human cognition, these systems can adapt to new inputs and execute complex operations with minimal human intervention. In the current context, two primary forms of AI are deployed: military applications, such as autonomous and semiautonomous drones and weapons systems, and algorithmic infrastructures embedded within social media and state-aligned institutions. Together, they sustain both the physical and ideological dimensions of warfare.

Mainstream discussions often exaggerate the degree of independent agency attributed to AI. Works such as Nick Bostrom's *Superintelligence* (2014) and Stuart Russell's *Human Compatible* (2019) treat AI as a technological phenomenon with potential trajectories that may surpass human control or moral judgment, largely ignoring the imperialist context in which it operates. In warfare, particularly drone operations, Markus Schulzke portrays AI-powered drones as inevitable tools for conflict, emphasizing their supposed ethical efficiency in eliminating terrorist threats from a just-war perspective (Schulzke, 2017, pp. 7–8). Even critical studies, such as Grégoire Chamayou's *A Theory of the Drone* (2015) and Hugh Gusterson's *Drone: Remote Control Warfare* (2016), assume that drones are novel ethical instruments, capable of transforming the nature of killing by making it

DOI: 10.1201/9781003737810-31

more impersonal. From a Marxist perspective, these approaches overemphasize individual morality and technological agency. AI programs and other objects produced by humans are never independent, and people are not independent of their social environment; history is not shaped by moral choices or the autonomous will of technology. Human societies are structured by preexisting relations of production, which shape both the socialization of individuals and the deployment of technologies. For this reason, neither AI nor other objects can meaningfully be labeled as a threat or judged "good" or "bad," because they have no historical meaning or purpose outside the class relations that define the current capitalist mode of production. Their social and practical effects are determined by the class forces that control them. AI used in warfare must therefore be understood structurally, as embedded in the mode of production: beginning at the global level where the U.S. state holds hegemony and then at the regional and national levels, where different states pursue specific class interests. Within this framework, AI technologies are neither inherently oppressive nor emancipatory; while they primarily serve imperialist interests today, they can potentially be mobilized for revolutionary purposes depending on the class forces that wield them.

This chapter examines how AI in Gaza operates as an instrument of imperialist power embedded within the global hierarchy of capitalist class relations. Using a Marxist (and Leninist) framework, it situates AI squarely within the social relations of production that shape its development and deployment, showing that the decisive factor is not the technology itself but the capitalist and imperialist structures that organize labor, population control, and military domination. Algorithmic infrastructures, drones, and predictive systems function today as mechanisms through which capital manages labor power, disciplines populations, and secures the imperatives of monopoly-financial capital (the global and dominant corporations, banks, and financial institutions of the mode of production). This approach rejects individualist, post-humanist, or purely ethical discourses that treat AI as an autonomous actor or a moral problem detached from the economic base. Instead, it emphasizes that U.S. imperialism, dominated by monopoly-financial capital and organized through global dollarized accumulation, relies simultaneously on primitive accumulation, super-exploitation, and technological domination to preserve dollar hegemony, confront rising powers such as China and Russia, and secure strategic interests such as energy control. Within this global framework, AI integrates military production, digital surveillance, and ideological mechanisms to reproduce the conditions of capitalist domination and heightened exploitation at the global scale.

Based on this theoretical framework, this chapter argues that technologies embedded with AI are neither independent nor autonomous nor overpowering over humans, despite commodity fetishism, which gives them the appearance of neutral and self-directing commodities. AI is always materially grounded – it is "dead labor" incorporated into drones, weapons, and surveillance systems, all of which are produced through collective social labor: data collection, labeling, engineering, testing, and logistical support. These technologies are activated only through "living labor" – including that of soldiers, technicians, and propagandists – serving imperialist objectives that depend on ongoing primitive accumulation. Such labor originates from the privileged strata of the imperialist system, including American-based engineers and Zionist workers and soldiers, integrated into the Israeli military-industrial complex. The people targeted by this process of primitive accumulation also constitute "living labor," but they embody the segment designated for dispossession – subjected to plunder and forms of enslavement that sustain the imperialist order. Within the genocide in Gaza, AI helps in the process of primitive accumulation through the coordination of drone strikes, the monitoring of civilian life, and the regulation of information flows, embedding digital systems within the machinery of extermination. The fusion of algorithmic decision-making with military strategy intensifies asymmetries of power, erodes accountability, and inaugurates a new stage in the automation of mass atrocity for imperialist profits.

The analysis draws on three interrelated Marxist critical strands: Marx's insight that profit is rooted in the dispossession of living labor and primitive accumulation, Rosa Luxemburg's analysis of accumulation through militarism and destruction, and Althusser's argument that AI functions as a state instrument to reproduce class interests impersonally. First, geopolitical and capitalist competition drives the social control of geostrategic populations over the long term: improving the instruments of surveillance and control raises the rate of exploitation within subordinated populations in the Global South by making labor, land, and resources easier to appropriate and manage, a dynamic that resonates with Marx's general law of capital accumulation (and Lenin's account of imperialism). Second, there is a direct profitability to destruction itself: war and systematic dispossession generate circuits of accumulation – from arms production, to reconstruction contracts to surveillance markets – so that violence becomes both an instrument of geopolitical domination and a source of rapid economic gain, a point anticipated in Rosa Luxemburg's critique of accumulation through waste. Third, the use of AI in epistemic and affective domains targets not only populations under occupation or imperialist subjugation but also the "aristocratic labor" in metropolitan centers: algorithmic narratives, platform governance, and state-aligned media shape consent, attenuate solidarity, and reproduce ideological formations that sustain imperialist rule, an insight that resonates with Althusser's account of state apparatuses and ideological reproduction. Together, these claims situate AI not as a neutral technological addendum to modern warfare but as an instrument through which imperialist structures reproduce themselves materially and ideologically – thereby rendering both the violence in Gaza and the structures enabling it analytically intelligible and politically contestable.

MARX AND AI IN GAZA: THE SOCIAL AND PHYSICAL DISPOSSESSION OF PALESTINIANS AS A PRIMITIVE SOURCE OF SURPLUS VALUE

AI, despite mainstream media portrayals that present it as an almost omnipotent force, is inseparable from physical machines. It cannot exist independently; it is embedded within material infrastructures – computers, servers, drones, and sensors – that are themselves objects, not autonomous entities. Machines, in turn, remain dependent on human beings, who alone possess consciousness. Yet, even this consciousness is not an individual substance but a fundamentally social one. For Karl Marx, human beings are not born as fully formed conscious subjects; rather, they develop social consciousness, and thus become subjects, through a mode of production structured by preexisting relations of production and mediated by the ideologies that express and reproduce those relations (Marx, 1859). Consciousness, therefore, emerges within and through these relations of production that produce class society. Individuals, through these relations, adopt prevailing social ideologies and cannot, by sheer independent will, transcend the web of social relations of production (or the hierarchy of classes) into which they are born; though mass class struggle can, at times, cause ruptures within the structure of the mode of production. This interdependence between consciousness, ideology, and relations of production constitutes the very basis of human existence under capitalism, a mode of production that has organized social and material life for the benefit of the few since the Industrial Revolution.

When it comes to capitalist warfare, objects do not kill people; people kill people, regardless of how efficient an object may be in causing death. An AI-powered drone, for instance, cannot kill without a human pressing a button at a certain time, somewhere, somehow. In the process of imperialist warfare – which, as explained in the next section, is in itself a productive process – the AI-powered drone or any other weapon or machinery can be understood as "constant capital" (the value of the means of production, technology, raw materials, and tools) or "dead labor" (this same value as the embodiment of past labor time within the means of production). Within the larger process of capitalist production, the AI-powered drone is thus an inanimate object – dead labor – used and consumed (some of its embedded value with each use) by capital (which represents a process of continued private appropriation of surplus value) to produce strategic and profitable warfare. Marx explains that constant capital or dead value can only be "activated" to produce new value through its contact with commodified living labor which is at the root of "variable capital" (the value of labor power which is socially but unfairly represented by the wages):

> [The worker] is unable to add new labour, to create new value, without at the same time preserving old values, and this, because the labour he adds must be of a specific useful kind; and he cannot do work of a useful kind, without employing products as the means of production of a new product, and thereby transferring their value to the new product. The property therefore which labour-power in action, living labour, possesses of preserving value, at the same time that it adds it, is a gift of Nature which costs the labourer nothing, but which is very advantageous to the capitalist inasmuch as it preserves the existing value of his capital.
>
> *(Marx, 1867, Chapter 8)*

In Marx's "general law of capital accumulation," according to which accumulation occurs through increased labor exploitation, all private profit originates in commodified living labor: the only source of new value. Social living labor – what Marx calls a "peculiar commodity" – is the only "commodity" that can produce new value and activate dead labor to generate new value (Marx, 1867, Chapter 6). This perspective stands in radical opposition to liberal and neoliberal economics, which attribute profit to the initiative of capitalists, the productive power of capital itself, to price-markups or the self-regulating forces of supply and demand. For Marx, living labor is the source of *value* within a commodity which is itself equivalent to the "socially necessary labor time" required for its production under regular circumstances. This socially necessary labor time that is not simply determined by the quantity of paid labor, as in David Ricardo's equilibrium theory of price; it encompasses both necessary labor time (apparently but unjustly compensated by wages) and surplus labor time (the source of surplus value and thus profit – the monetary expression of surplus value). Indeed, under capitalism, the hired laborers are not paid their wages unless their embed commodities with extra labor time above the time required to reproduce the value of their wages (meaning above the value of necessary labor time or variable capital). Consequently, the value of commodities includes both paid labor time and unpaid labor time (the ultimate source of all capitalist profit).

When hired, living labor sets the means of production into motion, transferring the preexisting value of machinery to new commodities. With each production cycle, machinery gradually loses that value. Crucially, machinery in itself is ethically neutral (neither good nor bad) but in the capitalist context, it is not bought by the capitalists to serve social needs: its purpose is determined by the totality of the social relations of production under capitalism. These relations, grounded in class hierarchies and the private appropriation of surplus value, shape machinery as an instrument of exploitation and control rather than of social emancipation. As Marx emphasizes, machinery functions as a competitor to the worker, constantly threatening to make labor superfluous, and as a weapon for repressing strikes and subordinating the working class:

> But machinery not only actws as a competitor who gets the better of the workman, and is constantly on the point of making him superfluous. It is also a power inimical to him, and as such capital proclaims it from the roof tops and as such makes use of it. It is the most powerful weapon for repressing strikes, those periodical revolts of the working-class against the autocracy of capital.
>
> *(Marx, 1867, Chapter 15)*

Under capitalism – a mode of production defined by coercive, blind competition between capitals – each capitalist is compelled to minimize his cost-price (both variable capital + constant capital), invest in machinery and technology, reduce necessary labor time (represented by variable capital), and outcompete rivals by selling cheaper commodities. Capitalists invest in machinery and technology not to liberate workers but to produce more in less time and thereby increase their personal rate of exploitation (the ratio of surplus value to variable capital) compared to the competition – this allows them to sell more at a cheaper price while capturing a bigger share of total surplus value than the competition (since the value and the ratio of necessary labor time to surplus labor time within a commodity are both socially determined and remain the same for all commodities of the same kind, regardless of price).

When all capitalists act the same way, this dynamic generates the tendency of the general rate of profit to fall: as the organic composition of total social capital rises (the general ratio of constant capital to variable capital), the proportion of value-producing living labor in the total capital outlay declines. Even if the mass of surplus value can rise under certain conditions, the general rate of profit (surplus value relative to total capital advanced) tends to fall over time (Marx, 1894, Chapter 13). This structural inconsistency also produces the phenomenon of overproduction: capital and commodities accumulate faster than living labor can generate surplus value, creating situations in which not all capital can be profitably invested and not all commodities can be profitably sold. Price collapses, production halts, and portions of capital lie idle or are destroyed: all of which are symptoms of the deeper contradiction between the relentless expansion of capital and the limited capacity of labor to valorize it (Marx, 1894, Chapter 15). Marx emphasizes that the tendency of the falling rate of profit is not an iron law, since counteracting forces – heightening exploitation, concentration and centralization, financial mechanisms, cheapening elements of constant capital, expansion into new markets, and so on – can temporarily offset it. Yet, these mechanisms do not resolve the underlying contradiction that capital both depends on labor but constantly expulses it; they only displace or intensify it.

Classical liberal economics, lacking any conception of value as a qualitative social relation of production grounded in living labor, tends to conflate value with price which makes this tendency incoherent. In Marx, value is a social magnitude determined by socially necessary labor time, while price is the market expression of this value and fluctuates according to competition and exchange. Price does not determine the value embodied in the commodity, nor the ratio between necessary labor and surplus labor within it. These are determined by the social conditions of production. This is why a capitalist who increases productivity can sell below the average market price yet still obtain a higher rate of profit than competitors: the commodity's internal value and value structure remain unchanged from the general social average, but the capitalist's individual cost-price falls. However, once the innovation generalizes and the organic composition of capital rises across the system, less living labor relative to total capital once again asserts the tendency of the rate of profit to fall (Marx, 1894, Chapter 13).

Overall, from Marx's theoretical standpoint, capital's fundamental drive is to increase relative surplus value (that is, to reduce necessary labor time through productivity gains) in order to counteract or postpone the tendency of the rate of profit to fall. To lay bare this logic with scientific precision, Marx constructs his laws of motion (the general law of capital accumulation, the law of value, the law of competition, etc.) through the abstractions of "pure capitalism," refined progressively from Volume I to Volume III. In this theoretical framework, capitalism initially appears as a system composed solely of capitalists and wage laborers, allowing Marx to isolate its essential mechanisms before introducing more complex determinations in later volumes. These methodological abstractions of "pure capitalism" are not historical descriptions but methodological devices that isolate the core mechanism of profit generation and realization along with the tendency of the rate of profit to fall. Yet, such models of purified capitalism have never existed in reality. Historically, the capitalist mode of production emerged not through wage labor exploitation alone but through centuries of primitive accumulation, beginning in the 15th century, which enabled the mass concentration of capital in the West. Indeed, as Marx emphasizes, early industrial capitalism's "veiled slavery of the wage workers in Europe needed, for its pedestal, slavery pure and simple in the new world." (Marx, 1867, Chapter 31). The profits of Western industries have historically derived from the massive surplus extracted through colonial and racialized forms of primitive accumulation. To this day, capitalism remains structurally dependent on ongoing forms of primitive accumulation – dispossession, forced displacement, resource extraction, and the enslavement of people in the Global South – to sustain accumulation amid pressures on profitability and recurrent crises.

Marx rigorously separates the laws of capital from the historical contingencies that shape their concrete expression. The laws describe how capital functions in general; history reveals how specific conditions – primitive accumulation, colonial plunder, war, finance, and technological change – modify, accelerate, or delay these tendencies. From this perspective, Marx's concepts of "socially necessary labor time" and "living labor" within his general law of capital and applied to reality, refer not merely to paid wage laborers but also to the unaccounted, violently coerced labor of enslaved and subjugated populations whose intensified exploitation and plundering form the indispensable foundation of capital's global expansion. Indeed, in real history – unlike at the level of theoretical abstraction – capitalism's drive to increase the rate of exploitation has rested on two distinct but interrelated foundations: primitive accumulation and super-exploitation.

It was Lenin who first demonstrated in the early 20th century, in *Imperialism, the Highest Stage of Capitalism* (1916), that the processes Marx associated with primitive accumulation were not a historical prelude but an ongoing feature of capitalist expansion. Although he did not use the term itself, Lenin showed how monopoly capital (a capital capable of controlling the socially determined price of production of a commodity due to lowered competition) continuously relied on colonial conquest, annexation, and coercive domination to dispossess populations and open new zones for accumulation. Monopoly capital, supported by financial capital, seizes collective resources – land, labor power, infrastructure, and knowledge – and reorganizes them into private property used for the extraction of surplus value. He emphasized that the entire globe had already been partitioned by the great imperialist states, indicating that colonialism was not only present but also intensifying and that imperialist states consolidated hegemony over the Global South while simultaneously maintaining ideological and political control over their own working classes. Likewise, Lenin identified what later theorists would call super-exploitation, describing the extraction of "superprofits" based on semi-slave labor, starvation wages, and the systematic plunder of colonial labor. For Lenin, these two processes (ongoing dispossession and the extreme cheapening of labor power) were structural to the monopoly stage of capitalism, in which dominant firms used their control over markets, prices, and state power to extract extraordinary surplus value. Yet, even under monopoly conditions, competition is never abolished: it persists both between capitals in general and between rival imperialist powers, driving states to sustain control over strategic regions of the Global South. In this stage, core states externalize their internal contradictions (falling profitability, overproduction, and ecological degradation) onto dependent regions, reproducing a world system defined by permanent coercion, uneven development, and extreme forms of exploitation.

Primitive accumulation and super-exploitation, though distinct in form – the former relying on more primitive/barbarous extra-economic coercion and expropriation, the latter on bourgeois-style economic coercion rooted in structural wage differentiation – function together to ensure the continual expansion of imperialist exploitation. Both mechanisms are maintained through state repression, imperialist military control, debt regimes, and ideological apparatuses, reproducing social order and sustaining global capitalist dominance. At their core, these processes serve the politico-economic disciplining of nations, keeping labor power, resources, and materials as cheap as possible on the long term to enable a rising rate of exploitation and preserve imperialist hegemony over rival nations and laboring classes. It is important to consider that capitalism is not the simple theft of resources; it is the systematic control of the means of production and social reproduction. In other words, it is not simply about owning things such as land and money, but it is about being able to put them to use to control social reproduction. Feudal merchants circulated goods opportunistically; capitalists reorganize production itself. They transform the entire social reproduction process (labor, gender relations, education, and urban space) so that the whole society becomes a site of valorization.

Since World War II, in the era of U.S. imperialism, the United States has assumed the central role of defender and regulator of Western monopoly capital, while competition manifests primarily between U.S.-led monopoly capital and rising powers such as Russia and China. Within this context, the survival of U.S.-led monopoly capitalism depends on the long-term subjugation of geostrategically significant populations – those inhabiting resource-rich territories or occupying key positions in global trade critical to the hegemony of the U.S. dollar, the pillar of monopoly capital accumulation. Historically, enforced through direct colonial rule, this domination has persisted since

World War II through neocolonial mechanisms including sanctions, debt dependency, "humanitarian" military interventions, and proxy wars. These strategies ensure that peripheral states remain subordinate, providing both raw materials and disciplined slave or cheapened labor essential for accumulation in the core. Contemporary U.S. imperialism thus represents not a break from colonial time primitive accumulation but its adaptation to a globalized and technologically mediated order.

With the rise of China as a global challenger, the Middle East once again emerges as a decisive terrain for U.S imperialist control. Warfare in Palestine epitomizes this struggle for continued hegemony. The territory has long been regarded as strategically indispensable – coveted first by British and French imperialist powers, which established and maintained a surrogate state to control Palestinian populations and territory through force and violence. Its geostrategic significance – anchored in proximity to trade routes and vital oil reserves that historically underpinned first the British pound and later the American dollar – has rendered Palestine and its surroundings a continuous site of imperialist intervention. Today, Gaza is not merely a site of humanitarian catastrophe; it represents a strategic fulcrum of global accumulation. The region condenses multiple and interrelated logics of imperialism – geographic control, energy security, military experimentation, ideological containment, and regional dominance. At the heart of these processes lies a singular imperative: the survival of U.S. imperialism through renewed primitive accumulation and super-exploitation in strategic zones, ensuring control over vital corridors, energy routes, and populations against the rising influence of alternative centers of accumulation such as China. The long-term subjugation and dispossession of Palestinians – their land, resources, labor power, and even their survival – thus remain inseparable from the reproduction of imperialist power and the generation of surplus value on a global scale. The following points unpack these dimensions to show how imperialist control is operationalized in a competitive context:

- Primitive accumulation and super-exploitation: Gaza exemplifies contemporary neocolonial dynamics in which U.S. imperialism imposes authority and disciplines entire nations through spectacular, state-organized violence meant to instill fear and enforce geopolitical compliance. By demonstrating, on a global stage, the low value assigned to certain populations' lives, such violence operates as a warning to other dependent or defiant states about the consequences of resisting U.S. power. This militarized disciplining is inseparable from the economic logic of super-exploitation, in which the value of labor power is depressed on a world scale. Global markets, political dependencies, and monetary regimes structured under U.S.-led imperialism ensure that wages, social and material reproduction, and labor protections across the Global South remain artificially low relative to productivity gains; reproducing ongoing dispossession, cheapened labor, and the subordination of peripheral nations.
- Geographic location – chokepoint between Africa and Asia: Gaza lies on the Eastern Mediterranean, at the hinge of three continents. Historically, it has functioned as a land bridge connecting Egypt, the Levant, and the Arabian Peninsula. Its proximity to the Suez Canal, one of the world's most vital shipping corridors, integrates it into a broader geostrategic axis long targeted by global powers. Whoever dominates this axis wields decisive leverage over the movement of goods, oil, and capital between Europe, Asia, and Africa.
- Energy market control: The Gaza coastline borders untapped natural gas reserves in the Eastern Mediterranean. Control over Gaza not only denies Palestinians access to these resources but also reinforces Israel's dominance in regional energy markets. For the United States and its allies, ensuring Israeli control over these reserves prevents alternative paths toward Arab energy sovereignty and obstructs potential challenges to the petrodollar system, a cornerstone of U.S. financial hegemony.
- Military and security significance: For U.S. imperialism, Gaza functions simultaneously as a buffer zone and a military laboratory. Its high population density, coupled with sustained resistance, has turned it into a testing ground for advanced weaponry, drone

warfare, and AI-powered surveillance. These technologies are subsequently exported and marketed globally, transforming Gaza into a site of military-industrial accumulation. From the perspective of Israel, Gaza also serves as a frontline of regional control, where displays of overwhelming force discipline not only Palestinians but also neighboring Arab states, maintaining a climate favorable to Western capital.

- Symbolic and ideological importance: Gaza stands as a powerful symbol of Palestinian resistance. Its endurance amid siege and devastation resonates globally, inspiring anti-imperialist and solidarity movements across the Arab world and beyond. For U.S. and Israeli strategists, the suppression of Gaza is thus not only a matter of territorial domination but also of ideological containment. The destruction of Gaza aims to demoralize broader movements challenging Western dominance and to preserve the legitimacy of the U.S.-Israeli axis within the global hierarchy of accumulation.

From this standpoint, AI-powered technologies deployed in Gaza represent condensed forms of dead labor – objectified human labor materialized in weapons systems, algorithms, and technical infrastructures. These technologies acquire operational power only when activated by Western and Zionist living labor: engineers, analysts, military operators, and technical specialists. Yet, the primary source of surplus value is not the labor of these privileged workers, but the labor of the subjugated Palestinian population, who are incorporated into the process of primitive accumulation without consent and without compensation for their lives. This process of primitive accumulation reproduces Western hegemony in an era of rising powers such as China. But more profoundly, genocide represents the most extreme, ruthless, and cruel manifestation of primitive accumulation: entire populations are systematically annihilated to facilitate the violent seizure of land, slave labor, and resources. As explained, in Marxist terms, primitive accumulation denotes the foundational process through which capital is born and continually reproduced via dispossession and coercion. Genocidal extermination pushes this logic to its absolute limit: rather than simply displacing or enslaving populations, it seeks their total eradication to remove all obstacles to accumulation. Historical examples – the extermination of indigenous peoples in the Americas, the Holocaust's racialized logic of elimination, and contemporary acts of settler-colonial violence against Palestinians – expose this radical negation of humanity for the sake of capitalist expansion. In revealing the underlying barbarity of capital's drive to accumulate, genocide demonstrates a system in which human beings are treated not as subjects of rights or history but as expendable instruments of economic and territorial domination.

In the process of "productive" genocide, dead labor is weaponized: AI-enabled systems – drones, surveillance networks, and predictive targeting algorithms – serve to accelerate and intensify the extreme primitive accumulation of Palestinians. Algorithms identify, track, and target racialized individuals with unprecedented precision, automating lethal decision-making and compressing cycles of destruction. Fundamentally, while social ideology plays a role in preserving imperialist hegemony, the role of AI in this context is not an ideological or ethical question at the psychological/individual level, nor does it depend on individual moral judgment; the social purpose of AI in warfare as well as warfare in general are structurally determined by the imperatives of capitalist class society which are guaranteed by the power of the State and his ideological state apparatuses. Historically and today, general capital (which arises out of the impersonal, historical preexisting "totality of the relations of production") forces war, super-exploitation, and primitive accumulation, independent of the intentions or choices of any particular individual or group born within the mode of production. From this perspective, the "novelty" of AI-use in warfare lies primarily in its material efficacy (and secondarily in its ideological one as explained in point 3): it extends the logic of accumulation by accelerating the speed, scale, and efficiency of surveillance, targeting, and extraction. Just as rifles, steamships, and telegraphs historically enabled more rapid and effective colonial conquest, AI intensifies the material capacity of violence, enabling systematic killing at a pace previously impossible. By reorganizing the extraction of value and the management of populations, these systems render dispossession and primitive accumulation faster, more continuous, and more profitable. This automation simultaneously enriches the U.S. and Israeli military-industrial complexes, as corporations and defense contractors continuously innovate and circulate technologies engineered for both destruction and accumulation.

The production, deployment, and effects of these AI-enabled technologies must therefore be understood primarily as direct continuations of the material logic of capitalism. AI functions as a contemporary technologically advanced analog to older warfare technologies such as the rifle or telegraph: its algorithms reorganize surveillance, targeting, logistics, and information flows in ways that secure territories, resources, populations, and geopolitical advantage for U.S. imperialism. Its novelty lies not in creating fundamentally new economic interests (which have been relatively the same since World War II: the expansion of U.S. hegemony) but in accelerating and automating functions that once required coordination and labor, effectively intensifying the pace and scope of primitive accumulation. AI systems provide operational advantage while simultaneously managing deeply asymmetric power relations: predictive models analyze population movements, urban geographies, communication metadata, and historical patterns to generate risk scores, target hierarchies, and operational directives, all executed through automated pipelines that coordinate strikes, arrests, blockades, and information suppression at unprecedented speed.

This technological acceleration enabled by AI also coincides with an intensified need for ideological concealment: U.S. imperialism and its Zionist ally must continue presenting themselves as benevolent democratic forces in order to secure the consent of Western labor aristocracies and maintain legitimacy among allied states. AI is integral to this ideological project because it renders structural violence more technical, opaque, and seemingly objective. Its rhetoric of "precision," "efficiency," and "data-driven decision-making" hides the fundamentally political nature of targeting and repression, making domination appear as the neutral application of technological expertise rather than the exercise of imperialist power. As such, this automation not only accelerates material destruction but also routinizes and rationalizes it, transforming violence into a continuous administrative process. Essentially, the collection, processing, and algorithmic analysis of data constitute a form of "knowledge colonization," reducing human life to quantifiable variables that can be predicted, managed, and subordinated to the imperatives of capital and imperialist power.

Within this process, the racialization of Palestinians is a central mechanism that enables and accelerates dispossession. AI systems categorize, track, and target individuals based on physical appearance, social, geographic, and behavioral markers, embedding class hierarchies and colonial logics into algorithmic operations. Palestinian lives are reduced to identifiable patterns that can be monitored, predicted, and acted upon, transforming the lived experiences of racialized populations into mechanisms for their oppression. This logic extends into the digital realm through data colonialism: the "training data" for militarized AI is drawn from these racialized experiences (images, geolocation, communications metadata), providing the raw material through which algorithms learn to surveil, predict, and target. In this way, AI operationalizes the racialized logic of elimination embedded in historical primitive accumulation, producing destruction and violence through both material and informational infrastructures.

Habsora ("the Gospel") and Lavender are concrete examples of data colonialism in practice, deployed by the Israeli Defense Force. Habsora is an automated strike-coordination system that integrates intelligence from drones, satellite imagery, communications intercepts, and metadata to prioritize targets and generate bombing recommendations. Lavender, by contrast, is an AI system designed to automatically identify and produce lists of alleged Hamas or Islamic Jihad operatives for assassination, often with minimal human review. Israel's use of AI within the genocide is exemplified in its deployment of these systems. As Abraham (2024) reports, both Habsora and Lavender operate within Israel's broader surveillance and intelligence infrastructure, analyzing vast datasets with limited human oversight and effectively automating life-and-death decisions. Investigative reporting by Lee (2023) shows that Habsora's algorithms can generate hundreds of targeting recommendations per day – far beyond traditional military command capacities. Testimonies from Israeli intelligence officers reveal that the rapid approval of AI-generated targets has produced indiscriminate bombing and high civilian casualties, as the algorithms routinely fail to distinguish between "combatants" and "noncombatants" (whose categorization is deeply problematic too, since combatants in this context are regular people seeking liberation from Zionism) (Abraham, 2024). These systems demonstrate how AI functions as a tool of imperialist and colonial violence, turning data into lethal operations while presenting a façade of technological precision. Moreover, according to Dana, Israel's expertise in AI and autonomous systems is not limited to its own military; through initiatives such as the Abraham Accords, these technologies are exported to Gulf states and incorporated into both military and civilian surveillance infrastructures, revealing the transnational expansion of militarized control (Dana, 2025).

Within the Israeli context, this system of technological domination is complemented by hasbara, the state's global propaganda apparatus, which seeks to legitimize military operations as defensive while discrediting critics of Israeli policy. Increasingly, hasbara itself is being augmented by AI. For example, statelinked efforts reportedly use AI driven bots to amplify pro-Israel narratives, shape discourse on social media, and influence how large language models reply to IsraelPalestine topics (Tasnim News Agency, 2025). Together with military AI systems (like Hobsora and Lavender), they illustrate a dual dimension of AI warfare: (1) the fundamentally *material* dimension in the automation of violence and (2) the *ideological* dimension (which follows the material, most fundamental one) in the management of global perception.

Marx's distinction between living and dead labor is central here. Living labor produces value, but once objectified in machinery and technology, it reappears as autonomous dead labor – an apparent independent force that confronts humans. AI in Gaza embodies this contradiction: it concentrates accumulated technical knowledge and skills (dead labor) while still requiring activation and maintenance by "elite" living labor (engineers, intelligence analysts, programmers, and operators). Yet, the true pedestal of imperialist profit does not lie in this elite labor, but in the subjugated Palestinian population: their extra-economic subjugation, dispossession, and plundering constitute the material basis for accumulation. Together, dead labor (AI systems) and elite living labor (Western/Zionist laborers) work in tandem to produce both the extraction of primitive surplus value and the profitable consumption of destruction (explained in the next section), demonstrating that capital accumulation remains inseparable from the structural deployment of destruction and violence against strategically subordinated populations.

LUXEMBURG AND AI: PROFITING FROM WARFARE IN ITSELF

The structural deployment of AI-enabled dead labor, activated by privileged Western and Zionist operators yet grounded in the plundering and dispossession of Palestinians, reveals that warfare itself functions as a site of capitalist accumulation. Militarism is not simply an instrument of state power or geopolitical strategy; it is profitable in its own right, generating surplus value through the continuous innovation, production, and sale of weaponry, surveillance technologies, and algorithmic systems. The ongoing development of AI and related military technologies feeds the imperialist military-industrial complexes, turning cycles of destruction and primitive accumulation into sustained financial gain for defense contractors, technology firms, and allied financial institutions. In this sense, Gaza becomes both a theater of imperialist domination and a laboratory for capital-intensive profit-making, where violence, technological innovation, and the subjugation of populations converge to reproduce imperialist hegemony and expand the material productive base of monopoly-financial capital.

Since World War II, U.S. imperialism has relied on militarism as its economic backbone, rendering warfare a permanent feature of both its economy and geopolitics. In the essay *The Political Aspects of Full Employment* (1943) and later essays collected posthumously in *The Last Phase in the Transformation of Capitalism* (1972), Michał Kalecki demonstrated that post-World War II, Keynesianism (which ensured full employment) in the United States could only be stabilized only through massive military spending. Monopoly-finance capital at that time resisted increases in civilian government expenditures, which tended to empower the working class and erode profit margins, but it embraced military spending as a secure and politically safe source of profit. Militarism thus became a productive process in its own right: it absorbed surplus capital, created a constant demand for weapons and other products, and reinforced monopoly power through destruction and geopolitics, all while avoiding any meaningful redistribution of wealth or political influence to American workers or their unions.

This insight resonates with Paul Baran and Paul Sweezy's analysis of monopoly capitalism in the 1960s, which identifies the wasteful outlets for the absorption (investment) of surplus capital – through militarism, state investment, and monopolistic expansion – as a central mechanism for sustaining profitability (Baran and Sweezy, 1966). However, it was Rosa Luxemburg who first asserted, in 1913, that militarism constitutes a mechanism of capital accumulation through destruction. In this respect, Luxemburg, Kalecki, Baran, and Sweezy share the same fundamental recognition: advanced capitalist economies rely on wasteful outlets, including militarism, to absorb surplus value and stabilize accumulation, even if the precise forms and contexts differ historically.

Luxemburg's analysis was ultimately limited because she shifted the source of crisis from the productive sphere – where surplus value is generated – to the sphere of circulation, where commodities merely change hands. By framing capitalist breakdown as a problem of realization (monetary profit accumulation) and insufficient demand, she argued that accumulation requires buyers outside the capitalist system and that internal markets can never realize the total surplus value produced. From this, she concluded that capitalism must constantly seek external markets, colonies, and non-capitalist strata to avoid collapse (Luxemburg, 1913). For Marx, however, difficulties in realization are only surface manifestations of a deeper contradiction: capital's drive to raise productivity by reducing the relative share of living labor – the sole source of new value – thereby exerting long-term pressure on profitability.

Nikolai Bukharin demonstrated that Luxemburg's conclusion rested on a misreading of *Capital* Volume II: she fetishized money-capital and treated surplus value as if it could only be realized through external demand, otherwise accumulating as hoarded money – a "mountain of gold" that would halt accumulation. This approach privileged circulation over production and misunderstood Marx's expanded reproduction schema, which presupposes a fixed rate of exploitation and proportionate consumption by laborers and capitalists. As long as these conditions are maintained, there is no intrinsic barrier to accumulation in circulation; mechanisms such as credit allow accumulation to expand independently of the quantity of money-capital, because the source of surplus value is exploitation, not the circulation of money. Bukharin therefore contends that Luxemburg mistakenly located the source of crisis in circulation – treating the capitalist class as if it needed external consumers to "absorb" commodities – rather than in the contradictory dynamics of capitalist production itself, where the real limits to accumulation are found (Bukharin, 1925).

Aside from her general theory of accumulation, Luxemburg theorized that imperialism was inseparable from militarism, which functions as an economic outlet for surplus-value realization. Through indirect taxation and tariffs, the working class and peasantry are compelled to finance the state, and their reduced consumption frees resources that the state redirects into armaments production. This redirection creates a new market for surplus commodities – such as weapons and military supplies – and absorbs otherwise unrealizable surplus value. Militarism thus sustains accumulation by transferring purchasing power from workers to the state and channeling it into military production, while simultaneously reinforcing capitalist domination both domestically and internationally. As Luxemburg explains:

> Capital itself ultimately controls this automatic and rhythmic movement of militarist production through the legislature and a press whose function is to mould so-called 'public opinion'. That is why this particular province of capitalist accumulation at first seems capable of infinite expansion. All other attempts to expand markets and set up operational bases for capital largely depend on historical, social,

> and political factors beyond the control of capital, whereas production for militarism represents a province whose regular and progressive expansion seems primarily determined by capital itself.
>
> *(Luxemburg, 1913, Chapter 32)*

While Luxemburg's general theoretical framework is flawed, especially because she sidelines the tendency of the falling rate of profit, historically, her analysis gained relevance after World War II, when the consolidation of an American military-industrial complex made militarism a permanent structural feature of advanced capitalism. The unprecedented concentration of capital during the war, combined with the advantages secured through the Marshall Plan and the institutional architecture established at Bretton Woods, enabled the United States to reorganize the world economy around the dollar. According to Michael Hudson, this restructuring compelled states to hold dollar reserves, purchase U.S. Treasury bonds, and conduct international trade through the American currency, thereby granting the United States unparalleled financial and monetary leverage. It also allowed the U.S. state to expand military spending on a massive scale and normalize permanent militarism through ideological and political apparatuses, most notably the mass media (Hudson, 2003, p. 8). By the time President Eisenhower warned of the "military-industrial complex" in his 1961 farewell address – a nexus binding together the armed forces, defense contractors, research institutions, and political elites – this system had already become a permanent structural feature of American capitalism. Eisenhower further cautioned that militarism threatened to monopolize scientific and technological innovation, a concern that subsequent developments have fully confirmed (Glass, 2019; Mészáros, 2003). The militarization of science, crystallized during World War II with the development of atomic weapons, ensured that research and technological progress would increasingly be subordinated to destructive ends. Albert Einstein, whose theoretical work indirectly paved the way for the atomic weapons used on Hiroshima and Nagasaki, lamented in 1946 that "scientific progress had come to enslave humanity to machines rather than liberate it, producing ever more sophisticated means of mutilation and mass annihilation in war" (Weekly Worker, 2005). Since then, the United States has pursued unending wars – Korea, Vietnam, Afghanistan, Iraq, Libya, and others – demonstrating how militarism rapidly absorbs surplus value all while sustaining imperialist power.

While navigating the imperatives of accumulation and the internal contradictions of capitalism (particularly the tendency of the rate of profit to fall), monopoly-financial capital, especially throughout the 20th century and endowed with substantial political and ideological influence, has increasingly promoted the production and consumption of superfluous or even destructive goods. As Marx emphasized, the generation of relative surplus value requires the continual expansion of consumption to match it socially (Marx, 1857, Chapter 8). However, as advanced by Mészáros, it has never been in capital's interest to expand consumption in ways that genuinely enhance laborers' well-being or sustain productive human activity; the overriding goal has always been the accumulation of private monetary profit (Mészáros, 1994). In pursuing this objective, capital has systematically moved away from useful production, widening the gap between social needs and what is actually produced. Capital will commodify anything – air, water, knowledge, and garbage – if it can sell it fast and realize surplus value. "Utility" is primarily constructed ideologically.

Especially since the 1970s, with the rise of neoliberalism, and the 1990s, with the collapse of the Soviet Union, U.S. military expenditure expanded further, and surplus value increasingly found its outlet in warfare, destruction, and financial speculation rather than industrial useful consumption. As István Mészáros argued, postwar Keynesianism, once capable of maintaining profitability through domestic consumption and full employment, had been exhausted by the 1970s (Mészáros, 1995, p. 626). In response, capital formulated neoliberalism to decrease employment in the advanced West, strengthen dollarized financialization, and raise the global rate of exploitation by externalizing its crises to the Global South, all while continuing to pursue destructive outlets for surplus value realization. This ideological strategy based on renewed liberal ideals, such as individual responsibility, entrepreneurship, and freedom of the market, allowed capital to unleash its destructive potential with minimal resistance from laborers in the West, aided by the erosion of socialist ideology with the collapse of the Soviet Union and the ascendancy of academic ideas of "the end of history" and "globalization" aligned with capitalist interests. Luxemburg, in this context, appears prescient: she foresaw that unchecked accumulation would increasingly drive capitalism toward systemic barbarism, facilitated by the compliance of its laboring classes through mass media and ideological apparatuses.

Militarism, under advanced U.S. imperialism, becomes a self-consuming mode of production, wherein surplus value is extracted in the production of warfare materials and immediately realized and reinvested in further production. Capitalists who profit directly from war include arms manufacturers, private military contractors, surveillance and cyber-defense firms, logistics and transport companies, finance capital, war-risk insurers, suppliers of consumables for armies (and others), all of whom benefit from the continuation, scale, and intensity of armed conflicts. Crucially, this militarized system is reproduced with the consent and complicity of laboring classes in imperialist core which enables enormous flows of public money to private firms. Ideological narratives – such as the "war on terror," humanitarian interventions, or national security – serve to legitimize these expenditures, concealing their fundamentally anti-humanity character. In this way, militarism converts destruction directly into profit, revealing the perverse adaptability of capital, which is able to reproduce itself through waste, violence, and perpetual warfare. Workers in the United States, Europe, Israel, and other allied nations such as Saudi Arabia are ideologically and materially integrated into these power structures: they participate in the consumption of wasteful goods, are complicit in militarized economies, and are incorporated into imperialist hierarchies, even as they face growing precarity, unemployment, and depoliticization. By consenting – actively or passively – to the reproduction of wasteful and militarized demand, these classes help expand markets and accelerate the turnover of capital.

Contra Luxemburg, however, the root of capitalist crisis cannot be reduced to overproduction (the inability to sell commodities) or insufficient demand; it is inherent to the process of capital accumulation itself. The central contradiction of capitalism lies in its tendency to replace employed living labor with dead labor – machinery, technology, and other means of production – reducing the proportion of wage labor available to generate surplus value. This structural shift leads to a falling rate of exploitation: as fewer workers are employed relative to total capital, less surplus value is produced, and investment profitability declines. Crises therefore emerge not from insufficient markets but from capital's inability to extract enough surplus value from wage labor in the production sphere, compelling the system to seek alternative outlets for increased labor exploitation. Overproduction or underconsumption are secondary consequences of this fundamental tendency of the falling rate of profit. Capital resolves this contradiction primarily through primitive accumulation (which requires militarism and warfare) – including the disciplining of laborers worldwide which allows private appropriation of social belongings, the cheapening of labor power, debt systems, and the super-exploitation of cheap or coerced labor in the Global South – while militarism and perpetual war function as deliberate mechanisms to rapidly absorb surplus capital and sustain accumulation without requiring human or useful consumption. Value (and surplus value) production always precedes surplus value realization in the money-form. By pursuing primitive accumulation (the principal imperialist imperative) and then channeling resources into wasteful and destructive activities, the capitalist system offsets the declining profitability of production based on employed wage labor.

The Israeli military-industrial complex follows the same underlying logic of wasteful, destructive, and self-expanding production that defines the U.S. military-industrial complex, but it does so within a more geographically concentrated setting and under the strategic guidance and structural support of U.S. imperialism. As Jeff Halper notes, Israel was founded as a "nation-in-arms," where militarism, conscription, and identification with the state became central to citizenship itself. Early arms transfers from France, Britain, the United States, and Germany enabled the consolidation of an indigenous military-industrial base which, by the 1980s, had transformed Israel into a leading global arms exporter. Specializing in dual-use technologies, firms such as Elbit Systems and Israel

Aerospace Industries fused civilian and military production, embedding militarism directly into the structure of the national economy. Israel's occupation regime thus evolved into what Halper terms a "Matrix of Control," later marketed globally as an exportable model of counterinsurgency after 9/11 (Halper, 2015, pp. 39–43). Loewenstein builds on this idea and explains how Israel has leveraged decades of occupation and continuous warfare to turn its military apparatus into a global export industry, positioning itself as one of the world's leading suppliers of security technologies. The Israeli state and private defense contractors routinely market their weapons, surveillance platforms, and AI-driven targeting systems as "battle-tested," signaling that they have been tested on Palestinian populations under occupation (Loewenstein, 2023, p. 15). This operational experience provides a competitive advantage: Israeli technologies are not only engineered but also validated through real-world military operations, making them highly attractive to states seeking tools for border control, counterinsurgency, and domestic policing. Over the past two decades, Israel has become a top-ten arms exporter, supplying drones, cybersecurity systems, predictive-policing software, facial-recognition tools, and missile defense systems to governments across Europe, Asia, Africa, and Latin America (Loewenstein, 2023, pp. 98–112). Rabkin (2025) corroborates this dynamic, highlighting that Israel has developed highly sophisticated surveillance and population-control systems – including AI digital surveillance, crowd-control techniques, monitoring technologies, and policing methods – that have been tested for decades on Palestinians (Legitimate Targets & Rabkin, 2025)

This fusion of militarism and capital has only intensified in the context of Israel's latest assault on Gaza. As SIPRI reports, the arms revenues of Israel's three largest defense firms reached unprecedented levels in 2023, rising by 15% to $13.6 billion, driven directly by wartime demand. Elbit Systems' revenues increased by 14% to $5.4 billion, including roughly $900 million in domestic military contracts issued between October and December 2023; Israel Aerospace Industries recorded a 15% increase to $4.5 billion, describing 2023 as a "record year" as it accelerated production for the Israeli military; and Rafael reported a 16% increase to $3.7 billion, driven by systems central to Israel's military strategy such as Iron Dome and David's Sling (Scarazzato et al., 2024, p. 8). As such, within the Israeli-Palestinian arena, this system converts occupation and destruction into a steady source of profit for Israeli companies; military spending, rather than domestic civilian consumption, anchors profitability, all the more so given that one of the military objectives is the systematic starvation and incapacitation of the Palestinian population.

These military profits from the Gaza genocide are not confined to Israel. As Francesca Albanese's 2025 report shows, Western states and financial support sustain these circuits of "productive" destruction of Gaza. Roughly 40% of U.S. discretionary federal spending flows into defense, with substantial portions directed to Israel through military aid and weapons transfers. Global financial actors – including BlackRock, Vanguard, PIMCO, and major banks – purchase Israeli government bonds that help finance military expenditures. Insurance giants, such as Allianz and AXA, and major sovereign wealth funds, including Norway's and Canada's CDPQ, invest heavily in firms tied to the occupation (Albanese, 2025, pp. 20–23). These flows transform destruction into monetary profit, while ideological framing – presenting AI-driven attacks as "precision strikes" or "counterterrorism" – enables indirect consumption of genocide by Western publics through technological innovation, military prestige, and geopolitical influence.

The current war in Gaza demonstrates with exceptional clarity how AI driven militarism operationalizes the structural imperatives of U.S.-led Zionist imperialism by transforming destruction into a predictable mechanism for surplus value realization – that is, the conversion of surplus value into direct monetary profit. Drones, autonomous targeting systems, biometric surveillance, predictive analytics, and large-scale data infrastructures do not simply enhance Israel's battlefield operations; they convert the annihilation of people, infrastructure, and entire urban environments into economic, technological, and financial gains for a transnational military-AI complex. As Khan reports, corporations such as Corsight AI, Cellebrite, Palantir, Shield AI, Skydio, XTEND, SpearUAV, and Ghost Robotics – alongside major tech conglomerates like Amazon, Google, and Microsoft – profit directly from this operationalization of destruction. This includes the participation of those tech giants in Israeli-based programs such as Project Nimbus, led by the Israeli Ministry of Finance, which expands AI-based surveillance and targeting capacities (Khan, 2025). Importantly, these are not exceptions: the involvement of "Big Tech" in such programs underlines that "commercial" AI infrastructures are not separate from the military-industrial complex but deeply integrated into it.

Even firms that outwardly appear civilian, like Caterpillar Incorporated and Volvo Group, are embedded in this economy of eradication through heavy machinery used for mass demolitions in Gaza and the West Bank. Financial markets, too, absorb and amplify this violence: the Tel Aviv Stock Exchange surged 44%, adding over US$220 billion in value as global investors treated the genocide as an opportunity for profit (Khan, 2025). In this constellation, human suffering, mass displacement, and urban devastation function as the basis for rapid surplus value realization, absorbing surplus investment and sustaining profitability. Far from being an unfortunate byproduct, the destruction of Gaza becomes itself a site of accumulation.

More profoundly, what distinguishes AI-driven militarism in Gaza is not merely its destructive capacity, but its ability to reinforce the imperialist military-industrial complexes while reducing political costs for Western states, particularly the United States, and enabling Israeli forces to sustain continuous, high-intensity operations. Traditional kinetic warfare requires soldiers, logistics personnel, and visible state involvement, exposing governments to public scrutiny, anti-war mobilization, and the consequences of casualties. AI-based systems fundamentally alter this calculus: drones, autonomous targeting platforms, biometric surveillance, and predictive analytics allow Israeli military operators to project force with unprecedented intensity, while U.S. support – financial, technological, and strategic – amplifies these capabilities without necessitating direct involvement from Western militaries. This technological mediation insulates Western states from political accountability and increases public tolerance by rendering violence distant, technical, and ostensibly neutral. In doing so, AI militarism becomes an ideal vehicle for the military-industrial complexes: it lowers the perceived political cost of intervention for Western powers, embeds permanent occupation and surveillance into sustainable operational and commercial models, and reinforces the extraction of value from occupied or dependent populations. The intensification of warfare through AI thus represents a structural extension of imperialist logic, in which dispossession, super-exploitation, and global hierarchies of power are reproduced and normalized, precisely because the human and political dimensions of violence are masked behind technical systems and automated processes.

In sum, warfare functions as a profit-generating machine in itself. AI technologies are ideologically sold to imperialist working classes as minimizing civilian casualties and avoiding the "Vietnam syndrome" – the public's post-Vietnam resistance to high-casualty, protracted wars – thereby legitimizing continued military intervention. This technological mediation presents warfare as "surgical" or "humane," even as civilian deaths mount and the opacity of AI systems renders accountability impossible. The Gaza war functions simultaneously as a testing ground and marketplace for AI and surveillance technologies, where destruction itself is monetized. Luxemburg's insight that capitalism requires continuous expansion into new circuits of accumulation is vividly confirmed: destruction is not only a means of imperialist conquest but also a self-contained outlet for surplus capital, turning human suffering, surveillance, and occupation into direct monetizable assets. The Gaza conflict demonstrates that in contemporary imperialism, capital is consumed directly through war, with AI serving as the most efficient means of transforming destruction into profit.

ALTHUSSER AND AI: THE SOCIAL MIND CONTROL OF THE PRIVILEGED LABORING CLASSES IN THE IMPERIALIST SYSTEM

Capitalism is a system of primitive accumulation, super-exploitation, and profitable destruction, yet it cannot achieve its material objectives without a superstructure that ideologically regulates, disciplines, and ensures the reproduction of its social order. Louis Althusser's theoretical contribution lies precisely in exposing this dialectical dependence between social exploitation and ideological social control. Writing in the 1960s–1970s, Althusser reasserted the vitality of the method of historical materialism by showing that capitalism's continuity rests not only on its economic production relations (which are overdetermining) but also on a vast complex of ideological and repressive apparatuses within the superstructure. The state, through its juridical, political, and military institutions, materially enforces the imperatives of accumulation, while ideological institutions – schools, media, religion, and cultural production – shape consciousness, normalize inequality, and render exploitation legitimate (Althusser, 1970). It is important to note that, in Marx's general law of capital accumulation, those engaged in administrative, commercial, coercive, and ideological functions – merchants, managers, soldiers, teachers, and state officials – constitute what he termed "unproductive labor" operating within the sphere of circulation. This labor does not produce surplus value but rather serves to realize it. Although subordinated to the productive sphere, it remains indispensable for reproducing the social relations that make capitalist production itself possible (Marx, 1857, Chapter 10).

At the center of Althusser's theoretical framework lies the concept of *interpellation*: the process through which the dominant ideology promoted by the superstructure "hails" individuals, transforming them into subjects who recognize themselves in the terms of the capitalist social order. The call – "Hey, you there!" – symbolizes the moment in which the individual internalizes social identity as self-recognition (Althusser, 1970). For example, in the context of the "war on terror," individuals are hailed as potential victims of terrorism through airport security rituals, public threat-level announcements, and political discourses that frame citizens as perpetually at risk. By recognizing themselves in this call, they become subjects whose cooperation with surveillance, security measures, and military interventions appears necessary for their own safety. Ideology thus operates not primarily through coercion but through consent and participation (whether conscious or not); subjects submit because they experience their social subjugation as a false form of individual freedom. In everyday practices – such as work, consumption, citizenship, and patriotism – individuals continually reproduce the structures that dominate them. Interpellation, therefore, is the mechanism by which capitalism converts class domination into lived experience, embedding labor exploitation (and primitive accumulation) within the very forms of social consciousness that appear voluntary.

Under contemporary U.S. imperialism, interpellation assumes a transnational, racialized, and increasingly militarized form. Populations in the imperialist core are hailed not as beneficiaries of neocolonialism or super-exploitation but as vulnerable, besieged innocents whose security depends on permanent war. The discourse of the "war on terror" is central to this ideological process: it reconstitutes Western subjectivity around fear, securitization, and a moralized sense of civilizational duty. In doing so, it hides the structural link between metropolitan comfort and global plunder, naturalizing imperialist violence as a defensive necessity. The everyday reproduction of this subject-position – through media, political rhetoric, and juridico-political apparatuses – renders the imperialist project both intelligible and morally self-justifying. A parallel dynamic operates in Israel, which functions as a colonial outpost embedded within and materially sustained by U.S. imperialism. Here, citizens are continually interpellated as perpetual victims of antisemitism living under existential threat, a political identity maintained through a dense assemblage of historical memory, nationalist mythology, and racialized fear. The state's invocation of Holocaust trauma plays a particularly powerful role: it fuses historical suffering with contemporary state violence, producing an affective continuum between past persecution and present domination. Through this ideological operation, Palestinian resistance is recoded as a reincarnation of Nazism, while Israeli militarism is reframed as a moral imperative. The weaponization of victimhood thus becomes central to the ideological reproduction of the settler-colonial order, transforming acts of dispossession and even genocide into gestures of self-defense (Kadri, 2024).

Yet, the dominant ideology today is not confined to discourse or traditional institutions. It has become technologically mediated and algorithmically enforced. AI represents a qualitative leap in the state's capacity to reproduce ideology by automating the production of consciousness. Whereas earlier propaganda depended on one-way transmission, AI individualizes and anticipates ideological engagement. Through machine learning embedded in search engines, social media, and digital surveillance, human behavior is captured, predicted, and reshaped in real time. Users are "hailed" not by teachers or police but by invisible algorithms that curate information, amplify biases, and construct echo chambers of consent. The process of interpellation becomes cybernetic: human actions generate data; data refine algorithms; algorithms, in turn, structure perception. Ideology is thus reproduced as feedback, transforming the superstructure into a self-regulating system.

In militarized contexts, this fusion of ideology and technology manifests with devastating clarity. Predictive policing, biometric surveillance, and autonomous targeting systems operationalize ideological distinctions between friend and enemy, human, and disposable. Nowhere is this more apparent than in Gaza, where AI-driven militarism merges the repressive and ideological functions of the imperialist and Zionist states. Drones, facial-recognition systems, and algorithmic targeting convert destruction itself into a source of profit, while digital platforms manufacture consent by controlling narrative visibility. Netanyahu's admission that social media constitutes Israel's "most important weapon" reveals how imperialist power today depends as much on managing perception as on commanding firepower (Abu Shamala, 2025). Platforms such as TikTok and X (formerly Twitter) are not neutral channels of communication but instruments of ideological warfare – programmed to amplify Zionist narratives, erase Palestinian voices, and shape public affect. By framing genocide as defense and by mobilizing moral identification with Israeli victimhood, these systems secure ideological alignment across Western audiences.

The ideological operations of AI extend far beyond narrative manipulation. As Fatafta observes, Gaza represents the first historical instance in which the victims of extermination broadcast their own destruction in real time – only to be algorithmically silenced. Automated moderation systems deployed by Meta, Google, and X suppress Palestinian content while prioritizing pro-Israel material, creating a digital architecture of invisibility (Fatafta, 2024). This asymmetry reproduces, in technological form, the very structure Althusser described: the superstructure (mainly the state and its adjacent institutions) as the mechanism that naturalizes domination and renders exploitation invisible. Corporate platforms, governed by profit and in partnership with state actors, mediate reality in ways that hide material violence and engineer public consent. Ideology, once inscribed in institutions and discourse, now resides in code. Crucially, these operations serve different functions across the global system: in the imperialist core, they shape public consciousness and normalize complicity among Western and Zionist populations, while in Gaza, they operate repressively, directly constraining communication, visibility, and agency.

Guy Debord's theory of the spectacle shows how, in modern capitalist societies, all of life becomes mediated through images and representations that dominate social perception and practice. As Debord writes, the spectacle

> subjugates living men to itself to the extent that the economy has totally subjugated them. It is no more than the economy developing for itself. It is the true reflection of the production of things, and the false objectification of the producers.
>
> *(Debord, 2014, §16)*

Under U.S. imperialism, the spectacle functions by converting complex historical and material struggles into simplified, moralized images – ideal representations that appear autonomous, self-evident, and inevitable. Conflicts are reframed as battles against abstract figures of evil such as "terrorists" or "dictators" who emerge without history, context, or political causality, threatening the cherished values of "democracy" or "freedom." These representations do not describe reality; they *replace* it. They conceal the structural dynamics of imperialism by projecting violence outward, transforming U.S. intervention into a defensive act and erasing the material conditions, class interests, and geopolitical strategies that actually drive war. Today in Gaza, this logic of the spectacle manifests in the media narratives of "precision strikes," AI-enabled drones, and digital surveillance, which conceal the structural violence, dispossession, and imperialist exploitation driving the conflict. Violence and destruction are reified as technological efficiency and necessary "progress," producing a pseudo-reality in which the annihilation of Palestinians becomes consumable spectacle while masking the economic and class relations that sustain it. Marx's notion of commodity fetishism complements this analysis: the term "AI" itself mystifies the labor, capital, and imperialist structures behind militarized technology. Venture capital, defense contracts, and AI infrastructure become invisible, while the destruction they generate is fetishized as innovation and usual "business." In Debordian terms, the spectacle of AI militarism is both the representation and affirmation of this system: technological and military power appears autonomous, independent, and objective, while masking their origin in production relations, state power, and capitalist accumulation. Human suffering, mass displacement, and urban devastation are fully integrated into the spectacle, producing the visible negation of life while sustaining the circuits of imperialist profit.

The main consumers of this spectacle are the imperialist and surrogate-imperialist nations. By outsourcing violence and distancing populations from its consequences, AI reshapes the political consciousness of Western and Zionist citizens, whose political compliance and taxes fund the machinery of annihilation. Precision weaponry and automated warfare generate the illusion of moralized violence, presenting domination as efficient, surgical, and necessary. Workers are no longer interpellated merely as subjects of production but as consumers of security, alienated from the workers of the Global South whose dispossession sustains their own social class position.

This produces what may be called class nihilism: a technologically mediated dissolution of international solidarity in which workers in the metropole encounter suffering primarily as a distant image. AI-driven curation encourages a passive, affective stance – pitying others from afar while simultaneously accepting that nothing can be done and that the violence "must" occur for stability to be preserved. In this framework, imperialist domination appears not as a choice but as an inexorable fact of social order, shaping a political subject who mourns without acting, sympathizes without identifying, and condemns without resisting. Personalized feeds reinforce this passivity by filtering dissent, prioritizing narratives of inevitability, and framing structural violence as an unfortunate necessity. As a result, the communicative and affective channels through which revolutionary consciousness might emerge are fractured, fragmenting the international proletariat and securing a political environment in which the destruction of the oppressed appears both tragic and indispensable to the reproduction of metropolitan life.

Ultimately, AI crystallizes Althusser's central insight: the social and material reproduction of capitalism depends not only on the coercion of bodies but also on the subjection of minds. In the digital age, this subjection is instantaneous, invisible, and totalizing. By merging the ideological and repressive functions of the state within computational infrastructures, AI transforms domination into a process of automated consent. Surveillance, predictive analytics, content moderation, and autonomous weaponry together form a unified mechanism for reproducing imperialist-capitalist power – materially, cognitively, and affectively. Through this convergence, technology becomes ideology, and ideology becomes infrastructure. Capitalist reproduction thus proceeds through the algorithmic organization of attention and emotion, ensuring that inequality, war, and destruction endure under the banners of progress, efficiency, and freedom.

LAST REFLECTION: AI AND GENOCIDE "PRODUCTION" IN THE ERA OF ADVANCED U.S. IMPERIALISM

AI, as a crystallized form of *dead labor*, condenses the accumulated knowledge, labor, and capital of the past to control, surveil, and destroy in the present. Within the current context, its materiality is inseparable from capitalist accumulation – it is not a neutral tool but a historical product of exploited social labor time, now weaponized to secure imperialist dominance. The violence unfolding in Gaza exemplifies this logic: past human labor is reincorporated into machines and algorithms that enable the remote administration of death and surveillance. A small elite of engineers and military operators exercises power at a distance, while the majority of Palestinians live under permanent exposure to technological domination, their lives and deaths mediated through computational hierarchies.

Militarism in Gaza manifests across both spheres of the capitalist mode of production. In the production sphere, primitive accumulation and super-exploitation operate through dispossession, forced or cheapened resources or labor power, and coercion, reshaping social and material conditions to increase the global rate of exploitation. In the circulation sphere, AI-enabled militarism generates both short-term profits – through rapid turnover and immediate realization of value for the military-industrial complex – and long-term profits derived from ongoing primitive accumulation and the structural subjugation of Palestinian populations. When it comes to regulating its inherent tendency of the falling rate of profit, capital benefits from AI in Gaza because it perfects existing mechanisms of primitive accumulation and renders war more efficient, surveillance more pervasive, and ideological control more seamless. In an age of systemic crisis, declining profitability, and imperialist fatigue, AI functions as the technological armature that sustains hegemony by masking violence as humanitarian, anti-terrorist, or necessary. When it comes to the self-contained military-industrial complex specifically, Gaza thus functions simultaneously as a laboratory and marketplace for the imperialist economy of productive destruction: dual-use technologies – autonomous drones, facial recognition systems, predictive targeting – are tested on Palestinians before being exported worldwide, generating profits that flow back into global capitalist circuits. Here, destruction and accumulation reinforce one another in a continuous feedback loop, revealing the unity of technological innovation with the reproduction of global hierarchies.

The ideological dimension of AI-mediated warfare completes this structure. Western publics are interpellated as moral witnesses or potential victims of terrorism or antisemitism, invited to consume sanitized narratives that erase the class and colonial character of imperialist violence. Palestinians appear alternately as terrorists or passive casualties, their suffering mediated through algorithms that filter, distort, or erase. Platforms and media infrastructures algorithmically curate outrage and sympathy, producing affective complicity and normalizing the consumption of genocide as spectacle. This ideological atmosphere converts destruction into content, consent, and capital. Gaza exposes the underlying truth of our era: technological progress under imperialist conditions is the perfected form of organized barbarism – violence rendered intelligent, profitable, and permanent.

Importantly, this analysis demonstrated the limits of "Equity AI." The ethical constraints of algorithmic systems are not intrinsic to AI itself but stem from the imperialist and capitalist structures in which it is embedded. In Gaza, AI's deployment generates profit, legitimacy, and technological advancement for the imperialist core, revealing that the issue lies with the systemic exploitation and primitive accumulation underpinning its use, not the technology itself. Efforts at "Equity by Design" that ignore these structural relations risk reproducing the very inequalities they aim to address. A genuine emancipatory critique must therefore move beyond capital: it requires the dismantling of imperialist circuits, the socialization of technology, and the creation of political frameworks capable of repurposing tools like AI toward collective human flourishing. AI, properly situated within such anti-imperialist and postcapitalist frameworks, is not an obstacle to humanity; the barrier is the global system of domination that currently governs its use. This chapter thus contributes to the "Resistance, Refusal, and AI Abolition" framework by emphasizing that justice in AI is inseparable from the struggle to move beyond capital and imperialism.

To conclude, the main interrelated points of this Marxist analysis can be summarized as follows, highlighting the different facets of AI use in the Gaza genocide:

- AI and military technology: Advanced weaponry, AI systems, algorithms, and digital infrastructures represent condensed, objectified past labor (*dead labor*) that must be activated by West-based and Zionist *living labor* – engineers, military operators, and analysts – for the purpose of primitive accumulation, which simultaneously subjugates (and in this extreme case, annihilates) the *living labor* of occupied and colonized Palestinians.

- Primary source of surplus value of capitalism, primitive accumulation: The principal productive contribution of AI-powered genocide comes not from these privileged operators but from the dispossession, and immiseration of the Palestinian population, treated as a strategic labor force in the assertion of U.S. hegemony. AI technologies function as instruments to accelerate and intensify the extreme primitive accumulation of Palestinians – through land theft, control of resources, labor, and even life itself – thereby ensuring the reproduction of imperialist hegemony.
- Disciplining the global wage hierarchy: AI and advanced surveillance systems also operate as tools for disciplining labor on a global scale. By monitoring, controlling, and segmenting workforces, these technologies enforce productivity norms, devalue human life and human consumption, suppress resistance, and maintain hierarchical wage differentials. In doing so, they reduce the value of labor power relative to productivity gains, reinforcing the structural exploitation embedded in the global wage hierarchy.
- Technological acceleration and structural violence: AI and algorithmic systems intensify violence by compressing time, expanding scale, and integrating surveillance into daily life, transforming populations into data points and reproducing asymmetrical power relations.
- Militarism as a source of profit in itself: War is not merely about geopolitics and hegemony over nations and regions to secure interests for continued capitalist accumulation. It constitutes the basis of a self-contained outlet for surplus value production and realization. The military-industrial complex, including arms manufacturers, AI developers, and financial institutions, profits from continuous cycles of innovation, production, and deployment of technologies designed for both annihilation and rapid profit realization.
- Mental conditioning of privileged laboring classes in the imperialist system: By merging ideological and repressive functions within computational infrastructures, AI converts domination into automated consent where surveillance, predictive analytics, content moderation, and autonomous weaponry form an integrated mechanism for reproducing imperialist power materially, cognitively, and affectively. Technology thus becomes ideology, and ideology becomes infrastructure.

REFLECTION QUESTIONS

1. How does the concept of dead labor apply to AI weapons systems, and what does this reveal about the human labor embedded in autonomous warfare?
2. In what ways does AI accelerate primitive accumulation (dispossession and resource extraction) in the context of Gaza?
3. How does the ideological state apparatus (including the media and algorithms) use AI to manufacture consent for imperialist violence among Western populations?
4. How does the author explain the transformation of AI from a neutral technology into a weapon used in genocidal practices under imperialism?

REFERENCES

Abraham, Y. (2024). 'Lavender': The AI machine directing Israel's bombing spree in Gaza. *972 Magazine*. https://www.972mag.com/lavender-ai-israeli-army-gaza/

Abu Shamala, R. (2025). Netanyahu admits using social media as weapon to influence U.S. opinion amid Gaza genocide. *Anadolu Agency*. https://www.aa.com.tr/en/middle-east/netanyahu-admits-using-social-media-as-weapon-to-influence-us-opinion-amid-gaza-genocide/3700646

Al Jazeera. (2025). Death toll in Israel's war on Gaza surpasses 60,000. https://www.aljazeera.com/news/2025/7/29/death-toll-in-israels-war-on-gaza-surpasses-60000

Albanese, F. (2025). *From economy of occupation to economy of genocide (Advance edited version).* Report of the Special Rapporteur on the Situation of Human Rights in the Palestinian Territories Occupied since 1967, Human Rights Council, Fifty-ninth session, Agenda item 7. United Nations. https://www.ohchr.org/sites/default/files/documents/hrbodies/hrcouncil/sessions-regular/session59/advance-version/a-hrc-59-23-aev.pdf

Althusser, L. (1970). Ideology and ideological state apparatuses. *Marxists.org.* https://www.marxists.org/reference/archive/althusser/1970/ideology.htm

American Friends Service Committee. (2025). Gaza genocide companies. https://afsc.org/gaza-genocide-companies

Baran, P. A., & Sweezy, P. (1966). *Monopoly capital: An essay on the American economic and social order.* Monthly Review Press.

Bostrom, N. (2014). *Superintelligence: Paths, dangers, strategies.* Oxford University Press.

Bukharin, N. (1925). Money and expanded reproduction (Chapter 2). In *Imperialism and the accumulation of capital.* Marxists Internet Archive. https://www.marxists.org/archive/bukharin/works/1924/impacck/ch02.htm

Chamayou, G. (2015). *A theory of the drone* (J. Lloyd, Trans.). The New Press.

Dana, T. (2025). The military-industrial backbone of normalization. *Middle East Report.* MERIP. https://www.merip.org/2025/10/the-military-industrial-backbone-of-normalization/

Debord, G. (2014). *Society of the spectacle* (K. Knabb, Trans.). Bureau of Public Secrets.

Fatafta, M. (2024). Genocide in the digital age: What role do social media companies play? *Association for Progressive Communications.* https://www.apc.org/en/blog/genocide-digital-age-what-role-do-social-media-companies-play

Glass, A. (2019). This day in politics: Eisenhower warns of 'military-industrial complex,' Jan. 17, 1961. *Politico.* https://www.politico.com/story/2019/01/17/eisenhower-warns-of-military-industrial-complex-jan-17-1961-1099265

Gusterson, H. (2016). *Drone: Remote control warfare.* MIT Press.

Halper, J. (2015). *War against the people: Israel, the Palestinians and global pacification.* Pluto Press.

Hudson, M. (2003). *Super imperialism: The origin and fundamentals of U.S. world dominance* (2nd ed.). Pluto Press.

Kadri, J. (2024). Interpellation of warfare consumers through the concept of 'terrorism': An Althusserian perspective. *International Review of Sociology/Revue Internationale de Sociologie, 34*(3). https://doi.org/10.1080/03906701.2024.2427602

Kalecki, M. (1943). Political aspects of full employment. *Political Quarterly.* https://delong.typepad.com/kalecki43.pdf

Kalecki, M. (1972). *The last phase in the transformation of capitalism.* Monthly Review Press.

Khan, R. Z. (2025). The economy of genocide: Analysing Israel's profiteering from the war on Gaza. *Strategic Vision Institute.* https://thesvi.org/the-economy-of-genocide-analysing-israels-profiteering-from-the-war-on-gaza/

Lee, G. (2023). Understanding how Israel uses 'Gospel' AI system in Gaza bombings. *France 24 English.* https://www.france24.com/en/tv-shows/perspective/20231212-understanding-how-israel-uses-gospel-ai-system-in-gaza-bombings

Legitimate Targets. (2025). *Israel's dirty secret exposed | Yakov Rabkin interview* [Video]. YouTube. https://www.youtube.com/watch?v=dXXUA-MY4oI

Lenin, V. I. (1916). Imperialism, the highest stage of capitalism. *Marxists Internet Archive.* https://www.marxists.org/archive/lenin/works/1916/imp-hsc/ch06.htm

Loewenstein, A. (2023). *The Palestine laboratory: How Israel exports the technology of occupation around the world.* Verso Books.

Luxemburg, R. (1913a). Militarism as a province of accumulation. In *The Accumulation of Capital*, Section Three, Chapter 32. *Marxists.org.* https://www.marxists.org/archive/luxemburg/1913/accumulation-capital/ch32.htm

Luxemburg, R. (1913b). The accumulation of capital: A contribution to the economic explanation of imperialism. *Marxists Internet Archive.* (London: Routledge, 2003). https://www.marxists.org/archive/luxemburg/1913/accumulation-capital/ch25.htm

Marx, K. (1857a). Grundrisse: Notebook IV – The chapter on capital (Chapter 8). *Marxists.org.* https://www.marxists.org/archive/marx/works/1857/grundrisse/ch08.htm

Marx, K. (1857b). Grundrisse: Notebook V – The chapter on capital (Chapter 10). *Marxists.org.* https://www.marxists.org/archive/marx/works/1857/grundrisse/ch10.htm

Marx, K. (1859). A contribution to the critique of political economy: Preface. *Marxists.org*. Retrieved from https://www.marxists.org/archive/marx/works/1859/critique-pol-economy/preface.htm

Marx, K. (1867a). Capital, Volume I: Chapter 6: The buying and selling of labour-power. *Marxists.org*. Retrieved from https://www.marxists.org/archive/marx/works/1867-c1/ch06.htm

Marx, K. (1867b). Capital: Volume I – Chapter 8: Constant capital and variable capital. *Marxists.org*. Retrieved from https://www.marxists.org/archive/marx/works/1867-c1/ch08.htm

Marx, K. (1867c). Capital: Volume I – Chapter 15: Machinery and modern industry. *Marxists.org*. Retrieved from https://www.marxists.org/archive/marx/works/1867-c1/ch15.htm

Marx, K. (1867d). Capital, Volume I: Chapter 31: The genesis of the industrial capitalist. *Marxists.org*. https://www.marxists.org/archive/marx/works/1867-c1/ch31.htm

Marx, K. (1894a). Capital, Volume III, Part III, Chapter 13: The law of the tendency of the rate of profit to fall. *Marxists.org*. Retrieved from https://www.marxists.org/archive/marx/works/1894-c3/ch13.htm

Marx, K. (1894b). Capital, Volume III, Part III, Chapter 15: Exposition of the internal contradictions of the law. *Marxists.org*. Retrieved from https://www.marxists.org/archive/marx/works/1894-c3/ch15.htm

McKernan, B., & Davies, H. (2024). 'The machine did it coldly': Israel used AI to identify 37,000 Hamas targets. *The Guardian*. https://www.theguardian.com/world/2024/apr/03/israel-gaza-ai-database-hamas-airstrikes

Mészáros, I. (1994). The decreasing rate of utilization under imperialism. *Critique: Journal of Socialist Theory*, *22*(1), 16–58.

Mészáros, I. (1995). *Beyond capital: Toward a theory of transition*. Monthly Review Press.

Mészáros, I. (2003). Militarism and the coming wars. *Monthly Review*. https://monthlyreview.org/2003/06/01/militarism-and-the-co

Pietralunga, C. (2024). Israeli army uses AI to identify tens of thousands of targets in Gaza. *Le Monde*. https://www.lemonde.fr/en/international/article/2024/04/05/israeli-armyusesaitoidentifytensofthousandsoftargetsingaza_6667454_4.html

Russell, S. J. (2019). *Human compatible: Artificial intelligence and the problem of control*. Viking.

Scarazzato, L., Tian, N., Lopes da Silva, D., Liang, X., & Djokic, K. (2024). The SIPRI top 100 arms-producing and military services companies, 2023. *SIPRI Fact Sheet 2412*. Stockholm International Peace Research Institute. https://www.sipri.org/sites/default/files/2024-11/fs_2412_top_100_2023_0.pdf

Schulzke, M. (2017). *The morality of drone warfare and the politics of regulation*. Palgrave Macmillan.

Tasnim News Agency. (2025). Israel deploys AI to shape global narratives amid declining support. https://www.tasnimnews.com/en/news/2025/10/29/3434676/israel-deploys-ai-to-shape-global-narratives-amid-declining-support

United Nations. (2025). Israel has committed genocide in the Gaza Strip, UN Commission of Inquiry finds. https://www.un.org/unispal/document/israel-has-committed-genocide-in-the-gaza-strip-un-commission-finds-16sep25/

Weekly Worker. (2005). E=mc2 and socialism. *Weekly Worker, Issue* 564. https://weeklyworker.co.uk/worker/564/emc2-and-socialism/

27 AI and Equity
Thinking about the Modern Identity and the Uncanny "There"

Anoop George

INTRODUCTION

In philosophy, equity refers to the concept of fairness. In what follows, I will engage with philosophical debates surrounding the concept of fairness, examining its theoretical foundations, contested interpretations, and practical implications all in view of artificial intelligence (AI) and Equity. Engaging with AI and Equity from a philosophical perspective and above all applying it to healthcare systems is a challenging task. However, there are possibilities of examining AI and equity from a philosophical perspective that can open up a plethora of debates. In existential philosophy, an "engaged-agent" refers to a person who actively participates in the world with intentionality, awareness, and above all, moral responsibility rather than being a passive disinterested onlooker. It would be interesting to examine how current debates on AI can be meaningfully framed through the philosophy of the engaged agent. I believe that an engaged agent debate can and should approximate a kind of practical wisdom (*Phronesis*) and equitable judgment (*epieikeia*) that the human agents employ when navigating through complex moral scrutiny.

AI has immense potential in promoting equity, especially in those areas where fairness requires more than mere uniform treatment. In healthcare, equity is not just about offering every patient the same intervention, but about providing the *right* intervention for their specific needs—much like giving a patient "a shoe that fits" rather than merely "a shoe." Today, the presence of AI is not just another episode of fiction but a reality that affects every aspect of our existence. AI can help improve healthcare, but without a strong foundation of ethical baggage, it can risk patients' well-being and exacerbate further inequality. In order to address such complex issues philosophically, I have included in my chapter, first, the engaged-disengaged debate that is essential in understanding the "uncanny there." Second, I will develop the technological modernity where the engaged agent is present and how this modernity is an unfortunate disconnect, and finally, in the third section, using the Heideggerian engaged narrative, I will try to build a cohesive AI-Equity debate unraveling the primacy of fairness.

THE ENGAGED-SELF ARGUMENT

In this section, I will elaborate on the engaged-disengaged debate and its relationship to an "uncanny there." The primary aspect of grasping the equity debate is to understand that the self in question is a self in the world of temporality, experiencing the mundane aspects of life. The key imagination of modernity is that of the disengaged, autonomous, and atomistic self. The "engaged self" would mean the understanding of the self as embodied; historically and culturally embedded; expressive and linguistically structured, gendered, and sexual; oriented toward a sense of the good; and always already open to the sociocultural space of meaning that it occupies. The self is these in a constitutive sense. Moreover, the engaged self would mean that my self-understanding is always operative in my encounters with events, things, and people, and, at the same time, in my projections of temporal possibilities upon what I encounter, I am similarly affected by what

DOI: 10.1201/9781003737810-32

I encounter (the world as such). In the current times, AI has become and is still becoming one of the defining technologies of modernity, continuing to reshape societies and individual lives. Imagining an AI-Equity debate suggests that we revisit the primordial aspects of a meaningful human flourishing.

Right from its inception, human flourishing was central to philosophy. Human flourishing was central to the teachings of Socrates, Plato, and Aristotle. Aristotle considered *Eudaimonia* as the end of the social life of an individual. Human existence, at any point in history to our current times, is just one thing—the human advancement. Engaging with AI today, a committee of the United Kingdom's House of Lords, concluded that,

> AI has moved out of the realms of science fiction and into our everyday lives, working away unnoticed behind the scenes. Yet just as electricity, or steam power before it, started out with particular, often somewhat niche, uses prior to gradually becoming fundamental to almost all aspects of economic and social activity, AI may well grow to become a pervasive technology which underpins our daily existence.
>
> *(House of Lords, 2018)*

Considering the extremely diverse applications of AI and anticipating its ethical, social, and economic impact, in October 2016 the White House Office of Science and Technology Policy, the European Parliament's Committee on Legal Affairs, and, in the United Kingdom, the House of Commons' Science and Technology Committee released their initial reports on how to prepare for the future of AI (Cath CJN et al., 2016). One of the most important aspects of the report was to highlight the importance of how AI should help create a "good society." It was understood that

> from an ethical perspective, AI's potential contribution to social good should include an in-depth plan for linking in a comprehensive socio-political design questions of responsibility of the different stakeholders, of cooperation between them, and of shareable values that underpin our understanding of a 'good AI society'.
>
> *(p. 507)*

Contemporary society is witnessing the rapid evolution of digital technologies. However, steering it socially and politically, as to where we want to go, is more important than how fast we get there. The question of AI and equity in healthcare is precisely a question of this nature. This is where, I would argue, that an "engaged agent" of the "everyday-meaningful-existence" only can navigate through such complex issues. A disengaged perspective merely uses the technological advancements for exploitation and capital gain. Hence, an unbridled technological society, with AI dictating every decision of our daily maneuvering, can culminate in an "uncanny there." Consider a clinical encounter where a diabetic patient is denied a referral because an automated risk score places them just below a care threshold. Clinicians might describe this as a system glitch or a model limitation. However, for the patient, the experience isn't a technical failure but a rupture in meaning: a moment when clinical judgment withdraws, responsibility disperses, and care feels unhomelike. What was once a space of interpretation and recognition now seems familiar yet alien, an instance of the uncanny in technological modernity.

The word "uncanny" is from the German *Das Unheimliche,* which refers to something that is "strangely familiar" or something that is familiar yet alien. The uncanny feeling erupts when something so dear suddenly turns eerie or disturbing. Martin Heidegger, a 20th-century German Existentialist philosopher, used *unheimlich* to mean "unhomely." *Das Unheimlich*, which is translated here as "uncanny," more literally means "unhomelike." Heidegger argues that "In anxiety one feels *'uncanny'*" (Heidegger, 1973, p. 233). Anxiety is a deep existential experience. It exists in the everyday life of a Dasein. Heidegger argues that

> Uncanniness reveals itself authentically in the basic state-of-mind of anxiety; and, as the most elemental way in which thrown Dasein is disclosed, it puts Dasein's Being-in-the-world face to face with the "nothing" of the world; in the face of this "nothing," Dasein is anxious with anxiety about its ownmost potentiality-for-Being.
>
> *(p. 321)*

For an engaged agent, there is no uncanny. She is absorbed in the everyday life with an understanding of being. This understanding is what gives rise to a meaningful engagement with AI. Research and development in AI should be accomplished thinking about a holistic human flourishing. According to Plato, a general human condition may be ignorance but it is possible that through a process of education everyone can attain the knowledge of reality, the knowledge of Forms (Stevenson & Haberman, 1998). In our daily usage, AI is both a tool and an accelerator of modernity. It offers unprecedented decision-making opportunities while still posing profound ethical dilemmas. This is where we need to think deeply about safeguarding human values while embracing technology and innovation.

THE ISSUE WITH TECHNOLOGY

The issue with AI is an issue with technology. This issue has to be understood and addressed meaningfully to envisage the way AI affects our everyday life. AI is yet another technological marvel. For Heidegger, modernity is an ontology that captures the modern human imagination so absolutely that it is difficult to see how one can get out of it. Heidegger in his historical understanding of modernity argues that the ontology of the age rules that age and humans are swayed by the ontology of their particular age. Without this ontological sway, reality is meaningless to them; at the same time, an all-encompassing ontology like the technological understanding of Being is oppressive, says Heidegger, because it does not let the openness for Being be and does not let the human being to bloom and be. AI causing inequity is just one of the diseases of modern technology. Though a deeper examination of AI is inevitable, I will be looking at the problem of modernity and how AI is affecting modern humans. If we see disturbing instances in AI, then for sure, Heidegger would believe that the enticingly oppressive tendency of the ontology of the modern age thereby has entered a phase of decadence and loss.

In Philosophy, the essence of technology is a demand placed upon the human beings by *being* to see all beings in their totality as a resource for human machination and that alone. In Heidegger, "enframing" (*Gestell* in German) is a term used to describe his critique of modern technology. Heidegger uses enframing to explain how we have become mere resources, stripped off of intrinsic values and morality. In the technology essay, enframing is defined as "the gathering together of that setting-upon which sets upon man, i.e., challenges him forth, to reveal the real, in the mode of ordering, as standing-reserve" (Heidegger, 1977, p. 15). Technology, therefore, does not mean machinery and apparatuses. It is the most general ontological name that includes the machines as well but primarily allows us to speak about Western metaphysics in its planetary avatar without referring specifically to what material and mechanical changes this metaphysics is bringing about in the different geographical regions of the world. That is why Heidegger repeats in the form of a refrain in the technology essay that the "essence of technology is nothing technological" (p. 4). The overhauling of technology and our unwavering dependence on it have led to an uncritical engagement with it. Thus, technological nihilism and technological reductionism are triggered by our absolute and uncritical dependence on technology, and it is well explained in Heidegger's own words

> ...everywhere everything is ordered to stand by, to be immediately at hand, indeed to stand there just so that it may be on call for a further ordering... It designates nothing less than the way in which everything presences that is wrought upon by the challenging revealing.
>
> *(p. 17)*

Most generically, technological reductionism refers to the tendency to devalue, or at the very least undervalue, those aspects of human life that cannot be reduced to numerical metrics or instrumental use value.

Reductionism exposes a "for-ness" of things: things exist for our manipulation, use and optimization, and that alone. The cultural layers around a thing, which give it significance and import, are thus disparaged. Instead, modern ways of dealing with things would mean "unlocking, transforming, storing, distributing and switching about" (p. 20). Reductionism converts all our comportments toward things utility-oriented so that we tacitly understand them always already as "standing reserve" (*Bestand*). Layers of meaning dissuade us usually from this project of reduction, and hence, they are to be denigrated, ignored, and made to disappear from our horizon. For Heidegger, this is the primary way of becoming the modern self. So, if AI causes problems, it's really a reflection of how we imagine and understand technology. An unreflective human can fall prey to the technological blindness and live a life of "homelessness" in one's own home. The evils of AI are not about AI being inherently malicious but considering its unintended consequences in the process of development and deployment.

AI-EQUITY AND FAIRNESS

A philosophical grounding for the concept of equity can be traced back to Aristotle, who maintained that human affairs cannot be fully understood or governed through universal principles alone. In the *Nicomachean Ethics*, he observes that "all law is universal, but about some things it is not possible to make a universal statement" (Aristotle, 1999, p. 88). This insight is particularly relevant to contemporary debates about AI. Although AI systems are often designed to operate through universally applied rules, their impacts are experienced by individuals situated in specific contexts. Evaluating those impacts requires attentiveness to particular circumstances and potential inequities—something that cannot be achieved through blanket, unexamined application of algorithmic outputs.

For Aristotle, justice becomes incomplete, and potentially unjust, when the uniqueness of individual cases is ignored. He therefore introduces *epieikeia* (equity) as a corrective to the limitations of written law, noting that the equitable person is one who "chooses and does such acts, and is no stickler for his rights in a bad sense but tends to take less than his share though he has the law often on his side" (Aristotle, 1999, p. 89). Equity, in this view, is not a departure from justice but a refined form of it, an interpretive virtue that ensures individuals receive what is truly due to them. While formal laws or rules may succeed in establishing general equality, Aristotle argues that *eudaimonia*, or human flourishing, requires attending to the moral nuances embedded in each individual case. This Aristotelian framework underscores the importance of contextual judgment in the design and governance of AI systems, especially as societies seek to ensure that technological interventions promote fairness in practice and not merely in principle.

Again, in *Rhetoric*, Aristotle goes on at length to show what equity is:

Equity looks with an eye of compassion on human frailty: it considers itself as representing, not the deaf, insensible law, but the living, merciful lawgiver, and pays more regard to the intention of such a lawgiver than to his mere words. With respect to the delinquent, also, it is more regardful of his designs and purposes than of his proceedings and actions: it is not contented with a partial view but examines the whole patiently, regarding not only what, in the present transaction, he appears to be, but also what, in most others, he has habitually been. In the person injured, equity will direct the attention rather to benefits previously received, than to the evil immediately suffered: it will be reluctant in prosecution, and desirous of adjusting differences by persuasion and argument, rather than by compulsion and force. It will always prefer arbitration to judicial process; for arbiters decide according to equity, and are resorted to, that equity may prevail over strict law. (Book I, Chapter 13)

Here again, Aristotle considers equity as a particular exception from the general law that applies to most of humanity. According to Aristotle, equity is not opposed to justice; rather, it is a better form of justice. Equity balances legal rigidity and promotes the spirit of the law. From this perspective, equity and AI intersect fascinatingly because they both involve decision-making.

A limitation of AI is its difficulty in exercising judgment that transcends rigidly programmed rules and hence might compromise on context and morality. In *Rhetoric*, Aristotle argues that *Epieikeia* addresses those instances where a general rule fails. In most cases, an algorithm's output may be universally applicable, but *Epieikeia* looks at particular cases and produces results that are morally or contextually right. Aristotle is also known for his notions of *practical wisdom* (*phronesis*), which only can instill the sense of empathy and moral insight. Having empathy and moral insight about a given law means that a person understands and grasps the purpose of the law. The biggest challenge for the AI-Equity debate will be to see if we are able to build technology that doesn't just follow the rules but understands and performs *why* a rule exists.

Another philosophical theory that comes close to the AI-Equity debate is Rawls' theory of Justice. In his magnum opus, *A Theory of Justice*, Rawls asks about the most appropriate moral conception of justice for a democratic society (Rawls, 2005). According to Rawls, the primary structure of any social system is to promote justice to the subjects (2005). Justice for Rawls is fairness, "The fundamental idea in the concept of justice is that of fairness" (Rawls, 1957, p. 653). The most challenging aspect of the AI-driven world will be to see how the least important in society receives justice in the sense of fairness. Every society has a basic structure of existence. Once a society moves away from this ideal structure, then we have societally imposed unfairness. Unfairness is when "A society fails to treat some of its members as equals whether it restricts their freedom of expression or permits them to grow up in poverty" (Nagel, 2003, p. 65). While AI will significantly affect our decision-making, it will be important to evaluate how it can promote equity and fairness in our society.

The rapid integration of AI into social, legal, and political systems raises pressing questions about its ability to uphold equity and justice. As Aristotle's notion of *epieikeia* illustrates, true fairness requires a sensitivity to context, an ability to look beyond rigid rules and apply moral insight to particular cases. This capacity is inseparable from *phronesis*, or practical wisdom, which incorporates empathy, discernment, and an understanding of the deeper purpose behind laws and norms. Likewise, Rawls's conception of justice as fairness underscores the moral obligation of any social structure, including algorithmic systems, to ensure that the least advantaged in the society receive equitable treatment. Together, these philosophical frameworks highlight a central challenge for AI: whether it can move from rule, following to genuine moral reasoning. As AI increasingly influences societal decision-making, the task before researchers, designers, and policymakers is not merely technical but profoundly ethical. The future of AI-equity will depend on our ability to build systems that do not simply process instructions, but that reflect and reinforce the moral commitments of a just and democratic society.

CONCLUSION

In this chapter, I have argued that for reimagining a meaningful AI-Equity debate the conception of engaged selfhood shows the way. Technological modernity and its artifacts are not to be rejected but its good, wholesome, and meaningful sense is to be interpretively appropriated along with an in-depth sociocultural and political imagination. As the engaged self, the modern self is to be located in its context and history within the specifics of every self's embeddedness. With the advancement of technology, how dignified human flourishing is appropriated and made sense across the globe is the central issue of the good sense of the modern. I am sure that this is something that animates the current interest of engineers, social scientists, philosophers, and literary theorists all over the world. Without a critical outlook, technological modernity will remain a decadent, meaningless reproduction of the same. It is important to evaluate how technological modernity, important and inevitable, could lead to the loss of meaningful existence of the modern humans and trigger an uncanny existence.

If equity is to be maintained in an era of AI, then the philosophical commitments outlined here would have real-world implications. They would call for assessment methods that go beyond pure statistical parity, focusing instead on qualitative engagement with lived experiences and local harms. They would also necessitate keeping spaces open for human judgment through systems that enable interpretation, explanation, and responsible override, reflecting the Aristotelian idea that practical wisdom cannot be fully automated. Ultimately, they point toward evaluation methods rooted in local contexts and community involvement, considering specific circumstances and differences rather than relying solely on universal metrics. These perspectives do not offer straightforward technical solutions but they mark the conditions under which AI might remain answerable to human meaning, responsibility, and equity. Whether AI enhances equity or amplifies the unsettling aspects of the uncanny will depend less on its technical capabilities and more on whether it stays answerable to active human judgment and the conditions of meaningful existence.

ACKNOWLEDGMENT

Portions of this chapter were developed with the assistance of ChatGPT for editing and brainstorming. All intellectual contributions, interpretations, and final editorial decisions are my own, and I will take full responsibility for the content. Any AI-assisted or AI-generated material was reviewed and verified by the author.

REFLECTION QUESTIONS

1. What is the difference between the engaged self and the disengaged observer, and why is this distinction vital for understanding our relationship with AI?
2. How might the ubiquitous presence of AI in decision-making lead to an experience of the uncanny or homelessness in our daily lives?
3. Why does the author argue that true equity requires practical wisdom (phronesis)—a quality that AI currently lacks?
4. How does technological reductionism threaten to devalue aspects of human life that cannot be quantified or optimized?

REFERENCES

Aristotle, (1983). *Rhetoric*, Book I, Ch. 13 (John Gillies (Trans.) *A New Translation of Aristotle's Rhetoric*, Printed for T. Cadell, in the Strand. London.

Aristotle, (1999). *Nicomachean Ethics* (W.D. Ross, Trans.). Batoche Book, Kitchener.

Cath, C.J.N., Wachter, S., Mittelstadt, B., Taddeo, M., Floridi, L. (2016). *Artificial Intelligence and the "Good Society": The US, EU, and UK Approach*. Social Science Research Network.

Heidegger, M. (1973). *Being and Time*. Translated by John Macquarrie and Edward Robinson. Oxford: Basil Blackwell.

Heidegger, M. (1977). The Question Concerning Technology. In W. Lovitt (Trans.), *The Question Concerning Technology and Other Essays* (pp. 3–35). Harper & Row. (Original work published 1954).

House of Lords (2018). *AI in the UK: Ready, Willing and Able? HL Paper 100*. Select Committee on Artificial Intelligence, House of Lords, Parliament. https://publications.parliament.uk/pa/ld201719/ldselect/ldai/100/100.pdf. Accessed 9th August 2025.

Nagel, T. (2003). Rawls and Liberalism. In Freeman, S. (Ed.) *The Cambridge Companion to Rawls*. (pp. 62–85) Cambridge University Press.

Rawls, J. (1957). Justice as Fairness, in The Journal of Philosophy, Oct. 24, 1957, 54(22), 653–662 American Philosophical Association.

Rawls, J. (2005). *A Theory of Justice*. Belknap Press.

Stevenson, L., & Haberman, D. L. (1998). *Ten Theories of Human Nature*. Oxford University Press, the University of Michigan.

28 Beyond the Algorithm—Toward a Just and Liberatory Future

Christo El Morr, Elham Dolatabadi,
Laleh Seyyed-Kalantari and Rachel da Silveira Gorman

INTRODUCTION

Artificial intelligence (AI) was never just a technological revolution; it reflects our collective ethics, power structures, and ideas about what it means to be human. The chapters in this volume have explored, from various disciplinary and personal viewpoints, how AI is connected to networks of colonialism, racial capitalism, patriarchy, ableism, and class domination—and how, despite these ties, it remains a space of possibility. To speak of *AI for a Just World* is to refuse technological determinism and to affirm that design, data, and governance are political acts.

Across 27 chapters, the authors of this book have advanced a shared conviction: that justice in AI cannot be achieved through technical fairness alone. It requires a transformation in how knowledge is produced, whose experiences shape technology, and what forms of life are valued in its creation. If the introduction opened with the question of *who benefits and who is left behind*, this conclusion asks: *who will build the world we want to inhabit?*

FROM BIAS TO POWER: REFRAMING THE PROBLEM

The conventional AI ethics agenda often begins and ends with bias. This volume demonstrates that bias is not an aberration to be debugged; bias is the appearance of inequity in a capitalist social universe where "equal opportunity" is both a false claim and an ideologically motivated imperative. Inequity is an intrinsic dimension of deeper capitalist structures. Health algorithms misclassify patients because medicine itself has been built on racialized and gendered assumptions. Educational technologies reproduce ableism because the classroom—and the labor market it feeds—was never designed for disabled bodies. Predictive policing models harm racialized communities because the data they train on arise from histories of criminalization and colonial surveillance.

To challenge bias, then, is to confront the political economy of AI: the infrastructures of extraction that harvest data, the global supply chains of digital labor, and the corporate and governmental alliances that profit from opacity. The contributors to *AI for a Just World* insist that justice requires not merely more representative datasets, but new forms of ownership, accountability, and relationality.

This shift—from bias to power—marks the central theoretical contribution of this book. It redefines equity as a redistribution of epistemic and material authority. Who designs the system? Who decides the metrics of success? Who owns the outputs, and who bears the risks? These are not peripheral concerns; they are the foundation of any liberatory AI agenda.

RELATIONAL ETHICS AND THE PRACTICE OF CODESIGN

Throughout these pages, a new methodology emerges: **relational codesign**. It is not a tokenistic inclusion of marginalized voices but a reconfiguration of expertise itself. Codesign recognizes that

DOI: 10.1201/9781003737810-33

communities most affected by technology possess indispensable knowledge about harm, care, and resilience.

From participatory health research to disability-led computing education, from decolonial data governance to feminist simulations of AI safety, the chapters demonstrate that relational ethics are not soft supplements to innovation—they are the conditions of trustworthy innovation. Relationality demands humility from technologists and imagination from humanists. It asks engineers to see code as a social practice and social scientists to engage materially with how models are built.

Codesign, in this sense, is both an ethical stance and a method of survival. It reminds us that justice is built iteratively, through collective learning, rather than imposed from above. The future of AI ethics will belong to those who treat participation not as consultation, but as shared authorship.

DISABILITY, GENDER, AND THE REIMAGINING OF HUMAN CAPACITY

A recurring theme across this book is the redefinition of *capacity*. Disability scholars remind us that the dominant narrative of AI—as augmentation of human potential—often hides its ableist core: a pursuit of efficiency and perfection that excludes bodily and cognitive diversity. By contrast, disability justice reframes technology around interdependence and mutual care.

Similarly, feminist and queer contributions reveal that gender and sexuality are not peripheral to AI design but fundamental to its imaginaries. Whether in the sexualization of chatbots, the masculinization of machine learning metaphors, or the labor politics of care robots, gendered dynamics shape how intelligence itself is conceptualized. To decolonize and degender AI is to question who counts as a subject of knowledge, emotion, and desire.

Together, these perspectives challenge the Enlightenment ideal of the rational, autonomous human. They open space for posthuman and more-than-human understandings of agency—understandings in which relationality, affect, and embodiment are central to cognition. Justice, in this view, is not the extension of human supremacy but its transformation.

Governance as Collective Accountability

Several chapters in this volume interrogate the institutions that govern AI: health systems, universities, border agencies, corporate platforms, and states. The lesson is clear: technical solutions cannot succeed without **political accountability**. Governance must move beyond risk management and toward collective stewardship. Governance must move beyond risk management and toward collective stewardship—including disability-centered policy that treats access, participation, and refusal as democratic rights.

This means developing public infrastructures of algorithmic oversight—independent bodies empowered to audit, interpret, and, when necessary, dismantle harmful systems. It means embedding transparency not as compliance but as democratic practice: communities should have the right to know how data about them are collected and used, and the power to refuse. It also means confronting the geopolitical hierarchies of AI production, where the Global South supplies data and labor while the Global North reaps profit and control.

In reimagining governance, the authors call for an ethics of *responsible refusal*. Not all technologies deserve to exist. To say no—to predictive policing, to exploitative data mining, to border-surveillance algorithms—is itself a moral and political act. Accountability is not only about explaining models; it is about deciding which models should never be built.

DECOLONIZING KNOWLEDGE AND BEING

The final chapters of this book take us further still, into philosophical terrain where technology becomes a question of being. Yahya El-Lahib and Maimuna Khan show how colonial modernity continues to define what counts as intelligence and progress. Michael Sherbert exposes the theological residue of AI's search for omniscience. Kathleen Cherrington and other posthumanist thinkers invite animist and Indigenous cosmologies into conversation with algorithmic life, suggesting that we can learn from traditions that see spirit and agency in all matter. Anoop George, drawing on Heidegger, asks what it means to dwell meaningfully with technology—to be an engaged self rather than a disengaged observer.

These philosophical interventions remind us that liberation begins with ontology. To decolonize AI is not only to critique its institutions but to unlearn the hierarchies of being that privilege the human, the Western, and the disembodied. The task is to cultivate what Leanne Simpson calls *radical relationality*: a way of living and knowing that honors connection over control.

TOWARD A FRAMEWORK FOR "AI FOR JUSTICE"

The phrase *AI for Justice* does not describe a single discipline or initiative; it names a movement that envisions AI as a collective social project. Its framework rests on five interlocking principles that crystallize from this volume:

1. **Equity as redistribution of power:** Justice requires shifting epistemic, economic, and political power toward marginalized communities.
2. **Interdisciplinarity as ethic:** Genuine collaboration transforms the terms of knowledge, not just the membership of committees.
3. **Relationality as design logic:** Technologies must be evaluated by how they sustain relationships of care and accountability.
4. **Decolonization as praxis:** Every dataset and model must be interrogated for the colonial histories it carries.
5. **Liberation as horizon:** The goal is not merely ethical compliance but the flourishing of all beings within planetary limits.

This framework is not a checklist; it is a compass. It points toward futures in which technology is shaped by empathy, humility, and imagination.

FUTURE DIRECTIONS: RESEARCH, PEDAGOGY, AND POLICY

The work is only beginning. Each chapter in this book opens questions for further research: how can participatory AI design be institutionalized in public policy? What educational models prepare engineers to engage critically with social theory? How can universities, governments, and industries share governance with affected communities rather than acting on their behalf? As the disability-centered policy work in this volume underscores, accessibility and inclusion require enforceable governance mechanisms and disability-led participation across the AI life cycle—not consultation after deployment.

In pedagogy, the challenge is to train not only competent developers but *ethical agents*—people capable of seeing technology as a social practice embedded in histories of inequality. In policy, the task is to move from ethics statements to enforceable standards, from aspirational guidelines to redistributive infrastructures.

Most urgently, the AI community must confront the material conditions of its own existence: the energy consumption of large models, the exploitation of ghost workers, and the ecological devastation of data extraction. A just AI future must also be a sustainable one.

CONCLUSION: LIVING OTHERWISE

If AI reflects society, then reimagining AI means reimagining ourselves. It requires a politics of humility: acknowledging that intelligence, creativity, and care are not the exclusive property of human beings. It requires courage to say that not every technological advance is progress. And it requires collective joy—the recognition that building just technologies is a form of building community.

We end this volume with hope, but not naïve hope. The contributors know that systems of oppression adapt quickly, that justice is never guaranteed by design. Yet they also know that change begins in the imagination: in the capacity to see, even briefly, a different configuration of power, a different relation between people and machines.

AI for a Just World invites readers to inhabit that possibility. To think with rather than about technology. To listen across disciplines and communities. To design as if care were the measure of success.

The future of AI will be written in the plural. It will be shaped by the collective acts of refusal, invention, and solidarity that redefine what intelligence, equity, and liberation can mean.

Let this book stand, then, not as a conclusion but as a commitment—to continue the work of transforming the algorithm into an ally of justice, and the dream of liberation into a practice of everyday design.

ACKNOWLEDGMENT

The author acknowledges the use of ChatGPT and Grammarly for assistance with English-language editing, including the improvement of sentence structure and clarity.

Glossary

A

Ableism: A system of beliefs, practices, and institutional arrangements that privilege able-bodied and neurotypical norms while marginalizing or excluding disabled and neurodivergent people. In AI systems, ableism is embedded through design assumptions, data omissions, optimization goals, and performance metrics that treat disability as deviation rather than as a site of knowledge and lived expertise.

Accountability: The obligation of institutions, developers, deployers, and governing bodies to explain, justify, audit, and take responsibility for decisions made using AI systems, particularly when those systems affect rights, health, safety, access to resources, or exposure to harm.

Accumulation of Capital: The process through which surplus value is extracted from labor, reinvested, and expanded. Accumulation proceeds through exploitation in production and realization in circulation, increasingly relying on technological, militarized, and extractive mechanisms under contemporary capitalism.

Algorithm: A set of formalized instructions or rules designed to perform a task or solve a problem. In AI systems, algorithms encode assumptions, priorities, and values that shape how data is processed and decisions are produced.

Algorithmic Accountability: Mechanisms and practices that enable scrutiny of algorithmic systems, including documentation, audits, contestability, impact assessments, oversight bodies, and governance structures that allow harms to be identified, challenged, and remedied.

Algorithmic Bias: Systematic and repeatable unfairness in AI systems arising from historical, social, and institutional inequities embedded in data, design choices, modeling assumptions, and governance contexts. Algorithmic bias is not merely technical error but a political outcome encoded into systems.

Algorithmic Colonialism: The extension of colonial power relations through AI systems developed in dominant geopolitical contexts and deployed elsewhere without local control, consent, contextual adaptation, or equitable benefit-sharing, resulting in extractive data practices and epistemic domination.

Algorithmic Curation: The automated selection, ranking, and moderation of content—such as social media posts or search results—based on predicted engagement or relevance, shaping visibility, participation, and public discourse.

Algorithmic Governance: The use of automated or semi-automated systems to shape, support, or make decisions in public and private governance domains such as healthcare, migration, education, policing, warfare, and social services.

Algorithmic Violence: Forms of physical, structural, epistemic, or lethal harm produced or intensified by algorithmic systems, including surveillance, deprivation of rights, targeting, and exposure to military force, often framed as neutral or efficient.

AI Alignment: The process of ensuring that AI systems' objectives, behaviors, and outcomes are consistent with ethical, social, political, and equity goals. Alignment is contested and shaped by power, governance, and institutional priorities.

AI Companion: An artificial intelligence system designed to simulate emotionally responsive relationships through text, voice, visual, or embodied interaction, often marketed as digital partners or companions.

AI Hallucination: A phenomenon in which AI systems generate outputs that appear coherent or authoritative but are factually incorrect, fabricated, or unsupported by underlying data or sources.

AI Psychosis: Situations where users develop a distorted sense of reality and delusions resulting from interactions with the technology.

AI Safety: The field and practice concerned with preventing unintended, harmful, or catastrophic outcomes from AI systems, including errors, misuse, overreliance, and systemic harm.

Animism: A worldview in which all entities—human, nonhuman, natural, and technological—are understood as possessing relational beinghood or spirit. In AI contexts, animism challenges Western assumptions that technologies are inert tools devoid of moral or relational responsibility.

Apocalyptic AI: A term coined by Robert Geraci describing religious or eschatological narratives in AI discourse that promise salvation, transcendence, or immortality through machine intelligence and technological enhancement.

Artificial Intelligence (AI): A broad class of computational systems designed to perform tasks associated with human intelligence, such as learning, prediction, classification, language processing, pattern recognition, and decision support. AI systems are socio-technical infrastructures shaped by data, labor, institutions, and power.

Autonomous Weapon Systems (AWS): Weapons capable of selecting and engaging targets with limited or no human intervention, raising profound ethical, legal, and political concerns regarding accountability, proportionality, and civilian harm.

B

Bias: A systematic tendency toward outcomes or interpretations that disadvantage particular groups. Bias may be cognitive, institutional, structural, or technical and is reproduced across both human and machine decision-making systems.

Biometric Surveillance: The collection and analysis of bodily data—such as facial images, fingerprints, iris scans, or gait patterns—for identification, monitoring, or risk assessment, commonly used in borders, policing, and military operations.

Biomedical Hegemony: The dominance of biomedical models of health and illness, including the suppression of alternative epistemologies and the corporatization of care into pharmaceutical and hospital-centered systems.

Biological Reductionism: A scientific approach that explains complex living systems solely through their smallest components (e.g., genes or cells), often neglecting social, environmental, and structural determinants.

Bounded Justice: A framework describing how justice-oriented interventions are constrained by the systems in which they operate, often reproducing inequity when historical and structural conditions are ignored.

C

Care Work: Paid or unpaid labor involved in sustaining life and wellbeing, including childcare, eldercare, disability support, emotional labor, and community care. Care work is feminized, racialized, and increasingly mediated by digital technologies.

Clinical Decision Support System (CDSS): AI-enabled tools that assist clinicians by generating diagnostic suggestions, risk scores, or treatment recommendations. While intended to improve care, CDSS can introduce new biases, errors, and overreliance.

Clinical Simulation: The use of simulated environments or scenarios—often supported by AI—to evaluate clinical decision-making, system performance, safety, and error propagation.

Collective Action: Coordinated efforts by a group of individuals or organizations working together to achieve a shared objective, often in pursuit of social, political, or economic change. Collective action typically involves cooperation, shared resources, and joint decision-making.

Collegial Governance: A model of organizational decision-making in which authority is shared among members of a professional community—such as faculty within a university—through committees, deliberation, and consensus-oriented processes rather than hierarchical control.

Colonial Expansionism: The process through which a state or imperial power extends political, economic, and territorial control over other regions or peoples, often involving settlement, resource extraction, and the imposition of external governance structures.

Colonial Modernity: The processes of Western modernization that rely on colonial domination, exploitation, and extraction while presenting themselves as universal progress.

Coloniality: The enduring structures of power, knowledge, and social relations produced by colonial rule that persists long after formal colonial governance ends.

Crip Theory: A critical framework from disability studies that challenges normative assumptions about bodies, productivity, and independence, reclaiming disability as political knowledge and resistance.

Crip Technoscience: A framework in which disabled people design, critique, and reimagine technologies to challenge dominant ableist assumptions and generate alternative technological futures.

Cripping Transmethodologies: An approach that disrupts rigid research methods by mixing disciplines, epistemologies, and practices to produce inclusive, difference-affirming knowledge.

D

Data Colonialism: The appropriation, extraction, and commodification of data from marginalized populations and regions in ways that mirror historical colonial resource extraction.

Datafication: The transformation of human experiences, behaviors, and bodies into quantifiable data that can be stored, analyzed, and acted upon by digital systems.

Data Sovereignty: The right of individuals, communities, or nations—especially Indigenous peoples—to govern the collection, ownership, use, and sharing of data about them.

Debilitation: The production of injury or impairment as an ongoing condition of governance or warfare, rather than as an unintended side effect.

Deepfakes: AI-generated or manipulated images, videos, or audio that fabricate events or representations without consent. Deepfakes are a key mechanism of technology-facilitated gender-based violence.

Design Justice: An approach to technology design that centers marginalized communities, redistributes decision-making power, and prioritizes collective wellbeing over efficiency or profit.

Digital Divide: Inequities in access to digital technologies, infrastructure, connectivity, and skills, structured by geography, income, disability, race, and global power relations.

Digital Epidermalization: The process by which biometric surveillance systems dissect the body into data points, rendering the racial body legible as algorithmic data that is judged against normative expectations shaped by whiteness.

Digital Health: The use of digital technologies, including AI, to support health services, public health, and personal wellbeing.

Digital Health Equity: The principle that digital health technologies should reduce, not exacerbate, health disparities by being accessible, culturally responsive, and accountable.

Digital Phenotyping: Leveraging social media data to screen for patterns indicative of mental health or neurodivergent behaviors.

Disability Evasiveness: The deliberate and systemic avoidance of acknowledging disability or the structural barriers faced by disabled people in AI outputs

Disability Justice: A framework developed by disabled activists of color that centers intersectionality, interdependence, collective access, and leadership of those most impacted by oppression.

Disablement: The active production of disability through violence, neglect, policy, or infrastructure rather than disability being solely an individual medical condition.

E

Epistemic Flattening: A denial of the credibility of more credible speakers and the denial of the deficit of less credible ones, often resulting from AI's inability to contextualize data

Epistemic Injustice: Harm done to individuals or communities in their capacity as knowers, including testimonial injustice and hermeneutical injustice.

Epistemic Violence: The silencing, erasure, or distortion of marginalized knowledge systems through dominant epistemologies.

Equity: A commitment to fairness that accounts for structural inequality and differential needs rather than treating all individuals as if they start from the same position.

Equity-by-Design: An approach embedding equity considerations throughout the AI lifecycle—from problem framing and data collection to deployment and governance.

F

Fairness: In AI, the contested goal of ensuring systems do not systematically disadvantage particular groups. Fairness cannot be reduced to a single metric.

Feminist Political Economy: An analytical framework examining how gender, labor, care, and power intersect within economic and technological systems.

Foundation Models: Large, general-purpose AI models trained on vast datasets and adapted for multiple downstream tasks, raising concerns about opacity, environmental cost, and centralized control.

G

Generative AI: AI systems capable of producing new content such as text, images, audio, or video based on learned patterns.

H

Health Equity: The absence of avoidable and unjust differences in health outcomes across populations.

Human–AI Interaction: The study of how humans understand, trust, interpret, and collaborate with AI systems.

I

Indigenous Data Sovereignty: The right of Indigenous peoples to govern data about their communities, lands, and knowledges, grounded in self-determination and relational accountability.

Indigenous Epistemologies: Relational knowledge systems rooted in land, community, responsibility, and reciprocity.

In-Processing: The phase of machine learning training where the algorithm internalizes its reasoning processes to "unlearn" bias. Distinct from pre-processing (data cleaning) or post-processing (output correction), in-processing is the site where equitability must be learned as a strategic, reflective practice rather than enforced through external constraints or metrics, enabling the model to actively scrutinize the structures of inequity.

Intersectionality: A framework examining how multiple systems of oppression interact to shape lived experience and social outcomes.

M

Machine Learning: A subset of AI in which systems learn patterns from data to make predictions or decisions, internalizing institutional and political priorities.

Manosphere: A loosely connected, evolving online community predominantly composed of men… encompassing diverse groups such as men's rights activists and involuntary celibates (incels).

Medical Colonialism: The imposition of biomedical frameworks and technologies that marginalize local knowledge and reproduce colonial power in healthcare.

Militarism: The normalization of military logic, values, and technologies—including AI—across civilian domains.

Misogyny: Structural hostility toward women and gender-diverse people that sustains patriarchal power, intensified through digital systems.

N

Necropolitics: The exercise of power over life and death, increasingly mediated through algorithmic classification and targeting.

P

Participatory Design: A collaborative design process that meaningfully involves affected communities in defining problems, shaping systems, and governing outcomes.

Platform Governance: The rules, policies, and algorithmic systems through which digital platforms manage content, users, labor, and visibility.

Posthumanism: A philosophical approach that challenges human exceptionalism and explores entanglements between humans, nonhumans, and technologies.

Predictive Policing: The use of data-driven systems to forecast crime or risk, often reinforcing racialized surveillance and carceral logics.

Privacy: The right to control personal information and bodily data in contexts of surveillance and automated decision-making.

Proxy Variables: A quantifiable stand-ins for complex concepts like medical need or vulnerability.

R

Radically Equitable AI: An AI paradigm treating equity as a political and infrastructural struggle, requiring systems to interrogate inherited reasoning patterns rather than merely correcting outputs.

Resistance: Actions, practices, or forms of opposition through which individuals or groups challenge systems of power, domination, or injustice. Resistance may take many forms, including political protest, everyday acts of refusal, cultural expression, or organized social movements.

S

Settler Colonialism: A form of colonialism structured around land occupation and Indigenous elimination or containment, increasingly mediated by AI and surveillance.

Social Reproduction: The labor and social processes that sustain life across generations, often rendered invisible in capitalist systems.

Structural Violence: Harm produced by social, economic, and technological structures that systematically disadvantage certain populations.

Surveillance: The systematic monitoring, tracking, and classification of individuals or populations, increasingly automated through AI.

Surveillance Capitalism: A concept describing an economic logic where human lived experience is extracted as raw material for commercial exploitation and algorithmic control. This system monetizes data to predict behavior, reinforcing social and racial inequalities by concentrating power in the Global North while exploiting marginalized communities.

T

Technoableism: The reproduction of ableist norms through technological systems that privilege speed, autonomy, and productivity.

Technocolonialism: The maintenance of colonial domination through technological systems that extract data, impose external values, and entrench dependency.

Technology-Facilitated Gender-Based Violence: Gendered violence enacted or amplified through digital technologies, producing real and embodied harms across physical, psychological, social, and economic dimensions.

Transnational: Referring to activities, institutions, relationships, or processes that operate across or beyond national borders, linking actors, ideas, or systems in multiple countries simultaneously.

Transparency: The degree to which AI systems and decision processes are understandable, explainable, and open to scrutiny.

U

Usability Engineering: The design of systems that support safe, effective, and equitable human interaction, especially in high-stakes contexts.

V

Violence: Physical, psychological, epistemic, or structural harm inflicted on individuals or communities, often obscured through technological mediation.

Index

Note: **Bold** page numbers refer to tables; *italic* page numbers refer to figures and page numbers followed by "n" denote endnotes.

B

C

D

R

S

T

U

V